Learn FileMaker Pro 19

The Comprehensive Guide to Building Custom Databases

Second Edition

Mark Conway Munro

Apress®

Learn FileMaker Pro 19: The Comprehensive Guide to Building Custom Databases

Mark Conway Munro
Lewisburg, PA, USA

ISBN-13 (pbk): 978-1-4842-6679-3   ISBN-13 (electronic): 978-1-4842-6680-9
https://doi.org/10.1007/978-1-4842-6680-9

Managing Director, Apress Media LLC: Welmoed Spahr
Acquisitions Editor: Aaron Black
Development Editor: James Markham
Coordinating Editor: Jessica Vakili

Distributed to the book trade worldwide by Springer Science+Business Media New York,1 NY Plazar, New York, NY 10014. Phone 1-800-SPRINGER, fax (201) 348-4505, e-mail orders-ny@springer-sbm.com, or visit www.springeronline.com. Apress Media, LLC is a California LLC and the sole member (owner) is Springer Science + Business Media Finance Inc (SSBM Finance Inc). SSBM Finance Inc is a **Delaware** corporation.

For information on translations, please e-mail booktranslations@springernature.com; for reprint, paperback, or audio rights, please e-mail bookpermissions@springernature.com.

Apress titles may be purchased in bulk for academic, corporate, or promotional use. eBook versions and licenses are also available for most titles. For more information, reference our Print and eBook Bulk Sales web page at http://www.apress.com/bulk-sales.

Any source code or other supplementary material referenced by the author in this book is available to readers on GitHub via the book's product page, located at www.apress.com/978-1-4842-6679-3. For more detailed information, please visit http://www.apress.com/source-code.

Printed on acid-free paper

In loving memory of this noble beast.
She was my loyal companion for 13 years.
Rest in peace sweet girl.
I miss you.

Apache Munro
2007–2020

Table of Contents

xvii

About the Author

Mark Conway Munro is a software developer and the author of *AppleScript: Developer Reference* (2010, Wiley) and *Learn FileMaker Pro 16* (2017, Apress). After a 1988 introduction to FileMaker, Mark began using AppleScript and FileMaker for information management and process automation tasks. In 1994, Mark founded Write Track Media, a computer consultancy firm that develops custom database and workflow automation solutions. Mark builds time-saving custom systems for a diverse list of clients across industries, including education, entertainment, finance, news, publishing, manufacturing, and more. Understanding the virtue of using technology to free human focus from repetitive tasks so they can pursue a higher level of productivity, Mark is unwavering in his commitment to developing the highest-quality workflow management solutions.

About the Technical Reviewer

Brian Sanchez is a FileMaker developer, business workflow consultant, and a founding member of aACE Software. Brian's experience is wide reaching. For over 25 years, he designed and implemented custom apps for inventory tracking, digital catalogs built with FileMaker Go, plus asset management and pricing tools. His eclectic client list includes catering businesses, event training companies, schools, TV casting agencies, and European vacationing services. Brian holds multiple FileMaker certifications. His development philosophy is to build systems with such integrity in the code and architecture that the client never needs to call again – unless they're looking to upgrade the solution. Brian served as the technical editor of *Learn FileMaker Pro 16* (2017, Apress).

Foreword

In the 1990s and 2000s, I ran TECSoft, an AppleScript and FileMaker Pro development shop in New York City. Our specialty was database publishing – the powerful ability of Apple's AppleScript technology to intelligently extract data from FileMaker databases and to format it ready for print in page layout applications such as QuarkXPress and Adobe InDesign.

We worked closely with Apple and Claris, the predecessor of FileMaker Inc., to showcase the abilities of their technologies. In 1994, growing – and needing additional developer talent – we asked our pal Eric Silver, the then New York area sales rep at Claris, to be on the lookout for us. He told me about a FileMaker wizard he knew named Mark Munro working at Jack Morton, an AV production company in New York.

Mark was responsible for organizing Morton's production project data and managing their workflow. We met and he explained their workflow and showed me how he had organized it in FileMaker so that management was able to track projects from start to finish, track the various assets involved, and track and accurately bill their clients for the time and materials involved.

Mark's work was amazing, and I immediately realized we had come across FileMaker gold. All aspects of his company's workflow were logically organized in a functional workflow management tool and – most impressively of all – were clearly presented in an easy-to-follow interface. It is mind-bending to realize that Mark had accomplished this before FileMaker was a relational database.

We began working with Mark as a freelance FileMaker Pro and AppleScript gun slinger. We threw our most complicated and demanding projects at him – a huge workflow management and catalog publishing project at Sony Music and a very complex and mission-critical graphic file creation project with drop-dead deadlines for Associated Press, to name just a couple.

In short order, Mark had more than enough work to go out on his own as a full-time FileMaker and AppleScript developer. As TECSoft's focus turned to working with Apple delivering AppleScript seminars and training sessions, we created the TECSoft Developers Consortium (TDC) to handle the huge demand for FileMaker and

AppleScript integration projects our seminars generated. With Mark as TDC developer #1, we were able to create an international referral network of FileMaker Pro and AppleScript developers that became the largest FileMaker Pro and AppleScript brain trust on Earth.

Mark has now been running his own successful development company, Write Track Media, for over 25 years. What Mark possesses, more than any other developer I've worked with, is a true talent for organization. Mark's passion makes him eminently qualified to pass along his mastery of FileMaker's powerful organization tool. He just had to write this book.

—John Thorsen Jr.
Connected Hearth, LLC

Introduction

The previous edition of this book was published in 2017. In the introduction to *Learn FileMaker Pro 16*, I reminisced about my first encounter with the software working at Tannen's Magic Shop in Manhattan back in 1988 and highlighted the evolutionary changes that spanned the decades between. In the 3 years since that publication, the technological march forward has continued with improvements to the FileMaker application.

The product is now in version 19. The Apple subsidiary was renamed *Claris* to reflect an expanding product line with more diversity than the former FileMaker-centric offerings. The previous two versions of the desktop application – FileMaker Pro and FileMaker Pro Advanced – are now rolled into a single title that includes all development tools. Annual upgrades to the product have resulted in an accumulation of feature changes. To stay relevant and reflect the current software, a new edition was required.

In addition to revisions covering changes to the software, I was determined to make improvements to the original book. Some changes were in response to legitimate criticisms from readers. Although readers widely praised the first book, some thought there were too many pages focused on a function reference section that too closely resembles what is available in the online help guide. Others thought there were not enough real-world examples. I felt the original book could have been more succinct. I updated the text for feature changes and spent extra months completely rewriting each section and producing what is almost an entirely new book. I hope the effort shows.

I love hearing from readers and welcome any feedback or questions. If you enjoy the book, please consider posting a review on your favorite online bookseller's site and/or sharing on social media. Contact me directly by joining the *Learn FileMaker* FaceBook group and connecting to my professional network on LinkedIn or through my business website:

```
facebook.com/groups/LearnFileMaker/
linkedin.com/in/markconwaymunro
writetrackmedia.com
```

FileMaker is a highly capable tool used by millions worldwide. I hope you enjoy the book and that it helps you on your journey.

—Mark Conway Munro
December 2020, Lewisburg, PA

PART I

Using FileMaker

The FileMaker Pro desktop application merges a user interface and development environment into a single experience. These chapters focus on the user experience to serve as an introduction to the platform's features:

1. *Introducing FileMaker*

2. *Exploring the Application*

3. *Exploring a Database Window*

4. *Working with Records*

5. *Transferring Data*

CHAPTER 1

Introducing FileMaker

FileMaker Pro is a software platform used to create relational database applications for modern workflows. Published by Apple subsidiary Claris International Inc., the software is popular among novice programmers for its intuitive, low-code programming interface, while professionals appreciate access to advanced technologies, robust customization options, rich connectivity, and plug-in extensibility. A uniquely integrated architecture combines the full stack of data, logic, and interface layers into a seamless programming experience. Using the flagship desktop application, developers can collaboratively create a secure, multi-user, cross-platform solution and rapidly deploy it to mobile, cloud, and on-premise workflows. Solutions can range from simple spreadsheet-like worksheets to artfully designed, feature-rich, interface-driven solutions. FileMaker is used by independent consultants, employees of small businesses, and members of teams working at medium to large businesses, nonprofits, and government agencies. Although it is easy to learn, business leaders who can't invest the time themselves and don't employ a development staff can easily find a professional consultant to develop a system tailored to meet their needs. Whatever the skill set, FileMaker is an excellent choice for building custom databases. This chapter introduces FileMaker, discussing

- A brief introduction to databases
- The history of FileMaker in a nutshell
- Adapting to the integrated full stack
- Reviewing product line

A Brief Introduction to Databases

A *database* is a structured collection of information stored in a generic format that is easily accessible for a wide variety of uses. The modern world is full of databases, and we interact with them constantly through apps and websites. Most of these are focused on one specific data type with predefined properties and procedures. For example, a

M. C. Munro, *Learn FileMaker Pro 19*, https://doi.org/10.1007/978-1-4842-6680-9_1

calendar application allows a user to create and manage *events* with properties of *date,* *time, attendees, notes,* and *alerts.* Similarly, an email application allows management of *messages* with predefined properties of *sender, recipients, subject,* and *body.* These could each be thought of colloquially as an "event-base" and a "message-base" since, at their *base,* they store and provide access to *events* and *messages.* From a wider perspective, both events and messages are types of information; they are both forms of *data.* A calendar app accesses and manages an *event database.* A mail application does the same with a *message database.* Unlike these and countless other modern applications that provide front-end access to an out-of-sight database, an *open-ended database* application has no predefined data type; at its base is data, *any kind of data.* A database application like FileMaker allows a developer to create custom solutions that manage any data they define.

Applications such as a calendar or mail app provide a predefined database that is like a metaphorical filing cabinet, structurally locked and preconfigured by the vendor to accept a specific type of information. A user is free to enter information into this predefined framework but has little or no control over the framework itself. By contrast, a custom database is the metaphorical equivalent of that same filing drawer completely empty and unlocked so that *you* can define the content it accepts and decide how that information is stored, related, displayed, used, and shared. Every project starts fresh with the same blank slate waiting for you to define the framework and establish the capabilities that will be available to the user. So, don't make the mistake of thinking of FileMaker as a system for only managing contacts or projects. Similar to how a word processing document can contain a wide variety of different written content, a database built with FileMaker can store information about *anything* a developer defines it to manage: *companies, contacts, inventory, invoices, messages, notes, people, products, tasks,* and more.

The History of FileMaker in a Nutshell

The early history of FileMaker is a zigzag between various names, publishers, platforms, and numbering systems before eventually settling into a stable, modern track.

Nashoba Systems

FileMaker started its life in the early 1980s as Nutshell, an MS-DOS computer program developed by Nashoba Systems in Concord, Massachusetts, and distributed by electronics marketer Leading Edge. When the Macintosh computer was introduced in early 1984, Nashoba saw an opportunity and combined the Nutshell database engine with a graphic user interface to create a forms-based database product. Since Leading Edge wanted to remain a DOS-only vendor, Nashoba turned to a new distributor, Forethought, Inc. As a result, FileMaker version 1.0 was released in April 1985 for the Macintosh platform. In 1986, it was renamed *FileMaker Plus* to match the release of the Macintosh Plus. When Microsoft purchased Forethought in 1987, they tried to negotiate a purchase of FileMaker, which was outselling their own Microsoft File database application. However, Nashoba declined and began self-publishing the program, now named FileMaker 4. By today's standards, these early versions of FileMaker were incredibly primitive. However, it was very capable for its time, and the software filled an important need by providing an easy-to-use interface that became popular with the do-it-yourself crowd.

Claris International

In 1986, Apple formed Claris Corp. as a wholly owned subsidiary to develop and publish Macintosh software titles such as MacWrite and MacPaint. In 1988, Claris purchased Nashoba Systems to acquire FileMaker. By this time, Leading Edge and Nutshell had disappeared as other DOS and Windows database products dominated the market. In 1988, FileMaker II was released by Claris to match the naming scheme of their other products. After a few minor updates, the product was rebranded in 1990 under its modern naming and versioning format when FileMaker Pro 1.0 was released. Claris upgraded the product in 1992 with Windows support, making FileMaker Pro 2.0 the first cross-platform version. They began publishing a server application in 1994. It wasn't until 1995 with the release of version 3.0 that FileMaker became fully relational. By 1997, with version 4.0, FileMaker was a widely popular product and was outselling all other Claris products. Apple absorbed those in-house and renamed the subsidiary after their only remaining product.

FileMaker

In 1998, the company changed its name to FileMaker Inc. to reflect the new singular focus on the database product line. Over the subsequent decades, they transitioned the product from an early relational database to a feature-rich development platform. The product gained native support for Mac OS X and later to the modern macOS. Many features we take for granted today were added during this time. For example, a multi-table file architecture, the ability to open multiple windows in a single file, calculation variables, buttons, tabs, portals, web viewers, conditional formatting, built-in functions, and script steps. They continued improving the product by adding script triggers, integrated charts, filtered portals, themes, numerous new layout tools, recursive custom functions, and custom menus. More recent additions include support for *JavaScript Object Notation* (JSON), *client URL* (cURL), and *Structured Query Language* (SQL). Also features like add-on tables, self-lookup tables for master-detail layouts, automatic directory creation, *FileMaker URL* and *FileMaker API*. This era witnessed various adjustments to the product line to include desktop, server, and mobile versions and saw the version numbering scheme shift to whole numbers based on a consistent annual upgrade schedule.

Claris International Reborn

In 2019, FileMaker announced a resurrection of the Claris brand name and a rebranding of the company as Claris International Inc. The name was changed to better reflect plans for expanded offerings, such as the recently announced Claris Connect workflow integration service. In May 2020, Claris released FileMaker Pro version 19 with notable features like

- *Drag & Drop Installation (macOS)* — The macOS application is a bundle with embedded resources that can be dragged into the *Applications* folder for a one-step install.

- *Add-ons* — A revolutionary feature that allows a set of tables, relationships, layout objects, and scripts to be added to a database by dragging and dropping a widget onto a layout.

- *JavaScript* — Web Viewers and FileMaker scripts can now directly communicate with each other. JavaScript libraries can be used to add advanced interface elements in web viewers.

- *Keyboard Navigation in Layout Mode* — Quickly jump to other layouts using the keyboard or a new selection dialog.

- *Dark Mode Support (macOS)* — Changes the visual appearance based on settings in System Preferences.

- *Startup File* — Preference to automatically open a specific file when the application is launched.

- *New Functions and Script Steps* — *Near Field Communication* (NFC) features, convert paths to and from FileMaker format, access card dimensions, leverage the power of *Core ML* (Machine Learning), and more.

Adapting to the Integrated Full Stack

The FileMaker Pro desktop application employs an *integrated architecture* skillfully combining the full stack of a *presentation front end, process logic middleware,* and *data storage back end.* Unlike the traditional approach where these components are physically separated and built with different languages, FileMaker folds all three into a familiar, document-based user experience with an accessible low-code development environment. Experienced software developers familiar with multitier architectures that employ command-line languages may find this arrangement initially disorienting. They may even be tempted to hastily and unjustly dismiss it as something only for beginners. However, FileMaker expertly unites ease of use with powerful standards-based technologies, uniting the best of both worlds in a powerful application for those who look deeper than the façade. Although accessible to beginners, it is also a *very capable* and *extremely powerful* development tool.

FileMaker flattens the learning curve for beginners but also provides an astonishing flexibility in structural design options for advanced users. A database can be built as a self-contained solution, where the full resource stack of every table, layout, and script is all built inside of a *single document file.* Solutions built this way can be used like a document file, duplicated and modified like a word processing template, or passed on to a colleague like a spreadsheet file. They can be stored in your documents folder for personal use or shared across a network with other users. More complex solutions may benefit from the compact unified design but can optionally reach beyond the confines of the document container and become *modular solutions* made up of more than one file. Each module can incorporate tables from the others, opening up an enormous set of design choices. FileMaker databases can also interface with other ODBC/JDBC database systems and/or can act as a data source for other systems. This suggests a staggering number of possible design combinations.

Note   See Chapter 7 for information on adding an external table into a FileMaker database using *Open Database Connectivity* (ODBC) or *Java Database Connectivity* (JDBC).

While at the beginning of your FileMaker journey or when contemplating your first database, don't let the complexity of these options be a burden. It is not necessary to wrestle with them at first. However, be cognizant of the possibility to expand a solution beyond the confines of a single file and push further than the examples in this book. What starts as a single file with a handful of tables can evolve into a variety of different structural designs. A file can be combined with others, split into a *data-separation model* where interface files are linked to separate data files, and more. To summarize, a *database solution* can be constructed using any combination of any of the following:

- A custom single, self-contained, full-stack database

- A custom group of full-stack databases linked together

- A custom database acting as a back-end data source accessed by FileMaker databases, websites, or other platforms

- A custom database acting as a front-end interface, incorporating external tables from FileMaker databases or other platforms

- A custom database serving a specific data or interface function like printing specific reports, storing historical data, serving as an access point for mobile devices or web browsers, etc.

- A Claris starter template used as is or customized

- A module purchased from a third-party developer

- A file stored locally, hosted on a network server or in the cloud

Reviewing the Product Line

The FileMaker platform, summarized in Table 1-1, is made up of several applications, each designed to address a specific function in *developing, using,* and *sharing* databases.

Table 1-1. *A summary of each product in the FileMaker product line*

Product Name	Platform(s)	Develop	Use	Share
FileMaker Pro	Mac, Windows	Yes	Yes	Limited
FileMaker Server	Mac, Windows	No	No	Yes
FileMaker Cloud	Linux on AWS	No	No	Yes
FileMaker Go	iOS Devices	No	Yes	No
FileMaker WebDirect	Web Browser	No	Yes	No

Creating with FileMaker Pro

At the forefront of the product line is the flagship desktop application and the primary focus of this book, *FileMaker Pro*. This application is the modern incarnation of the legacy product, providing a multipurpose interface that can be used to *create, share,* and *access* database files on macOS and Windows computers. It is the *only* product that includes all the structural development tools required to define data models, design interface layout, and assemble scripts. It includes both front end, back end, and middleware in a single seamless low-code application programming interface.

The software provides front-end access to data through a familiar desktop document format that displays interface layouts (Chapter 3). A graphical schema editor makes it easy to define tables, fields, and relationships (Chapters 7–9). A layout editor allows rapid development of rich interfaces that render and integrate table content and interface objects (Chapters 17–22). A script editor skillfully balances object-driven construction with formula code, making it easy to create reusable sequences of automated events (Chapters 24–27). Credential management makes it simple to create secure accounts that limit user access and activity within the file using various types of internal or external authentication (Chapter 30).

Many advanced tools provide even more powerful control. Build a library of custom functions that can be reused anywhere in the file (Chapter 15). Override the entire menu bar with custom menus to take complete control of the user experience (Chapter 23). A script debugger helps identify problems and evaluate performance (Chapter 26). Save an entire database as XML, generate design reports with ease, and encrypt databases with AES 256-bit encryption to protect networked databases (Chapter 31).

Data can be shared and integrated in a variety of ways. Users and scripts can easily import and export data between databases and text-based data formats (Chapter 5). Network sharing allows workgroups to simultaneously access the same database in real time (Chapter 29). Numerous integration options are available to connect to external systems using AppleScript (macOS), Claris Connect, Dynamic Data Exchange (Windows), FileMaker API, JDBC, ODBC, SQL, and more.

Tip   Enable *Use advanced tools* under the *General* tab of application Preferences (Chapter 2) to access all advanced features.

Sharing with FileMaker Server and Cloud

Two product offerings are used exclusively to host databases on a network for team sharing: *FileMaker Server* and *FileMaker Cloud*.

FileMaker Server is a database-hosting software package offering scalable, secure, and reliable round-the-clock access to databases for authorized users. Hosted files can be simultaneously accessed by multiple users of FileMaker Pro, FileMaker Go, and FileMaker WebDirect or through other systems using hosted databases as a back-end data source. The server manages event scheduling for running database backups, system level scripts (shell script or batch file), and FileMaker scripts in a hosted database. Individual database scripts can be configured to run from the server rather than on a user's computer to offload tasks and save time. Administrators can access event and error logs to troubleshoot problems or view performance metrics to help optimize database performance. The server uses progressive downloading technology to begin streaming media content for immediate display without hesitation.

FileMaker Cloud is a Claris-managed cloud-hosting version of FileMaker Server with similar features plus full-time monitoring and support and the added ease of use for allowing remote access.

Note   Although this book is focused on using and creating databases, Chapter 29 introduces network sharing.

Accessing with FileMaker Go and WebDirect

Two offerings allow use or access to databases developed with the desktop application: *FileMaker Go* and *FileMaker WebDirect*.

FileMaker Go is an iOS-only app available free of charge from Apple's App Store that allows iPhone and iPad users to access databases when away from their desktop computer. Users can open a database stored locally on their iOS devices or access one remotely from a *FileMaker Server* or *FileMaker Cloud* server over Wi-Fi or cellular networks. Optionally, databases built for the desktop can be designed with custom scripts to detect a user's mobile device and switch to layouts designed specifically for smaller screens and touch navigation. Calculations and scripts can take advantage of iOS technologies including media capture through the camera, signature capture through the touch screen, barcode scanning, touch/face identification, and more. A database can access information about the device's battery, location, attitude, air pressure, acceleration, magnetic heading, steps, and more.

FileMaker WebDirect is the easiest way to share a database on the web. With a few settings, any database can allow access through a web browser *without* using coding tools like PHP, HTML5, CSS, or JavaScript. All the web programming required to present the database in a web front end is handled automatically by *FileMaker Server* or *Cloud*. Layouts are automatically rendered in the browser, and, except for certain incompatible script steps and the ability to work in multiple windows, most functionality is identical to that on a desktop or iOS device.

Summary

This chapter provided a brief introduction and historical overview of FileMaker, with a summary of the present-day product line. Next, we begin our exploration of the desktop application.

CHAPTER 2

Exploring the Application

FileMaker Pro is a desktop application for macOS and Windows with a dual-purpose interface that integrates features for *using* and *developing* databases. While other products in the line can *share* or *use* database, the desktop application is required to first create those databases. This chapter introduces the application, covering these topics:

- Introducing the Launch Center window

- Configuring application preferences

- Exploring menus (Browse mode)

- Accessing contextual menus

Introducing the Launch Center Window

The *Launch Center* is a multi-tabbed window used to create new databases, access existing databases, and link to educational resources. The window, shown in Figure 2-1, will automatically open when you launch the application. Later, it can be accessed by selecting any of the following items under the *File* menu, each corresponding to a tab section of the window:

- *Create New* – Opens the *Create* tab to create a database, convert files into a database, and access educational resources

- *My Apps* ➤ *Show My Apps* – Opens the *My Apps* tab to access databases from a FileMaker Cloud server (subscription required)

- *Favorites* ➤ *Show Favorites* – Opens the *Favorites* tab to access databases saved as favorites

- *Recent* ➤ *Show Recent* – Opens the *Recent* tab to access databases recently open

13

© Mark Conway Munro 2021
M. C. Munro, *Learn FileMaker Pro 19*, https://doi.org/10.1007/978-1-4842-6680-9_2

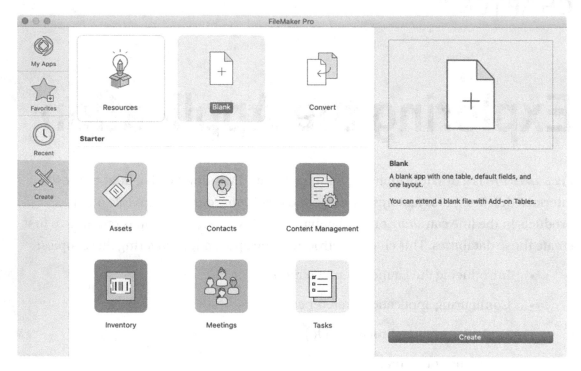

Figure 2-1. *The FileMaker Pro Launch Center*

Tip   For now, ignore these options as we continue exploring application features.
Learn more about creating files in Chapter 6.

Configuring Application Preferences

FileMaker's *application preferences* allow control and customization of key features of
the local user environment, and these should be reviewed after installation. Preference
settings are separated into five tabs: *General, Layout, Memory, Plug-ins,* and *Permitted
Hosts*. To begin, open the *Preference* window by selecting a platform-specific menu:

- macOS – *FileMaker Pro* ➤ *Preferences*

- Windows – *Edit* ➤ *Preferences*

Preferences: General

The *General* preference tab, shown in Figure 2-2, controls the user interface, username, update notifications, the availability of advanced tools, and startup file.

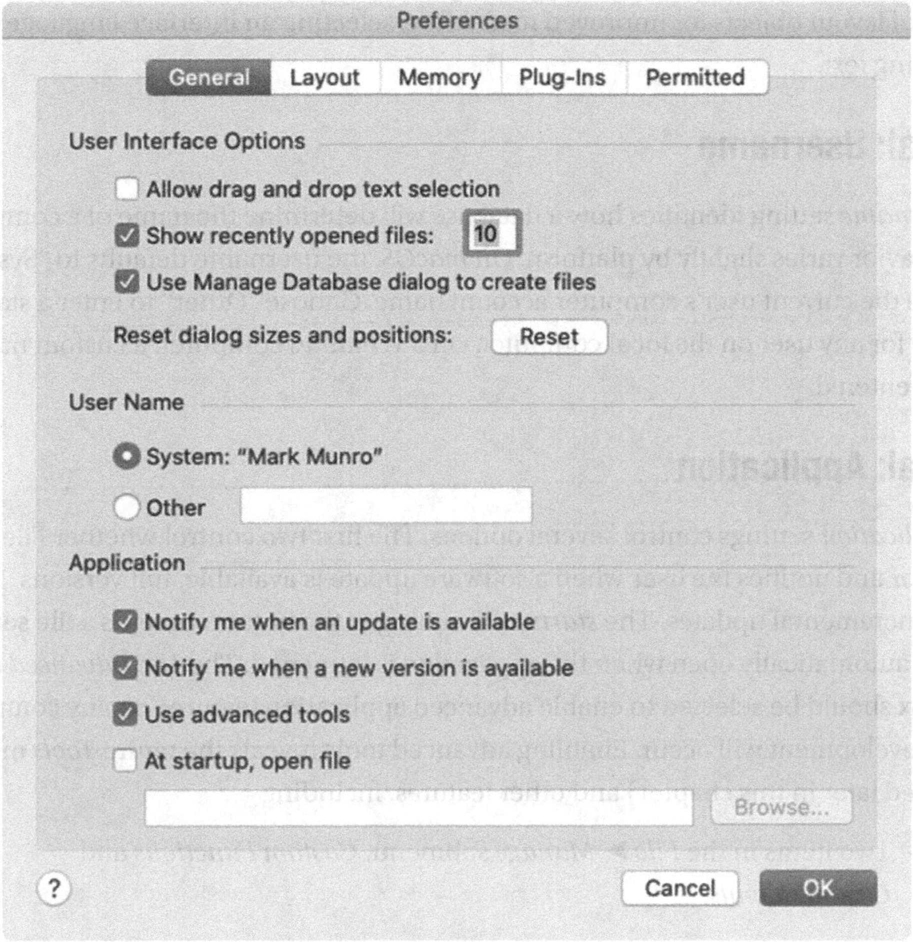

Figure 2-2. *The tab containing the application's general preferences*

General: User Interface Options

These *user interface options* control aspects of the application interface. The *Allow drag-and-drop text selection* checkbox enables dragging between fields, between layouts, and between fields and content from other applications. Take control of how many recently opened files appear in the *File* menu and *Launch Center* with the *Show recently opened files* options. Choose to enable opening the *Manage Database* window when creating a new file (Chapter 7), and click the Reset button to reset all application dialogs to default size and position.

There are a few Windows-only options, which are controlled by the operating system on Macintosh computers and not shown earlier. These include options to increase the size of layout objects for improved readability, selecting an interface language and sharpening text.

General: Username

The *username* setting identifies how a database will determine the name of a computer. The behavior varies slightly by platform. On *macOS*, the username defaults to "System" and uses the current user's computer account name. Choose "Other" to enter a static override for any user on the local computer. On a *Windows* computer, a custom name must be entered.

General: Application

The *application* settings control several options. The first two control whether FileMaker checks for and notifies the user when a software update is available, full versions and/or incremental updates. The *startup file* setting at the bottom accepts a file selection that will automatically open when the application is launched. The *Use advanced tools* checkbox should be selected to enable advanced application features on any computer where development will occur. Enabling advanced tools reveals the entire *Tools* menu (discussed later in this chapter) and other features, including

- Two items in the *File* ➤ *Manage* submenu, *Custom Functions* and *Custom Menus*

- Using copy-paste with tables, field definitions, and themes

- The ability to import tables

Tip   Enable advanced tools and then quit and relaunch the app.

Preferences: Layout

The *Layout* preference tab, shown in Figure 2-3, affects Layout mode behavior (Part 4).

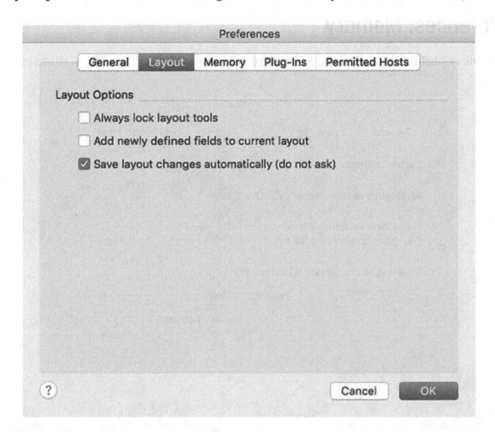

Figure 2-3. *The tab containing the application's layout preferences*

Selecting *Always lock layout tools* enables automatic locking of a selected layout tool until another layout tool is selected. Default behavior reverts to the cursor after an action with another tool. Disabling this may be preferable as there is a way to manually lock a tool selection.

The *Add newly defined fields to current layout* will add newly defined fields at the bottom of the current layout and will expand the layout to accommodate. This can be annoying since a carefully sized layout suddenly increases in height to accommodate roughly placed new fields with a default styling. It is usually easier to just manually add new fields to a layout after creating them.

The *Save layout changes automatically* option will automatically save changes made in Layout mode when switching back to Browse mode *without confirmation dialog*.

Consider turning this off to avoid saving accidental changes until you are confident in your knowledge of layout design.

Preferences: Memory

The *Memory* preference tab, shown in Figure 2-4, controls the file cache settings.

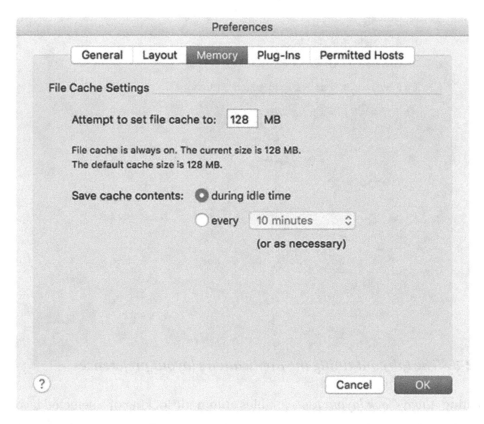

Figure 2-4. *The tab containing the application's memory preferences*

As changes are made to a database's structure or content, FileMaker stores changes in the RAM cache and periodically writes the accumulated data to the hard disk. The settings on the *File Cache* preferences tab control how often the cache is saved. The *Attempt to set file cache to* setting allocates an amount of memory for the file cache. Use a higher value for improved performance and a lower value for less risk of data loss after a crash. Choose when the cached data is written to disk by choosing a *Save cache contents* option: *during idle time* or *at a specified interval*. The default settings here are usually fine for most solutions.

Note   Relaunch the application for cache changes to take effect.

Preferences: Plug-Ins

The *Plug-In* preference tab contains a list of installed plug-ins (Chapter 28).

Preferences: Permitted Hosts

The *Permitted Hosts* preference tab lists any host computers whose SSL certificates cannot be verified. When a user attempts to connect to an unsecured host, FileMaker asks the user if they want to accept the connection and then adds it to this list. Any prior connections can be removed from the list here and will then require re-approval on the next connection.

Exploring Menus (Browse Mode)

The default Browse mode menu bar, shown in Figure 2-5, contains commands for data entry and switching to other modes, including the deeper developer interface used to define database structure and design layouts.

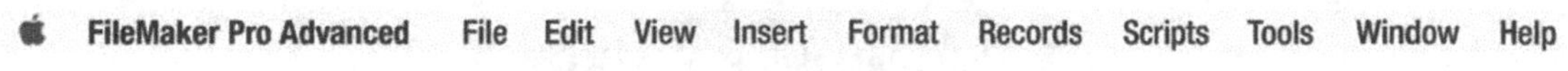

 FileMaker Pro Advanced   File   Edit   View   Insert   Format   Records   Scripts   Tools   Window   Help

Figure 2-5.   *The default Browse mode menu bar*

This section introduces the default Browse mode menus. There are many contextually sensitive items that are not enabled under various circumstances, e.g., no database is open, a script is running or paused, a modal window is open, or a user's login account (Chapter 30) doesn't grant them access to the feature. Similarly, some or all menus may be completely different under a variety of other conditions, including

- The *Launch Center* window or another file dialog is open.
- A window is in a non-Browse mode: Find (Chapter 4), Preview (Chapter 4), or Layout (Chapter 17) modes.

- A modifier key such as Option is held down.

- A developer dialog is open.

- The database is using a custom menu set (Chapter 23).

FileMaker Pro Menu

The *FileMaker Pro* menu, shown in Figure 2-6, is a macOS-only menu that contains access to information about the application, preferences, and some operating system features. These are used to get information about the application, open the preferences window, and hide or quit the app and may include services from the operating system and other applications. On Windows, this menu doesn't exist, so *Preferences* are available under the *Edit* menu, and an *Exit* item is added under the *File* menu to quit the application.

Figure 2-6. *The FileMaker Pro application menu*

File Menu

The *File* menu, shown in Figure 2-7, contains many file and developer-related functions. The menu's functions include accessing, configuring, printing, transferring data, and more.

The *Create New* item at the top opens the corresponding tab of the *Launch Center* window, providing access to resources, starter templates, and spreadsheet conversion functions and creating a new blank database. The next four submenu items each provide resource access with an option open a window or directly access a resource.

The *My Apps, Favorites,* and *Recent* submenus each correspond to a *Launch Center* tab providing access to databases in a cloud account, saved as favorite or recently accessed. The *Hosts* submenu provides access to hosted databases with an option to open a Hosts window that summarizes servers by cloud, favorites, and local with an option to add, edit, or remove hosts (Chapter 29).

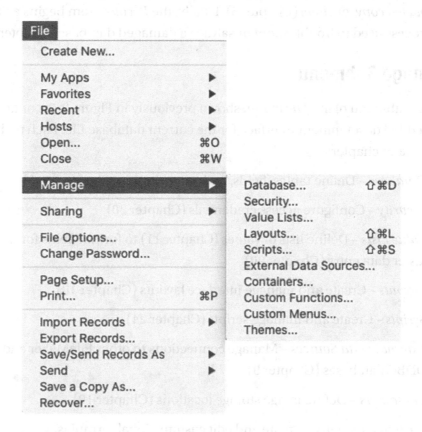

Figure 2-7. *The File menu and Manage submenu*

The *Manage* submenu provides access to development options (described later in this chapter), while the *Sharing* submenu provides control over who can access the current database across a network and the local application's ability to share open files (Chapter 29). *File Options* opens a dialog of settings for the current database (Chapter 6), and *Change Password* opens a dialog allowing a user to change the password for the current user account if that capability is permitted by their security privileges (Chapter 30).

At the top of the output options is *Page Setup* (called *Print Setup* on Windows) and *Print* which provide access to typical operating system dialogs used to configure the current window for printing. Next, the *Import Records* and *Export Records* options provide options for transferring data into or out of the current database (Chapter 5). The *Save/Send Record As* submenu allows records to be saved as an Excel or PDF file or a Snapshot link to a set of records (Chapter 29). The *Send* submenu has options for creating a manual email or creating an email with a FileMaker URL link to the current database (Chapter 31). The *Save a Copy As* menu can save the entire database as a *copy, compacted copy,* or *clone* (Chapter 6). Finally, the *Recover* item begins a database recovery process used to troubleshoot or salvage a damaged database (Chapter 6).

File: Manage Submenu

The *Manage* submenu of the *File* menu, shown previously in Figure 2-7, contains access to the embedded development interface for the current database file. Each of these is discussed in later chapters:

- *Database* – Define tables, fields, and relationships (Chapters 7–9)

- *Security* – Configure access credentials (Chapter 30)

- *Value Lists* – Define lists of values (Chapter 11) to format fields for faster data entry (Chapter 20)

- *Layouts* – Create and manage interface layouts (Chapter 18)

- *Scripts* – Create and manage scripts (Chapter 24)

- *External Data Sources* – Manage connections to other FileMaker and ODBC databases (Chapter 9)

- *Containers* – Define image storage locations (Chapter 10)

- *Custom Functions* – Create and edit custom global formulas (Chapter 15)

- *Custom Menus* – Create and edit custom menus (Chapter 23)

- *Themes* – Create and edit object styles (Chapter 22)

Edit Menu

The *Edit* menu contains standard features that are enabled when editing the contents of a field such as *Undo*, *Cut*, *Copy*, *Paste*, *Clear*, and *Select All*. These are ubiquitous computer functions and need no further description. However, a few others are worth mentioning. The *Find/Replace* menu contains functions for doing text replacements within a field for one or more records, while *Spelling* contains options for correcting text selected within a field or stepping through every field on the layout (Chapter 4). The *Export Field Contents* item opens a dialog to specify a name and location of a file in which to save the contents of the current field (Chapter 10).

View Menu

The *View menu, shown in Figure* 2-8, contains functions that control the view of the database. The first four items are viewing modes: *Browse* (default for data entry), *Find* to begin a search (Chapter 4), *Layout* to design interfaces (Chapter 17), and *Preview* to prepare for printing (Chapter 4). The *Go to Layout* submenu contains a list of layout choices allowing manual navigation between them. The three *View As* options invoke a new content view to the current layout. The togglable *Status Toolbar* item controls the visibility of the window's toolbar, while *Customize Status Toolbar* opens a customization dialog. *Formatting Bar* and *Ruler* each toggle the visibility of an additional horizontal extension of the toolbar, while the window magnification can be increased or decreased by 50% using *Zoom In* and *Zoom Out*. Most of these are discussed in Chapter 3.

Figure 2-8. *The View menu*

Insert Menu

The *Insert* menu contains contextually sensitive functions for inserting files or text into a field (Chapter 4, "Modifying Field Contents").

Format Menu

The *Format* menu contains submenus for standard text styling functions when editing field content including *Font, Size, Style, Alignment, Spacing,* and *Color.*

Records Menu

The *Records* menu, shown in Figure 2-9, contains functions for *creating, duplicating, deleting, navigating, including, excluding, sorting,* and *manipulating* (Chapter 4).

Figure 2-9. *The Records menu*

Scripts Menu

The *Scripts* menu provides access to the *Script Workspace* window and displays a list of individual scripts that have been configured to appear here (Chapter 24).

Tools Menu

The *Tools* menu, shown in Figure 2-10, contains access to key development functions and is only available when the *Use advanced tools* preferences is enabled.

Figure 2-10. The Tools menu

The top three items provide access to debugging features (Chapter 26). The *Custom Menus* submenu is used to define and select a custom menu set (Chapter 23). Analysis tools like *Save a Copy as XML* and *Database Design Report* are used to create readable documents listing internal structural resources (Chapter 31) for analysis or storage. *Developer Utilities* opens a dialog with file encryption and other features (Chapter 31). Finally, the *Tools Marketplace* provides a quick link to the online *Claris Marketplace* where you can download or purchase development tools from third parties.

Window Menu

The *Window* menu contains many window-related functions used to create additional windows for a database or choosing among multiple windows for any open database (Chapter 3).

Help Menu

The *Help menu* provides access to online resources including a help guide, learning resources, upgrades, the community website, and other application-related functions.

Accessing Contextual Menus

There are numerous *contextual menus* that appear within FileMaker's user and developer interfaces when the user right-clicks on regions or objects. These are summarized by field, record content area, web viewers, and windows. Each menu provides a specific shortcut to contextually relevant commands based on the context of the click. As you begin exploring databases in subsequent chapters, look for these time-saving menus as a faster alternative to searching the crowded menu bar.

Contextual Menus for Fields

There are six contextual menus for fields. These all contain cut-copy-paste functions with other functions varying by field type or window mode:

- *Text-Based Field (Browse Mode)* – Formatting, inserting, sorting, searching, charting, and exporting

- *Text-Based Field (Find Mode)* – Insert operator

- *Container Field (Browse Mode)* – Inserting file and exporting the contents of the field

- *Summary Field (Browse Mode)* – Formatting, charting, and exporting

- *Toolbar* ➤ *Quick Search Field (Browse Mode)* – Spell and grammar check, text substitutions, transformations, and speech functions

- *Any Field (Layout Mode)* – Text orientation, object style selection, specifying the field, configuring as a button, defining conditional formatting, configuring script triggers, formatting, and arranging

Contextual Menus for Record Content Area

The content area of a database window has a contextual menu that varies depending on the window mode:

- *Browse Mode* – Copy, create, duplicate, delete, sort, and save/send records
- *Find Mode* – Copy, add, and delete find requests
- *Preview Mode* – Copy the page, configure the page, and print
- *Layout Mode* – Paste, set background style, and open dialogs for theme and layout setup

Contextual Menus for Web Viewers

There two contextual menus for Web Viewers that vary by window mode:

- *Browse Mode* – One option to reload the content
- *Layout Mode* – Functions to cut-copy-paste, set style, configure as a button, configure the viewer settings, define conditional formatting, configure script triggers, and set various formatting options

Contextual Menus for Window Components

These three contextual menus appear on various window component:

- *Layout Part* (Layout mode) – Open the *Part Definition* dialog, and choose the style or fill color of the part
- *Ruler* – Choose points, inches, or centimeters as the unit of measure
- *Toolbar* – Open the toolbar customization dialog

Contextual Menus for Calculation Formulas

Every instance of the *Specify Calculation* dialog (Chapter 12) has a contextual menu that includes text manipulation functions that vary slightly depending on if text is selected or not.

Summary

This chapter introduced the basics of the *FileMaker Pro* desktop application, covering topics such as the default windows, preferences, and various menus. Next, we begin exploring a database window.

Exploring a Database Window

A *database window* is a view into an open database file. As a full-stack development environment, FileMaker's windows have different window modes for data entry and development. This chapter begins an exploration of a database window from a *user perspective*, covering these topics:

- Identifying window regions and modes

- Exploring the window header

- Managing multiple windows

Since we don't discuss creating database files until Chapter 6, to follow along with the exploration of the window interface, take a moment to download the Learn FileMaker sample files from the Apress website (*https://www.apress.com/9781484266793*), and open the *Chapter 3-5* file. This example contains a simple *Contacts* table with two layouts with a simple custom theme to render nice example pictures for the book.

Identifying Window Regions and Modes

A database window, shown in Figure 3-1, is divided into two primary regions: *toolbar* and *content area*. The *toolbar*, discussed later in this chapter, is the header containing two rows of controls that are uniform to all databases with some customization options. The *content area* includes the area below the toolbar that displays a custom user interface designed by a developer. In this example, the window is preconfigured with a few simple interface elements. When creating a new blank file (Chapter 6), this area would be completely blank and require a layout design (Chapters 17–22) which can be more graphically elaborate. This area displays one layout at a time but can switch between any number of layouts created in the file. The rendering method of content varies by the selected *window mode* and *content view.*

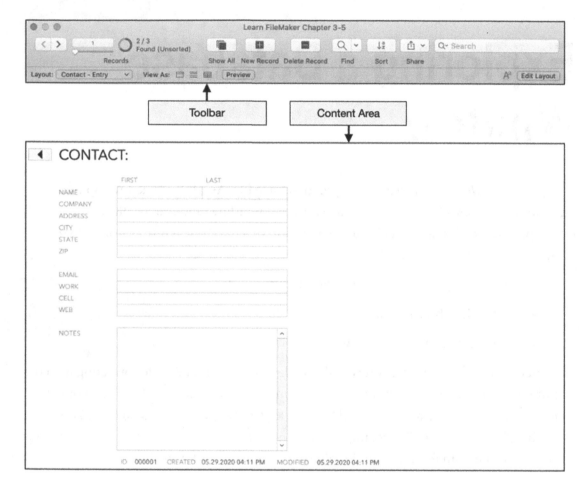

Figure 3-1. *The two window areas, toolbar (top) and content area (bottom)*

Defining Window Modes

A *window mode* is a display state that optimizes a window's interface for a specific functional purpose. FileMaker has four modes that are described across several different chapters: *Browse, Find, Preview,* and *Layout.*

Browse mode is the default window state and is used to interact with the content of a database and perform data entry–related tasks. In Browse mode, the content area of the window renders a set of records from a layout's table. Depending on the design of the layout and account permissions, a user can interact with the data to create, view, edit, delete, duplicate, search, sort, and omit records as well as interact with other objects.

Find mode is a window state used to enter search criteria. In Find mode, the layout transforms into a blank record-like *request* into which the user enters criteria defining a desired set of records prior to performing a search.

Preview mode is a window state that acts like a print preview, displaying the current layout and found set of records as they would appear on a printed page. The layout will appear similar to Browse mode but be presented in a nonfunctional state. So, fields will not be editable, and buttons that aren't hidden appear as non-clickable art. Also, objects may hide, slide, compress, summarize, and change formatting depending on how they are defined on the layout.

Layout mode is a window state used to create interface layouts. Special design tools are used to add and configure objects to the layout.

Each mode has a unique toolbar, menu bar, and content area rendering methodology. Depending on their access permissions (Chapter 30), a user can change the mode of a window by clicking a mode button in the status toolbar, selecting a mode from the *View* menu, or running a script that changes the mode. Using Browse mode is discussed in this chapter and in Chapter 4 along with using Find and Preview modes. Designing custom interface elements in Layout mode is explored in Chapters 17–22.

Defining Content Views

A *content view* is an interface setting that determines how records are displayed in the content area of a window in Browse mode. Depending on restrictions enforced by the layout settings (Chapter 18, "Views"), a user can choose to view records in up to three formats: *Form, List,* or *Table*. The current view of a layout can be changed by selecting a menu item under the *View* menu, clicking a *View As* icon in the toolbar, or running a script that changes the view.

In *Form view,* the window displays one record at a time rendered into one set of all the layout elements. To see other records in this view, use the navigation controls in the toolbar or custom interface elements designed to go to other records. This is analogous to looking at one sheet of paper pulled out of a file cabinet or a single page in a book.

In *List view,* the window displays a continuous list of records that are rendered by repeating the layout elements once for each. In this view, the user can scroll up or down to see other records. This is analogous to looking across a sequence of tabs on folders in a file cabinet or at a book's table of contents.

In *Table view,* the window displays a set of records in a spreadsheet-style format of columns and rows while excluding other graphical elements that are present on the layout. The user can rearrange and resize columns by dragging their headings. They can sort the records by clicking on a heading. New fields (columns) and new records (rows) can be created intuitively in a manner somewhat similar to a spreadsheet. An action pop-up menu is hidden within each field's heading and provides quick access to various features including sorting, summarization, field control, and view control. Table views aren't high on design and customized functionality, but they provide a more familiar environment for those used to working with spreadsheets and may be suitable for simple databases that don't require an elaborate interface.

Exploring the Window Header

There are three horizontal bars that can be displayed or hidden in the toolbar area of a window depending on the user's access privileges, preferences, and the settings established by the developer. These are the *Status Toolbar*, *Formatting Bar,* and *Ruler*.

Status Toolbar (Browse Mode)

The *Status Toolbar* is the most prominent area running along the top of the window containing controls pertinent to the current window mode. It is the only part of the window header that is visible by default. Unless hidden and locked by a script, users can toggle the visibility of the toolbar by selecting *View* ➤ *Status* from the menu.

Default Toolbar Items (Browse Mode)

The default toolbar configuration for Browse mode is shown in Figure 3-2. The top portions are customizable (discussed later in this section), and the bottom are static.

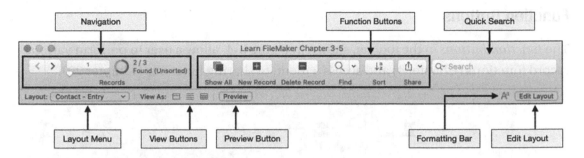

Figure 3-2. *The anatomy of the default Browse mode toolbar configuration*

Record Navigation Controls

The *record navigation controls* in the toolbar, shown in Figure 3-3, display information about the records being viewed and allow a user to move around within the found set of records (Chapter 4).

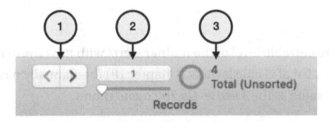

Figure 3-3. *The default Browse mode navigation controls*

The toolbar's navigation controls are

1. *Record Navigation Arrows* – Click to move to the previous or next record.

2. *Record Number & Slider* – The number of the current record. Move the slider or type a record number to jump to another record.

3. *Found Set Status* – Shows the total record count, the found set count (if a subset of the total), and the sort status. When viewing a subset, click the circle icon to toggle between found and omitted records.

Function Buttons

The *function buttons* in the toolbar, shown in Figure 3-4, allow a user to perform various record functions (Chapter 4) and access a menu of sharing functions (Chapter 29).

Figure 3-4. *The default toolbar buttons in Browse mode*

Quick Find Search Field

At the top right of the toolbar is a search field used to perform a *Quick Find* (Chapter 4, "Searching with Quick Find").

Layout Menu

The lower, non-customizable level of the toolbar starts with the *Layout* menu. In Browse mode, this displays a list of visible layouts (Chapter 18) for manually navigating to another layout, the same as the *View ➤ Go To Layout* menu.

Content View Buttons

Next in the lower bar are three *content view buttons* used to change the content as formatted in the window view as described earlier in this chapter. The view buttons enabled here are controlled by the current layout's view settings (Chapter 18).

Preview Button

The toolbar's *Preview button* changes the window into Preview mode (Chapter 4).

Formatting Bar Button

The *Formatting Bar button* toggles the visibility of a text-editing control bar between the status toolbar and the content area of the window (described later in this chapter).

Edit Layout Button

The *Edit Layout button* changes the window to Layout mode (Chapter 17).

Customizing the Toolbar (Browse Mode)

The controls in the top portion of the toolbar are customizable at the user-computer level. This means that a user can customize the inclusion and arrangement of controls in the toolbar, which affect all databases they open on their computer. With a database open, select the *View ➤ Customize Status Toolbar* menu to open a customization panel. On macOS, this is a graphical panel attached to the window as shown in Figure 3-5. On the lower left of this dialog is a *Show* menu that controls the button format in the toolbar. The choices are as follows: *Icon only, Text only,* or the default, *Icon and text*. On Windows, a less attractive list-based dialog appears with similar drag and drop options.

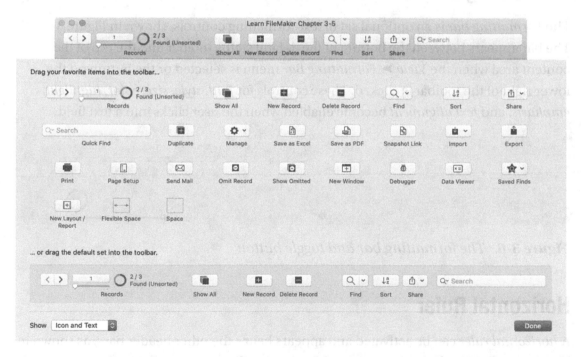

Figure 3-5. *The toolbar customization panel for Browse mode (macOS)*

Adding, Removing, and Rearranging Toolbar Items

To add an item to the toolbar, drag an icon from the customization panel up into the toolbar area and drop it. FileMaker will avoid duplication by automatically replacing an object already present in the toolbar when that same control is dropped elsewhere. To remove an item, drag it until it clears the toolbar area and release the mouse button. Items can be rearranged by dragging them around within the toolbar.

Restoring the Default Toolbar Set

To restore the default control set, drag the group in the rectangle at the bottom of the panel and drop it in the toolbar.

Formatting Bar

The *Formatting bar* is an optional set of text-formatting controls, shown in Figure 3-6. The bar appears between the bottom of the default status toolbar and the top of the content area when the *View ➤ Formatting Bar* menu is selected or the button on the lower right of the toolbar is clicked. These controls for *font, style, size, color, highlight, emphasis,* and *text alignment* become enabled when the user clicks into a text field.

Figure 3-6. *The formatting bar and toggle button*

Horizontal Ruler

A *horizontal ruler* can be activated and appears below the other header bars, as shown in Figure 3-7. The *View ➤ Ruler* menu toggles the visibility of this ruler. The *measurement unit* of the ruler can be changed using its contextual menu, with a choice of *centimeters, inches,* and *points*. The Browse mode ruler isn't useful until focus is inside a text field and it shrinks to the size of the field and shows tabs and margins. These settings can also be modified with layout tools (Chapter 19, "Exploring the Inspector Pane").

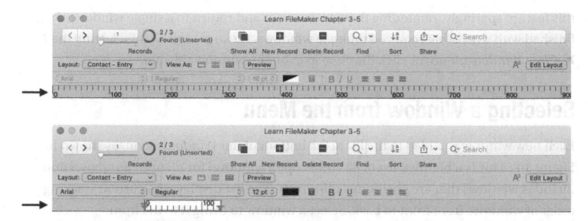

Figure 3-7. *A ruler visible (top) and when a field has focus (bottom)*

Using Multiple Windows

When a database is opened, a window automatically appears and displays a default layout. Users can navigate to other layouts within that window, or they can open additional windows to access multiple simultaneous views into the same file. They can view any combination of layouts and found sets of records. For example, a *Contact* record can be viewed in one window, a *Contact* list in another, and a *Company* list in a third. Opening a new window allows the preservation of a position in a found set in one window while performing work on other records in the same or different tables. Users and scripts can open and close windows as needed to complete a task more efficiently. Scripts can create new windows off-screen to perform work without disrupting the current view (Chapter 25).

Creating a New Window

Select the *Window ➤ New Window* menu to manually create a new window. The new window will open in front of and slightly offset from the current window. It will start as an exact duplicate with the same properties of the current window: *name (with suffix), mode, view, dimensions, toolbar visibility, layout, found set,* and *current record.* Once open, these can be changed by searching, navigating, moving, and resizing.

Multiple windows are great for viewing records side by side or alternating between different work. However, conflict warnings will occur if a user tries to edit a record that is busy with active focus in another window. So, it is a good idea to encourage users to use this feature sparingly, reminding them to close out and return to a single window when finished with a task that required multiple windows. Close a window by selecting the *File* ➤ *Close Window* menu, or click the close icon on the window title bar.

Selecting a Window from the Menu

Each new window is added to the list at the bottom of the *Window* menu, as shown in Figure 3-8. This is a blended list of all visible open windows for *all open databases* and includes windows that are positioned off-screen. The list displays the current stacking order of windows from front to back. Select a window to bring it to the front.

Figure 3-8. *The bottom of the Window menu lists all visible windows*

Hiding and Showing Windows

A window can be hidden from view while remaining open. This happens automatically when a database opens a database to access resources in it or when a script explicitly hides the window. A user can manually hide a window by selecting the *Window* ➤ *Hide Window* menu. Every hidden window is listed under the *Window* ➤ *Show Window* submenu, as shown in Figure 3-9. Selecting a window from this list will make it visible and bring it to the front. The *Bring All To Front* item makes all hidden windows visible. Windows off-screen can be brought back into view all at once and arranged neatly with onscreen windows using *Tile Horizontally*, *Tile Vertically*, and *Cascade Windows*. A window can be minimized to the macOS or Windows dock by selecting the *Minimize Window* menu item. When minimized, it is listed as an open window in the menu but must be selected to bring it back into view.

Figure 3-9. *The submenu containing hidden windows*

Summary

This chapter explored the anatomy of a window, toolbar controls, and managing multiple windows. In the next chapter, we begin working with records.

CHAPTER 4

Working with Records

A *record* is a primary unit of content in a table, one group of values that together represent a particular entity. Using the spreadsheet metaphor to analogize a database file to a spreadsheet file, a table is like a sheet, a field like a column, and a record is like a row. In a *Contacts* table, a record represents *a person,* while a record in an *Inventory* table represents *one product*. When working in a database, users spend most of their time performing tasks that involve creating, editing, deleting, omitting, searching, exporting, importing, printing, and viewing records. Although a database can contain many different tables each with its own collection of records, this chapter uses the *Learn FileMaker Chapter 3-5* sample file with a single *Contacts* table. This simplifies examples and provides the basic context necessary for later development of more complex custom solutions. This chapter explores user interactions with records, covering the following topics:

- Entering data
- Creating, deleting, and duplicating records
- Searching records
- Working with found sets
- Printing

Entering Data

A data entry task involves opening a record, focusing on a field, modifying field contents, moving from field to field, and then committing (closing) a record or reverting it.

© Mark Conway Munro 2021
M. C. Munro, *Learn FileMaker Pro 19*, https://doi.org/10.1007/978-1-4842-6680-9_4

Opening a Record

Opening a record transforms the fields on a layout from displaying information into an editable state ready for data input. To open the current record for data entry, click into any editable field on the layout, or type the Tab key to enter the first editable field.

Understanding Field Focus

A field has *focus* when it is currently ready to accept input. Only one field can have active focus at a time, and this fact is visually indicated by a text cursor blinking within the field. The visual appearance of the field may also change depending on the layout settings applied to its *in focus* state (Chapter 22, "Editing an Object's Style Settings"). A layout should be designed to provide some visual change to make clear to users that the record is opened and which field will receive their input. For example, the field borders might become visible, change thickness, or have a color applied. The field's fill color can also change. In the Learn FileMaker sample file, focus is indicated by a simple darker border, as shown in Figure 4-1. Focus can be shifted to other fields by either clicking on them with the cursor or typing the Tab or other key(s) that move focus to the next field in the *tab order* based on the field settings (Chapter 21).

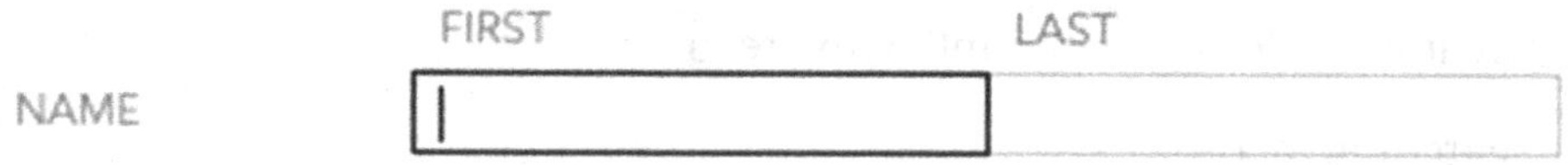

Figure 4-1. *A field in focus in the Learn FileMaker sample file*

Modifying Field Contents

Once a record is open and a field has focus, the value in the field can be changed in several different ways depending on the field's data type (Chapter 8) or the layout behavior and formatting options (Chapters 19 and 20). These may include *typing, cut, copy-paste, undo-redo, insert functions,* or *mouse clicks*.

The most common method of entering data into any data entry field is by simply *typing* on the keyboard. As long as a field is in focus, anything typed will flow in as its content.

Like most applications, FileMaker's *Edit* menu has commands for *cut, copy, paste, undo,* and *redo*. These functions only affect content stored in fields while they are in focus. Undo, for example, will step back text changes just made in the active field but does not reverse actions such as record creation or deletion and doesn't work after changes are committed when a record closes.

When *drag and drop* is enabled in the application preferences (Chapter 2), text can be dragged to rearrange it within a field. It can also be dragged from one field to another, between fields in different windows and between fields and text in other applications.

The *Insert* menu and similarly named submenu of a field's contextual menu contain functions for quickly inserting content into fields. Each is contextually enabled depending on the data type of the field in focus (Chapter 8) and the field's editable status on the layout (Chapter 19). Inserting different files is made possible by selecting the *Insert Picture, Insert Audio/Video, Insert PDF,* or *Insert File* functions. Quickly insert the *Current Date, Current Time,* or *Current Username* using other functions. The *From Index* option is used to select and insert a value into the current field from an indexed list of values entered into that field on any record. The *From Last Visited Record* option inserts the value of the current field from the last record viewed.

Finally, fields can also be configured with a *control style* that allows data entry with mouse clicks. For example, a *check box* style allows selection of boxes to enter a value, while a *calendar* style provides a graphical calendar for date entries (Chapter 20).

Closing a Record

After editing, a record must be *closed* to commit or revert changes. *Reverting* closes a record and omits all changes made during the session. A record can be reverted by selecting the *Record ➤ Revert Record* menu or running a script that performs the function of the same name. *Committing* a record closes the record while saving changes made during the session. During this process, FileMaker will perform data entry validations and report problems if any are detected. A record can be committed numerous ways. Manually commit a record by typing the Enter key or clicking on the layout's background, away from other objects. Other actions that will commit the current record include navigating to another record, creating a new record, closing the current window, closing the file, or running a script that uses the *Commit Records/Request* script step.

Tip   A layout can be configured to automatically save changes or present a confirmation dialog when committing (Chapter 18).

Creating, Deleting, and Duplicating Records

Users can *create, delete, delete all,* and *duplicate* records. All of these commands are accessible to users through the *Records* menu or a custom script. Some are also accessible through a toolbar icon or the *record contextual menu* on the background of a layout.

The *New Record* function will create a new blank record in the current layout's table of the front window and automatically open it with focus in the first field.

The *Delete Record* function will permanently delete the current record in the window after presenting a warning dialog to confirm the user's intent. A user can bypass this warning dialog and instantly delete a record by holding Option (macOS) or Shift (Windows) while selecting the *Delete Record* option. While this may be a useful tip for power users, it can be dangerous and shouldn't be shared with new users. It may be prudent to disable this ability using custom menus (Chapter 23). The *Delete All Records* function will delete every record being viewed in the found set.

The *Duplicate Record* function will create a duplicate of the current record with all local field values retained.

Tip   To reset the *Learn FileMaker Chapter 3-5* sample data, choose the *Reset Sample Records* under the *Scripts* menu.

Searching Records

A FileMaker table can contain a maximum of 64 quadrillion total records. While most tables will likely never reach that number, as the number grows, it becomes increasingly difficult to find a specific record. Scrolling through even a few hundred records to find one is unnecessarily time-consuming. Instead, a *record search* can quickly create a smaller temporary subset of records based on user-specified criteria. Searching helps users locate records for data entry work but also isolates a group of records for processes like printing or exporting. FileMaker offers several methods for searching records: *fast searches* using *quick find* or *field selection, Find mode* to build complex finds, *SQL queries* (Chapter 16), or *custom scripts* (Chapter 24).

Caution   Except for SQL Queries, all searches are *context sensitive* and executed from the perspective of a window's layout!

Performing Fast Searches

FileMaker offers two options for performing a single-criterion search: *Quick Find* and *Find Matching*.

Searching with Quick Find

The *Quick Find* feature searches for records in the current layout's table where some criteria are found in any field on the layout that is configured specifically for quick find inclusion (Chapter 19, "Inspecting the Data Settings"). To perform this type of find manually, enter a word or phrase into the search field located in the toolbar, shown in Figure 4-2, and then type the Enter key. The records visible in the window will be updated to only those with the matching value in a field, and the found/total record counts in the navigation area will reflect the difference. Click the magnifier icon in the quick find field to see a list of recent searches from any table in the file, and select one to repeat it for the current layout's table.

Figure 4-2.   *The Quick Find field in the toolbar*

Caution   After searching, the text remains in the search field but doesn't interact with the found set. If the user or a script changes the found set, the criteria linger as an obsolete reminder of the last search, no longer relevant to the records actually displayed.

Searching with Find Matching

A *find matching* type of search uses the text selection within a field as the criteria to quickly search for any records containing that value in the same field. There are three functions available by highlighting some text in a field and right-clicking to access the contextual menu, shown in Figure 4-3. Each of these functions will perform a predefined type of search by matching the selected value in the current field. The *Find Matching Records* option performs a new find for records where the field contains the selected value. The others modify the current found set; *Constrain Found Set* performs a narrowing find that retains only those records in the found set where the field contains the selected value, and *Extend Found Set* performs an expanding find that adds to the found set any records where the field contains the selected value.

Figure 4-3. *The find matching records functions of a field's contextual menu*

Using Find Mode

For more complex searching tasks, *Find mode* is a transitional window state that changes the menu, toolbar, and content area for flexible entry of search criteria, as shown in Figure 4-4. To begin, enter Find mode by selecting *Find Mode* under the *View* menu or clicking the *Find* toolbar icon.

Figure 4-4. *A window rendered in Find mode transforms to show find requests and search-related toolbar functions*

Status Toolbar (Find Mode)

The Find mode toolbar changes to search-specific buttons, either the default Find options or the user's customized set.

Default Toolbar Items (Find Mode)

The default toolbar for Find mode is shown in Figure 4-5. Similar to Browse mode, the top portion can be customized, and the bottom is static.

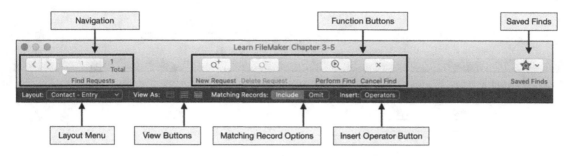

Figure 4-5. *The anatomy of the default Find mode toolbar*

Navigation Controls

The *navigation controls* in Find mode are similar to those in Browse mode except that they display information and navigation options pertaining to *find requests* instead of records.

Function Buttons

The *function buttons* in the Find mode toolbar are

- *New Request* – Create a new find request to enter alternate criteria

- *Delete Request* – Delete the current find request

- *Perform Find* – Execute the find and returns to browse mode with the resulting found set

- *Cancel Find* – Return the window to Browse mode with the previous found set

Saved Finds Menu

The *Saved Finds* button on the far right of the toolbar provides access to a menu of Finds explicitly saved for the current table. These can be selected to instantly perform a find instead of entering custom criteria. See "Working with Saved Finds" later in this chapter.

Layout Menu

The lower, non-customizable level of the Find mode toolbar starts with the *Layout* menu. This works the same as in Browse mode allowing a user to switch layouts. In Find mode, this can be useful if the user wishes to create a find using multiple fields that are only visible on different layouts. However, since a find requires a table context, at the time of execution, *only criteria entered on layouts for the same table as the current layout will be considered part of the request*. Therefore, use this only to access fields on layouts for a single table since others will be ignored.

Content View Buttons

The *Content View buttons* work the same as in Browse (Chapter 3), rendering content as a list, form, or table.

Matching Records Options

The *Matching Records options* are two togglable options that determine if records matching the current find request will be *included* or *omitted* from the resulting found set. See "Specifying a Matching Record Option" later in this chapter.

Insert Operators Menu

The *Insert Operators* menu contains search operators that can be inserted into a field with or without other criteria to enhance the search parameters. See "Using Search Operators" later in this chapter.

Customizing the Toolbar (Find Mode)

The Find mode toolbar is customizable at the user-computer level. Enter Find mode and select the *View ➤ Customize Toolbar* menu to open the customization panel attached to the window as shown in Figure 4-6. Although the available buttons are different, they can be added or removed as described for Browse mode in Chapter 3.

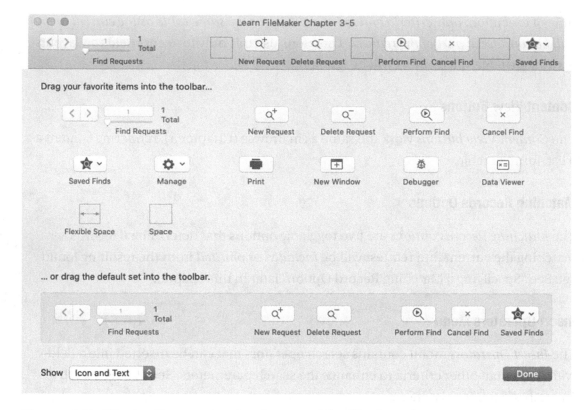

Figure 4-6. *The toolbar customization panel for Find mode*

Entering Criteria and Performing the Find

In Find mode, the window's content area is rendered as a blank version of the current layout, called a *find request.* This appears similar to a record but is used to enter search criteria. Unlike with the *Quick Find* and *Find Matching Record* functions where users search for one piece of information at a time, a find request allows criteria to be typed into more than one field. Users type criteria into specific fields to build more precise and complex search requests. Criteria can be typed, pasted, or inserted into fields and can be combined with search operators. For records to qualify as a match, they must match all of the values entered in a single request.

Once the desired criteria are entered into the appropriate fields, the search process can be performed by either typing Enter, clicking the *Perform Find* toolbar button, or selecting the *Requests ➤ Perform Find* menu. FileMaker will search the current table for matching criteria in the fields indicated and display a found set of the results. If there are no results, a dialog will offer the user an option to return to Find mode and edit the criteria or cancel the process and return to Browse mode.

Try searching the *Learn FileMaker* sample records for a resulting found set of contacts who work for a specific company, as shown in Figure 4-7, and follow these steps:

1. Enter Find mode.

2. Click into the *Company* field.

3. Type some or all of the desired value, e.g., "Widget."

4. Click the *Perform Find* button in the toolbar or type Enter.

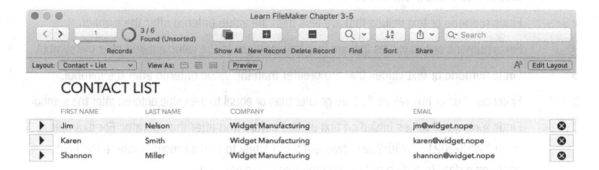

Figure 4-7. *The resulting found set of a search shows only matching records*

Experiment with different mixtures of criteria. For example, search for "Widget" in the *Company* field and "Karen" in the *First Name* field. Since the results must contain both values, only one record will be returned as a match.

Using Search Operators

A *search operator* is a character or set of characters that are used to narrow the focus of search criteria typed in a field. Without an operator, FileMaker defaults to a "begins with" type search, where matches are found at the beginning of words. So, searching for "Widget" or "Wid Manu" or "W M" would all find records with "Widget Manufacturing" in the field. Operators, described in Table 4-1, can be added to a field while in Find mode by typing them directly into a field, using the *Insert Operators* menu in the toolbar or selecting the *Operators* submenu from a field's contextual menu. To see operators in action, place an exclamation mark in the *Company* field to find all records with other records with the same value, or search the *First Name* field for *n to find records with names ending with that character.

Table 4-1. *A description of the available Find mode operators*

Operator	Description
=	By itself, finds records where that field is empty. In front of a value, matches a whole word within the field, excluding partial matches.
==	In front of a value, matches an entire phrase within the field.
!	Finds records that have duplicate values in the field, i.e., any record whose value in the field is also found in another record.
<	Finds numeric or text values that are less than the value entered after the symbol.
≤	Finds numeric or text values that are less than or equal to the value entered after the symbol.
>	Finds numeric or text values that are greater than the value entered after the symbol.
≥	Finds numeric or text values that are greater than or equal to the value entered after the symbol.
…	Finds a range of values based on text placed before and after the operator. For example, enter "1/15/2021…1/30/2021" (without the quotes) to find all records where the field contains a date including or between the two dates entered.
//	Finds records where the field contains today's date.
?	Finds records where the field contains an invalid value.
@	Finds records where the field contains a specific number of any character. For example, "@@" will find "He" or "It," while "@@@@" will find "Door" or "Test."
#	Finds records where the field contains a specific number of any number. For example, "#" will find "3" or "8" and "##" will find "33" or "81."
*	Use this in place of a character to create a search pattern indicating there must be some value present. For example, by itself, it will find every record with any value in that field (e.g., omitting empty), or typing "1/15/*" will find any records where the field contains a date of January 15 for any year.
\	Escapes the next character. This can be useful when searching for a literal operator by treating the operator as part of the search criteria and not as an operator. For example, to search for any records where the field contains a quote symbol, enter \".
` " "	Used to match the phrase exactly as typed between the quote marks.
* " "	Used to match the phrase typed between the quote marks anywhere in a field containing a lot of text.
~	Used to perform a relaxed search in Japanese text.

Manipulating a Previously Executed Find

Once a find has been performed, FileMaker offers three methods for further refining the results without having to start over with a new request: *modifying, extending,* and *constraining* the last find.

Modifying the Last Find

The *Modify Last Find* function re-creates the find request(s) and criteria of the last find performed in the current table providing an opportunity to edit the criteria and perform the modified search. This command is available in the *Record* menu, in the menu under the toolbar's *Find* icon, or as a step that can be included in scripts.

Extending the Last Find

The *Extend Found Set* command uses a new search to find and add matching records to the current found set. This can be accessed two ways. In Browse mode, highlight some text in a field, and select *command* from the contextual menu. The text selection is used to find records not in the found set and add them. In Find mode, enter criteria and select *the Request* ➤ *Extend Found Set* menu instead of *Perform Find.* The results will be added to the current found set. For example, if viewing a found set of records with a *State* of "NY," enter Find mode, type "CO" into *State,* and select *Extend Found Set.* The result will be an expanded list of contacts from *both states.*

Constraining the Last Find

The *Constrain Found Set* command uses a new request to remove records from the current found set. This can be accessed two ways. While in Browse mode, highlight some text in a field, and select *Constrain Found Set* from the field contextual menu. The selection is used find and retain only records from the found set with the matching value. In Find mode, enter criteria and select the *Request* ➤ *Constrain Found Set* menu instead of *Perform Find.* Records in the last found set without the matching criteria will be removed. For example, if viewing a result set of records with a *Company* of "Widget," enter Find mode, type "CO" in the *State* field, and then select *Constrain Found Set.* The resulting found set will retain only the contacts from the previous found set that are from Colorado.

Managing Multiple Find Requests

Find mode creates a single default find request. This can be expanded to create more complex searches. Each request provides one additional set of criteria defining values that indicate if a matching record should be included or omitted from the result. The results of all requests are combined into the final result. So, if one request specifies records with a *State* of "NY" and another specifies records with a *State* of "CO," the result will be a combined list of those two sets of records. A single request containing multiple field criteria acts as an "and" type search where a record must have all the values to be included in the result. In other words, it must contain the specified value in one field *and* the specified value in another. Conversely, multiple requests act as an "or" type search, where a record must match all the criteria of at least one request. In other words, it must contain specified values from one request *or* specified values from another request.

Users can *create, delete,* and *duplicate* find requests just like they can do with records except that they are accessed through a *Requests* menu, which replaces the *Records* menu while in Find mode. Some of these are also accessible through a toolbar icon or the *record contextual menu* on the background of a layout.

Specifying a Matching Record Option

Every new find request has a default *Matching Record option* set to "Include" which means that records matching the request criteria will be included in the results. If this option is toggled to "Omit" in the lower toolbar, then matching records will be excluded from the results of the previous request(s). In the examples shown in Figure 4-8, the first request will include every record with "Widget" in the *Company* field, and the second request will omit from that set any matches with a *First Name* of "Jim." The results will be all contacts working for Widget company except for Jim. Using this setting with multiple find requests makes it possible to construct and perform extremely complex include-omit multi-criteria searches.

Figure 4-8. *An example of a second find request set to omit results*

Working with Saved Finds

Find requests can be saved for future reuse. In Browse mode, the *Saved Finds* menu is accessible from the *Find* button toolbar and the *Records* ➤ *Saved Finds* menu. In Find mode, it is available through the *Saved Finds* toolbar button. This menu is used to *save* and *manage* saved finds as well as *perform* saved or recent finds.

The *Save Current Find* option will open a dialog to start the save process. A name can be entered, and optionally, the criteria can be edited. In Browse mode, the last executed find will be saved. In Find mode, the current find criteria entered will be saved.

The *Edit Saved Finds* option opens a dialog of the same name, shown in Figure 4-9, that is used to create, edit, duplicate, or delete saved finds.

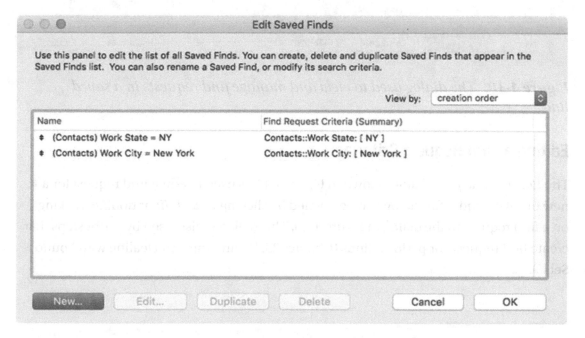

Figure 4-9. *The dialog used to view and manage saved finds*

Managing a Find Request

When saving or editing a find, a *Specify Options for the Saved Find* dialog opens displaying the name of the find. Clicking the *Advanced* button will open the stored criteria in a *Specify Find Requests* dialog shown in Figure 4-10. Each line in this dialog represents one request that makes up the find. Requests can be *created, edited, duplicated,* or *deleted* using the buttons on this dialog. Each request specifies an action (Find or Omit) and shows the criteria. Select a request and click *Edit* to open the editing dialog.

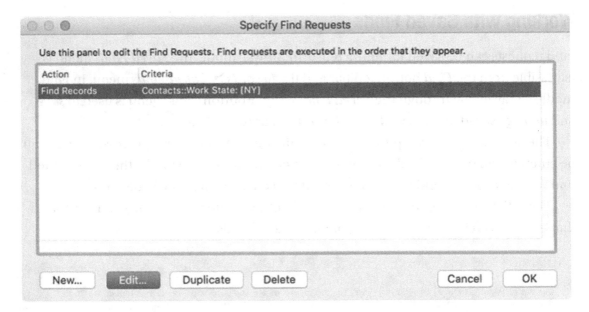

Figure 4-10. *The dialog used to view and manage find requests in a saved find*

Editing a Find Request Criteria

The *Edit Find Request* dialog, shown in Figure 4-11, is used to edit a find request for a new or saved find. This dialog can be opened by clicking *New, Edit* or double-clicking on a find request in the dialog in Figure 4-10. This dialog is also used by script steps that create find requests or perform finds (Chapter 25, "Searching and Dealing with Found Sets").

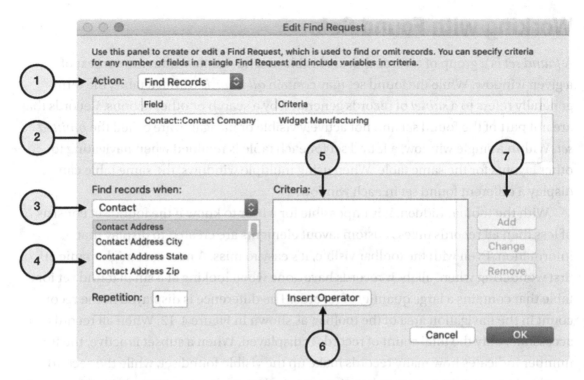

Figure 4-11. *The dialog used to edit a single request of a saved find*

In the dialog, you can edit the criteria of the request using the following controls:

1. *Action* – Choose *Find Records* or *Omit Records*, which indicates the matching records option for the request

2. *Criteria List* – Lists each field criteria defined to make up the request, displaying the selected row's details below

3. *Table* – Select a table occurrence to find a search field

4. *Fields* – Select the search field

5. *Criteria* – The value to search for in the selected field

6. *Insert Operator* – Click to choose and insert an operator

7. Criteria Buttons – Used to *Add* a new request, *Change* the currently selected request, or *Remove* the selected request

Working with Found Sets

A *found set* is a group of records that are visible and navigable within the context of a given window. While the found set may contain *all records* within a table, the term generally refers to a *subset* of records generated by a search or other actions. Records that are not part of the found set and not actively visible or navigable are called the *omitted set*. Within a single window, a found set for each table is retained when navigating to other layouts for the same table. When using multiple windows, the same table can display a different found set in each window.

With the toolbar hidden, it is impossible for a user to know if the found set consists of less than all records unless custom layout elements are created to display that information. Even with the toolbar visible, it's easy to miss. A new user might panic at first wondering where all their records have gone when looking at a small found set for a table that contains a large quantity of records. The difference is displayed in the record count in the navigation area of the toolbar, as shown in Figure 4-12. When all records are accessible, only the total count of records is displayed. When a subset is active, the first number indicates how many records make up the visible found set, while the second number indicates the total number of records including those that are omitted from the found set.

| All Records | Found Set of Records |

Figure 4-12. *The record count when viewing all records (left) or a found set (right)*

Changing the Records in the Found Set

The records in a found set can be changed by performing a find or one of several commands in the *Records* menu. The *Show All Records* command replaces the found set in the current window with all records in the table. The *Omit Record* command will move the current record from the found set to the omitted set. This can be used to fine-tune results by omitting individual records without the need to perform a new, more complex search. The *Omit Multiple* command allows the user to specify any number of records they wish to omit starting from the current record. For example, if the user is viewing the first record of a found set of 100 records and choose to omit 10 records, the first 10 records will be omitted leaving the remaining 90 records. However, if they are viewing record 50 of 100 and do the same thing, then records 50–59 will be omitted leaving records 1–49 and 60–100. Finally, the *Show Omitted Only* command replaces the current found set with the omitted set. Alternatively, click the circle icon in the navigation area of the toolbar to toggle between the found or omitted records.

Sorting Records in the Found Set

The *record sort status* is always indicated in the record navigation area of the toolbar as shown in Figure 4-13. Records always default to creation order, which is considered *unsorted*. They can be sorted based on a custom list of sort fields, which can be compiled from local or related fields using the *Sort Records* dialog, shown in Figure 4-14. The dialog can be opened by selecting the *Sort Records* command in the *Records* menu or the record contextual menu. It is also available by clicking the *Sort* button in the toolbar.

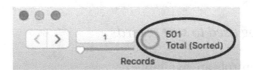

Figure 4-13. *The sort status is always displayed in the toolbar record count area*

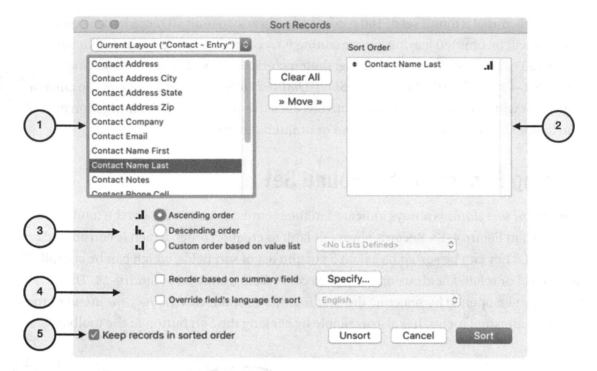

Figure 4-14. *The dialog used to sort records*

The following sort controls are available:

1. *Field Selector* – Select a field from the list which is based on the table or layout selected in the pop-up menu above.

2. *Sort Order* – Lists the current *sort fields* in the order they will be used to sort records. Add a field by double-clicking it in the field selector or with the *Move* button. Drag up or down to rearrange. Remove a field by double-clicking here or with the *Clear* button. To remove all fields, click *Clear All*.

3. *Sort Field Direction* – Choose the sort direction of the selected field: *ascending* (default), *descending*, or a *custom order based on a value list* (Chapter 11). The icons are displayed next to fields in the sort order list to indicate which option is assigned.

4. *Sort Option Checkboxes* – Enable advanced sort control:

   • *Reorder Based on Summary Field* – Select a summary field (Chapter 8) to reorder records based on the position of the sort field's value as sub-summarized by another sort field. For example, a list of contacts can be summarized by a state (sort field) but sorted by the number of contacts living in each state (summary field).

   • *Override Field's Language for Sort* – Select a language used to index text fields when sorting.

5. *Keep Records in Sorted Order* – Deselect to stop records from continuously resorting whenever the contents of a sort field is modified.

Modifying Field Values in a Found Set

Several commands can be used to modify field values across an entire found set: *Replace Field Contents, Relookup Field Contents, Find and Replace,* and *Spell-checking.*

Replace Field Contents

The *Replace Field Contents* command under the *Records* menu opens the dialog shown in Figure 4-15. This is used to define a value that will be inserted into the current field on every record in the found set, completely replacing the previous value. The replacement value can be the literal value contained in the field of the current record, a serial number starting from a specified number on the first record and incremented a specified amount for each subsequent record, or the result of a calculation (Chapter 12).

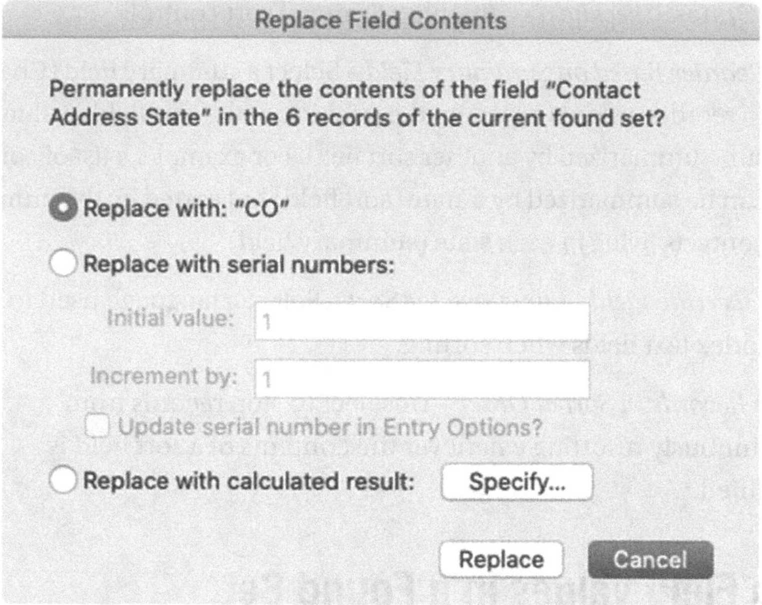

Figure 4-15. *The dialog used to define a replacement value*

Caution   The replace process can't be undone and should be used carefully. Use custom menus (Chapter 23) to hide this feature from users who don't require it, and create a custom script (Chapter 24) to perform developer-defined replacements safely.

Relookup Field Contents

When a field is defined to copy data from related records using the *Lookup* feature (Chapter 8, "Lookup for Field Dialog"), the copied values can be manually forced to update for every record in the found set using the *Relookup Field Contents* command.

Caution   The *Lookup* feature is a vestigial remnant from the days before better auto-enter options and relationships were available.

Find and Replace

FileMaker's *Find and Replace* function is reminiscent of those found in text editors. It can locate text within one or all fields for one or all records in the current found set and optionally replace matches with alternate text. The *Find/Replace* function from the *Edit* menu will open a dialog of the same name, shown in Figure 4-16.

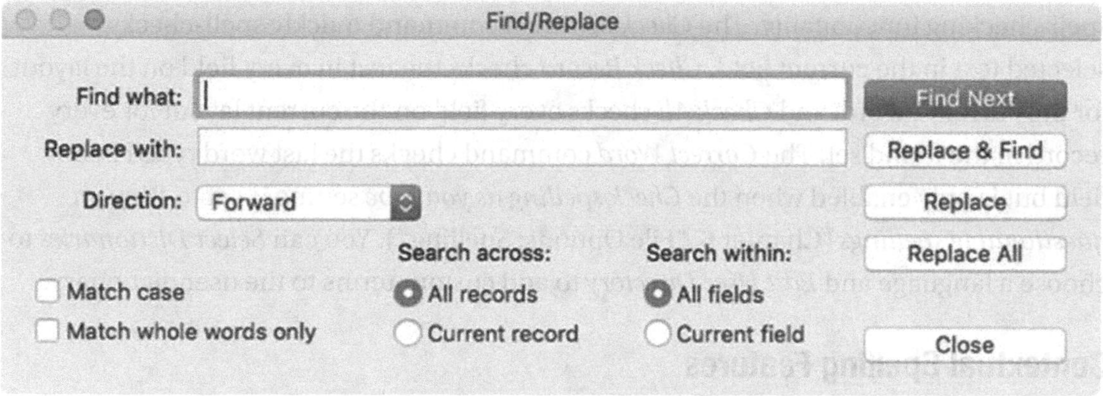

Figure 4-16. *The dialog used to find and replace text*

To begin, type text into the *Find what* field and optionally in the *Replace with* field. The *Direction* pop-up menu offers the choice of moving *forward* or *backward* through fields and/or records in a found set. Select the *Match case* checkbox for the find process to be case-sensitive, and select *Match whole words only* to only consider a match when the text in a field contains the entire, separate word(s) typed into the *Find what* field. The *Search across* radio buttons instructs the function whether it should search *all records* in the found set or limit itself to the *current record*. The *Search within* option controls if it should search *all fields* on the layout or just the *current field*.

Once configured, the *Find Next* button locates and highlight the next instance of the text in the *Find what* field in the current field, next field, or next record, depending on the other settings in the dialog. The *Replace & Find* button will either locate the first instance of a match, if one has not yet been made, or replace the currently highlighted matched text with the replacement text and then locate the next instance of a match. The *Replace* button performs the replace function if a find has already selected a matching instance of the search text. Afterward, the cursor appears immediately after the replaced text. The *Replace All* button replaces all matching instances of the search text based on the settings in the dialog.

Spell-checking

FileMaker has an integrated spell-checker that can process a piece of selected text, the contents of a field, every field on the current record, or all records in the found set.

Exploring the Spelling Menu

The *Spelling* submenu of the *Edit* menu has several commands for standard spell-checking functionality. The *Check Selection* command quickly spell-checks selected text in the current field. *Check Record* checks the text in every field on the layout for the current record, and *Check All* checks every field on the current layout for every record in the found set. The *Correct Word* command checks the last word typed in a field but is only enabled when the *Check spelling as you type* setting is set to *Beep on questionable spellings* (Chapter 6, "File Options: Spelling"). You can *Select Dictionaries* to choose a language and *Edit User Directory* to add custom terms to the user dictionary.

Contextual Spelling Features

When the *Indicate questionable words with special underline* file option is enabled, any questionable words in the active field will be marked with a red underline. This option applies to an entire file but can be turned off for individual fields on a layout (Chapter 19, "Inspecting the Data Settings"). When on, a list of suggested spellings and alternate words are available at the top of the text contextual menu for the selected word, shown in Figure 4-17.

Figure 4-17. *A contextual menu shows alternative spellings for questionable words*

Printing

The content area of a window can be previewed and printed using familiar operating system *Page Setup* and *Print* dialogs.

Using Preview Mode

Preview mode is a transitional window state that changes the menu, toolbar, and content area for the purpose of viewing a layout in preparation for sending it to a printer or saving as a PDF file. To preview a layout, select *Preview Mode* from the *View* menu, or click the *Preview* toolbar icon. The toolbar options will change to print related functionality, and the content area will become one or more non-interactive, non-editable pages rendered exactly as they will appear when printed. Any interactive objects such as buttons, tabs, slide controls, etc. will be displayed as a nonfunctional artwork. Depending on the settings of each layout object, some objects and data may be invisible, reformatted, slide into a new position, or be cut off at the page margins.

Status Toolbar (Preview Mode)

The Preview mode toolbar will change to print-specific buttons, either default options or the user's customized set.

Default Status Toolbar Items (Preview Mode)

The default toolbar for Preview mode is shown in Figure 4-18. Similar to Browse mode, the top portion can be customized, and the bottom is static.

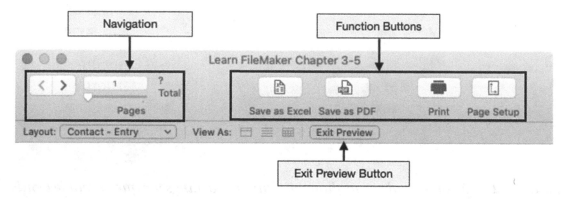

Figure 4-18. *The anatomy of the toolbar in Preview mode*

Navigation Controls

The *navigation controls* in the Preview mode toolbar are similar to those in Browse and Find modes except that they display information about and allow movement between *print pages* instead of records or find requests. At first, the page count may be displayed as a question mark if the entire document has not yet been rendered. Click through pages or scroll to the end to update.

Function Buttons

The function buttons included in the default Preview toolbar are

- *Save as Excel* – Export the records into an Excel file

- *Save as PDF* – Save the preview as a PDF file

- *Print* – Open the dialog to send the preview to a printer

- *Page Setup* – Open the dialog to configure page setup to change the rendering

Exit Preview Button

The *Exit Preview button* will end the preview and return the window to Browse mode.

Customizing the Status Toolbar (Preview Mode)

The Preview mode toolbar is customizable at the user-computer level. Enter Preview mode and select the *View ➤ Customize Toolbar* menu to open the customization panel attached to the window as shown in Figure 4-19. Although the available buttons are different, they can be added or removed as described for Browse mode in Chapter 3.

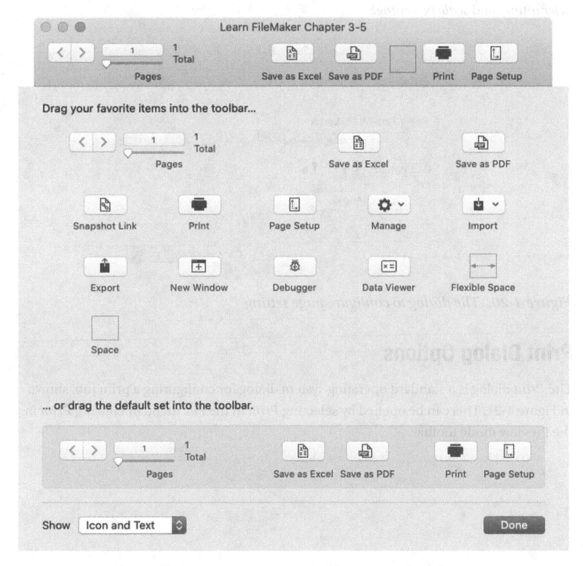

Figure 4-19. *The toolbar customization panel for Preview mode*

Page Setup

The *Page Setup* dialog (*Print Setup* in Windows) is a standard operating system dialog used to configure how the current layout will behave when previewing or printing, shown in Figure 4-20. This can be accessed in Browse, Preview, or Layout mode by selecting Page Setup in the File menu. Here you can choose a *printer, paper size, orientation,* and *scale percentage.*

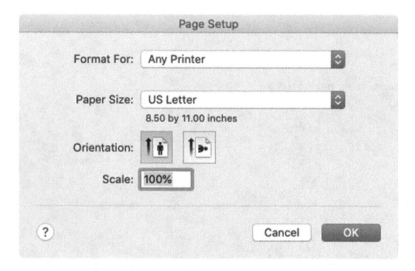

Figure 4-20. *The dialog to configure page setting*

Print Dialog Options

The *Print* dialog is a standard operating system dialog for configuring a print job, shown in Figure 4-21. This can be opened by selecting *Print* in the *File* menu or clicking *Print* in the Preview mode toolbar.

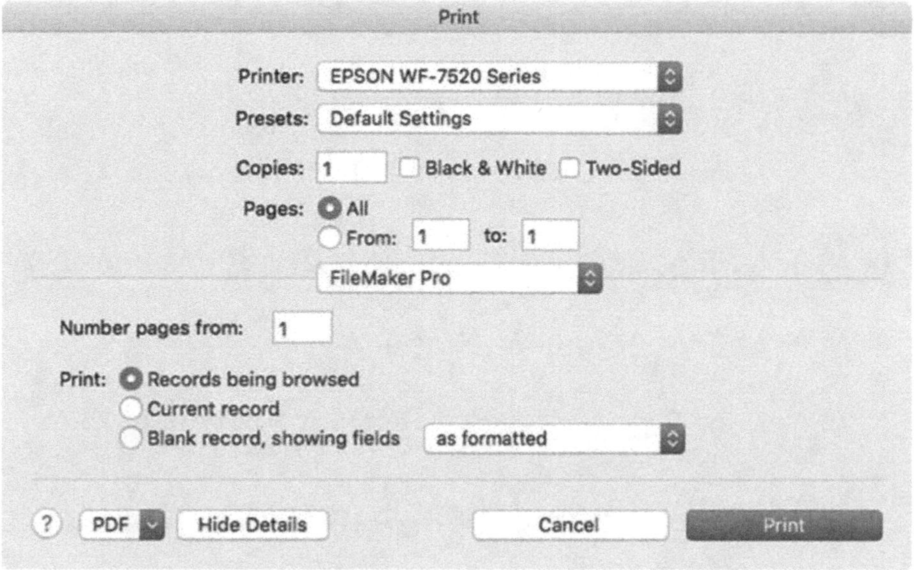

Figure 4-21. *The dialog for preparing a job to send to a printer*

While most of the options are identical to other applications, a few are specific to FileMaker. The *Number pages from* field accepts a page number that will be considered the first page for numbering purposes. Three print options determine how the content area of the window will be printed. Choose *Records being browsed* to include every record in the found set or *Current record* to include only the current record selected or in view when the Print dialog was opened. Choose *Blank record, showing fields* to print the *layout* without any record data. The adjacent menu controls how fields will be printed: *as formatted, with boxes, with underlines,* or *with placeholder text.*

Summary

This chapter explored how users interact with records to enter data, perform searches, and print. In the next chapter, we focus on importing and exporting records.

CHAPTER 5

Transferring Records

FileMaker has *import* and *export* functions that transfer records between two locations, manually or through an automatic scripted process. This allows sharing data to avoid retyping, moving template data into a content table for customizing, migrating old data into a newer version of a database, sending data to other systems, and more. This chapter discusses the following data transfer topics:

- Supported file types
- Importing records
- Exporting records

Supported File Types

FileMaker can *import and export records* in several formats, shown in Figure 5-1. In addition, *content imports* are supported from ODBC and XML sources, or a folder containing picture, movie, or text files.

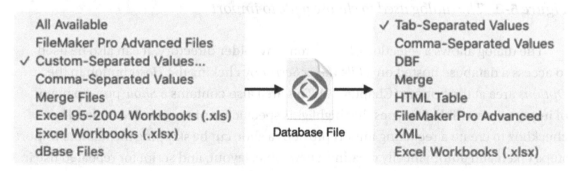

Figure 5-1. *The file types supported for record import (left) and export (right)*

© Mark Conway Munro 2021
M. C. Munro, *Learn FileMaker Pro 19*, https://doi.org/10.1007/978-1-4842-6680-9_5

Note   The new *Custom-Separated Values* import option allows a selection of delimiter and replaces the former *Tab-Separated Values*.

Importing Records

The *import records* function will create or update records in the table of the current layout. Records can be imported from various sources: a table within the same file, an external database, or one of various text-based data files. To explore the feature, import some contact data into the *Learn FileMaker Chapter* 3-5 database. First, download the free *us-500.csv* contacts sample file from www.briandunning.com/sample-data/. Then, select the *File* ➤ *Import Records* ➤ *File* menu to open the *Choose File* dialog, as shown in Figure 5-2.

Figure 5-2. *The dialog used to choose a file to import*

The dialog allows a selection of a file from any folder directory. It can also be used to access a database hosted on a *FileMaker Server* by clicking the *Hosts* button in the *Options* area at the bottom (Chapter 29). This area also contains a *Show* pop-up menu of import-compatible file types that highlights specific files in a crowded folder. The checkbox to create a recurring import provides a shortcut by skipping the manual import steps taken and automatically creating a new table, layout, and script for repeated use in the future. For now, select and open the downloaded CSV file.

Performing an Import

After selecting and opening the data file, a *Specify Import Order* dialog will appear, as shown in Figure 5-3. The dialog contains regions for browsing source data, specifying an import type, selecting a target table, and setting import options that vary depending on the type of import being performed. The default is an *add import*, where all imported records will be added as new records in the target table.

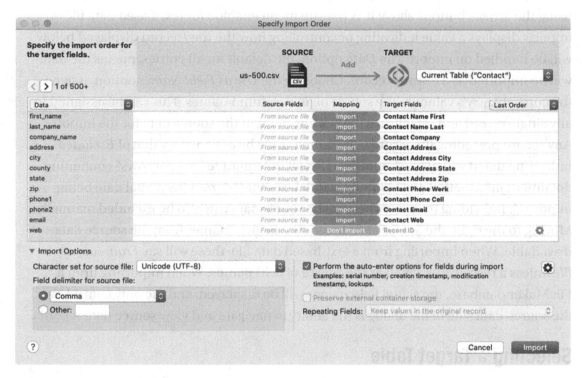

Figure 5-3. *The import field-mapping dialog*

Caution   This dialog design was introduced in FileMaker 18 and is completely different from earlier versions.

Browsing the Source Data

The *import source data* is displayed in a list on the leftmost column and is navigable using the arrows buttons above it. A pop-up menu enabled for text-based data file imports displays a value indicating or controlling how the row/record displayed below will be handled on import. The *Data* option, the default for all entries, means the data will be imported as a normal record. Choosing the *Use as Field Names* option assigns the current entry's values as the source of field/column names. This can be assigned to any single record and establishes the starting point in the source data for the import. Any record preceding the record will automatically be assigned a value of *Excluded*, indicating that it will not be imported. This allows multiple "header rows" containing document information and column titles to be excluded from the actual data being imported. Individual rows anywhere in the source data can also be excluded manually. Moving to the right, the *Source Field* list shows the field names from the source data if available. When importing from a text-based data file, these will say *From source file* unless a record is assigned as the source of field names. When importing from a FileMaker database, the actual field names will be displayed, and the only control over the source data side of the dialog is the ability to navigate and view source data records.

Selecting a Target Table

The *target table* is the destination table for incoming data and will default to the current layout's table. The *Target* pop-up menu, shown in Figure 5-4, provides one option for creating a new table as part of the import process. The menu is a standard FileMaker *table selection menu* that lists the *Current Table*, *Related Tables*, *Unrelated Tables*, and a *Manage Database* with an additional import-only option of *New Table*. Since an import must flow into the current layout's context, most of these options are disabled when importing. The only alternative to a target of the current table is to create a new table.

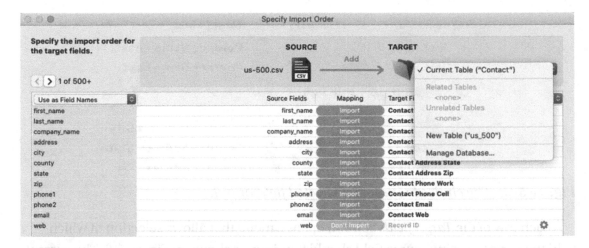

Figure 5-4. *The import target table pop-up menu*

Selecting the *New Table* option will configure the dialog to automatically, create a new table during the import and flow the data into it. The *Target fields* list will display new names as a numerically sequence with an "f" prefix unless a row has been assigned to *Use as Field Names*.

The *Manage Database* option is enabled and will open a dialog of the same name (Chapters 7–9) to create new fields in the target table so they can be included in the import without having to exit the import dialog.

Mapping Fields from Source to Target

The target table and import source file may have more or less fields than the other and in a different order. Therefore, it is necessary to indicate which source fields should be imported and match them to an appropriate target field. This process of *mapping fields* is the primary purpose of the *Specify Import Order* dialog.

Each selectable row of the central list shows columns for *Source Fields, Mapping,* and *Target Fields,* and these last two each open a menu of options. The *Mapping* column displays the import status of the corresponding two fields: *Import* or *Don't Import*. Click to reveal the menu of options, as shown in Figure 5-5.

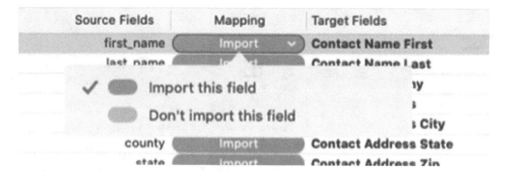

Figure 5-5. *The choice to import a selected field or not.*

Each row of the *Target fields* column opens a menu that allows selection of which field the corresponding source field should flow into, as shown in Figure 5-6. The current row's field will be highlighted in the list. An icon indicates each field's current import status: an arrow means they are already configured to receive input from the source, and a clear oval indicates they are not. Fields that don't accept data entry, like a calculation or summary fields, will be grouped at the bottom under a *Not for Importing* folder. Click to select the appropriate target field for the corresponding source field. Once all input fields are mapped to targets, it's time to configure import options.

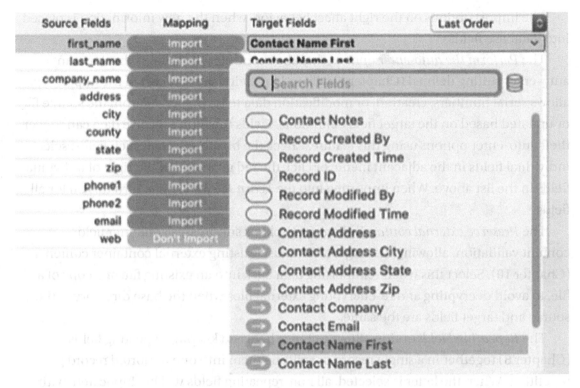

Figure 5-6. *The options available for arranging the list of target fields*

Setting Import Options

The *Import Options* section at the bottom of the *Specify Import Order* dialog, shown in Figure 5-7, controls various behaviors based on the type of import source.

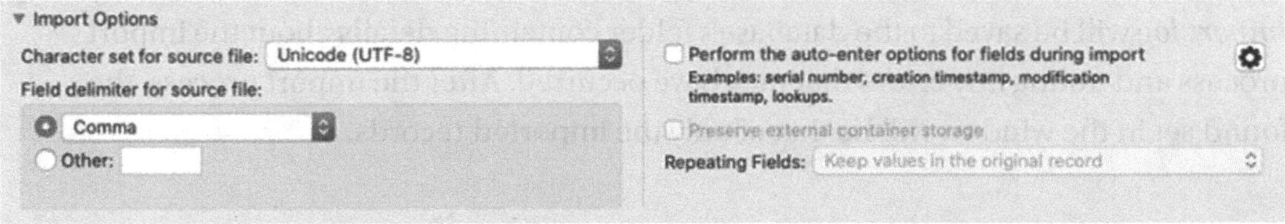

Figure 5-7. *The import options section of the dialog*

The *text-parsing options* on the left control how the import source is parsed and are only visible when importing from a text-based file. Here you can choose a character set and field delimiter: *comma, tab, semi-colon, space,* or a custom value.

The import options on the right affect behaviors when the new information is placed into database fields.

The *Perform the auto-enter options* checkbox controls which fields that have an auto-enter setting defined (Chapter 8) will update their values as part of the import. This allows serial numbers, creation, or modification data to be preserved from the source file or updated based on the target field definitions. Fields that don't receive data can trigger their auto-enter options using this feature. Check the box to select all such fields, select individual fields in the adjacent menu, or click the red gear icon to the right of individual fields in the list above. When importing into the *Learn FileMaker* file, turn this on for all fields.

The *Preserve external container storage* checkbox suppresses container field content validation, allowing the target table to use existing external container contents (Chapter 10). Select this when reimporting data back into an existing file or a copy of a file, to avoid decrypting and re-encrypting external files when the base directory of the source and target fields are the same.

The *Repeating Fields* option allows a choice between keeping repeating fields (Chapter 8) together in a single record or splitting them into one imported record per repetition. When the latter is selected, all non-repeating fields will be duplicated, with one record generated for each of the repetitions.

Finishing the Import

Once configured, click the *Import* button to perform the process. An *Import Summary* dialog appears reporting the number of records added or updated, the number of skipped records and fields, and how many tables were created, if any. A text file named *Import.log* will be saved to the database's folder containing details about the import process and noting any errors that may have occurred. After the import process, the found set in the window will be that of only the imported records.

Changing the Import Type

Besides the *add records* style import described earlier, there are two other types of import available: *update* and *replace*. Instead of creating records, these are used to overwrite existing records. An *import type selection* panel is accessible by clicking in the space between the source and target icons, shown in Figure 5-8.

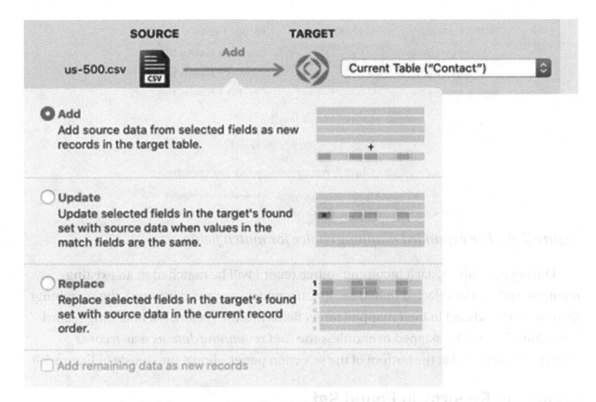

Figure 5-8. *The hidden panel to select a different import type*

Updating Matching Records in Found Set

An *update* import is a nonlinear data transfer that will import each record of the source data into an existing record based on match criteria. A *match field* is a new field mapping designation, shown in Figure 5-9, used to tag one or more fields as criteria for matching an incoming record to a record in the target table.

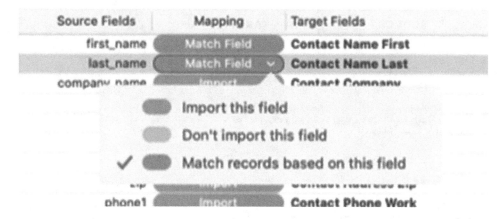

Figure 5-9. *The expanded mapping choice for match fields*

During the import, each incoming source record will be matched to an existing record based on the selected match field(s). If a matching record is found, the remaining fields will be updated in their mapped target fields for that record. If a matching record is not found, it will be skipped over unless the *Add remaining data as new records* checkbox is selected at the bottom of the selection panel, shown previously in Figure 5-8.

Replacing Records in Found Set

A *replace import* will use the incoming record values to overwrite fields on existing records based on their linear position in the corresponding sets without any concern for matching records. In other words, the values from the first record in the source data will be used to replace values in the mapped fields of the first record in the target set. This can be useful in a situation where you need to export a set of data, manipulate it outside of FileMaker, and then immediately replace some or all field values of those same records. When using this import type, typically, the source data and the target table's current found set should contain the same number of records. If the source record count is *less* than the target found set, records in the found set beyond that source's count will not be modified. If the source data count is *greater* than the target table's found set, the import will stop after the number of records in that found set are finished, unless the *Add remaining data as new records* checkbox is selected.

Setting Up an Automatic Recurring Import

Selecting the optional *Set up as automatic recurring import* checkbox in the *Choose File* dialog, as shown previously in Figure 5-2, will completely bypass the rest of the import process and create a new table, layout, and script that can be customized and used to automate the same process in the future. When selected, it opens a *Recurring Import Setup* dialog shown in Figure 5-10. This dialog remembers the path of the source data and has three configurable options. Select *Don't import first record* to skip importing the first record, and instead use it as field names. The other two fields allow entry of a layout and script name to override the default names entered based on the import file name.

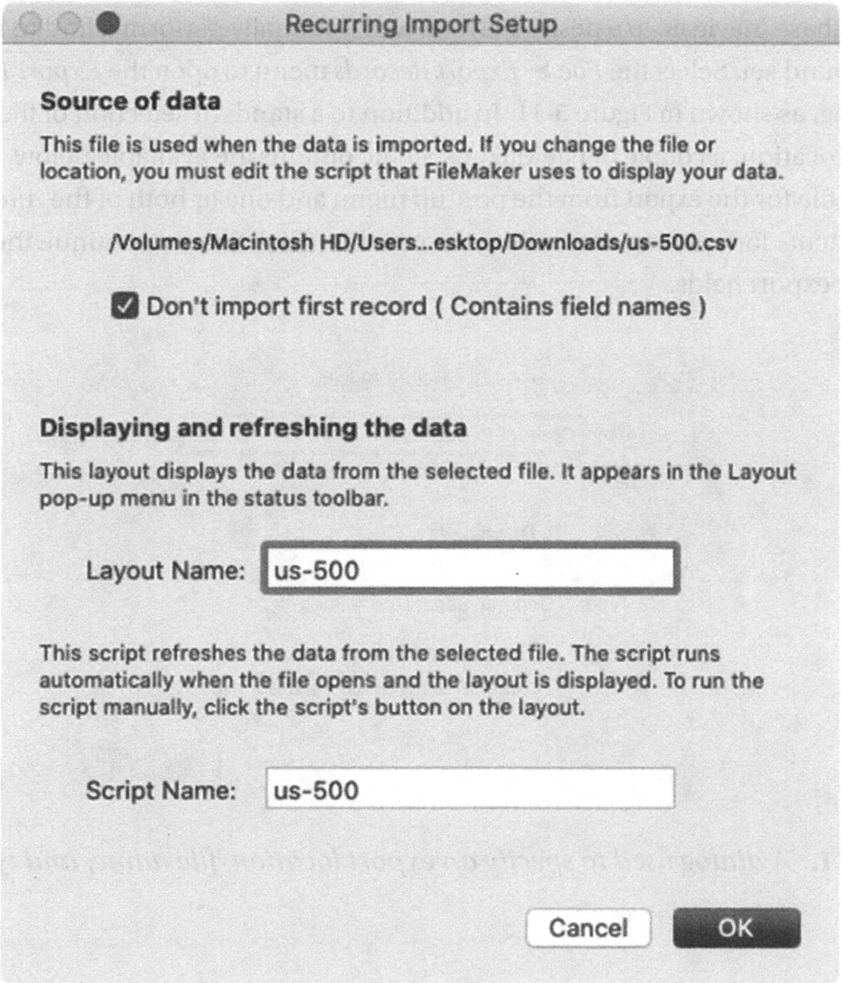

Figure 5-10. *The Recurring Import Setup dialog*

Once configured and continued, a new table will be created with the same name as the source data file with a field for every column of data it contains. A new layout is created with the specified name and every field displayed. A script is created with the specified name that will navigate to the new layout, delete every record, and import the records from the file thereby refreshing the data. All of these resources can then be renamed and customized as needed to suit a specific workflow.

Exporting Records

The *Export Records* function will save values from one or more selected fields from every record in the current found set to a file of a specified type. To begin an export, open a database, navigate to a desired layout, and optionally perform a find to isolate a desired found set. Select the *File* ➤ *Export Records* menu to open the *Export Records to File* dialog, as shown in Figure 5-11. In addition to a standard selection of file name and folder location, a couple of FileMaker specific options are available below. Select the *Type* of file for the export from the pop-up menu and one or both of the *After saving* action shortcuts for opening or emailing the new file. Click *Save* to continue the process and specify export fields.

Figure 5-11. *A dialog used to specify an export location, file name, and type*

Specifying Export Fields

The *Specify Field Order for Export* dialog, as shown in Figure 5-12, is used to select the fields that will be included in the export, the order they will be saved in the output file, and some formatting options.

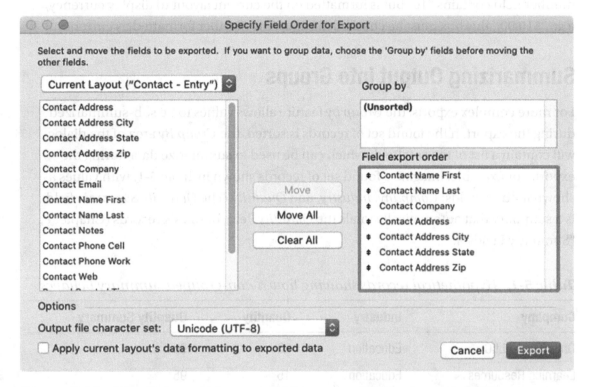

Figure 5-12. *The dialog used to specify the export field order and settings*

On the left, the *data source pop-up menu* is used to specify where to generate the field list below it. By default, this has the *Current Layout* selected, showing only the fields displayed on the current layout, both local and related. Select *Current Table* instead to show every field from the current layout's table occurrence, or choose a related table occurrence to include related fields in the export (Chapter 9).

Fields can be added to the export order by double-clicking in the list or using the *Move* or *Move All* button. The fields in the export list will be saved in the output file in the order they appear and can be dragged into the desired order. Remove fields from the export list by double-clicking, clicking the *Clear* or *Clear All* button, or typing the Delete key.

Once the field order is set, there are a few options available. The *Output file character set* pop-up menu specifies which character encoding will be used during the export. The *Apply current layout's data formatting* checkbox will cause any number, date, or time field to be exported with the data formatted as it is on the current layout rather than the format of the actual data entered (Chapter 19, "Data Formatting"). For example, if a number field contains "10" but is formatted on the current layout to display currency, e.g., "$10.00," this box must be checked to export the number formatted as currency.

Summarizing Output into Groups

For more complex exports, the *Group by* feature allows values to be sub-summarized during the export. If the found set of records is sorted, the *Group By* area of the dialog will contain a list of the sort fields which can be used to summarize data during the export. For example, imagine a found set of records shown in Table 5-1, with values as shown in three fields: *Company, Industry,* and *Quantity.* The *Quantity Summary* field is a summary that automatically totals the *Quantity* field for the six records (Chapter 8, "Summary Fields").

Table 5-1. *Hypothetical records showing how a non-grouped summary behaves*

Company	Industry	Quantity	Quantity Summary
Online Tutor, LLC	Education	20	95
Learning Resources	Education	15	95
Mutual Investors Corp	Finance	5	95
Dividend Party, Inc.	Finance	10	95
Knowledge Bound Co.	Publishing	35	95
Widget Books, Inc.	Publishing	10	95

If these three fields were exported, the values in the resulting file would look the same as they do in the table. However, the data can be exported as a *summary report* of the total quantity for each industry by first sorting the records by the *Industry* field. Begin an export, and when you reach the *Specify Field Order* dialog, the *Group by* area will have a checkbox for the *Industry* field. Add the *Industry* field and the *Quantity Summary* field to the export list. An extra third field will be added automatically: *Quantity Summary by Industry*. This last will be italicized to highlight the fact that it is not an actual field in the database, but a sub-summary of the quantity by industry, as shown in Figure 5-13.

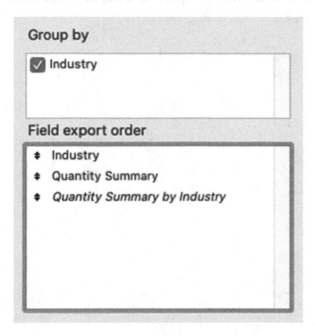

Figure 5-13. *An example of a field export order using the group by feature*

With this configuration, the export file would contain one row for each industry, the total quantity for all three industries (only on the first row), and the total of each industry in the third column, as shown in Table 5-2.

Table 5-2. *Hypothetical data exported using the Group by option*

Education	95	35
Finance		15
Publishing		45

Summary

In this chapter, we explored the basics of importing and exporting records. In the next chapter, we will move from the user perspective to the developer interface and begin defining data structures.

PART II

Defining Data Structures

The first step to building a custom database is to create a new file and begin defining its structural data schema, the *tables*, *fields*, *relationships*, *containers*, and *value lists* that provide a foundation upon which interfaces will be constructed.

## CHAPTER 6

Working with Database Files

A *database* is a structured collection of information stored in a digital format that is flexibly accessible for a variety of functions. A *FileMaker database file* is a document that contains both structural elements defined by a developer and data entered by users. A single file format has been shared by all versions of FileMaker between 12 and 19 and indicated by the file extension "fmp12." This chapter covers the basics of creating, configuring, and maintaining a database file, including

- Creating a new database file

- Configuring file options

- Designing and maintaining healthy files

Caution   While the "fmp12" extension indicates *file compatibility* between FileMaker versions 12 and 19, features introduced in newer versions are not backward compatible in older versions.

Creating a New Database File

A database file can be created from a starter solution, a blank file, or by converting a spreadsheet or other text-based file into a FileMaker database. All of these are performed from the *Create* tab of the *Launch Center* window, accessible by selecting *Create New* from the *File* menu.

© Mark Conway Munro 2021
M. C. Munro, *Learn FileMaker Pro 19*, https://doi.org/10.1007/978-1-4842-6680-9_6

Creating a Database from a Starter Solution

A *starter solution* is one of a set of templates provided by Claris as part of the FileMaker installation. Although this book is focused on starting from a blank file, these templates can be used as a starting foundation upon which to build a custom solution or serve as a "learn by example" tutorial. To begin, create a copy of the *Contacts* starter template by following the steps shown in Figure 6-1.

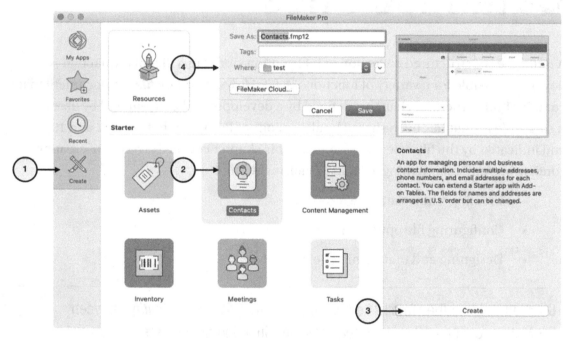

Figure 6-1. *The process of creating a new database from a starter solution*

1. Select the *Create* tab in the *Launch Center* window.

2. Click on the *Contacts* icon under the *Starter* heading.

3. Click the *Create* button.

4. In the *Save* dialog sheet attached to the top of the window, specify a name and save location.

Caution Starters are designed by Claris as examples. The structural and design choices they employ should not be taken as strict rules that must be unquestionably followed.

Creating a Database from a Blank Template

To create a new database from a blank template, select *Launch Center*, in the *File* menu, and follow the steps shown in Figure 6-2.

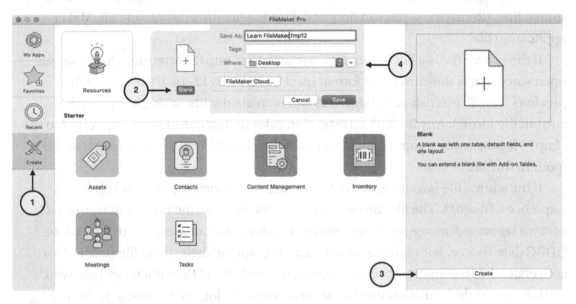

Figure 6-2. *The dialog used to create a new blank database file*

1. Select the *Create* tab in the *Launch Center* window.

2. Select the *Blank* icon.

3. Click the *Create* button.

4. In the *Save* dialog sheet attached to the top of the window, enter a name (type "Learn FileMaker" to follow along with the book's examples), choose a location, and click *Save*.

Caution   Files you create will appear different from screenshots in this book because a custom theme was used for visual clarity. Download sample files from Apress.com to follow the examples.

Converting an Existing File into a Database

FileMaker can automatically convert various files into a new database file. This includes older FileMaker databases, spreadsheets, or other text-based data files. To begin, select the *Convert* option on the *Create* tab of the *Launch Center* window, and then select a source file. Alternatively, you can drag and drop the file directly onto the FileMaker application file.

If the source file is a FileMaker database with the "fmp12" extension, it will simply open since that is the current file format used by versions 12–19. If the file has the previous "fmp7" extension, FileMaker 19 will recreate the file, saving a copy as the current file format. Any file with an extension prior to that must first be converted to the "fmp7" format using a copy of FileMaker 11 before FileMaker 19 can convert it to the modern format.

If the source file is a structured data file, there are various options available in a sequence of dialogs. The file can be one of various file types including *tab separated, comma separated, merge file, Excel workbooks* (*xls* or *xlsx*), *dbase,* or from an XML or ODBC data source. For example, assume an Excel spreadsheet. If the file selected for conversion has multiple tabbed worksheets, a *Specify Excel Data* dialog will ask which worksheet should be used as the data source. A save dialog will request a name and location for the new file. The source file's columns are used to automatically define a table with fields named *f1, f2, f3,* etc. A *Convert File* dialog similar to the *Specify Import Order* dialog (Chapter 5) opens allowing target table renaming and the option to use field names from a selected source record. Once finished, the new database file will have one table populated with the fields specified and with two layouts: a Form layout named "Layout #1" and a List layout named "Layout #2." The data structure and interface can then be customized to suit your purposes.

Configuring a Sandbox Table

Before exploring file basics, let's configure a rudimentary *Sandbox* table in the *Learn FileMaker* database. This process will provide a quick overview of building a table with fields and layouts, rapidly skimming over lessons that will be explored in more depth in later chapters. It also provides an experimental sandbox for tinkering and visualizing calculation results prior to later lessons on building layouts.

Tip   Walking through these lessons will provide a crash course in setting up a database. However, these steps are already done in the *Learn FileMaker Pro Chapter* 6 file available from Apress.com.

Changing the Default Table Name

A new database file will automatically have a default table with the same name as the file. So, the example database should already have one table named "Learn FileMaker" and a blank layout of the same name. This default behavior may be adequate when a database requires a table of the same name. For example, a database named *Contacts* or *Projects* will likely require a similarly named table. However, for our purposes and to gain a little practical experience, we will rename the default table to "Sandbox."

First, we need to make sure the *Manage Database* dialog is open. Depending on application settings (Chapter 2), the new file will open in Layout mode without opening the dialog or will open in Browse mode with the dialog open. If in Layout mode, open this dialog selecting the *File* ➤ *Manage* ➤ *Database* menu item. Then follow these steps, shown in Figure 6-3:

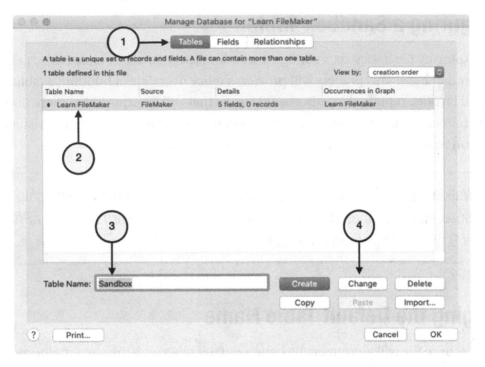

Figure 6-3. *Highlighting the process of renaming the default table*

1. Click on the *Tables* tab.

2. Make sure the default *Learn FileMaker* table is selected.

3. Type "Sandbox" into the *Table Name* field.

4. Click the *Change* button, and then click *OK*.

Adding Placeholder Fields

The renamed *Sandbox* table, probably already has five fields defined. Since version 17, FileMaker automatically creates default fields (Chapter 8, "Defining Default Fields"). For now, we will ignore these and create one field of each available data type to serve as an example for experimentation on topics presented in forthcoming chapters.

Creating Data Entry Fields

First, we will create six data entry fields that are capable of accepting input from a user. To get started, click on the *Fields* tab. Then, follow the steps shown in Figure 6-4:

1. Click in the white space under the default fields so no field is selected.

2. Type "Example Text" into the *Field Name* text area.

3. Select *Text* from the *Type* menu.

4. Click the *Create* button or type Enter.

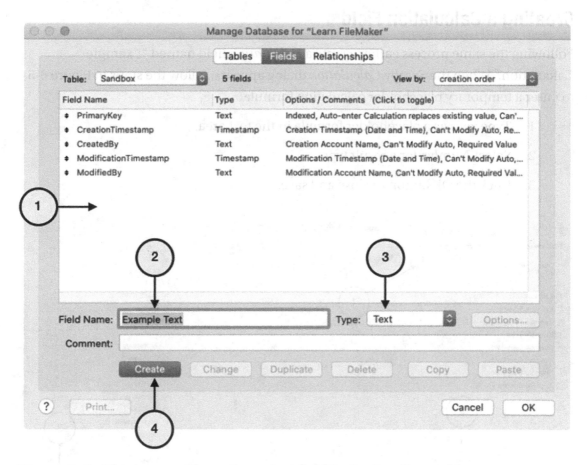

Figure 6-4. *The process of creating a text field in the Sandbox table*

For now, ignore other options and repeat this process for each of these field types:

1. Create a *Number* field named "Example Number"

2. Create a *Date* field named "Example Date"

3. Create a *Time* field named "Example Time"

4. Create a *Timestamp* field named "Example Timestamp"

5. Create a *Container* field named "Example Container"

Note   Field data types and options are discussed in Chapter 8.

Creating a Calculation Field

Following the same process earlier, create a *Calculation* field named "Example Calculation." When the *Specify Calculation* dialog appears, follow the steps in Figure 6-5 to enter a temporary placeholder calculation formula:

1. Type zero as a placeholder formula in the text area.

2. Select *Number* for a result type.

3. Click the OK button to close and save.

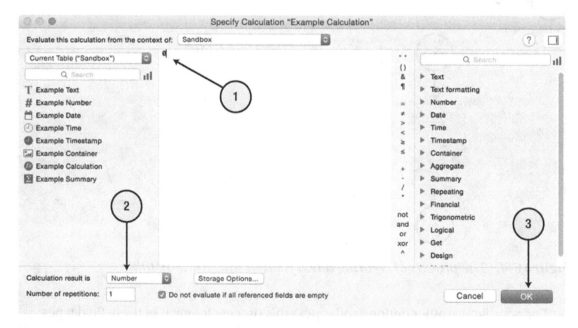

Figure 6-5. *The process of creating a placeholder calculation in the Sandbox*

Note   Calculation fields are discussed further starting in Chapter 12.

Creating a Summary Field

Again, repeat the process to create a *Summary* field named "Example Summary." When the *Options for Summary Field* dialog appears, follow the steps in Figure 6-6 to select a default summary process:

1. Click the *Total of* radio button.

2. Select the *Example Number* field from the *Available Fields* list.

3. Click the *OK* button to close and save.

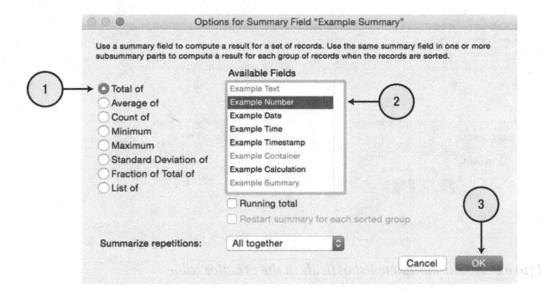

Figure 6-6. *The process of creating a summary field in the Sandbox*

Note   Summary field options are discussed further in Chapter 8.

Reviewing the Sandbox Fields

Once finished creating data entry, calculation, and summary fields, the *Sandbox* table should contain five default fields and the eight example fields shown in Figure 6-7. Click the OK button to close the *Manage Database* dialog, and save all changes made to the *Sandbox* table.

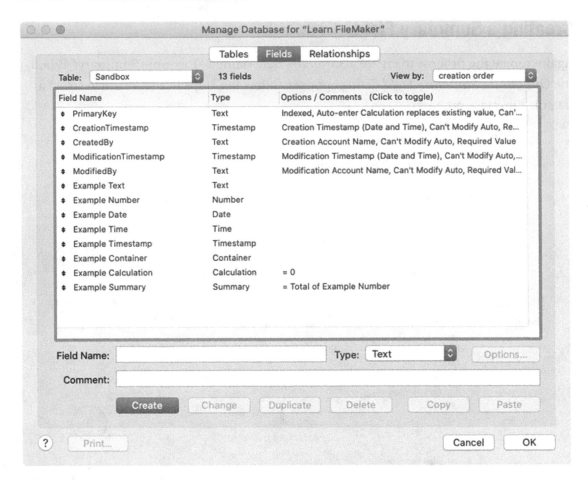

Figure 6-7. *The complete list of fields in the practice table*

Setting Up Placeholder Layouts

Continuing with a rapid setup of sandbox resources, let's set up two layouts: a *Form view* layout for data entry and a *List view* for scrolling through records.

Note   Content views were defined in more detail in Chapter 3.

Renaming the Default Layout as a Form View

A new database file will automatically have a default Form layout with the same name as the file. Initially there would have been a single *Learn FileMaker* layout. However, when the default table name was changed to "Sandbox," the layout should have changed as well. So, if following the instructions in this section, there should be a blank layout named "Sandbox." Since we will be building two layouts for the same table, we need to distinguish this one from the other layout by renaming it "Sandbox Form" following these steps:

1. Select the *View ➤ Layout* menu item to enter Layout mode.

2. Select the *Layout ➤ Layout Setup* menu to open the *Layout Setup* dialog.

3. In the *Layout Name* field on the *General* tab, change the name to "Sandbox Form" as shown in Figure 6-8.

4. Click the *OK* button to close the window and save the change.

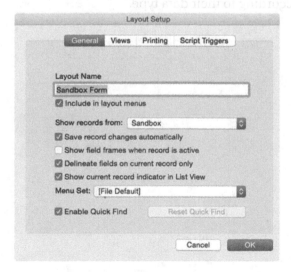

Figure 6-8. *The Layout Setup dialog with the new layout name entered*

Note   Layout settings are discussed further in Chapter 18.

Adding Fields to a Layout

If *Layout* preferences are set to automatically add new fields to the current layout (Chapter 2), then the eight Example fields will already be present on the default layout. If not, there are three ways to add fields to a layout. For now, use the *Field* tab of the *Objects* pane by following these steps in Layout mode:

1. Confirm that the *Field* tab is visible by selecting it under the *View* ➤ *Objects* ➤ *Fields tab* menu.

2. Select the entire list of fields by clicking in the field list and then selecting the *Edit* ➤ *Select All* menu item.

3. Click, hold, and drag the list of fields onto the layout, as shown in Figure 6-9. The fields should appear on the layout, neatly aligned and sized according to their data type.

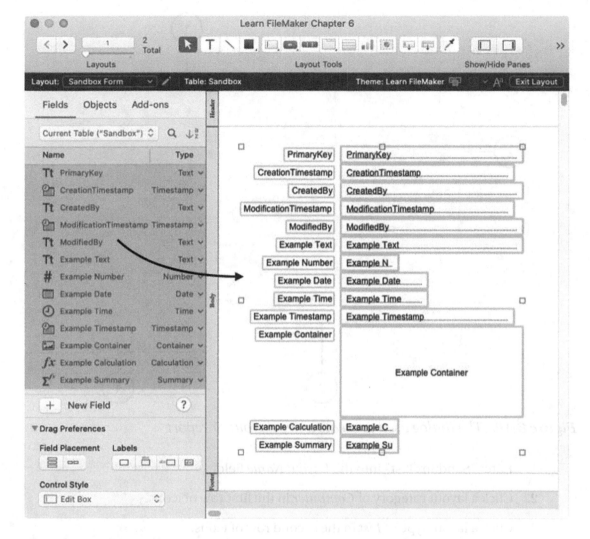

Figure 6-9. Drag selected fields from the Fields tab to the layout

---

Note   Learn about other ways to add fields to layouts in Chapter 20.

Creating a List Layout

Next, add a List view layout, by selecting the *Layout ➤ New Layout/Report* menu, and follow the steps in the dialog, shown in Figure 6-10:

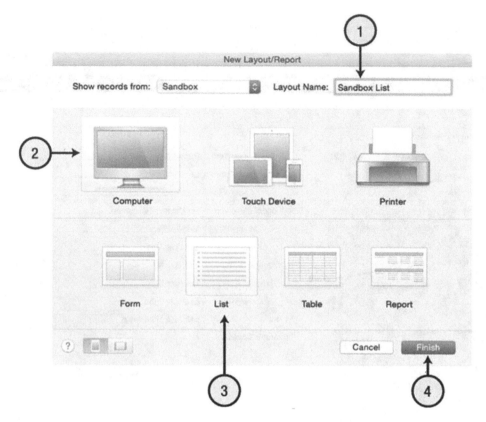

Figure 6-10. *The dialog used to create a new layout or report*

1. Enter "Sandbox List" into the *Layout Name* field.

2. Click a layout category of *Computer* in the first row of icons.

3. Click a layout type of *List* in the second row of icons.

4. Click the *Finish* button to close the dialog and complete the process.

Note   Other layout creation options are explored in Chapter 18.

When finished, an empty List view layout will appear with three parts: *Header, Body,* and *Footer.* Because a List view has a vertical orientation, the process of adding fields will change slightly, following the steps shown in Figure 6-11:

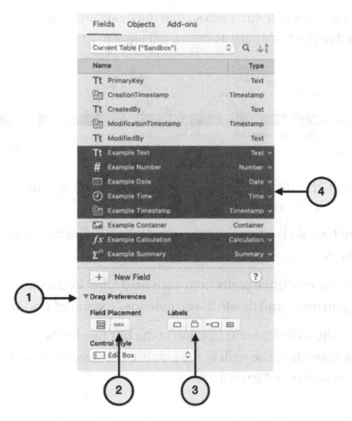

Figure 6-11. *Configure the Fields tab for dragging to a List view*

1. In the *Field tab* of the *Object* pane, confirm the *Drag Preferences* disclosure triangle is open and showing additional controls.

2. Select the *Horizontal* icon under *Field Placement*.

3. Select the *Labels* option to put labels above fields.

4. Select every Example field *except the container field* by clicking on each field while holding the Command (macOS) or Windows (Windows) key. We'll skip the container field on the List view since it will default to a large vertical footprint and attempt to expand the layout.

5. Next drag the selected fields onto the layout. Be sure to place them high enough so they land completely within the defined layout parts (horizontal white area).

6. Once placed, drag them down so that the fields are roughly centered in the *Body* part, as shown in Figure 6-12.

Figure 6-12. *The fields dropped into the Body part of the layout*

7. Position the labels squarely in the *Header* area using the mouse or arrow keys.

8. Remove the repetitive prefix from each field label by double-clicking on each, and delete the extraneous "Example" portion.

9. Finally, adjust the size and position of the last two fields so nothing extends to the right in the gray area beyond the visible layout, as shown in Figure 6-13.

Figure 6-13. *The List view with cleaned-up labels and fields*

Note   Manipulating layout objects is discussed further in Chapter 21.

Configuring File Options

The *File Options* dialog allows control over various behaviors of a database file. Unlike *application preferences*, these options are stored in the database file and are accessible only when a database is open. Select the *File ➤ File Options* menu to open the dialog which is divided into five tabs: *Open, Icon, Spelling, Text*, and *Script Triggers*.

File Options: Open

The *Open* tab settings, shown in Figure 6-14, control what happens when a database is first opened.

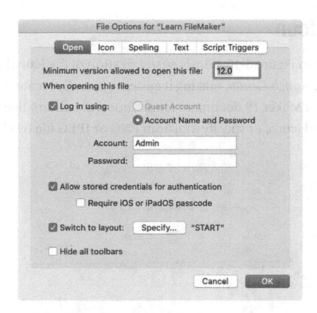

Figure 6-14. *The file options for open behavior*

The *Minimum version allowed to open this file* text field allows you to limit the file to only open for FileMaker versions at or above the version it is designed to support. Although all versions from 12.0 through 19.1 share the same file format, a database that uses features from newer versions should not be opened in an older version unless specifically designed with alternate functionality based on version. If a database uses features from newer versions, it is best to keep this set to the latest version. Enter both a *major* and *minor* version number into the field (e.g., "19.0" instead of "19").

The following four checkboxes control login and default interface functions:

- *Log In Using* – Specify automatic sign in credentials when a file opens. Do *not* use when a database requires tight security (Chapter 30).

- *Allow Stored Credentials for Authentication* – Controls if a user can opt to save credentials on their local device for automatic entry for future log-ins. Do *not* use for databases in a shared computer environment or where tight security is important.

- *Switch to Layout* – Specify a default layout when opened. This layout change runs prior to any *Script Triggers* (Chapter 27).

- *Hide All Toolbars* – Select to start with the toolbar hidden.

File Options: Icon

The *Icon* tab, shown in Figure 6-15, allows customization of the icon that represents the database in the *Launch Center,* making it easier to visually locate a desired file. The default icon is the FileMaker 19 document icon. Choose an alternative from the built-in list of Claris-provided icons, or specify a custom PNG or JPEG file by clicking *Custom*.

Figure 6-15. *The file options for assigning a custom icon*

File Options: Spelling

The *Spelling* tab, shown in Figure 6-16, controls automatic spell-check settings. The *Indicate questionable words with special underline* checkbox will enable a red dotted line under any potentially misspelled words in a field with focus unless that field or object has been configured in the *Inspector* to explicitly disable the feature (Chapter 19, "Inspecting the Data Settings"). With the *Beep on questionable spellings* selected, a sound will be played anytime a user types a word that the dictionary thinks is misspelled.

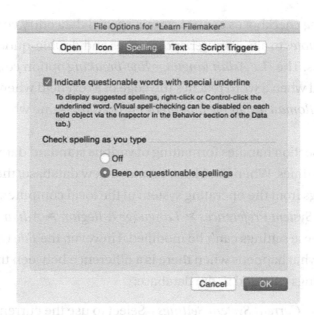

Figure 6-16. *The file options for spell-checking*

File Options: Text

The *Text* tab, shown in Figure 6-17, controls a few text entry options.

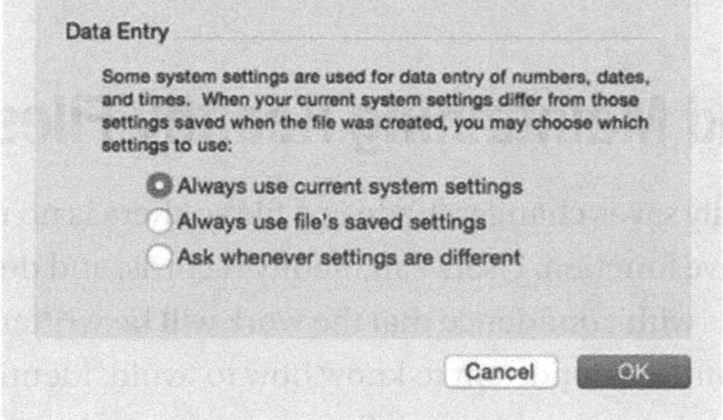

Figure 6-17. *The file options for text entry*

The *text handling* checkboxes control certain special data entry considerations. Enable *Use smart quotes* to always enter apostrophes and double-quotation marks in fields as curly quotes. The *Use Asian language line-breaking* option controls how line endings are handled when a word reaches the edge of a text field when using Asian languages, and *Use Roman language line-breaking* does the same when using Roman languages.

The *data entry* section handles formatting of various standard data like currency symbols, dates, and times. When FileMaker creates a new database, the file is encoded with regional settings from the operating system of the local computer. On macOS, these can be found in the *System Preferences* ➤ *Language & Region* ➤ *Advanced* panel. Once the file is created, these settings can't be modified. However, the *File Options* dialog allows selection of what happens when there is a difference between the user's operating system and the settings encoded in the database:

- *Always Use Current System Settings* – Select to use the current system settings of the computer instead of those saved in the database file.

- *Always Use File's Saved Settings* – Select to use the settings saved in the database file.

- *Ask Whenever Settings Are Different* – Select to ask the user at launch time which settings to use.

File Options: Script Triggers

The *Script Triggers* tab is used to configure database to automatically trigger scripts in response to interface events pertaining to the file (Chapter 27).

Designing and Maintaining Healthy Files

FileMaker automatically saves changes made in a file so there is no need or ability to explicitly perform a save function. Users can modify records, and developers can modify the structural elements with confidence that the work will be written to disk. However, things *can* go wrong, and it's important to know how to avoid, identify, and remedy problems in order to maintain healthy files. Before starting to design a custom database, take a moment to review some of the problems that can occur and how to help ensure they don't end in tragedy.

Avoiding Design and Training Deficiencies

Most database accidents are the result of some form of user confusion caused by a combination of lack of training, poor interface design, or careless scripting. A few specific problems involve users overwriting existing records, forgetting to commit a record, deleting records carelessly, or misidentifying a found set.

Overwriting an Existing Record

Overwriting existing content is a more common problem than you might think and occurs for a variety of different reasons, usually inexperience and mistaken assumptions made worse by a combination of poor interface design and inadequate training.

People lacking general computer experience or specific database knowledge often do not realize that they need to create a new record prior to typing data. Some assume that the window is like a web form that is used for entry but sends the data elsewhere for saving so they can type over and send again. Whatever the assumption, the best way to avoid this problem is with explicit training to ensure that everyone understands that they need to actually create a new record before typing information for a new entity.

Another cause of overwriting is when a user fails to duplicate a record and begin editing the original thinking it is a new duplicate record. The problem here is that the default *Duplicate* function doesn't produce any visual differences between the original and the duplicate record. The record count in the toolbar will increase, and if a field containing a unique record identifier is on the layout, it would contain a different value. Otherwise, the duplicate record will appear exactly the same as the original. If the user types or clicks in a way that doesn't actually produce a duplicate, they may accidentally begin typing over the original. Training can help them know where to look to visually confirm a new record has been created. However, a better way to avoid this is to use a custom menu (Chapter 23) that replaces the default function with your own custom script (Chapter 24). The script can create a duplicate record and then add the word "Copy" after the value in a key field, clear out fields that should be modified when creating a duplicate, and present a dialog to confirm the duplicate is ready for entry. Users will become accustomed to seeing these overt indicators and, in their absence, be more likely to realize that they failed to actually create a duplicate.

Similarly, an unnoticed failure to enter Find mode can result in inadvertent editing of a record when the user mistakes it for a temporary find request. The changes to the menu and toolbar in Find mode can easily be overlooked, and a find request appears very similar to a regular record. Newer versions of FileMaker have helpful indicators like a little magnifying glass icon that appears in every field in Find mode. Adding your own visual indicators to a layout can help further emphasize a successful switch in modes. Layout elements that hide or change formatting in Find mode can help (Chapters 17–22).

The reverse happens when a user fails to switch from Find back to Browse and then begins typing into find requests assuming they are new empty records. FileMaker has a "circuit breaker" dialog that appears after several find requests are created, reminding the user they are in Find mode. The custom visual indicators described earlier can also help avoid this problem.

A good developer must be able to switch mental focus to test an interface design from the perspective of a new user. It is important not to make biased assumptions that users possess your knowledge of a database you create in order to preemptively identify points of confusion before they cause a disaster.

Forgetting to Commit a Record

At the completion of a data entry task, an edited record must be *committed* for it to be saved and released for access by others. This happens automatically when a user navigates to another record or closes a file. They can also manually commit a record (Chapter 4, "Closing a Record"). If they leave a record open after completing the data entry task, it creates an annoyance for other users waiting to see, access, or edit the data. It can also cause conflicts for themselves if they try to access the open record in a second window on their own computer. Leaving records with uncommitted changes can even be *dangerous* and cause file damage (discussed later in this chapter). Encourage users to always commit records promptly after making changes and consider using conditional layout elements to visually indicate when a record has active focus. For example, a *Commit* button can be placed on a layout that only appears when a record is active, and a record heading text object can change color (Chapter 21).

Deleting Records Carelessly

Accidental record deletion can be the result of either the inexperience of new users or the overconfidence of experienced users. The delete confirmation dialog contains a generically minimalistic message that assumes the user is aware of the context. As a result, it does not adequately indicate which specific record(s) are about to be deleted, and this can be a major problem when the user has lost track of context or isn't paying attention. This is especially confusing on a List view when a user mistakenly assumes a different record is selected than the one they intend to delete. Also, when using multiple windows, they may think they are deleting a record in one window when they are really in another. Ironically, this problem can more often affect experienced users. While a new user may nervously read a dialog message and proceed with caution, an experienced user can become sloppy and click through a dialog with an unwarranted overconfidence. Record deletion is not something the *Undo* command can reverse so the only way to retrieve deleted records is to re-import them from a backup copy of the database. So, consider a few options to help avoid this problem.

A custom menu can override the delete functions and present a customized, informative warning dialog that clearly articulates *which record* is going to be deleted by including key identifying fields (Chapter 23, "Overriding a Menu Item Function"). Adding a second confirmation dialog can also help avoid accidents, especially when deleting a large found set. It is a little more inconvenient but can avoid the greater inconvenience of erroneous deletions. Alternatively, a custom dialog can require a user to type a word or phrase, providing an explicit confirmation of intent before a script continues with the deletion request. Also, consider placing strict limits on how many records can be deleted at once to avoid mistakes that wipe out an entire table's contents by having a custom script deny the request and present the record count in an informative dialog. Finally, security settings (Chapter 30) can completely restrict access to delete commands for users who aren't authorized to delete records.

Misidentifying a Found Set

When a user does not identify a found set, they may accidentally perform several functions that affect more records than they intend. If a user thinks the found set contains 10 records when it really contains 10,000, performing functions like *Delete All Records, Replace Field Contents,* or *Find/Replace* can create a disaster. Make sure that users understand what a found set is and how to confirm it prior to using these functions. Create more informative dialogs with custom menus (Chapter 23) and completely disable these features for users who don't require them with security settings (Chapter 30). Take extra care when creating scripts that run automatically since a poorly designed script can perform these same functions with even greater rapidity than humans, and the damage may not be immediately apparent.

Restraining File Size

Everything added to a database will increase the size of the file. Creating new tables, fields, layouts, and scripts increases file size. Entering hundreds, thousands, or millions of records increases file size. Indexed fields with large amounts of text and container fields with large files inserted both increase file size. This is a natural process that doesn't pose an immediate problem, especially since FileMaker limits databases to the amount of disk space available with a technical maximum of 8 terabytes. However, it is still a good idea to follow the adage "less is more" and design a database to be as efficient as possible both in its structure and content. Files with a large and convoluted structural design can be slower and confusing to developers and may be prone to other problems. There are two primary issues that can make a file larger than it needs to be: *inefficient design* and *fragmentation*.

Designing Efficiently

One way to maintain a slim file size and keep things operating efficiently is to design efficiently. Although there are numerous design approaches and these topics are not discussed until later chapters, the sooner you think about efficient design, the better.

When *container fields* store images or files internally, the database size will increase by the size of the item stored. Obviously, this can make a huge impact on the file size when storing hundreds or thousands of large images. If the database is hosted on a server or used locally but doesn't need to be a self-contained file, using *external container storage* (Chapter 10) is recommended and will greatly reduce the file size by storing files outside of the database file while rendering them as if they were internal so the user doesn't even notice a difference.

Another thing that rapidly increases the size of a file is field indexing, especially on lengthy notes fields. Indexing is important for certain functions and shouldn't be avoided. However, to the extent possible, try to minimize field indexes (Chapter 8, "Field Options: Storage").

Another way to keep a database slim is using a more sophisticated structural and interface design to avoid redundancy in tables, layouts, and scripts. Design *open-ended, dynamic resources* that can be used more broadly and with variable features and functions. A commonly used formula or a group of similar formulas can be moved into a single custom function (Chapter 15) to avoid repeating the same code. A table designed to store notes related to *Contact* records and a table storing notes related to a *Project* records could be combined. Layouts can be designed to provide global functionality, accessed from anywhere using a Card window attached to the main window (Chapter 25, "Managing Windows"). Scripts can be designed to accept parameters, flexibly process different information, and perform multiple variations on a single operational function.

A graphically rich interface design can improve the user experience but can also increase the size of the file and the length of time it takes to load and draw layouts. So, try to find a balance between a visually stunning display and a practical, efficient design. Use FileMaker's built-in layout objects instead of custom graphics where possible. When using custom icons, import them as SVG files into the file's icon library (Chapter 20, "Using an Icon Label"). Any custom graphics placed directly on the layout should be optimized for screen use, using lower resolution especially if they are not on print layouts.

It is worth mentioning that a monolithic hub-and-spoke relationship structure should be avoided in favor of a table occurrence group design (Chapter 9, "Using Table Occurrences"). Although a convoluted relationship setup primarily causes performance issues, it can also result in developer paralysis making better design in formulas, layouts, and scripts more difficult. Remember, an inefficient design in some areas might seem innocuous, but it can have negative repercussions elsewhere. Always strive for the best structural and interface design possible.

Finally, although it creates a more complex overall structure, spreading tables across multiple files can help reduce each file's size. There are various ways of doing this by mixing and matching different methods, briefly described in Chapter 1. For example, a *data separation model* can be used where one or more files provide a small footprint front-end interface that interacts with table content stored in one or more separate dedicated data files acting like a traditional back-end source. This allows record content to be distributed across one or more smaller files while still maintaining a single, unified interface.

Avoiding Fragmentation

As records are created and deleted through the course of normal data entry, empty space can accumulate within the file. This can also happen as developers add and remove resources. Over time, this artificially inflates the file's size and may impact performance and stability. Saving the file as a compacted copy (described later in this chapter) will safely re-create the file, fitting as much data into each block as possible to reclaim unused space by removing the bloat of empty "ghost" blocks.

Avoiding File Damage

Any digital file can become damaged. Since databases are typically accessed by many users simultaneously across a network and are continually reading from and writing to disk, they can be more vulnerable and at greater risk of data loss. Developers should be aware of what can cause damage, how to avoid it, ways to detect it, and the correct approach to repair it. Damage can range from a minor problem that initially goes unnoticed to a catastrophic inability to open the file.

There are many symptoms that may appear like a damaged file until other causes are ruled out. A field displaying a question mark instead of data can be evidence of corruption when it isn't a calculation returning the wrong type of data or a field width on a layout being too small to fit content. Records missing or appearing blank may indicate corruption. However, don't panic until confirming it isn't a mistaken found set, a layout formatting issue, or the result of accidental record deletion. Also, incorrect search results may indicate index corruption when it can't be remedied by adjusting the settings or recreating indices. Inadequate script design, inexperienced users, broken relationships, and networking issues can all create situations that can be mistaken for corruption.

Other symptoms clearly indicate damage. A database performing a consistency check when opened indicates the file wasn't closed properly and could have damage. If this happens randomly, without a crash event or force quit, it could indicate lingering damage. The FileMaker application randomly crashing when working in the database may be an operating system or networking issue, but it can also indicate corruption in the database. Finally, sometimes, a dialog will simply inform that the file is damaged, can't be opened, or should be recovered.

The best ways to avoid file damage is to share properly across a network, make sure that files are closed properly, and maintain hardware and software.

Share Properly

When sharing a database with others, *never place it in a directory that can be accessed by more than one person at a time*. This includes a folder on a file server or any type of cloud storage, e.g., Dropbox, Google Drive, etc. Two users opening the same database file directly from a folder will guarantee a corrupt file. Instead, use FileMaker's *peer-to-peer sharing,* or host the file on a *FileMaker Server* to ensure proper multi-user read/write management and greater protection from user crashes (Chapter 29).

Close Files Properly

Most file damage occurs when a database was improperly closed. This can result in the loss of data, corrupted data, and/or structural flaws. The proper close method is to close all database windows or to quit the FileMaker application by selected the *File* ➤ *Quit Application* menu. Some ways a database may be *improperly closed* include

- Computer power is interrupted, resulting in abrupt shutdown of an open database.

- A system-wide crash that also crashes FileMaker.

- A glitch that causes FileMaker to unexpectedly quit.

- If the network connection is dropped as it is when the user's computer goes to sleep while a hosted database is open.

- A hasty force quit of the application with databases open when a user mistakes a spinning cursor during a lengthy script process for a crash.

- A force quit is required to stop a faulty script endlessly looping with abort capability turned off.

- Trying to open or make a copy of a live database actively hosted by *FileMaker Server.*

Tip   Databases hosted on a FileMaker Server (Chapter 29) are cushioned from user computer crashes and force quit damage. Files run locally are more vulnerable.

Maintain Hardware and Software

Always maintain stable and up-to-date hardware and software, paying close attention to these details:

- Don't rush to upgrade anything. Perform extensive testing on a safe *copy* of your database prior to upgrading hardware or software.

- Keep host and user operating systems up to date.

- Keep the FileMaker application up to date, including all interim bug fix releases.

- Use an adequate uninterruptable power supply and surge protector on all computers to avoid sudden shutdowns in the event of a power loss, especially a database host server.

- Run regular hardware maintenance using a disk utility program, and don't let computers get outdated to the point of risking failure.

- Don't allow the disk of a host computer to run out of space.

- Use fast hardware and networking equipment with adequate cabling.

- Perform regular database maintenance.

Tip   Consider using FileMaker Cloud which handles most hardware and software maintenance functions automatically.

Exploring Maintenance Functions

There are several functions that can help maintain database integrity and troubleshoot file damage. Each must be performed *locally,* so files hosted on a network must be taken offline and manipulated directly in a copy of the *FileMaker Pro* desktop application. These functions are *Save a copy as, Consistency check,* and *Recover.*

Tip   Always make regular backups of your databases, and preserve an extra development copy of major structural changes. If damage occurs, the safest action is to revert to a recent backup or recover data from the damaged file and import it into a reliable backup.

Saving a Copy As

The *Save a Copy As* function, accessible under the *File* menu, will create a new copy of the open database as one of these four types selectable in the save file dialog: *Copy, Compacted, Clone,* or *Self-Contained.*

The *Copy of current file* option saves the database as an identical copy of itself without any changes. This is identical to the *Save As* function in most applications and can also be done by duplicating a closed file using the operating system file duplication command. It doesn't have any diagnostic function; it simply makes a copy.

The *Compacted copy (smaller)* option saves an optimized copy of the database with empty space removed, resulting in a smaller file size. Used periodically, this can maintain the health of a file, especially if a lot of content is deleted from a file or lots of structural changes have occurred.

The *Clone (no records)* option saves a copy of the database's *structure only*. This will include tables, fields, relationships, page setup options, field definitions, custom functions, layouts, scripts, and more, *without any records*. This can be used when troubleshooting a problem as it quickly isolates a file's structure from its content.

The *Self-contained copy (single file)* option saves a copy with external container data (Chapter 10) embedded in the file's container fields, making it fully self-contained.

Performing a Consistency Check

A *consistency check* will read every block that makes up a file, verify the internal structure of each block, and confirm it is properly linked to other blocks. This process does not read the data within blocks, check the file schema, or check higher-level structures; these functions are only performed by the full *Recover* process. Each time a database opens, FileMaker checks the file and automatically performs a consistency check if it detects that the file has been improperly closed. A manual consistency check can be performed on any closed file as a troubleshooting step when damage is suspected. Launch the *FileMaker Pro* application, and select the *File ➤ Recover* menu. In the file selection dialog, shown in Figure 6-18, select the file suspected of damage. Instead of clicking the *Select* button, which would begin the full *Recover* process, click the *Check Consistency* button.

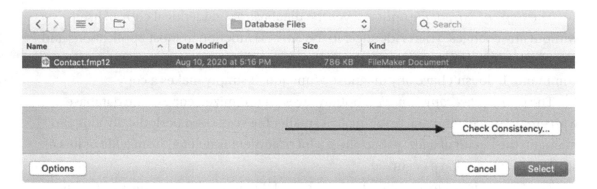

Figure 6-18. *Use the check consistency button instead of performing a full recovery*

FileMaker will immediately check the file and report the results in both a dialog and *Recover.log* file. If no problems have been reported, the file is probably safe to continue using. If damage is reported, it may recommend performing the recovery process. After the consistency check is complete, the file selection dialog remains open so you can choose to recover the file, perform a consistency check on a different file, or cancel.

Recovering a File

When a database is damaged or acting buggy, the *Recover* function can be used to rebuild a new copy of the file and regain access to its contents. This process is *aggressive* and will do whatever is necessary to restore access to a file. It will rebuild the file block by block and attempt to correct any corruption. However, if an object can't be repaired, it may be deleted. Because of its aggressive nature, the function should be used a diagnostic or recovery tool and *not* for regular maintenance. To perform the recovery process, launch the FileMaker Pro application, and select the *File ➤ Recover* menu. In the file selection dialog, locate the damaged file, and click the *Select* button. In the *Save* dialog, enter a name and select a save location for the new recovered copy of the file, and optionally specify advanced options (described in the next section). Then click *Save* to begin the recovery process.

FileMaker will rebuild the file to the specified save location and report the results. Based on the information provided, you can determine if the recovered copy of the file is safe for use or if you should transfer the content into a previously saved backup copy. If no stable backup is available, it is possible to meticulously review the recovery log to see what type of structural objects are reported as corrupt and then systematically delete resources and repeat the recovery process over and over until you isolate the corrupt resources. Then, each corrupted item can be deleted and recreated in the original file and the process repeated until the recovery process reports the file has no problems. However, preserving safe backups is the best practice.

Advanced Recovery Options

The *Advanced Recover Options* dialog, shown in Figure 6-19, controls how a recovery is performed.

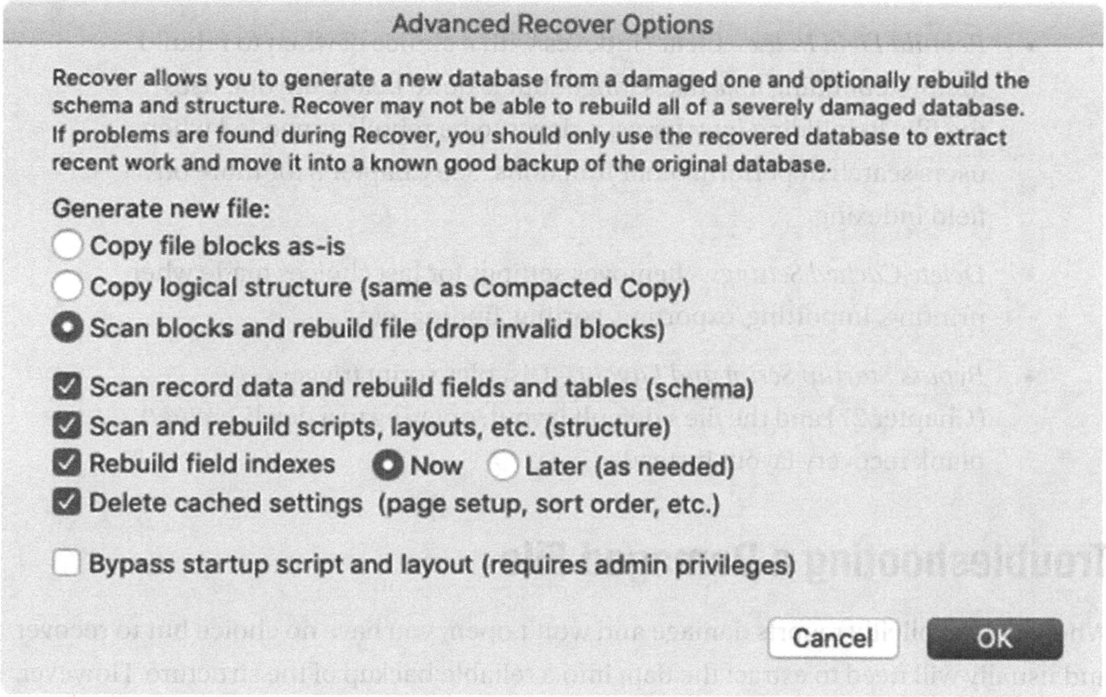

Advanced Recover Options

Recover allows you to generate a new database from a damaged one and optionally rebuild the schema and structure. Recover may not be able to rebuild all of a severely damaged database. If problems are found during Recover, you should only use the recovered database to extract recent work and move it into a known good backup of the original database.

Generate new file:
- ○ Copy file blocks as-is
- ○ Copy logical structure (same as Compacted Copy)
- ● Scan blocks and rebuild file (drop invalid blocks)

- ☑ Scan record data and rebuild fields and tables (schema)
- ☑ Scan and rebuild scripts, layouts, etc. (structure)
- ☑ Rebuild field indexes   ● Now   ○ Later (as needed)
- ☑ Delete cached settings (page setup, sort order, etc.)

- ☐ Bypass startup script and layout (requires admin privileges)

Cancel   OK

Figure 6-19. *The advanced options for recovery a file*

The *Generate new file* section controls which of three ways a new file will be created during the recovery process. Select *Copy file blocks as-is* to copy all file blocks exactly as they exist in the source file. The resulting file may still include damaged blocks. This is the equivalent of just saving a copy of the current file. The *Copy logical structure (same as Compacted Copy)* will copy all data in the source file without checking the blocks, but it will rebuild the tree structure. The resulting file may still include damaged blocks. This is the equivalent of saving a compacted copy of the current file. Finally, select *Scan blocks and rebuild file (drop invalid blocks)* to completely rebuild the file, including only undamaged and non-duplicate blocks. The resulting file may be structurally unsound and may only be suitable for data extraction into a reliable backup copy. This is the full recovery process. The following checkboxes control optional functions during recovery:

- *Scan Record Data and Rebuild Fields and Tables (schema)* – Rebuilds the file's database *schema* (tables, fields, and relationships), removing fields or records found to be at invalid locations within the file, and re-creates missing fields and table definitions.

- *Scan and Rebuild Scripts, Layouts, etc. (structure)* – Rebuilds the file's *structure* (layouts, scripts, themes).

- *Rebuild Field Index* – Clears indexes with a choice of when to rebuild them. Rebuilding *now* takes longer but is done before anyone uses the file. Rebuilding *later* forces indexes to be rebuilt as needed when users search or perform other functions. See Chapter 8 for more on field indexing.

- *Delete Cached Settings* – Removes settings for last choices made when printing, importing/exporting, sorting, finding, etc.

- *Bypass Startup Script and Layout* – Disables script triggers (Chapter 27) and the file's default layout, opening to a newly created blank recovery layout instead.

Troubleshooting a Damaged File

When a file explicitly reports damage and won't open, you have no choice but to recover and usually will need to extract the data into a reliable backup of the structure. However, when a file opens but exhibits severe intermittent crashing, there are several steps required to safely *locate the damage, determine the best course of action,* and *transfer records into a good structure.*

Locating Damage

The first troubleshooting step involves locating the damage by determining if it is in the *database structure* or *record data.* Depending on what you find, your recovery option and choice of file for future use may vary.

Checking the Database Structure

To determine if the *database structure* is damaged, follow these steps:

1. Create a troubleshooting copy of the original file, naming it something unique, e.g., "Broken Database."

2. Isolate the structure by making a copy without any record data. Open the *Broken Database* file, and perform the *Save a Copy as* command, selecting *Clone (no records)* option and naming it "Broken Database Structure." Then close the *Broken Database* file.

3. Next, compact the *Broken Database Structure* to preemptively fix any minor issues that might get in the way of troubleshooting. Open the *Broken Database Structure* file, and perform the *Save a Copy as* command, selecting *compacted copy (smaller)* option and naming it "Broken Database Structure Compacted." Then close the file.

4. To diagnose the structure, *Recover the Broken Database Structure Compacted* using default recovery settings (uncheck advanced options) and saving it as "Broken Database Structure Recovered."

If damage is found, you may be able to skip checking the record data and instead recover the original file and transfer record data from that into a reliable backup structure, ideally a preserved clone of a backup from a time prior to the introduction of corruption. If the corruption has been lingering awhile and you do not have access to such a file, you *can* use the recovered file generated previously as the structure. However, keep in mind that the recovery process may result in renamed or deleted objects that could not be recovered, so some work to remedy these may be required. For example, a field might be renamed "Recovered Field," or a "Recovered Blob" or "Recovered Library" table occurrence can appear in the relationship graph. These may or may not indicate corruption or data loss.

Caution   If the FileMaker recovery report explicitly states that a file is not safe for use, using it anyway is *not recommended*.

Checking the Record Data

Once the file structure has been ruled out as the source of corruption, follow these steps to determine if the *record data* is damaged:

1. Open the *Broken Database* troubleshooting copy, and perform the *Save a Copy as* command, selecting *compacted copy (smaller)* option and naming it "Broken Database Records." Then close the file.

2. Recover the *Broken Database Records* using default recovery settings by unchecking the `advanced options` and naming it "`Broken Database Records Recovered`."

Determining the Best Course of Action

If *no* damage is reported in both the file structure *and* record data, you can try to use the recovered file at the conclusion of the record data check. If random crashes continue to occur, consider transferring the record data into a safe structure anyway. If the structure *or* record data reported damage, immediately transfer the record data to safe structure.

Transferring Records into a Good Structure

To move record data from the recovered file into a reliable structure, follow these steps:

1. Make a copy of either the recovered file from the conclusion of the record data check (like the *Broken Database Records Recovered* described earlier) or the original troubleshooting copy.

2. Open the file.

3. Perform a *Find All* to confirm a found set of all records.

4. Export all records using the *Excel Workbooks (.xlsx)* type option. Be sure to check the *Use field names as column names in first row* option in the *Excel Options* dialog. In the *Export Options* dialog, take care to select all fields from the *Current Table* and not just the ones visible on the current layout.

> **Caution**   Exporting to a non-FileMaker format guarantees the data is cleanly separated from any structural corruption. However, container fields are not supported and can't be exported. Those must be manually restored in the new database. You may attempt to export to the FileMaker format instead but then need to double-check to confirm that no corruption follows the data in the transfer.

5. Repeat steps 3 and 4 for every table in the database.

6. Identify a stable copy of the database *structure*. Ideally use a clone that was created from a time prior to the corruption event. If that is not available, use a recovered copy (like the *Broken Database Structure Recovered* from the previous process) as long as the database structure is no longer reporting damage.

7. Import the records from the spreadsheet(s) into each table of the safe structure.

Summary

This chapter explored the basics of creating, configuring, and maintaining the health of database files. In the next chapter, learn how to create tables and begin developing an object model that will define the fields that can be populated when entering records.

## CHAPTER 7

Working with Tables

A *table* is the fundamental unit of a database's structural schema which forms a digital representative of some type of entity being modeled. Tables create a digital space and define a set of fields for storing data. This chapter explores the following topics:

- Introducing object modeling
- Introducing the Manage Database window (Tables)
- Planning table names
- Managing tables
- Adding tables to the example database

Introducing Object Modeling

An *object model* or *data model* is an abstraction that defines elements of data for database entries, describing how they relate both to each other and to properties of the real-world entities they represent. A model is like an architectural blueprint that informs FileMaker about the structure of the information a database will store and manage. The term is used because the information is sometimes called a *virtual model* of the real objects represented by that structure. *Data modeling* is the process of planning and creating a model of the various properties, relationships, and actions that make up a data model for a set of related entity classes that will be managed by a database. The elements of an object model are *tables*, *fields*, and *relationships*.

A *table* allocates a space for a particular type of entity being modeled within the database. These are analogous to a tab in a spreadsheet, as shown in Figure 7-1. The term is used to refer to both the structural definition of a table as a storage model and to the content collected within that structure. So, one may refer to a *table's fields* (defined structure) and a *table's records* (content entered). Objects modeled as tables can be broad categories (people or products), narrow subcategories (employees or cars),

© Mark Conway Munro 2021

M. C. Munro, *Learn FileMaker Pro 19*, https://doi.org/10.1007/978-1-4842-6680-9_7

properties of an entity (prices or components), actions (historical events or process steps), or any other thing one may need to manage. In the early planning stages, a model may take the form of a simple list of table names, e.g., *Company*, *Person*, and *Project*. Later, this expands into a field list for each table and details about how they all interconnect to form a relational hierarchy. Complex systems can contain models defining dozens or hundreds of tables.

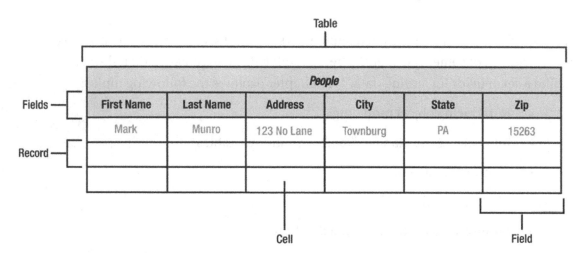

Figure 7-1. *The basic anatomy of a database table*

The spreadsheet metaphor continues for *fields, records,* and *cells.*

A *field,* similar to a column in a spreadsheet, is a defined container in which one piece of information about the modeled entity will be stored. In the example shown, each column heading names an individual field defining the column beneath it: *First Name, Last Name, Address,* etc.

A *record,* similar to a row in the spreadsheet, represents one individual entry stored within the table for one instance of the object being modeled. While the table in the example represents *people in general,* a row, or record, represents *one specific person.* The record is one instance of the table's defined field set, created to store information about a specific person.

A *cell* is the formal name of an intersection of a field and record. In FileMaker, these are commonly referred to less formally as *fields* with the implied understanding of the difference between an instance of a field definition for a specific record (*cell*) and the field definition itself (*field*).

Introducing the Manage Database Dialog (Tables)

Tables are created and configured from the *Tables* tab of the *Manage Database* dialog, shown in Figure 7-2. Once a database file is open, this dialog can be opened by selecting the *File* ➤ *Manage* ➤ *Database* menu in Browse or Layout mode or selecting *Database* in the *Manage* toolbar menu in Layout mode. It is also accessible from various developer menus throughout the development interface, such as the *Specify Import Order* dialog (Chapter 5).

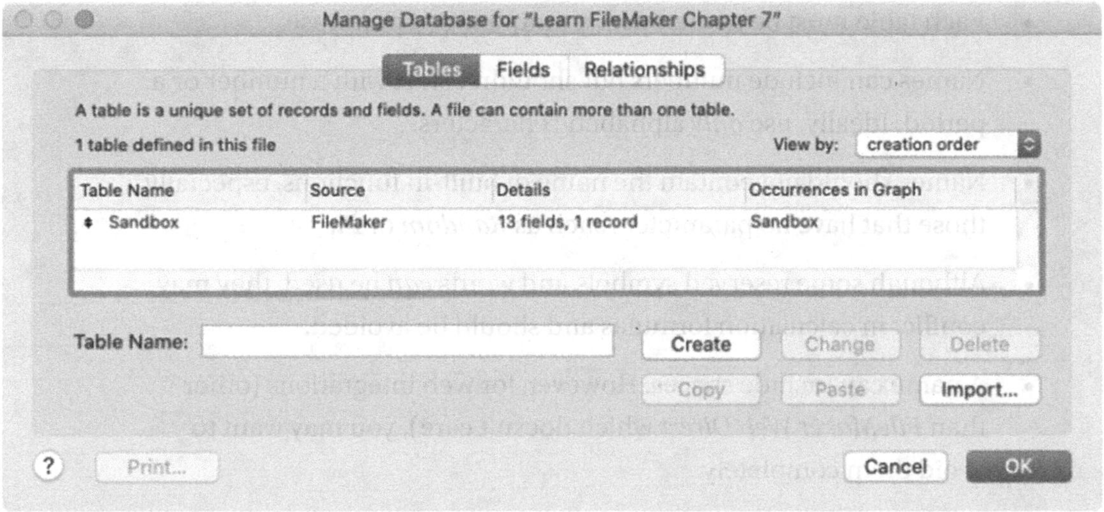

Figure 7-2. *The dialog used to manage tables*

The *Tables* tab displays a list of every table defined in the file. Each is made up of five properties listed in columns. The first column displays the *Table Name*. The *Source* column displays the source type of the table, either "FileMaker" or the name of an ODBC data source. *Details* includes a count of *Fields* defined as the table structure and *Records* of data content stored. Finally, *Occurrences in Graph* displays a comma-separated list of every instance of the table in the relationship graph (Chapter 9).

Tables in the list can be selected to *rename, delete,* or *copy* and *paste*. A double-click switches to the *Fields* tab for that table. The *Table Name* field below the list displays the name of the selected table and is used to change the name or enter a name for a new table. Clicking OK saves changes and closes the dialog. Clicking Cancel will close the dialog *without saving changes made in any tab*.

Planning Table Names

Table names can use a variety of different conventions depending on the preferences of an individual developer and any technical requirements for compatibility when the database is used as a source for inbound API, JDBC/ODBC, or WebDirect connections. Names composed of multiple words can be delimited with a space (*Project Resource*) and an underscore (*Project_Resource*) or have no space using "camel case" (*ProjectResources*). They can be upper- or lowercase or any combination of the two. Every table names must follow these rules:

- Each table must be named with a unique word or phrase.

- Names can include numbers but shouldn't start with a number or a period. Ideally, use *only* alphabetic characters.

- Names should not contain the name of built-in functions, especially those that have no parameters such as *Random* or *Pi*.

- Although some reserved symbols and words *can* be used, they may conflict in calculation formulas and should be avoided.

- A name can include spaces. However, for web integrations (other than *FileMaker Web Direct* which doesn't care), you may want to avoid them completely.

Beyond these technical considerations, take a moment to consider what constitutes a *good* table name. Every table should be clearly descriptive, concise but not cryptic, and exist harmoniously with other tables. Here are a few suggestions to consider when developing a list of table names:

- Names should clearly indicate the entity class modeled by the table, concisely as possible without being cryptic.

- Use full words instead of abbreviations where possible. If a word is too long, consult a thesaurus for a shorter alternative.

- Consider the full context of other tables in the file. A table named *Stuff* is fine in a database that manages only one kind of stuff. However, when modeling several kinds of stuff, use more descriptive names like *Inventory*, *Resources*, *Supplies*, etc.

- Use multiple words for clarity. When there are other tables for similarly named entities, make sure that their names are *differentiated enough* to avoid confusion.

- Be consistent, using the same format and keeping all names either singular or plural. For example, use either *Contact* and *Company* or *Contacts* and *Companies.*

- For large lists of tables, consider prefixes to organize them into conceptual groups so they sort neatly in developer selection menus, as shown in Figure 7-3.

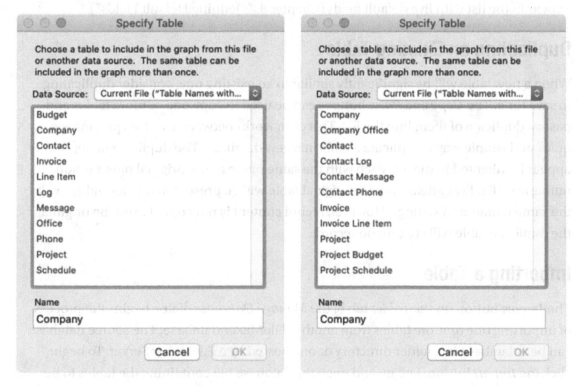

Figure 7-3. *A list of raw names (left) and the same with group prefixes (right)*

Managing Tables

Tables can be *added, renamed,* and *deleted* using the buttons on the *Tables* tab of the *Manage Database* dialog.

Adding Tables

There are *several* different methods for adding tables: creating a new table, duplicating an existing table, importing a table from another FileMaker database, or adding a table from an external ODBC data source. Tables can also be automatically created while importing records (Chapter 5, "Selecting a Target Table").

Creating a New Table

Manually create a new table from the *Tables* tab of the *Manage Database* dialog by typing a name into the *Table Name* text area and clicking the *Create* button. The new table will appear in the list with five default fields (Chapter 8, "Defining Default Fields").

Duplicating an Existing Table

When a new table will be significantly similar to an existing one, consider duplicating to save time. The *Copy* and *Paste* buttons can be used to copy one or more tables and paste a duplicate of them into the list. This even works between two files providing a quick and simple way to replicate a table in a new database. The duplicate table(s) will appear highlighted in the list, each with the same name as the original plus a unique numeric suffix. Every field from the original table will be present in the new table, with the same names and settings. However, record content is not copied from the original; the duplicate table will contain no records.

Importing a Table

The *Import* button on the *Tables* tab of the *Manage Database* dialog begins the process of importing one or more tables from another FileMaker database. The source database can be a database in a folder directory or one hosted by a FileMaker Server. To begin, click the *Import* button. Locate and open the database file containing the tables to be imported. Once opened, FileMaker will present an *Import Tables* dialog listing all the tables available for import from the selected database, as shown in Figure 7-4. Check the box next to the desired table(s) and click OK to import. Here too, only the structure will be imported so the tables will contain no records.

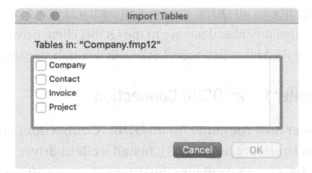

Figure 7-4. The dialog used to import tables from another FileMaker database

Adding a Table from an ODBC Data Source (macOS)

Open Database Connectivity (ODBC) is a standard application programming interface (API) that provides client applications a common language for interacting with other database systems. *Java Database Connectivity* (JDBC) is a similar API for accessing systems written in the Java language. FileMaker can use both ODBC and JDBC to communicate with a *Driver Manager* application that uses a client driver to communicate with an external data source, as shown in Figure 7-5.

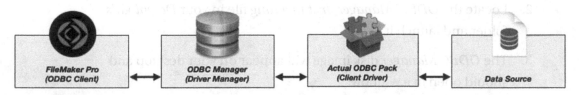

Figure 7-5. Connecting a FileMaker database to an ODBC data source

---

Caution   ODBC connections are only required to connect non-FileMaker databases, not for FileMaker database connections.

FileMaker can act as an ODBC client application or as an ODBC and JDBC data source. As a client application, FileMaker supports connections to external SQL data sources such as those from Oracle, Microsoft SQL, and MySQL. Once connected, tables from the external database can be added to the FileMaker database, and with a few exceptions, they act like a native FileMaker table. The process of configuring a computer and database for ODBC access is a relatively straightforward three-step process. First, prepare the host computer for an ODBC connection with a *Driver Manager* and *Client Driver*. Next, connect the FileMaker database to the ODBC client driver. Finally, insert and use ODBC tables in the FileMaker database. Let's walk through an example of this process.

Preparing a Computer for an ODBC Connection

To prepare a FileMaker host computer for an ODBC Connection, install the *ODBC Manager* application (freeware for macOS), install a client driver (such as *Actual Technologies ODBC Pack*), and configure the driver for a specific external data source. The *host computer* is the computer upon which the FileMaker database is installed (a computer running FileMaker Server rather than a client computer accessing it).

Installing the ODBC Manager Application

Download and install the freeware *ODBC Manager* application onto the host computer, by following these steps:

1. Download the *ODBC Manager* disk image from `www.odbcmanager.net`.

2. Locate the *ODBC_Manager_Installer.dmg* file in your *Downloads* folder and launch it.

3. The *ODBC Manager* disk image will appear on your desktop and should open in a window.

4. Double-click on the *ODBC Manager.pkg* file to launch the installer.

5. Step through the installer panels to complete the installation.

Once the installer has finished, the *ODBC Manager application* should be in your *Utilities sub*folder of the macOS *Applications* folder.

Installing the ODBC Driver

Next, download and install an ODBC driver, like the one described here from Actual Technologies, by following these steps:

1. Download the *Actual ODBC Pack* disk image, available at `www.actualtech.com/download.php`.

2. Locate the *Actual_ODBC_Pack.dmg* file in your *Downloads* folder and launch it.

3. The *Actual ODBC Pack* disk image will appear on your desktop and should open in a window.

4. Double-click on the *Actual ODBC Pack.pkg* file to launch the installer.

5. Step through the installer panels to complete the installation.

Note   The driver is a fully functional demo, limited to display only the first three rows resulting from any query. Purchase a license key from Actual Technologies web store to remove this limit.

Configuring Driver

Next, add and configure a driver for the specific database to which a connection will be made. Begin by opening the *ODBC Manager* application, shown in Figure 7-6.

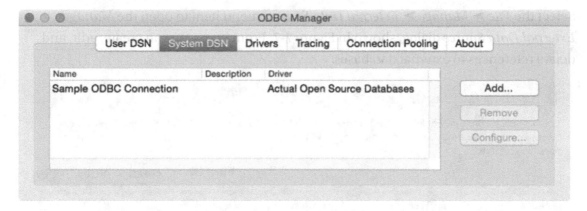

Figure 7-6.   *The ODBC Manager with a single connection*

Then follow these steps in the dialog:

1. Click on the *System DSN* tab.

2. Click the *Add* button.

3. In the panel that opens, choose a driver appropriate for the target database: *Actual access*, *Actual open source databases*, *Actual oracle*, or *Actual SQL server*.

4. Enter settings into the multi-panel driver specific configuration dialog. These vary but generally include the *server address*, *database name*, *username*, and *password*.

5. Click the *Done* button to close the configuration dialog.

6. The final panel of the configuration dialog allows you to test the connection.

7. Quit the *ODBC Manager* application.

Connecting a FileMaker Database to the ODBC Client Driver

Connect your FileMaker database to the ODBC driver you just configured. This is done by setting up an external data source in the database and then adding table(s) from the external source into the FileMaker relationship graph.

Setting Up External Data Source

Select the *File* ➤ *Manage* ➤ *External Data Sources* menu item to open the *Manage External Data Source* dialog, shown in Figure 7-7. From here, you can create, edit, and delete references to external databases.

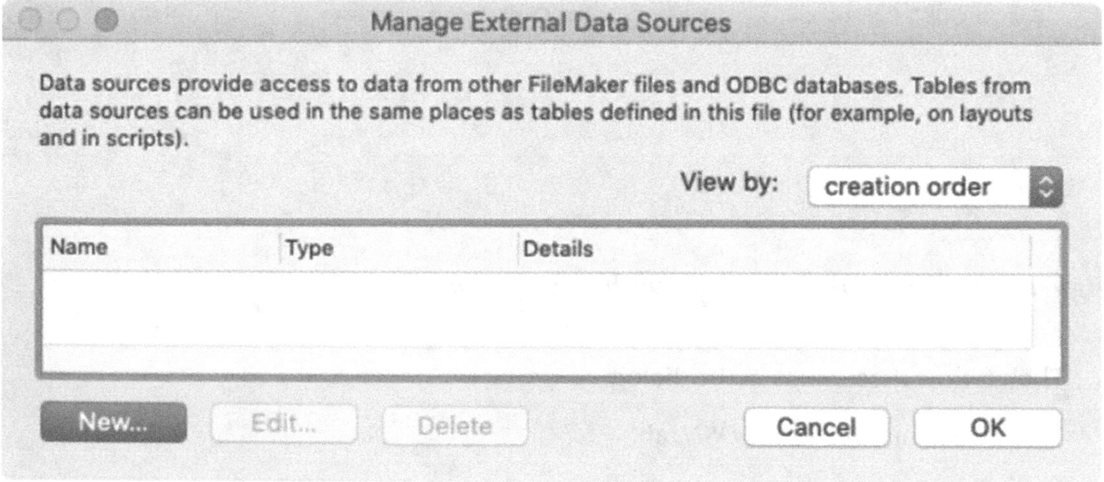

Figure 7-7. *The dialog to manage external data sources*

To add a new external source, click the *New* button to open the *Edit Data Source* dialog. At first, the dialog will ask for a *File Path List* because the *Type* is set to *FileMaker*. Once you select ODBC instead, the dialog will change, as shown in Figure 7-8.

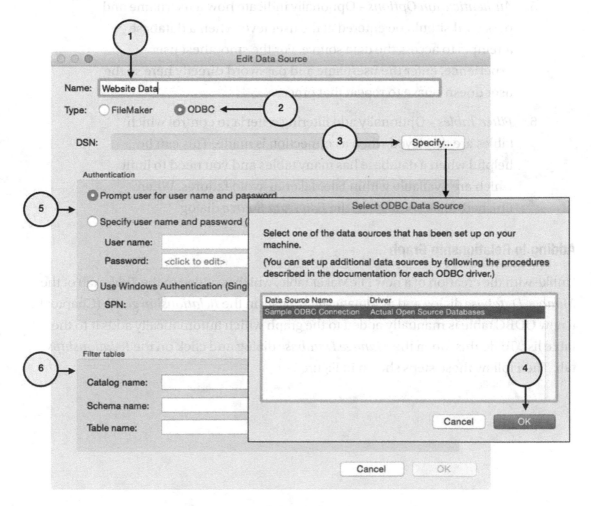

Figure 7-8. *The process for setting up an external data source*

Follow these steps to configure a connection to the ODBC driver:

1. *Name* – Enter a unique name for the data source for use within FileMaker.

2. *Type* – Select *ODBC* radio button.

3. *DSN* – Click the *Specify* button.

4. *Select ODBC Data Source* – Select the desired data source from the list defined in the *ODBC Manager* application, and then click to close the dialog.

5. *Authentication Options* – Optionally indicate how a username and password should be entered at the user level when a database attempts to access the data source. For the smoothest user experience, enter the username and password directly here so the user doesn't have to repeat that process.

6. *Filter Tables* – Optionally add filtering criteria to control which tables are displayed when a connection is made. This can be helpful when a database has many tables and you need to limit which are available within FileMaker to avoid failures. When finished, click OK to close the *Edit Data Source* dialog.

Adding to Relationship Graph

Unlike with the creation of a new FileMaker table, which is added to the *Tables* tab of the *Manage Database* dialog and automatically appears in the *Relationship graph* (Chapter 9), a new ODBC table is manually added to the graph which automatically adds it to the table list. To do this, open the *Manage Database* dialog and click on the *Relationships* tab. Then follow these steps shown in Figure 7-9:

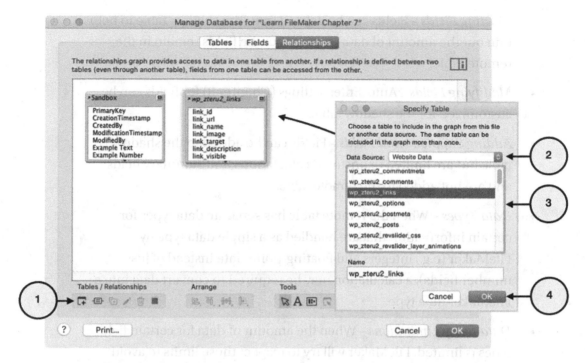

Figure 7-9. *The process for adding an ODBC source to the relationship graph*

1. Click the *Add* button.

2. In the *Specify Table* dialog that opens, select the ODBC connection in the *Data Source* menu.

3. Select the table.

4. Click the *OK* button to add the table to the occurrence graph and list of tables.

Defining an ODBC "Shadow Table" in FileMaker

When an ODBC table is added to the relationship graph, FileMaker automatically creates a *shadow table* in the *Tables* tab. This is an internal representation that mirrors the external table. These appear in the list on the *Tables* tab with italic formatting. Although this brings the external table into the database and allows interactions similar to a native FileMaker table, there are a few notable differences, including

- *Schema Lock* – The structure of the external data source is not available for modification from within FileMaker. The shadow table in FileMaker allows some modification, but this does not affect the remote table.

- *Deleting Fields* – Fields can be deleted from the shadow table to help thin out the amount of data queried, but the fields remain in the remote table.

- *Modifying Fields* – Auto-Enter settings (Chapter 8) for fields can be customized for the shadow table.

- *Adding Supplemental Fields* – Fields can be added to the shadow table but are limited to unstored calculations and summary fields and are not added to the remote table.

- *Data Types* – When the remote table has separate data types for certain information that are handled as a single data type by FileMaker (e.g., integers and floating-point data instead of just number fields), a calculation may be required to convert data into a FileMaker data type.

- *Data Entry Limitations* – When the amount of data for certain field types is limited, FileMaker will try to respect these limits to avoid problems, but special care may be required.

- *Data Updates* – Automatic refreshes of record changes in the external table are less frequent across the network than changes to native FileMaker tables. Use the *Refresh Window* script step to force an update and ensure that the data displayed is current.

- *Record Locking* – Unlike native tables, records open for editing are not locked, so users can be editing the same record simultaneously. A warning dialog will alert users if the record had been modified since they began editing and give them the ability to stop to avoid overwriting the other user's changes.

- *Indexing* – FileMaker can't index SQL fields, so searches in external tables should be limited to those fields already indexed by the remote table to avoid long delays.

Tip   Claris' technical brief "Introduction to External SQL Sources" contains more information about ODBC, JDBC, and the various connection options to and from FileMaker databases.

Renaming and Deleting Tables

A table selected in the *Tables* tab from the *Manage Database* dialog can be renamed or deleted. To rename, enter a new name in the *Table Name* text area, and click the *Change* button. To delete, click the *Delete* button. A *Delete Tables* warning dialog will appear to confirm you want to continue, as shown in Figure 7-10. The dialog includes a check box that, when selected, will also delete the corresponding table occurrence in the relationship graph (Chapter 9). If not selected, any table occurrences in the graph will become *<missing table>* placeholders. A deleted table's field definitions and records will always be deleted, while layouts will remain until manually deleted or reassigned.

Delete Tables

Permanently delete the selected 1 FileMaker table(s) and all of their fields and record data?

☐ Also remove occurrences of these tables in the graph

Delete   Cancel

Figure 7-10. *The warning dialog when deleting tables*

Adding Tables to the Example Database

Before continuing, add three tables to the *Learn FileMaker* database: *Company*, *Contact*, and *Project*. For now, create the tables and leave the automatically created default fields, table occurrences, and layouts in place. Once finished, the dialog should appear as shown in Figure 7-11.

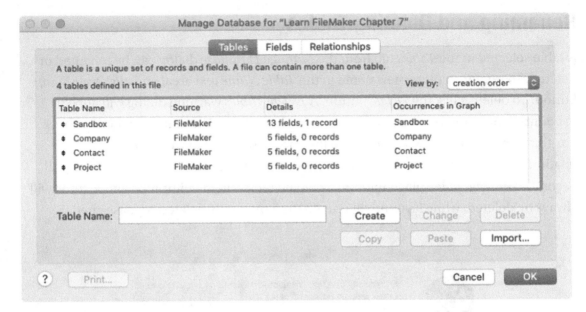

Figure 7-11. *The Learn FileMaker database tables with default fields*

Summary

This chapter explored the basics of working with tables, both natively in FileMaker and connecting to an external SQL data source. In the next chapter, we learn how to add fields to tables and configure their various properties.

## CHAPTER 8

Defining Fields

A *field* is a defined data entry space within a table. Using the spreadsheet analogy, a field is like a column, named and configured to contain a specific type of data. This chapter focuses on the following field-related topics:

- Defining field data types

- Introducing the Manage Database dialog (fields)

- Planning field names

- Defining default fields

- Managing fields

- Setting field options

- Adding fields to the example database

Defining Field Data Types

FileMaker supports eight different types of fields which fall into one of two categories: *entry fields* and *display fields*.

Entry Fields

An *entry field* is a field capable of data input by a user, script, or import process. FileMaker has six types of entry fields, each for a specific class of data: *text, number, date, time, timestamp,* and *container*.

M. C. Munro, *Learn FileMaker Pro 19*, https://doi.org/10.1007/978-1-4842-6680-9_8

Note   By definition, an entry field can accept input. However, a user's ability to do so in a given instance will depend on the field's layout presence (Part 4) and the user's security settings (Chapter 30).

Text Fields

A *text field* is used to store any combination of letters, symbols, or numbers as a string of any length up to ten million characters. The content of a text field can be plain text with layout settings controlling display format, or they can include embedded formatting information, richly styled with font, size, style, and color. When sorting records by a text field, the values will be sorted in alphabetical order. This means that numbers contained within the text will be sorted *as text* and evaluated one character at a time; e.g., a value of "10" will sort *before* "2," since 1 comes before 2.

Tip   Use a text field to store numbers that contain leading zeros.

Number Fields

A *number field* is used to store any numeric value ranging from 10^{-400} to 10^{400} up to one billion characters per field. A value in a number field can include non-numeric characters that are used to format numbers. For example, a number field can contain "5000" or "$5,000.00." While these additional characters don't adversely affect data entry, finding, or sorting, ideally only numerals should be physically entered into the field since currency formatting can be applied dynamically using field display layout settings (Chapter 19, "Data Formatting"). When sorting records by a number field, the values in the field will be sorted in numeric order, so a value of "10" will sort properly after "2."

Date Fields

A *date field* is used to store a formal date within a range from *January 1, 0001*, through *December 31, 4000*. Dates must be typed using the *short date format* matching the database setting for dates and times which was inherited from the computer upon which the file was created (Chapter 6, "File Options: Text"). In the United States, the default format is typically "<month>/<day>/<year>." For example, *January 15, 2017*, would be entered into a date field as "1/15/2017." Although all dates must be entered as short dates, a field on a layout can be configured to display the value in one of a variety of formats (Chapter 19, "Data Formatting"). When sorting records by a date field, the values will be sorted chronologically.

Two-Digit Date Conversion

FileMaker requires all dates to have four-digit years. Any entry in a date field with a two-digit year will automatically be converted to a four-digit year using a formula based on the year in which the data entry action occurs. This includes all entry methods: manual typing, importing, auto-enter formulas, or script step entry. The conversion process assumes that a date with a two-digit year is more likely to refer to a time further in the *past* than the *future*. Therefore, automatic conversion of a date's year from two to four digits will adjust so the date falls within either the *next 30 years* or the *preceding 70 years* based on the *current year* when the data is entered. So, in 2020, typing "1/1/51" or earlier will be automatically converted to "1/1/1951," while "1/1/50" will convert to "1/1/2050." A database managing dates that fall outside of a 100-year range or that don't fit this division pattern *must* be

- Entered with four-digit years
- Entered into a text field instead of a date field where they can remain two-digit years
- Entered into a field with an auto-enter formula or script trigger that converts the date to the appropriate four-digit equivalent *before* FileMaker imposes its automatic conversion

---

Caution   Prior to the year 2000, FileMaker allowed two-digit dates. When upgrading an old database, these will automatically receive a century of 1900 unless manually converted before upgrading!

Time Fields

A *time field* is used to store a formal time string. Times must be typed using the time format matching the database setting for dates and times which was inherited from the computer upon which the file was created. In the United States, the default format is typically "<hour>:<min>:<sec> <am|pm>" or "10:30:00 am." Times can refer to a time of day or an *amount of time*, which can be used to denote things like time allotted or elapsed. For example, "0:15:00" refers to 15 minutes. When sorting records by a time field, the values will be sorted chronologically by the amount of time.

Timestamp Fields

A *timestamp field* is used to unify a formal date and time in a single string. FileMaker allows timestamp values to range from *January 1, 0001, 12:00 AM*, through *December 31, 4000, 11:59:59 PM*. As with separate date and time values, a timestamp must be entered in a short format matching the database's settings for each component, which are inherited from the computer upon which the file was created. The two components are entered with a space between them: "*<date> <time>.*" For example, "1/1/2021 3:00 PM" or "8/1/2021 8:00 AM."

Tip   Dates, times, and timestamps are stored as numbers expressing time passed from a fixed point: dates as a number of days passed since January 1, 0001, and times as a number of seconds passed since midnight. For example, "8/1/2002" is stored as 737638, and "10:00:00 AM" is stored as 36000. Therefore, formulas can add or subtract a number of days to a date or seconds to a time.

Container Fields

A *container field* is used to store a document. Files can be placed into container fields by a variety of functions including *Insert, Copy/Paste,* or *Drag/Drop*. A database running on an iOS device can use the *Insert from Device* script step to insert music, photo, camera, microphone, or signature data into a container. Depending on the configuration of the database and field, the files displayed in containers can exist within the database structure or be linked to it from an external folder location (Chapter 10). Some file types have an *Interactive content* layout setting that allows for interactivity similar to their native applications (Chapter 19). For example, a PDF file can be stored in a field with a layout configuration that allows users to view and navigate through the pages of the document as if they were viewing it in Adobe Acrobat. Other file types with interactive options are *photos*, *movies*, and *audio files*.

Display Fields

A *display field* is a non-editable field that automatically displays a value determined by its settings. FileMaker has two types of display fields: *calculation* and *summary*.

Calculation Fields

A *calculation field* is defined with a formula statement that is evaluated by FileMaker to produce a result (Chapter 12). These are similar to cells in a spreadsheet with a formula applied with two major differences. First, the formula applies to the entire column, so each record uses the same formula to evaluate a result for the field. The formula can include variable conditions that evaluate differently for different records, but the overall formula itself remains the same for all. Second, it is *impossible* for a user to type into the cell, wipe out the formula, and enter data instead.

Summary Fields

A *summary field* is a field that automatically calculates a value based on another field's values across a set of records, based on the current user's context of a found set and sort order. For example, a summary field can calculate and display the total value of a field for every record in a found set or for subsets of records based on key sort fields. Summaries are configured with a combination of field options (explained later in this chapter) and layout part setup (Chapter 18).

Introducing the Manage Database Dialog (Fields)

Fields are created and defined in the *Fields* tab of the *Manage Database* dialog shown in Figure 8-1. Select *File* ➤ *Manage* ➤ *Database* menu and click on the *Fields* tab.

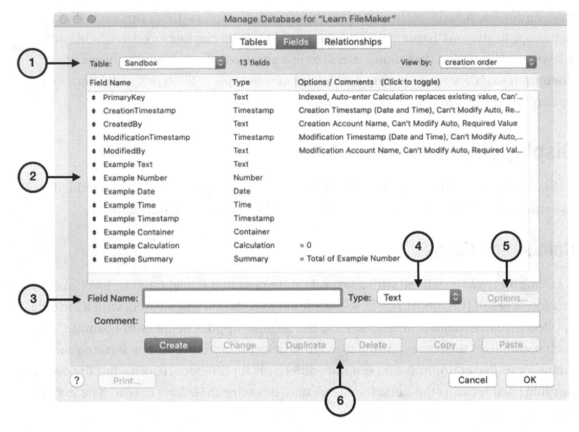

Figure 8-1. *The dialog used to manage fields*

The controls for field definitions include

1. *Table Pop-up* – Select a table to see its fields below.

2. *Field List* – Displays a list of fields defined in the selected table. Select one to configure, rename, duplicate, or delete.

3. *Field Name and Comment* – Enter a new name for the selected field or a name for a new field. Enter a short developer comment about the selected field.

4. *Type* – Select a type for a new field or to change the selected.

5. *Options* – Click to edit field settings based on type.

6. *Buttons* – Used to *create* a new field or *change, duplicate, delete,* or *copy-paste* selected fields.

Planning Field Names

Field naming should follow the same general guidelines as tables: they can have spaces, should avoid reserved words and symbols, and be descriptive of content without being excessively long. They can also be assigned name prefixes to form groups for sorting in the developer lists. However, with fields, this often requires a reversal of natural language flow, and that may be confusing for users in certain situations. For example, while *Company Name* and *Company URL* make sense, using *Name First* and *Name Last* instead of *First Name* and *Last Name* keeps the fields conceptually together in a list but may seem unnatural and may be confusing to users. While table names remain mostly hidden from users, field names are more visible when performing certain functions like *import, export, sort,* and more. On layouts, field labels can be renamed to avoid confusion. However, a user who is familiar with fields labeled *First Name* and *Last Name* may be confused by a dialog where those fields are suddenly called *Name First* and *Name Last*. When using this kind of naming technique, you may need to create a script driven processes for various functions to avoid users seeing the name differences. Alternatively, train users about the differences in names so they aren't confused.

Defining Default Fields

Starting with FileMaker 17, every new table is created with default fields that are pre-configured to automatically enter standard metadata. Once created, these can be edited, renamed, or removed as desired. The file that controls which fields are created for any future table is named *DefaultFields.xml* file and is located in a language subfolder of the FileMaker Pro application. These fields are

- *PrimaryKey* – Enters a Universally Unique Identifier (UUID) for each record

- *CreationTimestamp* – Enters when a record is created

- *CreationBy* – Enters the name of the record creator

- *ModificationTimestamp* – Enters when a record was last modified

- *ModificationBy* – Enters the name of the last modifier

Creating Your Own Standard Fields

Some developers define alternative and/or additional standard fields that they always add to tables in every database they create. A *standard field* is a field that can universally apply to any table, no matter what type of object is modeled by its content. They don't need to be limited to auto-entered metadata values like the preceding default fields. Instead, they can be any field that stores content or provides some type of function that can apply generically no matter the table's entity or purpose. As you develop more, ideas for standard fields may become plentiful although not every standard field should be forced into every table. Some *universal standards* will be easily applicable to every table. Other *group standards* may apply to only certain types of tables, while other *optional standards* may be applied sparingly as needed. Here are a few ideas for standardization across all tables:

- *Status* – A data entry status field that stores a progress value, e.g., *new, active, hold,* or *done.* The specific values may vary from one table to the next.

- *Notes* – A freeform notes field used to store information about the record itself or the entity represented by the record.

- *Errors* – A calculation used to automatically compile and display data entry error notifications on layouts, providing instant feedback to users about problems with key fields.

- *Title* – A calculation that combines fields to create a heading for display at the top of entry layouts or in the body of a List view or portal rows to help users quickly identify a particular record.

Tip   Custom standard fields can be copy and pasted into new tables or added to the DefaultFields.xml file for automatic insertion.

Grouping Standard Fields

Since a standard field will be used consistently in lots of tables and across many solutions, extra care should be taken when naming them. While grouping prefixes will help sort fields in lists, consider the addition of a *super grouping prefix*, a single word to separate fields into two "top level" groups: *standard* and *custom*. For example, a prefix of "Record" can indicate a standard field containing metadata, while a table-specific prefix indicates a custom field, e.g., using "Contact" to indicate a field specific to a table containing contacts, as shown in Figure 8-2.

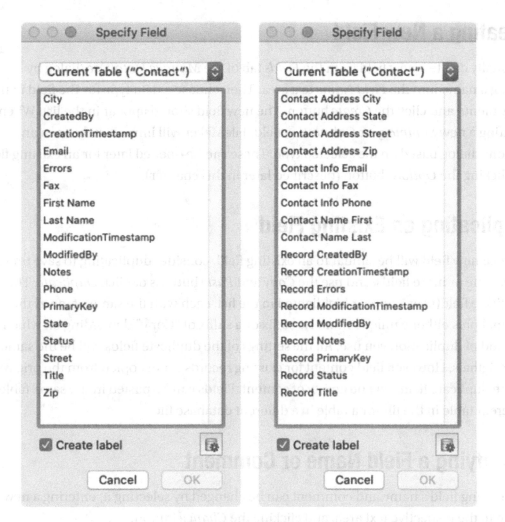

Figure 8-2. *Examples of unprefixed fields (left) and prefix-grouped fields (right)*

Although this approach may at first appear visually cluttered, as a list expands to include dozens or hundreds of fields, some kind of name-group organization can be beneficial.

Managing Fields

From the *Fields* tab of the *Manage Database* window, fields can be created, duplicated, renamed, modified, and deleted.

Creating a New Field

Manually create a new field from the *Fields* tab of the *Manage Database* dialog by typing a name into the *Field Name* text area. Then choose a data type for the field in the *Type* menu, and click the *Create* button. The new field should appear in the list. When creating a new *Summary* or *Calculation* field, FileMaker will immediately open an options dialog based on the selected type. These can be opened later for an existing field by clicking the *Options* button (described later in this chapter).

Duplicating an Existing Field

When a new field will be similar to an existing field, consider duplicating to save time. Select one or more fields, and use the *Copy* and *Paste* buttons or click *Duplicate*. The duplicate field(s) will appear highlighted in the list, each with the same name as the original plus either a unique numeric suffix or a suffix of "Copy" depending on which method of duplication you use. All the settings of the duplicate fields will be the same as the originals. However, field content for existing records is not copied from the original, so the duplicate fields will be empty of content. Fields can be pasted in the same table, a different table in the file, or a table in a different database file.

Modifying a Field Name or Comment

An existing field's name and comment can be changed by selecting it, entering a new value in the respective text area, and clicking the *Change* button.

Modifying a Field's Type

Once a field is created and has data entered, changing its type should be a rare occurrence. However, if necessary, due to a mistake or the need to structurally change a database, select the field, choose a new value from the *Type* menu, and then click the *Change* button. Depending on the original and new type, a dialog may warn that existing content in the field will be converted to the new type across all existing records. Changing from *text to* a *date* or *timestamp* will convert dates previously entered as text into formal dates and automatically convert years to four digits as needed (see "Two-Digit Date Conversion" earlier in this chapter). Changing a *container* to another data type will remove any non-textual data from the field. For example, the actual embedded file or image data would be removed leaving only the name or path of the file. Changing *to* a *calculation* or *summary* will result in the permanent loss of any previous manually entered input.

Deleting Fields

Fields can be deleted from a table by selecting them and clicking the *Delete* button. A warning dialog will confirm the deletion request. The selected fields(s) will disappear from the list immediately; however, the actual deletion doesn't occur until you click the OK button to close the *Manage Database* dialog. Click *Cancel* instead if you made an error and don't want to save the deletion change. FileMaker does a pretty good job of cleaning up instances of the field on layouts. However, you may need to manually delete any lingering *<missing field>* references on layouts in other files. Any references to a deleted field in script steps or formulas will need to be manually removed or reassigned.

Setting Field Options

In addition to a field's *name*, *type*, and *comment* properties, there are numerous options available for configuration depending on the type of field. To edit these options, select a field and click the *Options* button.

Options for Entry Fields

All entry fields have similar options that only vary slightly from one to the next. These are controlled through an *Options for Field* dialog with settings spread across four tabs: *Auto-Enter, Validation, Storage,* and *Furigana.*

Field Options: Auto-Enter

The *Auto-Enter options* tab of the *Options for Entry* dialog, shown in Figure 8-3, controls data that will be automatically entered into the field when a new record is created or when certain conditions are met.

Figure 8-3. *The Auto-Enter tab of the options dialog for entry fields*

Caution   Although all of the options are checkbox controls, the first five operate as radio buttons, allowing only *one* to be selected since they would overwrite each other.

Automatically Enter the Following Data into This Field

Some of these settings are limited or disabled for certain entry fields depending on the specific data type they contain. The options include auto-entering

- *Creation* – Select a value to be entered at record creation: *Date, Time, Timestamp, Name,* or *Account Name.*

- *Modification* – Select a value to be entered when a record is modified (same options as the preceding ones).

- *Serial Number* – Enter a serialized number at record creation or on first commit. The number is based on the value in the *next value* text area and automatically incremented each time by the value in *increment by*.

- *Value from Last Visited Record* – Enters a value into a new record from the same field on the last record the user viewed.

- *Data* – Enters the static text value in the adjacent text area.

- *Calculated Value* – Define a formula that generates a result entered into the field (Chapter 12). The *Do not replace* checkbox will cause the field to *not* evaluate the calculation if a value already exists from a preceding option or contains data previously entered by the user.

- *Looked-up Value* – Copies a value from a related field.

Caution   A calculated value set to not replace existing values will evaluate once when a record is created and will not reevaluate again if a value was generated, including when duplicating a record.

Lookup for Field Dialog

A *lookup field* automatically copies a value from a specific field from a related record immediately after a key field defining the relationship is updated. This is used to place a copy of a value locally from a related record so that it will remain in place even if the related record is deleted. This feature is a vestigial remnant from the pre-relationship days that will likely be deprecated in future releases. Instead, consider using either an auto-enter calculation or direct placement of a related field on a layout. To configure a lookup, click the *Looked-up value* checkbox on the *Auto-Enter* tab of the *Options for Field* dialog. This will open a *Lookup for Field* dialog, shown in Figure 8-4.

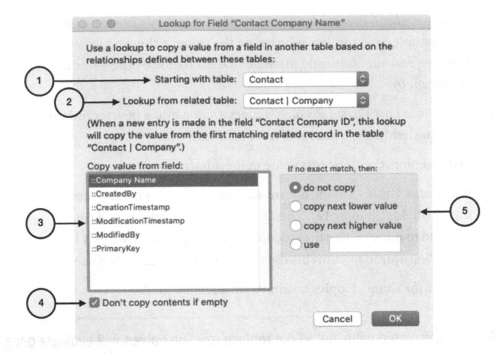

Figure 8-4. *The dialog for configuring lookup settings*

The dialog contains the following controls:

1. *Starting with Table* – Select a table occurrence for the field being defined to serve as the starting context if multiple table occurrences exist for its table (Chapter 9)

2. *Lookup from Related Table* – Select a table related to the starting table to identify the relational conduit through which a field value will be copied

3. *Copy Value from Field* – Choose a field from the selected lookup table occurrence whose value should be copied into the field being defined when the lookup happens

4. *Don't Copy Contents if Empty* – Select to halt the lookup if the selected field is empty, in favor of any existing value

5. *If No Exact Match Then* – Choose an action to perform if no related record is found

Prohibit Modification of Value During Data Entry

This checkbox at the bottom of the *Auto-Enter* tab of the *Options for Field* dialog makes the field non-editable at the data level *regardless* of a user's security settings or the field's configuration on a layout. After any auto-enter option(s) have been performed, the field's value will be non-editable unless this setting is changed. This is useful for default fields such as the primary key and record metadata or any other entry fields that you want to be read-only after an initial automatic entry is complete.

Field Options: Validation

The *Validation* tab of the *Options for Entry* dialog, shown in Figure 8-5, defines entry requirements for the field, allowing the database to automatically validate input and enforce rules. If one or more requirements are specified, FileMaker will validate data entered into the field. When a field fails a validation check, the user is notified and given a choice for corrective action.

Figure 8-5. *The Validation tab of the options dialog for entry field*

Validation Control

The options at the top of the *Validation* tab control when input is validated and whether a user can override a validation warning. Select *Always* to cause the field to validate when data entry is performed and when importing into the field or *Only during data entry* to validate *only* during data entry and not during import.

Caution   Fields set to always validate will cause FileMaker to *not* import a record if validation fails. These will be reported with the total incidence of import errors without providing any additional detail!

Check the *Allow user to override* box to change the validation warning options as shown in Figure 8-6. With the override option *off*, the warning dialog has two buttons. The *Revert Field* button will remove the data entry changes, restoring the previous saved value, while the OK button returns the user to the uncommitted record where they can edit their entry to comply with the validation requirements before attempting to commit again. With the override option *on*, the *Revert Field* option remains and is joined by a new message offering to override the warning. Clicking the No button returns the user to edit the uncommitted record, while clicking Yes ignores the validation warning, accepts the changes as entered, and continues committing the record.

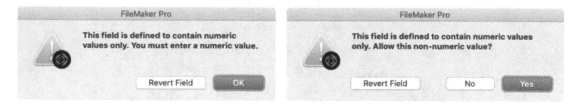

Figure 8-6. *The warning with allow override off (left) and on (right)*

Validation Requirements

The following validation requirements can be imposed on data entered into the field:

- *Strict Data Type* – Restricts values to one of the following options: *Numeric Only, 4-Digit Year Date,* or *Time of Day.*

Tip   The *4-Digit Year* option here requires entry of a full year *before* FileMaker performs its automatic conversion and can be used to avoid inadvertent conversions for dates outside of that span.

- *Not Empty* – Requires a value in the record.

- *Unique Value* – Requires the input to be unique for the field across *all* records in the table.

- *Existing Value* – Requires the input to already exist in the same field for at least one other record in the table.

- *Member of Value List* – Requires the input to be present in the specified value list (Chapter 11).

- *In Range* – Requires the input to be within a range specified, which can be text, date, time, or numeric values.

- *Validated by Calculation* – Allows a custom validation formula (Chapter 12). The formula *must* evaluate to *true* (non-zero) for the entry to pass the validation test.

- *Maximum Number of Characters* – Requires input of a character length equal to or less than the number specified (for non-container fields only).

- *Maximum Number of Kilobytes* – This option replaces the preceding one for container fields, specifying an upper limit on the size of a file that can be placed into the field.

Display Custom Message if Validation Fails

When the validation of a field fails, FileMaker will generate a dialog message like those shown previously in Figure 8-6. The default message will include details about the specific validation failure, which can be helpful when multiple validation criteria are applied to a single field. The *Display custom message* option allows the entry of an alternative custom static message for a field.

Exploring Validation Alternatives

Some developers use FileMaker's validation options sparingly and prefer alternatives. Many data entry errors can be anticipated and *automatically corrected* using an *Auto-Enter Calculation* formula to clean up and replace the value entered. For example, the *GetAsNumber, Filter, Trim,* and *Substitute* functions can automatically remove undesirable characters that are typed in a field (Chapter 13). Keeping paragraph returns out of a field can be done by making the Return key move to the next field for fields on layouts using *Behavior* settings in the *Inspector* pane (Chapter 19). When an error can't be easily avoided or auto-corrected, an error-detecting calculation field can display a list of fields with detectable validation errors. This removes an obtrusive dialog and allows searching/sorting records with errors; however, users can ignore it. An *OnObjectValidate* script trigger (Chapter 27) assigned to a field can run a script that checks the field for detectable errors and stops the user from exiting the field until they are corrected. This allows a more elaborate, formula-driven dialog message to explain the problem. An *OnRecordCommit* script trigger can halt record commit until detected problems are corrected.

Field Options: Storage

The *Storage options* tab of the *Options for Entry* dialog, shown in Figure 8-7, controls how information is stored and indexed within a field.

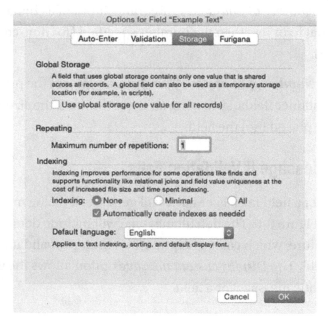

Figure 8-7. *The Storage tab of the options dialog for entry fields*

Global Storage

A *local field* is replicated as a unique instance of itself for each record like a cell in a spreadsheet where every record can contain a different value. The value placed within the field is considered *local* to a single record, which is separate and different from the same field on any other records. Local fields can only be displayed and accessed from the context of their parent table or a table related to that table. Every newly defined field starts out as local field but can be configured as global. A *global field* contains one value that will be shared across every record in the table and can be accessed from any context within the database. Using the spreadsheet analogy where a column represents a defined field and a row a record, a global field is like a column with the same value in every cell of that column for every row, except there is only *one value* that is the same from the perspective of any individual record.

In the *Storage* tab of the *Options for Field* dialog, the *Use global storage* checkbox converts a field to use global storage. FileMaker will present a warning dialog indicating that existing values within the field will be lost when the change occurs. Once a field is global, it can be used for a variety of special purposes, including

- Storing a fixed value that is available to *any* calculation formula or layout regardless of context, e.g., a tax rate

- Creating a *control field* like a menu of options, e.g., a pop-up menu of portal filtering or sorting options

- Providing temporary storage for scripts to place information that needs to interact with other calculation fields

- Storing static text or graphics that will be displayed on a multiple layout as iconography, branding, etc

- Storing print report headings or other temporary information

A global variable is preferable for most uses because it doesn't clog up the field definition list. However, it is limited to a single file. A global field in a table occurrence added to other files allows content to be shared globally between files to create a *solution-wide global*.

The value placed into a global field is retained from one session to the next *only* when entered on a non-hosted database that is open on a local copy of the *FileMaker Pro* desktop application. When opened across a network, values placed into a global field will not be saved between sessions and are not shared between users who access the file simultaneously. Each time the database is opened from a server host, the field will contain the value entered when it was last opened *locally* by the desktop application.

Tip   In ancient times, developers used global fields for a variety of functions that are now better managed with variables (Chapters 12 and 25), custom functions (Chapter 15), merge variables (Chapter 20), and script parameters (Chapter 24). Use global fields sparingly!

Repeating

A *repeating field* is a field defined to store multiple values for a single record. Instead of creating a separate field for each additional value of a certain type, a single field can be defined to *repeat* any number of times, e.g., a single phone number field can be defined to store multiple numbers as if they were separate fields. Any type of field can be made to repeat. For an entry field, indicate a number of desired repetitions in the text area provided on the *Storage* tab of the *Options for Field* dialog. For a *calculation* field, enter the number of repetitions in the *Specify Formula* dialog (Chapter 12). A *summary* field becomes repeating when the field it summarizes is repeating and the option to summarize repetitions individually is selected (described later in this chapter).

The *Maximum number of repetitions* entered in the *Storage* tab of the *Options for Field* dialog defines the number of separate values the field can contain. To allow user entry into two or more of these repetitions, the field must be configured to repeat on a layout (Chapter 19, "Inspecting the Data Settings"). There are a few implications to consider when using repeating fields, including

- Repeating fields are never scrollable on a layout.

- You can add more repetitions later, but the number displayed on a layout must be manually adjusted to include them.

- The *Hide* function (Chapter 21, "Hiding Objects") hides the entire field, including all repetitions displayed on the layout.

- A *Find* process will search in all repetitions, including those not displayed on the current or any layout. It is not possible to limit a find to just a specific repetition.

- A *Sort* process will *only* look at the first repetition.

- Calculations that use a combination of repeating and non-repeating fields may not work together without the usage of the *Extend* function (Chapter 12, "Creating Repeating Calculation Fields").

- An auto-enter calculation only works on the first repetition.

- Repeating values might not work properly in sub-summary parts of reports (Chapter 18) and may need to be condensed into a single value with an aggregating function such as *List* (Chapter 13).

Tip   Historically, repeating fields were used to achieve the function now provided by portals (Chapter 20). Use this feature sparingly!

Indexing

A *field index* is a hidden list of words or values automatically generated from a non-global field's content. This list is used when performing searches, determining the uniqueness of a field value, and connecting records through relationships. A field's index serves a function similar to a book index, quickly separating the individual terms and allowing faster location of them without having to visually scan through every page. FileMaker uses two kind of indexes, depending on the type of field and the option selected. A *value index* is created from every paragraph return-delimited line of text in a field. This is used to match related records and to search a field for matching values. Here, it helps to think of a "value" as a paragraph. This is used primarily for relationships, where each value is used to find a match in a related table. A *word index* is created from each unique word in a text field or a text calculation field. These are used for faster searching.

Caution   Indexing is required for some relational functions and improves search performance. However, it increases the file size of a database and should be used with conscious intent.

Indexing options in the *Storage* tab of the *Options for Field* dialog include

- *Indexing: None* – Prevents indexing completely. Use this for fields that don't require fast searching and won't be used to form relationships. Also, to cause a calculation to re-evaluate often.

- *Indexing: Minimal* – Create only a value index for the field.

- *Indexing: All* – Create a value index for non-text fields and both a word and value index for text fields.

- *Automatically Create Indexes as Needed* – Allow FileMaker to create indexes as needed, e.g., when a user performs a search on a previously unindexed field, this automatically switches *None* to *All* to generate and store an index.

- *Default Language* – Specify the language to use when indexing and sorting values in a text field. The default value will match the operating system of the computer upon which the file was created.

Tip   There may be situations where you want to customize the indexing settings to save file size. However, the default settings allow FileMaker to adjust them based on user and developer activity.

Container Storage Options

Container fields can't be indexed, so the *Storage* tab of the *Options for Field* dialog does not have the preceding options available when editing them and instead displays *container storage options* (Chapter 10).

Field Options: Furigana

The *Furigana* tab of the *Options for Entry* dialog specifies a phonetic translation of Japanese text typed into the field. For more information on Japanese functions, see Claris' documentation website.

Options for Display Fields

Options for *calculation* and *summary* fields are different than entry fields. Clicking the *Options* button or double-clicking will open an alternative dialog of options specifically focused for the field type.

For a calculation field, the *Options* button opens a *Specify Calculation* dialog where a formula can be entered and selection of the result data type, repetitions, storage options, and an evaluation context can be configured (Chapter 12).

For a summary field, the *Options* button opens an *Options for Summary Field* dialog for specifying the type of summarization, target field, and more. The *summarization type* selected determines what summary operation will be performed on the selected field for a group of records in order to arrive at a value which will be placed into the field being defined. The available summary operations that can be performed for a field across a group of records are

- *Total of* – Calculates the total value

- *Average of* – Calculates the average value

- *Count of* – Counts how many records contain a value

- *Minimum of* – Extracts the lowest available value

- *Maximum of* – Extracts the highest available value

- *Standard Deviation of* – Calculates the standard deviation from the mean of all the values

- *Fraction of Total of* – Calculates the ratio of the value to the total of all the values in that field

- *List of* – Creates a carriage return-delimited list of every non-blank value

Options for Summary Field Dialog

The *Options for Summary Field* dialog is divided into five general sections, shown in Figure 8-8.

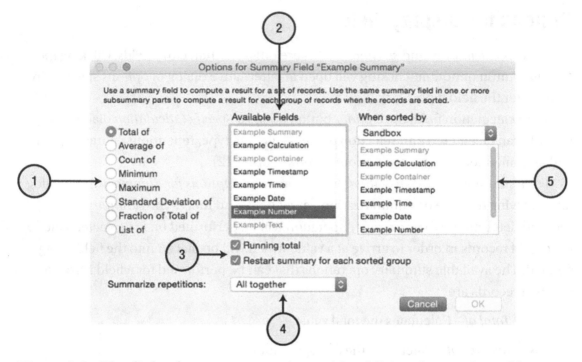

Figure 8-8. *The dialog for summary options with additional controls visible*

Caution   The options below provide an overview of summary settings and may seem too abstract until one sees a complex report built with sub-summary parts (Chapter 18, "Adding Layouts").

The dialog contains the following controls:

1. *Summarization Type* – Specify the type of summarization to use (listed in the previous section).

2. *Available Fields* – Choose a field from which to pull and summarize data. The list includes eligible fields from the table of the field being defined.

3. *Conditional Options* – This area will display either *one, two,* or *none* of the following options depending on which summarization type is selected: *Running total, Restart summary for each sorted group, Weighted average, Running count,* and *By population* or *Subtotaled.*

4. *Summarize Repetitions* – When a repeating field is selected, identify how repetitions will be handled. Select *Individually* to display a separate summary for each repetition, making the summary field repeating. Choose *All together* to add all repetitions for a record, and treat it as a single value in the summarization process.

5. *Conditional Secondary Field Choice* – Depending on the preceding selected options, a field selection may be required for one of these secondary functions:

   a. *When Sorted by* – Some operations allow a field to restart the summarization when a new sort value is detected. This creates summaries for multiple subgroups of records within a single found set. For example, you might want to summarize *sales per employee* or *revenue per client* using this feature. This option is available with the *Total of* or *Count of* summary type when the *Restart summary for each sorted group* option is selected or when the *Fraction of Total of* summary type is used with the *Subtotaled* option selected.

   b. *Weighted by* – When using the *Average of* summary type with the *Weighted average* option selected, a field can be selected that will be used to weight the results.

Adding Fields to the Example Database

At the end of the last chapter, we added three tables to the *Learn FileMaker* example database: *Company*, *Contact*, and *Project*. Now, using the lessons of this chapter, we can add a few fields to each of these. While these are not comprehensive lists these tables require in a real-world solution, they provide a few key fields to continue our exploration of building databases.

Defining Company Fields

In the *Company* table, create the following entry fields:

- *Company Name (text)*
- *Company Description (text)*

- *Company Industry (text)*

- *Company Website (text)*

- *Company Status (text)*

Defining Contact Fields

In the *Contact* table, create the following fields:

- *Contact Name First (text)*

- *Contact Name Last (text)*

- *Contact Company ID (text)*

- *Contact Address Street (text)*

- *Contact Address City (text)*

- *Contact Address State (text)*

- *Contact Address Zip (number)*

- *Contact Address Country (text)*

Defining Project Fields

In the *Project* table, create the following fields:

- *Project Company ID (text)*

- *Project Contact ID (text)*

- *Project Name (text)*

- *Project Description (text)*

- *Project Budget (number)*

- *Project Budget Summary (summary as a Total of the Project Budget field)*

Renaming and Modifying Default Fields

To follow along with the examples in the rest of the book and to gain some experience modifying field definitions, perform the following changes to the five default fields in all tables:

- *Rename PrimaryKey* to "Record ID" and *change its Auto-Enter from a Calculated value to a Serial number starting with "000001."*

- *Rename CreationTimestamp* to "Record Creation Timestamp."

- *Rename CreatedBy* to "Record Creation User."

- *Rename ModificationTimestamp* to "Record Modification Timestamp."

- *Rename ModifiedBy* to "Record Modification User."

Tip   Save time by doing these in one table and copy-paste them to replace default fields in other tables.

Summary

This chapter explored the basics of defining fields. In the next chapter, we turn attention to forming relational links between tables.

CHAPTER 9

Forming Relationships

A *relational database* allows connections to be defined between tables to automatically connect individual records based on field values. This chapter covers the following topics pertaining to relationships:

- Introducing relationships
- Managing data sources
- Introducing the manage database dialog (Relationships)
- Working with table occurrences
- Building relationships
- Adding notes to the graph
- Implementing a simple relational model

Introducing Relationships

A *relationship* defines a connection between tables that forms a context of bidirectional conduits that link individual records in one table to one or more individual records in another. As a digital model of real-world phenomenon, a database uses *tables* to represent entities, *fields* to store properties of entities, and *relationships* to reflect how those entities connect or interact.

Consider how the relationship between a company and employees would be modeled in a database. Each can be represented by a table: *Company* and *Contact*. Fields are created in each to store properties about the entities that are important for database work. For example, a company's *address, description, industry, name,* and *website* would be fields. Similarly, a contact's *email, name, phones,* and *title* would be fields. Next, looking at how these two relate in reality, we can identify the need for

© Mark Conway Munro 2021
M. C. Munro, *Learn FileMaker Pro 19*, https://doi.org/10.1007/978-1-4842-6680-9_9

a connection between them. Each company may employ one or more people, and conversely, each person is typically employed by a company. From this, we can define at least one relationship requirement in the database: each *Contact* record will require the option to be connected to a *Company* record. A person can be linked as an employee of a company, and conversely, a company can have one or more people linked as employees.

Every table created in a database adds a potential for more connections. For example, companies may need links to *inventory, projects, budgets, assets,* and *procedures,* while contacts may need links to *phones, emails,* and *web addresses.* Each of those imply more connections as the database grows. A project and budget may require links to *tasks, timesheets,* and *invoices.* The connections required will vary based on the database's purpose and the type of tables included in the object model. A relationship is defined when a developer decides a connection found in reality needs to be rendered in the digital object model and explicitly specifies the field criteria used to compare and match values between records.

Relationships make it possible to create navigable links between records in related tables. They also create a *relational context* between tables which can be used by calculations, layouts, and scripts to access or display field values from various tables. Relationships transform a bunch of isolated tables into an interconnected network of information that can be dynamically accessed, displayed, and manipulated in numerous ways. *Fields* use a relationship when they pull related values to perform lookups, auto-enter calculations, or validation (Chapter 8). *Formulas* use them to access or manipulate related fields to calculate results (Chapter 12). *Layouts* can display individual fields from related records or include a list of related records as a portal from another table (Chapter 20). Layout objects can use values from related fields in calculation formulas for conditional formatting, placeholder text, script parameters, tooltips, and hide functions (Chapter 21). Numerous *script steps* use relationships in formulas or when referencing a field (Chapters 24 and 25). Users can select fields from related tables in dialogs when manually exporting, importing, searching, and sorting.

Tip   While most relationships establish a connection between two *different* tables, it is possible to connect records to other records in the *same* table or to connect a record to itself, called a *self-join.*

Visualizing Relationships

A *match field* is any field used to form one side of the criteria for a relationship. Two match fields pair together with an operator to form a single criterion for defining a relationship. Any field can be used as a match field, although most relationships use keys. A *key field* is a field that uniquely identifies a record in a table. While many fields are candidates, a good choice for a key is one that is *both unique and unchanging*. For example, although a *Contact* record's email address field is unique to a person, it can change if the person's work changes or they move to a new service provider for a personal account. This makes it a poor candidate for a relational key because a change would sever the connection between previously linked records. Because of this, most developers establish a field that stores an automatically entered, anonymous, incremental, unique, and unchanging identification number as a standard practice in every table. This can be a simple auto-entered serial number (Chapter 8, "Field Options: Auto-Enter") or a more complex Universally Unique Identifier (Chapter 8, "Defining Default Fields"). These serve as a *primary key*, a key field that contains a value that identifies a record in the same table the field is defined. For example, a *Record ID* field in a *Company* table stores a primary key that identifies a specific company record, e.g., "1105" for Widgets Manufacturing. When a primary key is placed in a field where it identifies a record in another table in order to form a relationship, it is called a *foreign key* because it identifies a record foreign to the table containing it. Together, a primary key field and foreign key field form the basis for most relationships. Since these often create a hierarchical relationship, they are often referred to as a *parent-child connection*, as illustrated in Figure 9-1. In this example, the *Record ID* is the primary key of a *Company*, and the *Contact Company ID* field in *Contact* table contains a foreign key. When the values in both fields are equal, a relational link is formed between two records.

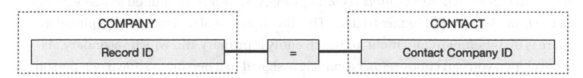

Figure 9-1. *An illustration of a single key field pair forming a relationship*

Each relationship must include at least one set of match fields but can include additional criteria. When more than one match field pair is defined, records will only link when *all* criteria match. The example illustrated in Figure 9-2 shows an additional set of fields, a *Company Contact Portal Filter* in *Company* and a *Contact Address State* in *Contact*. These second match fields would allow a user viewing a company record to select a state from a list, and that would be used to "filter" the list of contacts in a portal view, so it only displays those with an address in that state (Chapter 20, "Filtering Portal Records").

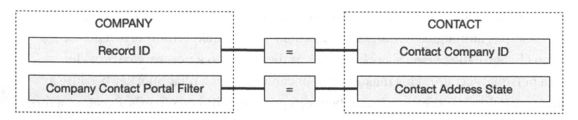

Figure 9-2. *An illustration of a relationship established by two match fields*

Relationships fall into one of the three general classifications named based on the number of matching records possible on each side: *one-to-one, one-to-many,* and *many-to-many*. FileMaker has a unique *multi-key option* that can be used to create one-to-many or many-to-many connections. These configurations can be enforced at the field validation level and/or through interface mechanisms that physically limit what can be selected or inserted into a key field. Another option is a *Cartesian join* that relates every record in one table to every record in another. These are set up at the relationship settings level with an operator.

One-to-One Relationship

A *one-to-one relationship* is a connection where a record in either table can only be matched to a single record in the other. The example in Figure 9-3 illustrates one set of matched records where a *Contact* record's primary *Record ID* is entered as a foreign key in the *Cubicle* record's *Contact ID* field. The directionality of assignment is optional as there is no inherent requirement for which entity is primary and which secondary. As a developer, you can choose *either* a cubicle assigned to a person as shown *or* a person assigned to a cubicle, depending on your preference or other logistical considerations. The setup requires both key fields to be validated to contain a single value that is unique across all records within their respective tables. So, in the example shown, each contact can only be assigned a single cubicle, and each cubicle can only be assigned one contact.

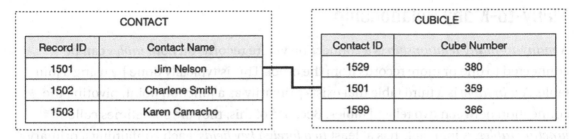

Figure 9-3. *Illustrating a one-to-one connection*

One-to-Many Relationship

A *one-to-many relationship* is a connection where a record in one table can be matched to one or more records in another. The example in Figure 9-4 illustrates one set of matched records where a *Company* primary *Record ID* has been entered as a foreign key into the *Contact Company ID* field of two records in a *Contact* table. This type of relationship is used often due to the number of real-world situations where an entity can relate to multiple entities. A company may have multiple offices, products, and employees. A person may have multiple phone numbers, email addresses, and web pages. A parent can have many children. This last example is why this arrangement is often referred to metaphorically as a *parent-child*-type relationship since, biologically, a child has only one father or one mother, but either one parent can have many children. The setup requires the primary key field to be validated to contain a single, unique value, while the foreign key field in the other table allows non-unique values. The directionality of assignment is dictated by the fact that the many side must contain the foreign key from the table containing the unique primary key.

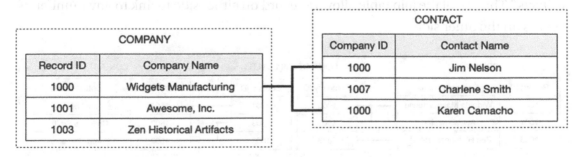

Figure 9-4. *Illustrating a one-to-many connection*

Many-to-Many Relationship

A *many-to-many relationship* is a connection where records on *both tables* can be connected to one or more records from the other. This is typically done by using a join table. A *join table* is a third table that exists primarily as a junction point, pivoting the connection between two related tables. Because of this, they are sometimes called *junction tables*. A join table has at least *two foreign key fields*, each containing a primary key from one of the two tables being joined. The example in Figure 9-5 illustrates such a relationship using a join table. The primary key from both *Table 1* and *Table 2* are each entered in a foreign key field on a single record in the join table, establishing a connection between the two tables.

Figure 9-5. *Illustrating a many-to-many connection through a join table*

An example of a many-to-many relationship is found connecting a company to contacts when there is a need to connect a person to their *current* employer while maintaining connections to their *past* employers, as illustrated in Figure 9-6. In this example, a *Company* table and a *Contact* table are connected through a join table named *Contact Employer*. The "Widgets Manufacturing" *Company* record has a connection to two join records that each connect to a contact record, one for Jim and one for Karen. While Jim's record has only a single connection to one join record, Karen's *Contact* record connects back to two companies: "Widgets Manufacturing" and "Zen Historical Artifacts." The use of the join table allows a record on either side to link to any number of records on the other side.

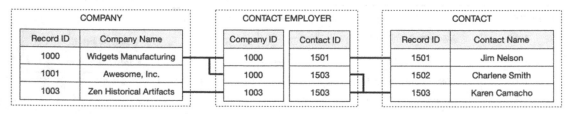

Figure 9-6. *Illustrating connections with a many-to-many relationship*

Technically, a join table is not a *single* relationship since it really consists of two one-to-many relationships. However, it is often referred to as *one relationship*, especially when a join table exists only to facilitate the wider connection of two regular tables. In those cases, the join table contains only the two fields and is completely hidden from view and has no user accessible interface. However, joins *can* include additional fields that are specific to the union of the two entities. For example, a phone number and email address for the contact at a particular company could be stored in a join table record. They can also have interfaces and even connections to other tables as needed.

FileMaker's Unique Multi-key Option

FileMaker has the unique ability to define a relationship using a key field containing multiple values. A *multi-key field* is a text or calculation field that contains a return-delimited list of keys used as a match field in a relationship. When a match field contains values separated by a return, each paragraph is treated as its own value and used to form a match, so the presence of *any* one value from one field found in the other will match and form a relational connection. Multi-key fields can be used to create a one-to-many relationship or a many-to-many relationship *without* the need for an intervening join table. The example in Figure 9-7 demonstrates this technique by showing a connection between two tables using a multi-key field as the match field on both sides. The field in the first record of *Table 1* finds *three* matching records in *Table 2* even though none of the fields contain all the same values. Matches are formed when at least one paragraph value is found on both sides. Setting up a multi-key, many-to-many relationship requires the match fields to be a text field (or a calculation field returning a text value) that allows multiple values and does not validate to require unique values. Although this example uses state names, any value, including serial numbers, can be used.

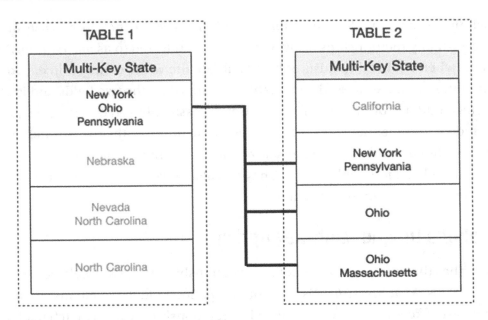

Figure 9-7. *An illustration of a multi-key field relational connection*

There are pros and cons to this technique. For example, there is no intersecting table in which to add fields or build layouts like with a join table so this isn't a good choice if that is required. However, relational connections are retained when duplicating a record since the keys are contained locally instead of in a separate join table. So, if the first record in *Table 1* in Figure 9-7 were duplicated, it would retain all the same connections to records in the other table.

Indexing Match Fields

A relationship forms a bidirectional conduit which allows either table to act as the local *starting context* (parent) for formulas and layouts from which the other related table is targeted (child). However, in order for the connection to produce results, *every match field used in the targeted (child) table must either be indexed or a global.* Since calculation fields can't be indexed when their formula contains related fields, a calculated match field on the targeted side must only include fields local to that table. Global fields can't be indexed but will still work on either side of the relationship. However, they are only really practical on the local (parent) side since they produce a match to every record when used on the target (child) side.

Using Table Occurrences

Instead of directly connecting tables, relationships are actually connections between an abstraction of a table. In FileMaker, a *table occurrence* is a representative instance of a table placed into a graphical worksheet called the *relationship graph*. Although the tables are technically linked, it is done through a specific occurrence instance of the table. This avoids circular connections between tables and enables multiple connections between the same two tables based on different criteria. It even allows *self-join connections* between a table and itself.

Every table is automatically represented in the relationship graph with a default table occurrence. Although this appears to be and can be thought of as the table, it is only an *occurrence* of the table. As a database grows, multiple connections involving the same table become necessary but risk becoming circular, as illustrated in Figure 9-8 (left). Here, the connections between *company-to-contact* and *company-to-project* are standard one-to-many relationships and don't pose a problem. However, when a *contact-to-project* connection is required, it would create an overall circular connection between the three tables which is forbidden. To resolve this, a new occurrence of the *Contact* table is created and used for the new relationship (right). Both instances of Contact represent the *same table* but from a *different relational context*.

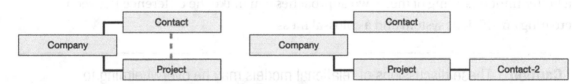

Figure 9-8. *A circular connection (left) is solved with a new occurrence (right)*

Context is a critically important concept in FileMaker. While a *table* is an isolated data structure defining and storing information in fields and records, a *table occurrence* specifies that data from a specific *relational context* and is used everywhere to control what tables are accessible from a given perspective. A calculation field's formula operates from a context that must be selected if there is more than one occurrence for the field's parent table. Value lists can be configured to filter values from a field to only those in an occurrence from a specific starting interface context (Chapter 11). Each layout requires an occurrence assignment that controls which fields can be displayed and establishes the context for object formulas. Numerous script steps automatically execute from the *user context*, based on the occurrence assigned to the layout active in the current window at the time they execute.

As more occurrences are added, they can be chained together in sequences. In the previous example, there is a connection from *Company* to *Project* to *Contact-2*. Each step between occurrences is often referred to as a "hop," referring to the number of occurrence steps to get from a starting occurrence to a target. A calculation, layout, or script step can access fields through any number of hops along a single relational chain, but reaching across too many can become problematic. In the preceding example, a formula in *Company* can access fields from *Contact-2* but *only* for the first related *Project* record because it has to reach through that relational conduit. A more direct route to the other *Contact* occurrence directly connected to the *Company* occurrence provides access to all company contacts.

As the relational model grows in complexity, it can quickly become a monolithic mess that is both confusing and technically dangerous. Developers with less experience tend to rapidly connect more and more occurrences into one gigantic multipronged chain of occurrences, a single mass that is referred to as a *hub-and-spoke monolith*. Instead, the recommended approach is to build multiple separate *table occurrence groups*. Given the reliance on relational context everywhere in a database's development, a better understanding of these two approaches can make the difference between creating an efficient system and a colossal mess.

Caution   These discussions of relational models may be overwhelming to beginners, especially prior to creating layouts. However, it will be worth the effort to avoid mistakes later.

Avoiding Hub-and-Spoke Monoliths

A *hub-and-spoke monolith* is a relational model where table occurrences are linked into a massive interconnected group, as illustrated in Figure 9-9. This structure tends to be adopted as an intuitive default by most new developers. They start by connecting a handful of default table occurrences. Then, as they attempt to add new relationships that would be circular, FileMaker prompts them to create new occurrences, and they leave the default name of the table with a numeric suffix. Soon, they have dozens or hundreds of poorly named occurrences interconnected in one massive group.

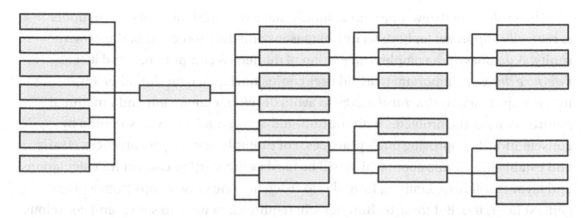

Figure 9-9. *Illustrating a hub-and-spoke monolithic relationship model*

Although this is not inherently problematic and can be a valid choice for simple databases, there are good reasons to avoid hub-and-spoke models completely. There is no easy way to tell which occurrences have been or should be used as a starting context, and as a result, hundreds or thousands of calculations, interfaces, and scripts zigzag around the structure, creating a conceptual gridlock. It quickly becomes confusing to keep track of which occurrence matches a certain context, e.g., trying to choose between *Contact-1*, *Contact-2*, *Contact-3*, and *Contact-4* in a formula requires time-consuming detective work. False starts and backtracking are necessary to correct a layout that is originally assigned the wrong context and only discovered after placing dozens of objects that now need to be reconfigured. Adding new features begins to feel like a tedious chore, and the ability to conceptualize the whole structure requires an enormous effort. As the grip of the convoluted structure tightens, the mind-numbing confusion is just the beginning. A small oversight can result in the loss of data when a script performs a function from the wrong context or a user types into a field through the wrong relationship because of an interface error caused by developer fatigue. Calculations reaching out in every direction across an excessive number of hops begin to make simple tasks dramatically slower and may return incorrect results. Eventually, technical problems appear as users struggle with unbearably slow performance and may even experience random application crashes. The temptation to blame the technology becomes overwhelming, but it is really the fault of a poor structural design chosen by an inexperienced developer.

The professional developer understands that a well-designed relational model is *critically important* for both technical reasons and the protection of their own sanity. A database is a complex integration of numerous components, and just as *interface design* is important to avoid user confusion, equal care should be taken in one's approach to *structural design* to avoid developer confusion and functional failure. Many of the problems with the hub-and-spoke model can be softened by conscientiously improving one's practices. For example, naming occurrences clearly and establishing a rule about which will be used as the starting context for calculations and layouts will help. Limiting formulas to reach out one or two hops from a given context helps too. But these techniques still require extra work to set up and conscious effort to follow. In the end, the best solution is to *avoid this model completely and instead use occurrence groups*!

Embracing Table Occurrence Groups

The *table occurrence group* relationship model establishes a *primary table occurrence* for every table and a rule that these are *never* directly interconnected to each other. Any connection between two tables *must* be established by connection from a primary occurrence to a new *secondary occurrence* of a table to avoid any direct connections between primaries. This is also called an *anchor-buoy* model since each primary occurrence acts as an independent anchor to which related secondary occurrences can be attached where they are said to float away from it. In the setup illustrated in Figure 9-10, a column of primary tables (gray) stands in a disconnected column on the left. Each secondary table (clear) that connects to these is a duplicate copy of a primary table. Using this model and following a few rules can solve most of the confusion and potential for technical complications found with the hub-and-spoke method.

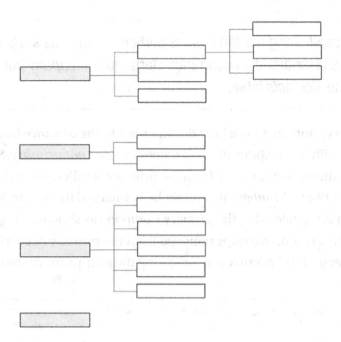

Figure 9-10. *Illustrating a table occurrence group relationship model*

Each primary occurrence on the left establishes the foundational anchor for an *occurrence context group*. These should be named with the actual table name to make clear that they represent the primary root occurrence, e.g., *Company, Contact, Project, etc.* When building interfaces, only these primary occurrences should be used as the context for calculation fields and layouts. The physical separation between groups limits how far and in which direction a field or interface formula can reach out to access related fields since they are limited to related secondary occurrences related within their small "island" group.

Each secondary occurrence "floats" off to the right from a primary. These should be named in a way that indicates the starting context group they connect to and include path information about how they relate back to the root primary occurrence of that group. This can take various forms but ideally starts with the name of the primary occurrence, with a delimiter indicating a hop to a new occurrence, and then the name of the secondary occurrence table. For example, a secondary *Contact* occurrence connected to the primary *Company* occurrence might be named "Company | Contact." The secondary part of the name could include additional information used to identify the nature of the relationship, e.g., "Company | Contact Employees" indicating that this *Contact* occurrence is used from company contexts and links to contacts that are a company's employees.

Tip   Consider capitalizing the table name portion for emphasis. *Company |
CONTACT* makes clear that the occurrence starts from *Company* but is actually an
occurrence of the *Contacts* table.

The "secondary" nomenclature here doesn't refer to the *distance* from the primary
but indicates a classification status of occurrences that are *not primary*. So, any
occurrence any number of hops away from the primary is called secondary. For example,
an occurrence of a *Phone Number* table might be connected to a secondary *Contact*
occurrence which is connected to the primary *Company* as shown in Figure 9-11. It is a
third occurrence in a chain, two hops removed from the primary occurrence, but is still
referred to as a "secondary" occurrence indicating the non-primary status of both.

Figure 9-11. *An example of two secondary occurrences extending from a primary*

Tip   Although secondary occurrences can extend further, it's a good idea to limit
each branch to about two or three hops if possible.

To illustrate this setup, consider two contextual groups anchored to *Company* and
Contact tables, as shown in Figure 9-12. The primary *Company* occurrence would
be used as the context for every company calculation and layout. The three tables
connected to it may be used within formulas (Chapter 12) and to define a portal on
a layout (Chapter 20) accessing related *Contact, Project,* and *Invoice* records. The
protruding *Phone* occurrence, two hops from *Company*, is added if the contact portal
needs to display a phone number for a contact or if a calculation or script needs to
access that information from the context of a *Company*.

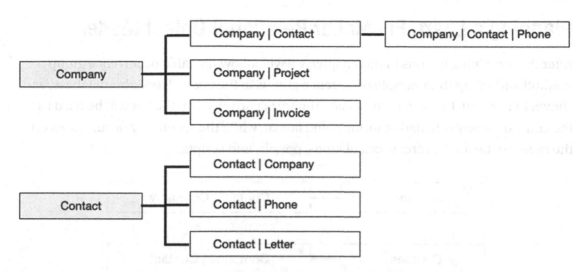

Figure 9-12. *An illustration of two hypothetical occurrence groups*

Similarly, the primary *Contact* occurrence would be used as the context for every contact calculation field and layout. The attached *Company* occurrence could be used to display the contact's employer name on a layout and used by scripts to navigate from a contact record to its related parent company. The *Phone* and *Letter* occurrences can provide the context for portals on contact layouts.

Using the occurrence group method will necessitate some redundancy in the relationship graph, and it may initially seem counterintuitive as unnecessarily increasing the number of occurrences. However, if implemented properly, eventually, the benefits prove themselves, and you will be thankful you took the time to implement it. The *separation between groups* streamlines performance and makes it easier to conceptually navigate the structure. Limiting all formulas and layouts to a primary occurrence starting context makes it easier to reach targets and avoids confusion. A naming scheme that includes the path from the primary keeps occurrence groups sorted in the selection menus throughout the development interface, synchronizing the orderly relational structure in a list and making the selection of a target table even easier.

Planning a Learn FileMaker Relational Object Model

After the remaining lessons in this chapter, we will follow the table occurrence group method and set up three simple occurrence groups in the *Learn FileMaker* database, as shown in Figure 9-13. Each of the three primary occurrences on the left will be used as the context for any calculation formula and layout, while the secondary occurrences on the right can be used to create calculations, portals, and scripts.

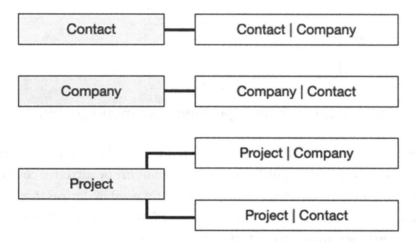

Figure 9-13. *The plan for table occurrences in the Learn FileMaker database*

Managing Data Sources

A *data source* is a defined reference to other FileMaker and ODBC databases. When building a self-contained database that doesn't access external tables, there is no need to define data sources since the implied source will always be the current file. However, when creating a multi-file database or integrating ODBC tables (Chapter 7), additional data sources will be required.

Introducing the Manage External Data Sources Dialog

External data sources are created, edited, and deleted from *the Manage External Data Source* dialog, shown in Figure 9-14. This dialog can be accessed by selecting the *File* ➤ *Manage* ➤ *External Data Sources* menu. It is also accessible at the bottom of the

Data Source pop-up menu found on the *Specify Table* dialogs that appear in various locations of the development interface. Once open, click *New* to open the *Edit Data Source* dialog and define a new connection to an external data source.

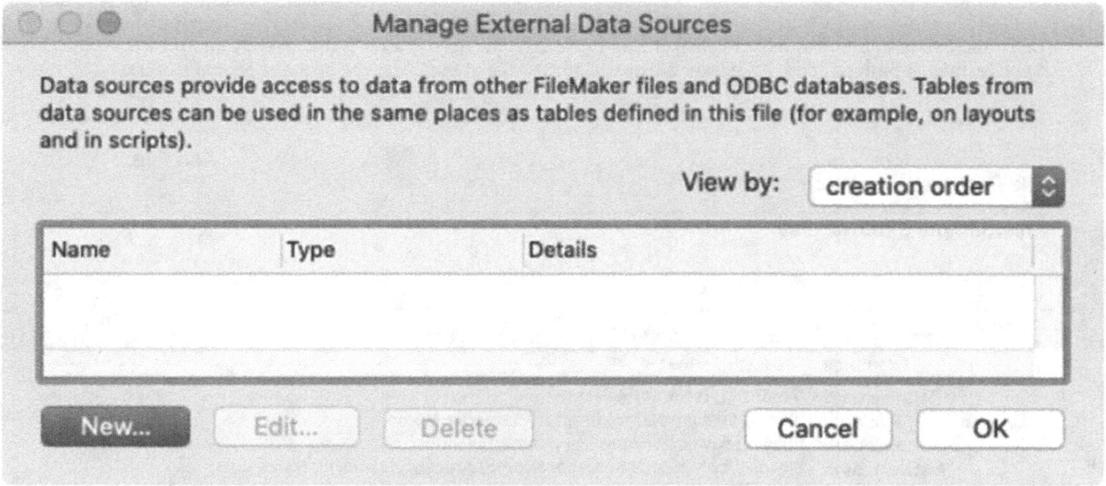

Figure 9-14. *The dialog used to manage external data sources*

Exploring the Edit Data Source Dialog

Creating or editing a data source is performed in an *Edit Data Source* dialog, shown in Figure 9-15. This dialog is opened from the *Manage External Data Source* dialog by clicking *New*, selecting a data source and clicking *Edit*, or double-clicking directly on a data source in the list.

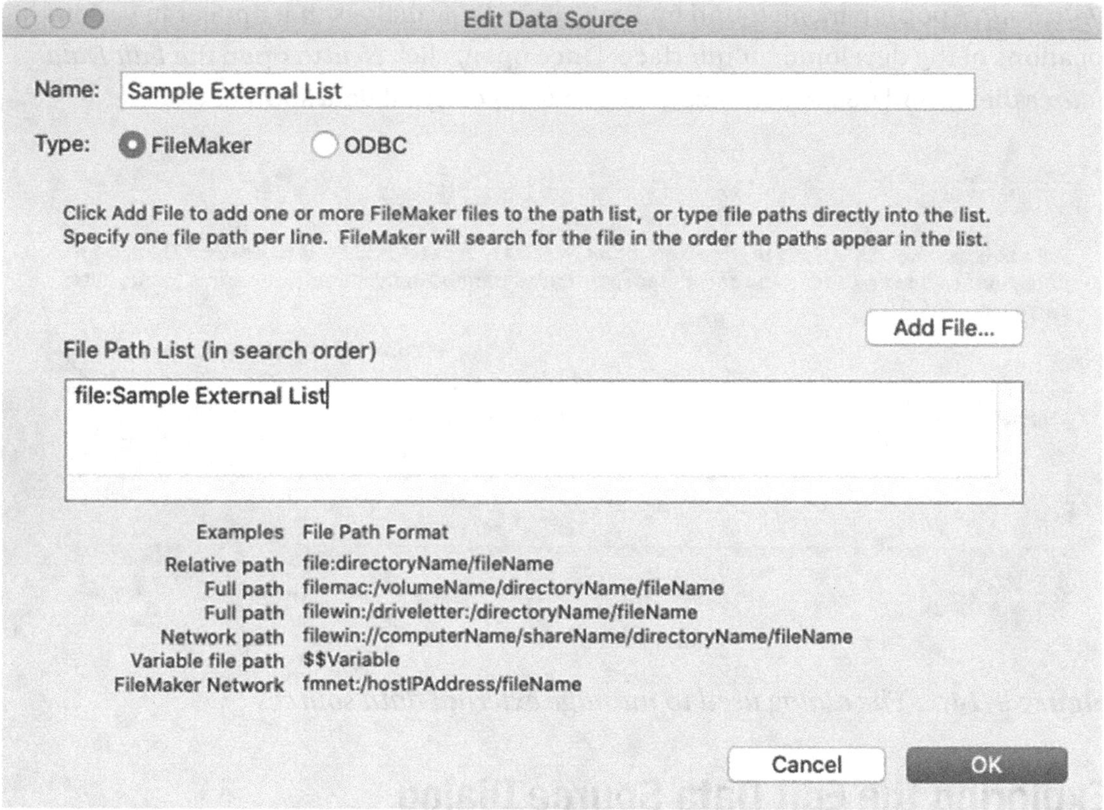

Figure 9-15. *The dialog used to edit a selected data source*

The Name entered is used to identify the source in menus throughout the development interface. The *Type* option offers two choices based on the data source being targeted and will change the interface depending on which is selected. The remainder of this section assumes a selection of *FileMaker*. The *File Path List* is used to specify one or more paths to the target data source (Chapter 24, "Specifying File Paths"). FileMaker will link to the first path that points to an existing database file. Click Add File to add a path automatically for a selected file, or type one manually. For details on configuring an *ODBC* type data source, see Chapter 7, "Adding a Table from an ODBC Data Source."

Introducing the Manage Database Dialog (Relationships)

Like tables and fields, table occurrences and relationships are created in the *Manage Database* dialog. Select *File* ➤ *Manage* ➤ *Database* to open the dialog, and make sure the *Relationships* tab is selected, as shown in Figure 9-16. The scrollable white area is the *relationship graph* where table occurrences are added and interconnected to define relationships. Each table should already be present in the graph but with no relationships connecting them. The row of buttons beneath this is used to perform various tasks within the graph area.

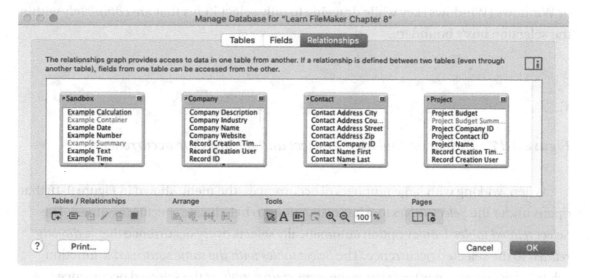

Figure 9-16. *The dialog used to manage relationships*

Working with Table Occurrences

A *table occurrence* is a graphical representation of an instance of a table displayed in the relationship graph. Before defining relationships between occurrences, let's review the basics of *selecting, interacting, arranging, viewing, formatting, editing, adding,* and *deleting* occurrences.

Selecting Table Occurrences

A selected occurrence will be highlighted with a blue shaded border, and its size, position, and formatting can be modified. Occurrences can be selected using a variety of different methods with the *Object Selection Cursor* activated, as shown in Figure 9-17. To select a single occurrence, click directly on it in the graph. To select multiple non-clustered occurrences, hold the Shift key and click on each desired occurrence. A second click on a previously selected occurrence while holding the key will deselect it. To select multiple occurrences clustered together in a group, click on the background and then hold and drag until the selection rectangle encompasses the desired occurrences. Every occurrence touched by the selection box will be selected. Hold the Command (macOS) or Windows (Windows) key while dragging to only select items that are *completely* within the selection box's boundary.

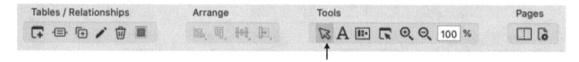

Figure 9-17. *The cursor tool used to select and manipulate occurrences*

When working with large numbers of occurrences, the menu shown in Figure 9-18 that opens under the *Select Tables* tool has two options to help locate specific instances. The *Select related tables 1-away* option automatically selects every occurrence that is *directly related* to the selected occurrence. The *Select tables with the same source table* function selects every occurrence that shares the *same source table* as the selected occurrence, which can be helpful trying to find other instances of a table in a complex graph.

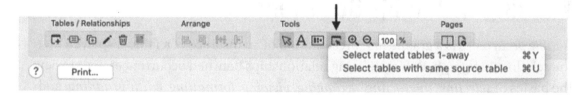

Figure 9-18. *The tool for selecting similar tables*

Interacting with Table Occurrences

With the cursor tool selected, an occurrence box can be moved, collapsed, expanded, resized, and scrolled from the points highlighted in Figure 9-19.

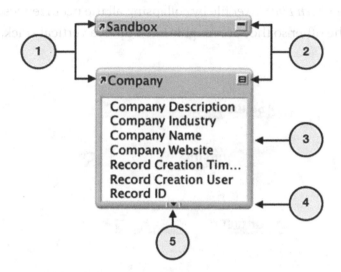

Figure 9-19. *Occurrence manipulation points when collapsed (top) and expanded (bottom)*

1. Click and hold the *heading* of an occurrence to drag the box, and reposition it within the graph. Hover the cursor over the arrow icon to reveal an informative metadata popover.

2. On the right of the heading is an expansion toggle button icon. A single-click will toggle the state of the occurrence between one of three states. Without any relational connections, one click collapses the box, and another click expands it. With relationship connections, an intermediate state collapses halfway showing only match fields used to form relationship(s) to other occurrences (not shown).

3. Drag the thin bar on the sides and bottom to resize the width or height, respectively.

4. Drag the bottom corners to resize the width and/or height depending on the direction.

189

5. When fully expanded, this arrow icon that appears at the top, bottom, or both is used to scroll up or down the list of fields. Individual clicks will move up or down one field at a time; holding will continuously scroll the list until released.

Practice in the *Learn FileMaker* file by collapsing all the occurrences and moving them one above the other so they are roughly lined up in a vertical stack, as shown in Figure 9-20.

Figure 9-20. *The four table occurrences collapsed and arranged in a stack*

Arranging and Resizing Occurrences

The *arrange* tools are used to align and resize groups of selected occurrences based on a selection from a hidden menu under these four icons, shown in Figure 9-21:

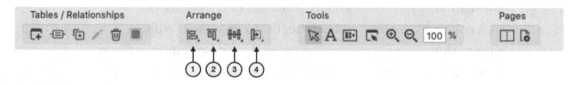

Figure 9-21. *Arrange tools contain menus for arranging and resizing occurrences*

1. Horizontally aligned by *left, center,* or *right edges.*

2. Vertically aligned by *top, middle,* or *bottom edges.*

3. Distribute *horizontally* or *vertically*.

4. Resize the *width*, *height*, or both, to *smallest* or *largest*.

Viewing Options

The *tools* section includes four controls that modify the magnification of the relationship graph, shown in Figure 9-22:

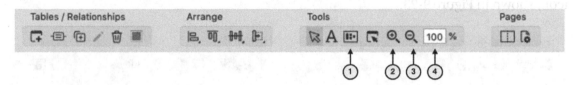

Figure 9-22. *The tools used to adjust the magnification of the relationship graph*

1. *Adjust Magnification* – Adjust the magnification to make every table occurrence fit in the view without scrolling.

2. *Magnification* – Click to activate, and then click in the graph to increase the zoom by 25%.

3. *Reduction* – Click to activate, and then click in the graph to decrease the zoom by 25%.

4. *Percentage* – Manually set the magnification percentage from 1 to 400.

Formatting Table Occurrences

The only *formatting* tool for table occurrences is a color menu accessible by clicking on the color tool located to the right of the *Delete icon* in the *Tables/Relationships* section. Color coding can be used in many ways to visually group table occurrences. Apply a color to all primary table occurrences and another to secondary or apply a color to each occurrence group. Colors can indicate the type of operator used to connect a secondary occurrence to a primary one, or color can denote the function of the occurrence, e.g., one color for those used as child portals, another for parent tables, etc. Colors can also be used to indicate the development status of each occurrence, e.g., highlighting those being worked on or deprecated. Whatever specific scheme you choose, coloring occurrences can help you visually navigate a complex relationship graph.

Editing Table Occurrences

Table occurrences are edited using the *Specify Table* dialog. This dialog is opened by double-clicking an occurrence or by selecting one and clicking the *Edit Selection* button icon, shown in Figure 9-23.

Figure 9-23. *The tool used to edit an existing occurrence*

Introducing the Specify Table Dialog

From the *Specify Table* dialog, shown in Figure 9-24, the *data source, table*, and name *can* all be modified for the occurrence. When selecting a different table, the name will always update to that table unless it has been edited since opening the dialog.

Figure 9-24. *The dialog used to specify which table is assigned to an occurrence*

Adding Table Occurrences

Table occurrences can be added to the graph for any table that exists in any data source defined in the current file. This can be done by *creating a new table occurrence* or *duplicating an existing one*.

Creating a New Occurrence

To create a new table occurrence, start by clicking the *Add Table* button icon, shown in Figure 9-25. This will open the *Specify Table* dialog described earlier. Optionally, choose a data source if the table you want to add is in a different file. After the occurrence is created, it can be resized and positioned as desired.

Figure 9-25. *The tool used to add a new table occurrence*

Duplicating an Existing Occurrence

To duplicate the selected occurrence(s), click the *Duplicate Table* button icon, shown in Figure 9-26. There are many great reasons to duplicate existing occurrences instead of creating new ones. When an occurrence already exists for the new target table, duplicating it saves the step of assigning the table manually. A duplicate also retains the size and formatting of the original, saving you the time required to modify the default styling of a new occurrence. Duplicating a group of related occurrences will retain all relational connections between them.

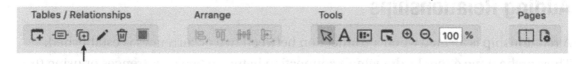

Figure 9-26. *The tool used to duplicate an existing occurrence*

Deleting Occurrences

Table occurrences can be deleted by selecting and typing the Delete key or clicking the *Delete* tool shown in Figure 9-27. Remember that this will only delete the *occurrence* of the table and *not* the actual *table*. However, any resources that use the occurrence as a context will be affected by the deletion. So, layouts and scripts may require updating after deleting occurrences assigned to or used within them.

Figure 9-27. *The tool used to delete an existing occurrence*

Printing the Relationship Graph

The *Pages* tools shown in Figure 9-28 provide control over *page breaks* and *page setup* in preparation for printing the relationship graph.

Figure 9-28. *The tools used to prepare the graph for printing*

Building Relationships

Once occurrences are present in the graph, they can be linked to define relationships.

Adding Relationships

A relationship is formed when a connection between two occurrences is established. This can be done either by dragging a connection between two occurrences or using the *Add Relationship* button.

Dragging a Connection Between Occurrences

The most intuitive way of creating a connection between two occurrences is to use the cursor to drag a connection from a field in one occurrence to a field in another, thereby establishing a relationship based on those two match fields. To begin, locate the two occurrences in the graph that will be connected, and click the icon in the upper-right corner of both until they are fully expanded. Scroll until the desired match field for the relationship is in the visible region of each list. Click and hold on a match field from one occurrence. As you begin to drag the cursor toward the other occurrence, a line will appear connected to the first match field, shown in Figure 9-29. Once the cursor is on top of the desired match field in the other occurrence, release it and the line connecting the two will be established.

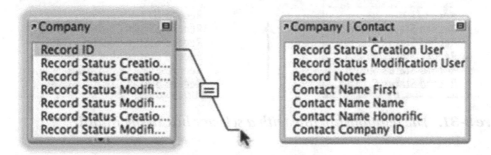

Figure 9-29. *Dragging a new relational connection between occurrences*

Tip   Save time by quickly dragging a connection between *any* two fields currently visible and then edit the relationship (described later) and select the desired fields in dialog's larger and more easily scrollable lists.

Using the Add Relationship Button

The other way to create a new relationship is by clicking the *Add Relationship* button in the toolbar, shown in Figure 9-30. Clicking this button opens an empty *Edit Relationship* dialog (discussed later in this chapter) with both tables set to *<unknown>*. Since the connection is empty, occurrences and match fields must be manually selected.

Figure 9-30. *The tool used to create an empty relationship*

Manipulating Relationships

A *relationship* is represented in the graph by a line connecting two occurrences with a selector box in the middle, as shown in Figure 9-31. The box will display the operator used to form a match between the two fields, with the default being an equal sign.

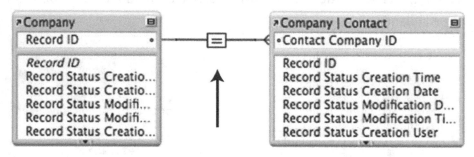

Figure 9-31. *The relationship line with a selector box in the middle*

On each end of the line where it connects to an occurrence is an indication of the relationship type, shown enlarged in Figure 9-32. A straight line, like that on the left, indicates a *one* connection, and the "crow's feet" on the right side indicates a *many*. Therefore, in this example, there is a *one-to-many relationship* connection from *Company* to *Contact*. FileMaker determines this by looking *only* at the auto-enter settings for the fields. Since the *Record ID* field in *Company* is configured to auto-enter a unique serial id for each record, it is displayed as a one. On the other side, the field has no restrictions, so it assumes a many.

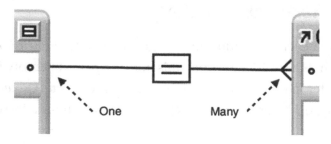

Figure 9-32. *End-of-line symbols indicate the type of connection on each side*

Caution   The end-of-line indicators only reflect field definition restrictions, not entry options on layouts or script functions.

When moving occurrences, the relationship lines will stay connected on both sides, regardless of one box's position relative to the other box. The line will split into three straight, pivoting segments, as shown in Figure 9-33. After moving a box far enough, the line will snap to the other side of the occurrence box in order to maintain a connection.

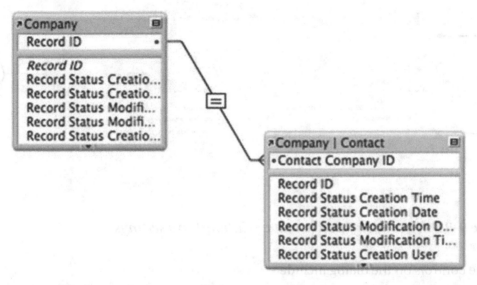

Figure 9-33. *The line splits into straight segments when an occurrence is moved*

Introducing the Edit Relationship Dialog

Relationships are edited in the *Edit Relationship* dialog, shown in Figure 9-34. This can be opened by either double-clicking the relationship connection box or by selecting the relationship and clicking the *Edit Selection* tool.

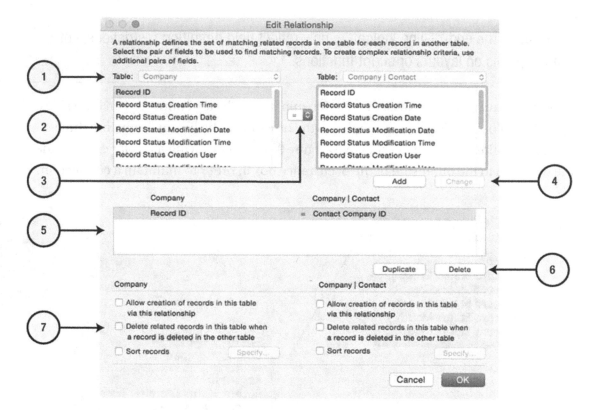

Figure 9-34. *The dialog used to edit a relationship's settings*

The controls on the dialog include

1. *Table Occurrence* – Select an occurrence for each side of the relationship when creating a new relationship. If editing an existing relationship, these are non-editable and can only be edited directly on the occurrence box in the graph.

2. *Selected Match Field* – Select a pair of match fields to be added or changed in the list below.

3. *Comparative Operator* – Select an operator to control how the match fields will be compared.

4. *Selected Match Field Buttons* – Click to *add* the selected fields as new criteria to the list below or *change* to update the fields in the selected combination below.

5. *Link Field(s)* – Lists the criteria defining the relationship.

6. *Link Field Buttons* – Click to *duplicate* or *delete* the selected link field.

7. *Relationship Options* – Specify certain behaviors for each side of the relationship.

Selecting a Comparative Operator

A *comparative operator* is used to specify how match field values will be compared to detect a relational match. The available operators are shown in Table 9-1.

Table 9-1. *A list of comparative operators available for relationships*

Operator	Description
=	Match when values in both fields are equal to each another.
≠	Match when values in both fields are not equal to each other.
<	Match when the value in the left field is less than the value in the right field.
≤	Mach when the value in the left field is less than or equal to the value in the right field.
>	Match when the value in the left field is greater than the value in the right field.
≥	Match when the value in the left field is greater than or equal to the value in the right field.
X	Match *every* record on the left side of the relationship will be matched to all records on the right side, regardless of the actual values contained in the selected fields. This is often referred to as a *Cartesian Product*, *Cartesian Join,* or *Cross Join*, where a connection between two tables is unrestricted by any criteria and every record will be a match no matter the criteria.

Relationship Options

The settings at the bottom of the *Edit Relationship* dialog, shown in Figure 9-35, control three functions for behavior on each side of the relationship.

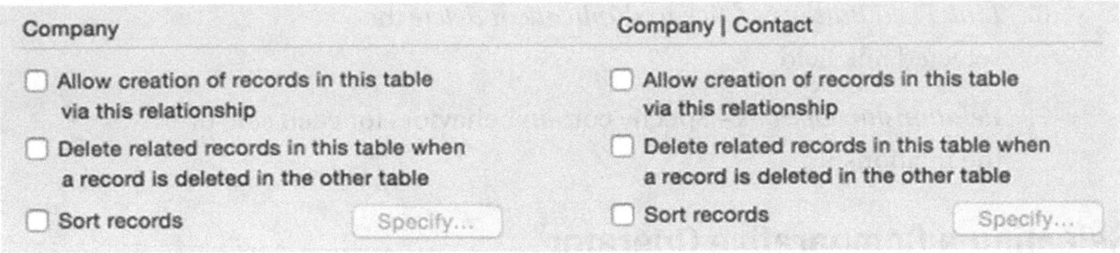

Company		Company | Contact	
☐ Allow creation of records in this table via this relationship		☐ Allow creation of records in this table via this relationship	
☐ Delete related records in this table when a record is deleted in the other table		☐ Delete related records in this table when a record is deleted in the other table	
☐ Sort records	Specify...	☐ Sort records	Specify...

Figure 9-35. *Relationship options for each occurrence*

Allowing Creation of Related Records

The *Allow creation of records* option makes it possible for users to create records in an occurrence by typing into a related field from the other occurrence placed on a layout. This is commonly used in portals to allow easy creation of new records (Chapter 20, "Creating Records in a Portal Directly").

Automatically Delete Related Records

The *Delete related records* option causes records in the table to be automatically deleted when a related record on the other side is deleted by a user or script. This is especially useful for deleting "child" records when their "parent" record is deleted. For example, when a *Company* record is deleted, any related *Contact* records can also be deleted if this feature is enabled on the *Company | Contact* side. Only use this when the lack of a parent record creates problematic "ghost records," detached records that aren't accessible or usable without a parent. To retain related records and allow them to later be attached to a new parent record, leave this option disabled.

Sorting Related Records

The *Sort records* option enables a specific record sort at the *relationship level*. While a portal can be configured to sort records for display (Chapter 20, "Exploring the Portal Setup Dialog"), this feature sorts them at the relational root so they are sorted when a calculation or script reaches through a relationship to access related records directly. This is important when using the *List* function (Chapter 13) when the order is important.

Adding Notes to the Graph

A *relationship note* is a free-floating, colored box that can be added in the graph to contain developer notes. A note is created by selecting the *Text* tool, shown in Figure 9-36, and then clicking and dragging in the relationship graph. An *Edit Note* dialog, shown in Figure 9-37, allows entry and editing of the note text as well as specification of the font, size, text color, and background color of the note. The dialog will automatically open when creating a new note or when double-clicking on an existing one. Once saved, a note can be moved, resized, minimized, aligned, or deleted just like a table occurrence.

Figure 9-36. *The tool used to create a new note*

Tip   A note can be created without selecting the text tool by clicking and dragging on the background while holding Option (macOS) or Alt (Windows).

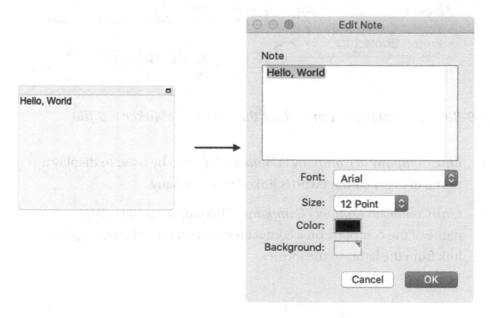

Figure 9-37. *A note (left) and the dialog used to edit it (right)*

Implementing a Simple Relational Model

Now the previously described simple relationship model can be implemented in the *Learn FileMaker* database. Align the four primary table occurrences into a vertical stack. First create two duplicates of the *Contact* occurrence, and name one "Company | Contact" and the other "Project | Contact." Then make two duplicates of the Company occurrence, and name them "Contact | Company" and "Project | Company." Then arrange them and form the following relationships between these, shown in Figure 9-38:

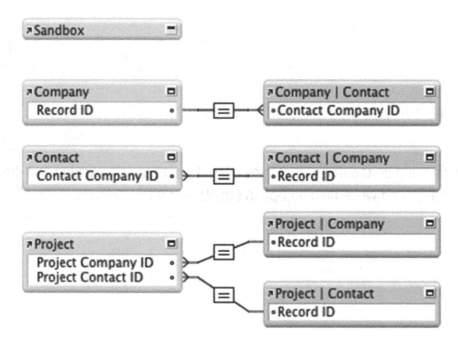

Figure 9-38.   *The relational model for the Learn FileMaker test file*

- *Link Company to Company | Contact* – This can be used to display a portal of every contact who is linked to a company.

- *Link Contact to Contact | Company* – This can be used to display the name of the company on a contact record and provide a navigable link from the latter to the former.

- *Link Project to Project | Contact* – This will link a project to a contact record as the primary contact.

- *Link Project to Project | Company* – This will link a project to a company record, allow displaying the name on a project record, and provide a navigable link between them.

Summary

This chapter introduced data sources, table occurrences, and relationships. In the next chapter, we will explore managing container fields and storage options.

CHAPTER 10

Managing Containers

A *container field* is a type of field that can store and display a document file. Formally, the content of a container is referred to as a *binary large object* or *basic large object*, both commonly expressed as the acronym "BLOB," which is a collection of binary data representing an image, audio, or any file type (except folders) stored as a single data entry in a database. In FileMaker, container fields have a variety of options that influence how files are inserted into a field, where that material is actually stored (internally or externally), and how it is displayed when placed on a layout. This chapter provides an overview of the options for defining container fields, covering the following topics:

- Inserting files into containers
- Extracting files from containers
- Explaining container storage options
- Using managed external storage

Inserting Files into Containers

When a container field is visible and accessible to a user on a layout, a document file can be inserted using a function from the *Insert* menu, by *dragging and dropping* or *copying and pasting*. Depending on the field definitions and layout settings for a container field, each method has different options and limitations that may impact how the document is inserted and the size of the database file.

Tip To follow along with these examples, open the *Sandbox Form* layout of the *Learn FileMaker* database.

© Mark Conway Munro 2021
M. C. Munro, *Learn FileMaker Pro 19*, https://doi.org/10.1007/978-1-4842-6680-9_10

Using the Insert Menu

The *Insert menu* contains four options for inserting a file into a container field with focus, shown in Figure 10-1. These options are also available in the field's contextual menu and as script steps. Choosing any options will open a *Choose File* dialog, automatically optimized for the type of file corresponding to the menu item.

Picture...
Audio/Video...
PDF...
File...

Current Date   ⌘ –
Current Time   ⌘;
Current User Name   ⇧⌘N

From Index...   ⌘I
From Last and Advance   ⇧⌘'

Figure 10-1. *The options for inserting a file into a container field*

- *Picture* – Insert and display a picture's content.

- *Audio/Video* – Insert an audio or video file. This is only enabled when the field's layout settings allow *Interactive content*, which allows the file to be played directly from within the field without having to open the file in another application.

- *PDF* – Inserts a PDF file. This is only enabled when the field's layout settings allow *Interactive content*, which allows the file's pages to be viewed directly from within the field without having to open it in another application.

- *File* – Inserts any type of file into a field. The file will appear as it does in a directory folder, represented by an icon with no option to view or interact with its content.

Note   For more on layout settings, see Chapter 19, "Data Formatting Options for Containers."

Dragging and Dropping

Using *drag and drop* to insert a file from a directory into a container field on the current layout is the most intuitive method available. When dropping a file, FileMaker will automatically use the appropriate storage method based on dropped file's type and the configuration of the field. For example, if you drop an image, it will be inserted and displayed as if you selected the *Insert Picture* menu. If you drop a PDF or audio file into a field that has not been configured for *Interactive content*, the file will be placed into the field and displayed as a preview of the first page of the PDF or as a file icon. However, if the field is configured for interactivity, the file will be inserted as if you chose the menu corresponding to the file type and will be fully interactive. When dropping, there is no way for a user to manually specify external storage (discussed later in this chapter). Instead, the field's defined method of storage will be automatically applied.

Copying and Pasting

Using *copy and paste* to insert a file into a container is another convenient option. The clipboard can contain an *actual file* copied from a folder, the *content of an image* copied from a picture file opened in photo editing software, or a properly formatted *text reference* to a file. The result of pasting is identical to that of dragging and dropping, and there is no way to manually specify external storage (unless pasting a text reference).

Extracting Files from Containers

When a container field on a layout is editable, a user can save a copy of the contents from the record into a folder directory of their choosing using the *Export Field Contents* function. This is available under the *Edit* menu, in the field's contextual menu, and as a script step. When selected, a dialog of the same name will open, allowing the user to choose a folder in which to export the document. The file name will default to the name of the document in the container but can be renamed in this dialog. The dialog includes the option to automatically open the file and to create an email with the extracted file as an attachment.

Tip   This feature can also be used to save selected text from a field into a text file.

Explaining Container Storage Options

A container field can be configured to store files in one of two ways: storing the *actual file* inside of the database file or storing a *reference* to a file located *outside* the database file.

Storing Files Internally

When a new container field is defined, it defaults to store content internally. This means that the entire content of a file is replicated *inside the database file*. This has some advantages and disadvantages.

A huge advantage is that internal storage maintains portability of the database since all elements are stored in a single document file. This may be important when accessing the database locally in a manner similar to a word processing or spreadsheet document. Although portability isn't an issue for shared databases hosted on a server (Chapter 29), internal storage ensures that the files stored in container fields are universally accessible regardless of any given user's lack of ability to access external files on an unmounted file server or an inaccessible coworker's computer. Since the file is literally copied into the database structure, if a user can access that, they can access the container content.

The downside to internal storage is that each file inserted into a field increases the size of the database file. This is not inherently a problem since a FileMaker database *can* be up to 8 terabytes in size. However, as the size of the file grows, performance can become degraded, especially when many users share access to a database over a network.

Generally, if the number or size of files stored in container fields is excessive, it's a good policy to insert file references into the fields and store the actual file externally. The user won't notice a difference in how they interface with the content if it is done correctly.

Storing a Reference to an External File

A *container field file reference* is a text string that stores an external file's location, type, and other information which varies by type. For example, a *container image reference* includes the dimensions of the original image, a path to the file relative to the database, and an absolute path to the image. This example shows a reference to an image file located on a user's desktop:

```
size:731,960
image:../../../../../../../../Desktop/Flower Picture.jpg
imagemac:/Macintosh HD/Users/john_smith/Desktop/Flower Picture.jpg
```

Storing references in container fields maintains a lean, efficient database. Although the insertion process only stores a reference in the field, that external file will still be rendered in the interface as if it were stored internally, based on the field's settings. From the user's perspective, there is no difference when the field displays its content on a layout.

There are two methods for using external files: *custom-managed* and *database-managed*.

Using Custom-Managed References in Any Directory

The traditional approach to using external references in container fields is *custom-managed external storage* where the external location of a referenced file can be any directory. After the reference is inserted, the file remains unchanged in the folder where it was selected.

The choice to use a *reference insertion* instead of *file insertion* is made when a user or script inserts a document into a container by selecting a *Store only a reference to the file* checkbox option at the bottom of the *Insert* dialog, shown in Figure 10-2.

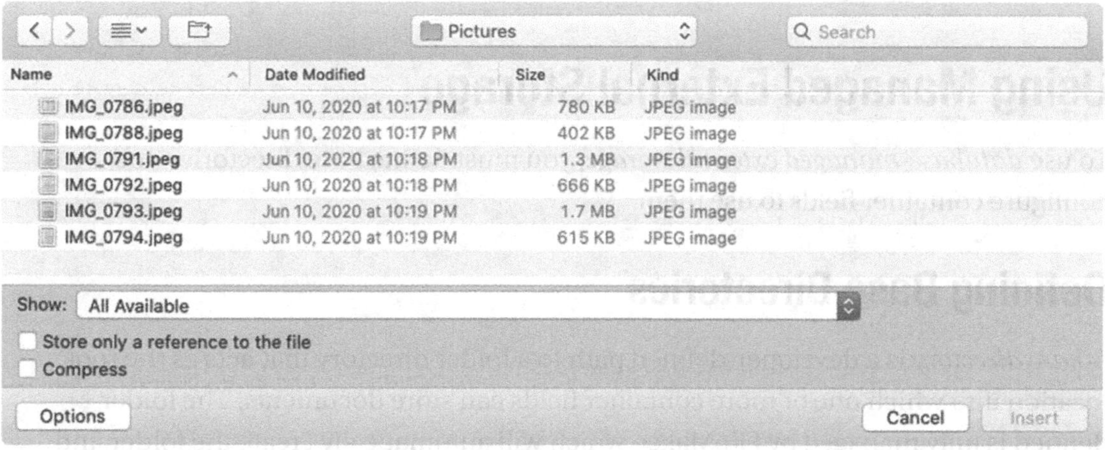

Figure 10-2. *The option to store a reference as an override to the field's settings*

This option works fine for many situations, but it is not without risk. If the choice is left up to the user, the result is likely to be a mixture of some insertions as files and others as references. Also, some references may be located in a directory that is not accessible to other users. For example, inserting a reference to a file on the user's desktop will produce a missing file error when other users attempt to view or access the container field. Similarly, a document located on a file server that is not accessible or not currently mounted will show as a missing file. These problems can be alleviated with custom scripts controlling container insertions, limiting insertions to *only files* or *only references,* and requiring referenced files to be stored on a universally accessible volume like a network file server. However, even with all of these techniques used, there is still a disadvantage. If the server volume, folder directories, or files are moved, renamed, or deleted, the reference link will be broken. For the best results, use reference storage with a managed directory on a FileMaker Server.

Using Database-Managed References in a Central Directory

The best choice for container field storage, especially for networked databases, is to use *database-managed external storage* where the database *automatically* saves an external copy of every inserted file into a managed folder and inserts a reference to it in the field. In this setup, no users have access to the actual folder directory that contains the files. Instead, FileMaker acts as a broker between the user and the stored material. This keeps documents safely stored and linked to records. Each field can be individually configured to control how managed files are stored.

Using Managed External Storage

To use *database-managed external storage*, you must define base directories and configure container fields to use them.

Defining Base Directories

A *base directory* is a developer-defined path to a folder directory that acts as the root location into which one or more container fields can store documents. The folder defined is fully managed by FileMaker, which will automatically create the folder and then manage an internal directory structure of subfolders and files depending on the settings defined for the base directory and individual fields. Every database file contains one default directory, automatically defined with the same name as the database and a formula prefix of *[database location]* meaning that the external container directory will be stored in the same folder as the database file.

Note   If a database file is renamed, the default base directory will not change but can be manually updated for consistency.

Exploring the Manage Containers Dialog

External containers are defined in the *Manage Containers* dialog which can be opened by selecting the *File* ➤ *Manage* ➤ *Containers* menu. This dialog has two tabs: *Storage* and *Thumbnails*.

Exploring the Storage Tab

The *Storage* tab of the *Manage Containers* dialog, shown in Figure 10-3, contains a list of defined base directories. This is where you *create*, *edit*, and *delete* base directories. You can initiate a transfer of documents using the *Transfer Data* button, which becomes highlighted after a field's assigned base directory is changed and documents are detected in the old location (see "Changing a Field Container Settings" later in this chapter).

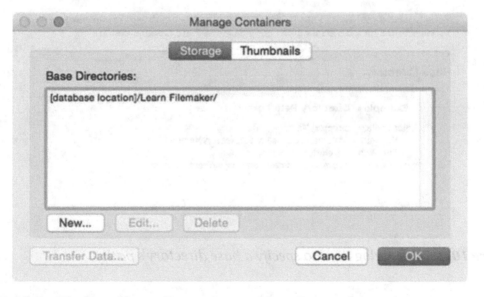

Figure 10-3. *The list of base directories used for managed containers*

Caution   Base directories can't be edited when a database is hosted on a FileMaker Server. Take the file offline and open with the FileMaker Pro desktop application to edit.

Creating a New Base Directory

The number of base directories in a given database file is completely up to the developer. The default directory can be shared by every container field in every table in the file. Alternatively, every table or even every field can be assigned a separate directory. To create a new base directory, click the *New* button. This will open a *New Base Directory* dialog, shown in Figure 10-4. This window contains a single text area into which you can either type a directory path or drop a folder to automatically insert its path. A path must be formatted as shown in the examples.

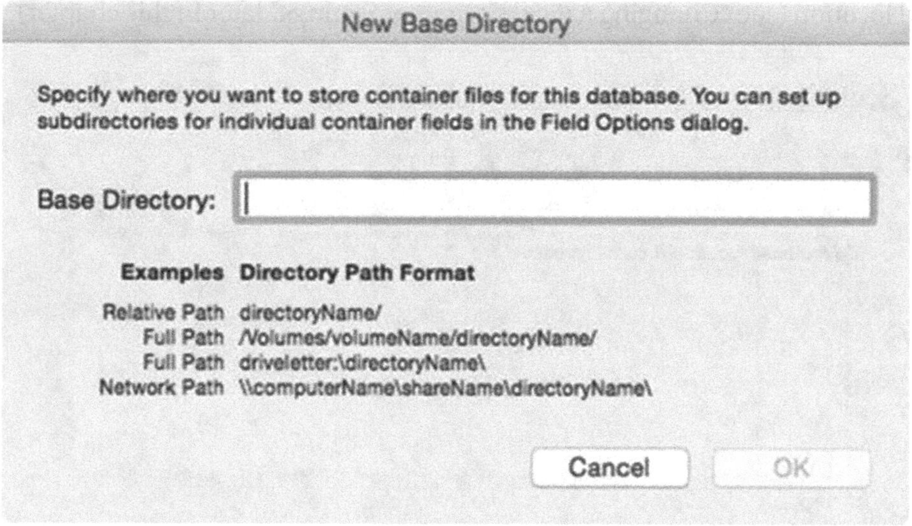

```
                          New Base Directory

    Specify where you want to store container files for this database. You can set up
    subdirectories for individual container fields in the Field Options dialog.


    Base Directory: |


           Examples  Directory Path Format
       Relative Path  directoryName/
          Full Path  /Volumes/volumeName/directoryName/
          Full Path  driveletter:\directoryName\
       Network Path  \\computerName\shareName\directoryName\


                                            Cancel        OK
```

Figure 10-4. The dialog used to specify a base directory's path

Editing a Base Directory

A directory path can be edited as long as it doesn't yet contain any managed files. If empty, double-click or click the *Edit* button in the *Manage Containers* dialog to open the selected base directory in the *Edit Base Directory* dialog (same as the *New Base Directory* dialog shown in Figure 10-4). If the directory does already contains files, create a new base directory, point any field using the old one to the new one, transfer the existing container documents, and then delete the old directory.

Deleting a Base Directory

When a base directory is no longer used, it can be deleted as long as it doesn't contain any managed files. Select it in the list and click the *Delete* button. FileMaker requires at least one base directory defined in a file, so a delete request will be rejected if there is only one in the list.

Note   FileMaker will delete the definition of the base directory from the list, not the actual external folder.

Exploring the Thumbnails Tab

The *Thumbnails* tab of the *Manage Containers* dialog, shown in Figure 10-5, controls automatic thumbnail generation which can speed up interface rendering of containers, especially when transferred across a network. To activate thumbnails, select the *Generate and store thumbnails for images* checkbox to allow FileMaker to automatically generate and display a thumbnail for images when a layout attempts to display them. Then choose between the two storage options. *The Permanent storage* option will cause thumbnails to be cached both on-disk and in-memory, with the on-disk portion retained when the database is closed. Use this for the fastest performance. *The Temporary storage* option will cause thumbnails to be cached in-memory only. When the database is closed, the cache is discarded. This will be slightly slower but save hard drive space.

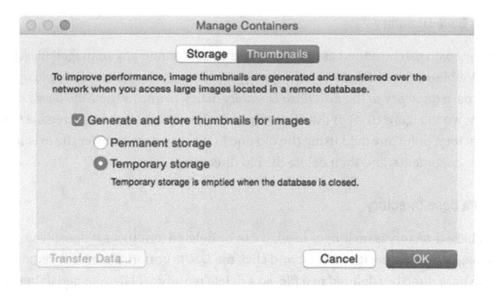

Figure 10-5. *The dialog used to specify a thumbnail generation*

Defining a Field's External Storage Directory

Once a base directory is defined, it can be assigned to container fields. The external
storage settings for a container field are configured on the *Storage* tab of the *Options for
Field* dialog, shown in Figure 10-6. Open the *Manage Database* dialog, click on the *Fields*
tab, and double-click on a container field. Then select on the *Storage* tab.

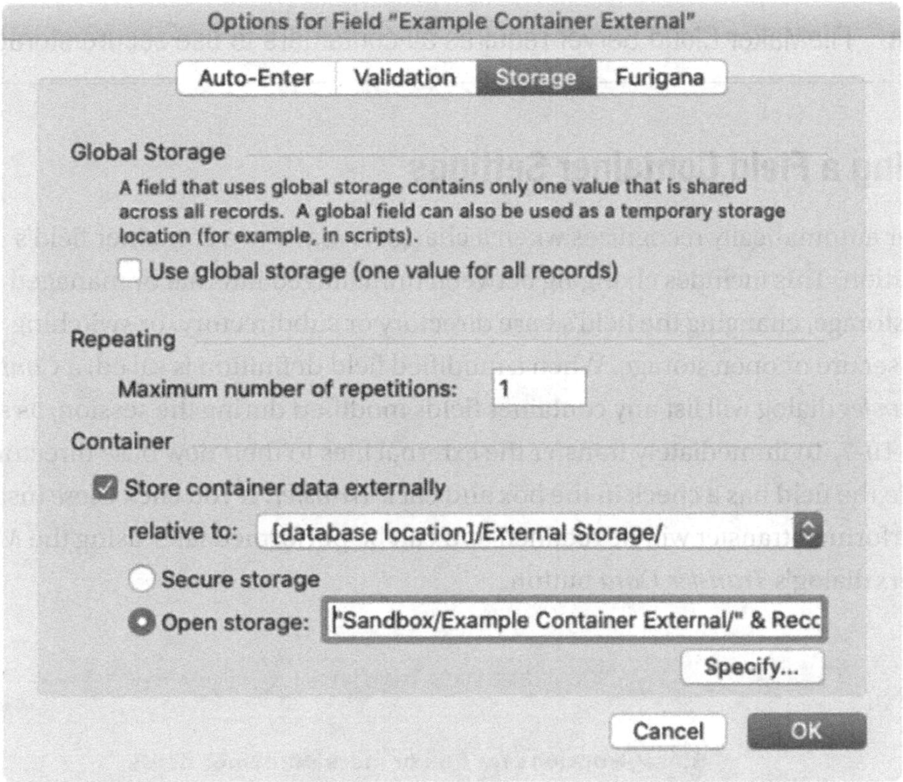

Figure 10-6. *The container field storage options*

Enable the *Store container data externally* checkbox and choose a base directory from the pop-up menu. Once a directory is selected, choose a storage methodology. The *secure storage* option will encrypt documents and automatically distribute the files randomly across automatically created subdirectories in a subdirectory within the base directory. This option automatically avoids conflicts between files with the same name stored in any field that is using the same base directory. The *open storage* option keeps document data in the original file format and uses a developer specified subdirectory which is required to avoid conflicts between similarly named items stored for different tables and fields. If using the same base directory for many fields across different tables in the database, use a formula to generate a subdirectory that includes the appropriate subfolders to avoid overwrite conflicts between records. Click the *Specify* button to enter a subdirectory formula like the following example which creates a hierarchy of folders for *table, field,* and *serial number* to ensure one container item per folder:

```
"Sandbox/Example Container/" & Record ID & "/"
```

Caution   FileMaker Cloud Server requires all containers to use secure storage.

Changing a Field Container Settings

FileMaker automatically recognizes when a change is made to a container field's configuration. This includes changing between unmanaged internal or managed external storage, changing the field's base directory or subdirectory, or switching between secure or open storage. When a modified field definition is saved, a *Container Data Transfer* dialog will list any container fields modified during the session, as shown in Figure 10-7. To immediately transfer the external files to their new base directory, make sure the field has a check in the box and click *Transfer*. If you click *Close* instead, the unperformed transfer will be retained and can be performed later using the *Manage Containers* dialog's *Transfer Data* button.

Figure 10-7. *The dialog indicating the need to transfer container field content*

Summary

This chapter explored inserting and extracting files from container fields as well as various methods of managing containers. In the next chapter, we explore how to define value lists.

CHAPTER 11

Defining Value Lists

A *value list* is a return-delimited sequence of values. Lists can be created by formulas (Chapter 13, "Aggregating Data") or by defining one as a centralized resource. A predefined list can be a set of static values or values dynamically compiled from the contents of a field gathered directly from a table or through a relationship. Once defined, these lists can be assigned to a field to enable selection-based data entry by means of *drop-down lists, pop-up menus, checkboxes,* and *radio buttons* (Chapter 20, "Configuring a Field's Control Style"). Using value lists as the control style for a field increases data entry speed and ensures accuracy and consistency. This chapter covers the following topics regarding defining value lists, including

- Introducing the Value Lists dialog
- Using custom values
- Using a list from another file
- Using values from a field

Introducing the Value Lists Dialogs

Predefined lists are configured using the *Manage Value Lists* dialog, shown in Figure 11-1. This dialog can be opened by selecting the *File ➤ Manage ➤ Value Lists* menu, clicking the pencil icon in the *Inspector pane* for fields assigned a list-based control style (Chapters 19 and 20) or with the *Open Manage Value Lists* script step. This dialog is used to *create, edit, duplicate,* and *delete* lists.

© Mark Conway Munro 2021
M. C. Munro, *Learn FileMaker Pro 19*, https://doi.org/10.1007/978-1-4842-6680-9_11

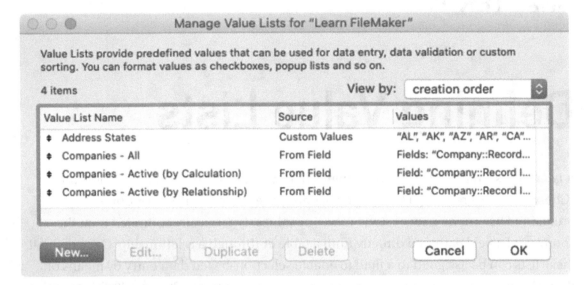

Figure 11-1. *The dialog used to manage value lists*

Tip   Value lists can be copied and pasted between two files.

List settings are defined in the *Edit Value List* dialog. This dialog opens when creating a new list or editing an existing list in the dialog in Figure 11-1. After entering a name for the list, there are three options for how values are generated:

- *Use Values from Field* – Generate a list from field values, defined in a *Specify Field* dialog

- *Use Value List from Another File* – Select a value list from a different FileMaker database for use in this one

- *Use Custom Values* – Manually define a return-delimited list of values in the field below

---

Caution   Examples in this section only *define* a list. See Chapter 20, "Configuring a Field's Control Style," to learn how to assign a list to fields on layouts.

Using Custom Values

A value list defined with manually entered *custom values* can be used for quick data entry of a set of static values, e.g., a *category, country, group, location, status*, and more. This defines a list of information that doesn't exist elsewhere in the database and is typed directly into the editing dialog. For example, create a simple example status list that can be assigned to fields such as *Company Status*. In the *Manage Value Lists* dialog, click the *New* button to open the *Edit Value List* dialog, and then perform these steps shown in Figure 11-2:

1. Enter a name for the value list, e.g., "Record Status."

2. Select the *Use custom values* option.

3. Enter values into the text area, e.g., "Active" and "Inactive."

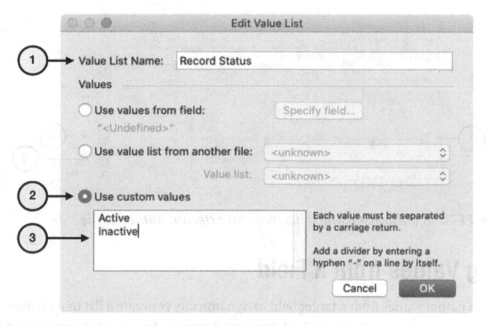

Figure 11-2. *A value list using custom values*

Using a List from Another File

A value list in one database can be defined to subscribe to a list defined in another database. This helps to eliminate redundancy in multi-file systems by defining a list once and sharing it in other files. The following example assumes a second file named

"Sample External List" with a value list named "Address States." From the *Learn FileMaker* database, open the *Manage Value Lists* dialog, and click the *New* button to open the *Edit Value List* dialog. Then enter a name and follow these steps to configure the list as shown in Figure 11-3:

1. Select the *Use value list from another file* option.

2. If the other database is already defined as an external file source, it will show up in the first pop-up menu. If not, it can be defined by selecting *Add FileMaker Data Source* from that menu and then locating and selecting the other database.

3. Once the file has been selected, the following *Value list* pop-up menu will become activated, allowing a selection from lists defined in the external file. Select the target list and close the dialog.

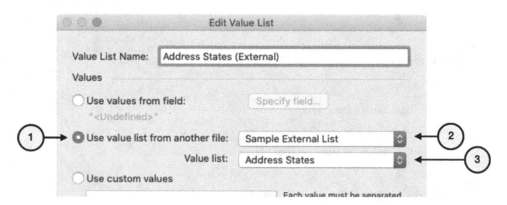

Figure 11-3. *A value list using a list from an external database file*

Using Values from a Field

A list can gather values from a target field to dynamically generate a list that changes based on record content. By using field data as the source, the value list content can be easily edited by authorized users, developers, or scripts and dynamically adjust the value over time. This is particularly useful when creating a list to aid users in assigning a record in one table to a record in another, e.g., assigning a *Company* record as the parent of a *Contact, Project, Invoice*, etc. Instead of remembering or finding a company's primary key and typing it manually or copy-pasting, a pop-up menu or drop-down list control style allows a user to select a company by name, and the primary key is entered for them automatically. By default, lists using field values are *context-insensitive*, meaning they will include values from *every record* in the field's table and are usable from *any context*. However, a list can also be configured to conditionally limit the values by declaring a *starting context* and pulling values through a relationship instead, thereby limiting the list to a single table's layouts.

Introducing the Specify Fields Dialog

Start by creating a new value list, assign it a name, and select the *Use values from field* radio button. This will automatically open a *Specify Fields* dialog, shown in Figure 11-4.

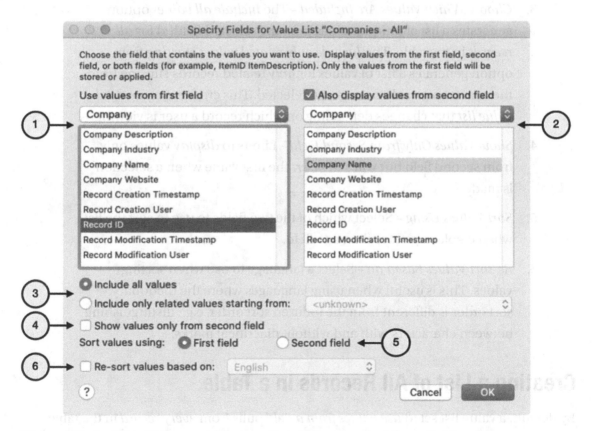

Figure 11-4. The dialog used to specify a list generated from field values

To define the list, specify the field(s) that will be used to generate values and indicate which values to include and how they will be displayed, using these controls in the dialog:

1. *Use Values from First Field* – Choose a table occurrence and field to specify the *first field* that will be used in the list. This value will be inserted in a field when a selection is made.

2. *Also Use Values from Second Field* – Optionally, choose a *second field* from the same occurrence or one related to it. This value is *displayed* in lists for identification purposes but not inserted when a selection is made. For example, if the first field uses a company primary key number, the second field can display the human-readable company name.

3. *Choose Which Values Are Included* – The *Include all values* option generates a list of unique values from the selected field(s) for *all records* in the table. The *Include only related values starting from* option generates a list of values for *only* related records starting from the context of a table occurrence selected. This creates a *contextual value list* that changes depending on which record a user is viewing.

4. *Show Values Only from Second Field* – Limits to *display* values only from second field but will still *insert* the first value when a selection is made.

5. *Sort Values Using* – Select which of the two fields to use to sort the list when displaying more than one field.

6. *Re-sort Values Based on* – Select a language to use when sorting values. This is useful when using languages where the dictionary sort order is different from the indexed sort order, e.g., distinguishing between characters with and without diacritical marks.

Creating a List of All Records in a Table

By default, a value list set to *use values from a field* pulls from *every record* in the table and can therefore be used on any layout in the database without concern for the relational context of the layout's table (Chapter 17, "Understanding Contextual Access").

The example previously shown in Figure 11-4 creates a value list using the *Record ID* and *Company Name* fields for all records in the *Company* table. Once configured and saved, this list can be assigned to a field as a *pop-up menu* or *drop-down list* in any table (Chapter 20, "Configuring Field Control Style"). For example, in the *Contact* table, the *Contact Company ID* field is used to store a foreign key that connects a contact record to a company. To allow a user to quickly enter this, the value list can be assigned to that field as a pop-up menu on the *Contact Form* layout.

Creating Conditional Value Lists

A *conditional value list* contains filtered choices that represent only a subset of the available record values. By offering a smaller list of only relevant values, users can more easily locate the value they need. This can be used in numerous ways. For example, when assigning a *Company* as the parent to a *Contact*, a conditional list can be limited to only include active company records. Similarly, assigning a *Product* to an *Invoice* can limit the list to only include products based on the value of a category field or the type of company receiving the invoice. When selecting a *Template* to use to generate an *Email* record, this can filter the list to only approved records for categories that are relevant to the type of email being generated.

There are two ways to create a conditional value list: *using a dedicated relationship* and *using a calculation field*. For the examples to follow, we will use the *Company Status* field in the *Company* table of *Learn FileMaker* database to create a value list that is conditioned to only display company records that have an "Active" status.

Using a Dedicated Relationship

A *relationship-driven conditional value list* is compiled through a relationship (Chapter 9), thereby creating a list containing a subset of values from only matching records. Creating a conditional value list using a relationship involves the selection of a *starting occurrence* which represents the interface context that will be used when pulling values from the selected list fields. Usually, this is the occurrence assigned to the table of the layout where the list will be used. However, it can also be any occurrence that is related to the layout's occurrence. The relational criteria from the *starting occurrence* to the *list occurrence* controls which matching records are included in the list and which are excluded. As an example, build a value list in the *Learn FileMaker* file that includes only *Company* records where the *Company Status* field contains a value of "active." Since the value list requires a relationship to work, we will declare a *use context* as the *Contact* table, i.e., the value list will be usable from any layout assigned to the *Contact* table. To begin, perform a few preparatory steps.

First, create a calculation field in the *Contact* table named "Contact Company Status Match" with a formula of "Active" and with a calculation result type of text (Chapter 12). Since the formula result will be the same for every record and since it will be a local key in the relationship (Chapter 9, "Indexing Match Fields"), it can be set to store a global value.

Next, in the relationship graph, create a new occurrence of the *Company* table, and name it "Contact | Company for Active List," and position it to the right of the *Contact* table. This will be the occurrence from which the list will pull values.

Finally, connect this new occurrence to *Contact* with a relationship as shown in Figure 11-5. Now, from the perspective of the *Contact* table (the starting occurrence), the *Company* values pulled through this relationship will be only those with a *Company Status* value of "Active."

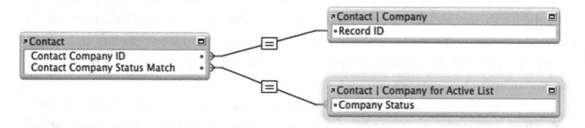

Figure 11-5. *The new relationship for the conditional value list*

Once finished, create a new value list set to *Use values from field* and specify the fields as shown in Figure 11-6:

1. Choose fields from the new occurrence created earlier.

2. Select the *Include only related values starting from* option.

3. Select *Contact* as the starting occurrence.

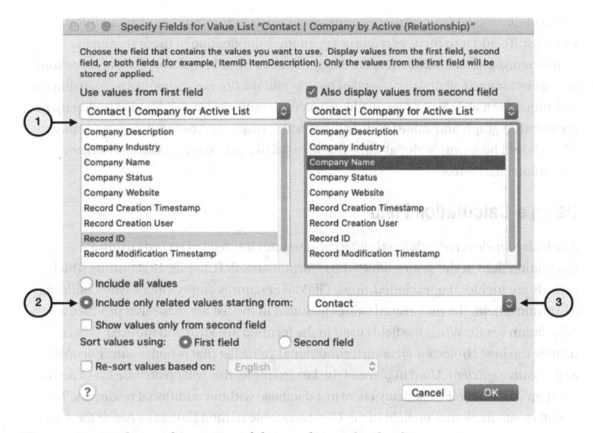

Figure 11-6. *The configuration of the conditional value list*

Once saved, assign the value list to the *Contact Company ID* field on a *Contact* layout as the source for a pop-up menu or drop-down list (Chapter 20, "Configuring a Field's Control Style"). Then, when clicking in that field, it should display a list of only the active companies.

Caution   If the value list is empty, confirm that some Company records that have an "Active" status.

Although there are many valid uses for this technique, a relationship-driven value list is not always the best choice. Since the filtering mechanism is a relationship, it is inherently context sensitive. To implement the same feature on layouts for other tables, it would require a duplicate set of resources. For example, to add the same list of active companies to a *Project* table would require a link calculation match field created there, a new dedicated table occurrence connecting *Project* to *Company,* and an additional value list. To add it to *Invoices* requires yet another duplication of these resources. Implementing such a value list in six different tables would require one set of those four resources for each, giving you a total of *twenty-four additional components*. So, using this technique for a widely used feature like an active company list would quickly clog up the relationship graph and value list definitions with extraneous resources to accommodate what should be a simple global value list. In cases like this, use a *calculation-driven conditional list* instead.

Using a Calculation Field

A *calculation-driven conditional value list* generates a subset of records using a calculation field in the source table whose formula result (Chapter 12) controls which records are included or excluded. Since FileMaker ignores empty values when building a list from a field, the only record values included in the list are those that produce a calculation result. When the fields used in the formula are local and indexed, this is usually the best choice for creating a conditional value list that is both *context neutral* and *resource efficient*. Used in place of the last example, this will create one list of active companies that can be used *anywhere* in a database without additional resources. To begin, create a calculation field in the *Company* table named *Company Name for Active List* that returns a *text* result and has a formula of

```
Case ( Company Status = "Active" ; Company Name ; "" )
```

Then create a value list that uses the *Record ID* as the first field and the aforementioned calculation field as the second field, as shown in Figure 11-7. When creating a list this way, only the second field needs to be conditionally generated from a calculation. Once created, this list can be used from *any* layout context, regardless of the source table and without requiring a dedicated relationship.

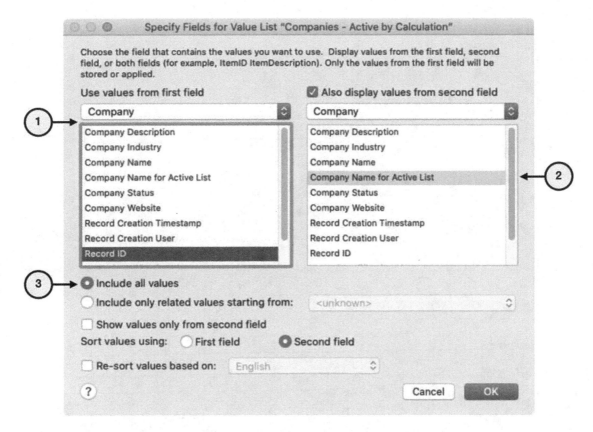

Figure 11-7. *The configuration of a calculation-driven conditional value list*

1. Select *Record ID* from the *Company* table as the first field.

2. Select the *Company Name for Active List* calculation field as the second field.

3. Select the *Include all records* option.

Summary

This chapter explored how to create predefined value lists a variety of different ways. Assigning these to layout objects is discussed further in Chapters 19 and 20. In the next chapter, we begin learning how to write formulas.

PART III

Writing Formulas and Using Functions

Formulas are used throughout the development interface in field definitions, custom functions, layout objects, custom menus, and script steps. These chapters cover the basics of writing formulas:

## CHAPTER 12

Writing Formulas

A *calculation formula* is an equation made up of one or more statements expressing operations that, when performed, produce a result. Formulas can *analyze, compare, concatenate, condense, convert, expand, format, parse, replace,* or *summarize* any of FileMaker's supported data types. They can range in size from a simple mathematical equation to an extremely complex collection of interrelated expressions and nested logical clauses involving values of any data type. This chapter introduces the basics of writing formulas, covering the following topics:

- Introducing formulas

- Defining formula components

- Exploring the calculation interface

- Writing formulas

- Adding calculations to the Learn FileMaker file

Introducing Formulas

Formulas are used in numerous places in the development interface. The *Replace Field Contents* dialog has an option to insert a formula result (Chapter 4). Many programming dialogs or panels have *Options, Specify, Fx,* or *Pencil icon* buttons that access a formula dialog. The same applies to a *Specify* option in some pop-up menus. When defining a calculation field, a formula is entered. Regular fields accept formulas to generate an auto-enter value and a validation result (Chapter 8). Custom functions define global formulas (Chapter 15). The *Inspector* pane in Layout mode accepts formulas to hide objects and create placeholder text and tooltips (Chapter 19). Many layout objects accept formulas to determine their name or other criteria, including *Button Bars, Buttons, Popovers, Tabs, Portals, Charts,* and *Web viewers* (Chapter 20). Custom menus can use formulas to determine a name and visibility (Chapter 23). Script parameters

© Mark Conway Munro 2021
M. C. Munro, *Learn FileMaker Pro 19*, https://doi.org/10.1007/978-1-4842-6680-9_12

can be generated with a formula (Chapter 24), and numerous script steps can or must be configured with formulas (Chapter 25). Security privileges can be configured to use formulas to determine access to schema resources (Chapter 30). The developer *Data Viewer* dialog has an *Edit Expressions* dialog that accepts formulas to continuously monitor a result (Chapter 31). All of these open a *Specify Calculation* window, as shown in Figure 12-1. This dialog is where formulas are constructed.

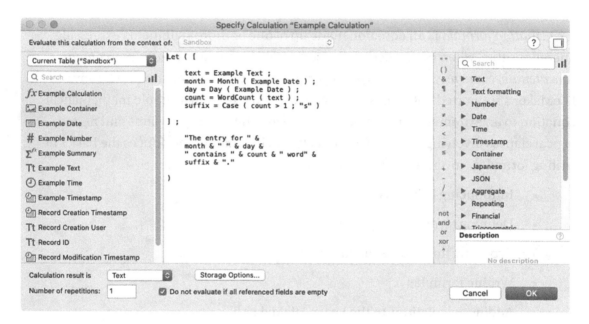

Figure 12-1. *A dialog used to define a calculation formula*

How Formulas Work

A calculation formula is created by assembling various text components into a written statement that express how a result should be produced. When saving a new or modified formula, FileMaker scans the statement to check for syntax errors, e.g., such as broken references, missing functions, or incorrectly structured statements. When a problem is detected, the save process is halted, the error is highlighted in the statement, and a dialog message explains the details of the error. This process is repeated until there are no errors detected, and the code can be successfully compiled and saved. Once saved, a formula remains in an idle state, until it is *called* by any process which prompts an evaluation of its statement to produce a result.

A formula can be called numerous ways. A field's auto-enter formula is called when a record is created or when fields used in the formula are altered. When a layout object is rendered, any formulas used by it will be called. This applies to objects that use formulas to generate a *name*, *hide condition*, *contextual formatting*, or other interface-related properties or conditions. A script step's calculation element is called when the step is executed as the script runs. A formula can be called by another formula, e.g., a calculation field including another calculation field in its formula or a custom function calling another custom function or a calculation field.

When called, the formula's statement is *evaluated*, which means that the code is converted into a result by working through each operation in a specific order of precedence. Formulas are always evaluated from the *context* of a specific table occurrence. A formula used in a *field definition* requires a manually selected context of any table occurrence for the table in which the field exists. A formula associated with an *interface element* will use the context of the table occurrence of the layout upon which the object is being rendered. A formula used in a *script step* will use the context of the table occurrence of the layout displayed in the current window at the time it is executed. Formulas used in *custom menus* also use the current layout's table as a context.

The *result* of a formula is returned to the calling process which handles it in a way appropriate to its function. For example, a *calculation field* contains the result of its formula and displays it when placed on a layout. A *layout object* name may change its displayed name, visibility, or appearance based on the result. The *Set Variable* script step places the result of its formula into a variable. The *Show Custom Message* script step will place a result into a dialog presented on screen. The type of object and the aspect of its configuration that called the formula determines the destination or use of the result.

When a formula is unable to create a result due to an execution error, it will return a question mark. For example, if a formula is using a field that has been deleted or is inaccessible from the current context, the formula may return an error. Similarly, using a custom function that has been deleted or providing a result as a data type inconsistent with the expectations of the calling process will return an error.

Defining Formula Components

A formula expression can be built using any combination of *comments, constants, field references, functions, operators, reserved keywords,* and *variables.*

Comments

A *comment* is a text string inserted into a formula that is completely ignored when the code is evaluated. Comments can be used to break code into sections or act as integrated documentation for developers, providing details about the functions it performs, how it works, a record of changes, or notes about unfinished work. A comment may be placed at the top of the formula or anywhere between individual statements or sections of code. There are two styles of comment available: *end-of-line* and *multiline*.

Creating End-of-Line Comments

An *end-of-line comment* starts at any double forward slash and continues until the next paragraph return. Any text placed between the slashes and the end of line indicated by the return will be ignored by FileMaker when the formula is evaluated. The following example has several end-of-line comments. The first and second paragraphs are both comments and demonstrate that each line requires a new set of slashes to produce a comment. The third paragraph has a comment starting in the middle of the paragraph, after a formula adding two numbers. The formula portion of this line will be evaluated, while the comment portion will be ignored. The result will be the total of the two numbers: *four*.

```
// This is a comment
// To continue on a second line you must use another set of symbols
2 + 2    // This comment starts in the middle of a line, after a formula
```

Creating Multiline Comments

A *multiline comment* uses an *initiating* and *terminating* symbol to indicate the start and end of a comment. These are used to "comment out" an entire block of paragraphs. To enter a multiline comment, use a forward slash and asterisk to indicate the *start* of the comment and the reverse, an asterisk and forward slash, to indicate the *end* of the comment. Any text between these two will be completely ignored by FileMaker when the formula is evaluated. In the following example, the formula has two block comments that will be ignored with a formula between them that will be evaluated, again producing a result of the total of the two numbers: *four*.

```
/*
This is a comment
The comment continues on additional lines
3 + 4 including this entire line
Until you terminate it here
*/
2 + 2
/*
This is another comment with returns as spaces
The comment continues on additional lines until terminated
*/
```

Constants

A *constant*, sometimes referred to as a *literal*, is a static, unchanging value literally typed into a formula. The value can be any of FileMaker's data types: *text*, *number*, *date*, *time*, or *timestamp*. A quantity, city name, event date, and start time are all examples of constants when typed *literally* into a formula. Numeric constants can be typed directly into a formula, while other text-based constants like dates, times, and strings must be contained within quotation marks so that it is interpreted as a literal value instead of as a field reference, function name, or variable. The following shows examples of each type of constant, as they might appear in a formula:

```
150
"New York"
"1/15/2017"
"10:15:00"
"1/15/2017 10:15:00"
```

A date and time constant entered as literal strings are seen as text and must be converted into actual date and time values in order to be treated as such. This is done using a built-in function: *GetAsDate*, *GetAsTime*, and *GetAsTimestamp*.

```
GetAsDate ( "1/15/2021" )
GetAsTime ( "10:15:00" )
GetAsTimestamp ( "1/15/2017 10:15:00" )
```

Tip   Learn more about built-in functions in Chapter 13.

Field References

A *field reference* is a pointer to a field that allows field values to be dynamically accessed by a calculation. A formula that contains only a reference to a *First Name* field will result in the value contained in that field for the current record based on the evaluation context. Complex formulas can use field references in conjunction with other components to produce various results by combining, comparing, parsing, or otherwise manipulating the values fields contain.

Depending on the type of calculation and the location of the field relative to the evaluation context, a reference is considered either local or related. A *local field* is a field that exists within the table of the current context. For a calculation field, the current context is that field's table so any fields referenced that are also in that table are considered local to the calculation. For a formula used outside of a calculation field, the context will always be the table occurrence assigned to the window's layout at the time of evaluation. A reference to a field in a table outside the formula's operating context table is considered a *related field*.

References are typed or inserted into a formula without quotation marks. When a field reference is used in a formula other than a calculation field, it must include a table occurrence to specify the relational context from which values should be pulled. This is done by combining an occurrence and field name with a double colon delimiter. For example, a reference to a *First Name* in an occurrence named "Contact" would be formatted as *Contact::First Name*. FileMaker will warn you that a "specified table can't be found" when a reference is missing the required table occurrence.

Caution   A few examples early in this chapter mention built-in functions which are not explained until later, here or in subsequent chapters.

Keeping Field References Dynamic

Field references are automatically *dynamic* and will update to reflect field or table occurrence name changes. It is possible and sometimes desirable to construct a field reference by appending text constants; however, this should be avoided because it creates a reference to a field that is not dynamic. For example, if a formula needs to conditionally pull from one of two fields, you might be tempted to construct the reference as text and then use the *GetField* and *Case* functions to construct a reference and retrieve the field value, like this:

```
GetField ( "Contact::" Case ( aValue = 1 ; "First" ; "Last") & " Name"
```

Using the *Case* function (Chapter 13), this example constructs a reference to either the *First Name* or *Last Name* field in a *Contact* table depending on the *aValue* variable and then gets the field value. This code will work fine until you change the name of the table occurrence or either of the two fields. While it may be unlikely that you ever rename certain field names, there are many instances where name changes might be desired. Referencing fields with static constants like this can be disastrous if a name changes. Doing so requires you to manually locate and update every referencing formula or never changing any field name. Instead, consider using techniques that keep field references dynamic even when they need to vary. In this modified example, the *Case* statement chooses one of two full, dynamic references instead of a text-based construction.

```
Case ( aValue = 1 ; Contact::First Name ; Contact::Last Name )
```

For complex situations where listing every possible field reference in a statement isn't practical, use the *GetFieldName* function to convert a dynamic field reference into a text string (Chapter 13, "Converting a Field Reference to Text"), and then manipulate the result to produce a new field reference (Chapter 13, "Working with Text").

Functions

A *function* is a predefined, named formula that is evaluated to return a result. Functions are like subroutines in other programming languages since they allow some specific functionality to be off-loaded to a process outside of the current formula to help avoid redundancies. Within FileMaker, there are two kinds of functions: *built-in functions* (Chapters 13 and 14) and *custom functions* (Chapter 15). In this section, we will introduce calling functions using simple pattern to illustrate their use in formulas. See those other chapters for more specific information.

Calling a Function from a Formula

A function call can be placed into a formula by typing its name or selecting it through the interface (described later). Generally, functions are named with two or more capitalized words, phrased without spaces that concisely describe the process they perform. So, a function call is simply that name placed into a statement, shown in pattern here:

```
FunctionName
```

Calling a Function with Parameters

A *function parameter* is a value that can vary with each call to the function. Some functions use parameters to allow input provided by the calling formula. Parameters may contain material for manipulation or instructions about the process(es) to be performed. Parameters are listed after the function name, enclosed within a set of parentheses. If a function accepts more than one parameter, they are listed in order, separated with semicolons after the function name. Examples of both are shown here:

```
ExampleFunction ( parameter )
ExampleFunction ( parameter1 ; parameter2 ; parameter3 )
```

The value of a parameter in a function call can be a constant, field reference, literal, nested function, or variable expression as illustrated in these examples, each calling a hypothetical function that has a single parameter.

```
ExampleFunction ( "Hello, World" )
ExampleFunction ( 5000 )
ExampleFunction ( Invoice Tax Rate * Invoice Subtotal )
ExampleFunction ( AnotherFunction ( 15 ) )
```

Optional Parameters

Some built-in functions have *optional parameters* that can be included or ignored as needed. When inserting a function call into a formula, FileMaker will denote optional parameters with braces as shown in this pattern.

```
ExampleFunction ( parameter1 {; parameter2 ; parameter3} )
```

In this case, the braces indicate that *parameter1* is required, while *parameter2* and *parameter3* are optional. Before compiling the formula, the braces must be removed along with any optional parameters that *won't* be used. The following examples show one call to the same hypothetical function without optional parameters and a second call to the same function with optional parameters included.

```
ExampleFunction ( parameter1 )
ExampleFunction ( parameter1 ; parameter2 ; parameter3 )
```

Nesting Function Calls

A parameter can accept an expression as a value, including calls to *other functions*. In this example, *ExampleFunction2* will be evaluated first, and the result will be used as the parameter for *ExampleFunction1*.

```
ExampleFunction1 ( ExampleFunction2 ( parameter ) )
```

Operators

An *operator* is a symbol used to express a type of operation within a formula. FileMaker has many different operators: *comparison, logical, mathematical,* and *textual.*

Caution   For clarity, examples in this section use simple formulas containing only constants. However, they can be used with any combination of formula components.

Comparison Operators

A *comparison operator* is a symbol used to compare two values, either a literal value or the evaluated result of two expressions. The result of an expression using a comparison operator will be a *Boolean value*, represented respectively by a 1 (*true*) or 0 (*false*).

Equal To

An *equal to* symbol is used to compare two values for similarity. The equation will evaluate true if the values are identical and false if they are not.

```
100 = 100          // result = 1
150 = 100          // result = 0
"New York" = "New York"  // result = 1
"New York" = "NY"        // result = 0
GetAsDate ( "1/15/2021" ) = GetAsDate ( "1/15/2021" )      // result = 1
GetAsDate ( "1/15/2021" ) = GetAsDate ( "7/20/2021" )      // result = 0
GetAsTime ( "9:30:00" ) = GetAsTime ( "9:30:00" )      // result = 1
GetAsTime ( "9:30:00" ) = GetAsTime ( "12:15:00" )      // result = 0
```

Not Equal To

Comparing two values for dissimilarity can be performed using either a *not equal to* symbol or a *less than* and *greater than* symbol side by side. An equation will evaluate false if the values are identical and true if they are not, as demonstrated in these examples:

```
100 ≠ 100          // result = 0
150 ≠ 100          // result = 1
"New York" <> "New York"  // result = 0
"New York" <> "NY"        // result = 1
GetAsDate ( "1/15/2021" ) ≠ GetAsDate ( "1/15/2021" )      // result = 0
GetAsDate ( "1/15/2021" ) ≠ GetAsDate ( "7/20/2021" )      // result = 1
GetAsTime ( "9:30:00" ) ≠ GetAsTime ( "9:30:00" )      // result = 0
GetAsTime ( "9:30:00" ) ≠ GetAsTime ( "12:15:00" )      // result = 1
```

Tip   The *not equal to* symbol can be created by typing an equal sign while holding the Option key on macOS.

Greater Than

A *greater than* symbol is used to compare the relative alphabetical, chronological, or numerical positions of two values. The equation will evaluate to true if the value on the left is greater in position compared to the value on the right.

```
150 > 100          // result = 1
```

```
100 > 100           // result = 0
"Bear" > "Automobile"      // result = 1
"Atlanta" > "New York"     // result = 0
GetAsDate ( "1/15/2021" ) > GetAsDate ( "1/10/2021" )      // result = 1
GetAsDate ( "1/15/2021" ) > GetAsDate ( "7/10/2021" )      // result = 0
GetAsTime ( "12:30:00" ) > GetAsTime ( "9:15:00" )         // result = 1
GetAsTime ( "9:30:00" ) > GetAsTime ( "10:45:00" )         // result = 0
```

Greater Than or Equal To

Comparing the relative positions of two values can be performed using either a *greater than or equal to* symbol or a *greater than* symbol followed by an *equal* sign. The equation will evaluate true if the value on the left is greater in position or the same value compared to the value on the right, as shown in these examples:

```
100 ≥ 100           // result = 1
100 ≥ 150           // result = 0
"Bear" >= "Automobile"      // result = 1
"New York" >= "Ohio"        // result = 0
GetAsDate ( "1/15/2021" ) ≥ GetAsDate ( "7/20/2016" )      // result = 1
GetAsDate ( "1/15/2021" ) ≥ GetAsDate ( "7/10/2021" )      // result = 0
GetAsTime ( "12:30:00" ) ≥ GetAsTime ( "12:30:00" )        // result = 1
GetAsTime ( "9:30:00" ) ≥ GetAsTime ( "10:45:00" )         // result = 0
```

Tip   The ≥ symbol can be created by typing a *greater than* symbol while holding the Option key on macOS.

Less Than

A *less than* symbol is used to compare the relative positions of two values. The equation will evaluate true if the value on the right is greater in position than the value on the left.

```
100 < 350           // result = 1
100 < 100           // result = 0
"Automobile" < "Car"      // result = 1
```

```
"New York" < "New York" // result = 0
GetAsDate ( "7/20/2016" ) < GetAsDate ( "1/15/2021" )      // result = 1
GetAsDate ( "7/10/2021" ) < GetAsDate ( "1/15/2021" )      // result = 0
GetAsTime ( "9:15:00" ) < GetAsTime ( "12:30:00" )         // result = 1
GetAsTime ( "10:45:00" ) < GetAsTime ( "9:30:00" )         // result = 0
```

Less Than or Equal To

Comparing the relative positions of two values can be performed using either a *less than or equal to* symbol or a *less than* symbol followed by an *equal* sign. The equation will evaluate true if the value on the left is greater in position or the same value compared to the value on the right, as shown in these examples:

```
100 ≤ 100        // result = 1
100 ≤ 50         // result = 0
"Automobile" <= "Bear"    // result = 1
"Ohio" <= "New York"      // result = 0
GetAsDate ( "7/20/2016" ) ≤ GetAsDate ( "1/15/2021" )      // result = 1
GetAsDate ( "7/10/2021" ) ≤ GetAsDate ( "1/15/2021" )      // result = 0
GetAsTime ( "12:30:00" ) ≤ GetAsTime ( "12:30:00" )        // result = 1
GetAsTime ( "10:45:00" ) ≤ GetAsTime ( "9:30:00" )         // result = 0
```

Tip   The ≤ symbol can be created by typing a *greater than* symbol while holding the Option key on macOS.

Logical Operators

A *logical operator* is a keyword used to build compound conditions by joining two or more separate expressions into a single expression or, in one case, to negate a single expression to reverse a Boolean result. The result of an expression using a logical operator will be a Boolean.

Tip   Use parenthesis to help visualize the separate expressions on either side of a logical operator and ensure proper execution order.

AND

The AND operator is used to combine two separate Boolean expressions into a combined equation that will evaluate true only if the result of both expressions are true.

```
( 150 > 100 ) AND ( "Bear" > "Automobile" )        // result = 1
( 150 > 100 ) AND ( "Bear" = "Automobile" )        // result = 0
```

OR

The OR operator is used to combine two separate Boolean expressions into a combined equation that will evaluate true if the result of at least one of the two expressions is true.

```
( 150 > 100 ) OR ( "Bear" < "Automobile" )        // result = 1
( 150 < 100 ) OR ( "Bear" = "Automobile" )        // result = 0
```

XOR

The XOR operator is used to combine two separate Boolean expressions into a combined equation that will evaluate true if the result of only one of the two equations is true. If both equations are true, it will return false.

```
( 150 > 100 ) XOR ( "Bear" < "Automobile" )        // result = 1
( 150 > 100 ) XOR ( "Bear" ≠ "Automobile" )        // result = 0
( 150 < 100 ) XOR ( "Bear" = "Automobile" )        // result = 0
```

NOT

The NOT operator is a unique logical operator that will negate the result of any expression to its right, thereby reversing the Boolean result of that expression. If the expression evaluates true, putting this operator in front of it will reverse it to return false and vice versa.

```
NOT ( 150 > 100 )                       // result = 0
NOT ( "Tuesday" < "Monday" )            // result = 1
```

A reversal can also be achieved by comparing the Boolean result of an expression to 0. In this example, the false (0) result from the parenthesized expression is reversed by the subsequent comparison to 0:

```
( 150 < 100 ) = 0                       // result = 1
```

Mathematical Operators

A *mathematical operator* is a symbol used to perform or control arithmetic computations with one or more values or expressions. The mathematical operations can be performed not only on numbers but on other data types such as dates, times, and timestamps.

Note   For mathematical operations, dates and times are converted to a number (Chapter 8, "Defining Field Data Types").

Addition

The *plus* symbol is used to add the value on the right to the value on the left.

```
100 + 50                     // result = 150
GetAsDate ( "1/5/2021" ) + 5   // result = 1/10/2017
GetasTime ( "1:15:00" ) + 300  // result = 1:20:00
```

Subtraction

The *minus* symbol is used to subtract the value on the right from the value on the left.

```
100 - 50                     // result = 50
GetAsDate ( "1/5/2021" ) - 2   // result = 1/3/2017
GetasTime ( "1:15:00" ) - 300  // result = 1:10:00
```

Multiplication

The *multiply* symbol is used to multiply the value on the left by the value on the right.

```
100 * 50                     // result = 5000
GetAsDate ( "1/5/2021" ) * 2 // result = 1475590
```

Division

The *division* symbol is used to divide the value on the left by the value on the right.

```
100 / 50                     // result = 2
GetAsTime ( "1:15:00" ) / 2    // result = 2250
```

Raising to a Power

The *power of* symbol is used to raise the value on the left to the power of the value on the right.

```
100^2
```

Precedence

A set of *parentheses* is used to change the order of *evaluative precedence* (discussed later in this chapter). FileMaker will evaluate formulas from left to right after first evaluating expressions that are enclosed within parentheses, working from the inside out and based on an order of precedence. Although these two equations perform the same mathematical operations on the same numbers in the same order, the results are drastically different due to the control of precedence imposed with parentheses:

```
100 * 2 + 50 / 25              // result = 202
( ( 100 * 2 ) + 50 ) / 25      // result = 10
```

Text Operators

A *text operator* is a symbol used to construct an equation that combines text items into a single item and performs other text-related functions. These include quoting, concatenating, paragraph returns, and backslashes.

Quoting Text

A pair of *quotation marks* is used to indicate a literal text constant. Text entered into a formula without quotation marks will be interpreted as a *field*, *function*, or *variable*. Date and time constants must be enclosed in quotation marks.

```
"John"
"1/15/2021"
```

Concatenate Text

The *ampersand* symbol is used to join text values into a single value.

```
"John" & " " & "Smith"         //result = John Smith
```

Paragraph Return

The *paragraph return* symbol is used to insert a carriage return into a text value and can be placed in a calculation. Although a single return character can be placed outside of quotes as shown in the second example, putting multiple returns together outside quotes will produce an error and fail to compile. All three examples in the following return the same result:

```
"John Smith" & "¶" & "Jim Smith"
"John Smith" & ¶ & "Jim Smith"
"John Smith¶Jim Smith"
// result = John Smith¶Jim Smith
```

Tip   The paragraph return symbol can be created by typing a "7" while holding down the Option key on macOS.

Backslash

Quotes are operators and are not actually part of the value they contain. The backslash symbol is used to force an operator to be used literally instead. This is referred to as *escaping a string* since it allows operator use in a string without causing errors. For example, a backslash preceding a quote symbol will force the quote symbol to be treated as text and become part of the result. Without the backslash, FileMaker will interpret the formula as having a syntax error and not allow it to be saved.

```
5"                  // result = syntax error, will not compile
"5\""               // result = 5"
"Hello, World"      // result = Hello, World
"\"Hello, World\""  // result = "Hello, World"
```

Tip   FileMaker's built-in *Quote()* function will automatically enclose an existing value into quoted text.

Reserved Name

FileMaker will allow a reserved keyword or function name to be used as a table name or field name. However, when referencing these in a formula, an error may occur because FileMaker has no way to distinguish between it as a field reference instead of an operator or function call. For example, you can name a field "AND," but when referring to it in a formula, it must be wrapped in curly brackets with a preceding dollar sign in order for it to be interpreted as a field and compile:

${AND}

Tip   Avoid using reserved names as table or field names!

Understanding Operator Precedence

Operators in a calculation formula are evaluated in the following order of precedence:

1. Comments

2. Space, backslash, paragraph return, reserved name

3. Parentheses

4. NOT

5. Power of (^)

6. Multiplication, division

7. Addition, subtraction

8. Ampersand

9. Equal to, not equal to, greater than, less than, greater than or equal to, less than or equal to

10. OR, XOR

Reserved Words

A *reserved word* is a word, term, or symbol used by FileMaker for function names, predefined parameters, and operators and to construct SQL statements. These should not be used as names for tables, fields, custom functions, and other objects to avoid problems when writing formulas. Claris provides a list on their site by searching "Reserved words in FileMaker Pro" or following this address:

https://support.claris.com/s/article/Reserved-words-in-FileMaker-Pro-1503693036814

Variables

A *variable* is a developer-named letter, word, or phrase that stores a value which can be used in a calculation formula and other places in the development interface.

Types of Variables

FileMaker has three different variable types, each with a different naming requirement and scope: *statement, local,* and *global.* Although variables can be named using a variety of different formats, there are a few general naming considerations to keep in mind. Variable names should avoid reserved words and field names to avoid confusion and conflicts in formulas. As with names elsewhere, variable names should be concise to avoid clutter but with enough descriptive clarity to indicate what data it contains. Overall, be consistent in case; choose either *camel-case* (`variableNameExample`), *dot-delimited* (`variable.name.example`), *underscore-delimited* (`variable_name_example`), or some other format of your choosing.

Statement Variables

A *statement variable* is a variable initialized within *Let* or *While* statements (Chapter 13). These only exist when the statement is being actively evaluated. Except for the normal restrictions, FileMaker imposes no special naming requirements to a statement variable. Names can be as short as a single character or a lengthy, multi-word phrase like any of the following examples. Since statement variables are limited to the statement in which they are defined, they can't conflict with similarly named variables in other formulas or within the same formula outside of the statement containing them. Therefore, standardized names can be reused from one formula to the next without concern for conflict.

```
X
data
firstName
first_Name
dateToProcess
table.name
```

Local Variables

A *local variable* is a variable that persists temporarily during the evaluation of a formula, custom function or the execution of a script. A local variable can be initialized within a *Let* or *While* statement (Chapter 13) and with the *Set Variable* script step (Chapter 25) and has a variety of uses. Store information at one position in a script for use later in the same script, share information between a script and a custom function, or store information from one iteration to the next in a recursive custom function (Chapter 15). FileMaker requires that local variables be named with a single dollar symbol prefix. Beyond that, the name can be as short as a single character or a lengthy, multi-word phrase and can use any of a variety of delimiters, as shown in the following examples. Since local variables are limited to the formula or script in which they are defined, they can't typically conflict with similarly named variables in other scripts. However, multiple calls to custom function from the same script will retain any local variables used by that function.

```
$x
$data
$firstName
$recordNumber
$dateToProcess
$date.to.process
$date_to_process
```

Global Variable

A *global variable* is a variable that is accessible from any formula anywhere within a single database file and will persist until the file is closed. Like local variables, a global variable can be initialized within a *Let* or *While* statement and the *Set Variable* script step. Global variables can be used to store custom preference settings that control custom functionality, stage data being prepared for some purpose, or log troubleshooting information to help track down problems with complex, multi-script processes or iterative formulas.

Tip   Limit global variables to information truly used *universally* within the file! Avoid using them to exchange data between scripts; use parameters instead (Chapter 24).

FileMaker requires that global variables be named with a double dollar symbol prefix. Beyond that, names can be as short as a single character or a lengthy, multi-word phrase and can use any of a variety of delimiters, as shown in the following examples. Since they are global, they must each be uniquely and carefully named to avoid confusion and conflicts with other global variables used for different purposes in the same file. However, since they are not shared between files, standardized names can be reused from one file to the next without concern about them overwriting each other.

```
$$x
$$data
$$firstName
$$recordNumber
$$dateToProcess
$$date.to.process
$$date_to_process
```

Tip   The *Data Viewer* (Chapter 26, "Exploring the Data Viewer") can be used to monitor global variables anytime and local variables during the execution of a script.

Exploring the Calculation Interface

To experiment with formulas, use the *Example Calculation* field of the *Sandbox* table in the *Learn FileMaker* database. To begin, follow these steps:

1. Open the *Learn FileMaker* database.

2. Switch to the *Sandbox* layout.

3. Select the *File ➤ Manage ➤ Database* menu item.

4. Click on the *Fields* tab.

5. Confirm *Sandbox* in the *Tables* pop-up on the upper left.

6. Click on the *Example Calculation* field.

7. Click the *Options* button.

Exploring the Specify Calculation Dialog

All formulas are written in a *Specify Calculation* dialog, shown in Figure 12-2.

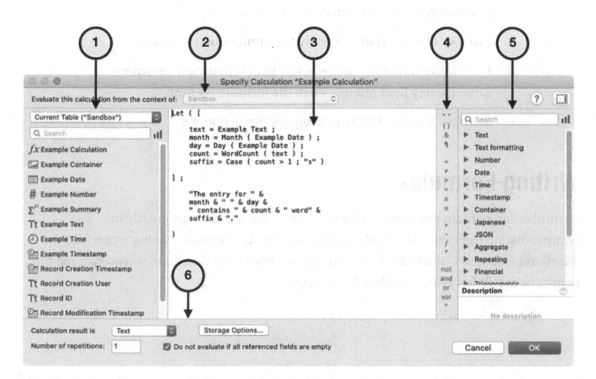

Figure 12-2. *The dialog window used to specify a calculation formula*

1. *Field Selector Pane* – Select a table occurrence and choose a field to insert a field reference into the formula.

2. *Context Indicator* – For calculation fields only, choose an occurrence to serve as the context for the formula if more than one occurrence exists for the field's table.

3. *Formula Text Area* – This is the formula's code. Type, drag-drop, copy-paste, or insert content by clicking on the panes to the left and right to build the formula.

4. *Operators* – Use these buttons to quickly insert an operator.

5. *Functions Pane* – A list of built-in, custom, and plug-in provided functions that can be inserted into the formula. They can be organized hierarchically or alphabetically.

6. Settings for calculation fields only:

   - *Calculation Result Is* – Select a data type for the result for field calculations. Other formulas automatically specify by object or function type, e.g., button names must be text.

   - *Number of Repetitions* – Specify the number of repetitions.

   - *Do Not Evaluate Checkbox* – Select to automatically return no value if every field referenced in the formula is empty.

   - *Storage Options* – Open a dialog of storage options.

Writing Formulas

Formulas can contain any combination of components and range greatly in complexity. All the examples in this section assume the formula is being typed into the *Sandbox::Example Calculation* field in the *Learn FileMaker* database, so you can see the results in that field on the *Sandbox Form* layout.

Constant-Only Formula

A *constant-only* formula is a formula that evaluates to a literal value without performing any actual operations. It is basically a statement containing a single value that will always evaluate to a result of the same value. These have a practical value as a way of storing static information such as a current tax rate or value(s) used as a relationship match field to connect to a subset of related records of a certain type. For now, it will serve as the most basic example to get us started writing simple formulas. Type "Hello World" into the formula area, and select a calculation result data type of *text*. The dialog should now look as shown in Figure 12-3. After saving the formula, the *Example Calculation* field on the layout should now display the text `"Hello World"` for every record. The result is the same because the formula returns a static value. For it to vary from one record to the next, the formula would require components that vary from one record to the next, such as field references.

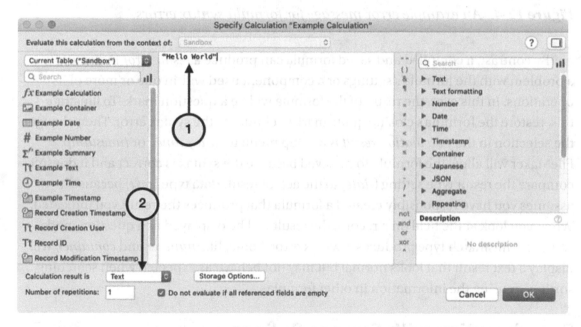

Figure 12-3. *A simple calculation formula with a static result*

Creating Intentional Errors

Before moving forward, it is important to understand the difference between a syntax error and a result error. A *syntax error* is an error with the format or language of the code which causes it to fail when attempting to compile and save the formula. To illustrate this with the simple constant formula, remove the final quotation symbol from the previous formula. When you attempt to save the calculation, FileMaker will display the error dialog message shown in Figure 12-4. When a syntax error is detected, FileMaker will not allow you to save the formula until it is correctly formatted. Not every syntax error message will be this specific, but it usually gives you enough information to help determine the nature of the error.

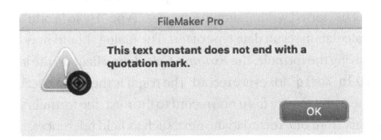

Figure 12-4. *An example error message for formula syntax errors*

By contrast, a compiled and saved formula can produce a *result error* indicating a problem with the formula's settings or a component used within one or more of its operations. In this case, the result of the formula will be a question mark. To illustrate this, restore the formula's closing quote mark to eliminate the syntax error. Then change the selection in the *Calculation result is* pop-up menu to *date*, *time*, or *timestamp*. FileMaker will allow the formula to be saved because the syntax is correct and it doesn't compare the result type setting (*date*) to the actual result data type (*text*) because it assumes you have responsibly created a formula that produces the result you indicated. When you look at the field on a record, the result will be displayed as a question mark. Not every mismatch type produces a syntax error. Some, like *number* and *container,* will display a text result that looks normal but may not behave as expected when searching, sorting, or using the information in other formulas.

Experimenting with Storage Options

Like entry fields, calculation fields have *storage options* that control how the result of a formula is stored, shown in Figure 12-5. The settings for *global storage* and *indexing* work similar to *entry* fields (discussed in Chapter 8) with an additional option for indexing. The *Do not store calculation results* checkbox forces a calculation to never index results and instead automatically recalculates anytime the field is accessed or displayed. This box is unchecked by default when a new field is created.

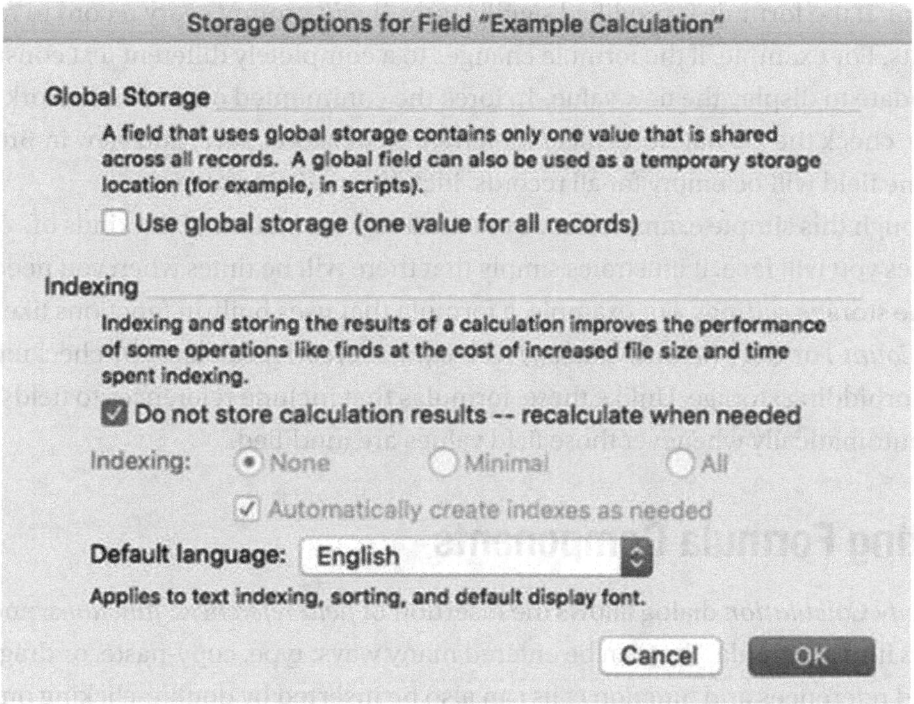

Figure 12-5. *The Storage Options dialog with indexing disabled*

To demonstrate the effect of storage, start with the "Hello World" formula configured to return a *text* result and the *Do not store* box unchecked. Save the formula and confirm that the field displays correctly in Browse mode. Then, open the formula again and type two forward slashes in front of the text to convert the entire formula into a comment, as shown in this example.

```
// "Hello World"
```

Without making other changes, save the formula and again view it in Browse mode. Don't be surprised if it still displays the value "Hello World" as if nothing changed. This is due to the existing records containing a stored result. If you select the *Record* ➤ *New Record* menu, the new record will correctly display a blank value in the field reflecting the fact that the formula is commented out. With the checkbox set to not recalculate the results, the previous value remains in older records and appears unchanged until something triggers an update.

Like other field types, calculations use index settings to pre-process data in a way that will speed up searches or establish relationships. However, this setting allows a calculation field to not recalculate an updated result when nothing else triggers it to reevaluate. If the formula is modified significantly, it *will* prompt every record to refresh the results. For example, if the formula changes to a completely different text constant, it will update to display the new value. To force the commented out example work correctly, check the *Do not store calculation results* checkbox, save, and view in Browse mode. The field will be empty for all records, including existing records.

Although this simple example isn't a practical representation of the kinds of challenges you will face, it illustrates simply that there will be times when you need to adjust the storage settings. For example, a formula that uses built-in functions like *Get (FoundCount)* or *Get (RecordNumber)* will *require* forced recalculate by checking the box forbidding storage. Unlike these, formulas that include references to fields *will* update automatically whenever those field values are modified.

Inserting Formula Components

The *Specify Calculation* dialog allows the insertion of *field references*, *functions*, and *operators* into a formula. Text can be entered many ways: type, copy-paste, or drag-drop text. Field references and function calls can also be inserted by double-clicking on an item in the panes on either side of the dialog.

Using Auto-complete

The formula area of the dialog combines text-based entry with dynamic assistance that detects key phrasing and presents an *auto-complete suggestion interface*, as shown in Figure 12-6. As you type, the list of available components refreshes to include a mixture of every built-in function, custom function, and field that starts with the letter or phrase typed. In the example, the letter "E" causes a list of three functions and a bunch of fields. As you continue typing – "Ex," "Exa," and "Exam" – the list continuously filters until you see only a list of our example fields.

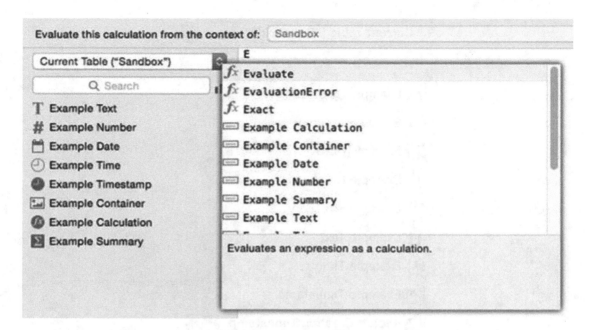

Figure 12-6. *An example of the auto-complete function when typing into formulas*

When the auto-complete list appears, you have the option to ignore it while continuing to type or to select an item for rapid insertion. An item can be located in the list by scrolling, vertically navigating with the arrow keys, or continuing to type enough text until the desired item is the default selection at the top of the list. Once located and selected, insert it into the formula by either double-clicking or typing the Enter key.

Using the Field Selection Pane

The *field selection panel*, shown in Figure 12-7, is used to locate and insert a field reference.

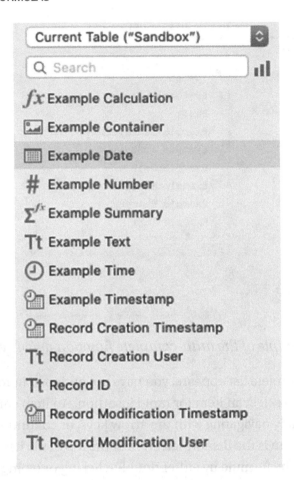

Figure 12-7. *The field selection pane on the left side of the dialog*

The pop-up menu at the top is used to select which table occurrence's fields are listed below. The default selection is based on the current context. When editing a calculation field, the default will be the table containing the field being defined, and the occurrence list will be separated into related and unrelated occurrences to help distinguish which relationships can be used. When editing a formula for a layout object, script step, or other item, the list defaults to the current layout's table and lists all occurrences alphabetically leaving you responsible for safely selecting a valid relationship based on the appropriate context that will be active at the moment of execution. Once an occurrence is selected, the field list updates and can be searched or sorted. To insert a reference into the formula, double-click it.

Using the Function Selection Pane

The *function selection panel,* shown in Figure 12-8, is used to locate and insert a function into a formula. It includes a list of *built-in functions* (Chapter 13), *custom functions* (Chapter 15), and *plug-in functions* (Chapter 28). The list of functions can be grouped by category (shown) or listed alphabetically using a menu hidden under the sort icon. Search by keyword in the text area or by selecting one category from the sort menu. After locating a desired function, double-click it to insert it into the formula. At the bottom of this pane is a short description and a help button to open the online documentation for the selected function.

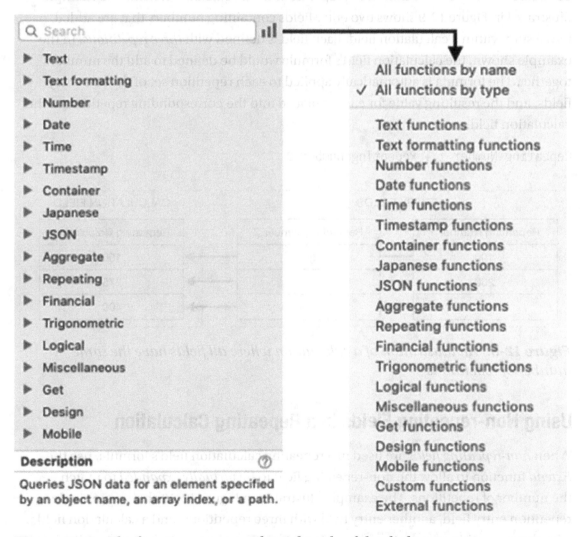

Figure 12-8. *The function pane on the right side of the dialog*

Creating Repeating Calculation Fields

A calculation field can be defined as repeating by entering a number in the *Number of repetitions* at the bottom of the *Specify Calculation* dialog. A repeating calculation works like a repeating entry field (Chapter 8). However, there are a few techniques and built-in functions that may be necessary when working with repeating calculation fields.

Using Repeating Fields in a Repeating Calculation

Repeating calculations work as expected when all fields used in the formula are configured with the same number of repetitions as the calculation field. The example illustrated in Figure 12-9 shows two entry fields containing numbers that are added into a sum within a calculation field. Each field is defined with *three repetitions*. In the example shown, the calculation field's formula would be defined to add the numbers together. The formula is automatically applied to each repetition set of the two entry fields, and the resulting value for each is placed into the corresponding repetition in the calculation field.

```
Repeating Number 1 + Repeating Number 2
```

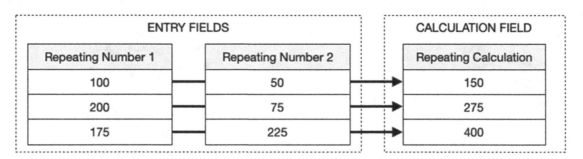

Figure 12-9. *An illustration of a calculation where all fields have the same number of repetitions*

Using Non-repeating Fields in a Repeating Calculation

When *non-repeating fields* are used in a repeating calculation field's formula, use the *Extend* function to allow the non-repeating field to be *virtually expanded* to match the number of repetitions. The example illustrated in Figure 12-10 shows one single-repetition entry field, another entry field with three repetitions, and a calculation field with three repetitions.

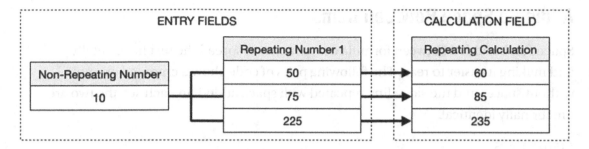

Figure 12-10. *An illustration of a mixture of repeating and non-repeating fields*

For the formula to successfully apply the value in the non-repeating field to each value in the repeating field and generate three results, the formula must extend the non-repeating field as shown in the following example. The single value will be treated as if it were three separate repetitions, each populated with the same value.

```
Extend ( Non-Repeating Number ) + Repeating Number 1
```

Other Repetition Functions

There are other built-in functions that are useful in both *repeating* and *non-repeating* calculations. The *Get (ActiveRepetitionNumber)* function returns a number indicating which repetition of the current field has the cursor focus. This can be used by interface-related calculations and script steps to determine where the cursor is located within a repeating field. The *GetRepetition* function can be used to extract the value from a specific repetition of a specified repeating field. The *Get (CalculationRepetitionNumber)* function returns a number indicating which repetition of a repeating calculation field is currently being evaluated. This allows the calculation field formula to know which repetition of its own field structure is currently being evaluated when each repetition needs to perform slightly different functionality.

Including Space for Visual Formatting

When compiling a formula, FileMaker will ignore any extra spaces, tabs, and paragraph returns that are outside of quoted text. This means you can add white space throughout a formula to spread out the code and make it easier to read. When writing formulas, consider a policy of always adding space between items to expand complex statements into an easier to read format.

Adding a Space Between Items

Space can be added between formula components to spread the text horizontally and making it easier to read. The following pairs of code show a cramped example without spaces and the same line repeated with space added. In each set, the two are functionally identical.

```
(150+50)/25
( 150 + 50 ) / 25
$FirstName&$Space&$LastName
$FirstName & $Space & $LastName
Get(CurrentDate)
Get ( CurrentDate )
```

Expanding Complex Statements

Formulas involving complex *Case*, *Let*, *Substitute*, *While,* and certain *JSON* functions (Chapters 13 and 14) can benefit from spaces, tabs, and carriage returns. While the exact format may vary depending on the complexity of the statement and the use of nested clauses, the following simple examples show a few patterns of the author's preferred format for separating and indenting complex statements to enhance their visual format:

```
// CASE Example
Case (
   Condition1 = result1 ;
   Condition2 = result2
)
// LET Example
Let ( [
   var1 = expression1 ;
   var2 = expression2
] ;
   calculation
)
// SUBSTITUTE Example
```

```
Substitute (
   Text ;
    [ searchString1 ; replaceString1 ] ;
    [ searchString2 ; replaceString2 ]
)
```

Managing Character Limits

FileMaker limits the overall text of each formula to 30,000 characters. When writing lengthy formulas, the natural tendency to *avoid* adding spaces, tabs, and paragraph returns to save space and avoid hitting that limit. However, there are techniques that can be employed to manage space *without* requiring code to become condensed and less readable. First, evaluate the reasons why the formula is so long. With some exceptions, lengthy formulas often have redundant elements and phrases. A lengthy field reference used repeatedly can be condensed into a shorter statement variable with a *Let* statement (Chapter 13). For example, a field reference of *Contact::Contact Name First* can be placed into a variable called something like "nameFirst" and used repeatedly, with each subsequent instance using far less space. Also, renaming variables to shorten their length without losing clarity can save space. Some parts of a formula can be offloaded to a custom function (Chapter 25), especially when the functionality is generic and used elsewhere in the database. Another option is to break a complex calculation into separate fields or script steps, rather than trying to force a huge process into one.

Tip   Make a habit of efficient coding with meticulous attention to clarity and an efficient technical design regardless of formula length.

Adding Simple Calculations to the Example File

To experiment with formulas, add a couple of simple calculations to tables in the *Learn FileMaker* database.

Company Contact Count

In the *Company* table, follow these steps to add a new calculation field called "Company Contact Count" with a formula that counts related contact records:

1. Open the *Manage Database* dialog and select the *Fields* tab for the *Company* table.

2. Create the new calculation field.

3. Select the *Company | Contact* table occurrence from the pop-up menu in the field selection panel.

4. In the formula area, begin typing "Count" and select the *Count* function from the auto-complete list.

5. Double-click on the *Record ID* field from the *Company | Contact* table occurrence. The formula should read

   ```
   Count ( Company | Contact::Record ID )
   ```

6. Make sure the result type is *number*.

7. Click to save and close the dialog.

8. Place the new field on the *Company* layout to confirm that it accurately counts the related contacts for each company. Remember that the count will vary from one record to the next depending on company assignments to contacts.

Contact Full Name and Address Label

In the *Contact* table, add a new calculation field named "Contact Name Full" and define the formula to concatenate the first and last names. This can be used on layouts and in calculations instead of constantly using the two fields in formulas separately.

```
Contact Name First & " " & Contact Name Last
```

Then, add another field named "Contact Address Label" and define the formula to contain the address formatted as a single text value. The formula will look like this:

```
Contact::Contact Name Full & "¶" &
Contact::Contact Address Street & "¶" &
```

```
Contact::Contact Address City & ", " &
Contact::Contact Address State & " " &
Contact::Contact Address Zip
// Result =
Karen Smith
521 Loft Street
Sleepytown, CA 55555
```

Tip   Use the *Case* or *List* functions (Chapter 13) to build a label without extra space caused by missing information in empty fields.

Summary

This chapter introduced the basics of writing formulas. In the next chapter, we will see many practical examples of formulas using a variety of useful built-in functions.

Exploring Built-in Functions

FileMaker includes a library of over 300 *built-in functions* that can be used in formulas to perform common functionality. This chapter explores many essential built-in functions, covering the following topics:

- Working with numbers, dates, and times

- Working with text

- Working with value lists

- Introducing Get functions

- Accessing fields

- Aggregating data

- Using statement functions

Note   Although most examples show literal values used as parameters, remember these can be variables, field references, nested expressions, and even nested calls to other functions.

Working with Numbers, Dates, and Times

There are numerous functions available for getting, generating, parsing, and manipulating numbers, dates, and times.

© Mark Conway Munro 2021
M. C. Munro, *Learn FileMaker Pro 19*, https://doi.org/10.1007/978-1-4842-6680-9_13

Using Number Functions

Beyond the obvious basic mathematical operations available, there are many built-in functions that provide more advanced numeric functionality: *Int*, *Random*, *Round*, *Mod*, *Set Precision,* and *Truncate*.

Int

The *Int* function returns the integer part of a number by dropping any digits to the right of the decimal without rounding.

```
Int ( 34.2653 )  // result = 34
Int ( -2.85 )    // result = -2
Int ( 10 / 3 )   // result = 3
```

Random

The *Random* function generates a pseudo-random number between 0 and .99999999999999999999. The result can be multiplied by any integer to generate a random number between 0 and that number.

```
Random                 // result = .69521348632189605699
Random                 // result = .49928041600104466902
Random                 // result = .16828354164749970145
Int ( 10 * Random )    // result = 8
Int ( 10 * Random )    // result = 3
Int ( 25 * Random )    // result = 4
Int ( 25 * Random )    // result = 16
```

Round

The *Round* function rounds a number to a chosen number of decimal places. It accepts a *number* and *precision* parameter, with the latter being the number of decimal places that should be included in the result generated from the former.

```
Round ( 10.1564 ; 2 )   // result = 10.16
Round ( 10 / 3 ; 0 )    // result = 3
```

Mod

The *Mod* function calculates a remainder from the result of a number being divided by a divisor. It accepts a *number* and *divisor* as parameters. This is can be used to convert units of measure, such as seconds to minutes, minutes to hours, or days to years.

```
Mod ( 100 ; 60 )           // result = 40
Mod ( 410 ; 365 )          // result = 45
Int ( 310 / 60 ) & " hours, " & Mod ( 310 ; 60 ) & " minutes"
// result = 5 hours, 10 minutes
```

SetPrecision

The *SetPrecision* function evaluates a math expression with a specified precision. This is not a rounding or truncating function but a way of expanding the decimal precision beyond the default of up to 16 digits returned by FileMaker. It accepts an *expression* and *precision* as parameters, with the latter being a number between 16 and 400 indicating the desired precision. Providing a precision value less than 16 will return the default of up to 16 digits.

```
22 / 7                              // result = 3.1428571428571429
SetPrecision ( 22 / 7 ; 20 )    // result = 3.14285714285714285714
SetPrecision ( 22 / 7 ; 30 )    // result = 3.142857142857142857142857142857
```

Truncate

The *Truncate* function shortens a number to a specified decimal precision without rounding. It accepts a *number* and *precision* as parameters.

```
Truncate ( 10.246913 ; 2 )      // result = 10.24
Truncate ( 22 / 7 ; 4 )         // result = 3.1428
```

Working with Dates and Times

Built-in functions allow *getting*, *creating*, *parsing*, and *calculating* date- and time-related information.

Getting Current Information

There are several *Get* functions that return the current date, time, or timestamp.

```
Get ( CurrentDate )               // result = 1/15/2021
Get ( CurrentTime )               // result = 2:05:10 PM
Get ( CurrentTimestamp )          // result = 1/15/2017 2:05:10 PM
```

Getting Coordinated Universal Time (UTC)

This function returns the current time in *Coordinated Universal Time* (UTC) to the nearest millisecond without regard to the current time zone. UTC was previously known as *Greenwich Mean Time* (GMT) and is the primary time standard used to regulate clocks. The result represents the current time of the computer running the script in the form of the number of milliseconds since "1/1/0001 12:00 AM," without regard to the user's current time zone.

```
Get ( CurrentTimeUTCMilliseconds )        // result = 63603934624024
```

   To calculate the time for a specific time zone, factor in the UTC time zone adjustment for the region. For example, when New York City is 4 hours behind UTC, this formula will return the time adjusted for that region:

```
GetAsTimestamp (
    Round ( ( ( Get ( CurrentTimeUTCMilliseconds )  + ( -4 * 3600000 ) ) / 1000 ; 0 )
)
```

Caution   Universal Time is not adjusted for daylight savings, so the preceding example will be off by an hour half of the year unless your formula adjusts for that change.

Creating Dates

The *Date* function accepts a numeric *month*, *day*, and *year* parameters and returns a date object. The following examples demonstrate how a date object is created. The first provides three values used to construct the date. The second shows that any of the parameters can be expressions which will be evaluated prior to the construction of the date.

The third example shows how the function will automatically shift to a new month, day, or year if the month or day provided falls out of range. For example, a month value of 13 causes the function to automatically return a date for January of the next year.

```
Date ( 1 ; 15 ; 2021 )         // result = 1/15/2021
Date ( 1 ; 15 ; 2021 + 10 )    // result = 1/15/2031
Date ( 13 ; 15 ; 2021 )        // result = 1/15/2022
```

The automatic date shift can be used to dynamically calculate the last day of any month regardless of the number of days in that month. Build a date for the following month with a negative one for the day. The result will be one day before the first of the month specified, i.e., the last day of the previous month.

```
Date ( 4 ; -1 ; 2021 )         // result = 3/30/2021
Date ( 7 ; -1 ; 2021 )         // result = 6/29/2021
```

Parsing Dates

Each of these parsing functions accepts a *date parameter* and returns a specific component indicated by the function name. The date provided can be a formal date from a date field or constructed with the *Date* function. It also accepts a literal text-based date.

```
Day ( Date ( 1 ; 15 ; 2021 ) )    // result = 15
Day ( "2/26/2021" )               // result = 26

DayName ( Date ( 1 ; 15 ; 2021 ) )    // result = Friday
DayName ( "6/27/1758" )               // result = Tuesday

DayOfWeek ( Date ( 1 ; 15 ; 2021 ) )    // result = 6
DayOfWeek ( "6/27/1758" )               // result = 3
DayOfYear ( Date ( 1 ; 15 ; 2021 ) )    // result = 15
DayOfYear ( "6/27/1758" )               // result = 178
Month ( Date ( 1 ; 15 ; 2021 ) )        // result = 1
Month ( "6/27/1758" )                   // result = 6
MonthName ( Date ( 1 ; 15 ; 2021 ) )    // result = "January"
MonthName ( "6/27/1758" )               // result = "June"
WeekOfYear ( Date ( 1 ; 15 ; 2021) )    // result = 3
WeekOfYear ( "6/27/1758" )              // result = 26
Year ( Date ( 1 ; 15 ; 2021 ) )         // result = 2021
Year ( "6/27/1758" )                    // result = 1758
```

The *WeekOfYearFiscal* function calculates a number representing the week of a year for a given date based on a specified starting date for a workweek. This is useful in accounting applications to calculate if a year has an extra pay period because a week is split across the calendar year boundary. These examples show how Friday, January 2, 2009, can be either the first week of 2009 or the fifty-third week of 2008 depending on the day number provided as the start of the week, indicated by the second parameter.

```
WeekOfYearFiscal ( "1/2/2009" ; 1 )     // result = 53
WeekOfYearFiscal ( "1/2/2009" ; 2 )     // result = 1
WeekOfYearFiscal ( "1/2/2009" ; 3 )     // result = 1
WeekOfYearFiscal ( "1/2/2009" ; 4 )     // result = 1
WeekOfYearFiscal ( "1/2/2009" ; 5 )     // result = 1
WeekOfYearFiscal ( "1/2/2009" ; 6 )     // result = 1
WeekOfYearFiscal ( "1/2/2009" ; 7 )     // result = 53
```

Creating Times

The *Time* function accepts a numeric *hour*, *minute*, and *second* parameters and returns a time object.

```
Time ( 9 ; 15 ; 55 )    // result = 9:15:55
Time ( 2 ; 8 ; 19 )     // result = 2:08:19
```

Creating Timestamps

The *Timestamp* function accepts a *date* and *time* parameter and returns a timestamp object. These examples show that timestamps will automatically add the appropriate AM/PM suffix to the time portion.

```
Timestamp ( "1/15/2021" ; "9:15:55" )
// result = 1/15/2021 9:15:55 AM
Timestamp ( Date ( 5 ; 10 ; 1990 ) ; Time ( 10 ; 30 ; 00 ) )
// result = 5/10/1990 10:30:00 AM
```

If the hours are out of normal range, as in military time, the function will automatically convert to civilian time, also with the appropriate AM/PM suffix:

```
Timestamp ( "1/15/2021" ; "15:15:55" )
// result = 1/15/2021 3:15:55 PM
```

Parsing Times

Each of these functions accepts a *time* or *timestamp* parameter and returns a specific component.

```
Hour ( "09:15:55 AM" )                    // result = 9
Hour ( "4/20/2021 03:30:00 PM" )          // result = 15
Minute ( "09:15:55 AM" )                  // result = 15
Minute ( "4/20/2021 03:30:00 PM" )        // result = 30
Seconds ( "09:15:55 AM" )                 // result = 55
Seconds ( "4/20/2021 03:30:00 PM" )       // result = 0
```

Calculating Time Elapsed

There are several ways to calculate the time elapsed from a start and end dates, times, and timestamps. These examples can be used with values stored in fields and variables or hard coded into formulas (as shown). The first example calculates the number of days elapsed, simply subtracting the latter from the former. The others demonstrate calculating time elapsed.

```
GetAsDate ( "1/30/2021" ) - GetAsDate ( "1/15/2021" )     // result = 15
Time ( 11 ; 15 ; 48 ) - Time ( 8 ; 10 ; 35 )              // result = 3:05:13
GetAsTime ( "4:15:00 pm" ) - GetAsTime ( "11:15:00 am" )  // result = 5:00:00
```

Although timestamps work the same, these will return the amount of time elapsed between the two date-time combinations. When these span across multiple days, the results may not be easily human readable, as demonstrated by the following example. See the "Converting Seconds into a Sentence" example at the end of this chapter to see how to convert time elapsed into a human-readable form.

```
GetAsTimestamp ( "8/1/2021 10:15 AM" ) - GetAsTimestamp ( "1/1/2021 10:00 AM" )
// result = 5088:15:00
```

Working with Text

There are numerous functions available for performing various operations on text values such as *analyzing, changing data type, formatting, modifying,* and *parsing.*

Analyzing Text

There are three functions available that are used to analyze text: *Length, PatternCount,* and *Position.*

Length

The *Length* function counts the total number of characters in the text provided, automatically converting non-text values to text before counting. For example, a number will be converted to text and the number of digits returned, e.g., 24 will return "2."

```
Length ( "Hello World" )        // result = 11
Length ( "Two¶Paragraphs" )      // result = 14
Length ( 359 )                   // result = 3
```

Remembering that formal date objects are different than a date string, notice the difference in the following examples. The first example converts the date into a number and then to text and then counts the number of digits. A date string will simply count characters, producing a different value.

```
Length ( 1/15/2021 )        // result = 17
Length ( "1/15/2021" )      // result = 9
```

PatternCount

The *PatternCount* function counts the number of times a piece of text contains a search string. The first parameter specifies the text to be searched and the second the string whose pattern will be counted. The result is a number indicating the number of times the search string is detected inside the text.

```
PatternCount ( "Hello, World. How is your world today?" ; "world" )
// result = 2
PatternCount ( "15839" ; "4" )                          // result = 0
PatternCount ( "Jim¶John¶Jo" ; "Jo" )                   // result = 2
```

The function is *not case-sensitive* and searches for matches *anywhere* in the text, including as part of a word or paragraph.

```
PatternCount ( "The age of his page caused RAGE." ; "age" )    // result = 3
```

> **Tip**   The *PatternCount* function finds partial matches in paragraphs. Use *FilterValues* to find full paragraph values instead (see "Manipulating Value Lists" later in this chapter).

Position

The *Position* function finds the numeric starting position of the first character of a specified occurrence of some text in the provided text. The function accepts four parameters. The *text* parameter provides the text that will be searched and the *searchString* indicates what pattern of text to locate. A *start* parameter is a number indicating the character position, counting from the left, where the search will begin. Finally, the *occurrence* parameter is a number indicating the desired occurrence of a match found in the search string after the starting position that should be used as the result. So, if a string exists multiple times in the text, the last two parameters can be used to specify where to begin searching and/or which match of many should be returned.

```
Position ( text ; searchString ; start ; occurrence )
Position ( "Where is Waldo today?" ; "Waldo" ; 1 ; 1 )        // result = 10
Position ( "Where is Waldo today?" ; "Waldo" ; 1 ; 2 )         // result = 0
Position ( "Waldo is looking for Waldo?" ; "Waldo" ; 1 ; 2 )  // result = 22
```

Changing Data Types

There are several functions used to convert values into a different data type: *Boolean*, *date*, *number*, *text*, *time,* and *timestamp*. Each accepts a single value of any data which it attempts to convert into the desired type indicated by the function name.

GetAsBoolean

The *GetAsBoolean* function will convert any value into a Boolean. The result will be 1 (true) when the data provided converts to a non-zero result or a container field contains a value. Otherwise, the result will be 0 (false).

```
GetAsBoolean ( "Hello, World" )        // result = 0
GetAsBoolean ( "Hello" = "World" )      // result = 0
GetAsBoolean ( "100" )                 // result = 1
```

GetAsDate

The *GetAsDate* function will convert a value into a formal date object. The data provided can contain leading zeros or not, as shown in these examples:

```
GetAsDate ( "1/5/2021" )          // result = 1/5/2021
GetAsDate ( "01/05/2021" )        // result = 1/5/2021
```

Text-based dates that include a two-digit year will be automatically converted with the assumption that the date falls within the next 30 years or the preceding 70 years from the current date (Chapter 8, "Two-Digit Date Conversion"). Dates intended to fall outside of that range will get incorrect results if you don't use four-digit years. These examples assume a current date of January 5, 2021:

```
GetAsDate ( "1/5/17" )            // result = 1/5/2017
GetAsDate ( "1/5/95" )            // result = 1/5/1995
GetAsDate ( "1/5/50" )            // result = 1/5/1950
```

When a number is provided, it will be used to calculate the number of days that have passed since January 1, 0001. For example:

```
GetAsDate ( 737805 )              // result = 1/15/2021
```

GetAsNumber

The *GetAsNumber* function will convert a value into a number. This can be useful to ensure proper results when a value is compared to or sorted with other numbers. When providing numbers as text, they are converted back into numbers. For example:

```
GetAsNumber ( "1234" )            // result = 1234
GetAsNumber ( "015" )             // result = 15
GetAsNumber ( "13.75" )           // result = 13.75
```

When converting text, any non-numeric characters will be automatically ignored.

```
GetAsNumber ( "$25.09" )                  // result = 25.09
GetAsNumber ( "He ran 9.75 miles." )      // result = 9.75
```

In some cases, relying on automatic filtering of non-numeric characters might not provide in a desirable result.

```
GetAsNumber ( "3 men ran 9.75 miles." ) // result = 39.75
```

These examples assume a value of "03" is contained in a *Qty* text field and show the importance of converting text into a number prior to comparing it to other numeric values. Because of the leading zero on the text-based number in the field, the two values don't appear to be the same (in the first example) until the text is converted to a number (in the second example).

```
3 = Qty                        // result = 0
3 = GetAsNumber ( Qty )        // result = 1
```

Similarly, comparisons will fail when a value isn't numeric. The following examples assume a value of "20" is contained in a *Qty* text field. Since it is a text value, 20 will appear as a smaller value than 3 because the text is compared character by character rather than the entire value compared as a number. Once converted to a number, as shown in the second example, it evaluates correctly.

```
3 > Qty                        // result = 1
3 > GetAsNumber ( Qty )        // result = 0
```

GetAsText

The *GetAsText* function converts any value to a text string.

```
GetAsText ( 58.75 )                    // result = "58.75"
GetAsText ( 05:15:00 )                 // result = "5:15:00"
GetAsText ( 6/30/2016 5:20:49 PM )     // result = "6/30/2016 5:20:49 PM"
```

The function will even convert a container content into one of two values depending on how the file is stored (Chapter 10, "Explaining Container Storage Options"). When stored internally, the name of the file will be returned. When a file is stored as a reference, the result will be a metadata string that varies by file type but includes the file's name and path.

```
GetAsText ( Contact::Image )
    // result = Mark Munro.jpg
GetAsText ( Contact::Image )
    // result =
        size:191,175
        image:Mark Munro.jpg
        imagemac:/Macintosh HD/Users/admin/Desktop/Mark Munro.jpg
```

GetAsTime

The *GetAsBoolean* function converts a text-based time or timestamp value into a time object to ensure proper results when compared to or sorted with other times. Non-time values will result in an error.

```
GetAsTime ( "5:15:00" )         // result = 5:15:00
GetAsTime ( "Hello, World" )    // result = ?
```

GetAsTimestamp

The *GetAsTimestamp* function converts a text-based value into a timestamp object to ensure proper results when compared to or sorted with other times. When the text provided does not contain information for a full timestamp, the function will fill in the missing information. For example, when a date is provided without time information, the function returns a timestamp for midnight on the specified date. When a number is provided, the function returns timestamp for that number of seconds since the first of January in the year 0001.

```
GetAsTimestamp ( "1/5/2017 5:15:00" )   // result = 1/5/2017 5:15:00
GetAsTimestamp ( "1/1/2017" )           // result = 1/1/2017 12:00 AM
GetAsTimestamp ( 100000 )               // result = 1/2/0001 3:46:40 AM
```

Converting Text Encoding

There are three functions that are useful when preparing text for web-related uses or other uses.

Encoding Text for URLs

The *GetAsURLEncoded* function encodes text for use in a *Uniform Resource Locator* (URL). Any style information is removed from the text, and all characters are converted to UTF-8 format. Any non-letter or digit characters that are in the upper ASCII range are *percent encoded*, meaning they are converted to a percent symbol followed by the hexadecimal value of the character, e.g., spaces are converted to "%20". The function accepts a single text parameter.

```
GetAsURLEncoded ( "Hello World" )    // result = "Hello%20World"
GetAsURLEncoded ( "10% Surcharge" )  // result = "10%25%20Surcharge"
```

Converting to CSS

The *GetAsCSS* function converts formatted text into the *Cascading Style Sheet* (CSS) format, preserving the font, font size, font color, and font style attributes in a markup format. The style information must be applied directly to the actual text content as this function doesn't look at layout settings applied to change how a field displays text. The following example assumes a record in a *Contact* table with a field named *Contact Notes* that contains the word "Hello" where the font is "Arial," the font size is 18, the font style is bold, and the font color is red.

```
GetAsCSS ( Contact::Contact Notes )
// result = <span style="font-family: 'Arial';font-size: 18px; color:
#FF2712;font-weight:bold;" >Hello</span>
```

Converting Text to SVG

The *GetAsSVG* function converts text to the *Scalable Vector Graphics* (SVG) format, which supports more text formats than HTML and may represent text more accurately in certain cases. This example assumes a record in a *Contact* table with a field named *Contact Notes* that contains the same styled text from the previous example.

```
GetAsSVG ( Contact::Contact Notes )
// result =
<stylelist>
<style#0>"font-family: 'Arial';font-size: 18px;color: #FF2712;font-weight:
bold;",begin: 1, end: 4</style>
</stylelist>
<data>
<span style="0">Hello</span>
</data>
```

Modifying Text

There are many functions available for performing text modifications, including *changing case*, *filtering*, and *substituting* characters.

Changing Case

Three functions, each accepting a single text parameter, change the case of characters to *Upper, Lower,* and *Proper.*

```
Upper ( "Hello, World" )         // result = "HELLO, WORLD"
Upper ( "this is screaming" )    // result = "THIS IS SCREAMING"

Lower ( "Hello, World" )         // result = "hello, world"
Lower ( "THIS IS SCREAMING" )    // result = "this is screaming"

Proper ( "hello, world" )        // result = "Hello, World"
Proper ( "THIS IS SCREAMING" )   // result = "This Is Screaming"
```

Filter

The *Filter* function removes unwanted characters from a text value. Two parameters are required: the text to be filtered followed by a string of allowable characters. Any character not present in the second parameter will be removed from the text provided in the first.

```
Filter ( "Hello World" ; "1234567890" )                        // result = ""
Filter ( "1 Hello 2 World 3" ; "1234567890" )                  // result = "123"
Filter ( "Las Vegas, NV 89101" ; "1234567890" )                // result = "89101"
Filter ( "(212) 555-1234" ; "1234567890" )                     // result = "2125551234"
Filter ( "The total purchase is $5,000.00" ; "1234567890$.," )  // result =
                                                                  "$5,000.00"
```

Tip   See *FilterValues* later in this chapter to perform a similar function with entire paragraphs instead of individual characters.

Substitute

The *Substitute* function replaces a search string within a piece of text with a replacement string. When specifying one *search-replacement pair,* the function is called with three parameters as shown here.

```
Substitute ( text ; searchString ; replacementString )
```

These examples demonstrate the function making simple replacements where one search value is replaced with one replacement value:

```
Substitute ( "One Two Four" ; "Four" ; "Three" )
    // result = "One Two Three"
Substitute ( "Hello World? It is good to see you?" ; "?" ; "!" )
    // result = "Hello World! It is good to see you!"
```

To specify *multiple search-replace pairs* in a single statement, each set of search and replacement strings is contained within square brackets and separated by a semicolon as shown in the following pattern:

```
Substitute ( text ;
    [ searchString1 ; replacementString1 ] ;
    [ searchString2 ; replacementString2 ] ;
    [ searchString3 ; replacementString3 ]
)
```

The following example demonstrates two search-replace pairs, first replacing "Four" with "Three" and then replacing "Six" with "Four":

```
Substitute ( "One Two Four Six" ; [ "Four" ; "Three" ] ; [ "Six" ; "Four" ] )
// result = "One Two Three Four"
```

In this example, the result will be the text in the *Notes* field with all carriage returns and tabs removed:

```
Substitute ( Table::Notes ; [ "¶" ; "" ] ; [ "    " ; "" ] )
```

This example shows a crude method of clearing extra space in a piece of text using three substitutions – replacing a quadruple space, triple space, and double space with a single space in succession to ensure that most extra spaces are removed:

```
Substitute ( Table::Text Field ; [ "    " ; " " ] ; [ "   " ; " " ] ; [
"  " ; " " ] )
```

Tip   To guarantee all extra spaces are removed, repeatedly substitute double spaces with single spaces until none remain using the *While* function (described later in this chapter).

Parsing Text

Several text parsing functions can extract characters or words from the beginning, middle, or end of a text value. These include *Left*, *Right*, *Middle*, *LeftWords*, *RightWords*, and *MiddleWords*.

Extracting Characters

The *Left* function extracts a specified number of characters from the provided text starting from the first character on the left. If the number specified is greater than the number of characters in the text provided, the function simply returns the original value.

```
Left ( "Hello, World" ; 8 )        // result = "Hello, W"
Left ( "Hello, World" ; 100 )      // result = "Hello, World"
```

The *Right* function extracts a specified number of characters starting from the last character on the right.

```
Right ( "Hello, World" ; 5 )    // result = "World"
```

The *Middle* function extracts a specified number of characters from a specified position within a text string. Unlike the *Left* and *Right* functions, *Middle* requires a start parameter indicating where to begin pulling the specified number of characters.

```
Middle ( text ; start ; numberOfCharacters )
Middle ( "Good Morning Everyone." ; 6 ; 7 )   // result = "Morning"
Middle ( 123456789 ; 4 ; 3 )                  // result = 456
```

Extracting Words

The *LeftWords* function extracts a specified number of words from the text provided, starting from the first word on the left. The words returned will include any space and punctuation that fall *within* the range specified.

```
LeftWords ( "Hello, World. How are you?" ; 3 )    // result = "Hello, World. How"
LeftWords ( "Hello, World. How are you?" ; 2 )    // result = "Hello, World"
```

The *RightsWords* function extracts a specified number of words from the text provided, starting from the last word on the right.

```
RightWords ( "Hello, World. How are you?" ; 3 )  // result = "How are you"
```

The *MiddleWords* function extracts a specified number of words from the text provided, starting from a specified word anywhere in the text provided. The following example extracts two words starting from the third word:

```
MiddleWords ( "Hello World. How are you?" ; 3 ; 2 )    // result = "How are"
```

Working with Values

A *value* is a return-delimited list of text values where each paragraph is considered a single value unit. FileMaker provides several functions specifically for *counting, parsing,* and *manipulating* value lists.

Counting and Parsing Values

Several built-in functions can count and parse values in lists: *ValueCount, LeftValues, RightValues, MiddleValues,* and *GetValue.*

Caution   Unlike text counting and parsing, these functions work with values, i.e., entire paragraphs.

ValueCount

The *ValueCount* function counts the number of values in the text specified.

```
ValueCount ( "John¶Jane¶Jim¶Joe¶" )    // result = 4
```

LeftValues

The *LeftValues* function extracts a specified number of values from a list, starting from the first value.

```
LeftValues ( "John¶Jane¶Jim¶Joe¶" ; 2 )        // result = "John¶Jane¶"
LeftValues ( "159¶245¶396¶721¶" ; 3 )          // result = "159¶245¶396¶"
LeftValues ( "John¶Jane¶Jim¶Joe¶" ; 10 )       // result = "
John¶Jane¶Jim¶Joe¶"
```

RightValues

The *RightValues* function extracts a specified number of values from a list, starting from the last value.

```
RightValues ( "John¶Jane¶Jim¶Joe¶" ; 2 )    // result = "Jim¶Joe¶"
```

MiddleValues

The *MiddleValues* function extracts a number of values specified by the third parameter from a list of values in the first parameter starting from a value specified by the second parameter. In this example, one value is extracted, starting with the second.

```
MiddleValues ( "John¶Jane¶Jim¶Joe¶" ; 2 ; 1 )  // result = "Jane¶"
```

Caution   When extracting values from the *left*, *right*, or *middle*, a carriage return after the last value will be included and may need to be removed for use with other text functions.

GetValue

The *GetValue* function extracts a single value from a list by numeric position, without a trailing return character. If the number specified is greater than the number of values in the list provided, an empty string will be returned.

```
GetValue ( "John¶Jane¶Jim¶Joe¶" ; 3 )   // result = "Jim"
GetValue ( "159¶245¶396¶721¶" ; 2 )     // result = 245
GetValue ( "John¶Jane¶Jim¶Joe¶" ; 18 )  // result = ""
```

Manipulating Values

A few functions can manipulate values in a list, including *FilterValues*, *SortValues,* and *UniqueValues.*

FilterValues

The *FilterValues* function removes unwanted values from a list. The function accepts two parameters: *textToFilter* contains the values that will be manipulated, and *filterValues* indicates the desired values that are allowed to remain in the result. The result will be the original text with any values not specified in *filterValues* removed.

```
FilterValues ( textToFilter ; filterValues )
```

Any *filterValues* that exists more than once will be included, in the same order as they originally appear. Notice how partial paragraph matches are not included in the results. For example, even though "NYC" includes "NY," it is filtered out because this function matches *values* (entire paragraphs) and not partial strings.

```
FilterValues ( "NY¶IN¶OH¶PA¶NY¶IN¶NYC" ; "PA¶NY" )   // result = "NY¶PA¶NY¶"
FilterValues ( "10¶100¶10¶1000" ; "10" )              // result = "10¶10¶"
```

This formula can be used to safely detect a *full value match* in situations where *PatternCount* would fail because it finds *partial pattern matches*. This is shown in the following two examples, both checking to see if "age" exists in a list of values. In first example, *PatternCount* finds three text pattern matches, so it returns a true value even though there is no complete paragraph value match. In the second example, *FilterValues* filters out all three values because none exactly match. So, the second example correctly returns a *false* result, indicating that a *full value* of "age" is not present in the list.

```
PatternCount ( "Rage¶Page¶Sage" ; "age" ) > 0     // result = 1
FilterValues ( "Rage¶Page¶Sage" ; "age"  ) ≠ ""   // result = 0
```

SortValues

The *SortValues* function will rearrange the order of values in a list based on a specified data type. To sort values as text using the file's default locale, only a single parameter is required, the text to sort. Optional parameters allow specification of a *datatype* and/or *locale*. All three varieties are shown here:

```
SortValues ( values )
SortValues ( values ; datatype )
SortValues ( values ; datatype ; locale )
```

The *values* parameter is a list of return-delimited text values to be sorted. The *datatype* parameter is a number from 1 to 5 indicating the data type to use when sorting: 1, text; 2, numeric; 3, date; 4, time; and 5, timestamp. A positive number indicates an ascending sort, while a negative number sorts descending. The *locale* parameter indicates one of several dozen locales to use when sorting, e.g., *French*, *Norwegian*, *Ukrainian*, etc. The result of the function will be the list provided rearranged.

```
SortValues ( "New York¶Illinois¶Pennsylvania¶California" )
// result =
    California
    Illinois
    New York
    Pennsylvania
```

These three examples sort the same list of numbers different ways. The first sorts as text because no *datatype* is specified. The result puts 20 after 100 because "2" sorts alphabetically after "1," and the sort is performed one text character at a time. The second specifies a numeric sort and the third a descending numeric sort.

```
SortValues ( "100¶10¶200¶20" )         // result = "10¶100¶20¶200"
SortValues ( "100¶10¶200¶20" ; 2 )     // result = "10¶20¶100¶200"
SortValues ( "100¶10¶200¶20" ; -2 )    // result = "200¶100¶20¶10"
```

UniqueValues

The *UniqueValues* function returns a value list with any duplicate values removed. This function also accepts additional *datatype* and *locale* parameters that work the same as *SortValues*.

```
UniqueValues ( values )
UniqueValues ( values ; datatype )
UniqueValues ( values ; datatype ; locale )
```

These examples show the difference between results when treating the data as text (default) or specifying a numeric result. Notice that "10" and "10.0" are treated differently as text but the same when using a numeric *datatype*.

```
UniqueValues ( "15¶125¶10¶125¶10.0" )      // result = "15¶125¶10¶10.0"
UniqueValues ( "15¶125¶10¶125¶10.0" ; 2 )  // result = "15¶125¶10"
```

Introducing Get Functions

Get functions provide a single piece of information about the computer's system, the user's environment, the current database context, or the status of various processes. These are useful when creating conditional formulas or scripts that return different results or perform a different task based on some aspect of the current context or situation. They each require a single unchanging parameter, a keyword that indicates the desired information.

```
Get ( <StaticParameter> )
```

Tip   For a complete list of functions and fuller description of those listed here, see FileMaker's documentation.

Credentials and User Information

These functions get information about the user and their database account credentials (Chapter 30).

```
Get ( UserName )                     // result = Karen Camacho
Get ( AccountName )                  // result = k.camacho
Get ( AccountExtendedPrivileges )    // result = fmapp
Get ( AccountPrivilegeSetName )      // result = [Full Access]
Get ( AccountGroupName )             // result = dbmarketing
```

OS, Computer, and App

These functions get information about the user's computer and application, or the host computer.

```
Get ( ApplicationArchitecture )      // result = x86_64
Get ( ApplicationLanguage )          // result = English
Get ( ApplicationVersion )       // result = ProAdvanced 19.0.1
Get ( HostApplicationVersion )   // result = Server 19.0.1
Get ( HostName )                 // result = Production-FileMaker-Server.
local
```

```
Get ( HostIPAddress )              // result = 10.0.1.50
Get ( SystemDrive )                // result = Macintosh HD
Get ( SystemIPAddress )            // result = 10.0.1.27
Get ( SystemLanguage )             // result = "English"
Get ( SystemPlatform )             // result = 1
Get ( SystemVersion )              // result = 10.15.5
```

Records

These functions get information about the records in the current layout's table. The results shown assume the current table contains 500 records and the user is viewing the 15th record in a found set of 125.

```
Get ( FoundCount )          // result = 125
Get ( TotalRecordCount )    // result = 500
Get ( RecordNumber )        // result = 15
Get ( ActiveRecordNumber )  // result = 15
```

The difference between *RecordNumber* and *ActiveRecordNumber* is subtly confusing but useful for layout work. Formulas used in custom functions, custom menus, and script steps all operate from the *window context* and will always return the same value for both of these two functions because the *record number* will always be the currently *active record number*. Alternatively, a formula used on a layout object operates from the *record context* so the *RecordNumber* will always be different for each record, while the *ActiveRecordNumber* will always be the same for the entire found set. This can be useful with the *Hide* feature (Chapter 21, "Hiding Objects") where the following formula will hide a button or other object on every record except the current one.

```
Get ( RecordNumber ) ≠ Get ( ActiveRecordNumber )
```

Layouts

These functions get information about the current layout in the front window:

```
Get ( LayoutName )       // result = Sandbox – List
Get ( LayoutNumber )     // result = 2
Get ( LayoutTableName )        // result = Sandbox
```

```
Get ( LayoutViewState )          // result (Form View)  = 0
                          // result (List View) = 1
                          // result (Table View) = 2
```

Window

Many *Get* functions return window properties and dimensions.

Getting Window Properties

These functions provide information about the frontmost window's name, mode, style, or zoom level.

```
Get ( WindowName )       // result = "Learn FileMaker"
Get ( WindowMode )       // result (Browse)  = 0
                         // result (Find)    = 1
                         // result (Preview) = 2
                         // result (Printing) = 3
                         // result (Layout)  = 4
Get ( WindowStyle )      // result (Document) = 0
                         // result (Floating) = 1
                         // result (Dialog)  = 2
                         // result (Card)    = 3
Get ( WindowZoomLevel )  // result = 100
```

Getting Window Dimensions

Several *Get* functions access measurement from one of four dimensional domains, as shown in Figure 13-1. These are useful when setting a window position or size with script steps (Chapter 25).

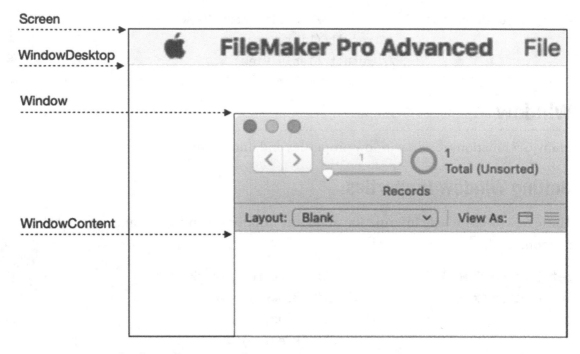

Figure 13-1. *The four domains of measurement accessible with Get functions*

Each of the four domains has a *Height* and *Width* function. Because a window can move around the desktop area, it has an additional *Top* and *Left* function.

```
Get ( ScreenHeight )              // result = 1440
Get ( ScreenWidth )              // result = 2560
Get ( WindowDesktopHeight )       // result = 1417
Get ( WindowDesktopWidth )        // result = 2560
Get ( WindowHeight )             // result = 613
Get ( WindowWidth )              // result = 840
Get ( WindowTop )                // result = 75
Get ( WindowLeft )               // result = 100
Get ( WindowContentHeight )       // result = 492
Get ( WindowContentWidth )        // result = 825
```

These functions can be used with the *New Window* and *Move/Resize Window* script steps (Chapter 25, "Managing Windows") to center a window at a specific point on screen by calculating a new *top* and *left* position based on the *height* and *width* in relation to the screen dimensions. First, get the center point of the screen in each direction by dividing the height and width in half. Then subtract half of the window's corresponding dimension from those respective measurements. The following formulas calculate these two measurements to center an existing window. When creating a new window, the measurements for the window would need to be manually entered since the window doesn't exist yet.

```
( Get ( ScreenHeight ) / 2 ) - ( Get ( WindowHeight ) / 2 ) // Top
( Get ( ScreenWidth ) / 2 ) - ( Get ( WindowWidth ) / 2 )   // Left
```

Accessing Fields

Any calculation can include field references that directly access field content (Chapter 12, "Field References"). Several functions allow additional access to various meta-information about fields or advanced access to the data contained within.

Discovering Active

While any function has *direct* contextual access to any local or related field, a few functions access information about the field currently active within the interface. This is useful when creating functionality that needs to be aware of the current user's activity to provide responsive and adaptable features.

```
Get ( ActiveFieldName )                 // result = Full Name
Get ( ActiveFieldContents )             // result = Mark Munro
Get ( ActiveFieldTableName )            // result = "Contacts"
```

Converting a Field Reference to Text

The *GetFieldName* function accepts a *field reference* and returns the entire reference as a *string*. This function can allow field name manipulations with dynamic references to avoid hard-coding names that may break in the future if a field or table name is changed (Chapter 12, "Keeping Field Names Dynamic").

```
GetFieldName ( Contact::Name First )        // result = "Contact::Name First"
```

Getting Field Content

There are two built-in functions that return the contents of a field in very specific ways. These are *GetField* and *GetNthRecord*.

GetField

The *GetField* function returns the contents of a field based on a *text-based field reference* instead of a *dynamic field reference*. This is useful when building a field reference dynamically or using a reference stored in a text field or variable. The parameter can be either the *name* of the field or a full text-based *reference* to the table and field, with the latter required for fields in a related table.

```
GetField ( "Contact Name Full" )              // result = Mark Munro
GetField ( "Contact::Contact Name Full" )     // result = Mark Munro
```

Since the function requires a *text-based reference*, providing a dynamic reference to a field will fail unless that field referenced happens to contain a text reference to third field. For example, if a field named "Referring Field" contains the text "Contact::Contact Name Full," then the function will accept a dynamic reference to the referring field and use its content to identify the target field and retrieve *its* content. This is the only instance where the function works as expected with a dynamic reference, as demonstrated in the following three examples. The first passes a *text reference to the referring field* and returns the actual contents of that field. The second passes a *dynamic reference to the referring field* so it uses the reference contained in the field to identify and successfully return the value of the full name field. Although the third also passes a dynamic reference, the field contains the name "Mark Munro" which does not contain a text reference, so it returns an error.

```
GetField ( "Contact::Referring Field" )   // result = Contact::Contact
                                          //          Name Full
GetField ( Contact::Referring Field )     // result = Mark Munro
GetField ( Contact::Contact Name Full )   // result = ?
```

GetNthRecord

The *GetNthRecord* function returns the contents of a field from a record within the found set, regardless of the current record. The *fieldName* parameter must contain a dynamic reference to a field and the *recordNumber* parameter the numeric position of a record in the current found set, together specifying the desired value. This example would return the contents of the *Contact Name Full* field from the fifth record in the found set from the *Contact* table.

```
GetNthRecord ( Contact::Contact Name Full ; 5 )
```

This function can be used with an iterative process to "step" through a found set and gather information across numerous records much faster without having to change the context of the active record. Use the *While* function (this chapter), a recursive custom function (Chapter 15), or a looping script (Chapter 25, "Iterating with Repeating Statements").

Getting Selected Text

Two *Get* functions allow a calculation to extract the currently selected text within the field with current active focus. The *Get (ActiveSelectionSize) function* returns the number of characters selected, and *Get (ActiveSelectionStart)* returns the character position at which a selection of text within a field begins. Together, these make it possible to extract a selection and replace it with another value. The following examples use functions discussed previously in this chapter to demonstrate how to access selection ranges assuming the *Contact Notes* field has focus (although the *Get (ActiveFieldContents)* function can be used instead to pull contents from any field). In three different steps, we get the selected text, the text before the selection, and the text after it. Once these three are held in a variable as separate values, the selection can be modified and then reassembled for placement back into the field using a *Set Field* (Chapter 25) or used in some other way.

The *Middle* function is called with a reference to the field as the first parameter. This example will extract the selected text from the active field:

```
Middle (
    Contact::Contact Notes ;
    Get ( ActiveSelectionStart ) ;
    Get ( ActiveSelectionSize )
)
```

The *Left* function can extract characters before the selection.

```
Left (
    Contact::Contact Notes ;
    Get ( ActiveSelectionStart ) - 1
)
```

The *Right* function extracts the text remaining after the selection.

```
Right (
    Contact::Contact Notes ;
    Length ( Contact::Contact Notes ) - Get ( ActiveSelectionStart ) - Get (
    ActiveSelectionSize) + 1
)
```

Aggregating Data

Aggregate functions can summarize fields and perform statistical computations on numbers, dates, and times. Each of these functions can accept a single repeating field or a list of non-repeating, repeating, or related fields: *Average, Count, List,* and *Sum.* Due to the similarity in behavior and the number of different combinations of input possible, all the examples in this section use the same data as shown in Figure 13-2.

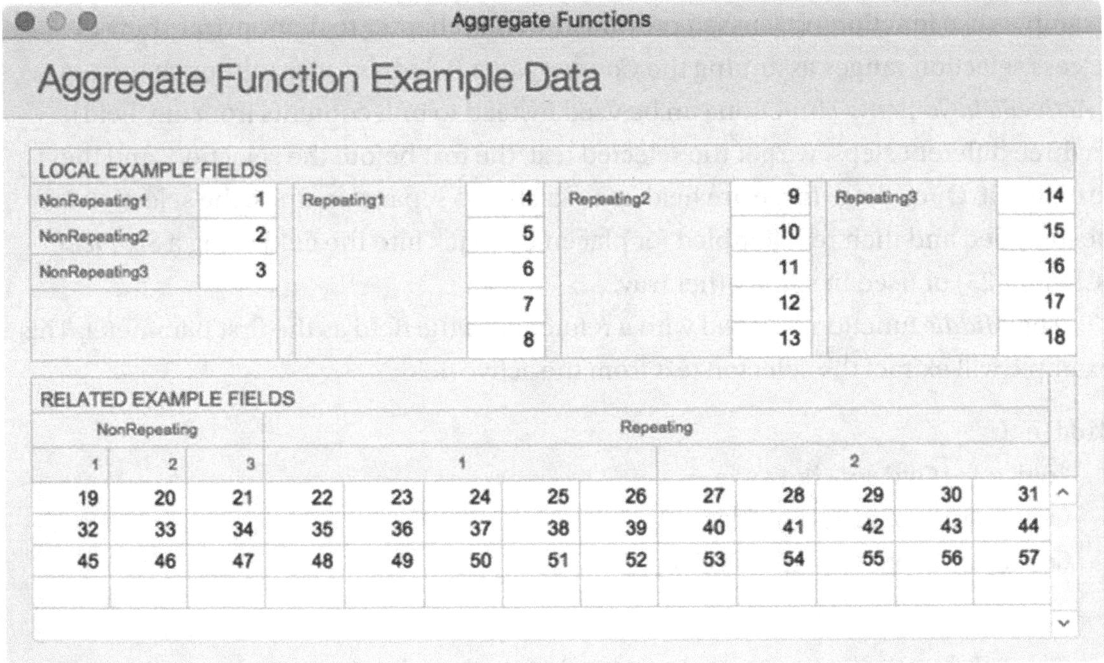

Figure 13-2. A set of fields, local and related, with simple values that are used for all the examples in this section

Average

The *Average* function calculates the average of all values in one or more fields. It can accept a single repeating or related numeric field or multiple numeric fields (repeating or not) with a semicolon delimiter.

```
Average ( field )
Average ( field1 ; field2 ; field3 ; etc. )
```

Using the Average Function with Local Fields

A *list of non-repeating local fields* will return the average based on all the values contained within the fields provided:

```
Average ( Example::NonRepeating1 ; Example::NonRepeating2 ;
Example::NonRepeating3 )
// result = 2
```

A *single repeating local field* will return the average based on all the values contained within that field:

```
Average ( Example::Repeating1 )
// result = 6
```

A *list of repeating local fields* used in a *non-repeating calculation* will return the average based on the first repetition from each field provided:

```
Average ( Example::Repeating1 ; Example::Repeating2 ; Example::Repeating3 )
// result = 9
```

A *list of repeating local fields* used in a *repeating calculation* returns the average for each repetition of the result based on the corresponding repetition from each field provided:

```
Average ( Example::Repeating1 ; Example::Repeating2 ; Example::Repeating3 )
// repetition 1 = 9
// repetition 2 = 10
// repetition 3 = 11
// repetition 4 = 12
// repetition 5 = 13
```

Using the Average Function with Related Fields

A *single related, non-repeating field* will return the average based on all the values from that field for each record related to the local record performing the calculation:

```
Average ( Related::NonRepeating1 )
// result = 32
```

A *list of related, non-repeating fields* returns the average based on the values from the fields provided for the first related record:

```
Average ( Related::NonRepeating1 ; Related::NonRepeating2 ;
Related::NonRepeating3 )
// result = 20
```

A *single related, repeating field* will return the average based on the values from every repetition from every record related to the local record performing the calculation:

```
Average ( Related::Repeating1 )
// result = 37
```

A *list of related, repeating fields* used in a *non-repeating calculation* will return the average based on the values from the first repetition of those fields from the first record related to the local record performing the calculation:

```
Average ( Related::Repeating1 ; Related::Repeating2 )
// result = 24.5
```

A *list of related, repeating fields* used in a *repeating calculation* will return the average based on the values from the corresponding repetition from each field provided from the first record related to the local record performing the calculation:

```
Average ( Related::Repeating1 ; Related::Repeating2 )
// repetition 1 = 24.5
// repetition 2 = 25.5
// repetition 3 = 26.5
// repetition 4 = 27.5
// repetition 5 = 28.5
```

Count

The *Count* function counts the number of values in one or more fields. Although the examples shown here count lists of numeric values, the function will count any type of data files. For example, both "8¶10¶2" and "Mon¶Tues¶Wed" contain three values.

```
Count ( field )
Count ( field1 ; field2 ; field3 ; etc. )
```

Using the Count Function with Local Fields

A *list of non-repeating local fields* will return the total non-blank value count based on all the values contained within the fields provided:

```
Count ( Example::NonRepeating1 ; Example::NonRepeating2 ;
Example::NonRepeating3 )
// result = 3
```

A *single repeating local field* will return the total non-blank value count based on all the values contained within that field:

```
Count ( Example::Repeating1 )
// result = 5
```

A *list of repeating local fields* used in a *non-repeating calculation* will return the total non-blank value count based on the first repetition from each field provided:

```
Count ( Example::Repeating1 ; Example::Repeating2 ; Example::Repeating3 )
// result = 3
```

A *list of repeating local fields* used in a *repeating calculation* returns the total non-blank value count for each repetition of the result based on the corresponding repetition from each field provided:

```
Count ( Example::Repeating1 ; Example::Repeating2 ; Example::Repeating3 )
// repetition 1 = 3
// repetition 2 = 3
// repetition 3 = 3
// repetition 4 = 3
// repetition 5 = 3
```

Using the Count Function with Related Fields

A *single related, non-repeating field* will return the total non-blank value count based on all the values from that field for each record related to the local record performing the calculation:

```
Count ( Related::NonRepeating1 )
// result = 3
```

A *list of related, non-repeating fields* returns the total non-blank value count based on the values from the fields provided for the first related record:

```
Count ( Related::NonRepeating1 ; Related::NonRepeating2 ;
Related::NonRepeating3 )
// result = 3
```

A *single related, repeating field* will return the total non-blank value count based on the values from every repetition from every record related to the local record performing the calculation:

```
Count ( Related::Repeating1 )
// result = 15
```

A *list of related, repeating fields* used in a *non-repeating calculation* will return the total non-blank value count based on the values from the first repetition of those fields from the first record related to the local record performing the calculation:

```
Count ( Related::Repeating1 ; Related::Repeating2 )
// result = 2
```

A *list of related, repeating fields* used in a *repeating calculation* will return the total non-blank value count based on the values from the corresponding repetition from each field provided from the first record related to the local record performing the calculation:

```
Count ( Related::Repeating1 ; Related::Repeating2 )
// repetition 1 = 2
// repetition 2 = 2
// repetition 3 = 2
// repetition 4 = 2
// repetition 5 = 2
```

List

The *List* function generates a return-delimited list of values for one or more fields, or other values.

```
List ( field )
List ( field1 ; field2 ; field3 ; etc. )
```

Using the List Function with Local Fields

A *list of non-repeating local fields* will return a carriage return-delimited list based on all the values contained within the fields provided:

```
List ( Example::NonRepeating1 ; Example::NonRepeating2 ;
Example::NonRepeating3 )
// result = 1¶2¶3
```

A *single repeating local field* will return a carriage return-delimited list based on all the values contained within that field:

```
List ( Example::Repeating1 )
// result = 4¶5¶6¶7¶8
```

A *list of repeating local fields* used in a *non-repeating calculation* will return a carriage return-delimited list based on the first repetition from each field provided:

```
List ( Example::Repeating1 ; Example::Repeating2 ; Example::Repeating3 )
// result = 4¶9¶14
```

A *list of repeating local fields* used in a *repeating calculation* will return a carriage return-delimited list for each repetition of the result based on the corresponding repetition from each field provided:

```
List ( Example::Repeating1 ; Example::Repeating2 ; Example::Repeating3 )
// repetition 1 = 4¶9¶14
// repetition 2 = 5¶10¶15
// repetition 3 = 6¶11¶16
// repetition 4 = 7¶12¶17
// repetition 5 = 8¶13¶18
```

Using the List Function with Related Fields

A *single related, non-repeating field* will return a carriage return-delimited list based on all the values from that field for each record related to the local record performing the calculation:

```
List ( Related::NonRepeating1 )
// result = 19¶32¶45
```

A *list of related, non-repeating fields* will return a carriage return-delimited list based on the values from the fields provided for the first related record:

```
List ( Related::NonRepeating1 ; Related::NonRepeating2 ;
Related::NonRepeating3 )
// result = 19¶20¶21
```

A *single related, repeating field* will return a carriage return-delimited list based on the values from every repetition from every record related to the local record performing the calculation:

```
List ( Related::Repeating1 )
// result = 22¶23¶24¶25¶26¶35¶36¶37¶38¶39¶48¶49¶50¶51¶52
```

A *list of related, repeating fields* used in a *non-repeating calculation* will return a carriage return-delimited list based on the values from the first repetition of those fields from the first record related to the local record performing the calculation:

```
List ( Related::Repeating1 ; Related::Repeating2 )
// result = 22¶27
```

A *list of related, repeating fields* used in a *repeating calculation* will return a carriage return-delimited list based on the values from the corresponding repetition from each field provided from the first record related to the local record performing the calculation:

```
List ( Related::Repeating1 ; Related::Repeating2 )
// repetition 1 = 22¶27
// repetition 2 = 23¶28
// repetition 3 = 24¶29
// repetition 4 = 25¶30
// repetition 5 = 26¶31
```

Sum

The *Sum* function adds a series of numbers into a total.

```
Sum ( field )
Sum ( field1 ; field2 ; field3 ; etc. )
```

Using the Sum Function with Local Fields

A *list of non-repeating local fields* will return the sum total based on all the values contained within the fields provided:

```
Sum ( Example::NonRepeating1 ; Example::NonRepeating2 ;
Example::NonRepeating3 )
// result = 6
```

A *single repeating local field* will return the sum total based on all the values contained within that field:

```
Sum ( Example::Repeating1 )
// result = 30
```

A *list of repeating local fields* used in a *non-repeating calculation* will return the sum total based on the first repetition from each field provided:

```
Sum ( Example::Repeating1 ; Example::Repeating2 ; Example::Repeating3 )
// result = 27
```

A *list of repeating local fields* used in a *repeating calculation* returns the sum total for each repetition of the result based on the corresponding repetition from each field provided:

```
Sum ( Example::Repeating1 ; Example::Repeating2 ; Example::Repeating3 )
// repetition 1 = 27
// repetition 2 = 30
// repetition 3 = 33
// repetition 4 = 36
// repetition 5 = 39
```

Using the Sum Function with Related Fields

A *single related, non-repeating field* will return the sum total based on all the values from that field for each record related to the local record performing the calculation:

```
Sum ( Related::NonRepeating1 )
// result = 96
```

A *list of related, non-repeating fields* returns the sum total based on the values from the fields provided for the first related record:

```
Sum ( Related::NonRepeating1 ; Related::NonRepeating2 ;
Related::NonRepeating3 )
// result = 60
```

A *single related, repeating field* will return the sum total based on the values from every repetition from every record related to the local record performing the calculation:

```
Sum ( Related::Repeating1 )
// result = 555
```

A *list of related, repeating fields* used in a *non-repeating calculation* will return the sum total based on the values from the first repetition of those fields from the first record related to the local record performing the calculation:

```
Sum ( Related::Repeating1 ; Related::Repeating2 )
// result = 49
```

A *list of related, repeating fields* used in a *repeating calculation* will return the sum total based on the values from the corresponding repetition from each field provided from the first record related to the local record performing the calculation:

```
Sum ( Related::Repeating1 ; Related::Repeating2 )
// repetition 1 = 49
// repetition 2 = 51
// repetition 3 = 53
// repetition 4 = 55
// repetition 5 = 57
```

Using Logical Functions

Logical functions are used to test conditions to produce variable results and perform other evaluative functions. These include four absolutely essential functions: *Case,* *Choose, Let,* and *While.*

Case

The *Case* function evaluates one or more expressions and returns a result corresponding to the first expression that returns a true result. If none of the expressions are true, an optional default result can be included. The function produces a conditional result similar to nested *if-then* functions, but it handles multiple statements with less verbiage. At a minimum, the function requires parameters consisting of one *test-result pair* where the *result* is only evaluated and returned if the *test* portion is true. The *test* parameter must contain a text or numeric expression that evaluates to a Boolean. The *result* parameter can be a literal result or an expression that generates any result.

```
Case ( test ; result )
```

Any number of additional test conditions can be added, and each will be evaluated in order until one evaluates true and causes the corresponding result to be returned.

```
Case ( test ; result ; test2 ; result2 )
Case ( test ; result ; test2 ; result2 ; test3 ; result3)
```

A final, untested result can be included at the end to serve as the result when no prior test conditions produce a true result. If no default is provided, the result will be nothing when all tests are false. In this example, if the *test* and *test2* conditions are both false, the result will be whatever is produced by the *defaultResult* statement.

```
Case ( test ; result ; test2 ; result2 ; defaultResult )
```

As these statements grow, consider adding tabs and carriage returns to reformat them vertically, putting each pair on its own line and making the statement easier to read and follow the logical execution of tests.

```
Case (
    test ; result ;
    test2 ; result2 ;
    test3 ; result3 ;
    test4 ; result4 ;
    defaultResult
)
```

This example builds a sentence and uses *Case* to optionally pluralize the word "widget" if the value in the *Qty* field is greater than one.

```
"Enclosed find " & Qty & " widget" & Case ( Qty > 1 ; "s" ) & " for
inspection."
// result examples (varying by Qty) =
//    Enclosed find 1 widget for inspection.
//    Enclosed find 8 widgets for inspection.
```

In this example, a field named *Elapsed* contains the number of days an invoice is past due and generates one of four different text results indicating its status. If the value is 32, the result will be "Past Due" because the first two tests were false and the third was true. Similarly, a value of 64 will result in "Delinquent," while a value of 20 will receive the "On Time" default result.

```
Case (
    Elapsed > 90 ; "Severe" ;
    Elapsed > 60 ; "Delinquent" ;
    Elapsed > 30 ; "Past Due" ;
    "On Time"
)
```

Note   FileMaker does include a built-in *If* function but that is largely shunned in favor of the superiority of *Case*.

Choose

The *Choose* function evaluates a single test condition to generate an integer and uses that number to select from a list of one or more result values. The *test* parameter must contain a text or numeric expression that evaluates to an integer. Any number of *result* parameters can be included and will be returned based on the number generated by the test. The results can be literal values or expressions that evaluate to any data result. The indexing is *zero-based*, so the first result listed will be returned if the test evaluates to a 0, the second result for a 1, etc.

```
Choose ( test ; result0 ; result1 ; result2 ; result3 )
```

In this example, a *Status* field contains a number from 0 to 4, and the *Choose* function is used to convert this into a textual status.

```
Choose ( Status ; "Low" ; "Guarded" ; "Elevated" ; "High" ; "Severe" )
```

This example uses a random number to pick one of four names.

```
Choose ( Random * 4 ; "Jim Thomas" ; "Shannon Miller" ; "Charlene Smith" ;
"Karen Camacho" )
```

Let

The *Let* function initializes one or more variables prior to performing an embedded calculation statement. The function accepts two expressions as parameters. The *variable declaration* parameter is made up of one or more variable names, each with an expression that produces its value, separated by an equal sign. Variables can be a mixture of any type: *statement, local,* or *global* (Chapter 12, "Types of Variable"). The expression for each can be a literal value, function call, or expression that produces any type of result that will become the corresponding variable's value. The *calculation parameter* can be any expression that produces the result of the overall statement.

```
Let ( variable = expression ; calculation )
```

When initializing more than one variable, square brackets must be added around the declaration parameter and a semicolon between each *variable-expression* pair.

```
Let ( [
   variable = expression1 ;
   variable2 = expression2 ;
   variable3 = expression3
] ;
   calculation
)
```

The *Let* function is useful when constructing complex formulas. Lengthy field names can be compressed into short variables to save space when they are used multiple times in a formula. Complex expressions made up of many nested functions or clauses can be separated into a cascade of shorter expressions that produce a variable's value in steps, making it easier to read and edit. This can also eliminate the negative performance impact of performing the same operation on large sets of related record, e.g., using the *Sum* function on a large set of related records multiple times.

For a simple example, a reference to a *Contact::Contact Last Name* field may be used in a *Case* statement several times, each repeating the full field reference. With a Let statement, the field's value can be inserted into a short variable named *lastName*, *name.last*, or just *last* that can be used in its place. This is illustrated in the following two examples that build a three-level folder path to a folder using the first letter of the last name, the first three letters of the last name, and the last name with a condition to use a placeholder when the last name isn't specified; for example, "Munro" would become "M:Mun:Munro:". Here we can see four references to the same field repeated in the formula to produce this result:

```
Case (
   Contact::Contact Last Name = "" ; "Missing Name:" ;
   Left ( Contact::Contact Last Name ; 1 ) & ":" &
   Left ( Contact::Contact Last Name ; 3 ) & ":" &
   Contact::Contact Last Name & ":"
)
```

Alternatively, using a *Let* statement, a single field reference is used to place the field's value into a short variable. Then, if that variable is empty, it is replaced with the missing placeholder. Finally, it is used to construct the path.

```
Let ( [
    last = Contact::Contact Last Name ;
    last = Case ( last = "" ; "Missing Name:" ; last )
] ;
    Left ( last; 1 ) & ":" & Left ( last; 3 ) & ":" & last & ":"
)
```

The preceding example uses a *cascading declaration* which uses the same variable to establish a value for one variable in a stepped succession that separates a complex statement into a more readable format. In the preceding example, the *last* variable was first set to the field name and then reset in a second declaration step if empty. This allows complex nested statements to be separated into steps that can be more easily read. In the following example, four functions are nested in a single line and can be very hard to read, especially in more complex formulas. Working from the inside out, this example first gets content from a *Notes* field, from which the *GetValue* function extracts the first paragraph, then uses the *TextFormatRemove* function to eliminate all formatting, and then uses the *Substitute* function to replace dashes with periods.

```
Substitute ( TextFormatRemove ( GetValue ( Contact::Notes ; 1 ) ) ; "-" ; "." )
```

In the modified example that follows, each of these steps is performed on a separate variable declaration in a *Let* statement. Since it is building a single value in steps, the same variable name can be used so each step replaces the previous value, in a downward cascading flow.

```
Let ( [
    result = Contact::Notes ;
    result = GetValue ( result ; 1 ) ;
    result = TextFormatRemove ( result) ;
    result = Substitute ( result ; "-" ; "." )
] ;
    result
)
```

This technique isn't necessarily the best for every situation. Even the preceding example looks a little more crowded using *Let* instead of nesting. One may argue that, in this case, adding returns and tabs to space out the nesting would be a better solution. However, in situations with statements more complex than this simple example, the Let statement can be used in this manner with great success.

While

The *While* function is a complex statement that repeats a series of logical steps as long as a specified condition is true. The function accepts four parameters. First, one or more *initialization variables* are declared as the first parameter. These set up values similar to a *Let* statement. A *condition parameter* is a Boolean expression that controls the looping action. As long as this result evaluates true and the maximum number of allowable iterations hasn't been reached, the function will repeat the logical steps. Next, one or more *logic variables* contain variable declarations that will be repeated over and over until the function terminates. These are also structured like the initial variables and a *Let* statement. Finally, the *result parameter* is an expression that generates the final result of the statement. This can include values stored in any of the initial variables or logic variables.

```
While (
   [ initialVariable ] ;
   condition ;
   [ logicVariables ] ;
   result
)
```

Removing Double Spaces with a While Statement

The following simple example demonstrates the basic structure of a *While* function. First, a *data* variable is initialized to the value of a *Notes* field in a *Contact* table. This is a statement variable that will be available within the *While* statement during execution. Next, a *condition* is established that will cause the function to repeat as long as the *data* variable contains any double spaces. The *logic* portion reinitializes the *data* variable with double spaces replaced with a single space. This will continue looping until there are no double spaces left, thereby correcting any number of extra spaces: double, triple, quadruple, etc. Finally, after the *condition* fails to find double spaces and terminates, the cleaned up *data* variable becomes the *result* and returns the text without any extra spaces.

```
While (
   [
      data = Contact::Notes
   ] ;
```

```
    PatternCount ( data ; "  " ) ;
  [
    data = Substitute ( data ; "  " ; " " )
  ] ;
    data
)
```

Place this formula into an auto-enter calculation (Chapter 8, "Field Options: Auto-Enter") that replaces an existing value to have any double spaces typed by a user automatically removed from the field. Just change the field reference to Self and the formula can be used for any field.

Tip   Consider creating a custom function to automatically clean text (Chapter 15) and use that for the auto-enter formula on any field.

Compiling a List of Related Records Using While

The following example pulls a list of names and titles from *Contact* records related to the current *Company* record and merges these values together to form a single contact list. In other words, a list of return-delimited *names* and a list of return-delimited *titles* become a return-delimited list of "name title" for each related record. The two lists are initialized into a variable, and these are counted, and two control variables are initialized. As long as the *current* value is less than or equal to the *count* of values, the logical variables will be repeated. There the entry for the *current* value is created and added to the *result* variable. Then the *current* variable is incremented by one. When all values have been processed, the statement exits and returns the accumulated results.

```
While (
  [
    names = List ( Company | Contact::Contact Name Full ) ;
    titles = List ( Company | Contact::Contact Title ) ;
    count = ValueCount ( names ) ;
    current = 1 ;
    result = ""
  ] ;
    count ≥ current ;
```

```
[
    entry = GetValue ( names ; current ) & " " & GetValue ( titles;
    current ) ;
    result = result & Case ( result ≠ "" ; "¶" ) & entry ;
    current = current + 1
] ;
    result
)
```

Caution   The *List* function excludes blank values. If even one related record in the preceding example is missing a value in one of the two fields, the merged results will be mismatched for every subsequent record.

Compiling a List of Local Records Using While

This example generates the same results as in the preceding example, but instead of looping through lists pulled from records in a related table, it loops through a found set of records in the current table by employing the *GetNthRecord* function (described previously in this chapter).

```
While (
    [
        count = Get ( FoundCount ) ;
        current = 1 ;
        result = ""
    ] ;
        count ≥ current ;
    [
        name = GetNthRecord ( Contact::Contact Name Full ; current ) ;
        title = GetNthRecord ( Contact::Contact Title ; current ) ;
        entry = name & " " & title ;
        result = result & Case ( result ≠ "" ; "¶" ) & entry ;
        current = current + 1
    ] ;
        result
)
```

Nesting Functions into Complex Statements

Built-in functions can be combined and nested to create statements as complex as necessary to produce any desired result. The examples in this section demonstrate the move from simple statements to more complex by combining various functions and statements.

Creating a Record Metadata String

This example gathers information about a record and creates a string displaying that information. Each result can be displayed on a layout in a field or a *formula-named object* like a button bar (Chapter 20). The *Let* statement pulls values from metadata fields and assembles them into a single value displaying the record serial number and created/modified dates and times.

```
Let ( [
   id = Record ID ;
   creator = Record Creation User ;
   created = Record Creation Timestamp ;
   modifier = Record Modification User ;
   modified = Record Modification Timestamp ;

   creation =
      Right ( "0" & Month ( created ) ; 2 ) & "." &
      Right ( "0" & Day ( created ) ; 2 ) & "." &
      Year ( created ) ;

   modification =
      Right ( "0" & Month ( modified) ; 2 ) & "." &
      Right ( "0" & Day ( modified) ; 2 ) & "." &
      Year ( modified)
] ;
   "ID " & id & " | " &
   "Created on " & creation & " by " & creator & " | " &
   "Modified on " & modification & " by " & modifier
)
// result = ID 55326 | Created on 07.01.2020 by Admin | Modified on
07.01.2020 by Admin
```

Creating a Record Count String

This example assembles a string that displays a record navigational string, including the *current record number* and total record count. If the user is viewing a found set, it includes that number as well.

```
Let ( [
    total = Get ( TotalRecordCount ) ;
    found = Get ( FoundCount ) ;
    current = Get ( ActiveRecordNumber )
] ;
    "Record " & current & " of " & found &
    Case ( found ≠ total ; " Found ( " & total & " Total )" )
)
// result (viewing all)        = Record 2 of 6
// result (viewing found set)  = Record 2 of 4 Found ( 6 Total )
```

Caution   When using the preceding example as a calculation field formula, turn indexing off under *Storage Options* to ensure constant updates.

Creating Sentence from Time Elapsed

This example creates a human-readable statement of time elapsed. First a *Let* statement begins initializing variables starting with *start* and *end* with a timestamp value. Although these are set to hard-coded values for this demonstration, they could be provided by a field, variable, or other function. The *end* is then subtracted from the *start* and converted to a number to establish the seconds *elapsed*. This number is then passed through four cascading steps to determine the number of *days*, *hours*, *minutes,* and *seconds* elapsed while, at each step, deducting the extracted amount from the *elapsed* seconds. These use the *Int* function which returns the integer part of a number without rounding by dropping any digits to the right of the decimal. Once these four values are calculated and placed into variables, the calculation portion of the statement produces the final result. This uses a sequence of four *Case* statements nested in a *List* statement which is nested in *Substitute* statement. Each *Case* checks to see if the corresponding value is not zero which is required for inclusion. If included, it constructs a sentence with a conditional suffix, e.g., "1 day" or "10 days." Each of these is added to a return-delimited value list using *List* which is then converted into a comma-space-delimited sentence using *Substitute.*

```
Let ( [
    start = GetAsTimestamp ( "8/1/2021 10:00 AM" ) ;
    end = GetAsTimestamp ( "8/2/2021 11:15:10 AM" ) ;
    elapsed = GetAsNumber ( end - start ) ;

    days = Int ( elapsed / 86400 ) ;
    elapsed = elapsed - ( days * 86400 ) ;

    hours = Int ( elapsed / 3600 ) ;
    elapsed = elapsed - ( hours * 3600 ) ;

    minutes = Int ( elapsed / 60 );
    elapsed = elapsed - ( minutes * 60 ) ;

    seconds = Int ( elapsed )

] ;
    Substitute (
        List (
            Case ( days ≠ 0 ; days & " day" & Case ( days > 1 ; "s" ) ) ;
            Case ( hours ≠ 0 ; hours & " hour" & Case ( hours > 1 ; "s" ) ) ;
            Case ( minutes ≠ 0 ; minutes & " minute" & Case ( minutes > 1 ;
            "s" ) ) ;
            Case ( seconds ≠ 0 ; seconds & " second" & Case ( seconds > 1 ;
            "s" ) )
            ) ; "¶" ; ", "
        )
)
// result = 1 day, 1 hour, 15 minutes, 10 seconds
```

Converting a Number to a Sentence

This example converts a number into a sentence using *Let, Case, Choose,* and other functions. In the variable declaration portion of the Let statement, a number is pulled from a field and placed into an *n* variable. The *Length* and *GetAsText* functions count the characters of the number and puts that into the *count* variable. Next, three variables are initialized with one digit of the number as needed based on the digits. The first (right) digit is placed into a, the second (middle) into b, and the third (left) into c using a combination of *Left, Middle, Right, GetAsNumber,* and *Case* functions. The calculation portion contains four *Case* statements that conditionally use the positional digit to insert a text representation of each value which are then concatenated to form the resulting sentence. Depending on the input number, the function will return a result from "1 Year" up to "Nine Hundred Ninety Nine Years."

```
Let ( [
|
 n = Example Number ;
 t = GetAsText ( n ) ;
 count = Length ( t ) ;

 a = GetAsNumber ( Right ( t ; 1 ) ) ;
 b = Case ( count > 1 ; GetAsNumber ( Left ( Right ( t ; 2 ) ; 1 ) ) ) ;
 c = Case ( count > 2 ; GetAsNumber ( Left ( t ; 1 ) ) )

] ;

 Case ( c > 0 ;
    Choose( c ; "";
       "One "; "Two "; "Three "; "Four "; "Five "; "Six "; "Seven "; "Eight
       "; "Nine "
    ) & "Hundred " ) &

 Case ( b > 1 ;
    Choose( b ; ""; "";
       "Twenty "; "Thirty "; "Forty "; "Fifty "; "Sixty "; "Seventy ";
       "Eighty "; "Ninety ")
    ) &
```

```
Case ( a > 0 and b ≠ 1 ;
   Choose( a ; "";
      "One "; "Two "; "Three "; "Four "; "Five "; "Six "; "Seven "; "Eight
      "; "Nine ")
   ) &

Case ( b = 1 ;
   Choose( a ;
      "Ten "; "Eleven "; "Twelve "; "Thirteen "; "Fourteen "; "Fifteen ";
      "Sixteen "; "Seventeen "; "Eighteen "; "Nineteen ") ) &
 "Year" & Case ( n > 1 ; "s" )
)
// result (if the number field contains 32) = Thirty Two Years
```

Summary

This chapter discussed many useful built-in functions. Remember that FileMaker has over *300* built-in functions that are available when writing formulas. A few more of these will be mentioned in the forthcoming chapters, and all are described in the online help guide accessible from the hint at the bottom of the *Functions* pane in the *Specify Calculation* dialog. In the next chapter, we will continue our exploration of built-in functions looking at the *JavaScript Object Notation* (JSON) functions.

CHAPTER 14

Using JSON

JavaScript Object Notation (JSON) is an open-standard, lightweight, data-interchange format originally specified by Douglas Crockford in 2000, standardized in 2013, and finalized to its current version in 2017. It was derived from the JavaScript Programming Language to fulfill a need for a language-independent, real-time, server-to-browser exchange protocol that didn't require plug-ins. *JSON objects* are formatted using a relatively simple key/value pair structure that is easy for humans and machines to read and write. As a result, it has become popular with *Representational State Transfer* (REST) web services as an indispensable tool for a variety of data exchanges. FileMaker added a set of built-in functions in version 16 that can be used to create and manipulate JSON data. These are essential when working with data in the format provided by external services and can also be employed when using JSON as an internal format for data exchange between scripts and other functions. This chapter introduces JSON, covering the following topics:

- Defining the JSON format
- Parsing JSON
- Manipulating JSON

Defining the JSON Format

A *JSON object* is a bracketed list of *elements* that combine an identifying *key* with an associated *value*. Similar structures are referred to many ways in other languages, including *array*, *dictionary*, *hash table*, *keyed list*, *record*, and *struct*. The *key* is always a text string that acts like a label to name and identify the element. An element's *value* contains some data content that is one of the following types:

- *JSONString* – A text string
- *JSONNumber* – A numeric value

© Mark Conway Munro 2021
M. C. Munro, *Learn FileMaker Pro 19*, https://doi.org/10.1007/978-1-4842-6680-9_14

- *JSONBoolean* – A true or false value

- *JSONArray* – An ordered list of comma-separated values contained within square brackets

- *JSONObject* – A JSON object nested in the element of a parent object

- *JSONNull* – A null value

- *JSONRaw* – A value that will be determined by the JSON parser

A JSON object with a single element containing an id number is formatted with the label in quotes, a colon followed by the value, all enclosed in curly brackets as follows. Here the key's value is a *JSONumber*:

```
{"id":5103}
```

In this example, the value contains *JSONText*, a person's first name:

```
{"First":"John"}
```

A multi-element object uses a comma to separate each uniquely named element. For example, an object containing data about a person may combine elements for *id*, *first name*, *last name*, and *title*, as shown here:

```
{"id":5103,"First":"John","Last":"Smith","Title":"Chief Technology
Officer"}
```

JSON doesn't care about white space around the elements, so the preceding object can be formatted in a multi-line format, as shown here:

```
{
    "id":5103,
    "First":"John",
    "Last":"Smith",
    "Title":"Chief Technology Officer"
}
```

A *JSON array* is a type of object that contains a list of unlabeled values or elements. These are formatted as comma-separated values enclosed in square brackets as shown in the following example of an array of numbers:

```
[1,2,3,4,5]
```

An array can contain other data types, including text as shown in this example:

```
["Karen","Charlene","Jeff","Susan","Howard"]
```

The value of an element can even be another object, creating a nested hierarchy of objects. This example shows an object with two *product elements*, each containing a nested *JSONObject* of product metadata:

```
{
    "Product1":{"name":"Widget 1","price":39.99,"vendor":15},
    "Product2":{"name":"Widget 2","price":55.48,"vendor":38}
}
```

An element value can also contain an array, as shown here where the *friends* and *colleagues* elements are each a *JSONArray* that contains a list of names.

```
{
    "friends":["Dan","Brian","Carolyn","Karen"],
    "colleagues":["Brian","Michael","Mary","Walker","Nadya"]
}
```

Similarly, arrays can contain objects. This example shows an array of two items, an object with two *Product* elements and another object with two *Employee* elements:

```
[
    {"Product1":"Widget 1","Product2":"Widget 2"},
    {"Employee1":"William"," Employee2":"Janice"}
]
```

While some systems and servers will return data in a JSON format defined by them, when creating JSON in FileMaker, the structure of an object can be whatever you define. Any number of objects, arrays, and data types can be mixed and matched, joined, or nested, using custom labels you define to create a unique structure based on the requirements of your custom system.

Tip   Validate JSON object formatting at `www.jsonlint.com`.

Parsing JSON

FileMaker provides three JSON functions that parse data, each requiring two parameters: a *json* object (or empty string) and a *keyOrIndexPath* that optionally references a specific element key, array index position, or a path to a nested element: *JSONGetElement, JSONListKeys, JSONListValues*.

Let's work through some examples from the assumption that the *Example Text* field in the Sandbox table contains the following JSON that contains vendor information:

```
{
    "id":350,
    "name":"First Class Widgets",
    "category":"Manufacturing",
    "contact":
        {
            "phone":"555-867-5309",
            "email":"sales@widgets.nope",
            "web":"www.widgets.nope"
        },
    "products":
        [
            {
            "aisles":[3,8]
            "id":1000,
            "name":"Widget 1",
            "price":39.99,
            },
            {
            "aisles":[2,4]
            "id":1001,
            "name":"Widget 2",
            "price":59.99,
            }
        ]
}
```

Using JSONGetElement

The *JSONGetElement* function will return the value of a specified element from the json data provided.

```
JSONGetElement ( json ; keyOrIndexOrPath )
```

Referring to an Element by Key

To refer to an element by key, use its label name in the *keyOrIndexOrPath* parameter. This example shows a call requesting the *name* element:

```
JSONGetElement ( Sandbox::Example Text ; "name" )    // Result = First
                                                     Class Widgets
```

This example requests the *contact* element, so the result is a JSON object.

```
JSONGetElement ( Sandbox::Example Text ; "contact" )
// Result =
    {
        "phone":"555-867-5309",
        "email":"sales@widgets.nope",
        "web":www.widgets.nope
    }
```

Referring to an Element by Array Index

When the object is an array, the *keyOrIndexOrPath* parameter should be a number in square brackets indicating the zero-based position of the desired element. By using an index position of 2, this example will extract the third value from an array of names as shown in this example.

```
JSONGetElement ( ["Michael","Mary","Walker","Karen"] ; "[2]" ) // Result =
                                                       Walker
```

Referring to an Element by Path

When parsing complex JSON with elements containing nested objects and arrays, a *path* can be used to refer to elements deeper than the first level. A *JSON path* is specified by denoting each key necessary to traverse the hierarchical structure down to the desired element, each separated by a period. Using the vender example, to get the *phone* element, we must specify that it is contained within the *contact* element, as shown here:

```
JSONGetElement ( Sandbox::Example Text ; "contact.phone" )
// Result = 555-867-5309
```

A *path* can reach down as many levels as necessary, and they can mix object keys and array index positions. In this example, we get the *price* of the *product* at the second position in the array by including the index position [1], as shown here:

```
JSONGetElement ( Sandbox::Example Text ; "products.[1].price" )
// Result = 59.99
```

Similarly, this example will extract the *second* array position from the *aisle* element of the first array position of the *product* element:

```
JSONGetElement ( Sandbox::Example Text ; "products.[0].aisles.[1]" )
// Result = 8
```

Using JSONListKeys

The *JSONListKeys* function returns a list of the name of every key in the object or a specified element.

```
JSONListKeys ( json ; keyOrIndexOrPath )
```

This example shows how to get a list of the keys in the example json:

```
JSONListKeys ( Sandbox::Example Text ; "" )
// Result =
    category
    contact
    id
    name
    products
```

The *keyOrIndexOrPath* parameter can be used to specify a nested element containing an object or array. This example will return a list of keys for the *contact* element:

```
JSONListKeys ( Sandbox::Example Text ; "contact" )
// Result =
    phone
    email
    web
```

Because arrays are unlabeled lists, the keys returned will be a list of the zero-based index positions of items, as shown here specifying the *product* element:

```
JSONListKeys ( Sandbox::Example Text ; "products" )
// Result =
    0
    1
```

Using JSONListValues

The *JSONListValues* function will return a list of the value of every key for an element containing an object or array.

```
JSONListValues ( json ; keyOrIndexOrPath )
```

This works the same as *JSONListKeys* except it returns the *values* instead of the *keys*, as shown in this example which returns the values of every element of the *contact* element:

```
JSONListValues ( Sandbox::Example Text ; "contact" )
// Result =
    555-867-5309
    sales@widgets.nope
    www.widgets.nope
```

Creating and Manipulating JSON

FileMaker provides three functions used to manipulate elements within a JSON object: *JSONSetElement, JSONDeleteElemnet,* and *JSONFormatElements.*

Using JSONSetElement

The *JSONSetElement* function sets the value of one or more elements in an object, creating them if necessary. The function call has four parameters, shown here:

```
JSONSetElement ( json ; keyOrIndexOrPath ; value ; type )
```

The *json* parameter can contain an object, array, or an empty string when creating a new object. The *keyOrIndexOrPath* and *value* are required and specify the element key that should be created or modified and the content it should contain. The *type* parameter can specify a data type of the *value* or be an empty string, and FileMaker will use a type determined by the content provided. The following example creates a simple object with a *name* element:

```
JSONSetElement ( "" ; "name" ; "First Class Widgets"; "" )
// Result = {"name":"First Class Widgets"}
```

Assuming the preceding result is placed into a variable named *data*, this example shows how to add an element to the existing object, in this case a *category* element:

```
JSONSetElement ( data ; "category" ; "Manufacturing"; "" )
// Result =
  {
    "name":"First Class Widgets",
    "category":"Manufacturing"
  }
```

Setting the value of an element that already exists in the object provided will replace the existing value with the new value.

```
JSONSetElement ( {"name":"Honda"} ; "name" ; "Ford"; "" )
// Result = {"name":"Ford"}
```

> **Tip**   Instead of writing JSON manually, always use the JSONSetElement function to create a new element to help avoid mistakes.

Specifying a Data Type

The previous examples leave the *type* parameter blank because the data provided is obviously text, and we can rely on FileMaker to choose the correct format. Often you will need to specify a type to ensure the correct result. For example, if the *value* starts with a numeric digit and no type is specified, FileMaker will automatically treat it like a number. This means that text with leading zeros or dates will be converted into a number unless you specify the correct data type. To illustrate the importance of specifying a type for text-based text strings, consider the difference in these results:

```
JSONSetElement ( "" ; "phone" ; "555-867-5309" ; "" )
// Result = {"phone":555}
JSONSetElement ( "" ; "phone" ; "555-867-5309" ; JSONString )
// Result = {"phone":"555-867-5309"}
```

Setting Multiple Values at Once

You can set multiple keys with a single call by using semicolon-delimited, square-bracketed sets of *keyOrIndexOrPath*, *value,* and *type* parameters, as shown in this example that sets two elements at once:

```
JSONSetElement ( "" ;
   [ "name" ; "First Class Widgets"; "" ] ;
   [ "category" ; "Manufacturing"; "" ]
)
// Result =
     {
        "name":"First Class Widgets",
        "category":"Manufacturing"
     }
```

Setting a Value by Path

When working with complex objects that need elements containing objects and arrays, it is necessary to specify a *path* that refers to elements deeper than the first level. This example sets the *name* element at the top level and then sets a *contact* element as an object containing a *phone* and *email* element:

```
JSONSetElement ( "" ;
   [ "name" ; "First Class Widgets"; "" ] ;
   [ "contact.phone" ; "555-867-5309"; JSONString ] ;
   [ "contact.email" ; " sales@widgets.nope "; "" ]
)
// Result =
{
   "name":"First Class Widgets",
   "contact":
     {
         "phone":"555-867-5309",
         "email":"sales@widgets.nope"
     }
}
```

Setting Array Values

JSONSetElement can target an index position in an array as described for *JSONGetElement*. The index value must be enclosed in square brackets to avoid the number being used to create or refer to a key instead of an array position, as demonstrated by the following examples. The first shows how to correctly create a value in an array. The second shows the incorrect result when failing to use brackets.

```
JSONSetElement ( "" ; "[0]" ; "Claris" ; "" )
// Result = ["Claris"]
JSONSetElement ( "" ; "0" ; "Claris" ; "")
// Result = {"0":"Claris"}
```

When setting an element in an existing array, the value at the index position will be replaced with the new value, even if it is a different data type. This example replaces the *number* in the third array position with some *text*:

```
JSONSetElement ( "[1,2,3,4]" ; "[2]" ; "Claris" ; "" )
// Result = [1,2,"Claris",4]
```

If an index position specified is beyond the range of existing values, FileMaker will insert one or more *null* placeholders to target the desired position.

```
JSONSetElement ( "" ; "[3]" ; "Claris" ; "" )
// Result = [null,null,null,"Claris"]
JSONSetElement ( "[1,2,3,4]" ; "[6]" ; "Claris" ; "" )
// Result = [1,2,3,4,null,null,"Claris"]
```

Arrays work the same as keys in paths. This example will change the *price* of the first *product* in the vendor example:

```
JSONSetElement ( Sandbox::Example Text ; "products.[0].price" ; "45.00" ; "" )
```

Using JSONDeleteElement

The *JSONDeleteElement* function will delete an element from an object. The function call has two parameters, shown here:

```
JSONDeleteElement ( json ; keyOrIndexOrPath )
```

The specified element will be completely removed, as shown in the following example which removes the *name* element, leaving only the *id* remaining:

```
JSONDeleteElement ( {"name":"Honda", "id":350} ; "name" )
// Result = {"id":350}
```

Deleting an index position in an array will automatically shift values to avoid an empty position.

```
JSONDeleteElement ( "[1,2,3,4,5]" ; "[2]" )
// Result = [1,2,4,5]
```

Deleting works with paths as well. This example will completely remove the first *price* from the first *product* of the vendor example, shifting the second price into the position of the first:

```
JSONDeleteElement ( Sandbox::Example Text ; "products.[0].price" )
```

Using JSONFormatElements

The *JSONFormatElements* function reformats an object by inserting extra space to render it in an easier to read format. FileMaker will always remove spaces from an object when performing any of the manipulation functions, so this function is useful when reviewing the results:

```
JSONFormatElements(
     {"id":5103,"First":"John","Last":"Smith","Title":"Chief Technology
     Officer"}
)
// Result
   {
      "id":5103,
      "First":"John",
      "Last":"Smith",
      "Title":"Chief Technology Officer"
   }
```

Summary

This chapter introduced JSON and explored the built-in functions used to create, parse, and manipulate objects and elements. In the next chapter, we will learn how to create custom functions.

CHAPTER 15

Creating Custom Functions

A *custom function* is a developer-defined formula that expands on the built-in functions within the database it is installed. Formulas can be off-loaded away from individual formulas and placed into a custom central library of easily accessible functionality. Unlike regular formulas, custom functions can be defined to accept parameters, can be recursive, and can be accessed directly from any formula or script in the database. A well-designed, open-ended, reusable custom function can reduce redundancies in formulas, simplify calculations, and save time. In this chapter, we discuss the process of creating and using custom functions, covering topics such as

- Introducing the Manage Custom Functions dialog
- Introducing the Edit Custom Function dialog
- Adding parameters to a custom function
- Accessing fields from custom functions
- Building recursive custom functions

Note Custom functions can only be created and edited with advanced tools enabled (Chapter 2).

© Mark Conway Munro 2021
M. C. Munro, *Learn FileMaker Pro 19*, https://doi.org/10.1007/978-1-4842-6680-9_15

Introducing the Custom Function Dialogs

Custom functions are created and managed from the *Manage Custom Functions* dialog, shown in Figure 15-1. To open it, select the *File ➤ Manage ➤ Custom Functions* menu. This dialog is used to *create, edit, duplicate, delete,* and *import* custom functions.

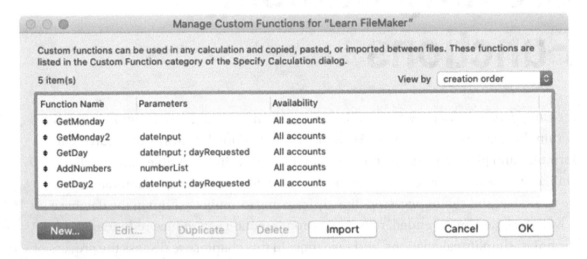

Figure 15-1. *The dialog used to manage custom functions*

Tip   Custom functions can be copied and pasted between two files or imported.

To begin, click *New* to open a new function in the *Edit Custom Function* dialog, shown in Figure 15-2. This dialog opens when creating a new function or editing an existing one. It is similar to a *Specify Calculation* dialog but with a few important differences.

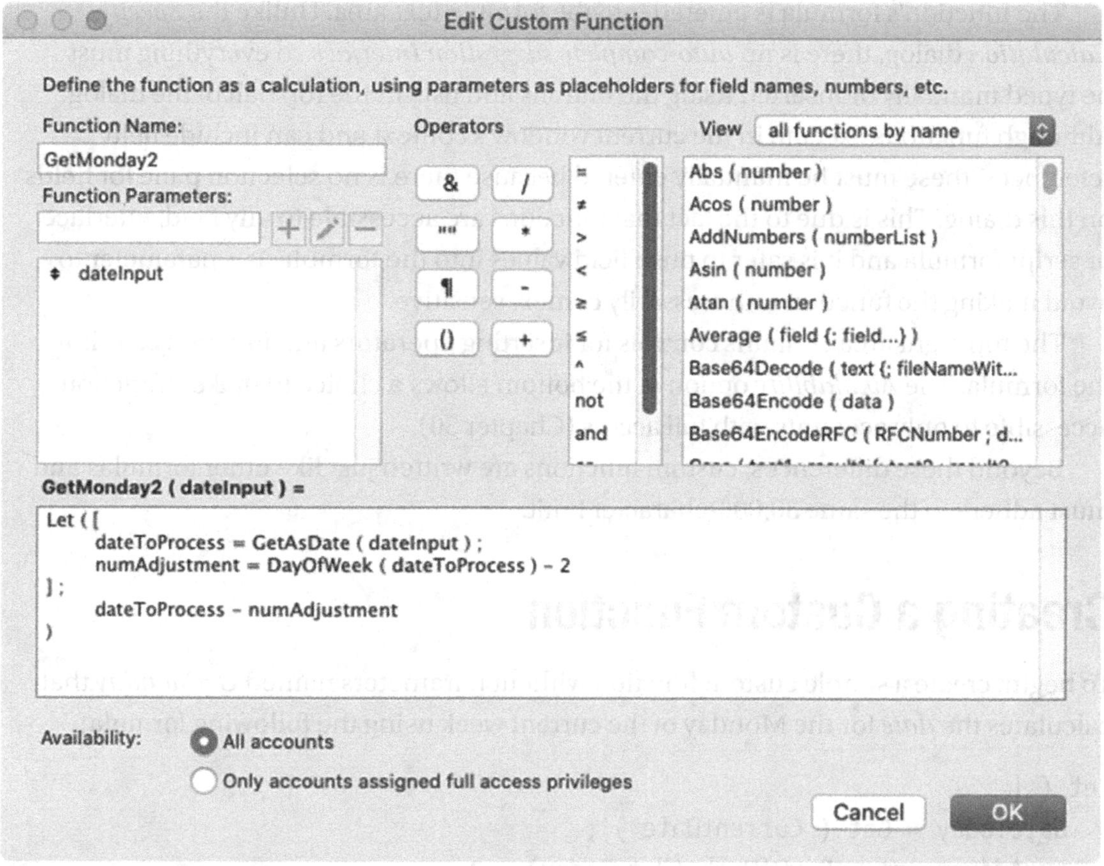

Figure 15-2. *The dialog used to define a custom function*

The *Function Name* field allows the function to be named so it can be called by other formulas in the same way built-in functions are called.

Several tools are used to define optional *Function Parameters*. Parameters are positional input variables that are assigned a value when another formula calls the function. These work like parameters on built-in functions except you define them. Create a new parameter by entering a name and clicking the *plus* icon. Select and rename an existing parameter and click the *pencil* icon to save that change. Parameters can be deleted by clicking the *minus* icon. Once in the list, they can be drag-arranged to specify their order. Since parameters are positional, values passed when the function is called are inserted into the variable at the corresponding position in the list. *Changing the order of an existing function's parameters will require rearranging the values in any existing call.* Once created, double-click a parameter in the list to insert it into the formula below.

The function's formula is entered into the formula text area. Unlike the *Specify Calculation* dialog, there is no *auto-complete suggestion interface* so everything must be typed manually or inserted using the buttons and lists in the top half of the dialog. Although functions execute in the current window's context and can include field references, these must be manually entered because there is no selection pane for fields on this dialog. This is due to the fact that functions are accessible to any field, interface, or script formula and it is safer to push field values into the formula as a parameter to avoid making the function unnecessarily context sensitive.

The top-right area contains controls for inserting operators and function calls into the formula. The *Availability* option at the bottom allows a choice to make a function accessible to only accounts with full access (Chapter 30).

Beyond these differences, custom functions are written just like other formulas and must adhere to the same 30,000-character limit.

Creating a Custom Function

To begin, create a simple custom function without parameters named *GetMonday* that calculates the *date* for the Monday of the current week using the following formula:

```
Let ( [
    dateToday = Get ( CurrentDate ) ;
    numAdjustment = DayOfWeek (dateToday) – 2
] ;
    dateToday - numAdjustment
)
```

The formula uses a *Let* statement to put today's date into a variable called *dateToday*. To determine the number of days today's date needs to be adjusted to land on a Monday, it converts *dateToday* using the built-in *DayOfWeek* function. Then, since we know Monday is always the second day of a calendar week, we subtract 2 from that number and put the result into a variable named *numAdjustment*. Finally, that adjustment number will be subtracted from today's date to arrive at the date for this week's Monday. For example, if today is a Friday, that is the *sixth* day of the week. Since we want to determine the corresponding Monday, which is the *second* day of the week, we subtract 2 from that number to arrive at the number of days we need to subtract from the current day in order to arrive at a Monday in the current week. No matter what day it is *today*, the result of this formula will always be the corresponding Monday's date.

To create this custom function, open the *Manage Custom Functions* dialog, and click the *New* button to open the *Edit Custom Function* dialog. Then follow the steps shown in Figure 15-3, first entering a name of "GetMonday" and then entering the formula. Click the OK button to save the function and then click OK in the *Manage Custom Functions* dialog.

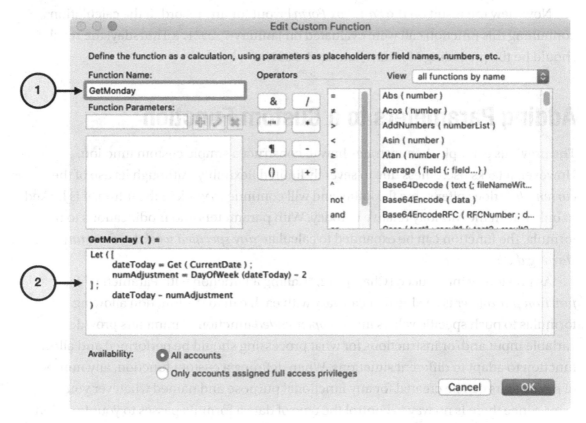

Figure 15-3. *The steps required to create the example custom function*

Once finished, the new function can be inserted into any formula using the same process used to insert a built-in function. Test this in the *Sandbox* table by following these steps:

1. Open the *Fields* tab for the *Sandbox* table in the *Manage Database* dialog.

2. Double-click the *Example Calculation* field or select it and click the *Options* button.

3. Change the field's formula to GetMonday.

4. Change the calculation result type to *date*.

5. Click OK to save the calculation formula and close the *Specify Calculation* dialog.

6. Click OK to save and close the *Manage Database* dialog.

Now view the result on the *Sandbox Form* layout for any record. If the calculation containing this function call were evaluated on January 7, 2021, a Thursday, the result should be the preceding Monday: January 4, 2021.

Adding Parameters to a Custom Function

The previous example demonstrates how to construct a simple custom function. However, it lacks usefulness due to severely limited flexibility. Although its use of the *current date* does offer some flexibility and will continue to work in the future, it is locked to only return the Monday relative to today. With parameters and modifications to the formula, the function can be expanded to calculate *any specified weekday from any starting date*.

As previously introduced (Chapter 12, "Calling a Function with Parameters"), a *function parameter* is a value that can vary with each call to the function allowing formulas to push specific values into an *open-ended* function. Parameters provide variable input and/or instructions for what processing should be performed and allow a function to adapt to different situations. When defining a custom function, any number of parameters can be created for any functional purpose and named whatever you want. Since there is no way to control the type of data a formula passes to your function as a parameter, be sure to choose a name that describes the intended data type(s) it is intended to receive. For example, a parameter named *input* is too vague, while *dateInput* or *startDate* clearly states what type of data is expected. For our example, we want to add two parameters to our function: an input date named "dateInput" and a desired result weekday named "dayRequested."

Adding an Input Date Parameter

First, create a duplicate of the previous function that we will expand to calculate the corresponding Monday from any starting date provided in a parameter named "dateInput." Open the *Manage Custom Functions* dialog, select the *GetMonday* function, and click the *Duplicate* button. Then click the *Edit* button to open the function in the *Edit Custom Function* dialog, and make the changes shown in Figure 15-4.

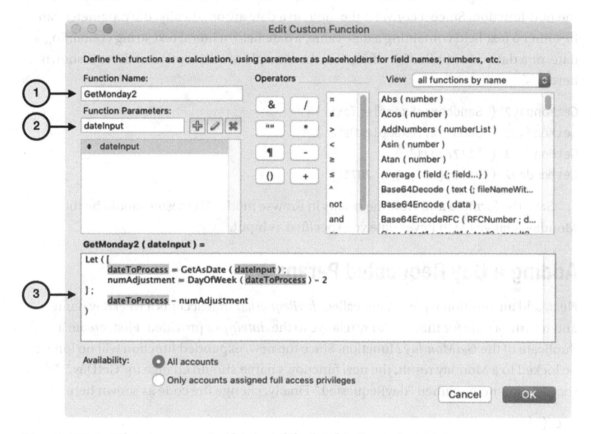

Figure 15-4. *The steps required to modify the duplicate function*

1. Change the name of the function to "GetMonday2."

2. Type the parameter name "dateInput," and then click the + button to create the parameter in the list below.

3. Modify the code so that the *dateInput* parameter is used in place of the current date and is converted to a date using the *GetAsDate* function. Also, rename the *dateToday* variable to *dateToProcess*:

```
Let ( [
    dateToProcess = GetAsDate ( dateInput ) ;
    numAdjustment = DayOfWeek ( dateToProcess ) - 2
] ;
     dateToProcess - numAdjustment
)
```

Save the function and modify the formula in the *Example Calculation* field to call the new function. Since it converts the input to a date automatically, the parameter can be either a text field containing a date value, a date field, a literal text string containing a date, or a date value built with a function. An example of each option of these is shown here:

```
GetMonday2 ( Sandbox::Example Text )
GetMonday2 ( Sandbox::Example Date )
GetMonday2 ( "1/7/2021" )
GetMonday2 ( Date ( 1 ; 7 ; 2021 ) )
```

Save the formula and view the results in Browse mode. The result should be the Monday relative to whatever date you specified as input.

Adding a Day Requested Parameter

Next, add an additional parameter called *dayRequested* that accepts a weekday name and returns a date for that weekday relative to the *dateInput* provided. First, create a duplicate of the *GetMonday2* function. Since the new, expanded function will no longer be locked to a Monday result, the new function's name should change to "GetDay." Add a second parameter named "dayRequested." Finally, change the code as shown here:

```
Let ( [
    dateToProcess = GetAsDate ( dateInput ) ;
    list = "Sunday¶Monday¶Tuesday¶Wednesday¶Thursday¶Friday¶Saturday" ;
    list = Left ( list ; Position ( list ; dayRequested ; 1; 1 ) ) ;
    dayNumber = ValueCount ( list ) ;
    numAdjustment = DayOfWeek ( dateToProcess ) - dayNumber
 ] ;
    dateToProcess - numAdjustment
)
```

The code will accept a day name (e.g., "Wednesday") in the *dayReqeusted* parameter and convert that into a day number (4) by finding that day's position in a list of day names. This is done by adding three steps to the formula. A new *list* variable is initialized to contain a paragraph return-delimited list of weekday names. In the next line, the *list* variable is modified using the *Left* and *Position* functions to reduce the list to only the day names prior to the one requested. So, if "Wednesday" was the day requested, list would contain "Sunday¶Monday¶Tuesday¶W." Finally, the *ValueCount* function is used to convert that list into the weekday number (4), which is placed into the *dayNumber* variable. This determines the *numAdjustment* value which is used to adjust the input date as in previous versions. Once the new function is saved, modify the formula in the *Example Calculation* to call the new function. In this example, the result will be the date of *Friday* for the week of *January 4, 2021*:

```
GetDay ( "1/4/2021" ; "Friday" )        // result = 1/8/2021
GetDay ( "1/4/2021" ; "Wednesday" )     // result = 1/5/2021
```

Adding a Default Date Option

As a further refinement, modify the function to automatically use a default date when one is not specified in the *dateInput* parameter. This provides a shortcut for any formula calling the function that wants to use the current date. Currently, if the function were used to calculate the Friday for the current date, right now, a calling formula would be required to explicitly include today's date in the call as shown here:

```
GetDay ( Get ( CurrentDate ) ; "Friday" )
```

Modifying the first line of the *Let* statement from the last example, a *Case* statement can automatically default to the current date when none is provided in the parameter. When a call passes an empty string instead of a date, this condition will allow the function to produce a result. Modify the first line of the *Let* statement as shown here:

```
dateToProcess = Case ( dateInput = "" ; Get ( CurrentDate ) ; GetAsDate
( dateInput ) ) ;
```

Now, a formula can request a day relative to the current date by passing in an empty string in the first parameter or for a specific date by providing one, as shown in the following two examples:

```
GetDay ( "" ; "Friday" )
GetDay ( "1/4/2021" ; "Friday" )
```

Stressing the Importance of Thorough Testing

Every formula should be carefully tested prior to live production use. Being accessible from anywhere in the database, a custom function requires greater care. This is especially true for complex functions that accept parameter input. A single test showing a function working may not be adequate since different input may cause conditions not anticipated by the formula. Instead, perform as many tests as possible with a variety of input to confirm that it will handle a full range of possible values in various combinations.

The testing requirements of each custom function will be different. Start by asking what variety of input might be received. There are many questions we might ask regarding the previous example. What if the date provided is at the *start* of the week: a Sunday or a Monday? What if the date is at the *end* of the week: a Friday or a Saturday? What if the day requested is the same day of the date provided? Will the function work under each of these circumstances? Will it operate correctly when requesting *any* day of the week relative to *any* date? Do all the anticipated data types – *date*, *timestamp*, and *text string with a date* – return an accurate result? To confirm this, we should devise a set of tests for each condition and confirm the results. To begin, convert the list of questions into a list of test scenarios that will adequately confirm the desired functionality with a large enough sampling of input. In our example, at the minimum, the following tests should be performed:

- *dateInput* – Run seven tests, one test for each day of the week as input, also, at least one test of each accepted data type.

- *dayRequested* – Run seven tests, one test for each day of the week.

This indicates the need for at least *16* tests. Rather than perform these tests manually, one by one, the following single calculation formula, entered in the *Example Calculation* field, covers them all at once by producing a single text result that lists all the various results:

```
Let ( [
    dateInput = Date ( 1 ; 17 ; 2021 )
] ;
    "Input = " & dateInput & " (" & DayName (dateInput) & ")¶" &
    "+1 Sunday=" & GetDay ( dateInput + 1  ; "Sunday" ) & "¶"
    "+2 Sunday=" & GetDay ( dateInput + 2  ; "Sunday" ) & "¶" &
    "+3 Sunday=" & GetDay ( dateInput + 3  ; "Sunday" ) & "¶" &
    "+4 Sunday=" & GetDay ( dateInput + 4  ; "Sunday" ) & "¶"
    "+5 Sunday=" & GetDay ( dateInput + 5  ; "Sunday" ) & "¶" &
    "Sunday=" & GetDay ( dateInput; "Sunday" ) & "¶"
    "Monday=" & GetDay ( dateInput ; "Monday" ) & "¶"
    "Tuesday=" & GetDay (dateInput; "Tuesday" ) & "¶"
    "Wednesday=" & GetDay ( dateInput; "Wednesday" ) & "¶" &
    "Thursday=" & GetDay ( dateInput; "Thursday" ) & "¶" &
    "Friday=" & GetDay ( dateInput; "Friday" ) & "¶" &
    "Saturday=" & GetDay ( dateInput; "Saturday" ) & "¶"
    "Timestamp=" & GetDay ( GetAsTimestamp ( dateInput )  ; "Sunday" ) & "¶" &
    "Text Date=" & GetDay ( GetAsText ( dateInput )   ; "Sunday" ) & "¶" &
    "Text TS=" & GetDay ( GetAsText ( GetASTimestamp ( dateInput ) )  ;
    "Sunday" ) & "¶"
)
// result =
    Input = 1/17/2021 (Sunday)
    +1 Sunday=1/17/2021
    +2 Sunday=1/17/2021
    +3 Sunday=1/17/2021
    +4 Sunday=1/17/2021
    +5 Sunday=1/17/2021
    +6 Sunday=1/17/2021
    Sunday=1/17/2021
```

```
Monday=1/18/2021
Tuesday=1/19/2021
Wednesday=1/20/2021
Thursday=1/21/2021
Friday=1/22/2021
Saturday=1/23/2021
Timestamp=1/17/2021
Text Date=1/17/2021
Text TS=1/17/2021
```

Caution   Be sure to change the Example Calculation result data type to "text" since this test formula returns text instead of a *date*.

This formula uses a *Let* statement to place a start date into a variable and uses that to perform repeated calls to the function and concatenate the results into a string result. The first six results show that, as the *dateInput* is incremented to cover each day of an entire week, the result for the requested Sunday remains the same. The next seven results show that using the same *dateInput* while requesting a different day of the week works since the results span a 7-day period. Finally, the last three results show that when the *dateInput* is a *timestamp*, *text-based date*, or *text-based timestamp*, the result remains the same. With this test completed and confirmed, it should now be safe to use this custom function.

Building Recursive Functions

A *recursive function* is a formula that is capable of generating calls that are self-referencing, i.e., calling and executing itself from within itself. In FileMaker, custom functions are the only formulas that can be recursive. Recursion is often confused with the iterative functionality found in looping scripts or in the new *While* function (Chapter 13). Although there are similarities and many tasks can be accomplished using either, recursion is actually very different. In a repeating, or *iterative process*, a piece of code is executed numerous times in succession; each iteration is completed *before* the next begins. By contrast, a *recursive process* creates and runs successive new instances of the same code *during execution of the preceding instance*, a difference illustrated in Figure 15-5.

Each instance queues up in memory forming what is known as a *call stack* until it reaches a termination point known as a *base case* where it stops calling itself and produces a result that cascades back up the stack, collapsing it.

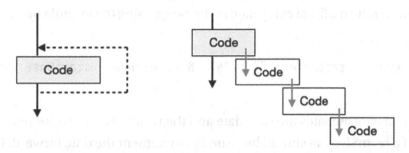

Figure 15-5. *The difference between iterative looping (left) and recursion (right)*

Both the iterative and recursive options are superior to hard-coded statements that restrict the number of iterations. For example, using *If* or *Case* statements requires each possible iteration to be explicitly stated in a fixed sequence. Similarly, a *Let* statement can perform a fixed number of cascading variable declaration. While this is fine for static choices that never change and don't vary in number, often a more dynamic approach is warranted.

A *looping script* is easy to set up and runs quickly. However, scripts can't be triggered from within a formula, so they are limited to interface-related actions and events. Also, they can be bulky to set up since they require iteration control variables along with lines to perform whatever functionality is required.

For an exclusively *formula-based* solution, the choices are the iterative *While* function or a recursive custom function. The *While* function has the advantage of working in any formula, while recursion is limited to custom functions. The nested hierarchy of the recursive stack can be more difficult to conceptualize, but using the *While* function is not without its own confusion. It can feel overly wordy in simple examples and mind-boggling in more complex ones. Using *While* may be a little faster and doesn't have the same memory impact. Although many programming challenges can be handled with either approach, when performing a complex, repeated process through hierarchical data, recursion is often the only practical choice.

Building Simple Recursive Functions

To grasp the basic structure of a recursive function, start with some simple examples. First, create a new function named "DateRange" that accepts *startDate* and *endDate* parameters and uses these to return a list of every date in the range using the formula here:

```
startDate &
Case (  endDate = startDate ; "" ; "¶"  & DateRange ( startDate + 1 ;
endDate ) )
```

The formula concatenates the start date and the result of a *Case* statement, which determines if a recursive call should be issued to increment the date forward. If the end date equals the start date, the formula returns an empty string, thereby providing a terminating base case. If the two dates are different, a paragraph return is included, and then the function calls itself with the start date incremented by one. Each recursive call repeats this process until the start date equals the end, creating a result as shown in the following example:

```
DateRange ( GetAsDate ( "1/1/2021" ) ; GetAsDate ( "1/5/2021" ) )
// result =
    1/1/2021
    1/2/2021
    1/3/2021
    1/4/2021
    1/5/2021
```

Create another function named "MergeValues" that accepts two return-delimited text value lists and returns a blended list. The code for this function shown in the following assumes two parameters, *column1* and *column2*:

```
Let ( [
    current = GetValue ( column1 ; 1 ) & " " & GetValue ( column2 ; 1 ) ;
    column1 = RightValues ( column1 ; ValueCount ( column1 ) - 1 ) ;
    column2 = RightValues ( column2 ; ValueCount ( column2 ) - 1 )
] ;
    current & Case ( column1 ≠ "" ; "¶" & MergeValues ( column1 ; column2 ) )
)
```

In this example, the *Let* statement is used to step through the task. The first value from both inputs is extracted and concatenated into a *current* variable with a space between them. Then, the two input parameters are reduced by one value using the *ValueCount* and *RightValues* functions to remove the first value. The result is the value in the *current* variable, and if there are values remaining, a paragraph return and recursive call continue the process. This example call has three labels and phone numbers as input and shows the corresponding result:

```
MergeValues ( "Work¶Home¶Cell" ; "555-2121¶555-3421¶555-2645" )
// result =
    Work 555-2121
    Home 555-3421
    Cell 555-2645
```

Controlling Recursion Limits with setRecursion

To avoid infinite regress for situations when a recursive function doesn't provide a terminating base case, FileMaker imposes a limit on the number of iterations a recursive stack can include. Any formula that exceeds this limit will return an error expressed as a question mark. Prior to FileMaker 18, the limit varied depending on the type of recursion used. Functions using *tail recursion*, where the recursive call is the final step at the end of the function's formula leaving no processing unfinished, had a limit of 50,000 total recursive calls, in contrast to *head recursion*, where the placement of a recursive call anywhere within the formula was previously limited to 10,000 total calls. However, in version 18, both tail- and head-recursive calls and the *While* function have a default limit of 50,000 iterations. Also introduced in that version is the *setRecursion* function which allows a developer to set the maximum number of iterations allowed higher or lower than this default limit.

```
setRecursion ( expression ; maxIterations )
```

This is a *conditioning function* which sets the iterative terms for processing the *expression* it encloses. Any recursive function calls or *While* statements included in the first parameter's statement will be limited to the number specified by the *maxIterations* parameter. This can be used to *increase* or *decrease* the maximum number of iterations allowed. For example, try calling the previous *DateRange* function with a start and end date more than 30 days apart from within a *setRecursion* statement limited to 30 iterations. This example fails because the recursive calls neccesary to finish the task exceed the limit of 30.

```
setRecursion ( DateRange ( "1/1/2021" ; "2/10/2021" ) ; 30 )
// result = ?
```

Next, increase the limit to an amount greater than the range of dates to see it functions properly. If the preceding example were modified with a limit of 60, it is more than enough to cover the range of dates specified, and a proper result will be delivered.

The following example shows the function increasing the limit to 250,000 in order to execute a simple *While* statement that increments a counter up to 200,000:

```
SetRecursion (
    While (
        counter = 0 ;
        counter < 200000 ;
        counter = counter + 1 ;
        counter
    ) ; 250000
)
```

Embedding Test Code Inside a Function

Earlier we discussed writing test code to quickly perform multiple tests of the *GetDay* custom function with a variety of different input. Recursion opens the possibility of storing that test code *inside* of the custom function it tests. While it may seem unnecessary to save test code at all, it may be prudent to retest a function anytime it is modified in the future. A *Case* statement can be used to detect a test request and perform an alternate set of code. In this example, the *dateInput* parameter will be used to determine if the call to the function was asking for *test results* or *normal operations* and run one or the other accordingly as shown in the following pattern:

```
Case ( dateInput = "Test" ; <<test code>> ; <<normal code>> )
```

Using this format, we can combine the previous example test code with the original function code to convert the formula into the following combined statement. To demonstrate this technique, create a new function called *GetDay2* with this new capability. In this example, if the *dateInput* receives a value of "Test," it will perform the test routine; otherwise, it will assume the parameter contains a date and will perform its normal function.

```
Case ( dateInput = "Test" ;
//    Test Code
   Let ( [
      dateInput = Date ( 1 ; 17 ; 2021 )
   ] ;
      "Input = " & dateInput & " (" & DayName (dateInput) & ")¶" &
      "1 Sunday=" & GetDay2 ( dateInput + 1  ; "Sunday" ) & "¶" &
      "+2 Sunday=" & GetDay2 ( dateInput + 2  ; "Sunday" ) & "¶"
      "+3 Sunday=" & GetDay2 ( dateInput + 3  ; "Sunday" ) & "¶" &
      "+4 Sunday=" & GetDay2 ( dateInput + 4  ; "Sunday" ) & "¶"
      "+5 Sunday=" & GetDay2 ( dateInput + 5  ; "Sunday" ) & "¶" &
      "+6 Sunday=" & GetDay2 ( dateInput + 6  ; "Sunday" ) & "¶" &
      "Sunday=" & GetDay2 ( dateInput; "Sunday" ) & "¶" &
      "Monday=" & GetDay2 ( dateInput ; "Monday" ) & "¶" &
      "Tuesday=" & GetDay2 (dateInput; "Tuesday" ) & "¶" &
      "Wednesday=" & GetDay2 ( dateInput; "Wednesday" ) & "¶"
      "Thursday=" & GetDay2 ( dateInput; "Thursday" ) & "¶"
      "Friday=" & GetDay2 ( dateInput; "Friday" ) & "¶" &
      "Saturday=" & GetDay2 ( dateInput; "Saturday" ) & "¶" &
      "Timestamp=" & GetDay2 ( GetAsTimestamp ( dateInput )  ; "Sunday" ) & "¶"
      "Text Date=" & GetDay2 ( GetAsText ( dateInput )  ; "Sunday" ) & "¶" &
      "Text TS=" & GetDay2 ( GetAsText ( GetAsTimestamp ( dateInput ) )  ;
      "Sunday" ) &
   )
;
//    Regular Code
   Let ( [
      dateToProcess  = GetAsDate ( dateInput ) ;
      list = "Sunday¶Monday¶Tuesday¶Wednesday¶Thursday¶Friday¶Saturday" ;
      list = Left ( list ; Position ( list ; dayRequested ; 1; 1 ) ) ;
      dayNumber = ValueCount ( list ) ;
      numAdjustment = DayOfWeek ( dateToProcess ) - dayNumber
 ] ;
      dateToProcess  - numAdjustment
   )
)
```

Summary

This chapter covered the basics of developing your own custom functions and the possibility of making them recursive. In the next chapter, we explore using the *Structured Query Language* (SQL) with the *ExecuteSQL* function.

CHAPTER 16

Introducing ExecuteSQL

The *Structured Query Language* (*SQL*) is a standardized programming language used to manage relational databases and perform numerous operational functions to the data they store. It was created in the 1970s and became the standard programming language for relational databases. The *American National Standards Institute* (ANSI) and the *International Organization for Standardization* (ISO) adopted an official SQL standard in 1986 and 1987, respectively. Since then, many updates to the standard have been released jointly by both organizations. Numerous companies now develop proprietary and open source SQL-compliant database systems. While FileMaker is not built on the standard, it has some support for performing SQL queries internally and externally. In version 9.0 (2007), FileMaker introduced the ability to create live connections to external ODBC data sources (Chapter 7). Version 12.0 (2012) introduced the *ExecuteSQL* function which can perform queries against FileMaker tables from any calculation within a FileMaker database. A *SQL Query* is a text-based statement used to instruct a database to perform an action. The most frequently used type of query and the only one supported by the *ExecuteSQL* function in FileMaker is the SELECT query, which contains data retrieval instructions for a desired result set. Experienced SQL programmers will appreciate the direct back-end access of this feature but may find the limitation constraining. Others may find the divergence from FileMaker's interface context–centric data access confusing. But the ability to perform a search, sort, and summarize data directly *within a calculation formula* in a completely *context-independent* manner is something many will appreciate. It isn't necessary to learn SQL or to use this command to create databases since it doesn't replace native FileMaker features. However, it is worth learning for situations where it complements those features more efficiently. This chapter explores the *ExecuteSQL* function, covering the following topics:

- Defining the ExecuteSQL function

- Creating SQL queries

- Accessing the database schema

© Mark Conway Munro 2021
M. C. Munro, *Learn FileMaker Pro 19*, https://doi.org/10.1007/978-1-4842-6680-9_16

Defining the ExecuteSQL Function

The *ExecuteSQL* function allows a formula to retrieve data directly from *any* table occurrence within the file's relationship graph *completely independent* of any relationship between it and the current interface context. A call to the function must include three parameters: *sqlQuery*, *fieldSeparator*, and *rowSeparator*. It can also accept one or more optional *arguments*.

```
ExecuteSQL ( sqlQuery ; fieldSeparator; rowSeparator )
ExecuteSQL ( sqlQuery ; fieldSeparator; rowSeparator ; arguments )
```

The parameters in the statement are defined as follows:

- *sqlQuery* – A text expression or reference to a field that contains a SELECT statement which specifies the location and criteria for fetching a desired record and field result.

- *fieldSeparator* – A text string containing the character(s) that should be used as a separator between fields in the result. If left empty, a comma is the default.

- *rowSeparator* – A text string containing the character(s) that should be used as a separator between records in the result. If left empty, a paragraph return is the default.

- *arguments* – One or more text values that are used as dynamic parameters in the query, replacing question marks typically in a WHERE clause.

The results of the function will be a text string with the value for each specified field for every matching record delimited by the specified or default separators. For example, using default separators, the result will be paragraphs representing records made up of comma-separated field values.

Caution   This is a *calculation function* and should not be confused with the similarly named script step!

Understanding the Limits of ExecuteSQL

The *ExecuteSQL* function has a few limitations that are important to note. There are features not supported that experienced SQL programmers may expect and others that experienced FileMaker developers may incorrectly assume.

- As mentioned in the introduction, the function is currently limited to the SELECT command only. It *does not support* any other common SQL functions that perform record changes or modify schema such as DELETE, INSERT, UPDATE, INSERT INTO, CREATE TABLE, DELETE TABLE, etc.

- FileMaker's relational connections are not recognized or required by the function. A SELECT statement must use a JOIN clause to dynamically create temporary relationships for use within the query.

- The function does not recognize the current layout context. Instead, it directly accesses a *table* based on the *occurrence* specified.

- Values *must* be sent to the function with SQL-92 compliant date and time formats with no braces. To apply the correct formatting in a query, use a DATE, TIME, or TIMESTAMP conditioning operator, or the value may be evaluated as a literal string. It will *not* accept the ODBC/JDBC formats for *date, time,* and *timestamp* constants contained in braces.

- The function will return *date, time,* and *number* data using the Unicode/SQL format rather than the date and time settings of the database file or operating system. So, these must be converted for use as dates in FileMaker.

- Sorting performed by the function uses the Unicode binary sort order.

Creating SQL Queries

At a minimum, the *sqlQuery* portion of the *ExecuteSQL* function requires a SELECT statement, which can include numerous optional clauses, and these can be used to perform numerous different data retrieval tasks.

Defining SELECT Statements

When calling the *ExecuteSQL* function, the *sqlQuery* parameter must contain a properly formatted SELECT statement. Minimally, this defines *what* to find and from *where*, following the pattern shown here:

```
SELECT <what> FROM <where>
```

Usually, the *what* is the name of one or more fields and the *where* is the name of the table occurrence from which to extract them. For example, the following example would return the contents of a *Name* field from every record in a *Contact* table occurrence:

```
SELECT Name FROM Contact
```

The preceding code shows an example of the simplest statement, requesting *one field from all records*. There are many optional clauses that are shown in the following and briefly defined in Table 16-1:

```
SELECT/SELECT DISTINCT <fields>
FROM <tables>
JOIN <table> ON <formula>
WHERE <formula>
GROUP BY <fields>
HAVING <formula>
UNION <select>
ORDER BY <fields>
OFFSET <number> ROW/ROWS
FETCH FIRST <number> PERCENT/ROWS/ROW/ONLY/WITH TIES
```

Table 16-1. *The definitions of each available clause of a SELECT statement*

Keyword	Clause Description
SELECT	Specifies one or more fields to select. Can include fields, constants, calculations, and functions. Use an asterisk to select all fields.
SELECT DISTINCT	Adding the DISTINCT operator will remove any duplicates from the result.
FROM	Specifies one or more tables from which to select the fields.
JOIN	Defines a table and relational formula to allow the results to include fields through a temporary relationship.
WHERE	Defines one or more criteria formulas that specify qualifications for records included in the result.
GROUP BY	Identifies one or more selected fields used to summarize the results.
HAVING	Defines one or more formulas that specify the criteria for the inclusion of a grouped result. HAVING is to a GROUP BY what a WHERE is to a SELECT.
UNION	Used to combine two or more SELECT statements into a single result.
ORDER BY	Identifies one or more selected fields to use to sort the results.
OFFSET	Specifies a starting point within the selected set for the records that will be included in the result.
FETCH FIRST	Specifies the number of records that should be retrieved from the starting point, either the first record or a record specified by OFFSET.
AS	Creates a shorter alias for a table name that can be used elsewhere in the statement as a prefix to identify a field's table, especially when there is more than one table involved, like when using a JOIN clause.

Formatting Requirements

There are a few formatting requirements to keep in mind when writing SELECT statements. These include

- *Command and Object Names* – The names of tables, fields, and statement commands within a query are *not* case sensitive. However, typing SQL commands and operators in upper case helps to visually differentiate them from field and criteria values.

- *Criteria* – Literal criteria, such as that used within a JOIN, WHERE, and HAVING clause, *are* case sensitive and will fail to locate matching values of a different case. Also, all textual criteria *must* be enclosed in single quotations.

- *Name Separators* – When listing multiple tables and fields, always use a comma-space delimiter between them.

- *Quotations* – Table and field names don't need to be enclosed in double quotations *unless they contain spaces*. Table names that begin with non-alphabetic characters must be enclosed in double quotations even when they don't contain spaces. Since the SELECT statement is itself contained in quotations, quotes used within must be escaped with a preceding backslash.

Using the SELECT Statement

Although the SELECT statement is the only one supported by the *ExecuteSQL* function, it is very capable. Before delving into the many different optional clauses, let's explore the basic statement and discuss techniques for using it effectively.

Selecting an Entire Table

The most basic query is one in which *every field* will be selected for *every record*. This can be performed with a simple statement.

```
SELECT * FROM <TableName>
```

The statement must *always* begin with the word SELECT followed by an indication of which fields to select and from which table. In this case, the asterisk informs FileMaker to select *all fields*. The <TableName> placeholder shown in the preceding example is replaced with the name of an actual table occurrence whose base table the function should access. The SELECT statement shown in the following example will fetch every field from the *Contact* table:

```
SELECT * FROM Contact
```

Put this in quotes and use it as the first parameter of an *ExecuteSQL* statement as shown in this example:

```
ExecuteSQL ( "SELECT * FROM Contact" ; "" ; "" )
```

Enter this formula in the *Example Calculation* field of the *Learn FileMaker* database. After confirming that the *Calculation result type* is set to return *text*, save the formula, and the result displayed in Figure 16-1 should appear in the field in Browse mode. Each paragraph of the result is a single record that contains a comma-separated list of every field value, both in creation order.

```
000001,15:30:14,2016-11-04,2016-11-04,3:30:14 PM,Mark Munro,Mark Munro,,James,Butt,,,6649 N Blue Gum St,New Orleans,70116,Orleans,LA
000002,15:30:14,2016-11-04,2016-11-04,3:30:14 PM,Mark Munro,Mark Munro,,Josephine,Darakjy,,,4 B Blue Ridge Blvd,Brighton,48116,Livingston,MI
000003,15:30:14,2016-11-04,2016-11-04,3:30:14 PM,Mark Munro,Mark Munro,,Art,Venere,,,8 W Cerritos Ave #54,Bridgeport,08014,Gloucester,NJ
000004,15:30:14,2016-11-04,2016-11-04,3:30:14 PM,Mark Munro,Mark Munro,,Lenna,Paprocki,,,639 Main St,Anchorage,99501,Anchorage,AK
000005,15:30:14,2016-11-04,2016-11-04,3:30:14 PM,Mark Munro,Mark Munro,,Donette,Foller,,,34 Center St,Hamilton,45011,Butler,OH
000006,15:30:14,2016-11-04,2016-11-04,3:30:14 PM,Mark Munro,Mark Munro,,Simona,Morasca,,,3 Mcauley Dr,Ashland,44805,Ashland,OH
000007,15:30:14,2016-11-04,2016-11-04,3:30:14 PM,Mark Munro,Mark Munro,,Mitsue,Tollner,,7 Eads St,Chicago,60632,Cook,IL
```

Figure 16-1. *An example of the result of a SQL query*

Note   Although the examples in this chapter assume the formula is used in a calculation field, these can be used in any formula.

Selecting Individual Fields

For situations where you don't need *every* field for *every* record in a table, the SELECT statement can specify individual fields.

Specifying a Single Field

To select a *single field* from a *Contact* table, change the asterisk to the name of the field, remembering to enclose it in escaped quotes if it contains spaces. The following formula selects the *Contact Address City* field from every record of the *Contact* table. This will result in a return-delimited list of city names. Notice that the list includes the field value for *every* record, so it will include many duplicates.

```
ExecuteSQL ( "SELECT \"Contact Address City\" FROM Contact" ; "" ; "" )
// result =
    Hamilton
    Ashland
    Chicago
    San Jose
```

```
Sioux Falls
San Jose
Ashland
...etc...
```

Specifying Multiple Fields

To select *multiple fields*, list each in a comma-space separated string:

```
SELECT <Field1>, <Field2>, <Field3> FROM <Table>
```

For example, to select the *Contact Address City* and *Contact Address State* fields from the *Contact* table, use the following formula. The result of this statement will be a comma-delimited list of city and state names.

```
ExecuteSQL (
"SELECT \"Contact Address City\", \"Contact Address State\" FROM Contact" ;
"" ; ""
)
// result =
   Hamilton,OH
   Ashland,OH
   Chicago,IL
   San Jose,CA
   Sioux Falls,SD
   San Jose,CA
   Ashland,OH
   ...etc...
```

Keeping References Dynamic

In the previous examples and others to follow, table and field names are typed directly into the query statement as static text. While fine for examples in a book, when writing queries for live production databases, consider using *dynamic references* so changes to the database structure don't break query containing formulas (Chapter 12, "Keeping Field References Dynamic"). The following example demonstrates the technique:

```
Let ( [
   reference = GetFieldName ( Contact::Contact Name First ) ;
   reference = Substitute ( reference ; "::" ; "¶" ) ;
```

```
    tableName = Quote ( GetValue ( reference ; 1 ) ) ;
    fieldName = Quote ( GetValue ( reference ; 2 ) )
] ;
    ExecuteSQL ("SELECT " & fieldName & " FROM " & tableName ; "" ; "" )
)
```

The *Let* statement in the preceding example converts a field reference into a string and places it into the *reference* variable. The *Substitute* function replaces the two colons with a paragraph return and places that result into the *reference* variable. In the preceding example, *reference* will contain this value:

```
Contact¶Contact Name First
```

Next, the *GetValue* function extracts the first and second paragraph from the *reference* variable and places them into the *tableName* and *fieldName* variables, respectively, while the *Quote* function wraps these in quotations to protect against spaces in the names. From there, those variables are used to construct the SELECT statement which becomes a parameter for *ExecuteSQL*. When structured this way, any changes to the table or field name will automatically be reflected here, and the query will continue to function as expected.

Getting Unique Values with SELECT DISTINCT

To automatically alphabetize results and remove duplicates, use the SELECT DISTINCT command. The following example will generate a list of alphabetically sorted, unique values from the *Contact Address City* field of the *Contact* table:

```
"SELECT DISTINCT \"Contact Address City\" FROM Contact"
```

The uniqueness of the result is based on the *entire record value*, not individual fields within it. For example, when selecting only the city, the results will include only one entry for "San Jose." However, if multiple fields are selected, like a street address and city shown in the following example, the results will include multiple entries for San Jose since the full record now includes other values. For example, "123 First Street,San Jose" is not fully equal to "1837 Fifth Ave,San Jose," so both would be included in the result.

```
"SELECT DISTINCT \"Contact Address Street\", \"Contact Address City\" FROM
Contact"
```

Reformatting SELECT Statements for Clarity

Unlike the preceding examples that are short and easy to read, SELECT statements can quickly grow in complexity and wrap to multiple lines. There are two techniques that can be used to reformat statements and avoid visual clutter: adding extra space and using a *Let* statement.

Adding Extra Space with Tabs and Paragraph Returns

FileMaker will ignore paragraph returns and tabs in the *sqlQuery* text string so these can be used to separate the statement into readable blocks, as shown in the following pattern. A combination of a tab and paragraph return separates each clause of the statement onto its own line, where it is indented to stand out from the enclosing statement. Following this pattern will make the statement easier to read:

```
ExecuteSQL ( "
    SELECT <field>
    FROM <table>
    JOIN <table> ON <formula>
    WHERE <formula>
    ORDER BY <field>
" ; "" ; "" )
```

When multiple fields, find conditions, or other components are used, those can be pushed onto their own line, further indented for additional clarity as shown here in this pattern:

```
ExecuteSQL ( "
    SELECT
        <field1>,
        <field2>,
        <field3>
    FROM <table>
    JOIN <table> ON <formula>
    WHERE
        <condition1> and
        <condition2> and
        <condition3>
```

```
ORDER BY
    <field1>,
    <field2>
" ; "" ; "" )
```

Using a LET Statement

Another method of eliminating the visual confusion of a complex query is the use of a *Let* statement. The entire SELECT query can be built in pieces using separate variables that are finally combined into a single variable and inserted into the *ExecuteSQL* statement, as shown in this example:

```
Let ( [
    sFields = "SELECT <Fields>" ;
    sTable = "FROM <Table> " ;
    sJoin = "JOIN <table> ON <formula> " ;
    sWhere = "WHERE <formula> " ;
    sGroup = "GROUP BY <fields> " ;
    SQL = sFields & sTable & sJoin & sWhere & sGroup
] ;
    ExecuteSQL ( SQL ; "" ; "" )
)
```

Tip   Create a custom function to accept a field reference and other criteria and return the query statement.

Exploring the Benefits of Aliases

An *alias* is a short text string that can act as a proxy for a table name elsewhere in a SELECT statement. When a SELECT statement contains repeated references to more than one table, as in a JOIN clause (discussed later in this chapter), aliases are used to identify the table containing a field. Although an alias can be made up of any number of characters, as a space-saving mechanism shorter is always better. To establish an alias, use the AS clause after the identification of a table, and follow it with a text alias, as shown in the following pattern:

```
SELECT <field> FROM <table> AS <alias>
```

For example, to create an alias c for the *Contact* table, format it like this:

```
SELECT <field> FROM Contact AS c
```

Once the alias c is established, it can be used as a prefix on any field name, in any clause, to identify the table to which a field belongs. While aliases are not required when selecting fields from a single table, the following example demonstrates how aliases work. Notice that the alias is defined at the end of the statement but can be used in previous clauses.

```
SELECT c.Notes FROM Contact AS c
```

When a field with spaces in its name is enclosed in double quotations, the alias prefix should precede the name outside of the quotes.

```
SELECT c.\"Contact First Name\" FROM Contact AS c
```

Although an alias is unnecessary in the following short examples, as a demonstration of the formatting with or without an alias, each of these will generate the exact same result:

```
SELECT Notes FROM Contact
SELECT Contact.Notes FROM Contact
SELECT c.Notes FROM Contact AS c
```

Note   Aliases will be used in more complex examples later in this chapter.

Inserting Literal Text in the Field List

Literal text strings can be inserted before, between, and after field names within the SELECT statement and will be repeated in the results for each record. Literals must be enclosed in single quotation marks and separated by a comma. This example demonstrates a 'Name: ' label inserted into the field results.

```
ExecuteSQL ( "
    SELECT
```

```
        'Name: ',
        \"Contact Name First\",
        \"Contact Name Last\"
    FROM Contact"
; " " ; "" )
// Result
    Name: Cynthia,Johnson
    Name: Karen,Camacho
    Name: Sandy,Robinson
    Name: Thomas,Smithfield
```

Concatenating Results

A query can include instructions for pre-processing separate field values into combined results using *concatenation*, the action of linking things together in a chain or series. Instead of receiving a result of raw comma-delimited set of field names which would require further parsing and manipulating, concatenation provides more useful results. This can be achieved using either the + or || operators, although the latter is both more reliable and less likely to be confused with the same operator used in mathematical calculations. The following example query shows first and last names being concatenated into a single string, with a space inserted between them:

```
ExecuteSQL ( "
    SELECT \"Contact Name First\" || ' ' || \"Contact Name Last\"
    FROM Contact
" ; "" ; "" )
// Result
Cynthia Johnson
Karen Camacho
Sandy Robinson
Thomas Smithfield
```

Alternatively, the plus-sign delimiter would produce the same results.

```
SELECT \"Contact Name First\" + ' ' + \"Contact Name Last\"
```

In the preceding two simple examples, the same result could also have been achieved by placing a space in the *fieldDelimiter* parameter. However, when more fields are selected, concatenation allows different delimiters between different sets of fields where the field delimiter is the same for every field. The following example shows a more realistic example of using both concatenation and a custom delimiter to return a contact's full name and mailing address as a three-paragraph result. The first-last name and city-state-zip are each concatenated, and then a custom field and record delimiter format the results into a list of mailing addresses.

```
ExecuteSQL ( "
    SELECT
        \"Contact Name First\" + ' ' + \"Contact Name Last\",
        \"Contact Address Street\",
        \"Contact Address City\" + ', ' +
        \"Contact Address State\" + ' ' +
        \"Contact Address Zip\"
        FROM Contact" ; "¶" ; "¶¶" )
// Result
    Cynthia Johnson
    123 Main Street
    Youngstown, OH 44504

    Karen Camacho
    42 Memory Lane
    Brooklyn, NY 11111

    Sandy Robinson
    631 Front Street
    Lafayette, IN 47901
```

Using the WHERE Clause

Adding a WHERE clause to a SELECT statement allows the query to target specific records based on search criteria. The <formula> portion can contain one or more expressions that define the criteria used to match records, typically including a field, an operator, and a search value.

```
SELECT <field> FROM <table> WHERE <formula>
```

Creating a WHERE Clause with a Single Expression

To limit the results to contacts from California, a WHERE formula would be composed of the field name (in quotes if required), an equal sign as the operator, and 'CA' in single quotes. The following example demonstrates this by requesting the first and last name of every contact within that state. Remember, when this is inserted into the *ExecuteSQL* function call, the entire statement would be enclosed in quotes, and the quotes around field names would need to be escaped with a backslash.

```
SELECT
    "Contact Name First",
    "Contact Name Last"
FROM Contact
WHERE "Contact Address State" = 'CA'
```

Creating a WHERE Clause with Multiple Expressions

For complex criteria, a WHERE clause can contain multiple search expressions separated by a comparison operator of AND or OR. For example, when searching for contacts living in a city that is common to many states, such as 'Milford,' use two expressions to specify both the city and the state. To do this, use the AND operator between the two expressions, requiring results to match both criteria.

```
WHERE "Contact Address City" = 'Milford' AND "Contact Address State" = 'PA'
```

Similarly, to find contacts from two different states, for example, from Pennsylvania or Ohio, use an OR operator to allow the results to include results from either expression.

```
WHERE "Contact Address State" = 'PA' OR "Contact Address State" = 'OH'
```

Using the ORDER BY Clause

The ORDER BY clause can be added to specify result sorting.

```
SELECT <field> FROM <table> ORDER BY <fields>
```

The following example returns a list of the last name of every contact sorted by state.

```
SELECT "Contact Name Last" FROM Contact ORDER BY "Contact Address State"
```

Combining the ORDER BY with a WHERE clause, the following example will return the last name of every contact living in a city named 'Milford' sorted by state.

```
SELECT "Contact Name Last"
FROM Contact
WHERE "Contact Address City" = 'Milford'
ORDER BY "Contact Address State"
```

Using the JOIN Clause

Adding a JOIN clause creates a temporary relationship between two table occurrences that exist only during the execution of the SQL query. These are used to select fields from two tables and return a blended result. A JOIN allows other clauses like WHERE or ORDER BY to refer to fields from either table or both. For example, *Contact* records can be selected where related *Company* records are located in a specific state and the resulting contact list can be sorted by company name. The JOIN clause contains the name of a table that should be related to the FROM table with a formula expressing the criteria that should be used to form the temporary relationship. The full formula pattern is shown here:

```
SELECT <field> FROM <table1> JOIN <table2> ON <formula>
```

The following example connects *Contact* and *Company* tables to select every contact's first name and their related company's name when the *Contact Company ID* field in *Contacts* (aliased con) equals the *Record ID* field in *Company* (aliased com). It assigns an alias to the tables and uses these as a prefix in the field list and the join clause.

```
SELECT
    con."Contact Name First",
    com."Company Name"
FROM Contact AS con
JOIN Company AS com ON
    con."Contact Company ID" = com."Record ID"
```

Using the GROUP BY Clause

Adding a GROUP BY clause generates an *aggregate value* based on one or more fields. This is a SQL equivalent of a native FileMaker summary field (Chapter 8); both generate a summarization of data based on a sort-grouping field. For example, if a *Contact* table had a field named *State* and another named *Invoices* that contained a total of a customer's invoice amounts, the following code *without* a GROUP BY clause will return a list of each contact record's *State* and *Invoice* amount as shown in the following example:

```
SELECT State, Invoices FROM Contact ORDER BY State
// Result =
  AK,1000
  AK,500
  AK,250
  AZ,500
  AZ,750
  Etc.
```

By using the *Sum* function on the *Invoices* field and adding a GROUP BY clause that specifies the *State* field, the following example would return a summary of invoice amounts, totaled by state. Notice that the ORDER BY clause is removed from this example. It is not required since the GROUP BY clause sorts the records in order to group and summarize the results.

```
SELECT State, Sum ( Invoices ) FROM Contact GROUP BY State
// Result =
  AK,1750
  AZ,1250
  CA,2500
```

Adding a HAVING Clause

Combining a HAVING and GROUP BY clause allows the statement to define which *grouped results* will be included, acting like a WHERE clause but for summarized results. Building on the previous example, the following example uses a HAVING clause to only include results for states where the *summary of Invoices* is greater than a certain dollar amount. Here, the summarized entry for AZ from the previous example has been removed because the summary total of 1250 was under the threshold of 1500 that is specified in the HAVING clause.

```
SELECT State, Sum ( Invoices ) FROM Contact GROUP BY State HAVING Sum (
Invoices ) > 1500
-- Result =
AK,1750
CA,2500
```

Using the UNION Clause

Adding a UNION clause can combine the results of two or more SELECT statements, whether from the same table with the same or different criteria or from different tables, as long as each selects the same number of fields and each field position is the same data type across them all. For example, if the first SELECT statement returns three fields with the data types of *text*, *number*, and *text*, a second SELECT statement must also return three fields with the same data types in the same order. The following is a simplified pattern of adding UNION between two SELECT statements that doesn't show other clauses which can be included in either or both statements.

```
SELECT <fields1> FROM <table1> UNION SELECT <fields2> FROM <table2>
```

By default, this clause automatically excludes duplicate entries from the merged result. Use UNION ALL to include all results, even duplicates.

Limiting the Results of a Query

The OFFSET and FETCH FIRST clauses can be used separately or in unison to control the number of results returned by a query.

Using the OFFSET Clause

The OFFSET clause is used to specify a number of records to exclude from the top of the result. This example will exclude the first 20 records and return results starting from record 21:

```
SELECT "Record ID" FROM Contact OFFSET 20 ROWS
```

Using the FETCH FIRST Clause

The FETCH FIRST clause limits the number of rows returned. This example will return only the first ten results:

```
SELECT "Record ID" FROM Contact FETCH FIRST 10 ROWS ONLY
```

Combining the OFFSET and FETCH FIRST Clauses

A combination of the OFFSET and FETCH FIRST clauses can fetch specific groups of records from the result. This allows subsets of results to be extracted in a sequence of small batches, often referred to as *paging results*, where each query returns one "page" of results at a time. The OFFSET portion indicates where the desired group begins, and the FETCH FIRST portion limits the number of records accessed from that starting point. This code shows several examples of accessing batches of records, ten at a time.

```
SELECT "Record ID" FROM Contact FETCH FIRST 10 ROWS ONLY
SELECT "Record ID" FROM Contact OFFSET 10 ROWS FETCH FIRST 10 ROWS ONLY
SELECT "Record ID" FROM Contact OFFSET 20 ROWS FETCH FIRST 10 ROWS ONLY
SELECT "Record ID" FROM Contact OFFSET 30 ROWS FETCH FIRST 10 ROWS ONLY
SELECT "Record ID" FROM Contact OFFSET 40 ROWS FETCH FIRST 10 ROWS ONLY
```

The first statement returns records 1 through 10, the second records 11 through 20, the third records 21 through 30, and so on. Using this technique, interface elements can allow a user to click back and forth through groups of results one "page" at a time.

Accessing the Database Schema

The *ExecuteSQL* function has the ability to access two system tables which provide meta-information about the database's schema: *FileMaker_Tables* and *FileMaker_Fields*. These tables can be used in a SELECT statement as if they were custom table occurrences to access information about the tables and fields that make up the database structure.

Selecting FileMaker_Tables

The *FileMaker_Tables* table contains one virtual record for every *table occurrence* defined in the relationship graph with the following fields of information:

- *TableName* – The name of the table occurrence

- *TableID* – An identification number for the table occurrence

- *BaseTableName* – The name of the base table for the table occurrence

- *BaseFileName* – The name of the file in which the occurrence's base table exists

- *ModCount* – The number of modifications made to the table structure since its creation

To select all five fields for every table occurrence in the database, use the following query formula in the *ExecuteSQL* function:

```
"SELECT * FROM FileMaker_Tables"
// Result =
    Company,1065101,Company,Learn FileMaker,20
    Company | Contact,1065105,Contact,Learn FileMaker,24
    Contact,1065102,Contact,Learn FileMaker,24
    Contact | Company,1065106,Company,Learn FileMaker,20
    Project,1065103,Project,Learn FileMaker,4
    Project | Company,1065107,Company,Learn FileMaker,20
    Sandbox,1065089,Sandbox,Learn FileMaker,134
```

This example specifies a result of only the *TableName* field:

```
"SELECT TableName FROM FileMaker_Tables"
// Result =
    Company
    Company | Contact
    Contact
    Contact | Company
    Project
    Project | Company
    Sandbox
```

This example limits the results to the actual table names using SELECT DISTINCT and the *BaseTableName*:

```
"SELECT DISTINCT BaseTableName FROM FileMaker_Tables"
//Result =
    Company
    Contact
    Project
    Sandbox
```

Selecting FileMaker_Fields

The *FileMaker_Fields* table contains one virtual record for every *field* defined in the database with the following meta-information available:

- *TableName* – The name of the field's table occurrence

- *FieldName* – The name of the field

- *FieldType* – The SQL data type of the file

- *FieldID* – An identification number for the field

- *FieldClass* – The class of the field: *Normal*, *Summary*, or *Calculated*

- *FieldReps* – The number of maximum repetitions defined

- *ModCount* – The number of modifications made to the field since it was created

This example returns all seven values for every field for every table in the database:

```
"SELECT * FROM FileMaker_Fields"
```

Since this system table contains fields based on *table occurrences*, the results will include duplicates if there is more than one occurrence for a given base table. An iterative process like a *While* function (Chapter 13), a recursive custom function (Chapter 15), or a looping script (Chapter 25, "Iterating with Repeating Statements") can get the name of every base table and then step through these to retrieve the fields for each, thereby avoiding any duplicates. The following example shows a simple *While* statement that demonstrates how to do this:

```
While (
[
   baseTables =
      ExecuteSQL ( "SELECT DISTINCT BaseTableName FROM FileMaker_Tables" ;
      "" ; "" ) ;
   result = ""
] ;
   baseTables ≠ "" ;
[

   current.table = GetValue ( baseTables ; 1 ) ;
   baseTables = RightValues ( baseTables ; ValueCount ( baseTables ) - 1 ) ;
   current.fields =
      ExecuteSQL (
         "SELECT * FROM FileMaker_Fields WHERE TableName='" & current.table
         & "'" ; "" ; ""
      ) ;
   result = result & current.fields
] ;
   result
)
```

Exploring Other SQL Features

FileMaker includes additional SQL functionality beyond the material covered in this chapter. Numerous functions can be embedded into a `SELECT` statement to manipulate the results, many providing functionality like FileMaker's own functions. There are commands available to manipulate dates, times, and strings. Numeric values can be aggregated or used in mathematical computations. Conditional actions can be embedded, and numerous operators can be used with field values and SQL functions to manipulate results. The *Execute SQL* script step allows more robust manipulation of external ODBC/JDBC data sources from external databases. Also, a FileMaker database can be used as an ODBC/JDBC data source and supports SQL queries from external databases. For more information about these topics, visit `www.claris.com` and search for the *FileMaker ODBC and JDBC Guide* or *FileMaker SQL Reference* documents.

Summary

This chapter introduced the basics of using the *ExecuteSQL* function and provided examples of many features of the SELECT statement. In the next chapter, we begin to explore layout design, giving users an interface access into your data structure.

PART IV

Designing User Interfaces

An interface provides an access point for user and script interactions with the data stored in the foundational table structure. It is the most prominent part of a database and arguably one of the most important. These chapters explore the basics of layout design:

Introducing Layouts

A *layout* is a developer-designed graphical template that defines how records, fields, and objects will be rendered to produce an interactive experience. Each database window displays one layout at a time. The layout active at a given moment in time is referred to literally as the *current layout*. When a database opens, this is a default layout selected based on how the database is configured. It may be a selected layout in *File Options* (Chapter 6), one opened by a *Script Trigger* (Chapter 27), or the last layout that was open when the file was closed while running on a local computer. Unlike the convenient predefined layouts in Claris starter solutions, a custom database begins with a single empty layout from which a developer must design an interface. This chapter begins exploring interface design by introducing layout basics, including

- Understanding contextual access
- Anatomizing a layout
- Planning layouts
- Using Layout mode

Understanding Contextual Access

Each layout is assigned a table occurrence and acts as an *interface context* that corresponds to the *relational context* of that assignment. This extends a specific relational perspective from the back-end data to the front-end interface, rendering an intersecting context point where users and scripts can create, delete, edit, find, print, and view records stored in the underlying table. The occurrence assignment determines which records and fields are accessible when the layout is current. Any field that is local to a layout's occurrence or is in an occurrence related to that occurrence can be placed on the layout, viewed by the user, and used in calculations embedded into layout objects, scripts, and menus.

© Mark Conway Munro 2021
M. C. Munro, *Learn FileMaker Pro 19*, https://doi.org/10.1007/978-1-4842-6680-9_17

The illustration in Figure 17-1 shows a user viewing a *Contacts – Entry* layout that displays records from the *Contacts* table through the context of the primary *Contacts* table occurrence. Any field from the *Contacts* table placed on that layout will render the value stored for the current record being viewed. Additionally, fields from the *Company* table can be placed on the layout by way of the *Contacts | Company* occurrence. This will automatically pull record(s) based on the relationship criteria between the two occurrences and only display matching records (Chapter 9). The *Contact – List* layout is assigned the same occurrence, so it displays records from the same relational context. Switching between these two contact layouts within the same window will retain the current record and current found set. By contrast, the *Company – List* layout shows records from the *Company* table through the primary *Company* occurrence but can't include fields from *Contacts* since those two occurrences aren't currently related.

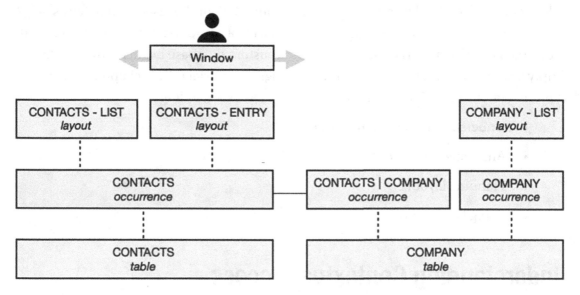

Figure 17-1. *An illustration of how tables, occurrences, layouts, and windows interconnect to present an interface*

Anatomizing a Layout

A *layout* is a configurable space that contains a stack of one or more horizontal regions that create a single screen or page. As discussed in forthcoming chapters, these *layout parts* come in a variety of types, each with inherent and configurable properties that determine their rendered appearance and behavior. Parts can be added, rearranged, and configured in various combinations depending on the functional needs of the layout. Fields and other objects placed onto parts have their own inherent and configurable properties. Together these elements define a layout. When rendered in Browse mode, a layout can be viewed in different ways when a user or script chooses from the developer-enabled *content views* or changes the window mode (Chapter 3). The illustration in Figure 17-2 shows the general anatomy using the example of a simple layout and the variety of viewing options that control how it is rendered for the user.

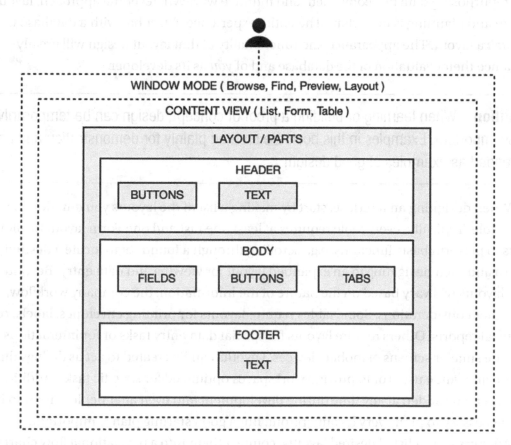

Figure 17-2. *An illustration of the anatomy of a layout*

Planning Layouts

Layouts will vary in complexity based on their purpose, the needs of a given workflow, budgetary restrictions, and the skills of the developer-designer. A quickly constructed spreadsheet-like table view can provide the ad hoc simplicity that adequately serves a specific need. In a modern workplace, populated with sophisticated professional users, a more elaborate design is usually more appropriate and may even be expected. Poorly designed layouts become a cluttered, confusing, visual nightmare that frustrates a user's ability to work. Such "solutions" tend to cause more problems than they solve. A well-designed layout can range from a modest but practical design up through an artistically expressed, robustly featured, efficiently visualized, graphical masterpiece that anticipates a user's needs and extends powerful, time-saving tools for manipulating and repurposing data in a convenient and intuitive way. Whatever the approach, layout design and planning is important. The entire experience a user has with a database is *through* a layout. The appearance and functionality of that layout design will greatly influence their evaluation of the database and of *you* as its developer.

Caution   When learning or building a proof of concept, design can be temporarily less important. Examples in this book are created plainly for demonstration and not intended as examples of good design!

When designing an interface, start by making a list of the layouts you envision for each table. Typically, every table requires at least one List and one Form layout to allow users to perform basic functions, e.g., scrolling through a found set to locate a desired record and then navigating to an expanded layout for viewing and data entry. Beyond that, layouts will vary based on the nature of the information, the company workflow, and other considerations. Some tables require layouts for printing envelopes, labels, or financial reports. Others require layouts for special data entry tasks or for interactions with the smaller screens of mobile devices. Layouts can be created to act as dialogs that inform and guide users or to provide workspaces optimized for specific tasks. Additional layouts can be added at any time during development and even after deployment, so it isn't necessary to plan every layout upfront. But a good starting plan is important.

After creating a list of desired layouts, connect them into a navigational flow chart to help visualize how the user will move around the interface. Even a rough sketch can be helpful, like the one shown in Figure 17-3. The diagram shows a rough representation of the *Learn FileMaker* database with an added menu layout and various placeholders for hypothetical future layouts. Remember, the navigational arrows are illustrating a general interface connection between layouts. In the actual interface, navigation functions may be much more complex depending on the number of tables, the relationships between them, the style of the navigational controls you develop, and other factors. For now, the diagram simply gives you a "big picture" overview of the flow. Once you have at least a rough plan prepared, enter Layout mode and begin exploring the environment used to design interfaces.

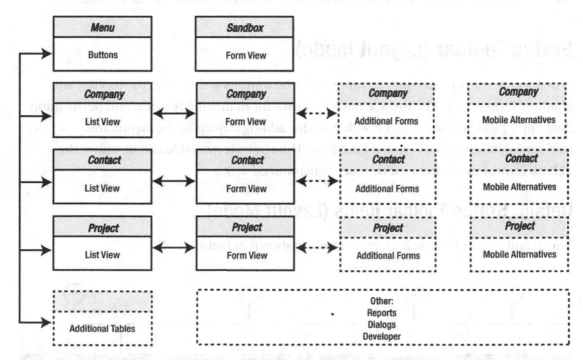

Figure 17-3. *A rough sketch of a simple layout flow with expansion placeholders*

Layout names can take whatever form you want. Ideally, they include the name of the table they represent and something to describe their general function. Although FileMaker allows layouts with the same name, keep the names unique to avoid confusion. The *Learn FileMaker* demo files use the name of the primary table for the main Form layout and the same plus a descriptor for other layouts, e.g., *Invoice, Invoice List,* and *Invoice Report*.

Using Layout Mode

Layout mode is an alternate window state in which the whole application environment is transformed to accommodate layout design work. In this mode, the toolbar buttons and menu items change to provide control over interface-related functions. Each side of the window has optional layout panes that provide access to fields, objects, add-ons, and configuration settings (Chapter 19). The entire content area becomes an editable workspace where you can add, configure, and style objects to control how things will be rendered in other modes (Chapters 20 and 21). Layout mode can be initiated selecting the *View* ➤ *Layout Mode* menu or clicking the *Edit Layout* button in the toolbar.

Status Toolbar (Layout Mode)

When a window is placed into Layout mode, the options available in the toolbar will change dramatically. The Browse mode controls for managing records, and performing data entry tasks will be replaced with tools for adding objects to the layout and performing other design-related functions. The controls available will be either the default Layout mode items or the user's customized set.

Default Status Toolbar Items (Layout Mode)

The default status toolbar for Layout mode is shown in Figure 17-4.

Figure 17-4. *The status toolbar for Layout mode*

1. Navigation controls

2. New Layout/Report button

3. Layout tools

4. Developer menu and pane toggling

5. Layout menu

6. Layout Settings button

7. Theme Selection

8. Screen and Device Dimension menu

9. Formatting Bar button

10. Exit Layout button

Navigation Controls

At the top left of the toolbar are navigation controls that appear and function similar to Browse mode (Chapter 3) except they refer to and control *layouts* rather than *records*. The total refers to the total number of layouts that exist in the current file, and the number in the text box indicates which layout is being viewed.

Caution   Although included here, recent versions of FileMaker *exclude* navigation controls from the default Layout mode toolbar. Customize the toolbar to add these essential tools.

New Layout/Report Button

The only function button present in the default toolbar is *New Layout/Report* which starts the process of creating a new layout (Chapter 18). Other function buttons, such as *Delete Layout* and *Duplicate Layout*, can be added by customizing the toolbar.

Layout Tools

The central row of icons are layout object tools, which are defined in Table 17-1. Most are *object-creation tools* that are used to insert a new instance of an object (Chapter 20). The majority of those are *draw-mode activation tools* that, once selected, allow object creation by clicking and dragging within the layout creation area. Each of these is a transitory selection which deactivates and reverts to the selection tool after an object is created. Double-click one of these to lock it and allow rapid creation of multiple objects of the same type one after another without having to reselect the tool. The tool will then remain active until another tool is selected. Many tools have dual modes: click to create a default object type or click-hold to reveal a menu of similar object types. Two of the object-creation tools are *drag-insertion tools* which are click-dragged from the toolbar onto the content area to initiate the creation of a field or layout part. Finally, two tools are *object manipulation tools* which are used to select an object or apply formatting.

Table 17-1. *Each layout tool defined*

Icon	Tool Description
▲	*Selection tool* – Select objects on the layout to move or configure them.
T	*Text tool* – Add or edit text on a layout or in object types like buttons, tabs, etc.
╲	*Line tool* – Draw a line on a layout. Hold the Shift key to lock for a straight horizontally or vertically line. Hold Option to lock to a 45-degree angle.
▣	*Shape menu* – Click to select the *Rectangle* shape tool or click-hold to choose from a menu of *Rectangle*, *Rounded Rectangle,* or *Oval*. Hold the Shift or Option key to maintain a uniform height and width while dragging its boundaries.
▭	*Field menu* – Click to select an *Edit box* mode or click-hold to choose a specific control style. Drag in the content area to create a field object and select a field assignment. Once created, the control style can be modified (Chapter 20, "Configuring Field Control Style").
▭	*Button menu* – Click to select the Button tool or click-hold to choose from a menu of *Button* or *Popover Button.*
▦	*Button Bar tool* – Draw a segmented bar that can contain multiple *Buttons* and/or *Popover Buttons.*
▭	*Multi-panel Object menu* – Click to select the *Tab Control* tool or click-hold to choose from a menu of *Tab Control* or *Slide Control*.
▤	*Portal tool* – Draw a portal, for viewing a list of records from a related table.
▮	*Chart tool* – Draw a graphical chart object.
▣	*Web Viewer tool* – Draw a web viewer object.
▨	*Field tool* – Drag a new field down onto a layout.
▨	*Part tool* – Drag a new layout part onto a layout (Chapter 18).
✐	*Format Painter tool* – Select to copy and apply format settings from one object to another.

Developer Menu and Pane Toggling

The *Manage Database* icon reveals a shortcut menu of developer options that are also accessible through the *File* ➤ *Manage* menu (Chapter 2). The two *Show/Hide Panes* buttons toggle a pane on each side of the window in Layout mode (Chapter 19).

Layout Menu

The lower, non-customizable level of the Layout mode toolbar starts with the *Layout* menu. Similar to the same menu in Browse mode (Chapter 3), this menu always lists *every layout* in the file and adds access to the *Manage Layouts* dialog (Chapter 18). It is used to quickly switch to edit another layout the same as selecting a layout from the *View ➤ Go To Layout* submenu.

Layout Settings Button

Next to the *Layout* menu, a button opens the Layout Settings dialog where options and behaviors can be set for the current layout (Chapter 18, "Configuring Layout Settings").

Theme Selection

The *Theme Selector* displays the name of the theme assigned to the layout with a button that will open a theme selection dialog. A *layout theme* is a collection of stylistic settings that, once assigned to the layout, can be quickly applied to objects and allows changes to be synchronized across the entire database (Chapter 22).

Screen and Device Dimension Menu

The *Screen and Device Dimension* menu allows a choice of dimensional guide overlays that show an orange border in the layout design area visually denoting the boundaries of specific screen sizes. Click the box portion of the icon to toggle the visibility of all the overlay boxes for selected dimensions.

Formatting Bar Button

The *Formatting Bar* button will toggle the visibility of a text-formatting control bar between the status toolbar and the design area of the window (Chapter 3, "Formatting Bar").

Exit Layout Button

The *Exit Layout* button will switch the window back to Browse mode with an optional dialog asking if you want to save changes depending on preference settings (Chapter 2, "Layout Settings").

Customizing the Status Toolbar (Layout Mode)

The toolbar in Layout mode is customizable at the user-computer level exactly as it is in Browse mode (Chapter 3, "Customizing the Status Toolbar") except that the buttons available are layout specific. To begin customizing, enter Layout mode and then select the *View* ➤ *Customize Toolbar* menu to open the customization panel attached to the window as shown in Figure 17-5. Once open, items can be added, removed, or rearranged in the same manner as in Browse mode.

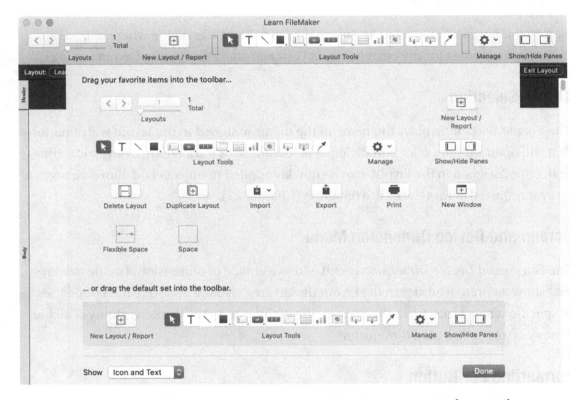

Figure 17-5.   *The toolbar customization panel for Layout mode (macOS)*

Menu Changes (Layout Mode)

The menus in Layout mode are similar to Browse mode but with a few notable changes. In addition to the *Records* menu being completely removed, the *Edit, View, Insert,* and *Format* menus are changed, and *Layouts* and *Arrange* menus are added.

Edit Menu

The *Edit* menu options change in Layout mode, as shown in Figure 17-6.

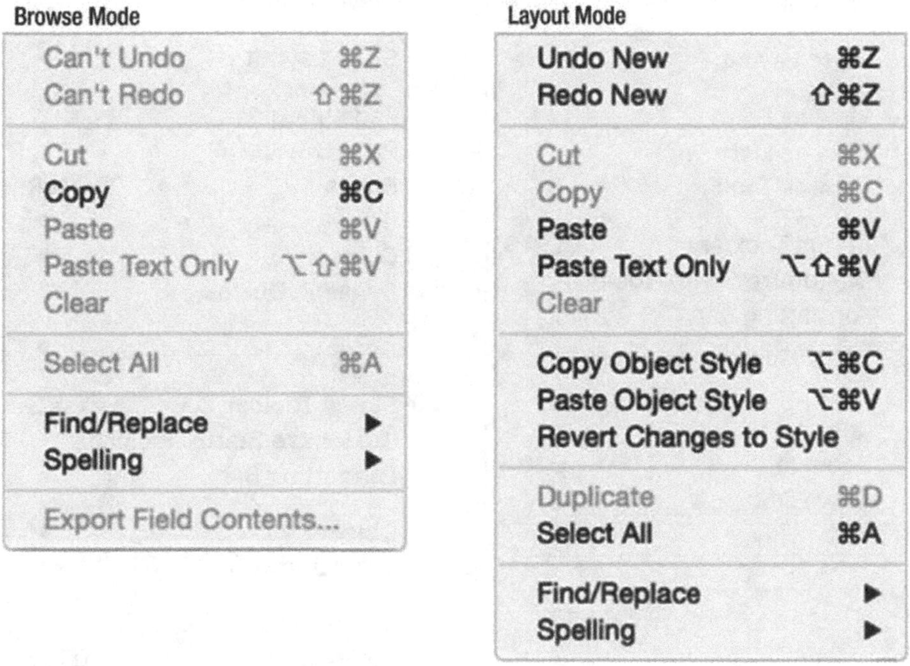

Browse Mode

Can't Undo	⌘Z
Can't Redo	⇧⌘Z
Cut	⌘X
Copy	**⌘C**
Paste	⌘V
Paste Text Only	⌥⇧⌘V
Clear	
Select All	⌘A
Find/Replace	▶
Spelling	▶
Export Field Contents...	

Layout Mode

Undo New	**⌘Z**
Redo New	**⇧⌘Z**
Cut	⌘X
Copy	⌘C
Paste	**⌘V**
Paste Text Only	**⌥⇧⌘V**
Clear	
Copy Object Style	**⌥⌘C**
Paste Object Style	**⌥⌘V**
Revert Changes to Style	
Duplicate	⌘D
Select All	**⌘A**
Find/Replace	▶
Spelling	▶

Figure 17-6. *The Edit menu in Browse mode (left) and Layout mode (right)*

- *Copy Object Style* – Copies style information of a selected object.

- *Paste Object Style* – Applies previously copied style information to the selected object.

- *Revert Changes to Style* – Reverts any formatting changes applied to the selected object back to the style assigned (Chapter 22).

- *Duplicate* – Duplicates the selected layout object(s).

- *Export Field Contents* – This function is removed in Layout mode.

View Menu

The *View* menu options change in Layout mode, as shown in Figure 17-7.

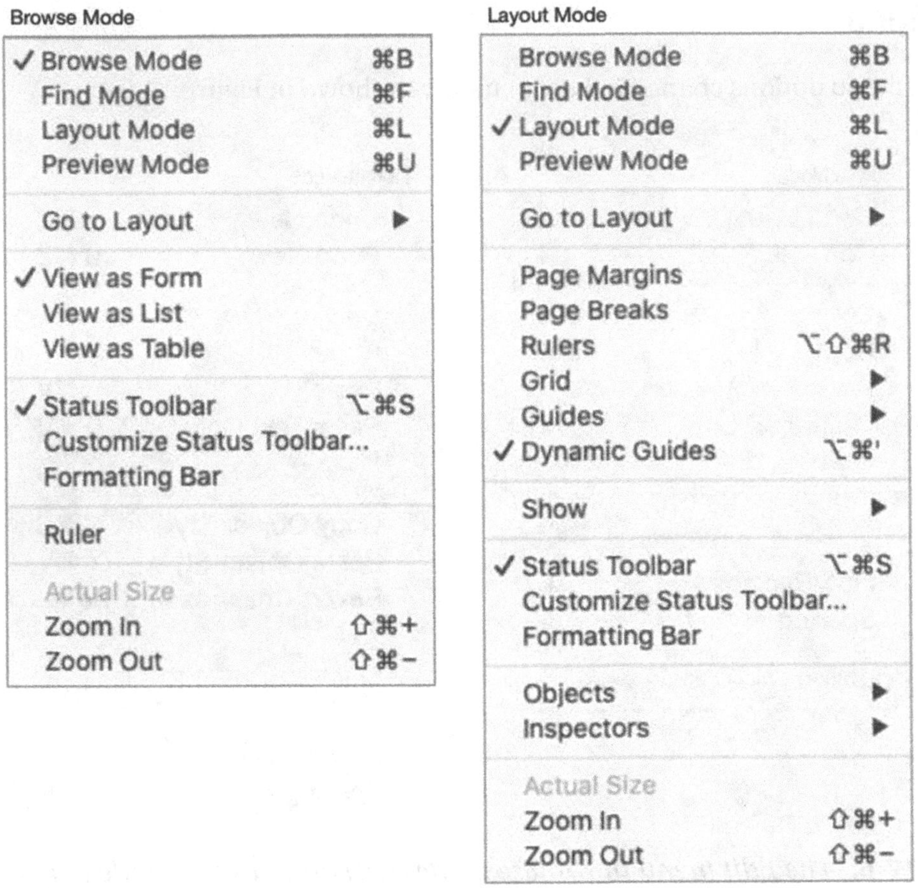

Browse Mode		Layout Mode	
✓ Browse Mode	⌘B	Browse Mode	⌘B
Find Mode	⌘F	Find Mode	⌘F
Layout Mode	⌘L	✓ Layout Mode	⌘L
Preview Mode	⌘U	Preview Mode	⌘U
Go to Layout	▶	Go to Layout	▶
✓ View as Form		Page Margins	
View as List		Page Breaks	
View as Table		Rulers	⌥⇧⌘R
		Grid	▶
✓ Status Toolbar	⌥⌘S	Guides	▶
Customize Status Toolbar...		✓ Dynamic Guides	⌥⌘'
Formatting Bar		Show	▶
Ruler		✓ Status Toolbar	⌥⌘S
Actual Size		Customize Status Toolbar...	
Zoom In	⇧⌘+	Formatting Bar	
Zoom Out	⇧⌘−	Objects	▶
		Inspectors	▶
		Actual Size	
		Zoom In	⇧⌘+
		Zoom Out	⇧⌘−

Figure 17-7. *The View menu in Browse mode (left) and Layout mode (right)*

- *Go to Layout* – Like the *Layout* menu in the toolbar, this submenu displays *all* layouts in Layout mode.

- *View as* – These three Browse mode functions are removed.

- *Rulers* – The menu, pluralized in Layout mode, toggles the visibility of both horizontal *and* vertical rulers.

- *Page Margins* – Select to activate page border guides superimposed on the layout background based on the current print settings.

- *Page Breaks* – Select to activate page breaks superimposed on the layout background.

- *Grid* – A submenu of two choices: *Show Grid* toggles the visibility of a grid of major and minor lines, reminiscent of graph paper superimposed on the background, and *Snap to Grid* toggles the magnetic attraction of objects to the grid.

- *Guides* – A submenu of two choices: *Show Guides* toggles the visibility of manually placed blue guide lines, and *Snap to Guides* toggles the magnetic attraction of objects to those.

- *Dynamic Guides* – Select to activate automatic guides that appear around and between an object when it is dragged around a layout.

Note   See further discussion of rulers, grids, guides, and dynamic guides in Chapter 21, "Layout Positioning Helpers."

- *Show* – A submenu listing special iconography and display options in Layout mode, including

  - Show *Sample Data* in place of field names.

  - Show *Text Boundaries* and *Field Boundaries* will make an object's dimension visible regardless of styling.

  - The remaining options toggle the visibility of a small icon called an *object badge* superimposed over objects indicating key features, each defined in Table 17-2.

- *Objects* – A submenu with an option to open an Objects pane tab: *Fields*, *Objects*, and *Add-ons*.

- *Inspectors* – A submenu with options to toggle the visibility of the Inspector pane and to create new floating Inspector windows.

Note   See further discussion of *objects* and *inspector panes* in Chapter 19.

Table 17-2. *A list of layout object badges*

Icon	Description
▭	The object is formatted as a button.
◆	The object has conditional formatting features applied.
🖨	The object will not be visible when printing.
▱	The object has placeholder text applied.
◁▭	The object is a popover button.
◉	The object has a Hide formula (Chapter 21).
🔍	The object is searchable with Quick Find (Chapter 4, "Searching with Quick Find").
🔍	The object is searchable with Quick Find but will be slower due to lack of indexing or other considerations.
✐	The object or layout responds to script triggers.
←	The object will slide left when printing.
↑	The object will slide up when printing.
T	The object has a tooltip text assignment.

Insert Menu

The *Insert* menu opens change radically in Layout mode, as shown in Figure 17-8.

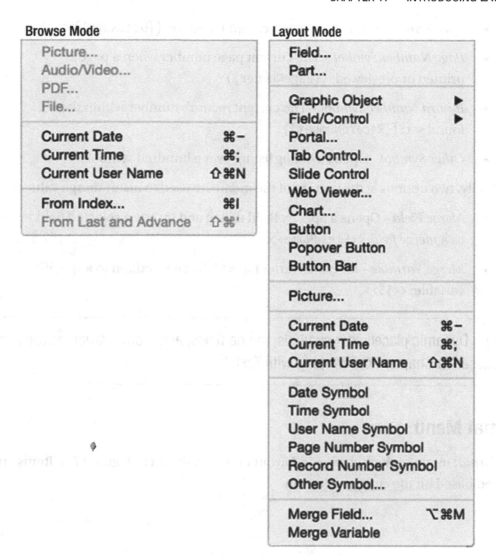

Figure 17-8. *The Insert menu in Browse mode (left) and Layout mode (right)*

The first two sections mirror the tools of the Layout mode toolbar, providing an alternate method of inserting any type of layout objects. In the middle are functions for inserting a *Picture* or placing static text of the *Current Date, Current Time,* and *Current Username*. Below these are functions used to insert *dynamic placeholder symbols,* specially formatted text that is automatically replaced with current values at the time a layout is rendered in non-layout modes. These symbols include

- *Date Symbol* – The current date; {{CurrentDate}}

- *Time Symbol* – The current time; {{CurrentTime}}

- *User Name Symbol* – The user's computer name; {{UserName}}

- *Page Number Symbol* – The current page number when a page is printed or previewed; {{PageNumber}}

- *Record Number Symbol* – The current record's number within the found set; {{RecordNumber}}

- *Other Symbol* – Opens a dialog listing over a hundred symbols

Finally, two options at the bottom of the menu are used to insert merge values:

- *Merge Field* – Opens a Specify Field dialog and inserts a selected field as a *merge field*; <<FieldName>>

- *Merge Variable* – Inserts a starter tag which can be edited to a specific variable; <<$$>>

Note   Dynamic placeholder symbols, merge fields, and merge variables are also discussed in Chapter 20, "Working with Text."

Format Menu

The *Format* menu options change in Layout mode, as shown in Figure 17-9. Items are enabled based on the current selection.

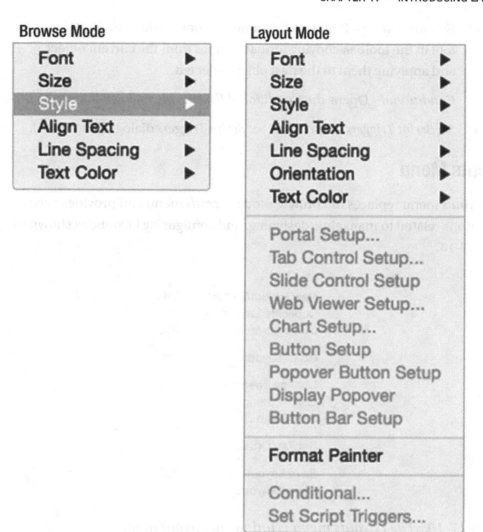

Figure 17-9. *The Format menu in Browse mode (left) and Layout mode (right)*

- *Orientation* – A submenu with two options: *Horizontal* is the default and *Sideways (Asian text only)*.

- *Setup Options* – This section of the menu contains a list of *Setup* menu items that are enabled based on the current object. Selecting one of these will open the corresponding setup dialog as if double-clicking on the object (Chapter 20).

- *Format Painter* – Performs the same function as the *Format Painter* tool in the toolbar, copying format settings from the current object and applying them to the next object selected.

- *Conditional* – Opens the *Conditional Formatting* dialog (Chapter 21).

- *Set Script Triggers* – Opens the *Set Script Triggers* dialog (Chapter 27).

Layouts Menu

The *Layouts* menu replaces the Browse mode *Records* menu and provides access to functions related to managing, designing, and configuring layouts, as shown in Figure 17-10.

Figure 17-10. *The Layouts menu is unique to Layout mode*

Note   See further discussion of managing layouts in Chapter 18.

The following functions are available in this menu:

- *New Layout/Report* – Starts the process of creating a new layout

- *Duplicate Layout* – Duplicates the current layout

- *Delete Layout* – Deletes the current layout after a warning

- *Go To Layout* – A submenu of options to go to another layout: *Next, Previous,* or by number

- *Change Theme* – Opens the Change Theme dialog to assign a different theme to the layout (Chapter 22)

- *Layout Setup* – Opens the Layout Setup dialog (Chapter 18)

- *Part Setup* – Opens the Part Setup dialog (Chapter 18)

- *Set Tab Order* – Opens a dialog to configure the Browse mode tabbing order (Chapter 21)

- *Save Layout* – Saves any unsaved changes while remaining in Layout mode

- *Revert Layout* – Discards any unsaved changes and reverts the layout to its previously saved state while remaining in Layout mode

Arrange Menu

The *Arrange* menu is unique to Layout mode and provides access to object arrangement functions, as shown in Figure 17-11. This includes functions grouping, locking, stacking order, rotation, alignment, distributions, and resizing and is described in Chapter 21.

Figure 17-11. *The Arrange menu items*

Summary

This chapter introduced Layout mode and identified changes to the window, toolbar, and menu. In the next chapter, we define layout parts and get started creating layouts.

Getting Started with Layouts

Continuing the introduction of layout basics, this chapter covers the following topics:

- Working with layout parts
- Adding layouts
- Deleting layouts
- Using the manage layouts dialog
- Optimizing layout performance

Working with Layout Parts

A *layout part* is a horizontal slice of the layout design area that contains objects which together are rendered into an interface. Every layout must have at least *one* part but can be made up of several parts as necessary for your design. There are several part types available, and these influence how components contained within will appear and behave. Depending on how a layout is created and the options selected during the process, each new layout usually has at least three default parts: *Header*, *Body*, and *Footer*.

Defining Layout Regions and Controls

There are several important regions and controls in layout mode, highlighted in Figure 18-1.

© Mark Conway Munro 2021
M. C. Munro, *Learn FileMaker Pro 19*, https://doi.org/10.1007/978-1-4842-6680-9_18

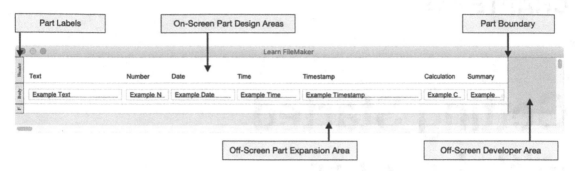

Figure 18-1. *A typical layout highlighting various regions and controls*

A *part label* is a small box attached to the left side of each part. These contain the part type name and are multipurpose buttons providing access to three functions. To open a configuration dialog, double-click on a part label. A single click while holding the Command (macOS) or Windows (Windows) key will toggle the label to a vertical or horizontal orientation. When horizontal, dragging a label will resize the part with more ease than clicking on the line between parts, although sometimes the Part Label can get in the way of layout objects. When horizontal, the opposite is true, as shown in Figure 18-1. A right-click on the label opens a contextual menu with options to open the part configuration dialog, choose a fill color for the part, or apply a style to the part (Chapter 22).

The *on-screen part design areas* are delimited horizontal slices of the layout space that runs from the left side of the window to the part boundary. This *stack* of parts makes up the layout design area and represents what will become the content area of the window when rendered non-Layout modes. New parts can be inserted below or between existing parts, expanding the part stack further down into the *off-screen part expansion* area below. Unused parts can be deleted from the layout as long as one remains.

The *part boundary* represents a vertical line that separates the visible *part stack* on its left from the *off-screen developer area* on its right. When viewed in other modes, everything on the left of this boundary will be rendered as the content area, while everything to the right will remain hidden off-screen. The off-screen area on the right can be used to store developer notes and other layout elements that are not accessible to users.

Tip   Fields configured for Quick Find (Chapter 4) placed in the off-screen area will still produce results.

Resizing a Part Area

Parts can be resized vertically and horizontally to any dimension that does not exceed the maximum limit of 32,000 x 32,000 points. To *vertically resize* a part, position the cursor at the line below the part area until the cursor changes into a short horizontal black line with two arrows on either size, pointing up and down. Then click and drag the cursor up or down to contract or expand the height of the part above the line. When the part labels are viewed horizontally, you can grab the label and drag to resize the part. To *horizontally resize* the entire part stack, position the cursor anywhere at the part boundary line until it changes into a short vertical black line with two arrows, pointing left and right. Then click and drag the cursor left or right to contract or expand the width of the part stack as needed. Alternatively, select a part label and adjust the width and height values in the *Position* settings of the *Inspector pane* (Chapter 19).

Defining Part Types

There are ten different part types available, each with specific inherent properties. These can be divided into two categories: *standard parts* and *summary parts*.

Defining Standard Parts

A *standard part* displays objects without any summarization function. Each layout is limited to a *single* instance of each standard part, and they *must* fall within an automatically enforced stacking order. There are seven different standard part types (in order):

- *Top Navigation* – Intended for on-screen navigation buttons and other controls. This will not print, and it will not zoom in or out when the window view settings are changed.

- *Title Header* – Appears at the top when printing, replacing a *Header* on the first page. This is not displayed in Browse mode.

- *Header* – Appears at the top, except when printing the first page if a *Title Header* is present.

- *Body* – Represents a single instance of a record. In List view, this part and every object placed within it will be repeated once for every

record in the found set. In Form view, it renders once for the current
record only.

- *Footer* – Appears at the bottom, except when printing the last page if a
  Title Footer is present.

- *Title Footer* – Appears at the bottom of the first page when printing,
  replacing a *Footer*. This is not displayed in Browse mode.

- *Bottom Navigation* – Intended for on-screen navigation buttons and
  other controls. This will not print.

Defining Summary Parts

A *summary part* is used to insert summarization values for groups of records and is
especially useful when creating report layouts. A summary field placed in a summary
part will display a value based on a group of records specified by the part type and its
settings. There are two types of summary parts, each with a *leading* and *trailing* variety
indicating a position relative to the *Body*. These are

- *Grand Summary* – A summary field here will display a summarized
  value for *all records in the found set*. It can be placed at the beginning
  (*Leading Grand Summary*) or end (*Trailing Grand Summary*) of a
  layout.

- *Sub-summary When Sorted by* – A summary field placed here will
  display summarized values for *one sorted sub-grouping of records*
  within the found set. It is used to calculate *subtotals* based on a
  specified break field and separates records into sorted groups. One
  or more sub-summary parts can be placed both above and below the
  Body, and they will only appear if records are sorted by the specified
  break field. A single sub-summary part will be repeated once for
  every group of records that result from the break field sort.

Managing Parts

In Layout mode, parts can be added, deleted, and reordered to create a custom layout.

Adding a Part Using the Toolbar Button

The *Part* tool, shown in Figure 18-2, can be click-dragged down into the layout area to add to the part stack. The cursor will turn into a clenched fist dragging a black horizontal line. Move this line into a position above or below an existing part that approximates the location within the stack to insert the new part and then release. The *Part Definition* dialog will open and allow the selection and configuration of a new part. Once finished and the dialog is closed, you can resize the part and begin adding objects.

Figure 18-2.   *The tool used to drag a new part into the layout part stack*

Tip   Dragging a new part this way is imprecise and changes the size of an existing part. To avoid this, use the *Part Setup* dialog described later in this chapter.

Configuring a Part

Parts are defined using the *Part Definition* dialog, shown in Figure 18-3. When a new part is created, this dialog automatically opens. Open it for an existing part by double-clicking a part label, selecting the *Layout* ➤ *Part Setup* menu, or choosing *Part Definition* from the part label's contextual menu.

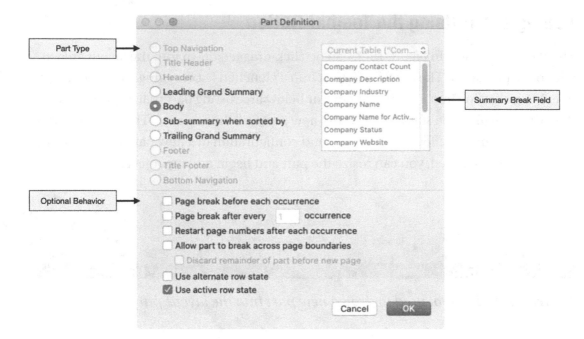

Figure 18-3. *The dialog used to define a layout part*

The *Part Type* options are automatically enabled or disabled based on the location within the stack of the part being defined. For example, a *Body* part can't change into a *Header* if there is already one defined, nor can you change it to a *Title Header* if it is in a stack below an existing *Header*.

The *Summary Break Field* on the right becomes enabled when defining a *Sub-summary* part. The field selection here indicates that the sub-summary part should be visible as a break between groups of records when those records are sorted by that field. These are often used to insert subtotals in financial reports. See the example for report layouts later in this chapter for more information about how sub-summaries work.

The first four option checkboxes control how the part will be handled when printing or viewing in Preview mode. Select *Page break before each occurrence* to automatically insert a page break before a *Trailing Grand Summary, Body,* or *Sub-summary* parts. The *Page break after every X occurrence* will insert a page break after the part has been displayed a specified number of times, limiting the number of times a *Body* or a *Sub-summary* part can be repeated on a single page. Use *Restart page numbers after each occurrence* to reset the page numbering after each instance of the part. Use this with a *Title Header* to create a title page that is not included in the numbering sequence or with a *Sub-summary* to restart numbering after each section. Finally, the *Allow part to break across page boundaries* allows a part to be split by a page boundary. Without this option selected, a part will not split between pages unless its contents won't fit on a single page. Instead, a blank space is left at the bottom of the current page, and the part begins on the next page. Enable this option to override this default behavior, and split at a page break to eliminate empty space. The adjacent *Discard remainder of part before new page* checkbox will truncate any remaining content for the part instead of displaying it on the next page, thereby clipping the content at the page break.

The two options at the bottom control the visual appearance of the part. The *Use alternate row state* checkbox enables the *Body* to be alternatively styled to visually delineate records. Enable *Use active row state* to have the *Body* visually indicate the current record (on-screen only) with special styling.

Tip   The appearance of the alternate and active row states can be edited by selecting these in the *Object State* menu of the *Inspector* pane (Chapter 22).

Deleting a Part

To delete a part and all the objects it contains, select the part label and type Delete.

Using the Part Setup Dialog

Parts can be managed with greater precision using the *Part Setup* dialog, shown in Figure 18-4. To open this dialog, select *Part Setup* from the *Layouts* menu or from the contextual menu available by right-clicking anywhere on the layout. The list displays every part defined on the current layout and is the *only* place where summary parts can be reordered above and below the body. To add a part, click the *Create* button. This inserts the part in the list and on the layout without resizing other parts as occurs when dragging a new part from the toolbar. To edit a part, select it and click the *Change* button to open the *Part Definition* dialog. Use the *Delete* button to delete the selected part. There is no cancel or undo option available in this dialog, so, if a mistake is made, click the Done button, and then select the *Edit* ➤ *Undo* menu to immediately reverse any changes made.

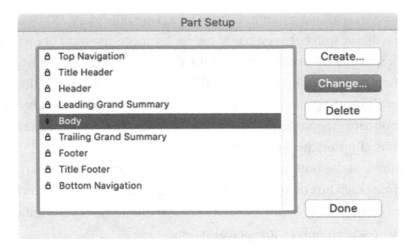

Figure 18-4. *The dialog allows more precise control over the part stack*

Adding Layouts

There are two ways to add layouts to a database file: creating a new layout and duplicating an existing layout.

Creating a New Layout

To create a new layout, select the *New Layout/Report* function from the *Layout* menu, or click the toolbar icon of the same name. This opens the dialog, shown in Figure 18-5, which will step through additional screens based on the selected target device type and function selected. The layout configuration can be modified afterward, and some find it easier to choose *Computer* and click *Finish* to bypass the rest of this setup assistant and then manually finish configuring. However, especially for initial configuration of complex report layouts, this dialog can be an enormous time saver, especially for new developers.

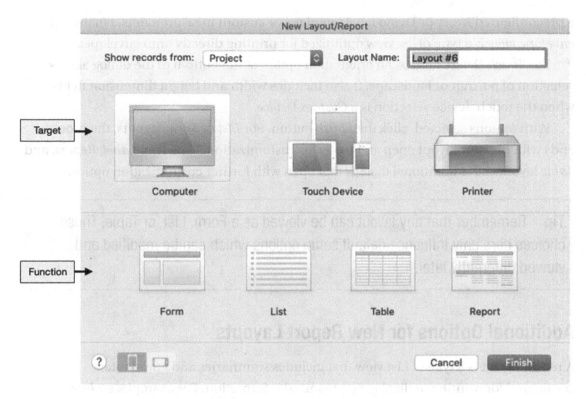

Figure 18-5. *The dialog used to create a new layout*

To begin, choose a table occurrence from the *Show records from* menu at the top, and enter a *Layout name* for the new layout. Select a target device type by clicking on one of three icons: *Computer, Touch Device,* or *Printer*. The *Touch Device* icon opens a pop-up menu with three choices: *iPad, iPhone,* and *Custom Device*. While any layout can be used on a combination of devices, these choices help determine default size and configuration options for the new layout to save a little time later.

Next, select a primary function to further control default settings. These choices vary depending on the target device selection. A *form layout* is generally used to view a single record for data entry tasks or entering find criteria. They can also be used for creating custom dialogs or print layouts. A *list view* is used to display a list of multiple records in a found set. A *table view* is a low-design list view that displays records and fields in a format resembling a spreadsheet. A *report view* is a type of list view that is optimized for either viewing or printing summarized lists of data using sub-summaries and a grand summary. A *label view* is a type of list view that is optimized for printing directly onto labels. These can be created *vertically* or *horizontally* and can be sized based on a preconfigured Avery or Dymo label template, or custom measurements. Finally, an *envelope view* is a type of list view optimized for printing directly onto envelopes.

For *Touch Device* targets, an orientation option at the bottom of the dialog allows selection of portrait or landscape. It also includes width and height dimension fields when the touch device selection is a *Custom Device*.

With options selected, click the *Finish* button. For *List* or *Form* layouts, the process ends with the new layout open and ready for customization. However, *Label, Report,* and *Table* layouts have additional dialogs that open with further customization options.

Tip   Remember that any layout can be viewed as a Form, List, or Table. These choices here only influence default setup options which can be modified and viewed differently later.

Additional Options for New Report Layouts

A report layout is a type of List view that includes summaries and grand totals, configured for printing or displaying organized information. For example, an *Invoice* report can present records sorted by year and month to summarize data into subtotaled groups as illustrated in Figure 18-6. Creating a report layout with the *New Layout/Report* dialog involves a sequence of up to *eight* separate dialogs that step through options to preconfigure parts, content, summarization, sorting, and more. Although a report layout can be created manually starting from a plain List view, these dialogs offer an enormous convenience by greatly reducing the laborious task of configuring the parts and settings required to build a complex hierarchical display of information.

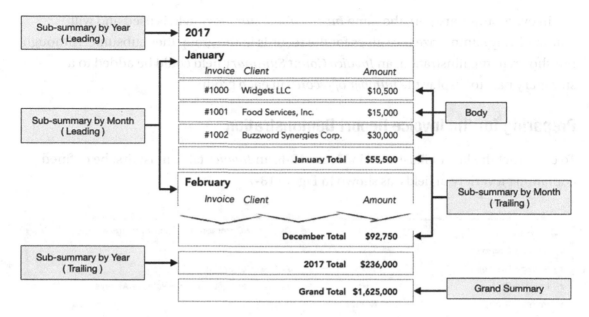

Figure 18-6. *An illustration of an invoice report summarizing sales by year and then by month*

The preceding report is made up of six layout parts, starting with a *Sub-summary when sorted by Year (Leading)*. When records are sorted first by *Invoice Year*, this part appears before each group of records whenever a new year is detected. Next, a *Sub-summary when sorted by Month (Leading)* does the same when records are sorted secondly by an *Invoice Month* field. Although the month name is displayed on the layout, for the months to be arranged chronologically, the actual sort and layout part must be based on a month number break field instead. The labels for column headings are placed in this summary part so they will appear above each group of individual records whenever a new month begins.

The *Body* part repeats once for every record in the found set. However, these are arranged into sorted groups based on the surrounding *Sub-summary* parts. So, January has one group of three records (shown), while other months like February will have their own group of records repeating the Body part (not shown).

Two additional *Sub-summaries* trail the *Body*: one sorted by month and another by year. These operate the same as the corresponding leading parts but appear after each sorted group. In this example, these are used to display summary fields that calculate subtotals of values for the records in the group above it. Finally, at the bottom is a *Grand Summary (Trailing)* which will provide grand totals, summarizing fields for the entire found set.

In every summary part, the same *Invoice Total Summary* field is used and will automatically summarize the values for the records in the group they subsume. Although not shown in the illustration, an *Invoice Count Summary* field could be added to a summary part to display the *number of records* in each group.

Preparing for the Invoice Report Demonstration

To construct the layout illustrated in Figure 18-6, an *Invoice* table must first be defined containing a variety of fields, as shown in Figure 18-7.

Field Name	Type	Options / Comments (Click to toggle)
✦ Invoice Company ID	Text	
✦ Invoice Number	Text	Auto-enter Serial
✦ Invoice Status	Text	Auto-enter Calculation, Evaluate Always
✦ Invoice Amount	Number	
✦ Invoice Date	Date	
✦ Invoice Month	Calculation	= Month (Invoice Date)
✦ Invoice Month Name	Calculation	= MonthName (Invoice Date)
✦ Invoice Year	Calculation	= Year (Invoice Date)
✦ Invoice Amount Summary	Summary	= Total of Invoice Amount
✦ Invoice Count Summary	Summary	= Count of Invoice Number

Figure 18-7. *The field definitions for an Invoice table required for the report*

The first few fields are used for data entry to store the *company ID, number, status, amount,* and *date* of an invoice. The three calculation fields convert the date into a *month number, month name,* and *year number.* These will be used to sort records and display values in summary parts. The two summary fields will be used to display the total count and the total dollar amount of invoices in the various sub-summary and trailing grand summary parts. Once these are configured, begin creating a new report layout by opening the *New Layout/Report* dialog and following these steps to begin a multi-dialog sequence of report configuration options:

1. Select the *Invoice* table.

2. Enter a *Layout Name* of "Invoice Report."

3. Click on the *Printer* icon.

4.   Click on the *Report* icon.

5.   Click the *Continue* button.

Dialog 1: Include Subtotals and Grand Totals

The first report configuration dialog will appear with two options, shown in Figure 18-8. The checkboxes provide the option to *Include subtotals* and to *Include grand totals*. Select both options to include these parts and to ensure that the *Specify Subtotals* and *Specify Grand Totals* dialogs (Dialogs 6 and 7) are included in the configuration process. Click *Next* to continue.

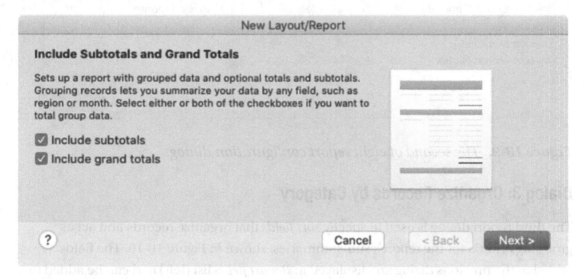

Figure 18-8.   *The first of eight report configuration dialogs*

Dialog 2: Specify Fields

The second report creation dialog is used to specify which fields will be placed on the report, as shown in Figure 18-9. While fields can be added after the layout is created, selecting certain fields now makes them available for summarization options in subsequent dialogs. Add fields from the list on the left to the right, by double-clicking or using the *Move* buttons. Fields can be dragged within the available list to determine their default order across the new layout. In our example, we include the *number*, *date*, *customer*, *amount*, *year*, and *month*, all from the *Invoice* table. Fields from a related table such as a *Company Name* could be included by selecting a different table occurrence in the menu above the *Available fields* list.

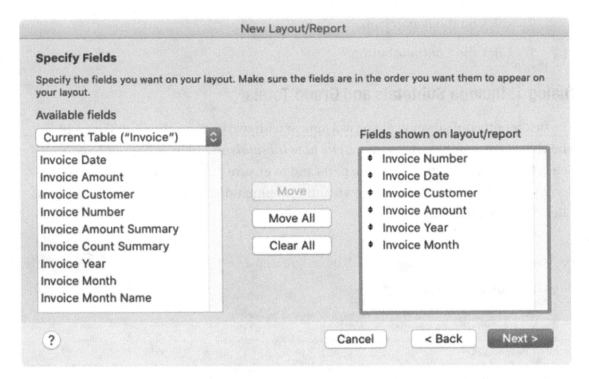

Figure 18-9. *The second of eight report configuration dialogs*

Dialog 3: Organize Records by Category

The third report dialog is used to specify *sort fields* that organize records and act as grouping criteria for the report's sub-summaries, shown in Figure 18-10. The fields added in the previous dialog are displayed in *Report fields* list (left) and can be added to and enabled in the *Report categories* list (right). Each selected field will be included as a summarizing category for groups of sorted records. Enable the checkbox to include the field in *both* the sub-summary layout part and the body of the report. In our example, the *Invoice Year* and *Invoice Month* fields are both added as categories and checked because they will be used to summarize groups of records.

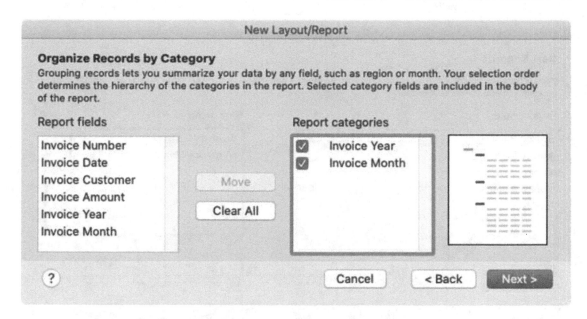

Figure 18-10. *The third of eight report configuration dialogs*

Dialog 4: Sort

The fourth report dialog is used to specify a sort order, as shown in Figure 18-11. This dialog contains an interface similar to the standard *Sort Records* dialog (Chapter 4, "Sorting Records in the Found Set"). Any fields added as *Report categories* in the previous dialog will automatically appear locked at the top of the *Sort order*. Having been selected to summarize groups, they are required in the sort order. Additional fields can be added below these to further sort records in the body of the report.

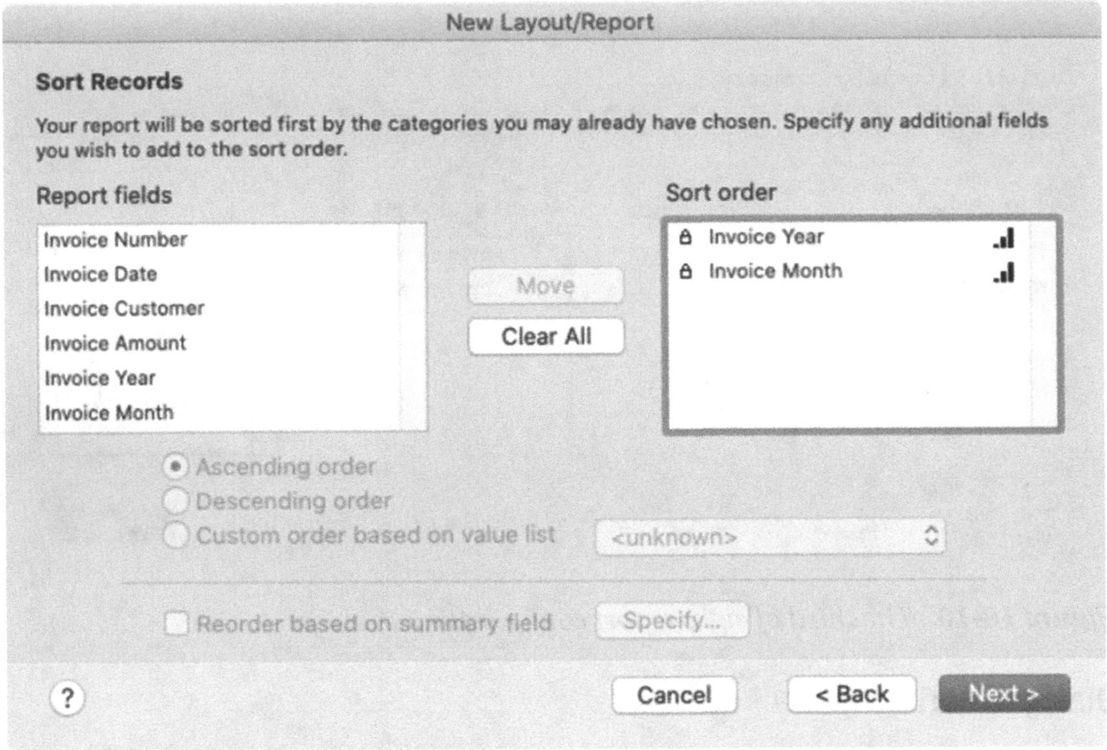

Figure 18-11. *The fourth of eight report configuration dialogs*

Dialog 5: Specify Subtotals

The fifth report dialog, shown in Figure 18-12, will only appear if the *Specify subtotals* checkbox was selected in the first dialog. This allows the addition of one or more *summary fields* that will be displayed above or below groups of records on a sub-summary part that groups by the selected field.

Select a *Summary field* for inclusion by clicking the *Specify* button. Next, a field can be selected from the *Category to summarize by* pop-up menu, which lists all the fields added as report categories in the third dialog. The *Subtotal placement* pop-up menu specifies where the subtotal will appear in relation to the group of records that it is summarizing: *Above Record Group, Below Record Group,* or *Above and Below.* Once these choices are made, click *Add Subtotal* to insert the field into the list below, and then repeat the process for additional fields. Multiple summaries can be added to create a more robust summarized hierarchy.

For our ongoing invoice example, the *Invoice Amount Summary* fields are added as subtotals that will appear *below* the record group, summarized twice for *Invoice Month* and *Invoice Year* so that they appear in both sub-summary parts. Optionally, this can be repeated to also include the *Invoice Count Summary*.

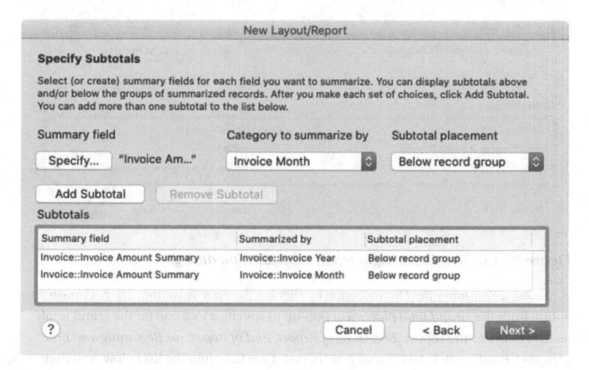

Figure 18-12. *The fifth of eight report configuration dialogs*

Dialog 6: Specify Grand Totals

The sixth report dialog, shown in Figure 18-13, will only appear if the *Specify grand totals* checkbox was selected in the first dialog. This works like the previous dialog but uses summary fields to display a grand total of *all records* on the report.

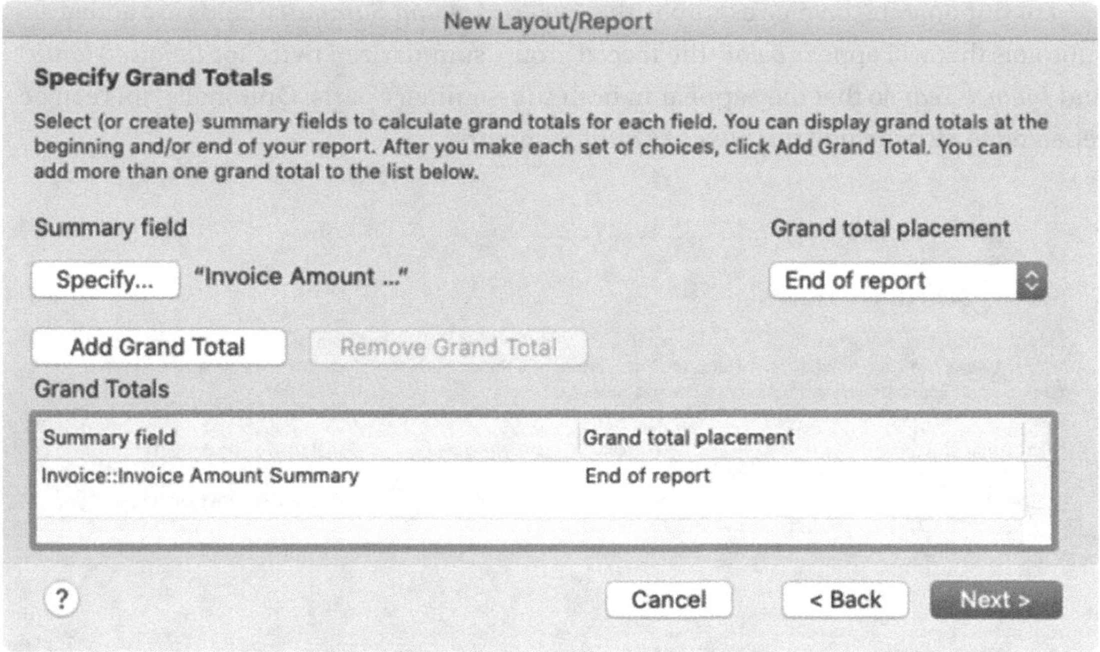

Figure 18-13. *The sixth of eight report configuration dialogs*

Select a *Summary field* for inclusion by clicking the *Specify* button. Then, choose an option from the *Grand total placement* pop-up to specify a location for the grand total relative to the entire report: *Beginning of Report*, *End of Report*, or *Beginning and End of Report*. Finally, click *Add Grand Total* to insert the field into the list below, and then repeat the process for additional fields.

In the invoice example, the *Invoice Amount Summary* fields are both added as grand totals that should appear only at the end of the report. Optionally, this can be repeated to also include the *Invoice Count Summary*.

Dialog 7: Header and Footer Information

The seventh report dialog, shown in Figure 18-14, allows insertion of optional placeholders for standard information automatically placed in six different locations on the layout. Each pop-up menu contains the same choices: *Page Number*, *Current Date*, *Layout Name*, *Large Custom Text*, *Small Custom Text,* and *Logo*.

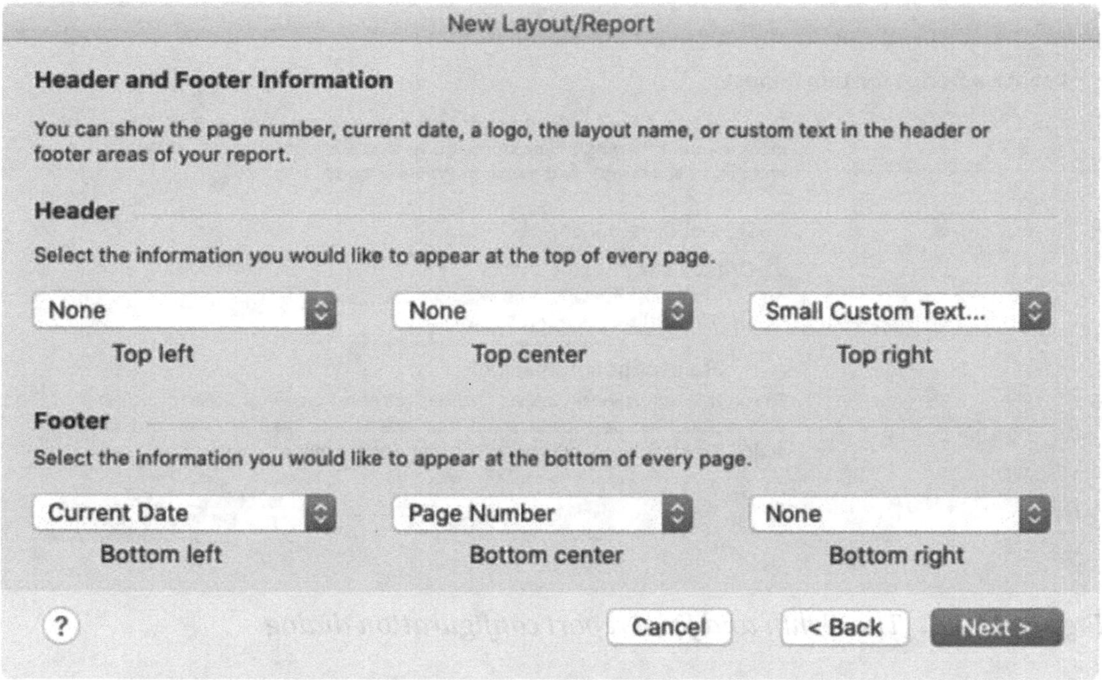

Figure 18-14.   *The seventh step is used to select standard header and footer info*

Dialog 8: Create a Script

The eighth and final dialog offers the option to automatically create a script for the new report layout. Without a script, a user is required to *manually* perform a find, navigate to the report layout, sort records, and print or preview the report. Scripts can be manually created to perform these steps (Chapters 24–28). This last dialog, shown in Figure 18-15, offers the convenience of an automatic head start.

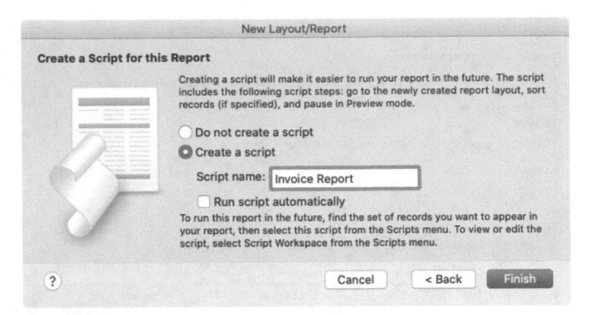

Figure 18-15. *The eighth and final report configuration dialog*

Click the *Create a Script* option, and optionally override the default *Script name*. Select the *Run script automatically* checkbox to assign an *OnLayoutEnter* script trigger (Chapter 27) that will run the script whenever a user navigates to the new layout. Then click the *Finish* button to create the script and complete the creation of the new layout and script.

The script created will include two or three steps, automatically configured depending on other options in this process. It will always include steps to *Enter Browse Mode* and *Go to Layout*. If sort fields were specified in the fourth dialog, it will include a step to *Sort Records* by the field(s) selected. Once created, the script can be further customized as needed. For example, as configured, it assumes the report should include every record in the found set. However, a step can be added to find a set of records based on the context of the current date, week, month, or year, or using any other criteria including that solicited from a user.

Refining the Report Layout

Once a report layout is created, it will usually require clean up and customization. The example in Figure 18-16 shows the layout based on the options selected in the preceding example. The height of parts can be tightened to save space, and the formatting of both backgrounds, labels, and fields is based on a theme and may not be appropriate, especially for printed reports. If a logo was included, the size and position might require adjustment. The field labels for the body fields automatically added at the top can be moved into a sub-summary just above the body so they are repeated directly above each group of fields. Also, the field labels automatically show the full name of the field and may overlap and include naming prefixes and may require editing.

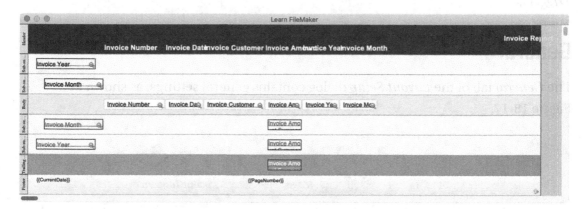

Figure 18-16. *An automatically created report layout typically requires refinement*

Duplicating an Existing Layout

To save time and maintain uniformity between layouts, consider designing a template for a typical List and Form view and then duplicating and customizing these for other tables. The current layout can be duplicated by selecting the *Layouts ➤ Duplicate Layouts* menu. Also, open the *Manage Layouts* dialog, and use the duplicate feature there (see "Using the Manage Layouts Dialog" later in this chapter). The new layout will have the same name as the original with the word "Copy" appended to it. Everything else about the layout will be the same as the original including all parts, theme, objects, formatting, settings, and the assigned table occurrence. Once duplicated, the new layout can be renamed, assigned to a new table occurrence, and further customized as needed.

Configuring Layout Settings

The *Layout Setup* dialog controls the behaviors, appearance, and functions of a layout. To open this dialog, enter Layout mode, and select *Layout Setup* from the Layouts menu or the toolbar. The dialog is divided into four tabs: *General*, *Views*, *Printing*, and *Script Triggers*.

General

The *General* tab of the *Layout Setup* dialog contains general settings, as shown in Figure 18-17.

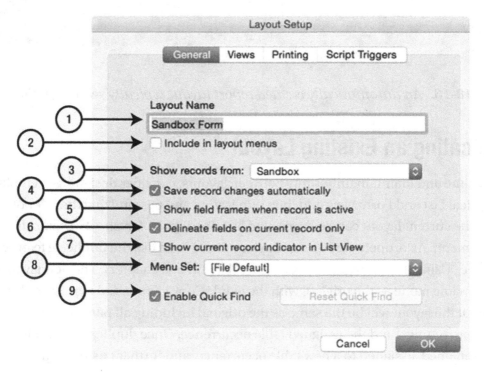

Figure 18-17. *The first tab contains general settings and options*

1. *Layout Name* – Edit the layout's name.

2. *Include in Layout Menus* – Enable for the layout to be a navigable option for users in the View menu and toolbar.

3. *Show Records from* – Select an occurrence for the layout's context.

4. *Save Record Changes Automatically* – Control if field changes are automatically saved when a user or script commits a record. If unchecked, a save dialog will be presented after each commit attempt.

5. *Show Field Frames When Record Is Active* – Enable to show special borders on every field when a record is active.

6. *Delineate Fields on Current Record Only* — Enable to cause only fields on the current record to have a border. Use this to avoid distraction on List layouts.

7. *Show Current Record Indicator in List View* – Enables a black bar on the left of the current record in a List view. This vestigial element should be disabled in favor of the *Use active row state* for the *Body* of a layout which allows style-driven control of objects for an active record (Chapter 22).

8. *Menu Set* – Set custom menus for the layout (Chapter 23).

9. *Enable Quick Find* – Enables the *Quick Find* feature (Chapter 4) for the layout. The button is used to reset all fields to their default *Quick Find* setting.

Views

The *Views* tab of the *Layout Setup* dialog, shown in Figure 18-18, contains three checkboxes controlling which content view types are available to a user (Chapter 3, "Defining Content Views"). The *Properties* button opens the *Table View Properties* dialog of settings that control how a layout appears in Browse mode when viewed in Table view.

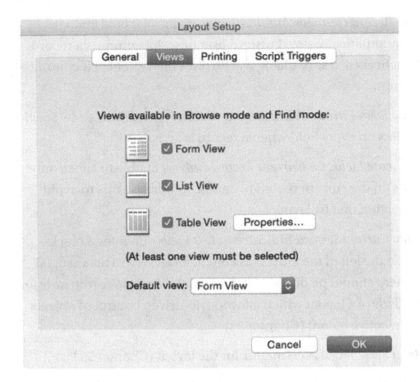

Figure 18-18. *The second tab controls view options*

Printing

The *Printing* tab of the *Layout Setup* dialog, shown in Figure 18-19, controls columns and page margins when printing the layout. Not to be confused with print and paper size settings accessible through the *Page Setup* and *Print* options in the *File* menu, these focus on spacing and columns of the *layout*, controlling the available printable area in which to place objects.

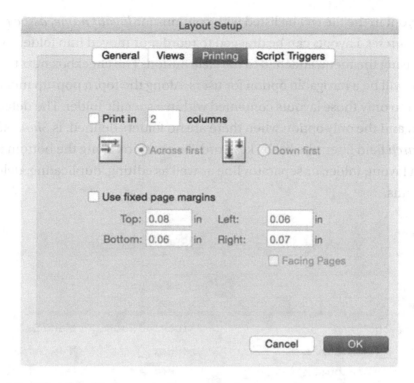

Figure 18-19.   *The third tab controls specific layout print options*

Script Triggers

The *Script Triggers* tab of the *Layout Setup* dialog is used to connect layout events to scripts (Chapter 27).

Using the Manage Layouts Dialog

The *Manage Layouts* dialog, shown in Figure 18-20, is used to reorder layouts, add separator lines, and group layouts into folders. It also integrates all management features used to *create, view, edit, duplicate, delete,* and *open* layouts. Open this dialog using the *Manage Layouts* option from the *Layout* pop-up menu in the toolbar or choosing the *File ➤ Manage ➤ Layouts* menu.

Every layout in the file will be listed with columns for *layout name, associated table,* and *menu set.* Layouts can be dragged to reorder or moved into folders, which are created using the menu attached to the *New* button. The checkbox next to a layout indicates if it will be a navigable option for users. Along the top, a pop-up menu quickly filters the list to only those layouts contained within a specific folder. The default value in the menu, and the only option when there are no folders defined, is *Show All.* The adjacent *Search* field filters the list by keyword. The buttons along the bottom allow creation of a layout, folder, or separator line as well as editing, duplicating, deleting, and opening layouts.

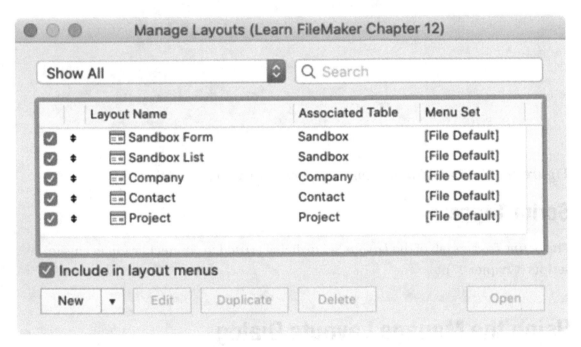

Figure 18-20. *The dialog used to manage layouts*

Tip Folders can be nested hierarchically. The folder structure defined here forms submenus in the Layout menus, making it easier for users to manually navigate a complex database.

Optimizing Layout Performance

Layouts can be designed as complexly as required for your project. Build simple, streamlined views or graphically rich, complex interfaces. However, here are a few principles to be mindful of to help ensure efficient performance:

- When multiple records are displayed at once, as in a List view or portal, try to minimize the number of objects, especially those involving complex functionality, e.g., lots of related fields or items performing SQL queries will slow down large lists.

- On a Form layout, try to minimize the number of advanced controls such as portals and panels.

- Divide complex layouts into multiple less complex layouts, and provide navigation buttons to quickly toggle between them.

- Minimize the use of objects with shadows, semi-transparent colors, gradients, large imported graphics, etc.

- Minimize the number of unstored calculations in fields, especially in lists.

- Use script triggers (Chapter 27) sparingly, and avoid connecting simple interface events with complex scripts that might create long lag times that interfere with a user's ability to work.

- Use themes and styles for object formatting (Chapter 22).

Summary

This chapter introduced the basics of creating and configuring layouts. In the next chapter, we will explore the controls used to construct and configure layout objects.

Exploring Layout Panes

Configuration tools for fields and objects are available in two panes, one integrated on either side of the window in Layout mode: an *Objects pane* and an *Inspector pane*. Both of these are visible by default in Layout mode but can be hidden when not required. In this chapter, we explore the controls available on these two panes:

- Objects pane
- Inspector pane

Exploring the Objects Pane

The *Objects* pane is an integrated region on the left side of a window in Layout mode that contains three tabs: *Fields*, *Objects,* and *Add-ons*. The visibility of this pane can be toggled using either clicking the *Show/Hide Pane* button in the toolbar or selecting an item from the *View* ➤ *Objects* menu.

Defining the Fields Tab

The *Fields* tab of the *Objects* pane, shown in Figure 19-1, was added in version 17 and replaced the previously detached *Field Picker* palette. This panel consolidates some *schema function shortcuts* with some *layout design functions*. It provides access to directly create fields, modify their data type, and access the field options dialog to edit a field's schema properties. Controls at the bottom allow pre-configuration settings that are applied when adding a field to a layout.

© Mark Conway Munro 2021
M. C. Munro, *Learn FileMaker Pro 19*, https://doi.org/10.1007/978-1-4842-6680-9_19

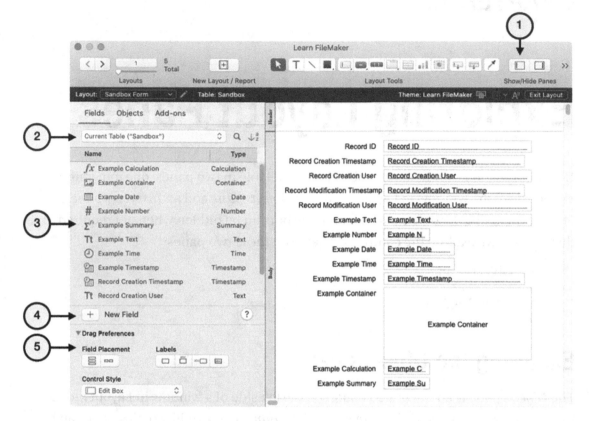

Figure 19-1. *The Fields tab of the Objects pane*

1. *Toggle Button* – Show and hide the pane.

2. *Table Occurrence* – Choose a table occurrence to access a field list other than the current layout's assigned occurrence. Click the adjacent search icon to reveal a hidden filter field.

3. *Fields* – Lists fields in the selected occurrence. Drag one or more to the layout to add an instance. Change the schema type or access a contextual menu to delete, rename, or open the *Field Options* dialog (Chapter 8).

4. *New Field* – Create a field in the selected occurrence's table.

5. *Drag Preferences* – Controls how fields are configured when dragged to the layout:

- *Field Placement* – Stack new fields *vertically* or aligned *horizontally* in a row.

- *Labels* – Include a label at a selected relative position .

- *Control Style* – Choose a data control style (Chapter 20) .

Defining the Objects Tab

The *Objects* tab of the *Objects* pane, shown in Figure 19-2, was added in version 17 and replaced the previously detached *Layout Objects* palette. This provides a hierarchical view of every object currently on the layout, making it easy to locate and select items, including those in groups or hidden behind other objects.

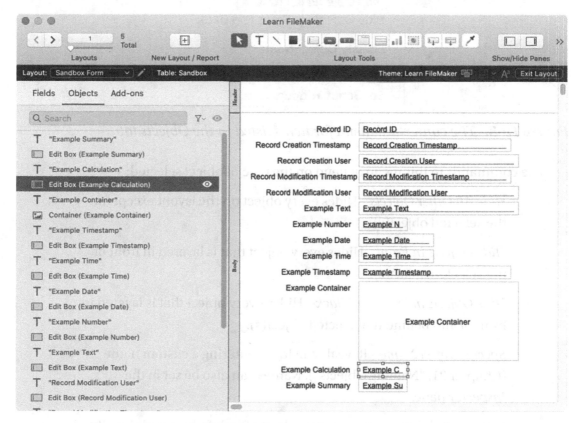

Figure 19-2.   *The Objects tab of the Objects pane*

Each object on the layout is listed here with a default name unless a custom name has been assigned. The default name displayed will vary by object type. For example, a label displays its text value, while a field shows its control style and field name.

There is a lot of functionality built into the object list. An object selected in the list will cause the corresponding object on the layout to be selected and vice versa. Grouped objects and multilayered objects like *portals*, *tab controls*, and *slide controls* show their nested hierarchy which can be expanded or collapsed in the list. A togglable *Hide* icon next to an item's name can temporarily make an item invisible in Layout mode to help declutter the design area for focused work. Finally, a contextual menu contains additional functionality, shown in Figure 19-3.

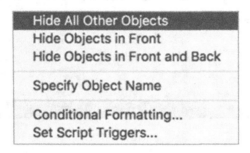

Figure 19-3. *The contextual menu for items listed in the Objects tab*

The commands in this menu depend on the type of object selected:

- *Hide All Other Objects* – Hides every object on the layout except for the selected object(s).

- *Hide Objects in Front* – Hides every object that is layered in front of the selected object(s).

- *Hide Objects in Front and Back* – Hides every object that is layered in front of and behind the selected object(s).

- *Specify Object Name* – Reveals a field for entering a custom name (Chapter 21, "Naming Objects"). Names can also be set in the *Inspector* pane.

- *Conditional Formatting* – Opens a dialog for defining conditionally applied styles (Chapter 21).

- *Set Script Triggers* – Opens the dialog for connecting layout events to scripts (Chapter 27).

Note   Objects hidden using this function are only temporarily hidden in Layout mode but continue to render normally in other modes.

Defining the Add-ons Tab

The *Add-ons* tab of the *Objects* pane, shown in Figure 19-4, is a new feature in version 19 that allows drag and drop insertion of preconfigured resource components. An *add-on module* is a collection of xml, json, and graphic elements that automate the insertion of specialty resources into a FileMaker database.

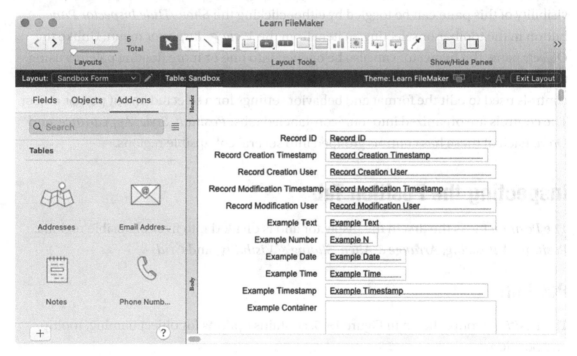

Figure 19-4. *The Fields tab of the Objects pane with some add-ons added*

Click the add (+) icon to open a panel containing a library of available modules. Select one and click *Choose* to add it to your file. The module will appear as an icon in the pane and, depending on the selection, may add some combination of tables, fields, relationships, scripts, and value lists to the database. Once added, drag the icon to any layout to instantly create a set of functional objects, pre-wired into the schema. The resources can be further customized to adjust to the formatting and functional needs of

427

the database. To remove, right-click on an add-on icon, and choose the *Uninstall Add-on* option. A warning dialog includes a checkbox option that can also automatically delete all the resources that were added to the database.

Caution   Some add-ons require a detectable primary key field in the current layout's table and will refuse to work if one can't be found.

Exploring the Inspector Pane

The *Inspector* pane is an integrated region on the right of a window in Layout mode. The visibility of this pane can be toggled by either clicking the *Show/Hide Inspector Pane* button in the toolbar or selecting an item from the *View ➤ Inspector* menu. Unlike the *Objects* pane, the Inspector can also be opened into one or more floating palettes using the *View ➤ New Inspector* menu, reminiscent of past versions. This pane is loaded with controls used to edit the format and behavior settings for a selected layout part or object. The controls are organized into four icon-labeled tabs: *Position, Style, Appearance,* and *Data*. Each of these has controls grouped into several collapsible regions.

Inspecting the Position Tab

The *Position* tab is the first in the Inspector and is divided into five collapsible regions: *Position, Autosizing, Arrange & Align, Sliding & Visibility,* and *Grid*.

Position

The *Position* group, shown in Figure 19-5, contains options for object naming, tooltip, and position.

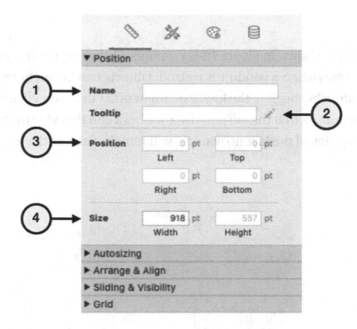

Figure 19-5. *The first group of settings on the Position tab of the Inspector pane*

1. *Name* – Add an optional object name (Chapter 21, "Naming Objects").

2. *Tooltip* – Add an optional string to be displayed as a floating tooltip when the user holds the cursor over the object in Browse mode. The icon opens a *Specify Calculation* dialog for formula-driven tips.

3. *Position* – Control positioning of a selected object within the design area precisely instead of dragging. These are proportionally locked, so changing one will automatically adjust the opposing value to maintain the *Width* or *Height*.

4. *Size* – Set an object's *Width* and *Height*.

Note   The unit of measurement for the position and size will match the current ruler's settings but can be changed by clicking the labels, which cycle through the options *centimeters*, *points*, and *inches*.

Autosizing

The *Autosizing* group, shown in Figure 19-6, contains anchoring control over how an object moves or grows when a window is resized. Objects can be anchored to the *Left*, *Top*, *Right*, or *Bottom* by toggling the lock icon on or off at the respective side of the box. A lock on any side means that the current distance between that side of the object and the corresponding edge of the layout/window will remain fixed as the window is resized in non-Layout modes.

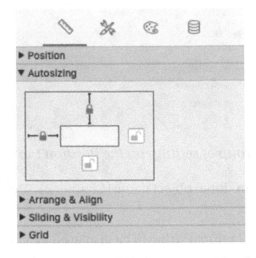

Figure 19-6. *The Autosizing settings on the Position tab of the Inspector pane*

Using these locks in different combinations can create many different positioning and sizing effects. Lock the *Top* and *Left* to cause an object to retain its size and remain stationary as the window is resized. To stick to the bottom right of the layout, anchor only the *Bottom* and *Right* sides. Objects will expand their size when two opposing anchors are active. For example, to expand an object's width as a window is resized, activate the *Left* and *Right* anchors. An object with no anchoring will float in the center of the window.

Arrange & Align

The *Arrange & Align* group, shown in Figure 19-7, contains six groups of buttons arranged in three rows that are used to adjust object alignment, distributed space, relative size, group status, arrangement, and locked status. Unlike other settings in the *Inspector* pane, these are not object properties but are tools used to arrange selected objects neatly to tighten an interface design.

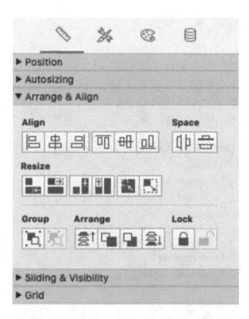

Figure 19-7. *The Arrangement controls on the Position tab of the Inspector pane*

- *Align* – Align objects by side: *Left, Center, Right, Top, Middle,* or *Bottom.*

- *Space* – Evenly distribute groups of objects *Horizontally* or *Vertically.*

- *Resize* – Sync the height and/or width of a group of objects based on the smallest or largest among them.

- *Group* – Convert individual objects into a single group or ungroup them.

- *Arrange* – Change the stack position of selected objects using *Bring to Front, Bring Forward, Send Backward,* and *Send to Back.*

- *Lock* – Change the locked status of objects. Locking protects from accidental modification.

Sliding & Visibility

The *Sliding & Visibility* group, shown in Figure 19-8, controls how objects behave when printing, saving as a PDF file, or viewing in preview mode. There are three primary options: *Sliding left, Sliding up based on,* and *Hide when printing.*

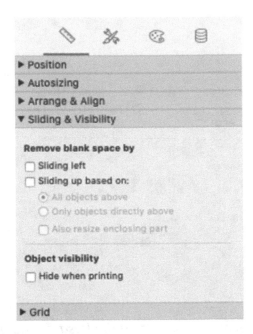

Figure 19-8. *The Sliding & Visibility controls on the Position tab of the Inspector pane*

The *Sliding left* option causes an object to shrink its width to the minimum required to display its content and to slide left as far as possible based on the other objects within the same horizontal plane.

The *Sliding up based on* option causes an object to shrink its height to the minimum required to display its content and to slide up as far as possible based on the other objects in the same vertical plane. When this object is selected, other options below will become enabled. Select the *All objects above* option to cause objects in a common horizontal plane to slide up *together* relative to objects resizing above them. Select the *Only objects directly above* option to cause objects in a common horizontal plane to slide up independent of each other relative to resizing objects directly above them. Select the *Also resize enclosing part* checkbox to cause the layout part enclosing the object to shrink vertically relative to the lowest object after all resizing is complete. For example, a notes field can be expanded on a large layout part to accommodate the potential for lengthy content will end up shrinking to only the space necessary to display the actual content.

The *Hide when printing* causes an object to be invisible when printing.

Grid

The *layout grid* is a sequence of evenly spaced horizontal and vertical lines overlaid on a layout background to form a regular grid of minor and major areas, shown in Figure 19-9. The grid is only visible in Layout mode to assist with precision manual placement and spacing of objects.

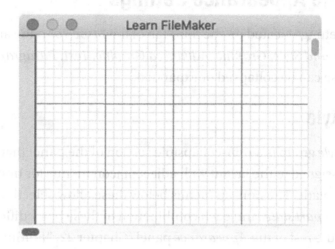

Figure 19-9. *The grid visible on the background of a layout*

The *Grid* group in the *Inspector* pane, shown in Figure 19-10, contains settings that control the layout grid, universally on every layout in the current file. The *Show grid* checkbox enables the grid in Layout view. Selecting *Snap to grid* forces objects to fall on grid lines when manually dragged to a new position. The major and minor grid spacing can be customized in the two fields.

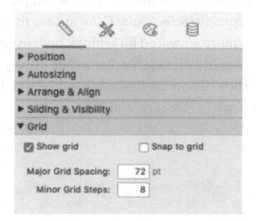

Figure 19-10. *The Grid controls on the Position tab of the Inspector pane*

Inspecting the Style Settings

The *Style* settings located on the second tab of the *Inspector* pane display and control the theme and style assigned to the layout and selected object (Chapter 22).

Inspecting the Appearance Settings

The *Appearance* settings located on the third tab of the *Inspector* pane are divided into six regions: *Theme and Style, Graphic, Advanced Graphic, Text, Paragraph,* and *Tabs.* All but the first of these can be collapsed or expanded.

Theme and Style

The *Theme and Style* group is a non-collapsible section of the panel that displays the theme and style assigned to the layout with adjacent icon menus for updating these when changes are made. The pop-up menus below these allow selection of an *object part type* and *object part state,* and each combination of these has a different set of format settings in the rest of the *Appearance* panel (Chapter 22, "Editing an Object's Style Settings").

Graphic

The *Graphic* group, shown in Figure 19-11, controls graphic settings of the chosen part type and state of selected objects.

The *Fill* menu contains four choices that conditionally change the options available below it: *None, Solid Color, Gradient,* or *Image.* The default option is *None* and means that the object will be transparent. Select *Solid Color* to have the option to choose a fill color or *Gradient* to access more advanced fill settings, both using familiar controls. The *Image* option allows selection of an image file that will be displayed as a background. A pop-up menu allows selection of how the image is handled with the following options: *Original Size, Scale to Fit, Scale to Fill, Slice,* and *Tile.*

The *Line* options include the selection of the object's border type: *None, Solid, Dashed,* and *Dotted.* A number of thickness and a color can be specified. The border icons allow selection of which dimensions of an object have a border: *All, Left, Top, Right, Bottom,* and *Between repetitions in repeating fields.* Finally, a *Corner Radius* is a number indicating the rounding points (pixels) for border corners that will be applied to the corners selected in the adjacent clickable quadrant selector.

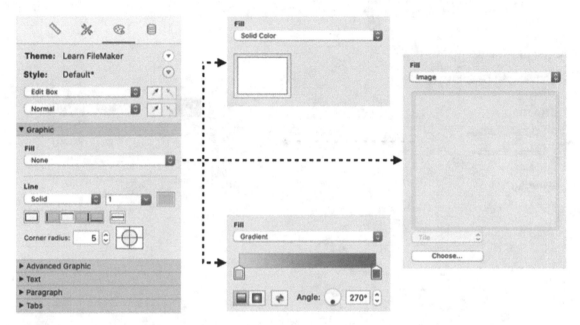

Figure 19-11. *The Graphic subgroup of the Appearance panel of the Inspector*

Advanced Graphic

The *Advanced Graphic* group, shown in Figure 19-12, controls advanced graphical settings of the chosen part and state of the selected object.

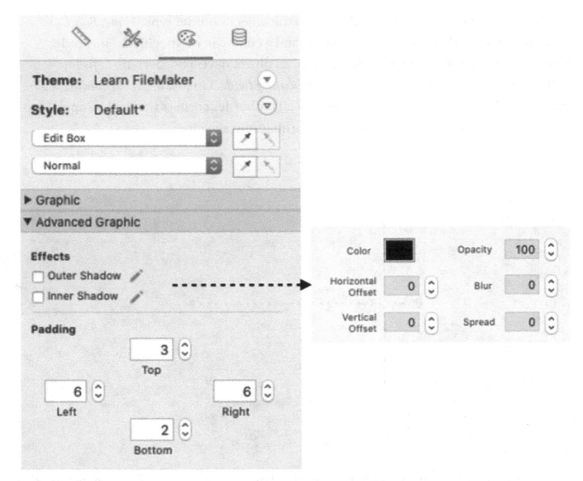

Figure 19-12. *The Advanced Graphic subgroup of the Appearance panel of the Inspector*

The *Effects* checkboxes enable an outer and inner shadow on the object using the adjacent icon button to open a panel with specific settings for *Color, Offsets, Opacity, Blur,* and *Spread*.

The *Padding* numbers control the amount of distance between the border of the object and its content. These settings may compete with the *Paragraph* group's settings for *indentation* and *spacing*, causing confusion if used simultaneously.

Text

The *Text* group controls standard text and style settings for the chosen part and state of the selected object. These include a selection of font *family*, *style*, and *size*, text settings for *color* and *style*, as well as baseline settings for *type*, *thickness*, *color*, and *offset*.

Paragraph

The *Paragraph* group, shown in Figure 19-13, controls paragraph alignment and spacing settings of a chosen part and state of the selected object.

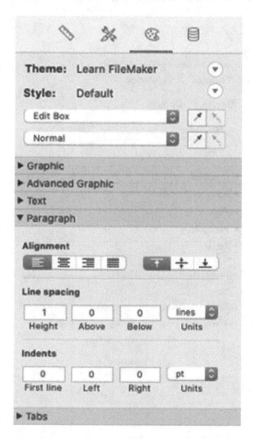

Figure 19-13. *The Paragraph subgroup of the Appearance panel of the Inspector*

The *Alignment* icons control the horizontal and vertical alignment of text within the object, e.g., a field's content, button's name, etc. The *Line spacing* options adjust the spacing of paragraphs, *height*, *space above*, and *space below*, based on a selected unit of measure. The *Indents* settings insert space for text on the *first line* of a paragraph and the entire *left* and *right* indent, all based on a selected unit of measure.

> **Caution**   Some of these settings may compete with the padding settings and may cause confusion if used simultaneously.

Tabs

The *Tabs* group, shown in Figure 19-14, controls tabbed indentation spacing of the text in the selected object. Click the buttons to add or remove *Tab positions* in the list. Click on a position to edit the measurement, and choose an *Alignment* and *Leader* character.

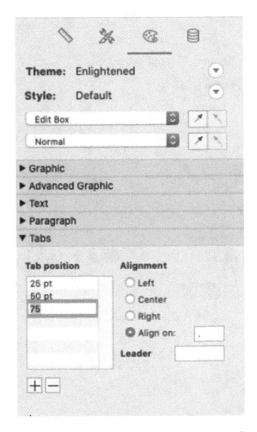

Figure 19-14. *The Tab subgroup of the Appearance panel of the Inspector*

Inspecting the Data Settings

The *Data* settings are located on the fourth panel of the *Inspector* and are divided into three collapsible regions: *Field*, *Behavior*, and *Data Formatting*.

Field

The *Field* group, shown in Figure 19-15, controls settings of a selected field.

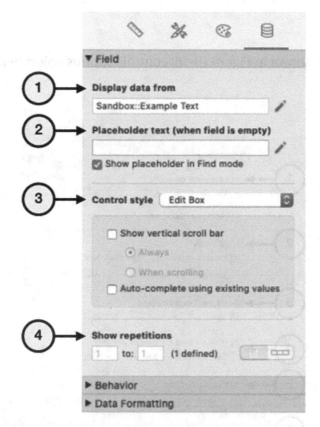

Figure 19-15. *The Field subgroup of the Data panel of the Inspector*

1. *Display Data from* – Choose a field to assign to the selected field object on the layout by clicking the adjacent button to open a *Specify Field* dialog (Chapter 20, "Exploring the Specify Field Dialog").

2. *Placeholder Text* – Enter text or click the icon to define a formula that will be displayed in a field when it is empty (Chapter 20, "Using Field Placeholders").

3. *Control Style* – Select an input style for the field. The settings in the shaded area below will vary depending on the selection (Chapter 20, "Configuring a Field's Control Style").

4. *Show Repetitions* – Controls which repetitions of a field are displayed on the layout and their vertical or horizontal orientation (Chapter 8, "Field Options: Storage").

Behavior

The *Behavior* group, shown in Figure 19-16, controls various object behaviors.

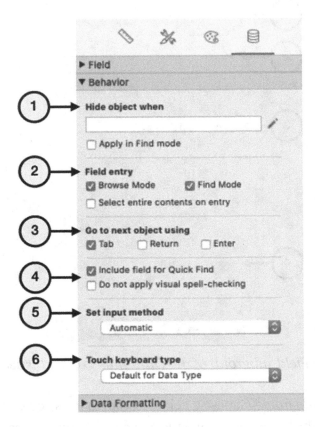

Figure 19-16. *The Behavior subgroup of the Data panel of the Inspector*

1. *Hide Object When* – Control when any object should be hidden. Enter a formula directly into the field, or open a dialog with the adjacent button. The checkbox enables hiding in Find mode.

2. *Field Entry* – Enable a field for user entry in Browse or Find modes. The checkbox below causes the entire contents of the field to be selected when a field acquires focus.

3. *Go to Next Object Using* – Select which key(s) jump to the next field/object. By default, FileMaker uses a *Tab* to jump fields and *Enter* to commit a record. Enabling Return here prevents the user from typing a return character in the field.

4. *Quick Find and Spell-Checking* – Control if a field is included in a *Quick Find* (Chapter 4, "Searching with Quick Find") and will visually highlight spelling errors.

5. *Select Input Method* – Choose a language for a field input.

6. *Touch Keyboard Type* – Choose a keyboard type for an iOS device: *ASCII, URL, Email, Numeric, Phone*, etc.

Data Formatting

The *Data Formatting* controls can be used to apply a transformation in how raw field content is rendered on-screen. Four icon buttons, shown in Figure 19-17, indicate the data type of the selected field: *number, date, time,* or *container*. These are conditionally enabled depending on the data type of the selected field. The *Format* pop-up menu contains options that vary by the data type selection, while the area beneath the menu varies based on the selection made within this menu.

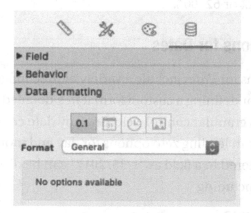

Figure 19-17. *The Data Formatting subgroup of the Data panel of the Inspector*

Data Formatting Options for Numbers

The *Format* menu options for *numbers* are

- *General* – Displays a numeric value as entered with no special formatting but may round or express it in scientific notation to fit within the boundaries of the field.

- *As Entered* – Displays a numeric value *exactly* as it was entered with no changes for any reason, displaying a question mark if the number extends beyond the boundaries of the field.

- *Boolean* – Transforms zero and non-zero values into a Boolean format. The default is *Yes* and *No*, but these can be replaced with other words or symbols.

- *Decimal* – Includes options for number of decimal places, notation, negative value formatting, choice of separators, and more, e.g., 1003.7568 can be displayed as 1,003.75 or #1003.

- *Currency* – Includes options for displaying monetary formats, e.g., 5.7534 can be displayed as $5.75, $5, etc.

- *Percent* – Includes option for displaying percentages, e.g., .62 can be displayed as 62% or 62.00%.

Data Formatting Options for Dates

The *Format* menu options for *dates* include a variety of preconfigured date formatting options with an option for defining a custom format in a detailed interface, shown in Figure 19-18. This allows granular control, selecting any date component, in any order, with any delimiter and with leading zero options for day and month numbers. Using these controls, a date entered in a field as "1/15/2017" can be displayed in any number of different combinations including

- January 15, 2017

- 01.15.2017

- 01.15.17

- 15 Jan 2017

- Sunday Jan 15, 2017

- Thursday 01/15/2017

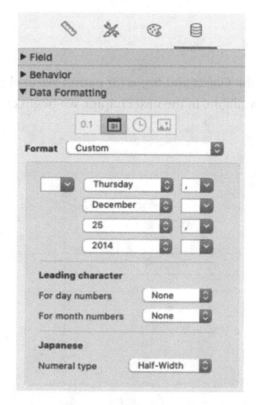

Figure 19-18. *The Custom options for formatting dates*

Data Formatting Options for Times

The *Format* menu options for *times* are similar to those available for date formatting. Choose from a variety of preconfigured time formats, enter a custom format, and choose military vs. civilian time, leading zeros for hours and minutes, and more.

Data Formatting Options for Containers

The *Format* menu options for containers control how an image should resize, relative to the field object: *Crop to frame, Reduce image to fit, Enlarge image to fit,* or *Reduce or enlarge image to fit.* Several additional settings are available below the menu. There is an option to *Maintain original proportions*, which keeps the image's aspect ratio fixed when it is reduced or enlarged to fit in a field. The *Alignment* controls provide positioning within the field. Other options control image optimization or enable interactive control over PDF, audio, and video files embedded in a field.

Summary

This chapter introduced the *Object* and *Inspector* panes. We explored the various tools and settings they make available. In the next chapter, we begin creating objects.

CHAPTER 20

Creating Layout Objects

A *layout object* is an interface element used to display information, accept data entry, and/or initiate a scripted process. An object can be one of eight types: *field, text, button, panel, portal, web viewer, chart,* or *shape.* This chapter introduces every type of layout object, covering the following topics:

- Inserting an object onto a layout
- Working with field objects
- Working with text
- Working with button controls
- Working with panel controls
- Working with portals
- Working with web viewers
- Working with charts

Inserting an Object onto a Layout

A new instance of any object can be inserted onto a layout, using the following methods:

- Select the toolbar icon shown in Figure 20-1. Then, click and drag on the design area to define the dimensions of the object.
- Select object type from the *Insert* menu to quickly place a new instance at a default size and position on the layout.
- Duplicate an existing object to a new instance by selecting it and choosing the *Edit ➤ Duplicate* menu.
- Select an existing object and use the *Copy* and *Paste* functions or option-drag to create a new copy of an existing object.

445

© Mark Conway Munro 2021
M. C. Munro, *Learn FileMaker Pro 19*, https://doi.org/10.1007/978-1-4842-6680-9_20

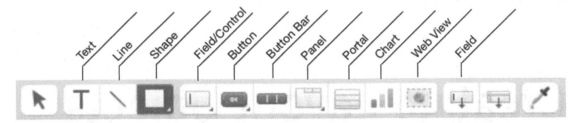

Figure 20-1. *The toolbar icons for adding objects to layouts*

Note   A couple of objects have different insertion methods that are noted throughout this chapter.

When an object is first added to a layout, it will be in a raw state and ready to be configured. Depending on the type, an object can be configured using different methods. Double-clicking on most object types will open a type-specific configuration dialog, usually focused on data configuration options rather than formatting or other behavioral control. A selected object can be manipulated using options in the *Formatting Bar* (Chapter 3), menus such as *Format* and *Arrange*, and the options in the *Inspector* pane.

Caution   The actual appearance of any object on a layout will vary depending on the object state, custom format settings, conditional format settings (Chapter 21), and the theme assigned to the layout (Chapter 22).

Working with Field Objects

In FileMaker, the meaning of the term *field* will vary greatly depending on the context of discussion. Take a moment to acknowledge the difference between four things that are usually blurred together under this single term, as illustrated in Figure 20-2:

- A *field definition* in a table's schema, its underlying data structure
- A *field cell* instance for a record of data
- A *field object* on a layout being designed
- A *field display* rendered on a layout in Browse mode

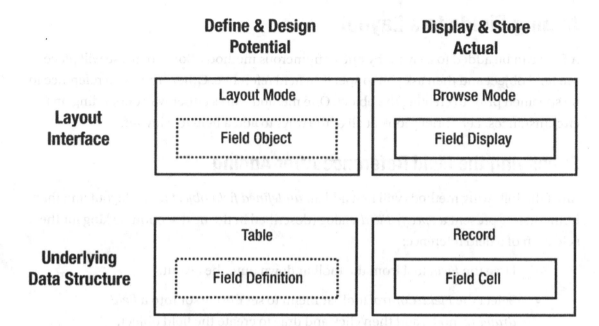

Figure 20-2. *An illustration of the various uses of the term "field"*

There is no inherent problem with referring to each of these as a "field," and one shouldn't feel obligated to use the formal terms shown. In fact, even this book will sometimes refer to these all by that term. However, take a moment to acknowledge the differences to avoid confusion.

A table's *field definition* is an individual unit of storage *potential* that establishes the data type and settings in the database schema. These are replicated as a *field cell*, one for each record created in the table's data content, making an *actual* unit of storage that will contain information. This is the spreadsheet metaphor: a field definition is like a *column*, a record is a *row*, and each instance of the field for a record is a *cell*. In FileMaker, since a user interacts with the data structure *through* a layout, the metaphorical spreadsheet is hidden from view, and the distinction is less important to them.

When designing a layout, a *field object* is a graphical element that defines the position, behavior, and appearance of where and how a field cell should be displayed. In Layout mode, the *field object* is assigned a *field reference* which is a pointer to a *field definition*. When viewed in Browse mode, that layout object is rendered as a *field display* showing information stored in the *field cell* for the record currently viewed; formatted, and behaving in accordance with the settings of both the *table's field definition* and the *layout's field object*.

Adding Fields to a Layout

A field can be added to a layout by one of numerous methods. Some of these will place the field object and then ask you to specify a field reference. Others require a reference to be specified prior to creating the object. One method works either way depending on the circumstances. Let's briefly look at all of the ways to add a field to a layout.

Specifying the Field Reference After Adding

All of the following methods will first add an *undefined field object* to the layout and then immediately present a *Specify Field* dialog (described in the next section) asking for the selection of a field reference:

- Drag the *Field* tool from the toolbar down onto the layout.

- Select the *Field/Control* toolbar menu to set the cursor into a *field drawing* mode, and then click and drag to create the field object. Click once to auto-select the default *Edit box* control type. Click and hold to select a control type from the menu.

- Select the *Insert* ➤ *Field* menu.

- Duplicate a selected field using the *Edit* ➤ *Duplicate* menu.

Specifying the Field Reference While Adding

All of these methods add a field with a reference already specified as part of the process:

- Drag one or more fields from the *Fields* tab of the *Objects* pane (Chapter 19).

- Copy and paste an existing field.

- Add fields in a dialog when creating a new layout (Chapter 18, "Creating a New Layout").

- Duplicate *multiple fields* using the *Edit* ➤ *Duplicate* menu, and their current assigned field will remain.

- Drag and drop an existing field while holding Option (macOS) or Windows (Windows) to create a new duplicate of the field object. This works within a single layout or between layouts in two windows.

When drag-duplicating fields between windows from two different files, the field assignment varies. If the receiving file has a field defined with the same name as the field being dragged in a table with the same name, it will be placed referencing that field. If the receiving file does not have matching field but does have a matching table name, the field will be placed with a `<Field Missing>` reference. If the receiving file does not have a matching field or table name, the field will be placed as a blank field object.

Exploring the Specify Field Dialog

Adding a field using any method that requires the selection of a reference will tentatively place a blank field object and open a *Specify Field* dialog, shown in Figure 20-3. At the top, select a table occurrence from the menu. The current layout's table occurrence will always be at the top with every other occurrence in the file included in one of two lists; related and unrelated. Any field can be added, but only those from the current table or a related table will work as expected. Once a field is located and selected, check the box to optionally create a label automatically, and click OK to add the field to the layout.

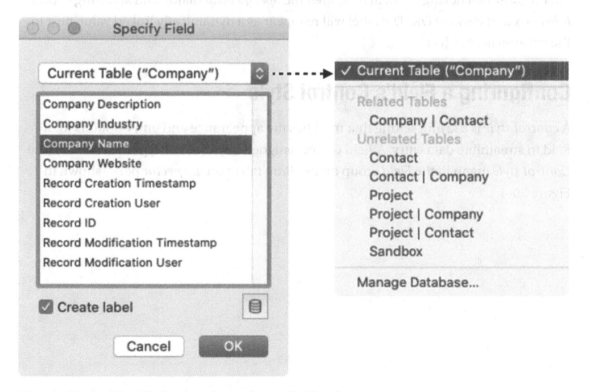

Figure 20-3. *The dialog used to select a field reference*

Editing the Reference of an Existing Field

To reassign the reference for an existing field object, open the *Specify Field* dialog by double-clicking on the field, choosing *Specify Field* from its contextual menu, or clicking the pencil icon next to the *Display data from* settings in the *Field* group of the *Data* panel in the *Inspector* pane.

Working with Field Labels

A *field label* is a text object placed adjacent to a field to help users identify its content. A label can be created manually by inserting a text object or automatically using the *Create label* option in the *Specify Field* dialog. Once created, these can be edited, moved, formatted, and manipulated like any other text object. Labels created automatically remain *dynamically linked* to the field name as long as they haven't been manually edited. In this case, if the field's defined name is modified in the schema, the label automatically updates to reflect the new name. A label for an existing field can be added later by double-clicking the field to reopen the *Specify Field* dialog and selecting *Create label* box and clicking OK. The label will reappear as a dynamically linked value next to the existing field object.

Configuring a Field's Control Style

A *control style* is a layout setting that modifies the appearance and entry options for a field to streamline data entry. A field can be assigned one of seven types available in the *Control style* menu in the *Field* group on the *Data* tab of the *Inspector* pane, shown in Figure 20-4.

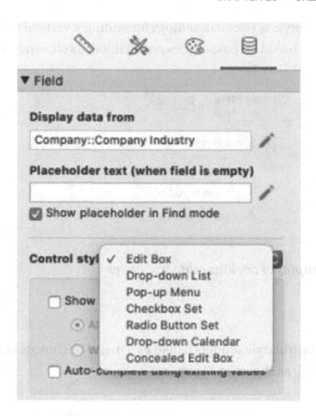

Figure 20-4. *The menu of available field control styles*

Edit Box

An *Edit box* is the default control style that renders a field as a box into which the user can perform freeform data entry tasks. These can vary in size from a single line of text to multiple paragraphs and can include a scroll bar to allow entries longer than the size of the field's frame, all shown in Figure 20-5. All container fields are automatically locked to an Edit Box control style.

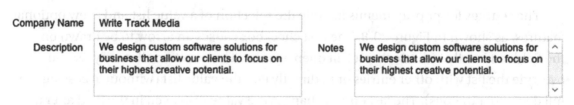

Figure 20-5. *Edit boxes; single line (top), multiline (bottom left), and with a scroll option (bottom right)*

Once this control style is selected, settings for adding a vertical scroll bar and auto-complete suggestions based on past entries are enabled, as shown in Figure 20-6.

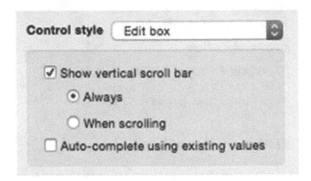

Figure 20-6. *Examples of various edit style boxes*

Pop-up Menu

The *pop-up menu* control style renders a field as a menu of choices based on a defined value list (Chapter 11), as shown in Figure 20-7.

Figure 20-7. *A pop-up menu at rest (left) and open (right)*

The settings for pop-up menus include the selection of a value list and a few optional features, as shown in Figure 20-8. The first checkbox causes an arrow to be drawn on the field to visually indicate that it will open a menu. The next two allow any user to override the list with other entries or to directly edit the value list (without accessing the full developer dialogs). The last option changes the value displayed in the field after a selection is made. When enabled, it displays the value list's *second value* instead of the value actually entered in the field. For example, if a list shows a *Record ID* and *Company Name*, the former is always entered in the field; with this option enabled, the latter is *displayed* as if it were the entry.

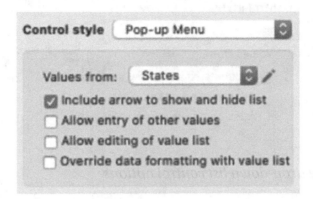

Figure 20-8. *The pop-up menu control options*

Drop-Down List

A *drop-down list* control style renders a field as a combination edit box with an attached menu of value list items, as shown in Figure 20-9. This allows a user a choice of either typing a custom value or choosing a preexisting value from a list.

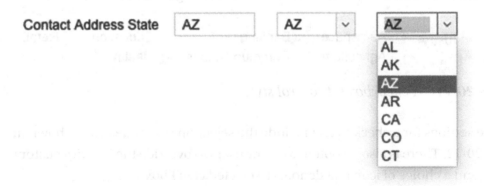

Figure 20-9. *A drop-down menu at rest without optional arrow (left), at rest with optional arrow (middle), and open (right)*

The settings for drop-down lists include the selection of a value list and a few optional features, as shown in Figure 20-10. The first checkbox enables an arrow icon that opens the list. Without this, the list springs open whenever the field gains focus.

Other options allow users to directly edit the values in the list or to auto-complete suggestions based on past entries in the field that start with the text a user is typing.

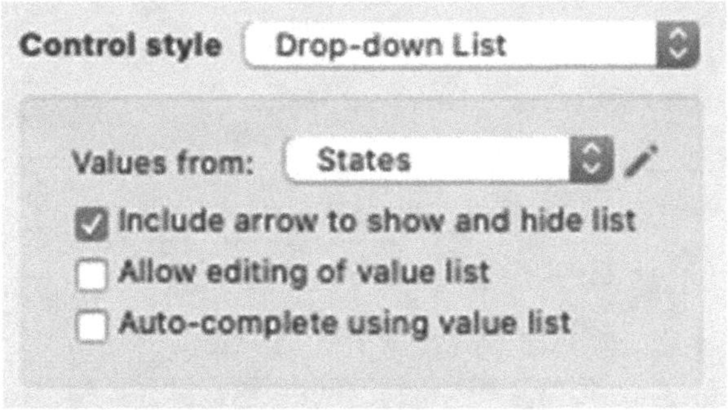

Figure 20-10. *The drop-down list control options*

Checkbox Set

A *checkbox set* control style renders a field as a set of check boxes, each with a text label, as shown in Figure 20-11. These allow a user to select one or more individual options from the assigned list. Checkbox sets are intended to facilitate the entry of multiple values into a single field. As the user checks boxes, the corresponding values are inserted into the field as a list of carriage return-delimited values, e.g., if "Banking" and "Retail" are checked, the actual value in the field will be Banking¶Retail.

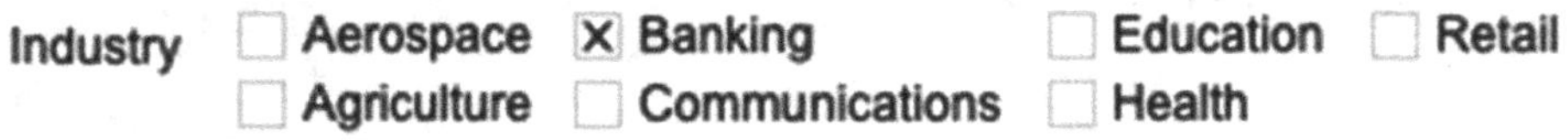

Figure 20-11. *A checkbox set control style*

The settings for a checkbox set include the selection of a value list, as shown in Figure 20-12. There is also an option to allow users to override the list with custom entries and a choice of icon that denotes a selected checkbox.

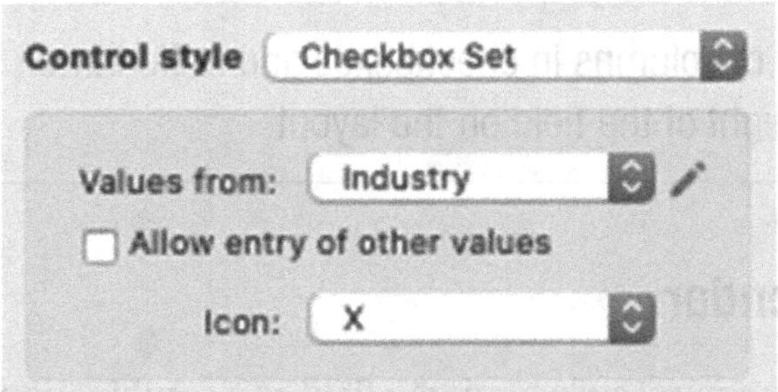

Figure 20-12. *The checkbox set control options*

Radio Button Set

A *radio button set* control style renders a field as a set of selection circles, each with a text label, as shown in Figure 20-13. These controls encourage a user to select a single option from the list. When a selection is made, the corresponding value replaces the previous value in the field maintaining only a single selection. The radio button format doesn't provide an intuitive method for removing a selection and leaving the field empty. To clear the selection, a user can click the current selection while holding the Shift key or click anywhere in the field and typing Delete.

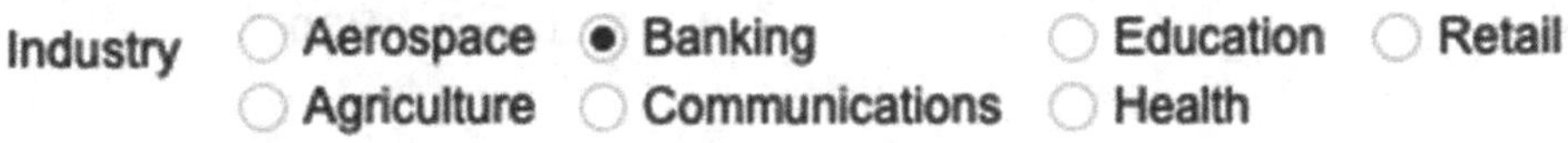

Figure 20-13. *A radio button set*

The settings for a radio button set includes a selection of a value list and option to allow users to enter custom values, as shown in Figure 20-14.

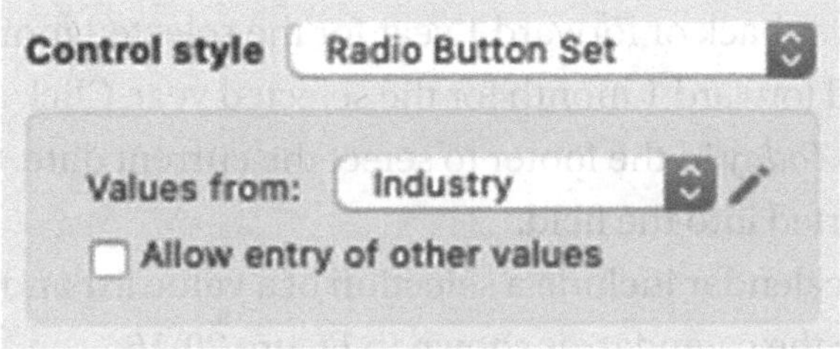

Figure 20-14. *The radio button set control options*

455

Note   The number of columns in checkboxes and radio button is automatically set by the width and height of the field on the layout.

Drop-Down Calendar

A *drop-down calendar* control style renders a field as a combination edit box with an optional calendar widget that opens attached to the bottom of the field, as shown in Figure 20-15.

Figure 20-15. *A drop-down calendar at rest without optional icon (left), at rest with icon (middle), and open with active focus (right)*

The calendar panel includes several controls that assist in quickly navigating to a specific date, including a few subtly hidden. Click on the month and year at the top to reveal a hidden pop-up menu that allows quick navigation to any month. The up/down arrow to the right moves back or forward 1 year for the selected month. The left/right arrows move back and forward 1 month for the selected year. Click a date in the calendar to select it, or click on *Today* in the footer to select the current date. Once a selection is made, the date is inserted into the field.

The settings for a calendar include a selection of a value list and option to include an icon to show and hide the calendar, as shown in Figure 20-16.

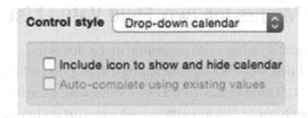

Figure 20-16. *The options for a drop-down calendar*

Tip   The calendar control style can be used with non-date fields. The selection will be entered into text fields as a text string and into timestamp fields as the date selected with the current time.

Concealed Edit Box

A *concealed edit box* control style renders the field as an edit box with each character displayed as a bullet, as shown in Figure 20-17. When the field has focus, it displays one bullet for every character entered but reverts to displaying eight bullets once focus shifts to another field or the record is committed.

Figure 20-17. *A concealed edit box without focus (left) and with focus (right)*

Caution   Concealed edit boxes are intended to provide *minimal security only*. The data stored in the field is *not* encrypted. It is obscured from view on layouts where the control style is applied but continues to be accessible to scripts and calculations, which can access and manipulate the data as they would any other field.

Using Pop-up Menus for Two-Field Value List

The pop-up menu control style has a unique feature that reduces the need for extra resources when used with a dual-field value list. By configuring the assigned value list to show only the *second field* (Chapter 11, "Using Values from a Field") and setting the field's control style as a pop-up menu with the *Override data formatting with value list* option enabled, the user only sees the second field even though the first will be entered into the field.

To illustrate this, add a value list for *Company* records to a *Contact Company ID* field in a *Contact* table that will insert a company *Record ID* and form a relationship between the contact and a company. To begin, set up a value list named *Company List,* as shown in Figure 20-18, which generates a list of the *Record ID* of every company record with the *Company Name* as the second field.

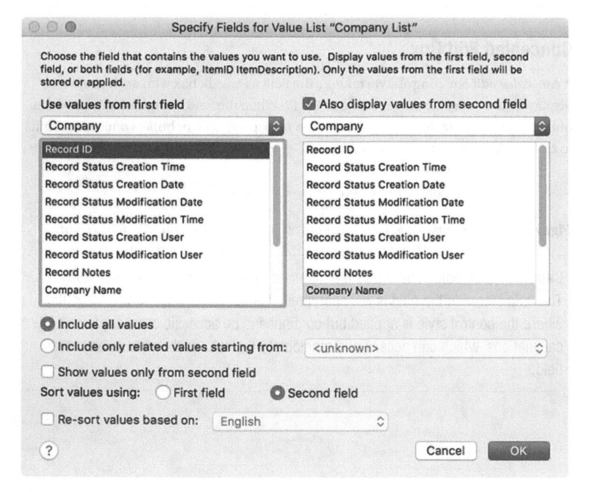

Figure 20-18.   An example of a dual-field value list sorting by the second field

Next, apply the value list to the *Contact Company ID* field as a drop-down list, as shown in Figure 20-19.

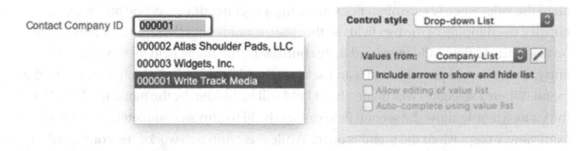

Figure 20-19. *The value list assigned to a field (left), configured as a drop-down list (right)*

By including the second field in the value list definition, the user can see and select a company by *name*. However, once selected and committed, the menu disappears leaving only the *id* visible. Traditionally, this problem would be solved by adding a relationship between the *Contact Company ID* field and the *Company* table's *Record ID* and then pulling the *Company Name* field through that relationship to display it nearby on the layout, as shown in Figure 20-20.

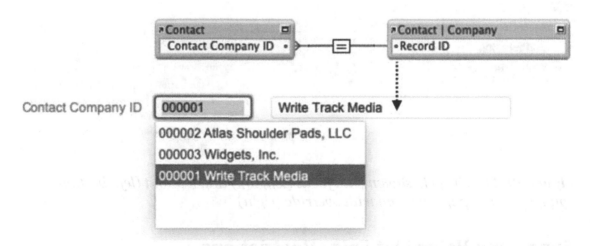

Figure 20-20. *The company name field (right) is pulled from the related occurrence (top, right)*

While this works to solve the problem, it has some drawbacks. It clutters the layout showing both the id and the name. It also makes the entry feel a little unnatural when you click on the id field, select by name, and the id goes into the field, while the name appears off to the side. Since ids are often not something a user needs to see, one might use a creative overlapping of the two fields so that the user only sees the company name field on top of the id field hidden behind it. By configuring the name field on top to not allow entry, a click would pass through it and activate the id field behind which then opens the menu. When a selection was made, the id field will be hidden by the name field. Making the value list only show the second field causes the id to almost completely disappear from view, except when the menu is open. While this approach works, the combination of a dedicated relationship and a clunky overlay of fields makes it less than ideal.

Instead, eliminate the whole mess and use a pop-up menu control style that overrides data formatting. Start by expanding the *Contact Company ID* field's width. Then, confirm that the value list is set to only show the second field (as shown previously). Finally, configure the field to display as a pop-up menu, and select the *Override data formatting with value list* option, as shown in Figure 20-21. Now the list will only show company names, and the field, while still *containing* an id, will override that with layout formatting to display the selected value from the value list, the company name. This works *without* overlapping fields or requiring extra table occurrences and relationships.

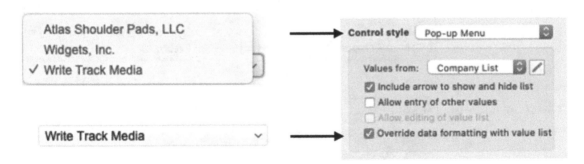

Figure 20-21. *The field shown with focus (left, top) and without (left, bottom), configured as a pop-up menu with override (right)*

Bypassing Value List Entry Restrictions

All four of the control styles that use value lists implicitly encourage compliance with certain data entry restrictions, either entering a *single value* or restricting entry to *value list items only*, as shown in Table 20-1. It is worth mentioning that *these are not strictly enforced rules and they can be bypassed by crafty users.* By the nature of their mechanism, both pop-up menus and radio buttons loosely exclude the possibility of a user entering multiple items or a value not present in the assigned list. Similarly, a checkbox set (without the setting to allow other values) appears to exclude choosing values not on the list. However, all of these "restrictions" can be overridden. In situations where it is important to restrict entry to options made available with a control style, it may be necessary to take explicit steps to make it impossible for users to bypassing the value list.

Table 20-1. *The implied restrictions for entry into value list driven control styles*

Control style	Single Item	Value List Items Only
Pop-up menu	Yes	Yes
Drop-down list	Yes	–
Checkbox set	–	Yes
Radio button	Yes	Yes

Halting Entry of Custom Values

The entry of values not present on a field's assigned value list can be done several ways. For example, when the field has focus, text in the clipboard can be pasted into the field. Also, any of the text-entering functions from the *Insert* menu can be used to insert predefined values. Users can drag a text selection from another field or even another application and drop it into the field. Importing records can bypass the interface as can many script steps. There are several ways to tighten up data entry, making it impossible to bypass the assigned value list.

Using Field Validation

One method to stop users from bypassing the assigned value list is to use validation at the field definition level (Chapter 8). This will apply to every use of the field on any layout (*including* those where a value list control style is not used) and will warn the user about the error. This is a good option for situations where universal coverage is desired.

Filtering Bad Values with a Calculation

Alternatively, an auto-enter calculation at the field definition level can automatically preprocesses data input to confirm that any entries made are appropriate and filter out those that are not. This provides greater flexibility since a custom formula can dynamically change behavior based on various conditions, e.g., make the field operate differently on different layouts or depending on various factors. Since the technique removes the erroneous entry silently without an error dialog, it is great for a nondisruptive correction and won't slow down a user's data entry. However, in some cases, it can be confusing, appearing like a bug to an inexperienced user who would have no idea what error they committed or that their entry was modified.

The following formula assumes a single value being entered and will automatically filter out any value entered that is not in the list. It uses a *Let* statement and the *ValueListItems* function to pull a list of all the items in a value list named "Company – Industry" into a variable named *itemsAllowed*. Then, the *FilterValues* function removes every item entered that isn't found in the list of items allowed. This formula could be expanded with a *While* statement to loop and reject one or more entries in a field containing multiple values, as one might with the checkbox control set.

```
Let (
    itemsAllowed = ValueListItems ( Get ( FileName ) ; "Company - Industry"
)
;
    FilterValues ( itemsAllowed ; Self )
)
```

Using a Script Trigger

Finally, the *OnObjectValidate* script trigger (Chapter 27) can be used to run a script that validates the user's entry and takes corrective action, automatically cleaning up and/ or informing the user about their error. It can even abort the validation process and force them to correct it before continuing. This is a good option for a layout-specific intervention that can auto-correct with a custom notification or inform and require a user change.

Halting Entry of Multiple Values

A checkbox set is the only value list–driven control style that intuitively allows the selection of multiple items from a value list. Other control styles always replace the existing value when a new value is selected and *appears* to restrict entry to a single selection. However, it is possible to select more than one item from pop-up menus, drop-down menus, and even radio buttons, using any of the following methods:

- Hold the Shift key while clicking on additional options.

- Use the *Paste* command to enter a return-delimited list.

- Drag a return-delimited list from another field or application.

- When the *Allow entry of other values* option is enabled on the field, a user can manually enter multiple values.

- Use a script step such as *Set Field*, *Insert Text*, *Replace Field Contents*, *Import Records*, and more.

Restricting Multiple Value Bypass

To forbid multiple values being entered in a field, use an auto-enter calculation or script trigger to bypass user entries.

Using Auto-Enter to Limit Field to a Single Value

An auto-enter calculation can automatically remove all values entered except for one. In the following example, only the last value entered will be retained. The first example in the following uses the *GetValue* and *ValueCount* function to also restrict the entry to the last value entered. The second example will always return the first value entered. All other values would disappear when this formula executes.

```
GetValue ( Self ; ValueCount ( Self ) )
GetValue ( Self ; 1 )
```

Using a Script Trigger to Limit Field to a Single Value

Use an *OnObjectValidate* Script Trigger that runs a script to detect the presence of multiple values and either automatically removes excess values or warns the user and halts the validation process until they correct the problem.

Using Field Placeholders

A *field placeholder* is a text value that will be displayed in the field when empty. This can be used in lieu of a field label or to provide users a short instructional call to action. Since the placeholder is applied to the field as a *layout object* and not to the *field definition*, each instance on a new layout must be configured separately. To avoid confusion, the placeholder value has its own *part style state* (Chapter 22) which allows formatting to change so users can distinguish a placeholder from actual field content. The example in Figure 20-22 shows three instances of the same *Company Name* field. The first shows the default state of a new field added to a layout without a placeholder. The second shows an example of a placeholder used instead of a label, displaying the field name. While this technique saves space, once actual data is entered into the field, the placeholder text vanishes, and no label will be shown. That may be confusing in cases where the content isn't easily identifiable. The third example shows the field with a permanent label and a descriptive prompt as a placeholder.

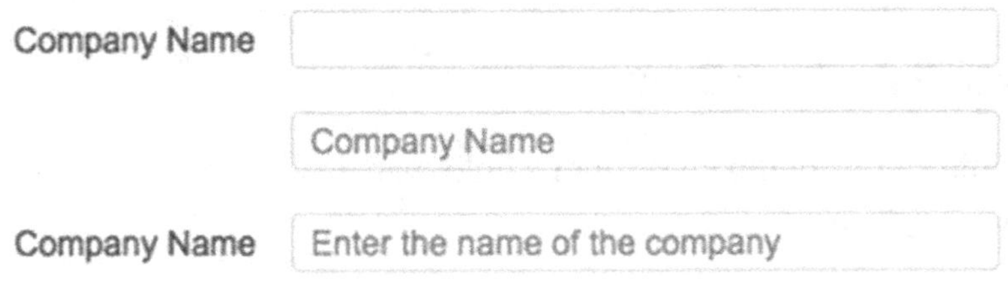

Figure 20-22. *An example without placeholder (top), with field name as placeholder (middle), and with a placeholder prompt (bottom)*

Note   A field formatted as checkbox or radio button can't have a placeholder text value.

Entering Placeholder Text

To define a placeholder, select a field and open the *Field* group on the *Data* tab of the *Inspector* pane. A static value can be typed directly into the *Placeholder text* box, shown in Figure 20-23.

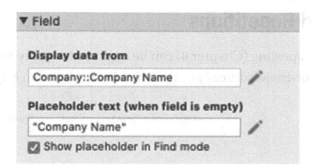

Figure 20-23. *The controls for defining a field's placeholder text*

Alternatively, click the pencil icon to enter a formula that generates the placeholder value. The placeholder text will be displayed when the window is in Browse mode. Enable the *Show placeholder in Find mode* checkbox to also show it in Find mode. When enabled in Find mode, a formula can vary the value displayed based on a *Case* formula that checks the *WindowMode*, as shown in this example:

```
Case (
   Get ( WindowMode ) = 0 ; "Enter a Company name" ;
   "Search for a Company name"
)
```

Replacing Display Calculation Fields with Placeholders

In the distant past, it was common for developers to use calculation fields to create variable field labels or to display conditional information about a record on layouts. For example, a field that concatenates meta-information about the record or shows dynamic error warnings would have been done by adding a calculation field in the table and used as a layout display mechanism. In the modern age, it is no longer necessary to clutter up the table's schema with calculation fields in order to display this type of read-only information through the interface. One method of doing this is with a single, non-editable global field placed in a central *System* table that can be replicated in numerous layout instances, each with a unique calculation-driven placeholder text value.

Tip   A transparently styled button bar's name calculation can be used as a read-only display mechanism. Using these as field labels allows the label to easily be switched into a button or popover panel.

Showing Field Repetitions

Fields defined to be repeating (Chapter 8) can be displayed on a layout with some or all defined repetitions, oriented vertically or horizontally, as shown in Figure 20-24.

Example Text	Rep 1
	Rep 2
	Rep 3
	Rep 4
	Rep 5

Example Text	Rep 1	Rep 2	Rep 3	Rep 4	Rep 5

Figure 20-24. *A five-repetition text field displayed vertically (left) and horizontally (right)*

When a field is added to a layout, it will automatically be configured to show a single repetition. To change this, select the field and use the *Show Repetitions* settings on the *Field* group of the *Data* tab of the *Inspector* pane, shown in Figure 20-25. The number of defined repetitions available for the field is displayed in parentheses. Enter the starting and ending repetition in the two fields to control *which* and *how many* repetitions are visible on the layout. The adjacent buttons toggle the orientation.

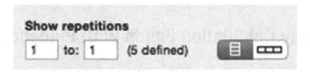

Figure 20-25. *The controls for defining how many repetitions appear on a layout*

Using these settings, each repetition of a field can be displayed individually as a separate field object or in groups in a single field object. To illustrate the various possible configurations, Figure 20-26 shows a total of seven field objects on a layout, five showing a different single repetition each, one showing repetitions 1–3, and another showing repetitions 3–5.

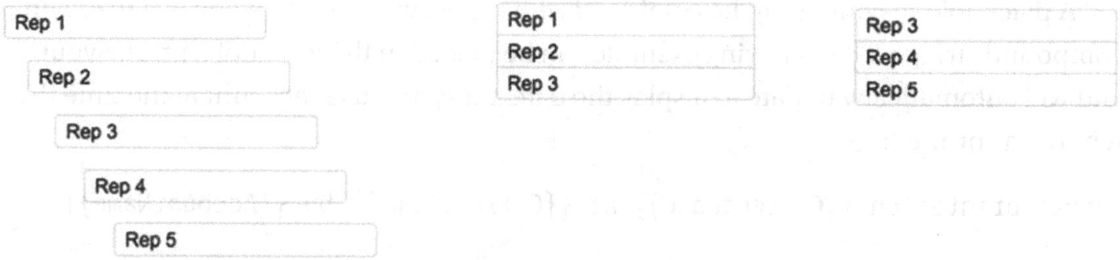

Figure 20-26. Repeating fields configured individually (left) or in groups (right)

Working with Text

A text object can be added to a layout in one of four types: *static text, dynamic symbols, merge fields,* and *merge variables.*

Creating Static Text

On a layout, *static text* is an object that contains an unchanging string of characters used for labeling or conveying a message to users. A static text object can contain rich formatting and multiple paragraphs. In Layout mode, create a static text object by choosing the *Text* tool in the toolbar and then click-dragging in the layout design area to define the object boundaries. When you release the cursor, begin typing. Once created, text can be edited and formatted by selecting the tool and clicking on the object or by double-clicking it.

Creating Dynamic Placeholder Symbols

A *dynamic placeholder symbol* is a special string in a text object that is automatically replaced with a predetermined value type whose content varies over time, e.g., a date or time. There are dozens of symbols available, each corresponding to a *Get* function (Chapter 13, "Introducing Get Functions"). These can be manually typed or added to a layout by selecting one from the *Insert* menu. The menu adds the symbol into the current text object with edit focus or as a new object. Symbols are made up of a keyword enclosed in double braces. For example, to have the *current date* rendered on a layout, create a text object with the value shown here:

```
{{CurrentDate}}
```

A placeholder symbol can be combined with other symbols and static text to create compound strings. The following example can be placed in the footer of a print layout and will automatically update to display the date, time, and user account at the time the report was printed:

```
Report printed on {{CurrentDate}} at {{CurrentTime}} by {{AccountName}}
```

Creating Merge Fields

Similar to dynamic function placeholders, a *merge field* is a symbolic tagging format that allows a field's content to appear on a layout within a non-editable text object. Use the *Insert* ➤ *Merge Field* menu to add one into the current text object with edit focus or as a new object. Merge fields are made up of a field name enclosed in two left-shift and two right-shift symbols and can also be typed manually.

```
<<FieldName>>
<<TableName::FieldName>>
```

When referencing a field local to the current layout's table, only the field name is required. A related field must include the name of the table occurrence to provide a contextual reference. The following example assumes placement on a *Contact* layout and will display the full name of a contact and the name of the related *Company* assigned to them:

```
Contact <<Contact Name First>> <<Contact Name Last>> at <<Contact |
Company::Company Name>>
// Result = Contact Karen Smith at Atlas Shoulder Pads LLC.
```

Caution   Empty fields used in a compound merge field string will show up blank in a string with other static text surrounding it to form a sentence that doesn't make sense!

Creating Merge Variables

A *merge variable* is a symbolic tagging format that allows a global variable (Chapter 12, "Variables") to be rendered as a text object on a layout. Like merge fields and dynamic symbols, merge variables can be used in any combination with other merge variables, text, symbols, and merge fields. Use the *Insert* ➤ *Merge Variable* menu to add one into the current text object with edit focus or as a new object. Merge variables are made up of a variable name enclosed in two left-shift and two right-shift symbols, following the pattern shown here:

`<<$$VariableName>>`

Working with Button Controls

A *button* is a layout object that embeds an action control into an object. Buttons work in Browse and Find mode and, depending on the type and configuration, can run a script, perform a single script step, or open a popover interface element. Buttons allow a developer to embed active controls into the interface for navigation, creating, deleting, or performing any number of other functions. These provide shortcuts for users and relieve them of the burden of manually repeating complex tasks. FileMaker has four options for buttons: three native button types – *buttons*, *popover buttons,* and *button bars* – and the ability to format *any object* as a button.

Working with Buttons

A *button* is a layout object in the form of a traditional graphical push button, like those shown in Figure 20-27. Buttons can be added to a layout using the toolbar icon or selecting the *Insert* ➤ *Button* menu. When a button is created, a *Button Setup* dialog opens which allows configuration of a *label* and *action*. The dialog can be opened for an existing button by double-clicking it or selecting the *Button Setup* command from the *Format* menu or the button's contextual menu.

Figure 20-27. *Examples of buttons*

Configuring a Button's Label

A *button label* is the identifying text and/or icon displayed within the boundary of the button that communicates to users what functionality it will perform. The label is defined in the top portion of the *Button Setup* dialog. A button can have a text label, icon label, or a combination of the two.

Using a Text Label

To define a button with a text label, choose the *label* option and enter the text for the label, as shown in Figure 20-28:

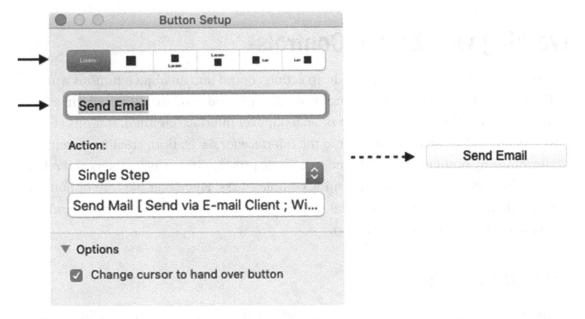

Figure 20-28. *A button configuration (dialog) rendering a named button (right)*

Tip A button label can include a merge field typed into the text area to create dynamic names. For more dynamic naming formulas, use a single segment button bar instead of a button.

Using an Icon Label

When defining a button with an *icon* label, the *Button Setup* dialog controls transform to allow selection and configuration of an image, as shown in Figure 20-29. Select an icon from the list of standard icons. The list can be expanded by clicking the plus icon below and choosing a PNG or SVG image. New images added here will be available anywhere within the current database file. Use the slider below the icon list to shrink or enlarge the size of the icon within the bounds of the button object.

Note   Unlike other controls, the size setting here will always be displayed in *points* regardless of units currently selected for the ruler

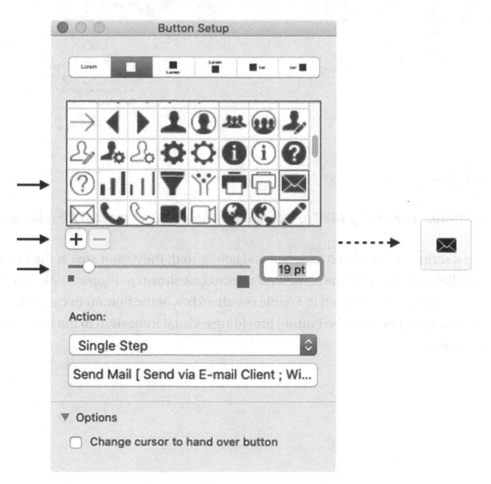

Figure 20-29. *A button configuration (dialog) rendering an icon button (right)*

Configuring a Button's Action

The bottom portion of the *Button Setup* dialog controls the button function.

Performing a Single Step

To configure a button to run a script step command, change the *Action* pop-up menu to *Single Step*. This will immediately open the *Button Action* dialog, shown in Figure 20-30. This is a limited version of the *Script Workspace* dialog (Chapter 24). Double-click a step from the list on the right to add it as the action assigned on the left, replacing an existing selection. Then configure as needed and click OK.

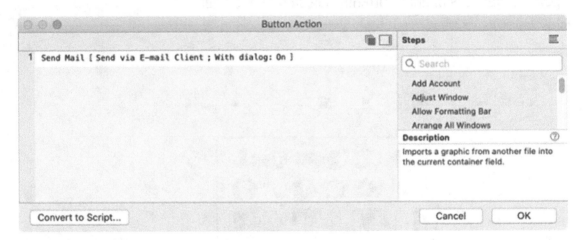

Figure 20-30. *The dialog used to select and configure a script step for a button*

Once a script step has been assigned and configured, the *Action* area at the bottom of the setup dialog will display the command selected, as shown in Figure 20-31. To change the command assigned, click on it. Enable the checkbox at the bottom to cause the cursor to change when over the button, providing a visual indication to the user that it is an active button.

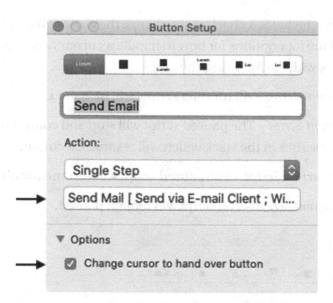

Figure 20-31. *The dialog configured to run a single step*

When using the *Single Step* option, only *one* command can be assigned to the button. To attach more complex functionality to a button, choose *Perform Script* instead of *Single Step*, or click the *Convert to Script* button in the *Button Action* dialog to quickly create a new script with any existing step configurations retained.

Performing a Script

To configure a button to run a script, change the button's action to *Perform a Script*. This will immediately open the *Specify Script* dialog (Chapter 24, "Exploring the Specify Script Dialog"), allowing the selection of a script and entry of an optional parameter. After choosing the script, the *Action* area at the bottom of the *Button Setup* dialog will display the script selected, parameter, and options, as shown in Figure 20-32. The assigned script can be clicked to open and directly edit the script steps. Click the adjacent script icon to choose a different script for the button. Click the script parameter button to open a *Specify Calculation* dialog and enter a formula for data that will be sent to the script as a parameter (Chapter 24, "Sending Parameters").

The *Options* area includes a checkbox to change the cursor. Also, a menu allows the selection of one of the four options for how to handle a currently paused script after the button's script runs, with the following choices:

- *Halt Current Script* – All running scripts will be halted.

- *Exit Current Script* – The paused script will stop and control reverts to any other scripts in the stack which will resume execution.

- *Resume Current Script* – The paused script will resume running.

- *Pause Current Script* – The script will remain paused.

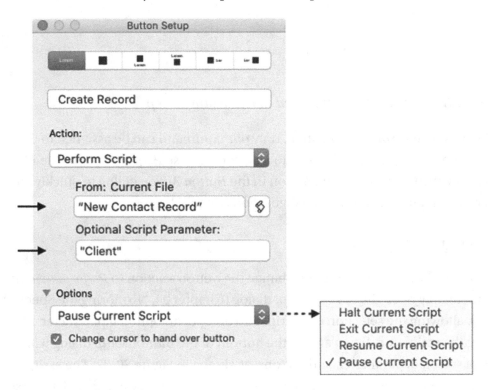

Figure 20-32. *The dialog configured to run a script*

Popover Button

A *popover button* is a type of button that a user clicks to open a floating panel that contains additional layout objects. This reduces visual clutter by storing groups of controls out of view until needed. Popovers can be used for a variety of different purposes such as expanding field inputs, documentation tips, or a menu of actions like the simple example shown in Figure 20-33.

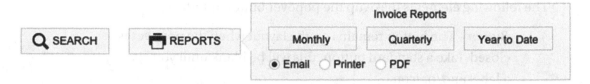

Figure 20-33. *A popover button containing an array of action buttons*

To create a popover, choose the *Insert* ➤ *Popover Button* menu, or click-hold the *Button* toolbar icon, and choose *Popover Button* from the menu, shown in Figure 20-34. Then click and drag in the content area to draw the boundaries for the object.

Figure 20-34. *Selecting the popover button tool from the toolbar*

Defining the Basic Popover Interface

Once it is created, a new popover appears as a button with a popover interface open, as shown in Figure 20-35.

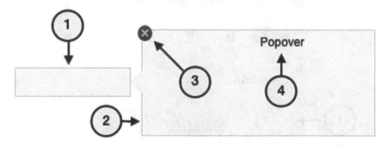

Figure 20-35. *A new popover button ready for editing*

The following elements make up the popover button interface:

1. *Button* – The button remains on the layout when the popover is closed. Like a standard button, this will be blank until you specify a label and/or icon.

2. *Interface/Design Area* – This area pops open when the user clicks the button. In Layout mode, this is a resizable design area where you can add layout elements as needed.

3. *Close Button* – This button, only visible when editing the popover in Layout mode, will close the popover interface.

4. *Title* – An optional title for the popover.

Tip   Click on the popover design area to show a gradient control bar and resize handles.

Exploring the Popover Button Setup Options

A popover's label and behavior settings are configured using the *Popover Button Setup* dialog, which automatically opens when it is created. This dialog, shown in Figure 20-36, can be opened later by double-clicking on a button or the popover interface design area or by selecting *Popover Button Setup* from the *Format* menu or the button's contextual menu.

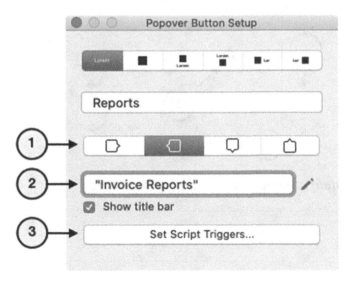

Figure 20-36.   *The dialog used to configure a popover's label and behavior settings*

476

The top portion of the setup dialog is identical to regular *Button Setup*, allowing control over the button's label and/or icon. The bottom portion contains settings specifically for the popover interface panel:

1. *Directional Control* – Choose a preferred open direction for the popover interface relative to the button icon. FileMaker will override this choice if needed to ensure that the popover interface never goes off-screen.

2. *Title* – Enter a title for the popover or click the adjacent pencil icon to generate one with a formula. Click the checkbox to have the title display for the user at the top of the panel when open.

3. *Script Triggers* – Click to open a dialog to configure script triggers (Chapter 27) for the popover interface.

Button Bar

A *button bar* is a layout object that defines a group of interconnected button segments, as shown in Figure 20-37. Create a bar by choosing the *Insert* ➤ *Button Bar* menu or using the corresponding tool in the toolbar. Each segment of the bar can be defined independently as a push button or a popover button. Clicking on a segment performs its defined action and then leaves that segment actively selected until another is selected, making them an odd combination of a button and mode indicator. This selection behavior can be overridden by configuring the default segment to 0 and refreshing the window after the script action has been performed.

Figure 20-37. *An example of a three-segment button bar with the second segment active*

Exploring the Button Bar Setup Options

Button bars are configured using the *Button Bar Setup* dialog, shown in Figure 20-38. This dialog automatically opens when a new bar is created and can be opened later by double-clicking on a button segment. It can also be opened by selecting *Button Bar*

Setup from the *Format* menu or the button's contextual menu. This dialog is a hybrid of the setting for a *button* and a *popover button* with a few controls specific to button bars.

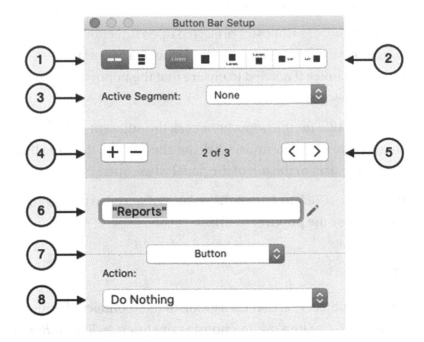

Figure 20-38. *The dialog used to configure a button bar*

The top portion contains controls for the overall bar, including

1. *Bar Orientation Control* – Select the direction segments should run: *horizontally* or *vertically*.

2. *Button Labeling Options* – Select a labeling option for all the segments (similar to buttons and popovers).

3. *Active Segment* – Specify which segment will be "active" by default. The menu allows selection of a segment by name and includes a *Specify* option for a formula-driven choice.

4. *Segment Control* – Add or remove segments from the bar.

5. *Segment Navigation* – Select a specific segment whose settings will be displayed for configuration below.

The bottom portion of the dialog applies to the currently selected segment:

6. *Button Labeling Specification* – Identical to buttons, enter a name and/or select an icon for the button segment's label depending on the labeling option selected previously.

7. *Segment Type* – Select a type for the current segment: *Button* or *Popover Button.*

8. *Action Menu and Specification* – This area provides action controls depending on the type selected previously with options identical to a button or popover.

Making Any Object a Button

In addition to formal buttons and button bar objects, any object or group of objects can be converted into a simple push button. Select the object, and click the *Format ➤ Button Setup* menu or the contextual menu option of the same name to open a simplified *Button Setup* dialog, as shown in Figure 20-39. Because the object is not a native button, the only configuration choices are an action selection and the option to change the cursor. Once converted into a button, the objects will no longer be receptive to input native to their type, e.g., fields will no longer accept data entry.

Figure 20-39. *The dialog used to assign an action to an object button*

Working with Panel Controls

A *panel control* is a layout object that contains multiple object groups, organized in separate panels, which can be alternately displayed within the area of the object. Panels save space by allowing part of a layout to be used for multiple purposes, one at a time as selected by a user. FileMaker has two such object types: *tab controls* and *slide controls*.

Tab Control

A *tab control* is a multi-panel layout object with labeled "tabs" reminiscent of file folders, as shown in Figure 20-40. When a user clicks on one of the available tabs, the corresponding panel becomes active and renders the other tabs inactive. Each panel can be designed with any number and different layout objects. A tab panel can even include other tab controls, making a hierarchical tab structure.

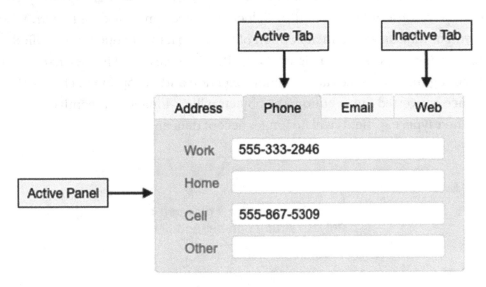

Figure 20-40. An example of a tab control with four tabbed panels

To create a new tab control, select the *Insert* ➤ *Tab Control* menu item, or click on the toolbar icon, and choose *Tab Control* from the menu, as shown in Figure 20-41.

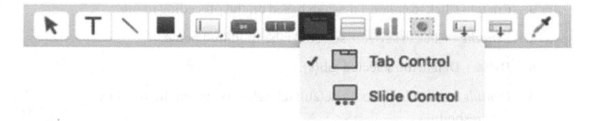

Figure 20-41. *Selecting the tab control tool from the toolbar*

Exploring the Tab Control Setup Dialog

Tabs are configured using the *Tab Control Setup* dialog, which automatically opens when a new tab control is created. This dialog, shown in Figure 20-42, can be accessed later by double-clicking anywhere on a panel of a tab control or by selecting the *Tab Control Setup* item from the *Format* menu or the tab control's contextual menu.

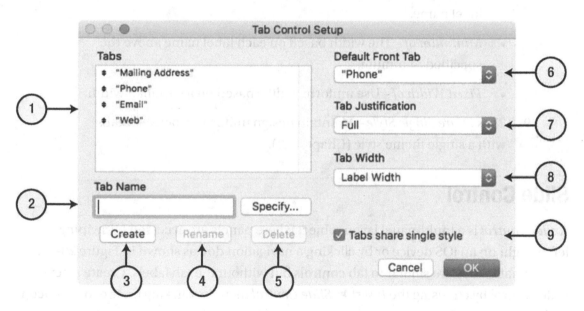

Figure 20-42. *The dialog used to define a tab control*

The controls available on the dialog are

1. *Tabs* – Lists each tab defined for the object. Drag to reorder.

2. *Tab Name* – Type a name when creating a new panel or edit the name of the selected tab. Click *Specify* to define a formula-driven name.

481

3. *Create* – Click to create a new tab based on the preceding name.

4. *Rename* – Click to save the selected tab's modified name.

5. *Delete* – Delete the selected tab(s).

6. *Default Front Tab* – Select a default tab selection when the window is refreshed.

7. *Tab Justification* – Select the justification of the tab's labels.

8. *Tab Width* – Select the width of the tabs:

   • *Label Width* – The width varies based on each label name.

   • *Label Width + a Margin of* – The width varies based on each label name plus the specified margin in pixels.

   • *Width of Widest Label* – Use uniform widths based on the longest label name.

   • *Minimum of* – The width based on each label name above the specified minimum.

   • *Fixed Width of* – Use uniform widths based on a specified width.

9. *Tabs Share Single Style* – Maintain design uniformity between tabs with a single theme style (Chapter 22).

Slide Control

A *slide control* is a multi-panel layout object where panels are accessed by swiping left or right on an iOS device or by clicking a navigation dot, as shown in Figure 20-43. Functionally, they are similar to tab controls but without the tab labels. Create a new slide control by choosing the *Insert ➤ Slide Control* menu or clicking on the toolbar icon and choose *Slide Control*.

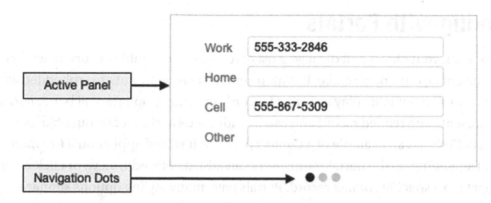

Figure 20-43. *An example of a three-panel slide control*

Exploring the Slide Control Setup Dialog

Slide controls are configured using the *Slide Control Setup* dialog, which automatically opens when a new control is created. This dialog, shown in Figure 20-44, can be opened later by double-clicking on the background of a slide control or choosing *Slide Control Setup* from the *Format* menu or the slide control contextual menu.

The setup dialog has panel controls used to add, remove, or navigate to a specific panel using the buttons. The checkboxes control iOS swipe gestures and the visibility of navigation dots so users on a macOS or Windows computer can click to other panels when swiping isn't an option.

Tip   Panels can also be reordered in Layout mode by dragging the navigation dots.

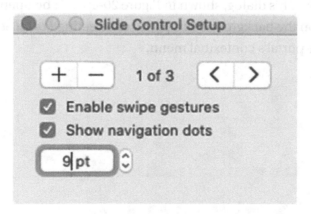

Figure 20-44. *The dialog used to configure a slide control*

Working with Portals

A *portal* is a layout object that displays a list of records from a table occurrence related to the current layout's occurrence. Portals resemble a List view but are embedded as an object on a layout to display a group of records with an optional scroll bar. A *portal row* represents one related record and can include fields and other layout objects. Figure 20-45 shows an example of a *Contact* portal as it would appear on a *Company* layout. Depending on the portal setup, users can add, delete, edit, view, or click a button to navigate to a specific contact record. Portals have many styling options similar to List views, allowing an *active row* to be styled differently and alternating styles to help visually separate inactive rows.

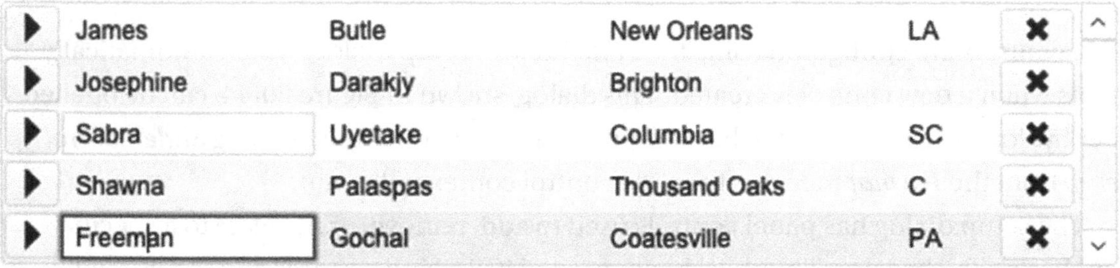

▶	James	Butle	New Orleans	LA	✖	∧
▶	Josephine	Darakjy	Brighton		✖	
▶	Sabra	Uyetake	Columbia	SC	✖	
▶	Shawna	Palaspas	Thousand Oaks	C	✖	
▶	Freeman	Gochal	Coatesville	PA	✖	∨

Figure 20-45. An example of a portal showing contact records

Exploring the Portal Setup Dialog

To create a new portal, choose the *Insert* ➤ *Portal* menu or select the tool in the toolbar. Portals are configured using the *Portal Setup* dialog, which automatically opens when a new portal is created. This dialog, shown in Figure 20-46, can be opened later by double-clicking anywhere on the background of a portal or selecting *Portal Setup* from the Format menu or the portal's contextual menu.

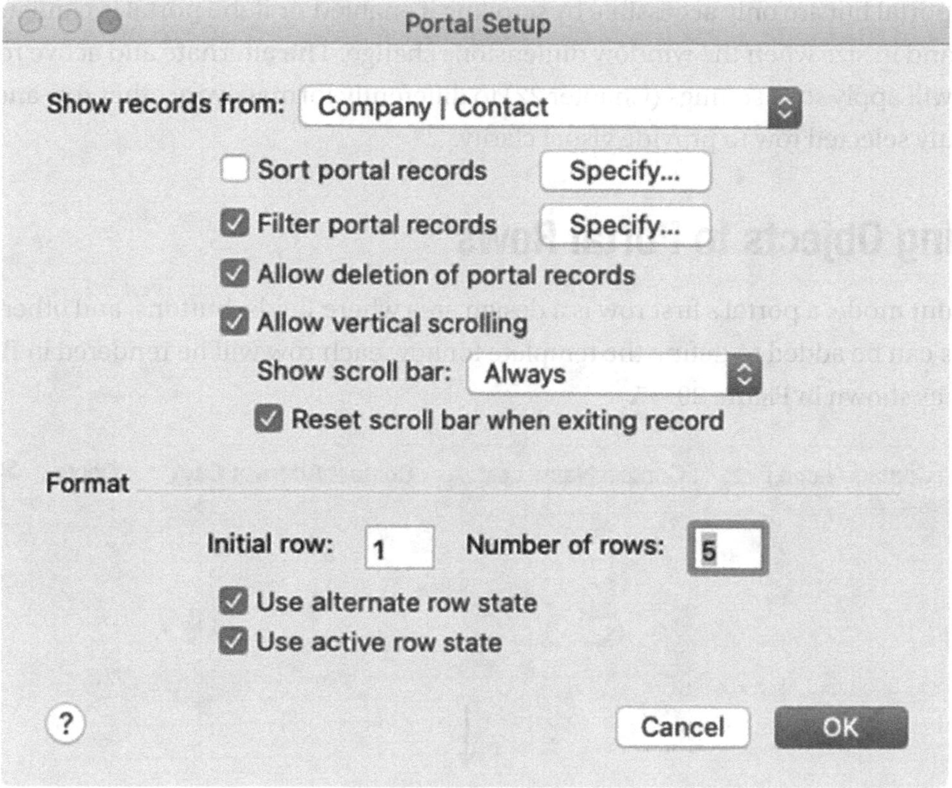

Figure 20-46.   *The dialog used to configure a portal*

The table occurrence selected from the *Show records from* pop-up menu acts as the *data source* for the portal. The four checkboxes and adjacent controls are used to configure sorting, filtering, and other functions available to the user in the portal. The *Allow deletion of portal records* checkbox allows users to delete a selected portal row with the Delete key. For a more intuitive experience and to avoid accidental deletions, disable this and create a custom *Delete* button in the portal row. Allow scrolling when the number of records exceeds the number of visible rows, optionally showing the scrollbar always or only when a user is scrolling. The *Reset scroll bar when exiting record* option will automatically scroll back to the first row when the record is committed instead of retaining the user's current scroll position.

The *Format* settings at the bottom allow control over which related records appear in the portal and which style options apply. The *Initial row* accepts a number indicating the first row that should be displayed with any related records preceding that being omitted from view. The *Number of rows* indicates how many related records to include in the portal at its minimum size. Any related records after the *first* will still be included in the portal but are only accessible by scrolling if enabled or if the portal is configured to expand in size when the window dimensions change. The alternate and active row states will apply style settings (Chapter 22) to differently format every other row and the currently selected row to provide visual clarity.

Adding Objects to Portal Rows

In Layout mode, a portal's first row is a design area where fields, buttons, and other objects can be added to define the template for how each row will be rendered in Browse mode, as shown in Figure 20-47.

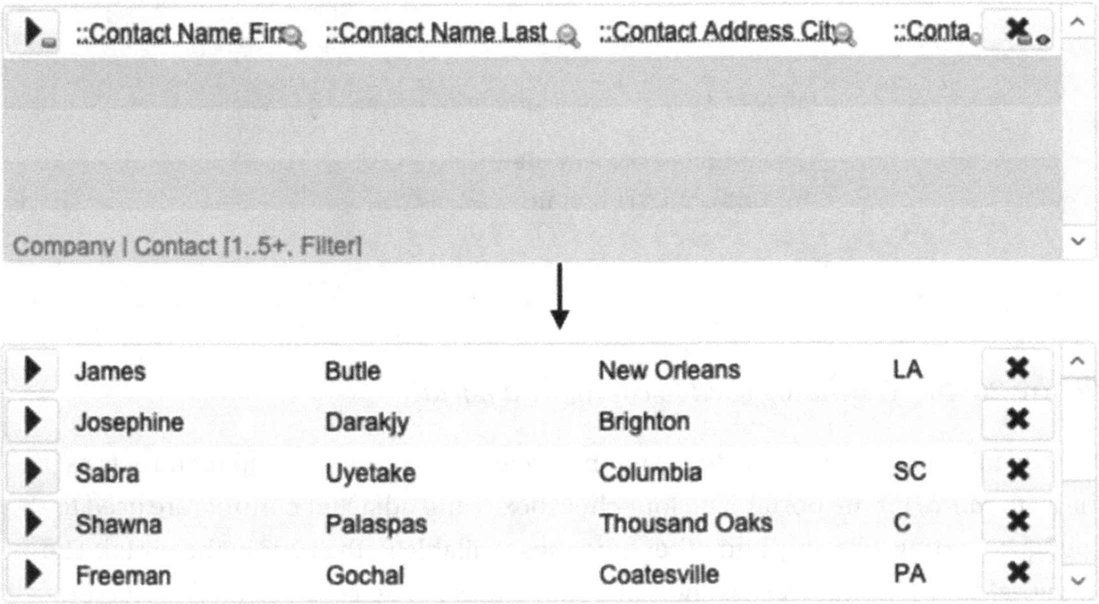

Figure 20-47. *Showing a portal in Layout mode (top) and Browse mode (bottom)*

Objects placed in the portal are rendered from the context of the current layout's occurrence and the relationship to the portal's data source occurrence. This is important to remember when choosing what objects to place inside a portal and how to configure them. Any *fields* added into the portal must be either from the portal's assigned occurrence or occurrences that are related to it in a direct line away from the layout's occurrence. Fields from tables beyond the portal's table will only display a value from the first matching record through the relationship conduit from the context of the record for each portal row. So, a *Contact* portal can include a field that hops across multiple relationships to show a field from an invoice line item from an invoice related to the contact, but it will only show the value from the first line item for the first invoice for the contact based on the relational connections along that chain. Any *object* in a portal must be thought of in the context of the portal's occurrence. When writing formulas for hide, tooltips, conditional formatting, script parameters, etc., the formula must be restrained to include fields based on the portal's context.

Creating Records in a Portal Directly

In Browse mode, portals automatically update anytime new matching records are created in the related source table. If one user is viewing a *Company* record on a layout with a *Contact* portal, any new contact record that is linked to that company will appear in the portal viewed by anyone. If the user viewing the company record wants to create a new related contact record from the *Company* layout, they would have to switch layouts, create the record, link it to the company, and then return to the original layout to see it in the portal – or run a script that performs those steps in sequence. Alternatively, a portal can be configured with a shortcut that allows users to create a new record directly in the portal by typing into an empty portal row at the bottom. This ability is configured at the relationship level instead of on the layout object. Open the *Manage Database* dialog and enable the *Allow creation of records* checkbox in the *Edit Relationship* dialog (Chapter 9) on the side of the relationship used as the portal's data source, in this case, *Company | Contact*. Once done, any portal assigned that occurrence will display one blank row, as shown in Figure 20-48. The blank row *only exists in the interface* and will be *programmatically ignored* with no effect on functions that summarize related records such as *Count, List, Max, Min, Sum*, etc.

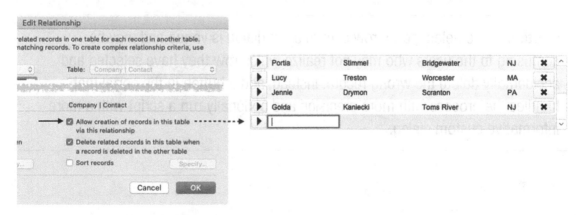

Figure 20-48. *The setting (left) that enables a blank portal row for creating new records (right)*

When the user types into any editable field in that blank row and then moves focus to another field or commits the record, a new record will be instantly created in the remote table. The new record will automatically populate each match field with the appropriate value required to relate it to the currently viewed parent record. Although the new record remains in the portal, it may sort to a new position based on the values in any sort field defined at the relationship level and/or specified in the portal's settings. Once finished, a new blank row will appear for the creation of additional new records.

Caution   This feature may confuse users since the empty row appears like an actual record with no field values. Users may try to delete it. Buttons can be hidden (Chapter 21) to make it less conspicuous, but some developers disable this and use a custom script to perform the sequence required to create related records.

Deleting Portal Rows

Portal rows are a representation of records from another table, and they will disappear from the portal whenever the related record is deleted. A portal can be configured to allow users to delete a record directly within the portal. Open the *Portal Setup* dialog, and select the *Allow deletion of portal records* option. Once enabled, a user can select a portal row and type the Delete key to delete the related record and remove it from the portal display. FileMaker will present a confirmation dialog asking if the user wants to continue with the deletion. If they confirm, the related record will be permanently deleted.

Caution   The delete portal row confirmation dialog is vague and may be confusing to the users who may not realize which row they have selected and accidentally delete the wrong record. Instead, add a button in the portal that handles the process with more precision and optionally run a script with a more informative custom dialog.

Filtering Portal Records

The relationship between the layout's occurrence and portal's occurrence automatically provides a baseline filter controlling the records displayed in a portal. Only records with a relational match of the current record's occurrence will be included. By contrast, the *portal filtering* option in the *Portal Setup* dialog allows a formula to further control which of the related records will actually be displayed in the portal. The filter formula is evaluated once for each available related record, and they are only displayed if the result is true.

The filter formula can be as simple or as complex as needed to determine if a record should be included. It can include field comparisons and can be based on a user's entry in fields exclusively for soliciting filtering preferences. For example, a field positioned near the portal can allow users to type any criteria that can be used to determine a subset of related records that will be displayed. In the example shown in Figure 20-49, a *Company* layout includes a *Contact* portal showing related people. The relationship limits the portal list to only people related to the current company. The value in the filtering field can be compared to the related *State* field in order to narrow the related to only contacts whose address matches the value entered by a user.

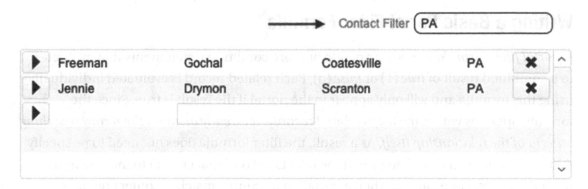

Figure 20-49. *An example of a portal filtering field*

Caution   Filtering only affects the *display* of related records and does not affect the actual relationship. Any calculation that accesses records through the relationship will continue to see all related records even when the portal displays a filtered set!

Setting Up Portal Filtering

To set up the filtering example, start with these steps:

1. In the *Company* table, create a text field named "Company
    Contact Portal Filter." Optionally make this field use global storage
    to avoid conflicts between users and preserve a user's entry across
    all records.

2. Place that field on the layout above the portal with a label that
    makes clear its function, like "Contacts Filter." Alternatively, use a
    placeholder calculation as a prompt.

3. Open the *Portal Setup* dialog.

4. Click the *Specify* button next to *Filter portal records*.

5. Enter a formula that indicates when a related record in the
    Contacts table should appear in the portal based on what the user
    has typed into the filter field (see following examples).

6. Then save the formula and close the *Portal Setup* dialog.

Writing a Basic Portal Filter Formula

A *portal filter formula* is made up of one or more conditional statements that evaluate
to a combined result of *true* (1) or *false* (0). Each related record is evaluated individually
using this formula and will only appear in the portal if the result is true. Since the
formula operates within the list of related records, *it already assumes the record matching
criteria of the relationship itself.* As a result, the filter formula does not need to re-specify
that criteria nor can it work to extend the results beyond that criteria to include non-
related records. For example, when a portal's data source matches contact records
assigned to the current company record, we can filter by contact address, but we can't
make the formula include contacts assigned to other companies.

When writing a formula for filtering, the formula should include a condition to
display all records for situations when no criteria is entered. So, start the formula with
the following code that provides a *true* result when the filter field is empty:

```
Company::Company Contact Portal Filter = ""
```

Next, add a second condition after an *or* operator that uses the *PatternCount* function, to specify a partial or full match between the related *Contact Address State* field and the text the user enters in the filter field. The following example formula allows a record to appear if no filter value is entered *or* if the value entered is found within the state field:

```
Company::Company Contact Portal Filter = "" or
PatternCount (
    Company | Contact::Contact Address State ;
    Company::Company Contact Portal Filter
) > 0
```

Save the formula and close the setup dialog to test the function. Start with a company record with a lot of contacts in the portal. When a state abbreviation is typed into the filter field, the record committed, and the window refreshed, the portal rows should only include those records matching the text entered. To have the portal update automatically as a user is typing into the filter field, use the *ObjectModify* script trigger (Chapter 27) to run a script that commits, refreshes, and re-enters the filter field constantly.

Expanding the Formula for Multiple Match Fields

The previous example assumed the user's filtering criteria would be a state. However, the filter formula can be expanded to detect matches across multiple fields. The following example adds conditions to find matches in *first name*, *last name*, *city*, or *state*:

```
Company::Company Contact Portal Filter = "" or
PatternCount (
    Company | Contact::Contact Name First ;
    Company::Company Contact Portal Filter
) > 0 or
PatternCount (
    Company | Contact::Contact Name Last ;
    Company::Company Contact Portal Filter
) > 0 or
PatternCount (
    Company | Contact::Contact Address City ;
    Company::Company Contact Portal Filter
) > 0 or
```

```
PatternCount (
   Company | Contact::Contact Address State ;
   Company::Company Contact Portal Filter
) > 0
```

Enhancing the Search Field

Once the filter field is operational, apply some formatting changes like those shown in Figure 20-50. The search field has its left corners rounded using the *Corner radius* settings of the *Appearance* tab of the *Inspector* pane. The label was removed in favor of a *Placeholder text* value of "Search by." Finally, a button has been added to the right of the field with opposing rounded corners, an icon assigned, and an *Action* defined to run a script that deletes the contents of the filter field and commits the record.

Figure 20-50. *A visually improved portal filter field*

Working with Web Viewers

A *web viewer* is a layout object that displays a web page directly on a layout. This can be configured with or without user interaction, and the content can be generated by any of the following:

- A web address hard-coded to point to a specific website

- A web address pulled from a database field or dynamically generated from a formula

- A Claris-provided address formula such as Google web search, Google maps, FedEx, or Wikipedia

- Custom HTML code from a field or formula, which can include hard-code elements, field data, and even images in fields

- A web address or custom HTML code provided by a script

Caution   Custom web addresses must begin with the correct URL scheme such as http://, https://, ftp://, or file://.

Exploring the Web Viewer Setup Dialog

To add a web page to a layout, select the *Insert* ➤ *Web Viewer* menu, or use the tool in the toolbar. The *Web Viewer Setup* dialog will appear, shown in Figure 20-51. This can be opened later by double-clicking on a web viewer or selecting the *Web Viewer Setup* from the *Format* menu or the viewer's contextual menu.

The *Choose a Website* list on the top left specifies the source data. Choose from a list of data-driven templates or select *Custom Web Address* to write your own URL or HTML formula. When using a template, the component fields on the right accept values that will be inserted into the URL. *The Web Address* area allows entry of a URL, HTML code, or a formula to generating either. The templates will insert a ready-made calculation with links to parameter fields on the top right. Enter addresses or formulas into the text area, or click the *Specify* button to enter a formula.

The checkbox options at the bottom control various viewer features. You can enable user interaction with the rendered web page, control display in Find mode, include a progress bar when loading, and include a status message. *The Automatically encode URL* option will *percent-encode* special characters in the address. For example, spaces are converted to %20 if this box is checked. Alternatively, the *GetAsURLEncoded* function can be used in a formula to handle encoding. The *Allow JavaScript to perform FileMaker scripts* option was added in version 19 to enable the HTML code to directly call native FileMaker scripts using a *FileMaker.PerformScript* JavaScript function (described later in this section).

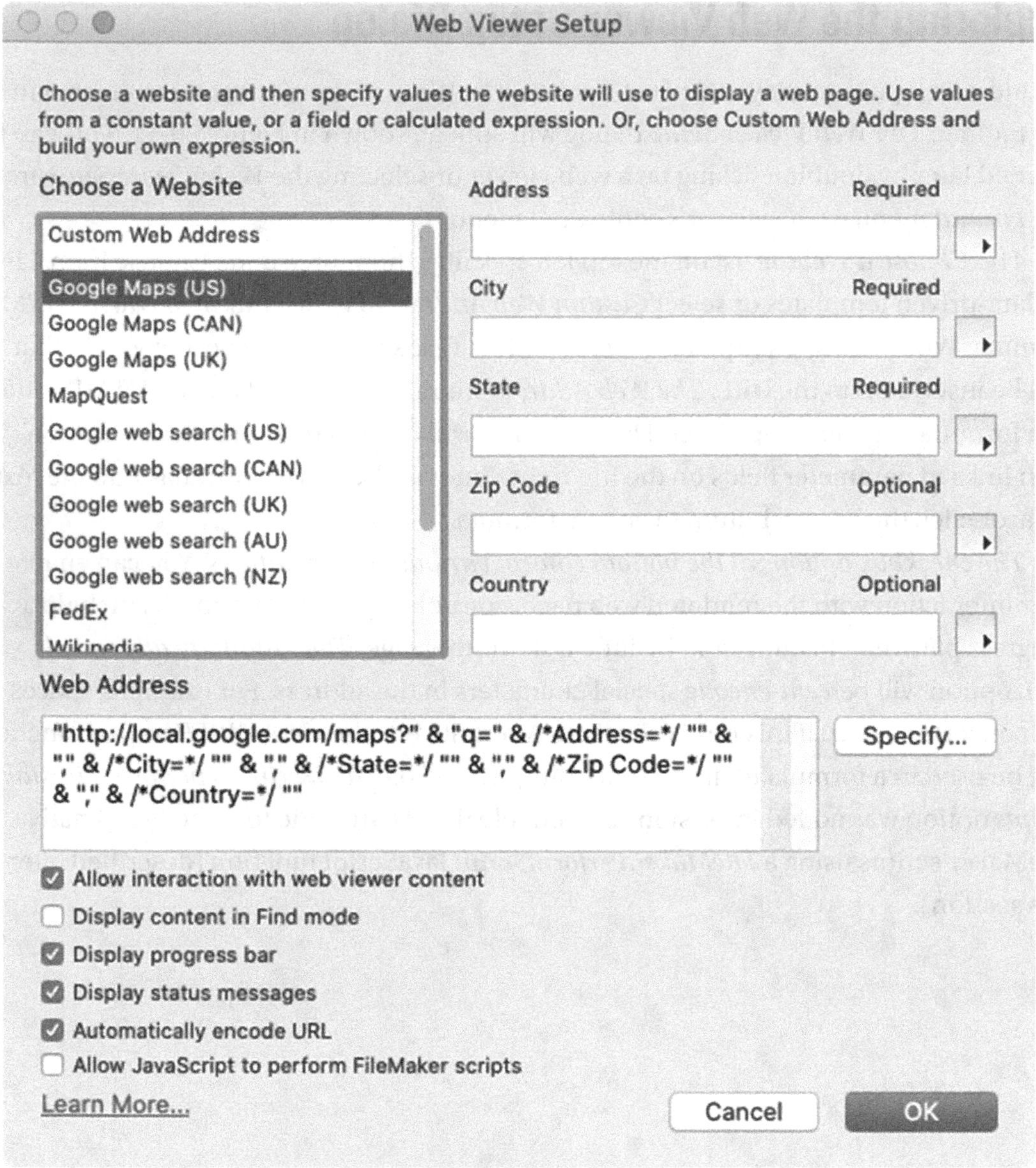

Figure 20-51. *The dialog used to configure a web viewer*

With the *Allow interaction with web viewer content* option enabled, users can interact with a web page as with any standard browser. They can click links to navigate to other pages and interact with rich content such as movies. Although very capable, viewers aren't intended to act as a full-featured web browser, and there may be some limitations. The *Open Link in New Window* function in the viewer's contextual menu in Browse mode will redirect the page out of FileMaker to the user's default browser application and allow a fuller web experience.

Building a Web Page Using Data from Fields

As an alternative to displaying a page based on a web address, a viewer can display HTML code to generate a custom page. FileMaker uses the *data universal resource identifier* (URI) scheme, which is a standard method of including data within the code of a web page instead of accessing external resources. The *data URI* is expressed with the following formula, with square brackets indicating optional elements:

```
data:[<media type>][;base64],<data>
```

This formula contains the following elements:

- `data` – This required prefix indicates the scheme being used, followed by a semicolon.

- `<media type>` – Optionally indicates the type of material contained in the data. A web page would use `text/html`, while an image would use `image/<type>`, for example, `image/png`. If no media type is specified, the data will be assumed to be text/plain.

- `base64` – This optional extension, delimited from the media type with a semicolon, is used to indicate that the data content is binary data, which is encoded in `ASCII` format using the `Base64` binary-to-text encoding scheme.

- `<data>` – Preceded with a comma, this placeholder would be replaced with a sequence of characters containing the content being described, HTML code or Base64 image data.

Note   Since version 15, the data and media type have been optional. The text can begin with `<html>` or `<!DOCTYPE html>` and render as expected in a web viewer.

Creating a Hello World Web Page

This code defines a simple *Hello, World* example web page formula for a web viewer:

```
"data:text/html,
<html>
<head>
</head>
```

495

```
<body>
<h1>Hello, World</h1>
</body>"
```

Add a `<style>` tag to control text formatting with *Cascading Style Sheets* (CSS). This example modifies the color of the h1 style to display the text in green:

```
"data:text/html,
<html>
<head>
<style>
h1 {
color: green;
}
</style>
</head>
<body>
<h1>Hello, World</h1>
</body>"
```

Add a `<script>` tag to include JavaScript functions as demonstrated by the following example that opens an alert dialog when the page loads:

```
"data:text/html,
<html>
<head>
</head>
<body>
<script>
alert('Hello, World!')
</script>
<h1>Hello, World</h1>
</body>"
```

Caution When calculating content for a web viewer in a formula, all text must be enclosed in quotation marks. Any quotes within that text must be escaped with a preceding backslash.

Including Text Fields in a Web Page

Using a formula-driven web page, inserting fields is done the same as in any formula (Chapter 12). Simply insert a field reference into the formula outside of the quoted text.

```
"data:text/html,
<html>
<head>
</head>
<body>
<h1>" & Company::Company Name & "</h1>
</body>"
```

Including a Container Field Image in a Web Page

Images from the Web can be included by inserting the URL in an <image> tag. However, to include an image stored in a field, use the *Base64Decode* function to convert the image into text.

```
"data:text/html,
<html>
<head>
</head>
<body>
<h1>" & Company::Company Name & "</h1>
<img src='data:image/imagemac;base64," & Base64Encode ( Company::Company
Logo ) & "'>
</body>"
```

Calling a FileMaker Script with JavaScript

In version 19, FileMaker added the ability for JavaScript in a web viewer to call a native FileMaker script. As long as the option in the *Web Viewer Setup* dialog is enabled, buttons and URLs in HTML code can call a *FileMaker.PerformScript* function with two parameters: *script name* and *parameter*. The following simple example assumes a script named "Test Script" exists that will generate a dialog using the *Show Custom Dialog* script step that displays the script parameter (Chapters 24 and 25). The code renders a button that calls a JavaScript function named *runScript()* that runs the FileMaker script. If configured correctly, clicking the button should cause FileMaker to open a dialog with a message of "Hello, World!"

```
"data:text/html,
<html>
<head>
</head>
<body>
<h1>Test FMP Script</h1>
<button onclick=\"runScript()\">Test FMP Script</button>
<script>
    function runScript() {
        FileMaker.PerformScript ( \"Test Script\", \"Hello, World!\" );
    }
</script>
</body>
</html>"
```

Caution   This JavaScript function only works on web pages rendered in a FileMaker web viewer. To enable HTML click access from outside the database, use the FileMaker URL (Chapter 29).

Working with Charts

A *chart* is a layout object that draws a graphical representation of data in one of several popular charting formats: *column, stacked column, positive negative column, bar, stacked bar, pie, line, area, scatter,* or *bubble*. These can be created using data from the current found set, a group of related records, or from calculated data. Charts are configured in a *Chart Setup* dialog that opens whenever a new chart object is inserted onto a layout. This dialog can be re-opened for an existing chart object by double-clicking on it or selecting *Chart Setup* from the *Format* menu or its contextual menu. The dialog is divided into two main sections: a *chart preview* area continuously updates a drawing of the chart as it is configured and a settings sidebar of togglable sections for various settings – *Chart, Styles,* and *Data Source*.

Creating a Chart Using Calculated Data

Using calculated data to generate a chart will pull information from either hard-coded calculated values or fields from the current record. To create a pie chart using hard-coded values, insert a chart object onto a layout, and then configure the settings as shown in Figure 20-52.

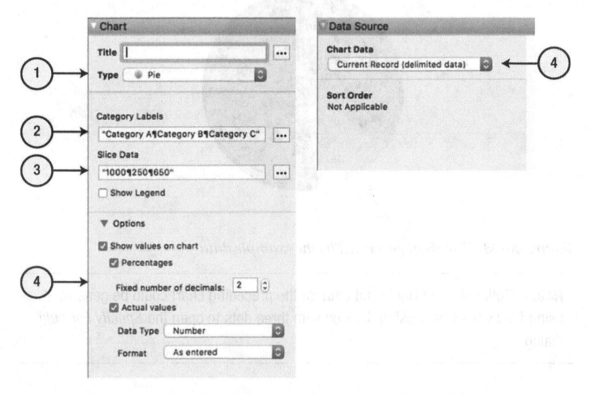

Figure 20-52. *The settings for a simple pie chart based on calculated data*

The following settings are required to generate a pie chart with three sections, as shown in Figure 20-53:

1. *Type* – Select *Pie* as the type and optionally enter a title.

2. *Category Labels* – Enter a return-delimited list of categories for the chart, e.g., Category A¶Category B¶Category C.

3. *Slice Data* – Enter a return-delimited list of numbers for each category slice of the pie, e.g., 1000¶250¶650.

4.   *Options* – Choose various optional settings for label format.

5.   *Chart Data* – From the *Data Source* settings group, select *Current Record (delimited data)* to instruct the chart engine to use data from the context of the current record only.

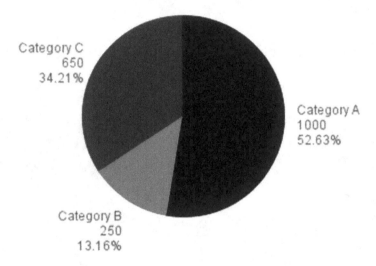

Figure 20-53. *The chart generated by the example data*

Note   Optionally, the labels and data for the preceding chart could be generated using field values by clicking the icon with three dots to open the *Specify Formula* dialog.

Creating a Chart Using the Found Set

Using the records in the found set as the data source, create a bar chart that displays the number of *Contact* records by state. To get started, insert a chart onto a layout, and then configure the settings as shown in Figure 20-54.

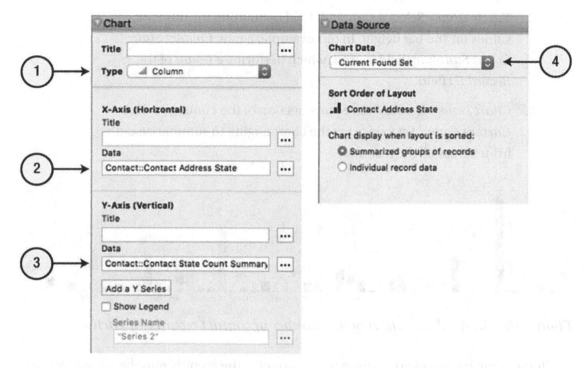

Figure 20-54. *Configuring a bar chart using data from the found set*

Caution Creating charts from found sets can be a little confusing. It is like creating a report with a sub-summary part since only records in the found set will be included and the current sort order controls how a summary field counts records into subgroups.

The following settings will create a chart as shown in Figure 20-55:

1. *Type* – Select *Column* as the type.

2. *X-Axis Data* – Select a field containing text that will act as the labels for the bars. To avoid duplicate values, FileMaker will automatically summarize these *if the found set is sorted by the field specified*. In our example, we sort by and point to the *Contact Address State* field.

3. *Y-Axis Data* – Select a summary field containing the numeric
    values for the bar height. In our example, a new *Contact State
    Count Summary* field is used, which performs a *Count* of the
    Record ID field.

4. *Chart Data* – On the *Data Source* section of the controls, select
    Current Found Set to instruct the chart engine to summarize data
    from across all the records.

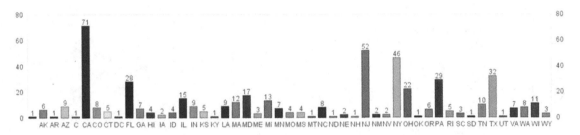

Figure 20-55. *A column chart of the number of contact records for each state*

Remember, for this chart to summarize correctly, the records *must* be sorted by the
x-axis, and the y-axis *must* be a summary field.

Summary

This chapter explored the various objects that are used when designing layouts. In the
next chapter, we learn how to manipulate, arrange, and configure objects.

CHAPTER 21

Manipulating Objects

After adding an object to a layout, it can be manipulated and configured in a variety of ways. This chapter introduces the many basic methods, covering these topics:

- Selecting objects
- Resizing objects
- Moving objects
- Arranging and aligning objects
- Hiding objects
- Conditional formatting
- Understanding tab order
- Naming objects

Selecting Objects

To *select* an object, click on it with the cursor or click on the layout near the object and drag the cursor over or around it. The object will become highlighted with an outline that includes eight *sizing handles*, as shown in Figure 21-1.

Figure 21-1. An object at rest (left) vs. a selected object (right)

© Mark Conway Munro 2021
M. C. Munro, *Learn FileMaker Pro 19*, https://doi.org/10.1007/978-1-4842-6680-9_21

To select more than one object at a time, either click on them one by one while holding down the Shift key or click on the background and drag the cursor so that the focal rectangle touches all the desired objects. Hold the Command (macOS) or Windows (Windows) key while dragging to require that an item be *completely* within the boundaries of the focal rectangle before it will be selected. When multiple objects are selected, they share one set of sizing handles, outlining the overall space of the group, as shown in Figure 21-2. Objects can be de-selected by clicking on the layout background or by selecting another object. To de-select one of a group of selected objects, click on the object while holding the Shift key.

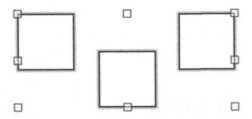

Figure 21-2. *Objects selected together will share sizing handles*

Caution   Shape objects with no fill can only be selected by clicking the border. Clicking in the center of an object will click through the object onto objects behind it or the background of the layout.

Resizing Objects

Objects can be resized by dragging one of the eight sizing in or out from the center of the object. Use the settings on the *Position* tab of the *Inspector* pane controls for precision resizing of objects, entering a new *Width* or *Height* and typing Tab or Enter to register the change. To uniformly resize groups of objects, use the *Resize To* functions, described later in this chapter.

Moving Objects

When one or more objects are selected, they can be moved to a new location by clicking and dragging them around the layout or using one of three other methods. The arrow keys will nudge a selection one pixel at a time in one directional plane. The settings on the *Position* tab of the *Inspector* pane allow objects to be precisely placed by entering a new measurement for *Left, Right, Top,* or *Bottom.* To move groups of objects relative to each other, use the *Arrange* and *Align* functions, described later in this chapter.

Layout Positioning Helpers

There are four features that are helpful when positioning objects manually: the *ruler, grid, guides,* and *dynamic guides*. These can be used individually or together to guide an object to a new location.

Ruler

The *ruler* is a horizontal and vertical strip running along the entire left and top of a window's content area that displays incremental markings based on a chosen unit of measurement: *inch, centimeter,* or *point*. The full ruler, as shown in Figure 21-3, is only visible in Layout mode when the *View ➤ Rulers* menu is active.

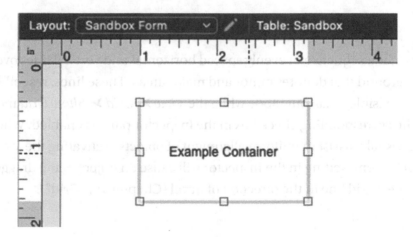

Figure 21-3. *The Layout mode ruler assists for precise positioning*

The ruler has several non-obvious features. At the corner where the horizontal and vertical rulers intersect, a button displays the current unit of measure. Click this to cycle through the available units for the ruler. The selected unit can also be changed from the ruler's contextual menu. The cursor's current position is marked in each ruler with a dotted line, and, when dragging an object, the rulers denote the boundaries of object with a white highlight.

When editing the content of a text object, the top ruler transforms into a gray bar with a text ruler overlay that spans only the width of text object, as shown in Figure 21-4. This ruler controls indentation, margins, and tabs within the text object in a similar manner to the text ruler accessible in Browse mode when editing a field.

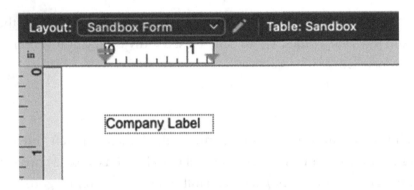

Figure 21-4. *The top ruler transforms when editing layout text*

Grid

The layout *grid* is a sequence of evenly spaced horizontal and vertical lines overlaid on a layout background that denotes minor and major areas. These lines, resembling graph paper, are only visible in Layout mode when the *View* ➤ *Grid* ➤ *Show Grid* menu item is active or the corresponding check box in the Inspector pane is enabled. When visible, the lines can visually assist in uniform alignment of objects. Activating the *View* ➤ *Grid* ➤ *Snap to Grid* menu setting in the Inspector will cause an object being dragged to be drawn to the next grid line in the direction of travel (Chapter 19, "Grid").

Guides

A layout *guide* is a movable blue line used to align objects and define regions of a layout. Multiple guides can be placed horizontally or vertically on the layout, as shown in Figure 21-5. Guides don't print and are only visible in Layout mode when the *View* ➤

Guides ➤ *Show Guides* menu is active. Click anywhere on the left or top ruler and then drag right or down, respectively, and release a new guide at the desired position on the content area. Guides can be repositioned by dragging them to a new position or removed completely by dragging them back to the ruler. When visible, guides can visually assist in uniform alignment of objects. Activating the *View* ➤ *Guides* ➤ *Snap to Guides* menu will cause an object being dragged to be drawn to the next available guide in the direction of travel.

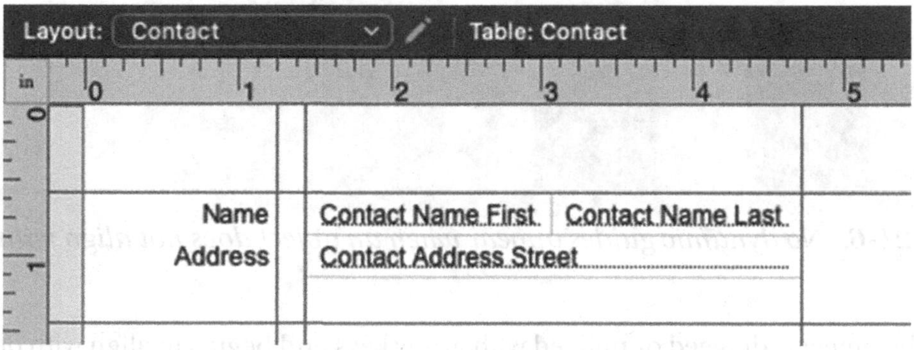

Figure 21-5. *A layout with several guides defining regions*

Dynamic Guides

As an object is moved around a layout, blue lines called *dynamic guides* automatically appear and disappear on or around nearby objects showing alignment and spacing patterns that would result if the object were dropped in its current location. By showing these spatial relationships of stationary objects relative to the position of the moving object, dynamic guides help to encourage a neat design when repositioning an object. Like the grid and guides, objects will be magnetically drawn to dynamic guides. Dynamic guides can be activated or deactivated with the *View* ➤ *Dynamic Guides* menu.

When first moving an object, no guides will appear when the current position does not align to any other objects on the layout, as shown in Figure 21-6.

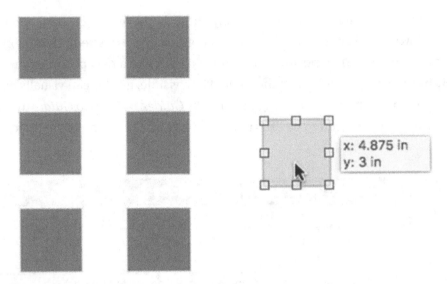

Figure 21-6. *No dynamic guides appear when an object does not align with other objects*

As the object is dragged or nudged with arrow keys and begins to align with other objects, one or more dynamic guides will appear, as shown in Figure 21-7. Alignments are shown for *left, right, horizontal center, top, bottom,* and *vertical center,* connecting to one or more other objects.

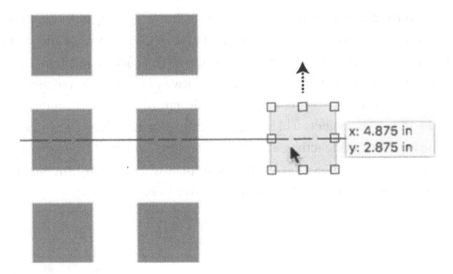

Figure 21-7. *As an object aligns with one or more objects, a guide will appear*

When the object is dragged into a position that creates a consistent spacing pattern, those are highlighted as well, as shown in Figure 21-8. These appear for *horizontal* and *vertical* distribution and are displayed simultaneously with alignment guides.

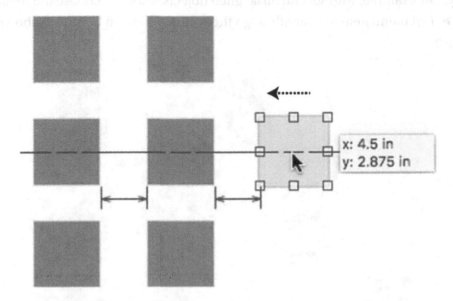

Figure 21-8. *Multiple guides can show alignment and distribution spacing*

Note   Examples in this chapter are shown with uniform square shapes for illustrative purposes only. Dynamic guides and all other features work the same with *any* combination of different object types, in non-uniform arrangements, and of varying sizes.

Arranging and Aligning Objects

When working on complex layouts with dozens or hundreds of items, moving, sizing, and spacing groups of objects can be a tediously repetitive manual chore. FileMaker has functions that assist in the task of *aligning, distributing, resizing, rotating, grouping,* and *locking* objects. These are all accessible from the Layout mode in the *Arrange* menu in the menu bar, a submenu of an object's contextual menu, and in the *Arrange & Align* group of tools on the *Position* tab of the *Inspector* pane. With the exception of *Rotate*, these functions all work with any combination of object type.

Align

The *Align* functions automatically align groups of selected objects horizontally or vertically. For example, with several misaligned objects selected, choose the *Arrange* ➤ *Align* ➤ *Left* menu item to instantly align them along their left border, as shown in Figure 21-9.

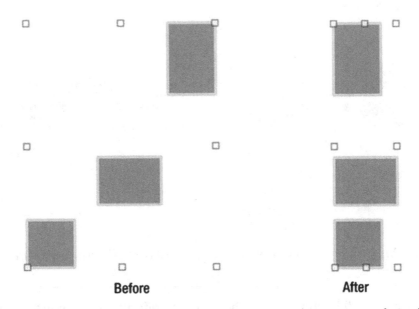

Before   **After**

Figure 21-9. *Transforming misaligned objects (before) to aligned (after)*

Resize To

The *Resize To* functions automatically resizes a group of selected objects to *Smallest Width, Smallest Height, Smallest Width and Height, Largest Width, Largest Height,* or *Largest Width and Height.* For example, with several non-uniformly sized objects selected, choose the *Arrange* ➤ *Resize To* ➤ *Smallest Width and Height* menu item to instantly resize every object to a uniform size and height based on the object with the smallest of each, as shown in Figure 21-10.

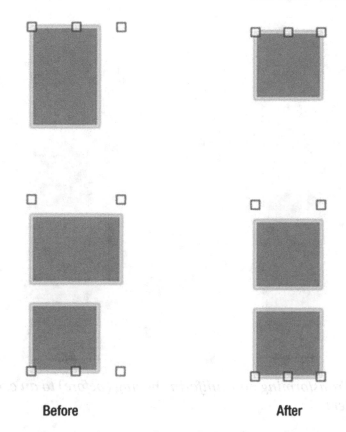

Before   After

Figure 21-10. *Transforming non-uniform objects (before) to a uniform size (after)*

Distribute

The *Distribute* commands will reposition a group of objects so that they are uniformly spaced horizontally or vertically using the outside measurements of the group along the respective axis. For example, with several non-uniformly spaced objects selected, choose the *Arrange* ➤ *Distribute* ➤ *Vertical* menu to instantly reposition every object uniformly spaced, as shown in Figure 21-11.

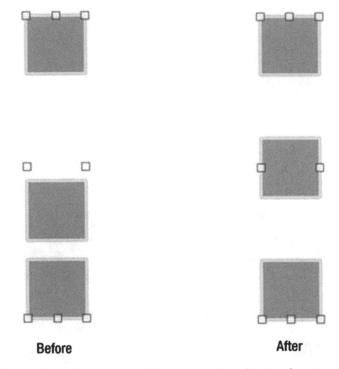

Before   **After**

Figure 21-11. *Transforming non-uniform spacing (before) to an even vertical distribution (after)*

Rotate

Many objects can be rotated in a clockwise direction in 90-degree increments by selecting the *Arrange* ➤ *Rotate* menu item, as shown in Figure 21-12. The exceptions are button bars, charts, popovers, portals, slide controls, tab controls, and web viewers.

Hello, World ·····························➤ Hello, World

Figure 21-12. *A text object (left) after two 90-degree rotations (right)*

Group

A set of selected objects can be transformed into a single *group object* by selecting the *Arrange* ➤ *Group* menu. Once joined together, the grouped objects can be moved or resized as a single unit but still manipulated individually within the group by clicking once on the group and a second time on an item within it. Objects such as buttons, button bars, charts, fields, web viewers, and more can be functionally edited while grouped by double-clicking directly on them. To ungroup formerly grouped objects, select the *Arrange ➤ Ungroup* menu.

Lock

Locking an object causes it to become non-editable in Layout mode. This helps avoid accidental deletion or movement of objects on complex layouts. A locked object can't be moved, resized, reassigned, reconfigured, or changed in any way until it is unlocked. Lock a selected object or group of objects by selecting the *Arrange ➤ Lock* menu. Once locked, the item will not respond to any editing attempts. Attempting to change some settings through the *Inspector* will produce a dialog stating that the change can't be made because of the object's locked status. However, in many cases, the command will just be silently ignored. An object can be unlocked with the *Arrange ➤ Unlock* menu. When selected, locked objects display an "x" icon in place of each sizing handle, as shown in Figure 21-13.

Figure 21-13. *A locked object indicated by its sizing handles*

Object Stacking

Objects exist within a front to back *stacking order*. When two objects are moved together, the one created more recently will appear on top of the first, obscuring it from view. There are four commands that change an object's position within the stack, as illustrated in Figure 21-14: *Bring to Front*, *Bring Forward*, *Send Backward*, and *Send to Back*.

Note   The object stacking order is reflected in the *Objects* tab of the *Objects* pane, where objects on top of the list are in front of those below.

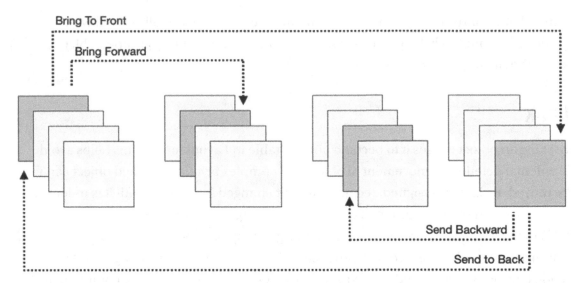

Figure 21-14. *An illustration of commands that affect an object's stack position*

Hiding Objects

Objects can be assigned a formula that determines when they should be rendered and when they should be hidden. Select the object and enter a *Hide objects when* formula in the *Behavior* section of the *Data* tab of the *Inspector* pane. When that formula returns a true result, the object will be hidden in non-Layout modes. The formula entered can be based on various criteria: the values in fields, conditions of the window, or details about the user's environment. A button can be hidden until data is entered in specific fields, e.g., hide a *Print* button until fields required for the report have a value, or hide an *Approve* button until key status fields have a value. Hide a *field* configured as a pop-up menu if the value list is currently empty. Hide data entry–specific buttons and objects when the window is in Find mode. A *chart* can be hidden until enough information has been entered into fields to actually draw something useful. A set of *portals* can be toggled depending on the type of record, showing a purchase order portal for vendor contacts and switching to a project portal for customer contacts. Use the feature to obscure information depending on a user's access privilege (Chapter 30) so they don't see blocked out fields saying "no access" and can't click buttons that produce access denied errors. A multi-segment *button bar* can toggle so only one segment shows at a time as a technique to toggle a button's icon and function.

Using Hide to Toggle a Button Bar

A two-segment button bar with a different *Hide* formula on each segment can create an *active label,* a button that changes icon and functionality depending on the corresponding field's value. For example, consider the label of a *Contact Company ID* field configured with a pop-up menu for assigning a company to a contact. If the desired company record exists, the user can simply select it in the field. However, if the company doesn't exist yet, a button can be created to create a new record and link it to the contact. Similarly, once a company has been assigned, it is customary to have a button that allows the user to navigate to the related company record assigned to the contact. A hide function can toggle which buttons are visible at a given time, but you still have three objects to contend with: a field label, a navigation button, and a create new button. Alternatively, all of these could be replaced with a single object: a two-segment button bar used as an active label that toggles between one or the other segment to allow creation of a new company (if one hasn't been selected) or navigation to the related record (if one has been selected).

The example illustrated in Figure 21-15 shows a two-segment button bar with no border used as a field label for a *Contact Company ID* field. The first button segment has a plus icon assigned and is configured to hide when the id field is not empty. This would run a script that creates a new related company record and assigns its id to the current contact record. The second segment has a navigation icon assigned and is configured to hide when the id field is empty. This would run a script that navigates to the selected *Company* record. Since the two hide formulas are binary opposites, only one label will be visible at any given moment in Browse mode.

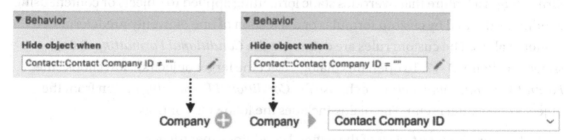

Figure 21-15. *A two-segment bar as a field label that always hides one segment.*

> **Caution**   A third segment could be added with no icon and no script as an inactive label in Find mode. The hide formulas would check the window mode and adjust the hide action accordingly.

Based on the preceding configuration, the label with a plus icon will only appear when no company is selected, and the label with the navigation icon will only appear when one is selected, both shown in Figure 21-16.

Company ⊕ [⌄]

Company ▶ [Write Track Media, Inc.   ⌄]

Figure 21-16.   *The label button when a company is empty (top) or selected (bottom)*

> **Tip**   Use hide to embed text objects with developer notes with a formula that always returns true (1) so they are only visible in Layout mode.

Conditional Formatting

Any layout object can be formatted using the tools in the *Inspector* pane. Fields can be formatted as an object, and the content they contain can be styled. *Conditional formatting* is a feature that overrides static formatting applied to objects or content using conditions defined by custom formulas or a selection of one of twenty predetermined content values. The custom rules are defined in the *Conditional Formatting* dialog, shown in Figure 21-17. To open this dialog, select the target object(s), and choose the *Format ➤ Conditional* menu, or choose the *Conditional Formatting* option from the object's contextual menu. The dialog includes the following controls:

1. *Condition List* – List of the defined conditions that trigger formatting. These will be evaluated in order from top to bottom. The checkbox indicates an active condition.

2. *Condition* – Define the criteria for the selected condition to determine when formatting will be applied.

3. *Format* – Select the formatting settings to apply when the selected condition evaluates true.

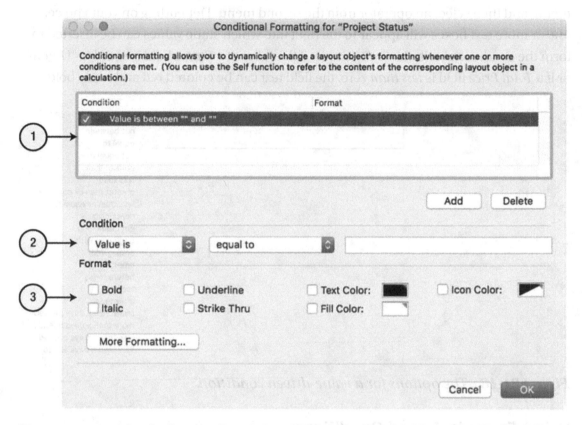

Figure 21-17. *The dialog used to define format overrides based on conditional criteria*

Condition Formula Options

A *contextual formatting condition* defines the circumstances under which a set of format settings will be applied to an object. The condition can be a selection of a predefined *value-based condition* or a custom *formula-based condition*.

Using Value-Based Conditions

A *value-based condition* determines when formatting should be applied by comparing the value of the object to static criteria using a selected operator, as shown in Figure 21-18. In the *Condition* section of the *Conditional Formatting* dialog, select *Value Is* in the first menu, and then select an operator from the second menu. Depending on your choice, one or more text boxes will appear to the right into which static values can be inserted to form the conditional criteria. For example, if the value of a *Status* field is *equal to* "Urgent" or if a *Total Price* field is *less than* zero, the field text can be colored red and made bold.

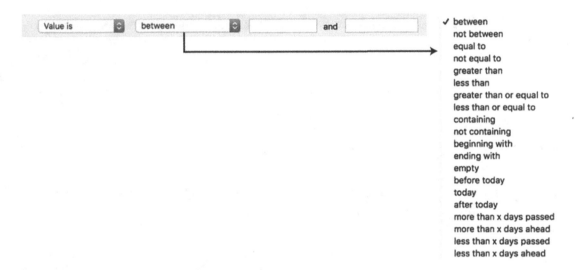

Figure 21-18. *The options for a value-driven condition*

Using Formula-Based Conditions

A *formula-based condition* determines when formatting should be applied by evaluating a custom formula and applying the styling if the result is true. In the *Condition* section of the *Conditional Formatting* dialog, select *Formula Is* in the first menu, as shown in Figure 21-19. Then, enter a formula directly into the field or click the *Specify* button to open the *Specify Calculation* dialog (Chapter 12). The formula can use any combination of built-in functions, custom functions, and fields to define the conditions under which formatting will be applied.

Figure 21-19. *The interface for a formula-driven condition*

Conditionally Formatting a Project Status Field

To illustrate a use of conditional formatting, consider an example of a *Status* field value controlling the formatting of itself and other fields in a list, like the example shown in Figure 21-20. By defining two conditions for each field, they are conditionally formatted bold when the status is "Active" or gray when it is "Hold." Records with a status of "Pending" are left unchanged with default layout formatting. The result is three format tiers that visually emphasize the urgency of records. Remember, these format changes are imposed on top of the default formatting for the fields set through the *Inspector* pane.

● ● ●	Learn FileMaker	
Project		
Number	Company	Status
1001	**Creative Musings LLC**	**Active**
1002	**Shoe Fits Wearables Co.**	**Active**
1003	**Widgets, Inc.**	**Active**
1000	**Write Track Media**	**Active**
1007	Shoe Fits Wearables Co.	Pending
1004	Write Track Media	Pending
1009	Creative Musings LLC	Hold
1008	Shoe Fits Wearables Co.	Hold
1006	Widgets, Inc.	Hold
1005	Write Track Media	Hold

Figure 21-20. *An example of conditionally formatted fields in a list based on record status*

In this example, the *Project Status* field is assigned a value list with three values: *Active*, *Pending*, and *Hold*. Because this field will be conditionally formatted based on its own value, it can be configured with two *value-based conditions*, shown in Figure 21-21. When the value is equal to "Active," it applies bold formatting, and when it equals "Hold," it colors the text a light gray.

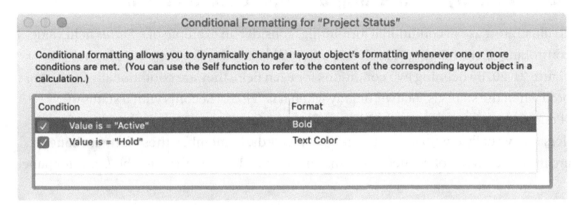

Figure 21-21. *The defined status field uses value-based conditions*

The other two fields in the list view need to each be configured with *formula-based conditions* because they need to look at another field value (the status field) to determine their formatting. The format settings are the same, but the specific condition formula is different, as shown for the *Company Name* field in Figure 21-22. Here the formula looks for "Active" or "Hold" in the *Project Status* field and then applies formatting.

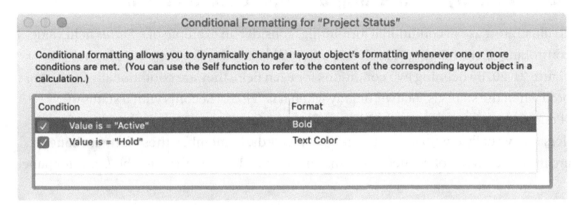

Figure 21-22. *The formula-driven conditions for other fields in the list view*

Understanding Tab Order

A layout's *tab order* defines the focus precedence when stepping from one object to another as the user types the Tab or other field-exiting keys defined for objects (Chapter 19, "Behavior"). This allows a user to "tab" through from *field to field* to *object to field, etc.*, using only the keyboard. The default order is left to right and top to bottom through every object that can accept focus. However, as objects are moved around on a layout or are added at a later time, the tab order will need to be reset to avoid bouncing focus back and forth haphazardly. When setting a custom order, objects that don't require data entry, like calculation fields or buttons, can be excluded.

Changing the Tab Order

In Layout mode, select the *Layout ➤ Set Tab Order* menu to place the layout into a *tab-order editing mode*, shown in Figure 21-23. Each object capable of receiving focus will have an arrow icon attached to one side. These contain the object's current tab order number and are editable text boxes. Delete an object's number to remove it from the tab order. Click inside a blank arrow to automatically assign the next available number in the tab order, and/or edit the number by typing over it. FileMaker enforces a unique number sequence by automatically changing object's value when its assigned number is typed elsewhere.

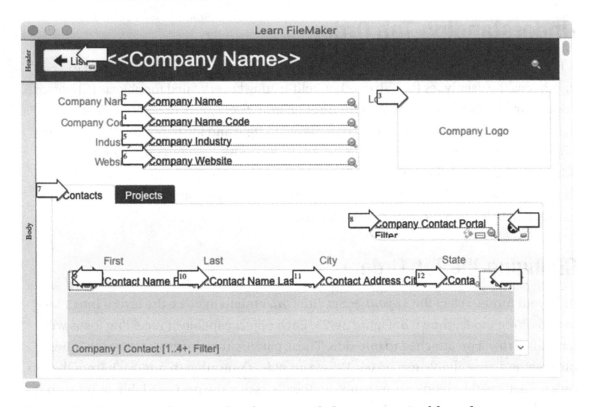

Figure 21-23. *A window in tab-editing mode has customizable order arrow fields*

Using Functions of the Set Tab Order Dialog

The *Set Tab Order* dialog shown in Figure 21-24 opens automatically when a layout is placed into tab-editing mode. This dialog is used to perform batch tab-order functions and to exit back to regular Layout mode.

Figure 21-24. *The dialog used to control batch tab-ordering functions*

1. *Add Remaining* – Add a default order to unassigned objects by selecting an option in the menu: *Objects*, *Fields only*, and *Buttons only*. Then click the *Add* button.

2. *Remove* – Remove objects from the tab order by selecting an option in the menu: *All fields* or *All buttons*. Then click the *Remove* button.

3. *Clear All* – Delete the tab order from every object on the layout, providing a clean slate for reassignment.

Tip   After moving any object on a layout, always return to Browse mode, and click through the fields to confirm a desirable tab order.

Naming Objects

The *object name* property is an optional static text identifier that can be manually assigned to a layout object or group of objects in layout mode. While these are somewhat of a formality, they are helpful when viewing elements in the *Objects* pane and necessary to allow certain functions and script steps to refer to non-field objects: portals, tab control, slide control, and web viewers. For example, the *GetLayoutObjectAttribute* and *Get (ActiveLayoutObjectName)* functions can *only* refer to an object by the name property. Similarly, scripts steps like *Go To Object*, *Refresh Portal*, and *Set Web Viewer* require an object name as a target reference.

An *object name* should not be confused with a *field name* as they are two separate things. Where a field name is a universal definition of a specific data container common to the field anywhere it is placed, an object name is a property unique to each layout instance of an object, including fields. An instance of a field can be assigned an object name different from its defined name, and each instance of the same field on any layout can have a different object name.

To assign an object name, enter Layout mode and select an object. In the *Position* group of the *Position* tab of the *Inspector* pane, click into the *Name* text area and type a name for the object. Names are not case sensitive, and they must be unique.

Tip   Objects pasted from other layouts with shared object names will be renamed to ensure unique naming between all objects. Always delete older objects prior to pasting new, and/or review any important names after pasting.

Summary

This chapter explored various options for manipulating layout objects, including selecting, resizing, moving, arranging, aligning, hiding, conditionally formatting, tabbing, and naming. In the next chapter, we will explore the themes and styles feature.

Using Themes and Styles

Object formatting can be applied directly to objects using the functions of the *Format* menu or in the *Appearance* tab of the *Inspector* pane. However, like many popular print and design applications, FileMaker allows you to save object style definitions and group them into a theme to create a more efficient design workflow. This makes it easier to maintain consistency in similar objects across multiple layouts and allows formatting changes to be instantly applied throughout. Using styles is also recommended as a best practice for improved system performance. This chapter covers the basics of using themes and styles, including

- Anatomizing styles
- Using themes
- Using styles
- Designing a custom theme

Anatomizing Styles

A *style* is a collection of appearance settings for a specific object type that can be applied to a new object with a single action. One or more styles can be defined for each object type, creating a library of design options. The applicable settings vary based on the type of object and only include properties pertaining to *appearance* rather than *data*, *position,* and other non-format related properties. Styles can include settings for *fill*, *border, corner radius, font, size, style, indents, line height,* and *tabs.*

In many ways, styles in FileMaker are *similar* to those found in word processing, desktop publishing applications, and cascading style sheets (CSS) since they enable the rapid application of formatting to new objects and facilitating global style updates to existing objects. However, they are also *different* in a couple important ways. First, they are a layout design mechanism used by developers to facilitate efficient layout design and are

© Mark Conway Munro 2021
M. C. Munro, *Learn FileMaker Pro 19*, https://doi.org/10.1007/978-1-4842-6680-9_22

not available to users when editing the text contents of a field in Browse mode. FileMaker has no user accessible, content applicable styles. Users can apply individual formatting changes to text inside of fields but there is no way to apply these in batches. Unlike CSS and desktop publishing, styles in FileMaker are discretely non-hierarchical and cannot inherit attributes from other styles. Further, because styles are applied to dynamic objects in an interactive interface, they have more dimension than those found in text-based applications. A style stores one group of every format setting for each possible *object state* for every *object part* forming a complex internal hierarchy, as illustrated in Figure 22-1.

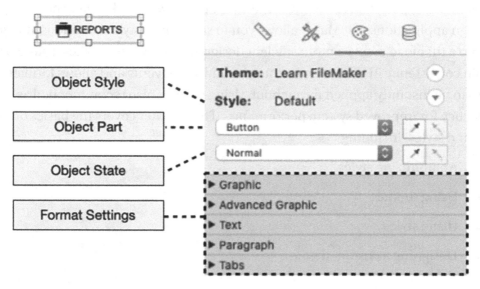

Figure 22-1. *An illustration of the hierarchy of an object style*

An *object part* is a component of an object (or the object itself) which can be separately styled. A *button* is made up of two parts: a *button* and an *icon*. A *portal* is also composed of two parts: a *portal* and a *portal row*. A *button bar* has four parts: a *button bar, divider, segment,* and *icon*. Each part has one set of format settings for every possible object state all defined as a single style.

An *object state* is the status of an object relative to a user. Most objects have at least four states. A *Normal* state means the object is visible but not actively engaged. An *Active* state indicates the object has active focus, e.g., a field in focus or the active segment of a button bar. The other two common states indicate the cursor's interaction with the object: *Hover* and *Pressed*. Some objects have additional states available based on their nature, e.g., *fields* have a *Placeholder Text* state, and a *button bar segment* has an *Inactive* state.

Each part-state combination can be assigned a group of format settings different from others. This enables a dynamic interface design where the overall appearance of an object changes based on the user's action. For example, when the user moves their cursor over a button, its border, shading, or text color can change to indicate that it is an active element that accepts a mouse click. Similarly, when the user clicks the button, it can deepen in color to visually indicate the pushing activity. The combination of parts and states creates an exponential number of format settings that can be defined for a given object. For example, a button has *eight* different groups of format settings, one for each of the four states for the two parts, as illustrated in Figure 22-2. Remember, this illustrates a *single style definition* that can be saved and then applied to any number of additional buttons with a single action.

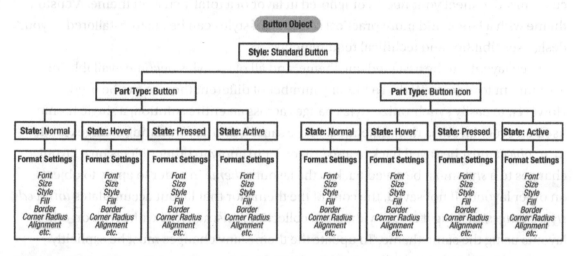

Figure 22-2. *Visualizing the number of format setting groups available for a button*

Styles are created and modified *through objects.* Each object type starts with one *Default* style. When an object's format is modified, the changes are applied to the *object* but do not affect the assigned *style.* Instead, they are held as *unsaved object changes.* To properly use styles, these changes must be explicitly saved back to the assigned style or saved as a new style. When saved to the existing style, the changes will be automatically applied to all other objects assigned that style on the current layout, as illustrated in Figure 22-3.

Figure 22-3. *Format changes must be saved to the style to update other objects*

A *theme* is a collection of styles for every object type that can be applied to layouts. FileMaker ships with dozens of built-in themes, some rather simple and others showcasing advanced styling features. Any of these can be used without modification, customized to meet your needs, or ignored in favor of a totally custom theme. A custom theme with a larger and more practical selection of styles can be custom-tailored to your design sensibilities and technical requirements.

Each layout can be assigned one theme, and all of its styles become available for assignment to objects. Within a file, any number of different themes can be used. However, to easily synchronize style changes across an entire solution, a single theme used on every layout is recommended. In the same way that formatting changes made to an *object* must be saved back to a *style* in order to apply to other objects on a layout, changes to a *style* must be saved back to the layout's *theme* in order to apply to objects on other layouts. If not saved, the copy of the theme for that layout accumulates *unsaved style changes,* making it an individualized collection, mismatched with styles on other layouts using the same theme. To update the theme, any changes must be explicitly saved back to the theme, as illustrated in Figure 22-4.

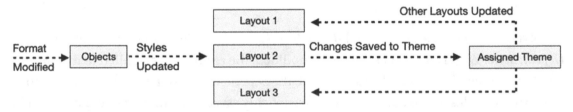

Figure 22-4. *Style changes must be saved to the theme to update other layouts*

Caution   Since style and theme updates must be explicitly saved, get into the habit of doing so *immediately* after making *any* format change to layout objects.

Using Themes

FileMaker automatically assigns a theme to every new layout based on a determination of the best option for the new layout type following a few basic rules. The default layout of a new database will always be assigned the *Enlightened* theme. A new *Computer* layout will always be assigned the same theme as the layout one is viewing when starting the layout creation process. New *Touch Device* layouts will be assigned the *Enlightened Touch* theme unless the built-in theme of the layout one is viewing has a built-in touch variant. For example, if viewing a layout assigned the *Luminous* theme, the new touch layout will be assigned the *Luminous Touch* theme. However, if viewing a layout assigned the *Cosmos* theme, the new touch layout will be assigned the *Enlightened Touch* theme since there is no available touch theme for it. Any new *Printer* layouts will be assigned the *Enlightened Print* theme. Once the new layout is created, you can assign another theme to the layout.

Caution   FileMaker does not look at custom theme names when determining the best default assignment for a new layout. Although you can create custom themes with a suffix of *Touch* and *Print*, they will not be automatically selected in the manner described previously.

Changing a Layout's Theme

After a layout is created, the theme assignment can be changed using the *Change Theme* dialog, shown in Figure 22-5. This dialog can be opened while in Layout mode by clicking the icon next to the *Theme* name listed in the second row of the toolbar and selecting *Change Theme* in the *Layout* menu, or the contextual menu on the layout's background.

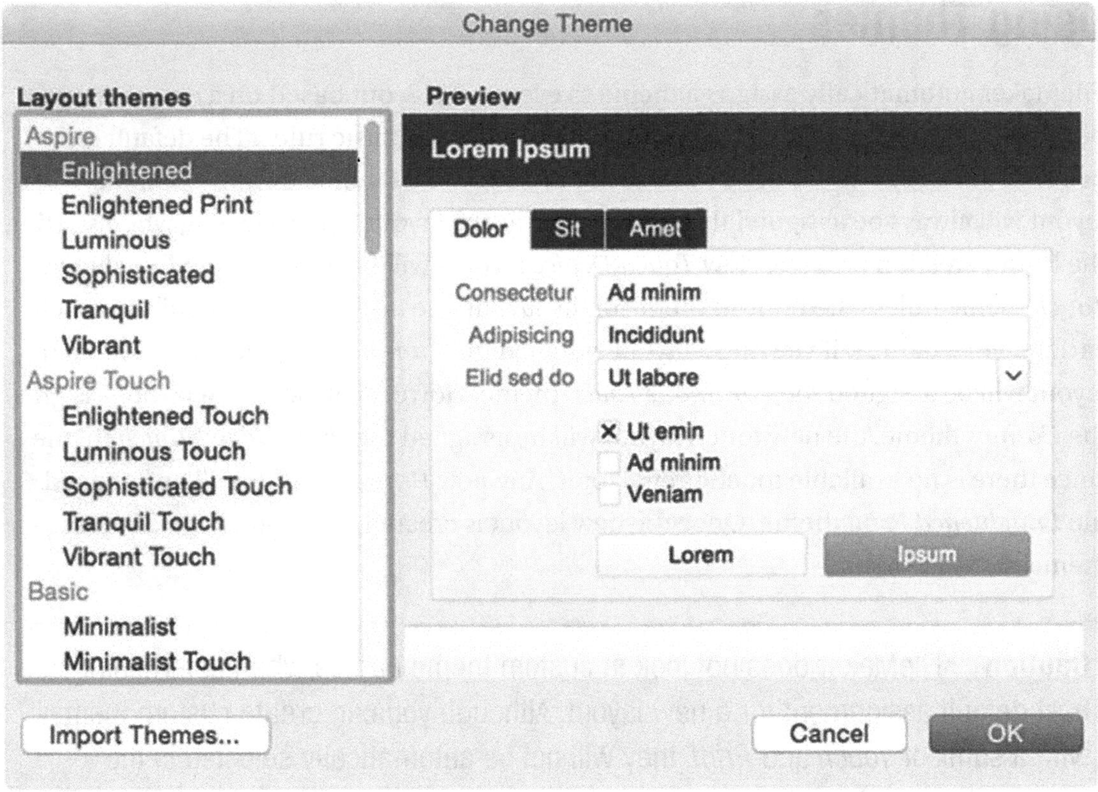

Figure 22-5. *The dialog used to select a theme assignment for the current layout*

This dialog categorizes a list of the available themes with the theme assigned to the current layout selected. Nothing is directly editable in the dialog. You can only select a theme or import themes for selection. When a different theme is selected and assigned, every object on the layout will be affected, depending on the styles available in the new theme compared to those assigned to objects from the old. If the new theme has a style with the same name as the one assigned an object, the object will retain that assignment and change the format settings for the style from the new theme. Style names are *not* case sensitive, so any name match will work. An object assigned a style name not found in the new theme will be assigned the *Default* style for the object's type from the new theme.

Most unsaved formatting changes will be lost during the theme transition. Some unsaved text formatting changes will be retained when the theme is changed, e.g., text size. To retain unsaved formatting changes, FileMaker has a rather clever two-stage undo process after a theme is changed. Immediately after assigning a new theme to a layout, the first use of the *Undo* command will retain the new theme assignment but restore any object attributes that were lost due to being unsaved in the old theme. A second use of *Undo* will fully restore the layout to the previous theme. This allows you to assign a new theme on a trial basis, go back a half step, and have an opportunity either to save previously unsaved changes into new or existing styles within the newly assigned theme or to revert completely to the old theme.

Tip   For the best experience, avoid changing themes after designing layout elements. Choose a theme and use it consistently throughout your database, constantly updating style changes.

Managing Themes

Themes are managed from the *Manage Themes* dialog, shown in Figure 22-6, which can be opened by selecting the *File* ➤ *Manage* ➤ *Themes* menu item. As you assign themes to layouts, they are added to this dialog.

Figure 22-6. *The dialog used to manage themes*

The dialog lists every theme that has been used on a layout within the database file, even if it is no longer in use. These remain until explicitly deleted. Built-in theme names will always be contained within square brackets. The *Import* button begins the process of copy custom themes from another database file. The *Rename* button allows the assignment of a new name to a custom theme. Built-in themes can't be renamed, but they can be duplicated to create a new custom named theme. Themes can be deleted as long as they aren't in use in the file.

Using Styles

Each object added to a layout is automatically assigned the type-appropriate *Default* style from the layout's theme. Default styles can't be renamed or deleted, but they can be updated with modified settings, and new completely custom styles can be added. A style can be assigned to a selected object by choosing it from the *Object Style* menu in the object's contextual menu or selecting a style from the *Styles* pane of the *Inspector* pane, both shown in Figure 22-7.

Figure 22-7. *Select a style from the object contextual menu (left) or the Inspector (right)*

Editing an Object's Style Settings

To modify an object's formatting and save it to the style and theme, follow the steps shown in Figure 22-8. First, select an object and then click on the *Appearance* tab of the *Inspector* pane. Then follow these steps: *select a part, select a state, edit any of the settings, save to a style,* and *save to the layout's theme.*

Let's walk through an example in more detail. Begin by selecting an *object part* from the pop-up menu just below the *Theme* and *Style*. This automatically displays the object type as the whole "part," and for objects composed of a hierarchy of components, it lists all available component parts. For example, when a *portal* is selected, the list will include *Portal* and *Portal: Row*, since each of these can have different formatting. In the example shown, a field formatted with a *pop-up menu* control style is selected, so there are three parts available: *Pop-up Menu, Pop-up Menu: Button,* and *Pop-up Menu: Icon.*

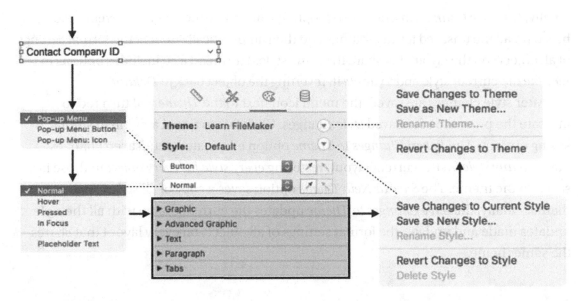

Figure 22-8. *The process for modifying an object's formatting and saving to a style*

Next, choose an *object state*. The default selection will always be *Normal* representing the object's part at rest. When you select a different state, the object's appearance on the layout changes to preview how it will appear in that state based on the current settings. Once you have selected the object part and state, begin modifying settings for the object using the formatting controls in the *Inspector*. Make any changes required to as many different settings for any state of any part until you have the object behaving as desired.

Tip   The eyedropper icons next to the object part and state menus allow format settings to be copy and pasted to save time.

When finished modifying the object format, the menu icon adjacent to the *Style* will turn red to indicate the presence of unsaved *object* changes. To consistently keep themes and styles in sync between objects and layouts, it is important to save these changes back to a style. Click the red icon to reveal the menu of action options. The *Revert Changes to Style* option will eliminate all unsaved changes and restore the object to previously saved settings. The *Save as New Style* option saves the object's current format settings as a new style which is then assigned to the object, leaving the previously assigned style unchanged.

Finally, the *Save Changes to Current Style* option will update the object's current style based on all the unsaved format settings and then automatically update the format settings of all objects on the layout that share the same style. The menu also includes options to *rename* the current style and to *delete* it, reverting the object back to *Default*.

After style changes are saved, the menu icon next to the *Theme* will turn red to indicate the presence of unsaved *style* changes. Click this to reveal a menu of similar saving options. The *Revert Changes to Theme* option eliminates all unsaved changes made to *any style* on the current layout, restoring *every style for every object* to those last saved to the theme. The *Save as New Theme* option saves a copy of all styles into a new theme. Finally, the *Save Changes to Theme* updates the current theme with all the style updates made and updates the format settings of all objects on every layout that shares the same theme.

Designing a Custom Theme

Your personal approach to custom theme design will be influenced by many factors. Two big ones are specific experience with FileMaker and a general knowledge of principles of interface design. Those familiar with both can leverage that experience to focus on innovation when designing their vision for an interface. Those with less experience will need to draw inspiration from others or experiment more speculatively. Other factors include the type of solution one plans to build, the target deployment platforms, a client's expectations, and budgetary constraints. There is no single approach that will work for every developer in every situation, and it can be challenging to plan a theme outside the context of a specific project. Without implying a one-size-fits-all approach, there are some specific things to think about when getting started.

Consider separating your theme design planning from any specific project, past or present, by creating an abstract design sandbox. This allows you to focus on creating a cleanly designed, original theme without any distracting baggage clogging up the file. You should still look back at as many different real-world examples as possible for inspiration to ground your choices in actual projects without being bound to any one of them. Select the best practices from many examples, compare, contrast, and then reinvent them into something new.

The sandbox file should contain one or two semi-realistic simple tables that can be used in the process, e.g., *Contacts* and *Company*, or *Invoices* and *Line Items*. Use one table as your design focus, and build a List and Form View layout for it, while the other can serve as a related table for portal design. Make additional layouts for dialogs, reports, iOS devices, etc. only as needed to define the styles necessary for a standard project. Remember to keep the fields and layouts limited to a minimum for now since you aren't designing an actual solution, just a *style prototype*. Stay focused on that goal at first.

Begin adding objects and experimenting with different formatting options. Focus on the unique formatting required on different layouts or when used for different functions. For example, a field on a List view may not be editable and can have a transparent fill and border, while one on a Form view that is editable may benefit from a visual indication that it is a field and accepts input, perhaps with a different fill color. Similarly, a separate style will be required for a text object used as a layout heading, field label, informational tips, prompts, report page numbers, and more. Think about all the different types of buttons you might use, such as a standard button, icon-only, text with icon, and more. Some may have borders and fill, others maybe only an icon with a transparent background, each requiring a separate style. Be sure to think about all the different control types for fields; each will require one or more defined styles since there is no general *Field* style category, only *Edit Box*, *Pop-up Menu*, *Calendar*, etc.

Since *any format difference* requires a separate style, fields and labels may need several variations depending on the type of solution you will build. For example, you might need one for each alignment (left, right, center) and another for each visual appearance (clear, bordered, filled). Take time to think about different object states and Window modes. Most styles will need to adapt to interactions, look good in appearance, inform correctly in different modes, etc. Try to find a reasonable balance between these objectives. On one hand, keep the list short to avoid being overwhelming. On the other hand, provide an adequate number of options that create a practical palette of design options to avoid any temptation to cheat and apply small formatting changes to objects without updating or creating another style.

When naming styles, choose a balance between a clear description of purpose and a concise easily readable string. Names must be unique across the entire theme regardless of object type, so it's a good idea to include the object type as a name prefix, e.g., avoid a conflict between a button and field style named "Bordered Right" by naming them "Button Bordered Right" and "Field Bordered Right." The *Default* style can't be renamed, so keep this as your most commonly used style choice for each object type or ignore it.

Once your style sandbox has enough styles that you feel adequately provides a solid foundation, move the theme to a live file and begin using it for real development. As you discover unanticipated style requirements, add or enhance the theme. If you do this purposefully and without haste, the result should be a well-designed, practical theme that can be imported and reused in other files.

Although this process may sound like a tedious overbearing chore, remember that the benefits of a solid theme will ultimately provide a good return on the time investment.

Summary

This chapter introduced the basics of using themes and styles to improve the efficiency of interface design. In the next chapter, we will explore customizing the application menus to create a unique user experience.

Customizing Menus

A database can override FileMaker's default menu bar with custom menus. The level of customization can vary based on your needs, ranging from changes to intercept a few functions to building a completely unique desktop experience. You can build one set of custom menus that dynamically change based on various conditions or create multiple sets that are installed contextually based on the layout. Customizing menus elevates a solution from a mere database *document* to a custom *application*. This chapter explores the basics of custom menus, covering the following topics:

- Getting started with custom menu basics

- Exploring the Manage Custom Menus dialog

- Creating a custom menu set

- Customizing menu items

- Installing a menu set

- Exploring the link between commands and menus

- Creating status-based custom menu

Getting Started with Custom Menus Basics

The *menu bar* in FileMaker is similar to any modern application: a horizontal strip running along the top of the screen (macOS) or the top of a database window (Windows). A database always displays the *active menu set*, which defaults to a non-modifiable set called *[Standard FileMaker Menus]*. Developers can create one or more additional menu sets that can be installed in place of the standard set under a variety of circumstances. Before delving into customization, review the objects and terminology of menus, as overviewed in Figure 23-1.

© Mark Conway Munro 2021
M. C. Munro, *Learn FileMaker Pro 19*, https://doi.org/10.1007/978-1-4842-6680-9_23

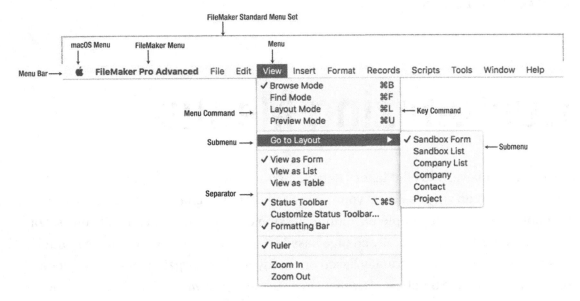

Figure 23-1. *The terminological overview of menu components*

A *menu set* is a named collection of menus that can be installed into the menu bar, thereby becoming the *active menu set*. A *menu* contains a collection of various items of different types, as illustrated in Figure 23-2.

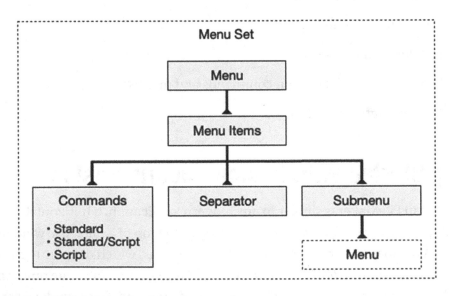

Figure 23-2. *The hierarchical structure of a menu*

Once defined, a *custom menu* can be added to one or more sets. Each menu can be created as one of the following four types:

- A totally custom menu created and built from scratch.

- Any of three *non-customizable* standard FileMaker menus with all their standard menu items: *Format*, *Scripts*, and *Window*.

- Any of eight standard FileMaker menus that can be duplicated and customized as needed (with a few exceptions): *FileMaker Pro*, *File*, *Edit*, *View*, *Insert*, *Records*, *Request*, and *Help*.

- A choice of about two dozen *standard submenus* that can be attached to the menu set as a stand-alone *menu* or as a submenu attached to a custom menu item. These include submenus such as *Open Recent*, *Import Records*, *Go to Layout*, *Manage*, *Sharing*, *Show Window*, and more.

A *menu item* is one of three types of objects added to a menu: *command*, *separator*, or *submenu*.

A *command item* triggers a function, either a standard FileMaker command or a custom script. Items can be completely customized with a unique name and script function, or they can inherit some or all properties of a standard FileMaker command (name, function, and key command).

A *separator* is a nonfunctional horizontal line used to separate groups of menu items to create a more visually pleasing organization of items.

A *submenu* is an item that springs opens a secondary menu of options subsumed under it. Submenus can cascade in a nested hierarchy, i.e., a menu item can open a submenu with an item that opens another submenu, etc. Each submenu is first defined as a separate menu which is then connected to the menu item that will open it.

Up to four standard menus can never be completely removed from the application. Even with a completely *empty* custom menu set installed, these four menus will persist. On a macOS computer, the *Apple* menu contains standard operating system functions and is completely unaffected by the custom menu set and can't be modified in any way. A *FileMaker Pro* application menu and a *Help* menu are always at opposite sides of the menu bar regardless of their presence in a custom menu set. The *Tools* menu is visible when *Advanced Tools* are enabled in preferences (Chapter 2), and these can't be modified at all.

Exploring the Manage Custom Menus Dialog

Custom menus are defined in the *Manage Custom Menus* dialog which can be opened by selecting the *Manage Custom Menus* option available in three places: the *File* ➤ *Manage* menu, the *Tools* ➤ *Custom Menus* menu, and the *Menu Set* pop-up menu in the *General* tab of the *Layout Setup* dialog. The dialog has two tabs, as shown in Figure 23-3: *Custom Menu Sets* and *Custom Menus*.

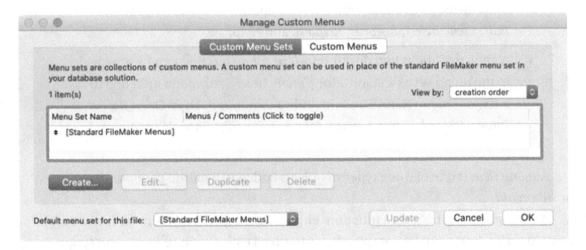

Figure 23-3. *The dialog used to define custom menus*

The *Custom Menu Sets* tab lists all the menu sets defined in the file. The default standard set is included by default and can't be removed. New sets can be *created*, *edited*, *duplicated*, and *deleted* in this dialog.

The *Custom Menus* tab presents a list of every defined custom menu with similar modification buttons. This list is empty until you begin creating menus. Any custom menus defined are available for connection to a custom set.

There is a confusing intersection of features between these two dialogs that can be intimidating and may discourage a novice developer. However, given the benefits of a totally custom menu system for advanced databases, it is worth the effort to grasp how it works, as illustrated in Figure 23-4. Although confusing at first, this presents an overview of dialogs and functions that will be described later in this chapter.

From the *Custom Menu Sets* tab, when you create or edit a set, the *Edit Custom Menu Set* dialog opens listing the menus that have been assigned to it. A menu there can be selected and edited, opening the *Edit Custom Menu* dialog, or a new menu can be added here by clicking the *Add* button which opens a *Select Menu* dialog. This dialog lists all the standard FileMaker submenus and any custom menus that have been created. Select one to add it to the menu set, or click the plus button to open the *Create Custom Menu* dialog to create a new menu which will be added.

From the *Custom Menus* tab, clicking *Create* opens the *Create Custom Menu* dialog which offers a choice of creating a new menu based on a standard menu or starting with an empty one. Once that choice is made, the *Edit Custom Menu* dialog opens.

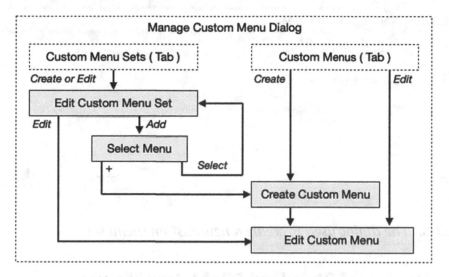

Figure 23-4. *The somewhat confusing intersection of dialogs for custom menus*

Creating a Custom Menu Set

Start a new menu set by opening the *Manage Custom Menus* dialog and clicking on the *Custom Menu Sets* tab. Click the *Create* button to open a new empty menu set in an *Edit Custom Menu Set* dialog, shown in Figure 23-5. Enter a name for the menu set and an optional developer comment.

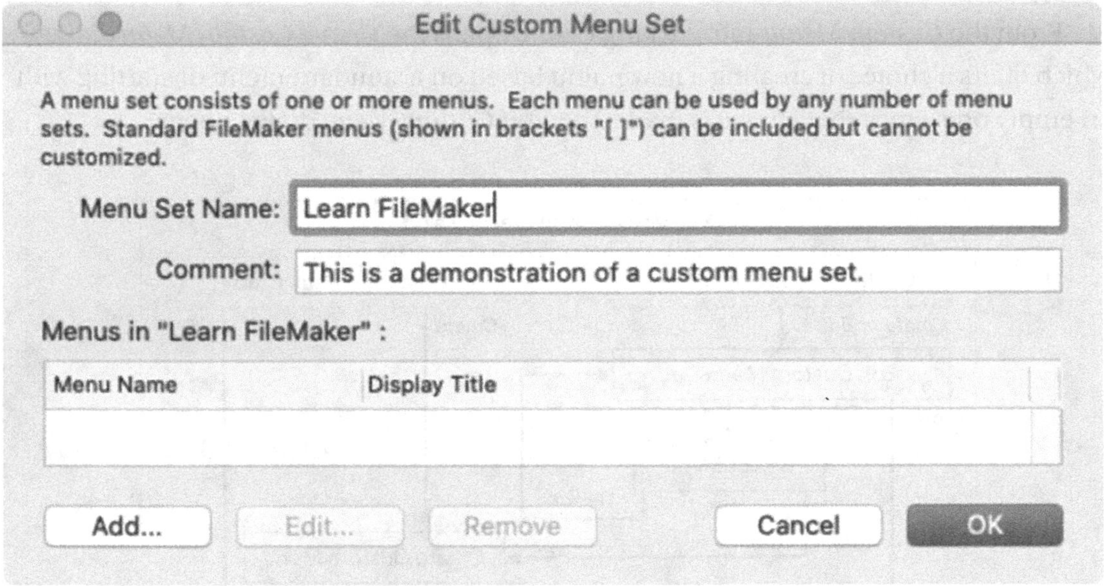

Figure 23-5. *The dialog used to create a new custom menu set*

Adding Copies of Standard FileMaker Menus

Add a copy of each standard FileMaker menu into the *Learn FileMaker Menus* set. To begin, click the *Add* button to open the *Select Menu* dialog, shown in Figure 23-6.

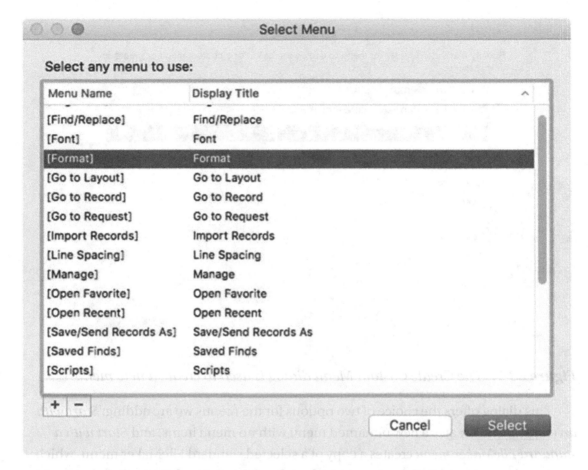

Figure 23-6. *The dialog used to select available standard and custom menus*

This dialog lists all available menus that can be added to a custom set. Until custom menus are created, this dialog will only list *standard submenus*. Hold down the Command (macOS) or Windows (Windows) key to allow for multiple selections, and then click on the three standard menus in the list: *[Format]*, *[Scripts]*, and *[Window]*. Once selected, click the *Select* button to add the three selected menus to the custom set. To add the remaining standard menus to the set, create a copy of each menu by once again clicking the *Add* button on the *Edit Custom Menu Set* dialog and then clicking the + button on the preceding *Select Menu* dialog. This will open the *Create Custom Menu* dialog, shown in Figure 23-7.

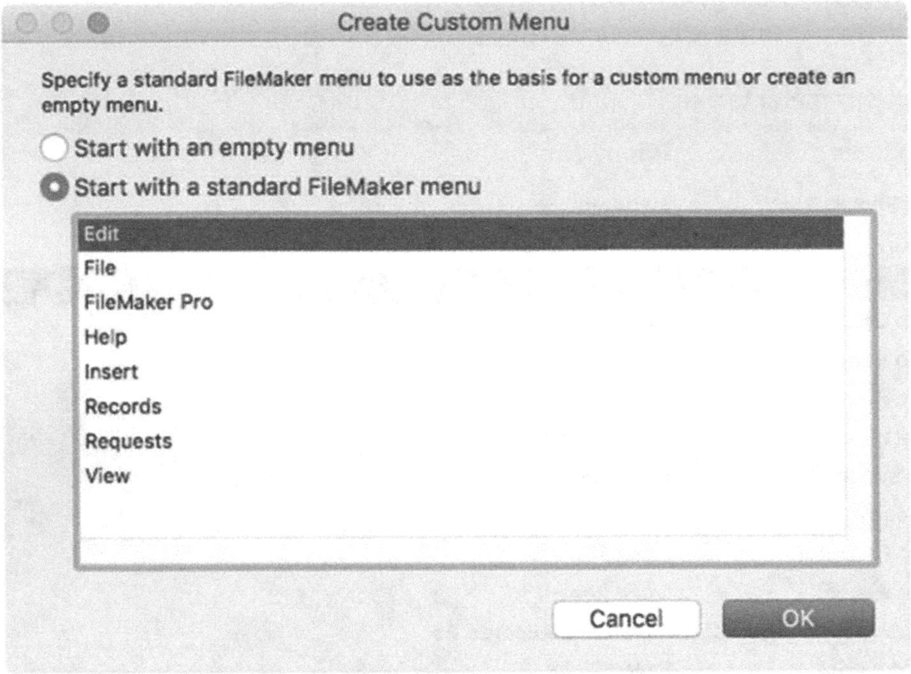

Figure 23-7. *The Create Custom Menu dialog is used to create a new menu*

This dialog offers the choice of two options for the menus we are adding: *Start with an empty menu* creates a new unnamed menu with no menu items, and *Start with a standard FileMaker menu* creates a copy of a selected standard FileMaker menu, which can later be customized. For now, add each of the eight standard menus listed, one at a time, by selecting them and clicking OK. Each copy will be created and opened in the *Edit Custom Menu* dialog. For now, just click OK in that dialog to save the new menu copy in its default state. Once finished, the *Select Menu* dialog should contain a list of all eight copies of the standard menus, shown in Figure 23-8.

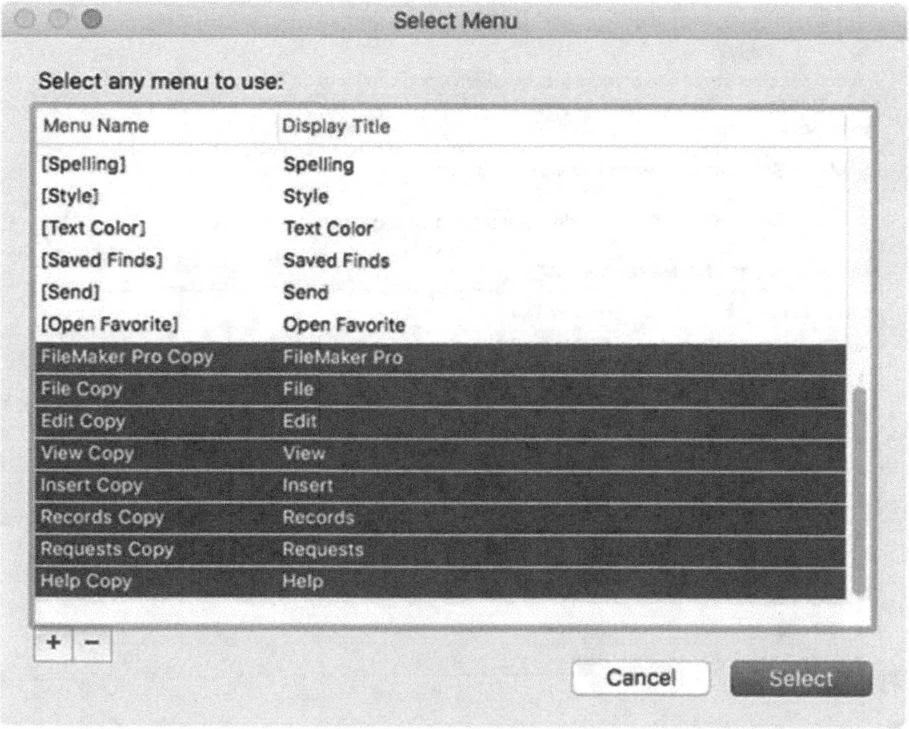

Figure 23-8. *The dialog after creating a copy of every standard FileMaker menu*

These copies have now been added to the database as custom menus but still need to be added to the custom menu set. Hold the Command (macOS) or Windows (Windows) key, select all eight of the standard menu copies, and then click the *Select* button. This will return to the *Edit Custom Menu Set* dialog, showing a list of all *11* menus we have added, shown in Figure 23-9.

Figure 23-9. *The new custom menu set*

Menus can be drag-arranged in the list with two exceptions: the *FileMaker Pro* menu will remain locked as the *first* in the list, and the *Help* menu will remain locked as the *last* menu in the list. Once the menus are in the desired order, click OK to save the changes, and close the *Edit Custom Menu Set* dialog. Then click OK to close the *Manage Custom Menus* dialog. Now you can manually install the custom menu set for the current layout by selecting it from the *Tools ➤ Custom Menus* menu (see more on installing later in this chapter). When the custom menu set has a check mark next to its name in this menu, it is installed. Since the custom set we created is simply a copy of the standard FileMaker menu set, you should notice no differences between the current menus compared to the standard FileMaker menus. Next, we can begin customizing the new menu set.

Customizing Menu Items

Whether editing standard menu items or configuring new empty menu items, the process of customizing a menu is essentially the same; open it in the *Edit Custom Menu* dialog, then modify settings, edit menu items, or add new items.

Exploring the Edit Custom Menu Dialog

Configuring menus and defining the items they contain are done from the *Edit Custom Menu* dialog, shown in Figure 23-10. This dialog is opened automatically when creating a new custom menu and can be opened from either tab of the *Manage Custom Menus* dialog. From the *Custom Menus* tab, select a menu, and click the *Edit* button or double-click directly on the menu. From the *Custom Menu Sets* tab, select a *menu set* and click the *Edit* button or double-click directly on the menu set. Then select a *menu* and click *Edit* button or double-click directly on the menu. The top of the dialog includes menu configuration controls, while the bottom section includes a list of the menu's items. From here, items can be created, duplicated, deleted, or have their properties and behavior customized.

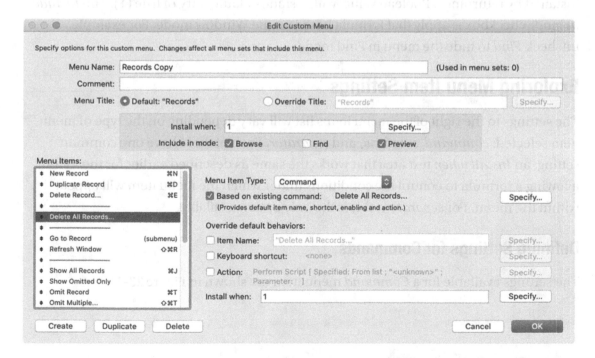

Figure 23-10. *The dialog used to configure a menu and define its items*

Configuring Menu Settings

The *Menu Name* accepts a custom name for the menu up to 100 characters. This name is only visible within the programming interface and is not necessarily the title that will appear in the menu bar. If following along, take a moment to rename the custom menus, removing the "Copy" suffix that was added when we copied the standard menus into our custom set.

The *Comment* field is used to store a description of the menu for developers, up to 30,000 characters.

The *Menu Title* controls the name of the menu when it appears in the menu bar. If the menu is a copy of a standard FileMaker menu, a *Default* option will be available, using the standard name. To override this or to enter a name for a custom menu, the *Override Title* option includes a field and a *Specify* button allowing entry of a static name or a formula to calculate a name. Custom menu names can be up to 30,000 characters in length; however, due to the dimensional limitation of screens as well as the nature of human perception, it is best to limit each menu name to a single word.

Control when a menu is installed in the menu bar using one of two sets of controls that work in concert. The *Install when* setting allows a formula to control when a menu is installed by returning a Boolean value, with a static default entry of true (1). The *Include in mode* checkboxes apply that formula based on the Window mode. For example, uncheck *Find* to hide the menu in Find mode.

Exploring Menu Item Settings

The settings to the right of the menu items list will vary depending on the type of menu item selected: *command, submenu,* and *separator*. Each of these have one common setting: an *Install when* text area that works the same as described earlier for the menu, allowing a formula to control the conditions under which the menu item will appear within the menu. For *separators*, this is the only option available.

Defining Settings for Commands

The settings available for a *Command* menu item are shown in Figure 23-11.

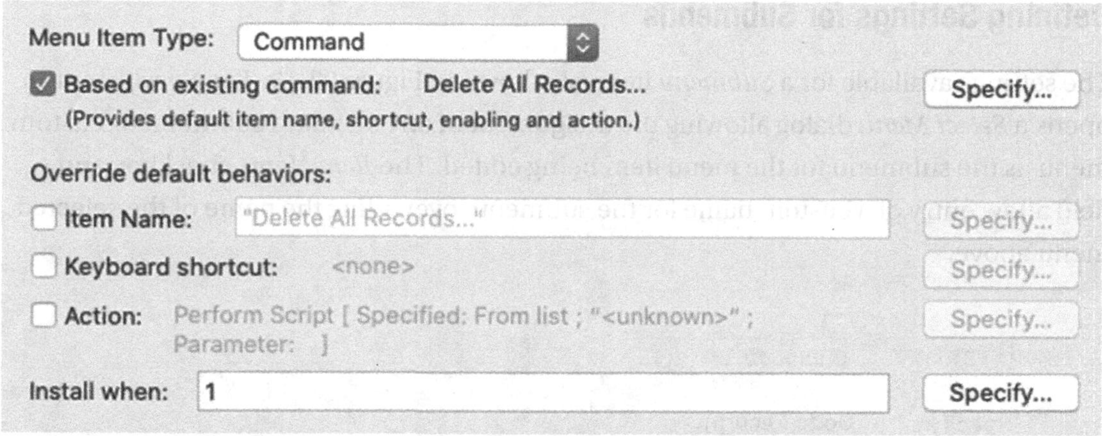

Figure 23-11. *The settings for defining a command menu item*

The *Based on existing command* can be enabled if the item's function will be an existing FileMaker command (with or without overrides). A *Specify FileMaker Command* dialog will open the first time the checkbox is enabled but can be opened later using the *Specify* button. This dialog presents a list of all available commands that can be selected to assign it to the menu item. For information about the benefits of basing an item on a command even when the menu item will perform a custom script, see "Exploring the Link Between Commands and Menus" section later in this chapter. The three checkboxes below this provide override controls for default behavior when based on a menu or custom settings when not.

First, enable the *Item Name* checkbox to override the default command name or to enter a name for a custom item. Names should be short action-oriented statements that clearly describe the function performed. For example, "Print Sales Report" and "Send Proposal Request" may be good names, while "Send to Accounting" doesn't make clear what is being sent, and "Get Approval" doesn't make clear the action being taken.

The *Keyboard shortcut* checkbox will override a default keyboard shortcut for a standard menu item or establish one for a custom item. A *Specify Shortcut* dialog appears the first time this box is checked or when the adjacent *Specify* button is clicked. While this dialog is open, any key combination typed will be captured as the shortcut for the menu item. Be sure to avoid any keyboard combinations that are reserved for operating system functions or standard FileMaker menus that will remain in use.

Finally, the *Action* checkbox allows a custom script or single script step to be assigned as the menu item's function.

Defining Settings for Submenus

The settings available for a *Submenu* item are shown in Figure 23-12. The *Specify* button opens a *Select Menu* dialog allowing the assignment of any standard submenu or custom menu as the submenu for the menu item being edited. The *Item Name* checkbox and field allow entry of a custom name for the submenu, overriding the name of the selected menu above.

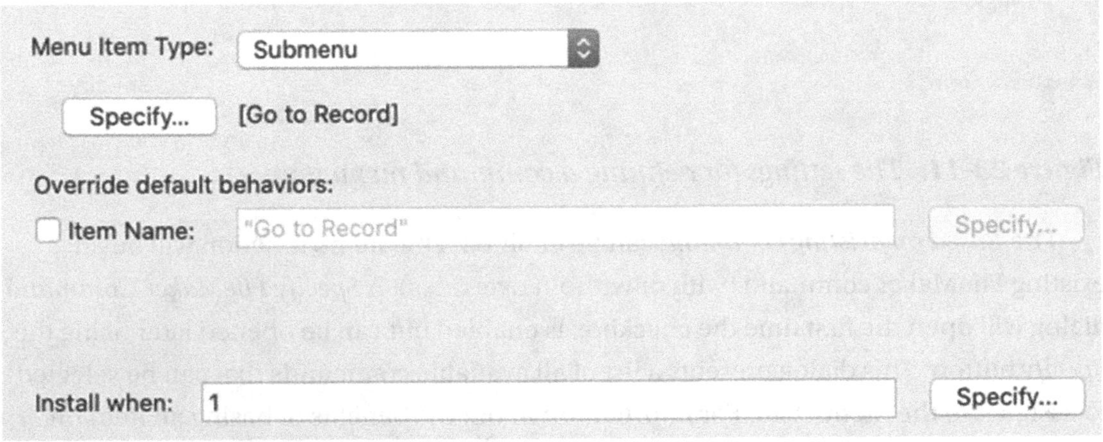

Figure 23-12. *The settings for defining a submenu*

Modifying a Standard Menu Item

Let's work through a few examples of customizing standard menu items: *renaming, overriding functionality,* and *conditional removal*. This section assumes a custom menu set was created with copies of all the standard FileMaker menus, as previously described.

Renaming a Menu Item

A standard menu item is named generically to be descriptive of *function* without specifying *context*. Regardless of the layout a user is viewing, a menu item is always named *New Record, Delete Record,* or *Duplicate Record*. This can become confusing when users are moving between different layouts, especially with multiple windows open. When they select *New Record,* it may result in a record created in a different table than the one they intended. With custom menus, the name can be set with a formula that looks at the current layout context to include the table name in the menu item, e.g., "New Contact Record" or "New Project Record."

To begin, Open the *Manage Custom Menus* dialog and click on the *Custom Menus* tab. Double-click on the *Records* menu to open the *Edit Custom Menu* dialog. Select the *New Record* menu item in the list and enable the *Item Name* checkbox to override the default name. Click *Specify* to open the *Specify Calculation* dialog if it didn't automatically open. Then enter a formula for the name. The exact formula may vary depending on your tables. If they are named clearly like the examples we have used previously – *Contact*, *Company*, and *Project* – then the following formula should produce the conditional menu items shown in Figure 23-13. This process can be repeated for many items in the *Records* menu, although having the first item in the menu specify the table provides a good contextual orientation for the remaining items and may be sufficient.

```
"New " & Get ( LayoutTableName ) & " Record"
```

Figure 23-13. *Examples of a conditionally named New Record menu*

Overriding a Menu Item Function

A custom script can be attached to a menu item to override to the function of a standard menu or provide a function for a custom item. For the former, consider the fact that the *Delete Record* and *Delete All Record* functions both present rather vague, generic dialog messages. Both dialogs ask the user to confirm the deletion process, but neither makes it clear exactly what will be deleted. The *Delete Record* process asks "Permanently delete this ENTIRE record?" with the assumption that the user is explicitly aware of which record they are about to delete. However, in a list view or when using multiple windows, it is possible that the user might become disoriented and accidentally delete the wrong record. Renaming the menu item as discussed in the last section can avoid this, but using a custom script with a more articulate dialog provides additional protection. A script using a *Show Custom Dialog* step (Chapter 25) can present a more specific confirmation prompt. For example, a message can include the table name and the contents of a field representing the record (e.g., a contact or project name), and/or a notification of related material will also be automatically deleted. Once you have established the desired message formula, create a script that performs the steps to ask the user, evaluate their response, and take the appropriate action or not. The following example script presents a dialog with whatever message formula you insert. The button the user clicks is placed into a *$button* variable which is used in an *If* statement to *Exit Script* if they click *Cancel*. If they didn't cancel, the script continues, performing a *Delete Record/Request* step without a default dialog.

```
Show Custom Dialog [ "Confirm Deletion Request" ; "<message formula>" ]
Set Variable [ $button ; Get ( LastMessageChoice ) ]
If [ $button = 1 ] // Cancel Button
  Exit Script
End If
Delete Record/Request [ with dialog:Off ]
```

Once written and tested, override the *Delete Record* menu item's *Action* to point to the custom script. The default message should now be replaced with the custom script dialog, as shown in Figure 23-14.

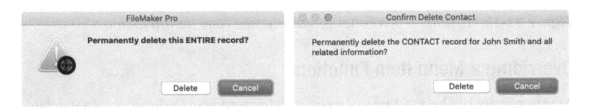

Figure 23-14. *The default delete dialog (left) and a custom example (right)*

Removing a Menu Item Conditionally

A menu can be conditionally hidden under specific conditions. For example, the *Delete All Records* menu item is useful for developers and knowledgeable users but potentially dangerous for certain other users. There is a real possibility that a user thinks they are deleting a small found set of records and inadvertently delete every record in the table. To avoid this, hide the menu by modifying the formula controlling when that item is installed. Click the *Specify* button next to the *Install when* setting for the menu item. Then enter a formula that evaluates to 1 (true) for any users, privilege sets, or extended privilege who are allowed to use the function and 0 (false) for everyone else. For example, the following formula will install the menu item only for developer users with *full access privileges* to the file (Chapter 30):

```
Case (
   Get ( AcccountPrivilegeSetName ) = "[Full Access]" ; 1 ;
   0
)
```

Hiding custom menus is a good idea when conditions would make a menu's function cause an error or be otherwise confusing for the user. For example, certain custom items shouldn't be accessible in Find mode, when viewing an empty found set or when a card-style window is open (Chapter 25).

Adding a Custom Menu

Adding a completely new menu can provide users with convenient access to custom scripts without cluttering a layout with dozens of buttons or clogging up standard menus with dozens of items.

A database with dozens of scripts that find groups of records in different tables by status or other criteria could be placed under the *Records* menu. Similarly, report scripts for invoices and other tables *could* be placed under the *File* menu near the *Print* item. This would integrate custom features into existing menus and may be desirable in these or other similar cases. However, when adding numerous such items, this adds clutter to already crowded menus and requires a user to know all the various locations in which to access these custom scripts. Instead, consider making custom menu items more conveniently located.

The *Scripts* menu (Chapter 24) *can* be used for this purpose since it allows scripts to be selectively included in a hierarchical folder-based arrangement of submenus. However, sometimes, it is beneficial or desirable to create one or more fully custom menus to provide a more professionally branded interface. This is especially important when the menu needs any kind of programmatic variability, since the default *Scripts* menu items can't dynamically change names, have custom key commands, or be conditionally hidden.

Adding one or more completely new menus solves these problems and satisfies a truly custom application experience. The setup will vary based on the number and variety of functions requiring a presence in the menu. Using the previous example, when faced with a large quantity of search and report scripts, a developer may add two menus: *Searches* and *Reports*. However, if the number of items in each is sparse or these are two among dozens of required custom menus, one might consider adding a single menu called *Actions* and having each category be a submenu. Alternatively, a single custom menu with a client's name is a great way to adding a personalized collection of custom actions.

Creating an Actions Menu

To create a new *Actions* menu, open the *Manage Custom Menus* dialog, click on the *Custom Menus* tab, and click the *Create* button. Then follow these steps:

1. Select *Start with an empty menu* and click OK.

2. In the *Edit Custom Menu* dialog, enter a custom name (e.g., "Actions"), an override title of the same name, and only include the menu in Browse mode. Then click OK.

3. Click the *Custom Menu Sets* tab of the *Manage Custom Menus* dialog.

4. Select the *Learn FileMaker* menu set and click *Edit*.

5. In the *Edit Custom Menu Set* dialog, click *Add*.

6. In the *Select Menu* dialog that opens, scroll to the bottom and select the *Actions* menu, and then click the *Select* button.

7. In the *Edit Custom Menu Set* dialog, drag the *Actions* menu to the desired location within the list of menus.

8. Click OK to close the *Edit Custom Menu Set* dialog and then OK to close the *Manage Custom Menus* dialog. If the custom menu set is active, the menu bar should have a new *Actions* menu, as shown in Figure 23-15.

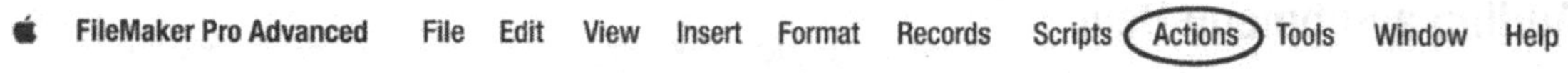

FileMaker Pro Advanced
File
Edit
View
Insert
Format
Records
Scripts
Actions
Tools
Window
Help

***Figure 23-15.** The new menu appearing in the menu bar*

Adding Items to the Actions Menu

With the new *Actions* menu added to the menu set, add menu items as needed.

Adding a Command Menu Item

To add a command item, return to the *Custom Menus* tab of the *Manage Custom Menus* dialog, and open the custom *Actions* menu. Then click the *Create* button to add a new menu item. To get started with a simple example, make an "About This Menu" item that displays a dialog by following these steps:

1. Enable the *Item Name* checkbox and enter a name of "About This Menu" into the adjacent text area.
2. Enable the *Action* checkbox.
3. In the *Specify Script Step* dialog, select the *Show Custom Dialog* step (Chapter 25), and configure it to display a message describing the menu's purpose and function.
4. Click OK to save back through all the dialogs.

Now the *Actions* menu should have a single menu item that displays a dialog describing its function, as shown in Figure 23-16.

Records
Scripts
Actions
Tools
Window
Help
About This Menu
Actions Menu
The Action menu contains the Widget Company database functions.
Cancel
OK

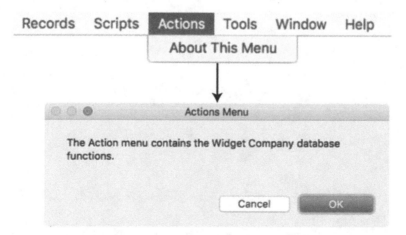

***Figure 23-16.** The custom menu item and resulting dialog*

Adding a Submenu Item

As menus become too crowded, organize groups of items. Using separators can help divide a long list of items into separate groups. For more complex situations, use submenus to organize items into subcategories and make it easier for users to locate a specific function. For example, a *Searches* submenu can list all the available search functions, while a *Reports* submenu can list all the reports, moving both of these groups of items from the main list of an *Actions* menu.

Tip   Consider using the "rule of seven" to determine when to divide menu items into groups using separators or submenus. As a group approaches or exceeds seven items, consider separating them from other groups.

First, create a new custom menu with some items. This will not be added directly to the menu set as a menu but will be attached as a submenu to an item of another menu. For example, create new custom menu called *Reports Submenu,* and add one menu item placeholder for each report script you envision creating, e.g., *Revenue This Year to Date, Revenue This Year*, and *Revenue Last Year*. For now, these won't actually run a script but will be used to illustrate setting up a submenu. Once they are created, return to editing the *Actions* menu and create a new item named "Reports" and configure it as a *submenu* pointing to the *Reports Submenu,* as shown in Figure 23-17.

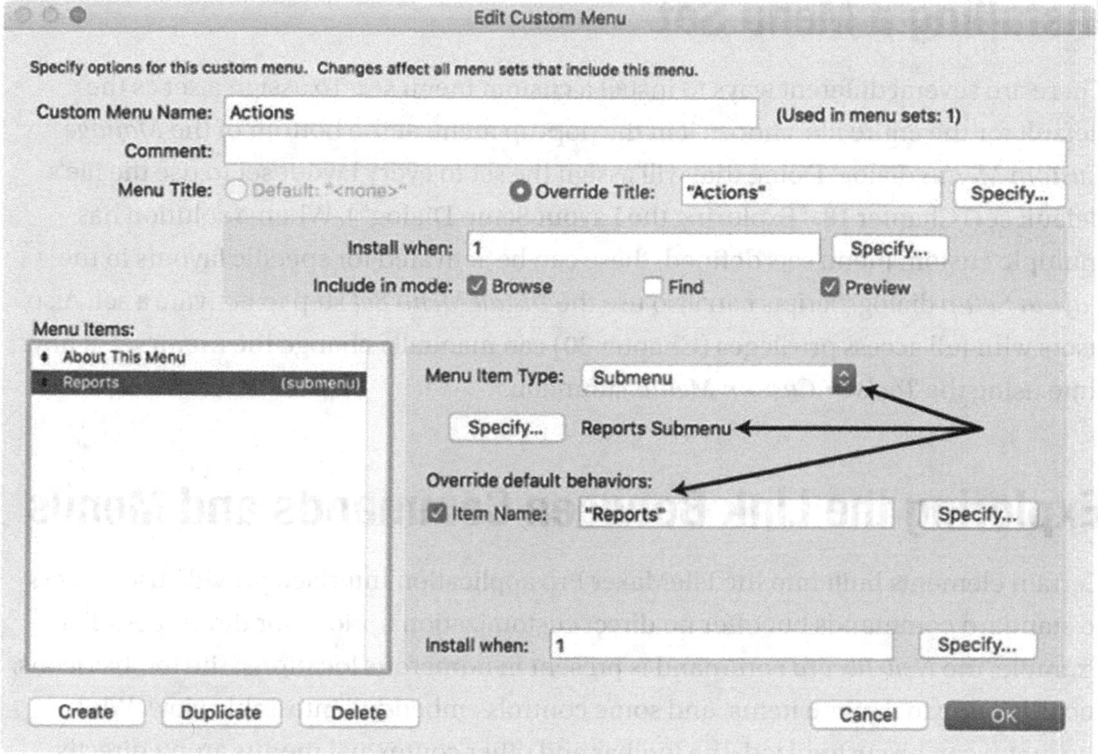

Figure 23-17. *An example of a submenu attached to an item in the Actions menu*

After saving your way back out of the dialogs, the *Actions* menu should now display a *Reports* submenu, as shown in Figure 23-18.

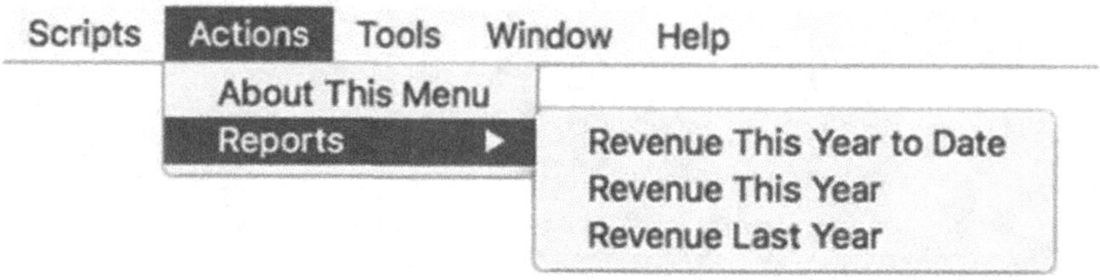

Figure 23-18. *An example of the submenu as it appears to users*

Installing a Menu Set

There are several different ways to install a custom menu set. To assign a set as the default for the entire file, choose it in the pop-up menu at the bottom of the *Manage Custom Menus* dialog. Doing that will assign the set to every layout set to use the file's default set (Chapter 18, "Exploring the Layout Setup Dialog"). When a solution has multiple custom menu sets defined, these can be activated for specific layouts in the *Layout Setup* dialog. Scripts can also use the *Install Menu Set* step to activate a set. Also, users with full access privileges (Chapter 30) can manually change the menu set at any time using the *Tools ➤ Custom Menus* submenu.

Exploring the Link Between Commands and Menus

Certain elements built into the FileMaker Pro application interface provide user access to standard commands but offer no direct customization options for developers. For example, the *New Record* command is present in numerous locations: the toolbar icons, record contextual menu items, and some controls embedded into Table view. While the menu can be customized, the toolbar and other contextual menus aren't directly modifiable. However, FileMaker handles this by linking those elements to commands *through the active menu set*, as illustrated in Figure 23-19. These static interface elements pull their *name, tooltip,* and *enabled status* from a *command-linked menu item* and route a click through the menu item to the command. This setup allows indirect customization of these standard interface elements when using custom menus.

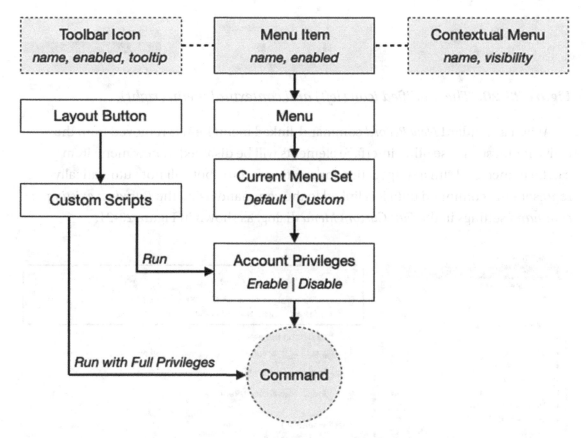

Figure 23-19. *The integration of a command with interface elements*

A good example of this is the *New Record* command, which is present in the *Records* menu and in all of the other locations mentioned. The core *New Record* command is enabled or disabled by a user's account privileges (Chapter 30), although these can be bypassed by a custom script running with full privileges (Chapter 24). The default menu item is linked to the command and is automatically enabled or disabled depending on the user's credentials. Other access points like the toolbar icon look to the *menu* for an item based on the *New Record* command to determine name, tooltip, and enabled status. A click on any of those interface elements is the equivalent of selecting the menu item directly. So, a command-linked menu item acts as the hub for the command, and this makes it possible to replace the default menu set with a custom one and still have control over these non-customizable interface elements. If the menu item's name is customized, the toolbar icon for that command is updated, as shown in Figure 23-20. If a custom script is assigned to the menu item, the toolbar icon runs that instead of the default command. Unlike these elements, buttons on a layout aren't linked through the command-menu structure and can only run commands through scripts.

Figure 23-20. *The modified icon (left) and contextual menu (right)*

When a standard *New Record* command-linked menu item is removed from the active menu set, these other interface elements will be disabled. A new menu item can be named and run a script action for creating records but will not automatically represent the command until it is linked to the command using the *Based on existing command* settings in the *Edit Custom Menu* dialog, as shown in Figure 23-21.

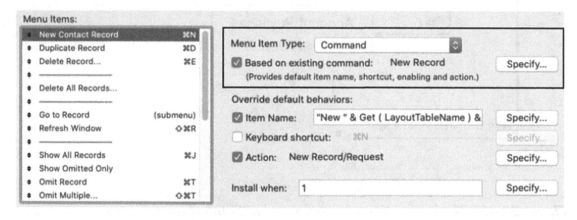

Figure 23-21. *A menu item's command link allows permission enabling and customization of standard interface elements*

A menu item's relationship to a standard command can take one of three forms. *If the item is linked to a standard command only, without* a name or script override, it will appear and perform the normal functionality associated with the command and influence other interface elements normally. *If the item is not linked to a standard command and assigned a custom name and a script,* it will perform the custom script as its function but any other command-related interface elements will be disabled or invisible. When these two are combined and an item *is linked to a standard command with a name or script override*, it will appear with a custom name, perform the assigned custom script, continue to be automatically enabled based on permissions, and extend these capabilities to standard interface elements.

Creating a Status-Based Custom Menu

Some standard menu items are *status based*, meaning they indicate the status of some mode of operation. The *View* menu has several examples, as shown in Figure 23-22. Some status-based menus are a single menu item that toggles an on-off setting. For example, the *Status Toolbar* menu item displays a check mark when the toolbar is visible and no check mark when it is not visible. The single menu item can be selected to toggle this choice back and forth. Other examples combine groups of menus to allow multiple choice status menus, where there are more than two options. One of the four available modes at the top of the *View* menu will always have a check mark next to it indicating it as the active window mode. Similarly, one of the three *View as* options will be marked indicating the current Content view selected for the active window.

Figure 23-22. *Status-based menus are denoted with a check mark when active*

When menu items are based on commands, they will continue to function this way. Beyond that, there is no built-in option to make one or a set of custom menu items status based, and there is no way to include a check mark in the proper position to simulate such a state. However, since an item's name can be the result of a calculation, it is possible to have a single menu item's name changed to indicate a current state and create a similar toggle effect each time a user selects the item. For example, a menu item can be configured to alternate between two names, e.g., "Enable Tooltips" and "Disable Tooltips." This can be accomplished by creating a global variable that stores a current status value and use that to generate the menu item's name. The custom script assigned as the menu's action looks at the variable's current value to determine how to toggle to the opposite state, which then changes the menu item's name.

To illustrate this method, let's create a custom menu item under the *Actions* menu that will have a *Name* formula shown in the following example. First, it uses a *Let* statement to initialize a *$$Mode_Tooltips* variable if it doesn't yet contain a value. This is done with a *Case* statement that checks the variable for an empty string and sets it to 0 or uses the current value if one is found. Then, it uses another *Case* statement to create a menu name that reflects the action that will be taken depending on the current value. If the variable has a value of 0 indicating tooltips are off, the name will be "Enable Tooltips"; if the global variable has a value of 1 indicating tooltips are on, its name will be "Disable Tooltips."

```
Let ( [
   $$Mode_Tooltips = Case ( $$Mode_Tooltips = "" ; 0 ; $$Mode_Tooltips )
] ;
   Case ( $$Mode_Tooltips = 1 ; "Disable Tooltips" ; "Enable Tooltips" )
)
```

The menu item's *Action* should be configured to run a script that uses the *Set Variable* script step (Chapter 25, "Setting Variables") to toggle the value in the variable using the following *Case* statement. To refresh the menu name for the current layout, the script will also need to perform the *Install Menu Set* step to reset the custom set.

```
Case ( $$Mode_Tooltips = 1 ; 0 ; 1 )
```

Once the menu is in place, every layout object that will be assigned a tooltip in the *Position* tab of the *Inspector* pane can use the following formula to determine if a tooltip should be displayed:

```
Case ( $$Mode_Tooltips = 1 ; "<tooltip text>" ; "" )
```

Now, when the user selects *Enable Tooltips*, the global variable is assigned a value of 1, tooltips begin appearing when the cursor hovers on objects, and the custom menu item's name changes to *Disable Tooltips* which will hide the appearance of tooltips.

Summary

This chapter introduced the options for creating custom menus for total control of the application interface. In the next chapters, we begin creating scripts that can be assigned to menus, buttons, and event triggers to automatically perform a sequence of actions.

PART V

Automating Tasks with Scripts

Scripts that automate repetitive actions can be assigned to buttons, menus, and interface events to improve data entry efficiency and reduce human errors. These chapters explore the basics of creating and debugging scripts:

CHAPTER 24

Introduction to Scripting

A *script*, sometimes called a *macro*, is a developer-defined action sequence stored for later execution. Once created, scripts can be connected to interface objects (Chapter 20), menu items (Chapter 23), and interface event triggers (Chapter 27). They can also be run by other scripts, external scripting languages like *AppleScript* (macOS) or *ActiveX* (Windows). There are options to run a script with a URL (Chapter 20), from JavaScript code in a web viewer's HTML (Chapter 20) or based on a FileMaker Server schedule. By performing complex tasks with a click, scripts can save users an enormous amount of time while improving consistency, reducing errors, and increasing productivity. Scripting transforms a database from a fancy spreadsheet to a fully functional custom application. It liberates users from having to manually perform mundane data entry chores and allows them to focus more attention on creative endeavors and customer engagement. FileMaker comes with numerous ready to configure script steps that can navigate, search, sort, print, export, communicate, and more (Chapter 25). Plug-ins can add new functions to the library of available steps (Chapter 28). This chapter introduces scripting, covering the following topics:

- Introducing the script workspace
- Writing scripts
- Performing other scripts
- Emphasizing the importance of context
- Managing script errors

© Mark Conway Munro 2021
M. C. Munro, *Learn FileMaker Pro 19*, https://doi.org/10.1007/978-1-4842-6680-9_24

Introducing the Script Workspace

Scripts are viewed, written, and managed within the *Script Workspace* window, shown in Figure 24-1. This window can be opened by selecting the *File* ➤ *Manage* ➤ *Scripts* menu item or the *Scripts* ➤ *Script Workspace* menu item. The workspace is divided into four sections: *toolbar, scripts pane, script content area*, and *steps pane*.

Caution   The workspace in a new database will hide elements until the first script is created. Click the + button to get started.

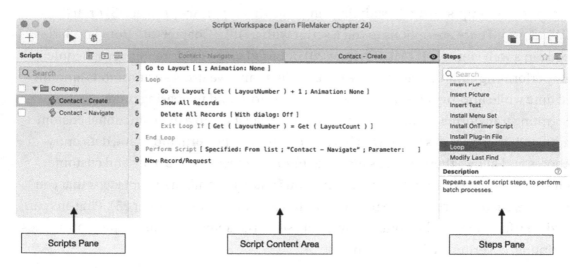

Figure 24-1. *The workspace for defining scripts*

Exploring the Workspace Toolbar

The *toolbar* of the *Script Workspace* window, shown in Figure 24-2, is a static toolbar of controls focused on script design and troubleshooting.

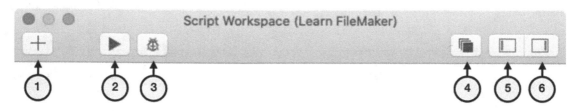

Figure 24-2. *The workspace toolbar contains several static buttons*

The following function buttons are available in the toolbar:

1. *Create Script* – Creates a new script, open for editing

2. *Run Script* – Runs the selected script directly from the *Script Workspace* using the context of the frontmost window behind it

3. *Script Debugger* – Opens the *Script Debugger* window and runs the selected script (Chapter 26)

4. *Compatibility* – Diminishes steps in the *Steps* pane and the content area based on compatibility with the selected device and software platforms

5. *Scripts Pane* – Toggles the visibility of the *Scripts* pane on the left side of the window

6. *Steps Pane* – Toggle the visibility of the *Steps* pane on the right side of the window

Exploring the Scripts Pane

The *scripts pane* on the left side of the window displays a list of every script defined in the file. The pane's visibility can be toggled by clicking the toolbar button. Scripts are displayed with an icon and name, as shown in Figure 24-3. In the pane, each script is an interactive region that hides an assortment of functionality.

Figure 24-3. *The scripts pane on the left side of the workspace window*

- A *single click* on a script name will select and open it in the content area where it can be viewed and edited. When unmodified, it automatically closes when another is selected.

- A *second single click* on a selected script will cause the name to become editable directly in the list. Edit the name and type Enter.

- A *double-click* will open the script in a locked tab where it remains open until explicitly closed.

- A *right-click* opens a contextual menu containing functions also present in the *Scripts* menu.

A *script folder* can be used to organize groups of scripts. Click the middle + icon at the top of the *script pane* to create a new folder, and then enter a name and type Enter. Once created, scripts can be dragged from the list into a folder. Folders can be dragged into other folders to create a nested hierarchy which can be collapsed or expanded to hide or show each folder's content. Similar to scripts, two successive single clicks on a folder make its name editable.

A *separator line* can be inserted anywhere in the list to create visual space between long lists of folders or scripts. Just click the line icon on the right at the top of the pane.

The checkbox makes a script, folder, or separator appear in the *Scripts* menu visible by default when viewing regular windows. If the checkbox is not visible, click the first icon at the top. Folders included in the menu form submenus, and scripts become menu items that can be selected by users to run a script.

Scripts, separators, and folders in the list can be deleted, duplicated, and more using the commands in the contextual menu and in the *Scripts* menu visible only when the *Script Workspace* is open.

Exploring the Script Content Area

The *script content area* at the center of the *Script Workspace* window displays open scripts and is used to view or edit the action steps that define the current selection. As shown in Figure 24-4, scripts are automatically opened into tabs, making it easy to jump back and forth between multiple open scripts. They can also be moved into separate windows using the contextual menu on the tabs or a function in the *Scripts* menu.

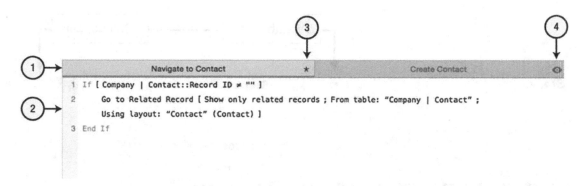

Figure 24-4. *The script content area of the workspace window*

1. *Script Tabs* – Hover the cursor over a tab to reveal and click a close icon. Right-click to open a contextual menu of functions. Drag horizontally to rearrange the tabs.

2. *Script Steps* – A numbered list of interactive lines, each representing one step in the scripted process.

3. *Unsaved Change Indicator* – This asterisk icon indicates the script has been modified since opening.

4. *Preview Mode Indicator* – Indicates the script is open in a temporary state with no changes.

Steps Pane

The *steps pane* on the right of the *Script Workspace* window contains a list of every available action step, as shown in Figure 24-5. This include *built-in* steps and steps from installed *plug-ins*. The pane's visibility requires a selected script and can also be toggled open or closed by clicking the toolbar button. The list can be toggled between an alphabetic or categorical arrangement using the icon at the top shown in the figure.

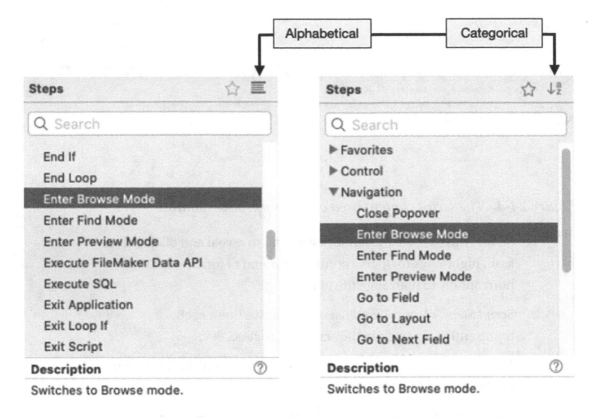

Figure 24-5. *The pane of steps can be alphabetical (left) or hierarchical (right)*

A script step can be inserted into the active open script by double-clicking on it or by right-clicking and choosing *Insert Into Script* from the contextual menu. That menu includes options to add or remove the step from the *Favorites* category (only available when steps are viewed in a categorical hierarchy) or to open the step in the online help guide. The *description pane* at the bottom provides a brief description of the selected step, and the help icon button opens the online documentation.

Menu Changes (Script Workspace)

The menu bar is radically transformed when working in the *Script Workspace*. Any active menu set (standard or custom) is replaced by a set specifically designed for working with scripts. Many inapplicable standard menus are removed completely, while the *Edit, View,* and *Scripts* menus are radically transformed.

Edit Menu

The *Edit* menu of the workspace contains a modified set of functions, as shown in Figure 24-6. Below standard functions such as *Cut*, *Copy*, and *Paste*, new items have been added for *Duplicate Step* and a toggling item to *Disable/Enable* selected script steps.

Figure 24-6. *The Edit menu when working in the Script Workspace*

View Menu

The *View* menu of the workspace contains a completely unique set of functions, as shown in Figure 24-7. This menu provides basic workspace functions for toggling pane visibility, managing tabs, and other functions, including many accessible through various buttons and contextual menus within the workspace.

Hide Scripts Pane	
Hide Steps Pane	
Hide Step Description Pane	
Hide Scripts Menu Management	
Close Tab	⌘W
Close All Tabs	⌥⌘W
Close Workspace	⇧⌘W
Select Next Tab	⌘}
Select Previous Tab	⌘{
Move Tab to New Window	
Compatibility	▶
Script Workspace Preferences...	

Figure 24-7. *The View menu when working in the Script Workspace*

Scripts Menu

The *Scripts* menu when working in the *Script Workspace* is completely transformed, as shown in Figure 24-8. It contains functions for *creating, importing, opening, renaming, duplicating, deleting, saving, reverting,* and *running* scripts, many also available in the toolbar or contextual menus. One notable function, *Grant/Revoke Full Access Privileges,* configures a selected script to run with *full access privileges* even when the current user does not have full access (Chapter 30). When a script has been granted full access, a small icon of a person appears next to its name in the list.

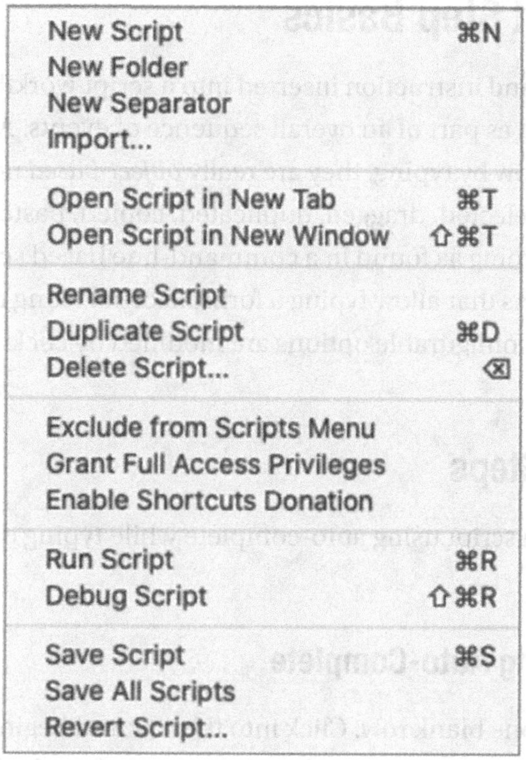

New Script	⌘N
New Folder	
New Separator	
Import...	
Open Script in New Tab	⌘T
Open Script in New Window	⇧⌘T
Rename Script	
Duplicate Script	⌘D
Delete Script...	⌫
Exclude from Scripts Menu	
Grant Full Access Privileges	
Enable Shortcuts Donation	
Run Script	⌘R
Debug Script	⇧⌘R
Save Script	⌘S
Save All Scripts	
Revert Script...	

Figure 24-8. *The Scripts menu when working in the Script Workspace*

Caution   The Scripts menu is macOS only. In Windows, these functions can be found in a modified File and Edit menus.

Writing Scripts

To create a script, click the + button in the toolbar or select the *Scripts* ➤ *New Script* menu item. The new script will appear in the *scripts pane* and open as a tab with editing focus on the label awaiting entry of a custom name. Enter a name and type Enter or click away from the tab to commit it.

Exploring Script Step Basics

A *script step* is a command instruction inserted into a script workflow that defines a specific action executed as part of an overall sequence of events. Although steps can be *inserted* into the workflow by typing, they are really *object-based* not *text-based*. Once inserted, steps can be selected, dragged, duplicated, copied, pasted, or deleted but are no longer editable by typing as found in a command-line based scripting environments. Some have active regions that allow typing a formula or selecting menu options directly in line. However, most configurable options are modified by clicking to open a pane or dialog.

Inserting Script Steps

Steps can be added to a script using auto-complete while typing directly or using the *steps pane*.

Inserting Steps Using Auto-Complete

A new script will have one blank row. Click into the row and begin typing a step name to activate an auto-complete suggestion interface. A list of available steps appears and is filtered as you type, as shown in Figure 24-9. To select a step, either click directly on a step, use the keyboard arrows, or keep typing until the desired step is at the top of the list. Once a step is selected, insert it by typing Enter or double-clicking on it. Once inserted, the step transforms from editable text into an interactive object.

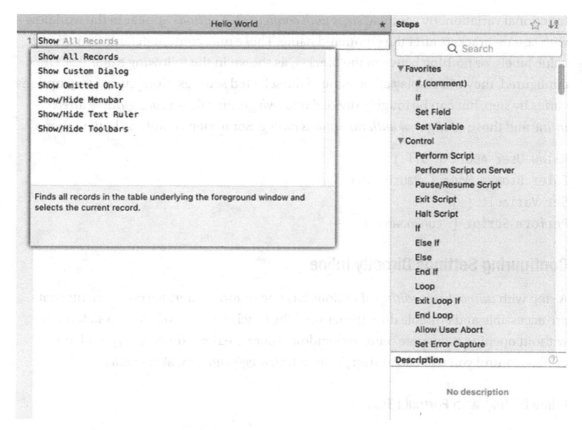

Figure 24-9. *The suggestions available for auto-complete*

Inserting Steps from the Steps Pane

To insert using the *Steps* pane, locate the desired step in the list by scrolling, using the arrow keys, typing a few characters of the desired step or using the *Search* field to filter the list. Once selected, insert the step into the script workflow by typing the Enter key, double-clicking on it or right-clicking on it and selecting the *Insert into Script* function from the contextual menu.

Configuring Script Steps

Script steps can be divided into two fundamental categories. *Steps without configurable options* will perform a predetermined function without any variability. These appear in the script workflow by name only, without any interactive options, and include commands like a *New Record/Request*, *Go to Next Field*, *Show All Records*, *Beep*, and more. They can be dragged around to position them in the workflow but offer no

577

functional variation. By contrast, *steps with configurable options* appear in the workflow with square brackets after the command name. These may contain default settings, value labels, or nothing between the bracket, as shown in the following examples. Once configured, they will display all or some of the selected settings. Configuring step options varies by step, but can be roughly divided into two groups: those *configurable directly inline* and those *configured with an options dialog*. Some steps combine both of these.

```
Allow User Abort [ Off ]
Enter Browse Mode [ Pause: Off ]
Set Variable [ ]
Perform Script [ <unknown> ]
```

Configuring Settings Directly Inline

A step with *inline direct editing* of options has one or more interface components that are accessible and editable directly between the bracketed area of the step statement without opening a separate panel or window. There are three different types of inline editing control you will encounter: *formula text*, *toggle buttons*, and *menus*.

Inline Editing with Formula Text

Many steps allow *inline formula editing* where a formula can be typed directly into the script step. These include steps like *If, Exit Loop If,* and *Exit Script*. When inline editing is available, a red box appears between the square brackets. With the cursor over this, the box deepens in color and gains a red outline. Click it to reveal an expanded formula text area, as shown in Figure 24-10.

Figure 24-10. *A formula step at rest (top), with hover (middle), and with active focus (bottom)*

Note   Inline formula editing is a convenience for entering a short formula but is impractical for longer formulas. Click the *fx* icon to open a full-sized *Specify Calculation* dialog.

The inline formula editor is fully featured like the *Specify Calculation* dialog (Chapter 12, "Exploring the Specify Calculation Dialog"). It includes auto-complete suggestions and allows for multiline formula entry and editing, both shown in Figure 24-11. After typing a formula, compile and save by clicking outside of the formula area or by typing either the Return or Enter key. If a syntax error is detected in the formula, the full *Specify Calculation* dialog will automatically open with an error notification dialog, forcing you to remedy the problem before saving.

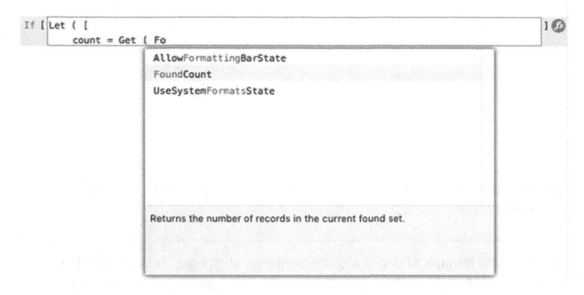

Figure 24-11. *An inline multiline formula showing the auto-complete interface*

Tip   To insert a carriage return in an inline formula, type Return while holding down the Option key (macOS) or Alt key (Windows).

Inline Editing with a Toggle Button

A step with an *inline editable toggle button* allows a choice between two possible options. These can be identified by a labeled value between the brackets that is logically binary and the appearance of a blue border outlining the current value when the cursor hovers over it, as shown in Figure 24-12. To toggle the current value, click it or press the space bar with the step selected.

```
Enter Browse Mode [ Pause: Off ]


Enter Browse Mode [ Pause: Off ]


Enter Browse Mode [ Pause: On ]
```

Figure 24-12. *A toggle button at rest (top), with hover (middle), and after click (bottom)*

Tip   When available in combination with a dialog or popover of configuration options, the toggle setting is generally only accessible inline and not included on a dialog with other options.

Inline Editing with Pop-up Menu

A step with an *inline pop-up menu* allows a choice between several possible options. These can be identified by a value between the square brackets and the appearance of a blue border outlining the current value when the cursor hovers over it. Click on it to reveal a pop-up menu of other values. Each of these states is shown in Figure 24-13.

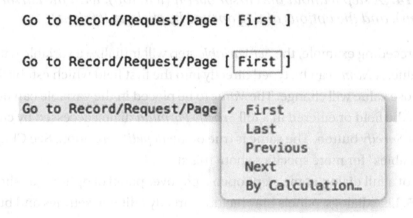

Figure 24-13. *A pop-up menu at rest (top), with hover (middle), and with active focus (bottom)*

Configuring Steps with an Options Dialog

A step uses a *dialog or panel* when the available configuration options are too numerous or in some way not conducive to inline editing. While many are unique to the step, some open standard dialogs, e.g., *Specify Field* and *Specify Calculation*. Some dialogs present a few simple options, while others summarize settings alongside buttons that open additional dialogs. Some open an independent dialog window, others open a popover panel that remains connected to the step. The method of opening an options interface also varies between steps. A step that has a configuration dialog will display a gear icon to the right of its statement when the cursor hovers over it. Clicking this icon will open the options interface, like the *Set Variable* dialog shown in Figure 24-14.

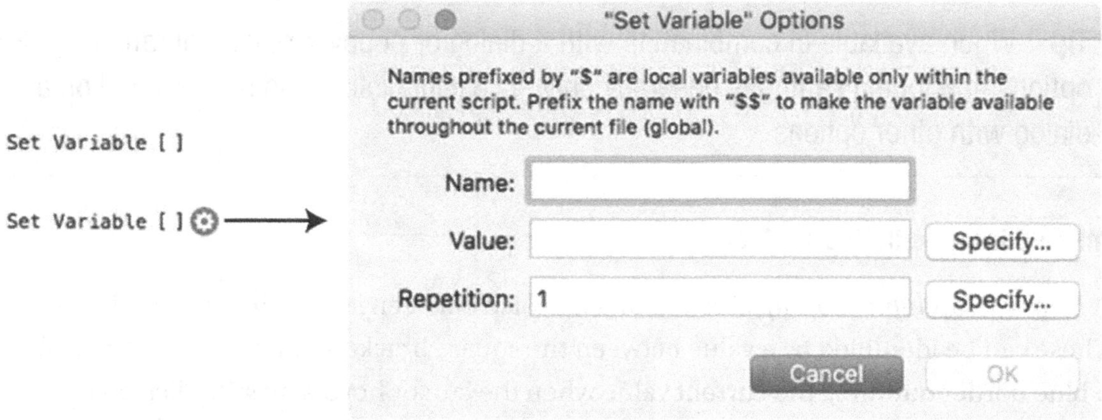

Set Variable [ ]

Set Variable [ ] ⊙ ——————————➤

"Set Variable" Options

Names prefixed by "$" are local variables available only within the
current script. Prefix the name with "$$" to make the variable available
throughout the current file (global).

Name: [   ]

Value: [   ]   [Specify...]

Repetition: [1   ]   [Specify...]

[Cancel]   [OK]

Figure 24-14. *A step without the cursor over it (left, top), with the cursor over it (left, bottom), and the options dialog opened by clicking it (right)*

In the preceding example, the *Set Variable* step will initialize a variable with a specified value. A *Name* can be typed directly into the first field which establishes the variable whose value will change. The *Value* to be placed in the variable can be typed directly into the field or entered in a full *Specify Formula* dialog accessed by clicking the adjacent *Specify* button. The same is true of the *Repetition* option. See Chapter 25, "Setting Variables" for more specifics about this step.

Instead of a full dialog, some steps open a popover panel of options, as shown in Figure 24-15. Like dialogs, panels may include directly editable settings and buttons that open other dialogs. In this example, the *Enter Find Mode* step opens a simple panel that contains a button which opens the standard *Find Request* dialog (Chapter 4, "Editing a Find Request"). Unlike dialogs, which typically have OK and Cancel buttons, changes made in these panels are saved immediately. A popover can be closed by clicking on the script workspace outside of the panel's boundaries or typing the Return or Enter key.

Enter Find Mode [Pause: [On]] ⊙

[ ] Specify find requests   [Specify...]

Figure 24-15. *A popover streamlines the selection of options for some steps*

Tip   Many steps have multiple active regions that combine configuration styles.

Specifying Targets

Many script steps require you to specify a target using dialogs. Some steps require a variable and present a version of the *Set Variable Options* dialog, described previously. A handful require a field selection using the *Specify Field* dialog (Chapter 20, "Exploring the Specify Field Dialog"). Many present a *Specify Path* dialog (described later in this chapter). In addition to these, many steps use the *Specify Target* dialog, shown in Figure 24-16, allowing specification of a field or variable. In recent versions, this dialog has replaced the *Specify Field* option for a lot of script steps. For example, most of the available *Insert* steps have been converted to this dialog, and many of the newer *Data File* steps us it as well. This dialog allows the selection of either a field or entry of a variable name, while the script step that opens it also provides access to a *Specify Calculation* dialog that determines the value to be inserted into that target.

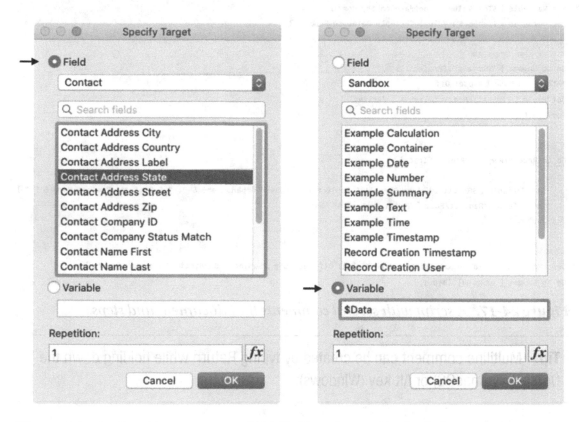

Figure 24-16. *Specifying a target field (left) and variable (right)*

Script Comments

A *script comment* is a text note placed into a script as a nonfunctional step. Comments appear as a line of text with a preceding pound or hash symbol. These are used to provide inline documentation, describing the function of a script or of a group of steps. When combined with empty comments, they help to separate sections of a script and avoid visual clutter, as shown in Figure 24-17. When a comment is added to a script without any content, it becomes a blank line.

```
# This script will demonstrate good commenting practices

# Setup & Declarations
Freeze Window
Allow User Abort [ Off ]
Set Error Capture [ On ]
Set Variable [ $To ; Value: "Joe@FakeCompany.com" ]
Set Variable [ $Subject ; Value: "Example Database Report" ]

# Find open projects
Go to Layout [ "Project" (Project) ]
Enter Find Mode [ Pause: Off ]
Set Field [ Project::Project Status ; "Active" ]
Perform Find [ ]

# Compile the report information
Go to Record/Request/Page [ First ]
Loop
    Set Variable [ $Result ; Value: $Result & Project | Company::Company Name & ": " & Project::Project Name & "¶" ]
    Go to Record/Request/Page [ Next ; Exit after last ]
End Loop

# Email the result
Send Mail [ Send via E-mail Client ; With dialog: Off ; To: $To ; Subject: $Subject ; Message: $Result ]
Go to Layout [ original layout ]
```

Figure 24-17. *A script with several comments that document and steps*

Tip   Multiline comment can be created by typing Return while holding down the Option key (macOS) or Alt key (Windows).

Specifying File Paths

There are many instances in the development interface where file paths must be specified. This can be found when managing data sources (Chapter 9) and script steps such as *Import Records, Export Records, Save Records as Excel, Save Records as PDF, New File, Open File, Read from Data File,* and more (Chapter 25). Paths are entered into a *Specify File* dialog, shown in Figure 24-18. The *File Path List* text area of this dialog can contain one or more return-delimited paths. If more than one is entered, FileMaker will check each one, in the order entered, until it finds a valid path pointing to an existing file.

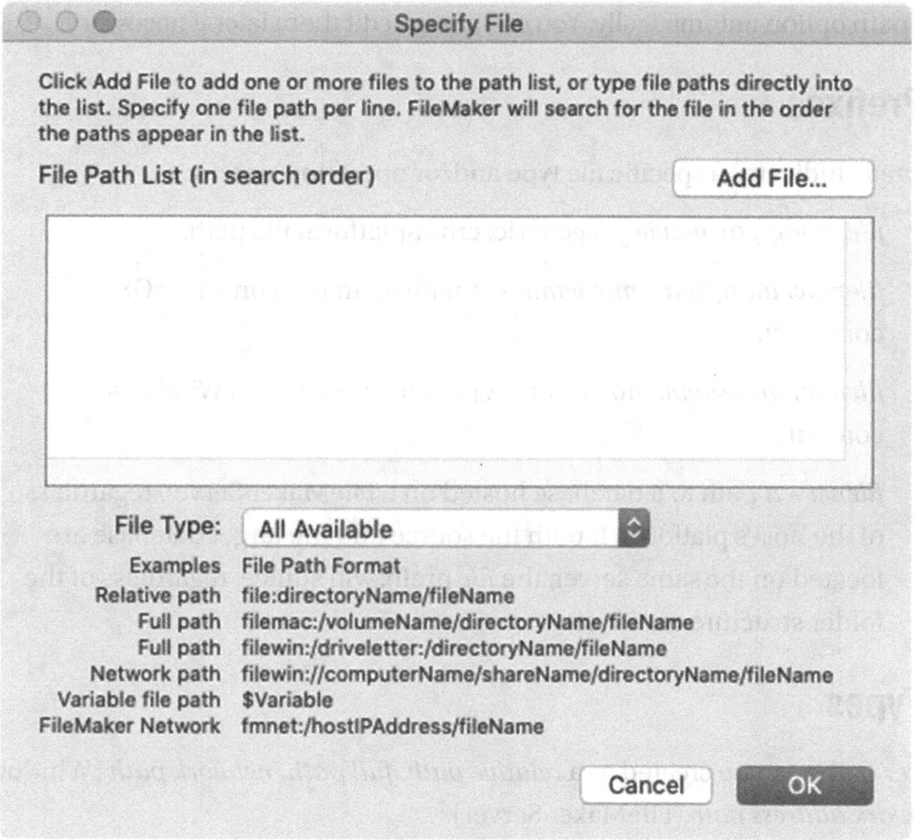

Figure 24-18. The dialog for specifying a file path

Formatting Paths

As indicated by the examples displayed on the dialog, paths can be entered using various formats to point to a file in a local directory, server folder directory, or at a FileMaker Server network address. Properly formatting a path can be tricky, especially when addressing files in a local directory relative to the database location. There are various prefixes that can be mixed and matched with different path format types. If a path is incorrectly entered or the target file is moved after a path has been defined, a file missing error will occur when FileMaker attempts to access it. To avoid mistyping a complex path, use the *Add Files* button and subsequent *Open File* dialog to select a file and allow FileMaker to formulate the best path option automatically. You can always edit them later if necessary.

Path Prefixes

A *path prefix* indicates a specific file type and/or operating system:

- *file, image,* or *movie* – A generic, cross-platform file path.

- *filemac, imagemac, moviemac* – A path to an item on a macOS computer.

- *filewin, imagewin, moviewin* – A path to an item on a Windows computer.

- *filenet* – A path to a database hosted on a FileMaker Server, regardless of the host's platform. If both the source and the target database are located on the same server, the *file* prefix will suffice, regardless of the folder structure on the server.

Path Types

FileMaker paths can be created as a *relative path, full path, network path* (Windows), and *network address path* (FileMaker Server).

Relative Path

A *relative path* specifies a target file from the context of the current database location. This format assumes the source and target database are both not hosted and have a portion of their directory location in common. In other words, they are running locally from a folder on the same hard drive. Although sometimes confusing, these paths have the benefit of allowing the location of the files to move with a parent folder structure as long as the relative location between the two remains the same. The formula for a relative path is

```
file:[pathDifferential]fileName
```

The prefix and *fileName* are required with the *pathDifferential* included when there is a difference between the two folders containing them. The following examples assume two files: a current database named "Test Source" that is targeting a database named "Test Target." If these two files are sitting in the same directory folder, there is no need to include any information about the difference between their locations, so the path will be simply be the prefix and the name of the target file.

```
file:Test Target
```

If the source file is moved to the macOS *Desktop* and the target to the user's *Documents* folder, the two files will have only part of their path in common:

```
Macintosh HD/Users/john_doe/Desktop/Test Source
Macintosh HD/Users/john_doe/Documents/Test Target
```

In this case, for the source file to point to the target file, it would need a differential of two periods and a forward slash indicating that we must move up the directory hierarchy one folder and then down into the *Documents* folder to locate the file as shown in the following path:

```
file:../Documents/Test Target
```

Leaving the source file on the *Desktop*, if the target was moved into a subfolder within the *Documents*, subfolder named "Target Subfolder," the file path would change to include the additional subfolder.

```
file:../Documents/Target Subfolder/Test Target
```

When the source is placed into a folder on the *Desktop named "Source Subfolder,"* the differential must change to indicate the need to move up the two levels before navigating downward into the target file's folder. For example, assume the two files are in the following folders:

```
Macintosh HD/Users/john_doe/Desktop/Source Subfolder/Test Source
Macintosh HD/Users/john_doe/Documents/Target Subfolder/Test Target
```

So, the file path would require two sets of *double-period, forward slash* hierarchy indicators to point up two levels to reach the common parent folder before heading back down into the folder structure to find the target, as shown in the following path:

```
file:../../Documents/Target Subfolder/Test Target
```

Full Path

A *full path* is a path to a target database in a folder that is specified from the context of the disk volume containing it. This establishes an absolute path that doesn't change. As long as the target remains in place, the path will work regardless of where the source database is located. Full paths can be used for macOS directories on the local startup hard drive, an external disk and for Windows local directories. The formula of an absolute path varies slightly depending on the operating system of the user computer.

```
filemac:/volume/directoryName/fileName
filewin:/driveLetter:/directoryName/fileName
```

For example, if the file is in the user's *Documents* folder on a macOS computer, the path would be formatted as shown here:

```
filemac:/Macintosh HD/Users/alex_smith/Documents/Test Target
```

The generic `file` prefix will also work for full paths and be completely cross-platform.

```
file:/Macintosh HD/Users/alex_smith/Documents/Test Target
```

Network Path (Windows Shared Directory Only)

A *network path* is a path to a target database file stored in a server directory in a Windows environment. The formula of a network path is

```
filewin:/computerName/shareName/directoryName/fileName
```

For example, a path might be

```
filewin:/Company_Server/Databases/Sales/Test_Target
```

FileMaker Server Network Path

A *FileMaker network path* is a path to a target database file hosted on a FileMaker Server computer (not any form of file sharing). The formula of a network path is

```
fmnet:/addressOrName/fileName
```

For example

```
fmnet:/192.100.50.10/Test Target
fmnet:/FileMaker-Server.local/Test Target
```

If the source database is hosted on the same server as the target, a simple relative path can be used as shown in the following. Using this method will "future-proof" a database as it will continue to work even if the server address changes.

```
file:/Test Target
```

Building Dynamic Paths

Unlike literal paths typed as text, a *dynamic path* can automatically change from one user's computer to the next. There are a few techniques that can help keep paths dynamic: *using variables, using functions,* and *excluding file extensions.*

Using Variables in Paths

Paths entered in the *Specify File* dialog can include variables that specify an entire path or a portion of a path. For example, a script using the *Set Variable* step (Chapter 25) can store a network address and file name for a commonly used target file in global variables and use them when constructing a path. Alternatively, an entire path can be placed into a single variable. Script steps requiring a path can use paths stored in local variables as well. These examples show how paths can use variables for part or all of the path:

```
fmnet:/$$ServerAddress/$$FileName
file:$$PathToExport
$PathToImportFile
```

When a script step is provided an invalid path, it usually errors with a rather cryptic message. Building paths in variables makes it possible to troubleshoot these problems since the value is accessible prior to being embedded in the script step. This is especially important when a path is being constructed dynamically across several script steps and may not adhere to proper formatting requirements in a non-obvious way. A *Show Dialog* step can display the variable for examination prior to the step that requires it. As a variable, it can also be monitored in the Data Viewer (Chapter 26, "Exploring the Data Viewer"). More often than not, simply looking at the path instantly reveals the cause of the error.

Using Functions to Generate Contextual Paths

Several of FileMaker's built-in functions automatically generate paths to standard folders on the user's computer. These can be used in formulas to construct dynamic paths that work regardless of the context of the startup disk or home directory name.

```
Get ( SystemDrive )      // result = /Macintosh HD/
Get ( DesktopPath )      // result = /Macintosh HD/Users/karen_camacho/
                            Desktop/
Get ( DocumentsPath )    // result = /Macintosh HD/Users/karen_camacho/
                            Documents/
Get ( PreferencesPath )  // result = /Macintosh HD/Users/karen_camacho/
                            Library/Preferences/
```

These functions return the path to the FileMaker application or current database file.

```
Get ( FileMakerPath )
// result = /Macintosh HD/Applications/
Get ( FilePath )
// result = file:/Macintosh HD/Users/karen_camacho /Desktop/Learn
FileMaker.fmp12
```

A *temporary folder* is an automatically generated hidden folder that only exists until the user signs out or the computer is restarted. Since these are not stored in an obviously accessible directory, they are ideal for use as a staging location when exporting files prior to sending an email or storing transitory data files.

```
Get ( TemporaryPath )
// result = /Macintosh HD/var/folders/rt/n62fc5vd0hn7js2v4098ydkw0000gp/T/
S10/
```

Excluding File Extensions

When targeting a FileMaker database, the file extension is *completely optional*. Since the FileMaker file extension may change in the future, consider omitting extensions in paths (or store them in a global variable), so the database can be easily updated later without having to find and edit every path. For example, all of these paths will locate the same file (with the last one assuming that the $$Extension variable contains ".fmp12").

```
filemac:/Macintosh HD/Users/john_smith/Documents/Test Target
filemac:/Macintosh HD/Users/john_smith/Documents/Test Target.fmp12
filemac:/Macintosh HD/Users/john_smith/Documents/Test Target$$Extension
```

Converting Paths

In version 19, two new functions make it easier to convert between an operating system path format and a FileMaker path. This eliminates the chore of programmatically parsing formulas to convert paths to a different format. Both functions accept two parameters: a *path* and a *format*. The *format* parameter for either can be one of three values indicating the respective source or target path format: *PosixPath*, *URLPath*, or *WinPath*.

```
ConvertToFileMakerPath ( "/Users/mmunro/Desktop/" ; PosixPath )
// result (macOS) = file:/Macintosh HD/Users/mmunro/Desktop/
// result (Windows) = file:/C:/Users/mmunro/Desktop/
ConvertFromFileMakerPath ( "file:/Macintosh HD/Users/mmunro/Desktop/" ;
PosixPath)
// result = /Users/mmunro/Desktop/
```

Performing Other Scripts

The *Perform Script* step allows a script to run another script. This makes it possible to build modular scripts that perform discrete tasks and then have higher-level scripts run them in a sequence. Scripts can call scripts that call other scripts, creating complex *hierarchical call stacks*. Scripts can even call themselves creating a *recursive call stack*. After adding the step to a script, it will appear with an unknown script specification, as shown in Figure 24-19. The step has two active regions. First, the *Specified* value indicates what type of reference to a script will be defined, a formula-driven text value indicating the *name* of the script or a *dynamic reference* selected from a list of available scripts. Depending on that selection, clicking on the script name region of the call opens the appropriate specification dialog, either the *Specify Formula* or *Specify Script* dialog.

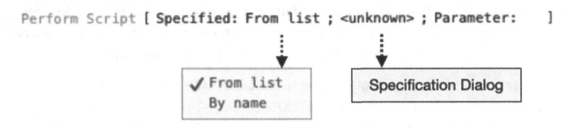

Figure 24-19. *The Perform Script step's options*

Tip   Hold the Command (macOS) or Windows (Windows) key when clicking on a *Perform Script* step's target script to automatically open the assigned script in a new tab.

Exploring the Specify Script Dialog

The *Specify Script* dialog is used to select a reference to a script that will be targeted as the action for a button, an interface event trigger (Chapter 27) or the *Perform Script* step mentioned previously. The dialog, shown in Figure 24-20, allows selection of a script from the current file or any FileMaker data source defined in the database (Chapter 9). An *Optional script parameter* can be defined to accompany the call to the selected script. When assigning a script to a button or as an event trigger, this dialog includes the three buttons that allow *adding, deleting, editing,* or *duplicating* a script directly from the dialog.

Figure 24-20. *Selecting a script for a button, script trigger, or script step*

The ability of a script to run other scripts allows for a more modular script design. Instead of building one monolithic script that performs dozens or hundreds of steps in a long complex sequence, a process can be broken into separate scripts, each focused on a certain task. This makes it possible to set up a hierarchy where some scripts perform open-ended, fundamental tasks that can be shared by many other scripts regardless of context. However, when creating a delimited mesh of shared script functions, be sure to manage the naming, organizations, and usage rules in a way to avoid confusing zigzagging cross talk back and forth.

Exchanging Data Between Scripts

A script call can include a *parameter* and receive a *result*, as illustrated in Figure 24-21 where Script 1 calls Script 2 with a parameter and then receives a result from that script's *Exit Script* step.

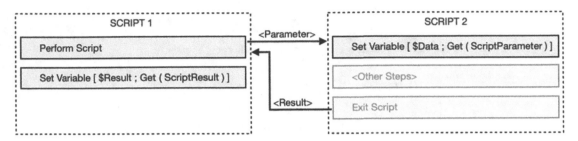

Figure 24-21. *Illustrating data exchange between two scripts*

Caution   Decades ago, global fields and variables were used to "park" data prior to script calls to facilitate an archaic data exchange. Before that, some used the clipboard for this purpose. However, parameters are now preferred for data exchange between scripts.

Sending Parameters

A *script parameter* is a text string sent to a script by a triggering object. Parameters are used to transmit any information that a script can use for any number of reasons. Instead of hard-coding field references or other values inside a script, parameters allow the triggering object to *push* information to the script that can vary from one call to the next. Parameters can be a single word, a sentence, a value list, a field name, a field value, or a JSON object containing a complex array of key-value pairs. They can be typed as literal values or constructed with a formula. To illustrate the use of parameters, create a script that displays an incoming parameter in a dialog using the *Show Custom Dialog* script step configured with this formula:

```
Get ( ScriptParameter )
```

Next create a button or a second script that uses the *Perform Script* function with a short message typed into the *Optional script parameter* field. When the button is clicked or script run, the targeted script should present a dialog displaying the message that was sent as a parameter.

Parsing a Parameter

A script parameter is a singular value. However, it can be arranged in a way to contain multiple values using a return-delimited value list, a reference to a repeating field, or a JSON object. When receiving structured information representing multiple components, a script will need to parse the values in order to deal with them separately. To accommodate this, use one or more *Set Variable* or *Insert Calculated Result* steps to parse and park the data into separate variables. This can be done with a *Let* statement and the *GetValue, GetRepetition,* or various JSON functions. The following example demonstrates how to parse a value list containing three values into separate variables:

```
Let ( [
   input = Get ( ScriptParameter ) ;
   $id = GetValue ( input ; 1 ) ;
   $name = GetValue ( input ; 2 ) ;
   $status = GetValue ( input ; 3 )
] ;
   ""
)
```

This example will parse values from a script parameter containing a reference to a field that is defined with four repetitions, using the *GetRepetition* function.

```
Let ( [
   field = Get ( ScriptParameter ) ;
   $id = GetRepetition ( field ; 1 ) ;
   $name = GetRepetition ( field; 2 ) ;
   $status = GetRepetition ( field; 3 ) ;
   $task = GetRepetition ( field; 4 )
] ;
   ""
)
```

While those two examples parse a fixed number of values in the parameter, it is possible to create more dynamic parsing functionality. If the number of values or field repetitions varies, a *While* function (Chapter 13) statement or *Loop* script step (Chapter 25) might be necessary to cycle through them. Also, a recursive custom function can step through each value, initializing it into a variable.

Exploring Script Results

A script run by another script can send back a result value using the *Exit Script* step. This step has a single parameter: a calculation formula that generates a text value. Like an input parameter, a result can be a single value or complex data structure. This example shows a simple result returning the word "Success" to indicate to the calling script that the target script reached the end of its steps without failure.

```
Exit Script [ Text Result: "Success" ]
```

A script can have multiple exit points, each returning a different value. In the following example, after a *Perform Find* step, a conditional *If* statement can exit the script if no records are found with a result that informs the calling script of this fact. When records are found, the script continues functioning until the end and returns the success indicator instead.

```
Perform Find [ ]
If [ Get ( FoundCount ) = 0 ]
   Exit Script [ Text Result: "No records found" ]
End If
Loop
   <steps to process records>
End Loop
Exit Script [ Text Result: "Success" ]
```

Perform Script on Server

When a database is hosted on a FileMaker Server (Chapter 29), scripts can be run locally on the current user's computer using the *Perform Script* step or can be offloaded to run on the server using the *Perform Script on Server* step. Running a complex script on the server tends to be faster since the client and server don't need to exchange as much information across the network. In instances where the local script doesn't require a response or any interface manipulation, the task can be fully handed off to the server, instantly freeing the user's computer to perform other script functions or manual work. However, before using this feature, it is important to realize that the context of the local computer's database window will *not* be known or accessible to the server when running the script. Therefore, any contextual information about the *current table, layout, record, found set*, *sort order*, or *window* required by the script being called must be included in a script parameter so the server can replicate the context before running. New scripts can be designed specifically to address this issue. When converting an existing script to run on the server, it may be necessary to split it into two: one script that loads the context information into a script parameter and another that will receive that information, reset the context on the server, and then perform the other script functions.

A script can be configured to run locally or on the server depending on certain conditions. For example, when the database is taken offline for maintenance, any scripts critical to the database at launch time must be able to run locally. For these, include a `condition` that allows the script to be run on the server when hosted and locally when not. The following example demonstrates a simple *If* step, choosing between running the script locally and on the server with the help of the *Get (HostApplicationVersion)* and *LeftWords* functions. If the host version starts with the word "Server," it indicates a hosted file, and the call will be performed using the *Perform Script on Server* step instead.

```
If [ LeftWords ( Get ( HostApplicationVersion ) ; 1 ) = "Server" ]
    Perform Script On Server [ <script name> ]
Else
    Perform Script [ <script name> ]
End If
```

Emphasizing the Importance of Context

Like calculations, *scripts are contextual,* and it is *important* to be cognizant of this fact as you develop your database. When a script step executes, it runs within the context of the table occurrence of the front window's current layout. This starts as the current layout when the script is triggered but may change when scripts begins changing layouts, performing finds or creating windows. A complex database may have scripts running scripts that run other scripts, and any of them might change the current context. If a script tries to access fields from a non-current context, it will cause errors and be confusing to users and possibly be destructive. If a script creates, deletes, or duplicates records while in the wrong context, it can be a disaster. Given this, it should be obvious that keeping track of context is a major imperative when designing scripts. When designing a script, keep focus on its intended context based on the steps it contains. Be aware of the expectation of different steps. While all script steps *operate contextually,*

597

they don't all have the same type of dependency. Some steps are *layout-table dependent* and access table values directly regardless of what is visible on the layout. Others are *layout-object dependent* and require direct interaction with something on the layout. In the next chapter, we will see examples such as *Set Field*, which doesn't require a field present on the layout, and *Insert Text* which does. Also, when calling other scripts in a complex mesh of interconnected workflows, try to design a naming and organization standard that helps you manage context by implementing rules for which scripts can call others and which can't.

Managing Scripting Errors

When an error occurs, a script may open a dialog informing the user of the problem. The message may or may not make sense to a user, depending on their knowledge and the type of error that occurred. A common example is a failure when the *Set Field* step tries to set a value for a field from a table not accessible from the current context. For example, if browsing a *Company* record, setting a field in the *Contact* table directly (not through a relationship) will result in the error message stating, "This operation could not be completed because the target is not part of the related table." Since this is a programming error, a user would have no idea what this means or what to do to reach a resolution. So, it is a good idea to design your scripts to capture errors and present more informative dialogs that notify users in a productive way.

To suppress error displays, use the *Set Error Capture* step with a parameter of *On*. This will cause the script to completely ignore any errors it encounters and continue processing. In many cases, this isn't ideal because an error at one step may cause major problems further in the workflow. So, it may be necessary to detect and handle specific errors with custom messaging or other steps. The *Get (LastError)* function can be used at various points in the script to determine if an error has occurred when the previous step(s) executed. The function will return a numeric value indicating either no error (0) or the number representing the error. An *If* statement can take conditional action in the event an error is detected.

To illustrate this technique, the following simple example attempts to set the *Contact::Name Last* field. If this script is run from the *Contact* table, there will be no error generated and no dialog presented. However, running it in a different table will generate an error and present that fact in a custom dialog. Depending on the error, its location, and other functions of the script, the *If* statement can include other steps to email a developer, perform alternative steps, halt completely, etc.

```
Set Error Capture [ On ]
Set Field [ "Contact::Name Last; "Smith" ]
If [ Get ( LastError ) = 103 ]
    Show Custom Dialog [ "Error 103: Set Field context error" ]
End If
```

Tip For a complete list of errors, search for "FileMaker Pro error code reference guide" on Claris.com.

Summary

This chapter introduced scripting basics, working in script workspace, and various step configuration interface options. We explored various formats for specifying file paths and discussed scripts running other scripts, passing parameters, receiving results, contextual awareness, and managing script errors. In the next chapter, we begin creating examples that perform common scripting tasks.

Common Scripting Tasks

FileMaker ships with over 180 built-in script steps that can perform just about any database task you can imagine. In this chapter, we work through a handful of real-world examples to provide a basic foundation upon which to base your own exploration of the remaining script steps, covering the following topics:

- Scripting basic functions
- Interacting with fields
- Accessing folders and files
- Working with records
- Using conditional statements
- Showing custom dialogs
- Searching and dealing with found sets
- Iterating with repeating statements
- Scripting portal functions
- Managing windows
- Using Insert from URL

Scripting Basic Functions

Let's begin by exploring a few basic script steps that perform common functions: controlling the ability of users to abort a script, setting variables, and navigational context changes.

© Mark Conway Munro 2021
M. C. Munro, *Learn FileMaker Pro 19*, https://doi.org/10.1007/978-1-4842-6680-9_25

Allowing User Abort

Any running script can be manually halted at any time by typing Esc (Windows) or a Period while holding the Command key (macOS). While this may not be a concern for scripts that perform a couple quick steps that finish before a user can attempt this, it introduces a danger with more complex scripts and may cause various problems. A partially completed process may not be so easy to start again without programming intervention. The user may become stranded on a staging layout not designed as an interface or have hidden windows left open but accessible through the *Windows* menu. A set of records may be half imported but not yet processed, and repeating the script could cause duplicates the second time around. The *Allow User Abort* script step can avoid these and countless other catastrophes by denying a user's ability to abort a script. The step has one setting with a default value of *On* to allow interruption of the script and an option to turn it *Off* to disable that ability.

The step can be placed at the beginning of a script or anywhere in the workflow. It can be turned on and off as needed at different points in the workflow to only protect sensitive steps that must be completed. Once configured, all subsequent script steps in the current script and any subscripts in the execution stack will inherit that setting unless reversed. If a parent script turns it off, all subsequent subscripts called by the parent will inherent that setting unless or until they explicitly change it. Similarly, if a subscript changes the setting, the parent script will inherit that setting when control is relinquished back to it.

A formula can check the status of the abort state using a *Get* function, which returns 0 (false) if abort is disallowed and 1 (true) if it is allowed. The following two examples show a script step turning the abort state *Off* and *On* with a formula below it checking the current state after each change:

```
Allow User Abort [ Off ]
Get ( AllowAbortState ) // result = 0
Allow User Abort [ On ]
Get ( AllowAbortState ) // result = 1
```

Caution   It is a good idea to always allow user abort when testing to avoid being locked into an endless loop or other situations that require a force quit to escape a programming error!

Setting Variables

The *Set Variable* step sets the value of a local or global variable (Chapter 12, "Variables") at a specific point in a script's workflow. Variables can be used within a script to "park" values at one step for use by another. They can store a value for later use, assemble data from multiple contexts, track iterations that control scripting behavior, and more. Remember that local variables are limited within the context of the running script. They are also *not inherited* by other scripts in the active execution stack, so subscripts called by a script or parent scripts calling it do not have access to local variables set within it. Insert the step into a script, and then open the *Set Variable Options* dialog, shown in Figure 25-1, by either double-clicking on the step or clicking the gear icon next to it.

The *Name* field is used to specify the name of the target variable. This can be a new variable or an existing one. The name is how the variable will be used in subsequent formulas, so choose something clear and descriptive. A single dollar sign prefix denotes a local variable, and a double dollar sign prefix denotes a global variable. If no prefix is entered, a single sign will be added automatically.

In the *Value* field, type the information to be stored in the variable when the step executes, either a static value, a field reference or a formula entered using the adjacent *Specify* button.

The *Repetition* field specifies which repetition of the named variable should receive the specified value. This allows a single variable to contain multiple separate values, similar to a repeating field (Chapter 8). The default is always one.

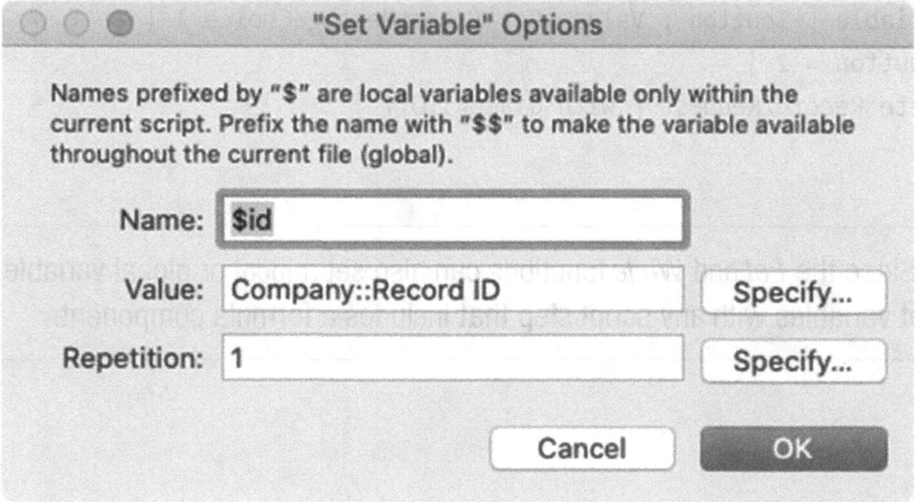

Figure 25-1. *The dialog used to set a variable*

Tip   Since you can create numerous variables with different names, the repetition feature should be reserved for managing an expandable number of programmatically determined values.

The following example could be used by a script assigned to a *Record* ➤ *Delete Record* custom menu item (Chapter 22) or a delete button. It provides a warning prior to deleting a company record although it could be expanded to work with any table. It uses the *Set Variable* step four times. It starts by setting a *$name* variable to the *Company Name* field of the current *Company* record and a *$count* variable to the number of *Contact* records related to it. Next, it uses these values to place a custom warning value into a *$message* variable for use in a *Show Custom Dialog* step. Finally, it places the user's button choice into a *$button* variable. The *If* step at the end limits the *Delete Record/Request* step to only execute when the button clicked in the message dialog indicates the user's approval.

```
Set Variable [ $name ; Value: Company::Company Name ]
Set Variable [ $count ; Value: Count ( Company | Contact::Record ID ) ]
Set Variable [ $message ; Value:
    "Are you sure you want to delete the company record for " &
    Quote ( $name ) &
    "? " & $count & " contact record(s) are connected to it!" ]
Show Custom Dialog [ "Confirm Delete Company" ; $message ]
Set Variable [ $button ; Value: Get ( LastMessageChoice ) ]
If [ $button = 2 ]
    Delete Record/Request [ with dialog: Off ]
End if
```

Tip   Since the *Let* and *While* functions can also set a local or global variable, you can set variables with any script step that includes a formula component.

Creating Navigation Scripts

Scripts can change a window's context by navigating to a different layout, record, or related record.

Go to Layout

The *Go to Layout* script step, shown in Figure 25-2, will switch the layout displayed in the current window. The step has two active regions.

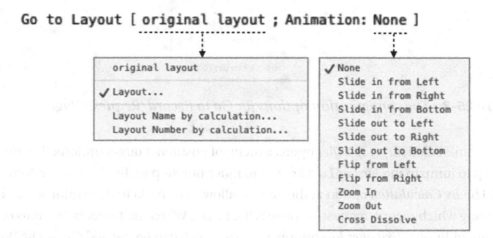

Figure 25-2. *The configuration options for Go to Layout*

The unlabeled *layout specifier* opens a menu of choices for how to identify the target layout. The default selection will be *Original layout* which instructs the script to navigate back to the layout that was active when the script started running. This saves development time when a script can be triggered from multiple locations in a database, automatically tracking and restoring the user's starting layout. Choose the *Layout* option to open a *Specify Layout* dialog, and choose a reference to a specific target layout. The *Layout Name by calculation* and *Layout Number by calculation* options open the *Specify Calculation* dialog allowing a formula to determine the name or number of the target layout.

The *Animation* region of the step is used in FileMaker Go to specify how the layout switch should be animated. This setting will be ignored when running the script on other platforms.

Go to Record/Request/Page

The *Go to Record/Request/Page* step, shown in Figure 25-3, is used to navigate through the content of a window, depending on the mode. It will navigate to a specified item by mode; record (Browse), find request (Find), or page (Preview). The step has one or two active regions depending on the option selected on the first setting.

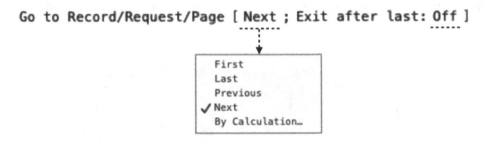

Figure 25-3. *The configuration options for Go to Record/Request/Page*

The unlabeled *target specifier* opens a menu of positional target options. These allow the step to jump to the *First* or *Last* item or to move one step to the *Previous* or *Next* item. The *By Calculation* option at the bottom allows a formula to determine a number indicating which record, request, or page is the target. When the target is *Previous* or *Next*, an additional *Exit after last* option appears, which can be toggled *On* or *Off*. When on, the step will automatically exit a *Loop* statement after reaching the last available record in the direction indicated by the first parameter. When on, *Previous* will exit after reaching the first record/request/page, while *Next* will exit after reaching the last.

Go to Related Record

The *Go to Related Record* step performs multiple functions as a single step. It finds and navigates to a set of related records on another layout and can optionally open the result in a new window. To illustrate, imagine a user is viewing a *Contact* record and wants to view the record for that contact's related parent *Company* in a new window. Instead of manually creating a new window, changing layouts, and performing a find, a button or script can use the *Go to Related Record* step to quickly carry out the task with a single click. In this example, *Contact* is the starting *source table*, and *Company* is the destination *target table*, each being on one side of a relationship between table occurrences (Chapter 9). The same relationship used to *display* a related company name on a contact layout will be used by this step as the conduit through which we *navigate*. By traveling "through" the relationship, the match fields used to form the relationship act like the search criteria for the record(s) that will be displayed in the target table.

Once the step is added to the script or assigned to a button, double-click it, or click the gear icon to open the *Go to Related Record Options* dialog, shown in Figure 25-4.

Figure 25-4. *The dialog used to configure going to a related record*

The *Get related record from* pop-up menu lists every table occurrence defined in the current database file's relationship graph. Select any occurrence related to the starting layout's table. In our example, we will start on a layout for the *Contact* table. To reach a layout for the *Company* table, we must pick an occurrence of that table that is also related to the *Contact* table. So, we select the *Contact | Company* relationship to travel from a *Contact* record to its related *Company* using that relationship's criteria.

The *Show record using layout* option specifies the target layout that will be the destination used to display the related record(s). This setting opens a menu with four options that are similar to the *Go to Layout* step. The *Current Layout* option will leave the user on the current layout. This is useful for targeting a self-join relationship, where the target records are in the same table as the source record. The *Layout* option opens a *Specify Layout* dialog for selection of a reference to a specific layout. The *Layout Name by calculation* and *Layout Number by calculation* options open the *Specify Calculation* dialog allowing a formula to determine the number or name of the target layout. The *Specify Layout* dialog will only display layouts for the target table from the current database file. If the target table is from an external data source, select the *Use external table's layouts* checkbox to instead show a list of layouts for the table from that external file.

The *Show in new window* checkbox and adjacent *Specify* button enable displaying the results in a new window instead of the starting window. These settings are identical to the *New Window* script step described later in this chapter.

The *Show only related records* option controls which records are included in the found set displayed in the target layout/window. When *disabled*, the step will attempt to preserve the found set already present in the target table. If the related record is present in that set, it will retain the set and drop the user on that record. If not, the step will find all records and take the user to the target record. When *enabled*, a different found set will be established in the target table depending on the radio button option selected. The *Match current record only* selection will result in a target found set of only the record(s) matching the related criteria for the *starting record*. This is like a *one-to-one* or *one-to-many* search, where the current starting record is used to find matching records in the target table. The *Match all records in the current found set* option will result in a found set of every record in the target table that has a match to *any* record in the starting found set. This is the equivalent of a *many-to-many* search, where the current found set is used to find matching records in the target table.

When this step is executed as the result of a click on a button in a portal, the settings control the target found set, but the record the user clicked determines which of those will be come the currently active record in that set.

Interacting with Fields

Several steps allow various interactions with fields. These include moving focus into a field, changing the contents of a field, and resetting the field's defined serialization settings.

Go to Field

Three script steps allow focus navigation to a field on the current layout: *Go to Next Field*, *Go to Previous Field,* and *Go to Field.* The first two of these have no parameter options; they will simply move active focus to the *next* or *previous* field on the current layout based on the field tab order (Chapter 21). If the current record is not open and no field has focus, these steps will open the record and place focus respectively in the first or last field in the tab order. The *Go to Field* step, shown in Figure 25-5, moves focus to a specific field. After inserting into the script, double-click anywhere on the step to open a *Specify Field* dialog and select a target field. The gear icon opens a panel with two options. Enable the *Select/perform* box to automatically select field contents, and/or open interface elements such as drop-down lists or calendars when entering the field. The *Go to target field* is an alternate way to specify the target field.

Figure 25-5. *The step used to move focus to a specific field*

Note   The selected field must be present on the current layout, and the user must have access to enter it. If no target field is selected in the script or the field is not accessible, the step will exit every field and commit the record.

Set Field

The *Set Field* step will replace the current value of a specified field for the current record with a new value. Click on the gear icon to open a configuration panel, as shown in Figure 25-6. The *Specify target field* option will open a *Specify Field* dialog and allow selection of a target field reference. The selected field doesn't need to be present on the layout. If no field is specified, the step will insert a value into a field if one on the layout has active focus. Click the *Specify* button to define a *Calculated result* which provides the value that will be placed into the field.

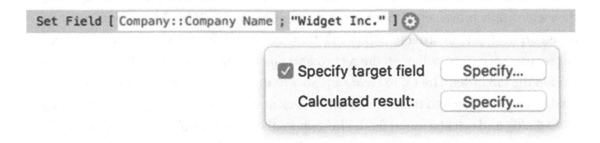

Figure 25-6. *The options for setting a field value*

Set Field by Name

The *Set Field by Name* step will change the value of a field specified *by name* for the current record displayed in the window. Unlike the *Set Field* step where a target must be a selected *dynamic field reference*, this step uses a formula to establish a *text-based field reference* which can vary as needed (Chapter 12, "Field References"). The options look exactly the same, except when you click to specify a target field, a *Specify Calculation* dialog opens and requires a formula that results in the target field name. The result must include a table occurrence to provide the necessary context to locate the field. This example targets the *Contact Address State* field for the current *Contact* record.

```
Set Field By Name [ "Contact::Contact Address State" ; "NY" ]
```

Since the field reference is text-based and created by a formula, it can be constructed with conditional variations. This example dynamically builds a reference to a standard *Record Notes* field for the table of the current layout, which would work in *any* layout where the assigned table contains a field of that name.

```
Set Field By Name [ Get ( LayoutTableName ) & "::Record Notes" ; "Hello
World" ]
```

Set Selection

The *Set Selection* step, shown in Figure 25-7, will select a portion of text within a field visible on the current layout. The step will target the field with active focus unless another target field is specified. Click to *Specify selection* to open a *Set Selection* dialog and enter two numeric values for *Start Position* and *End Position*. These can each be either static numbers or a dynamic calculation that analyzes the field's content and makes a selection based on custom criteria.

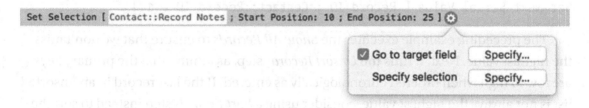

Figure 25-7. *The options for selecting text within a field*

Tip   To select the *entire* contents of the current field, use the *Select All* step instead.

Set Next Serial Value

The *Set Next Serial Value* step will update the next serial number value in a field's *Auto Enter* definitions (Chapter 8). Since the auto-enter settings automatically increment the *Next Value* setting each time a new record is created, this step is used infrequently. However, when importing records as part of a data migration or when resetting a new test copy of a database for live use, serial number fields may need an update to ensure that the next value assigned is uniquely one above the highest value assigned to date. If the field settings are out of sync with the record data, it might result in duplicate serial numbers. Using the script step to automate this process can save time when migrating a large solution with dozens of tables. The change is made to the field definition directly, so the specified field does not have to be visible on the current layout. In fact, when resetting this to a static number without the need to look at existing records, this step can be run for any table from *any context*.

The configuration options are similar to other steps that change field values. Click on the gear icon to open the panel, and then select a target field and enter a formula for the result which will become the next serial number for new records. After a migration script imports records into a table, add these steps to ensure that the primary key's next serial number is one greater than the current highest value.

```
Show All Records
Unsort Records
Go to Record [ Last ]
Set Next Serial Value [ Record ID ; Contact::Record ID + 1 ]
```

The preceding example executes the *Show All Records* to ensure that we don't miss the highest value. Next, it runs the *Unsort Records* step, assuming that the primary keys are low to high when ordered chronologically as entered. If the last record in an unsorted list is not always the highest value, consider using a *Sort Records* step instead to sort the records by the serial field. The *Go to Record* step jumps to the last record which should now have the highest current value. Finally, the *Set Next Serial Value* targets the *Record ID* field with the current value in that field for the current record plus one.

If the targeted key field is a text field with leading zeros, adding one will convert the result into a number without leading characters. To maintain a consistent number of characters in the field, the formula will need to add a calculated number of zeros to the result. If the field uses leading zeros to maintain six digits, the following formula ensures the appropriate result by adding six zeros to the left of the incremented id and then extracting six digits from the right.

```
Right ( "000000" & ( Contact::Record ID + 1 ) ; 6 )
// result = 000015
```

Accessing Folders and Files

In recent versions, FileMaker has added and improved various script steps that can access folders and files.

Get Folder Path

The *Get Folder Path* step, formerly named *Get Directory*, presents the user with a *Choose Folder* dialog. This allows a user to select a folder which can then be used by other steps that import, export, and save various resources. The step includes several configurable options, shown in Figure 25-8.

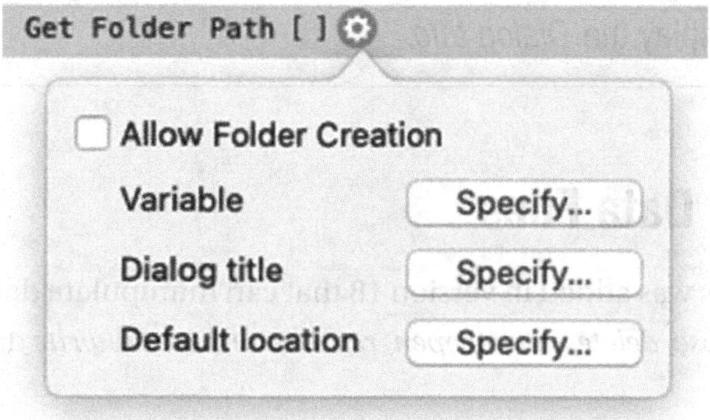

Get Folder Path [ ] ⚙

☐ Allow Folder Creation

Variable   Specify...

Dialog title   Specify...

Default location Specify...

Figure 25-8. *The options for selecting a directory*

The *Allow Folder Creation* checkbox enables the *New Folder* button in the *Choose Folder* dialog, making it possible for the user to create and select a new folder. The *Variable* button opens a limited *Set Variable Options* dialog that specifies the name of the variable into which the selected folder path will be placed. The buttons by *Dialog title* and *Default location* both open a *Specify Calculation* dialog to control the dialog's title prompt and default starting folder path.

When a script executes this step, the dialog opens and waits for user input. Once they choose a folder and click to dismiss the dialog, the path to that folder is placed into the variable specified. The path may need to be converted to a FileMaker format (Chapter 24, "Converting Paths") or have a prefix added in order to work with other script steps.

The following example uses *Set Error Capture* to suppress a warning dialog if the user clicks *Cancel* in the dialog. A default path is set to the user computer's documents path. After the *Get Folder Path* step, the *If* statement checks for a *LastError*. If the user cancels the dialog, the *If* statement uses the *Exit Script* step to stop the script. Otherwise, the user's folder selection in the *$pathToFolder* variable can be used later as the script continues.

```
Set Error Capture [ On ]
Set Variable [ $pathToDefault ; Value: Get ( DocumentsPath ) ]
```

```
Get Folder Path [ $pathToFolder ; $pathToDefault ]
If [ Get ( LastError ) = 1 ]
  Exit Script [ Text Result: "User Cancelled" ]
End if
```

Caution   The dialog's appearance depends on the operating system. For example, macOS doesn't display the *Dialog title*.

Manipulating Data Files

A new group of steps was added in version 18 that can manipulate data files. These can be used to *create, close, delete, detect, open, read, rename,* and *write* data files on the user's computer.

Creating a Data File

The *Create Data File* step will create a new empty file that automatically replaces any preexisting file with the same name at the specified FileMaker path. It accepts a file path parameter and has an option to automatically create folders to ensure the entire path exists. Once created, a script can open the file and write to it.

```
Set Variable [ $filePath ; Value: "file:/Macintosh HD/Users/mmunro/Desktop/
Hello.txt" ]
Create Data File [ "$filePath" ; Create folders: Off ]
```

Opening and Closing a Data File

The *Open Data File* step will open a data file and assign it a numeric *File ID* that will persist until the file is explicitly closed. This number acts as a reference pointer to the file and is required by other data file steps instead of a path, e.g., the *Close Data File* step accepts only a *File ID* that points to the file that should be closed. In the following example, the script assumes the file path created in the previous example is in a variable named *$filePath*. Using this path, it opens the file, places the id into a target variable named *$fileID*, and then immediately uses that id to close the file.

```
Open Data File [ "$filePath" ; Target: $fileID ]
Close Data File [ File ID: $fileID ]
```

Reading a Data File

The *Read from Data File* step will read data from an open data file and place the content into a *Target* variable or field. It accepts four parameters. The *File ID* requires a numeric file reference, typically the targeted result of the *Open Data File* step. The *Target* allows the selection of a field or entry of a variable into which the file's contents will be placed. A *Read as* inline menu allows the choice of character encoding, and an *Amount* option allows a formula to determine the number of bytes to read (leave blank for all). Building on the last example, this script has a step added between opening and closing the file, where it reads the contents as UTF-8 and places it into a variable named *$fileContents*. At the end, a *Show Custom Dialog* displays the text.

```
Open Data File [ "$filePath" ; Target: $fileID ]
Read from Data File [ File ID: $fileID ; Target: $fileContents ; Read as:
UTF-8 ]
Close Data File [ File ID: $fileID ]
Show Custom Dialog [ $fileContents ]
```

Confirming a Data File's Existence

When a referenced file does not exist, an error will be generated if a script attempts to open it. To avoid this, the *Get File Exists* step can first confirm the existence of a file and take an alternate course of action if it isn't found. The step accepts a *Source file* path and places a true (1) or false (0) value into a *Target* field or variable. This example will check for the file and, if it doesn't exist, will present a dialog and exit the script.

```
Set Variable [ $filePath ; Value: "file:/Macintosh HD/Users/mmunro/Desktop/
Hello.txt" ]
Get File Exists [ "$filePath" ; Target: $fileExists ]
If [ $fileExists = 0 ]
   Show Custom Dialog [ "Unable to locate the Hello.txt file!" ]
   Exit Script
End If
```

Writing to a Data File

The *Write to Data File* step will write data to an open data file. It requires the similar parameters as the read step but reverses the labelling of the target to a *Data source* and the character encoding to *Write as*. An additional optional checkbox to *Append line feed* adds a line feed character after writing data. This example will replace the previous file data with the words "Hello, World."

```
Set Variable [ $filePath ; Value: "file:/Macintosh HD/Users/mmunro/Desktop/
Hello.txt" ]
Set Variable [ $fileContents ; Value: "Hello, World" ]
Open Data File [ "$filePath" ; Target: $fileID ]
Write to Data File [ File ID: $fileID ; Data source: $fileContents ; Write
as: UTF-8 ]
Close Data File [ File ID: $fileID ]
```

To begin writing at the end of the existing data, use the *Get File Size* and *Set Data File Position* steps to determine the number of bytes in the file and to begin after that point. The first accepts a file path instead of a file id so the file doesn't have to be open for that step.

```
Set Variable [ $filePath ; Value: "file:/Macintosh HD/Users/mmunro/Desktop/
Hello.txt" ]
Set Variable [ $fileContents ; Value: "Hello, World" ]
Get File Size [ "$filePath" ; Target: $fileSize ]
Open Data File [ "$filePath" ; Target: $fileID ]
Set Data File Position [ File ID: $fileID ; New position: $fileSize ]
Write to Data File [ File ID: $fileID ; Data source: $fileContents ; Write
as: UTF-8 ]
Close Data File [ File ID: $fileID ]
```

Alternatively, reading from the file prior to writing will automatically begin writing after all existing data.

```
Set Variable [ $filePath ; Value: "file:/Macintosh HD/Users/mmunro/Desktop/
Hello.txt" ]
Set Variable [ $fileContents ; Value: "Hello, World" ]
Open Data File [ "$filePath" ; Target: $fileID ]
```

```
Read from Data File [ File ID: $fileID ; Target: $fileContents ; Read as:
UTF-8 ]
Write to Data File [ File ID: $fileID ; Data source: $fileContents ; Write
as: UTF-8 ]
Close Data File [ File ID: $fileID ]
```

Working with Records

Numerous script steps perform interactions with records. The *New Record/Request* step will create a new record in the current window, while the *Duplicate Record/Request* step will create a duplicate of the current record. These have no configurable options. The *Delete Record/Request* step will automatically delete the current record in the front window after presenting an optional confirmation dialog. Similarly, the *Delete All Records* step will delete every record in the found set after presenting an optional dialog. There are steps available to perform many of the record actions users can perform through the interface from the *Records* menu and toolbar options. Scripts can open, commit, copy, and revert records. There are steps for *Save Records as Excel*, *Save Records as PDF*, and *Save Records as Snapshot Link*. The *Truncate Table* step deletes all records in a specified table, regardless of the current found set or the current layout context. In addition, there are two steps used to move records in and out of a table: *Import Records* and *Export Records*.

Import Records

The *Import Records* step, shown in Figure 25-9, is used to import records into a table with or without human interaction, depending on the configuration settings.

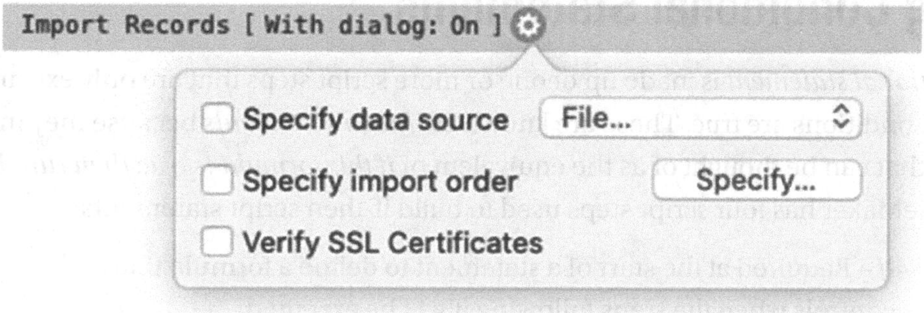

Figure 25-9. *The configuration options for automatically importing records*

The *With dialog* option can be turned *Off* to suppress dialogs when the step is performed, allowing a truly autonomous operation. However, if a *data source* or *import order* is not defined, this setting will be ignored, and the dialogs will appear, requesting the missing information. The *Specify data source* accepts a path for the file to import, and the *Specify import order* button opens the dialog of the same name used to map import data to fields (Chapter 5). Enable the *Verify SSL Certificates* when importing XML data from a server specified with a HTTP request.

Export Records

The *Export Record* step, shown in Figure 25-10, allows a script to automatically export records with or without human interaction, depending on the configuration settings. The *Specify output file* and *Specify export order* both open dialogs that respectively allow specification of a file path and field order. Two additional toggle options are accessible directly in the step line. The *With dialog* can suppress dialogs for autonomous operation as long as both panel options are configured. The *Create folders* option automatically creates folders to ensure the entire directory path exists.

Figure 25-10.   *The configuration options for automatically exporting records*

Using Conditional Statements

A *conditional statement* is made up of one or more script steps that are only executed if certain conditions are true. These are known as *if-then statements* because they include criteria that can be thought of as the equivalent of *if this formula is true then run these steps*. FileMaker has four script steps used to build if-then script statements:

- *If* – Required at the start of a statement to define a formula that controls when the steps following it will be executed

- *Else If* – Optionally placed between an *If* and *End If* step to start a new group of conditional steps based on a new formula

- *Else* – Optionally placed somewhere prior to an *End If* to denote a separate group of conditional steps that are performed only if all preceding conditions were false

- *End If* – Required to terminate the conditional statement started by the *If* step

As an example, assume an *Invoice Status* field has several possible values: *Unsent, Sent, Due, Past Due, Delinquent,* and *Paid*. A script created to email an invoice wouldn't apply to those already sent, and sending a reminder about an overdue status wouldn't apply to every invoice record. Further, some haven't been sent yet, some that have been aren't yet overdue, etc. A simple *If* statement can be set up to only send a reminder if an invoice has a past due status as shown in the following example:

```
If [ Invoice::Status = "Past Due" ]
   Perform Script ["Email Invoice Past Due" ]
End If
```

This can be expanded into a *compound conditional statement* that includes several conditions that each call a different script. If the invoice hasn't been sent, it runs a script to send it. If the status is past due or delinquent, it sends a reminder or a warning, respectively. Other statuses not included in the statement would send nothing.

```
If [ Invoice::Status = "Unsent" ]
   Perform Script ["Email Invoice" ]
Else If [ Invoice::Status = "Past Due" ]
   Perform Script ["Email Invoice Past Due" ]
Else If [ Invoice::Status = "Delinquent" ]
   Perform Script ["Email Invoice Collection Warning" ]
End If
```

A conditional statement can be placed inside of another conditional statement creating a *nested statement*. The statement hierarchy can be as complex as necessary to achieve the necessary objective. In this example, the first outer statement contains and controls which of the two inner compound statements get executed based on the status field.

```
If [ Invoice::Status = "Past Due" ]
   If [ Invoice::Days Past > 15  ]
      Perform Script ["Email First Warning" ]
   Else If [ Invoice::Days Past > 30  ]
      Perform Script ["Email Second Warning" ]
   Else If [ Invoice::Days Past > 45  ]
      Perform Script ["Email Final Warning" ]
   End If
Else If [ Invoice::Status = "Delinquent"]
   If [ Invoice::Days Delinquent > 15  ]
      Perform Script ["Email Collections Warning" ]
   Else If [ Invoice::Days Delinquent > 30  ]
      Perform Script ["Email Collections Notification" ]
   End If
End If
```

Tip   Avoid situations where excessive nesting makes it too difficult to follow how
a script will execute when scrolling pages of steps.

Showing Custom Dialogs

The *Show Custom Dialog* step is used to present a message to the user and can
also request input into three fields or variables. Dialogs can present an informative
notification, warn the user about a problem, confirm a certain action, present a choice
of action, request input, provide instruction, etc. With the step added to a script, the gear
icon opens a *Show Custom Dialog Options* dialog, which has two tabs: *General* and *Input
Fields*.

Configuring Dialog Properties

The *General* tab of the *Show Custom Dialog Options* dialog, shown in Figure 25-11, is used to configure the messaging properties of a custom dialog. The *Title* and Message fields can each receive static text typed directly or from a formula entered by clicking the corresponding *Specify* buttons. These produce the values that appear in the title bar and body of the dialog and should clearly convey a message or request an action.

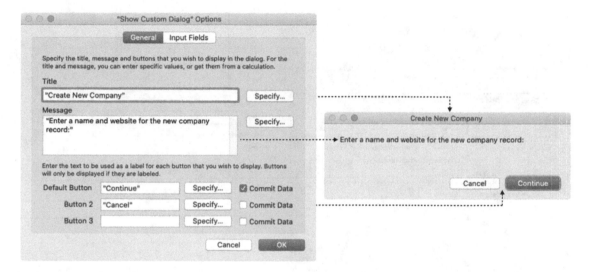

Figure 25-11. *The tab for configuring dialog properties (left) and an example dialog (right)*

Up to three button names can be defined for the custom dialog. These will appear in the dialog from right to left with the *Default Button* being highlighted as the default button which is responsive to the user typing the Enter key. If the current record has uncommitted changes at the time the dialog is presented, any buttons with the corresponding *Commit Data* checkbox enabled will cause the record to commit when a user clicks in the dialog. This is useful when the dialog requests information that is placed into fields.

Caution   Dialogs do not automatically resize, so lengthy messages may be obscured. Although users can resize, keep messages concise to avoid miscommunication.

Configuring Dialog Input Fields

A dialog can include up to three editable fields which are each linked to a target field or variable. This allows a dialog to present a request for input from the users and can be useful in numerous ways. A script can perform guided searches for specific fields, assist during record creation by prompting required input, require a key phrase to confirm a deletion action, and more. The *Input Fields* tab contains three sets of identical controls for this purpose, shown in Figure 25-12.

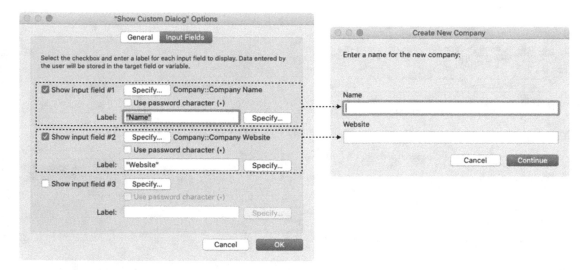

Figure 25-12. *The tab for configuring input fields on a dialog*

To include a field in the dialog, enable the corresponding checkbox. Then click *Specify* to select a target field or variable. The target acts as both the *source* and *destination* of the text for that text area in the dialog. When the dialog opens, any value in the target will be displayed in the input field as a default value which the user can customize. Their entry in the dialog updates the target's value which remains in place after the user dismisses the dialog.

The *Use password character* checkbox will render the field in the dialog as an obscured value, with each character appearing as a bullet point. Like the similar layout setting for fields (Chapter 20, "Concealed Edit Box"), this is a display feature only and does not alter or encrypt the text entered into the field. The value may still be visible on layouts unless the field is also configured to display as bullets. In any case, the script can access and manipulate the value like any other text string.

The *Label* field allows a field label to appear above the field in the dialog. By default, the field will be present on the dialog without a label. Type a static text label or click *Specify* to generate a label with a formula.

Tip   When a dialog requires more than three button or field options, or needs other controls like pop-up menus or checkboxes, use the *New Window* step to generate a dialog window from a custom layout.

Capturing a Dialog Button Click

A dialog naturally pauses a script until a user clicks a button. Once a dialog is dismissed, the script can access the index position of the button that was clicked using the *Get (LastMessageChoice)* function. The number corresponds to the button's configuration order, which will display from right to left on the dialog. This value can be used immediately or stored in a variable and used later in the workflow as shown in the example here:

```
Show Custom Dialog [ "Choose" ; "Please choose a function" ]
Set Variable [ $button ; Get ( LastMessageChoice )
```

If there are three buttons defined – OK, Cancel, and Help – and the user clicks OK, the *$button* variable will be set to a value of 1. The following example shows a formula that can be used in the preceding *Set Variable* step to convert the numeric value into the button name using the *Choose* function.

```
Let (
    number = Get ( LastMessageChoice )
;
    Choose ( number ; "" ; "OK" ; "Cancel" ; "Help" )
)
```

Creating a Related Record Using a Dialog

As a practical example of dialog with input options, create a script that starts from a *Contact* record and walks through the creation of a *Company* record which is then assigned to the contact. The script will automatically carry out a sequence that would be burdensome for a user: switch layouts, create a new company record, enter company info, capture the id of the new record, return to the original layout, and enter the new id into the contact's foreign key field for a company relationship. The exact order will change slightly for the scripted version. Instead of creating a record and entering data, a dialog will request the name for the new company in a variable and, if the user doesn't cancel, continue with the record creation and assignment steps.

```
Show Custom Dialog [ "Create a New Company" ; "Enter a name for the new
company:" ; $name ]
If [ Get ( LastMessageChoice ) = 2 ]
   Exit Script
End If
Freeze Window
Go to Layout [ "Company" (Company) ; Animation: None ]
New Record/Request
Set Field [ Company::Company Name ; $name ]
Set Variable [ $id ; Value: Company::Record ID ]
Go to Layout [ original layout ; Animation: None ]
Set Field [ Contact::Contact Company ID ; $id ]
Commit Records/Requests [ With Dialog: Off ]
```

Alternatively, if *Allow creation of records* (Chapter 9) is enabled for the *Company* side of the relationship, a single step dialog can request a name and push it into the related field, automatically creating the connection between the two.

```
Show Custom Dialog [ "New Company" ; "Enter a name:" ; Contact |
Company::Company Name ]
```

Confirming a Dialog Field Value

To avoid an empty field in the dialog, use a *Loop* statement to confirm a value before allowing the script to continue. When a user dismisses a dialog with a missing a value, the script loops back, presenting the dialog again until the user either enters a value or clicks Cancel. The following example places the dialog's prompt into a *$message* variable so it can change to a warning if subsequent loops are necessary. The *Show Custom Dialog* step is placed inside the *Loop* statement with an *Exit Loop If* step jumping out of the loop if the user cancels or if a name has been entered. If the *$name* variable is empty, the *$message* is modified to a more sternly phrased request before the loop repeats again. Once the user enters a name, then the script can continue to perform any other steps placed below these steps.

```
Set Variable [ $message ; Value: "Enter a name for the new company:"  ]
Loop
    Show Custom Dialog [ "Create a New Company" ; $message ; $name ]
    If [ Get ( LastMessageChoice ) = 2 ]
        Exit Script
    End If
    Exit Loop If [$name ≠ "" ]
    Beep
    Set Variable [ $message ; Value: "You MUST enter a name for the new
company:"  ]
End Loop
```

Searching and Dealing with Found Sets

There are several different steps available to perform searches. These can be used separately or used with steps that perform navigation, sorts, compilations, and other functions. The *Perform Quick Find* step uses the text result of a formula as the criteria to perform a search within any field on the current layout that has *Quick Find* enabled (Chapter 19).

The *Enter Find Mode* step places the window into Find mode, giving the user or script steps an opportunity to enter find criteria in fields before searching. It can *Specify find requests*, establishing a default starting criteria, and optionally *Pause* to wait for the user. Since the step does not actually perform a find itself, that must be initiated by the user or another script step.

The *Perform Find* step can be used in Find mode to execute the criteria entered by a user or script steps. Alternatively, it can be used in Browse mode as a stand-alone instant find step when using its optional *Specify Find Request* dialog to define search criteria (Chapter 4, "Working with Saved Finds").

A find script can take many forms. It may perform a find based on static unchanging criteria, build the criteria based on variables, solicit user criteria, or some combination of these. The following example uses one hard-coded criterion and one user entered.

After entering Find mode, it sets the *Invoice Status* field to "Paid" and then presents a dialog allowing the user to enter a date range into an *Invoice Date* field. When the dialog is closed, the search will resume, performing the find and showing a found set of all paid invoices whose date falls within the range specified.

```
Go to Layout ["Invoice List" ]
Enter Find Mode [ Pause: Off ]
Set Field [ Invoice::Invoice Status ; "Paid" ]
Show Custom Dialog [
    "Search Paid Invoices" ;
    "Enter a date range (m/d/yyyy...m/d/yyyy):" ;
    Invoice::Invoice Date ]
Perform Find
```

Tip   Help users enter date ranges by inserting a default range into the target field or variable prior to the *Show Custom Dialog* step.

Iterating with Repeating Statements

A *repeating statement* is made up of one or more steps that are executed repeatedly until a step exits the loop. FileMaker has three steps that are used to construct repeating statements:

- *Loop* – Required to begin repeating subsequent steps until a terminating step is executed

- *Exit Loop If* – Immediately terminates a loop when a formula entered is true, skipping to the step after the next *End Loop*

- *End Loop* – Required to mark the bottom of the repeating statement where control returns back to the start for the next iteration through the steps

Certain steps inside the statement can also terminate the loop. For example, both *Exit Script* and *Halt Script* will stop an entire script, including any active looping. Use the *Exit after last* option of the *Next* or *Previous* option of a *Go to Record/Request/Page or the*

Go to Portal Row steps to exit after the final record in the direction indicated is reached. A user can also halt a script by typing Esc (Windows) or Period with the Command key down (macOS) as long as *Allow User Abort* is *On*.

Caution   If no step causes the loop to terminate, the statement will run endlessly until a force quit which may cause file damage.

Looping Through a Found Set of Records

A script can step through a found set and perform actions to each record. The following example starts by navigating to the first record in a found set of invoices and then initiates a *Loop*. For each record in the set, it calls another script named "Send Invoice Email" that sends an invoice to the customer. Then, a *Set Field* step changes the *Invoice Status* field from "Open" to "Sent." Finally, it goes to the next record and repeats these steps until it reaches the end of the found set and exits the loop.

```
Go to Record/Request/Page [ First ]
Loop
    Perform Script [ Specified: From list ; "Send Invoice Email" ;
    Parameter: ]
    Set Field [ Invoice::Invoice Status ; "Sent" ]
    Go to Record/Request/Page [ Next ; Exit after last: On ]
End Loop
```

Another example in the following loops through a found set of open invoices and collects the value of several fields for each record. It extracts the id, date, company, amount, and a new *Invoice Status Overdue* field that calculates the overdue value for each invoice record with a status of "Sent" by looking at the number of 30-day increments that have passed since from the *Invoice Date*. These values are arranged as a columnar list stored in a variable named *$Body* which can later be used to create a report email or saved into a data file.

```
Go to Record/Request/Page [ First ]
Loop
    Set Variable [ $Body ; $Body &
        Invoice::Record ID & " " &
```

```
      Invoice::Invoice Date & " " &
      Invoice::Invoice Company Name & " " &
      Invoice::Invoice Amount & " " &
      Invoice::Invoice Status Overdue & "¶" ]
   Go to Record/Request/Page [ Next ; Exit after last: On ]
End Loop
// result =
   1001 04/15/2021 Fantastic Client 1000 Over 60 Days
   1001 04/15/2021 Fantastic Client 1000 Over 60 Days
   1002 05/19/2021 Creative Company 3000 Over 30 Days
   1003 06/1/2021 Fantastic Client 4500 Open
   1003 06/15/2021 Fantastic Client 958 Open
```

When the result of the preceding example is used as the body of an email message, the data can be formatted differently to make it more readable. The following example returns a similar report that is refined with overdue status as a heading above groups of invoices rather than being repeated for each invoice. Starting with the same found set of open invoices sorted by *Invoice Status Overdue*, the script uses a variable named *$Last. Status* to track the status value from the record in the last iteration. Anytime it encounters a new status value in the current record, it performs a conditional step to insert that into to the *$Body* variable with some extra paragraph returns. Then it puts the current status into the *$Last.Status* variable so it will be ignored on each subsequent iteration until a different value is detected.

```
Set Variable [ $Last.Group ; "" ]
Go to Record/Request/Page [ First ]
Loop
   Set Variable [ $Group ; Invoice::Invoice Status Overdue ]
   If [$Group ≠ $Last.Group ]
      # Add header row
      Set Variable [ $Body ; $Body & Case ( $Body ≠ "" ; "¶" ) & $Group &
      "¶" ]
      Set Variable [ $Last.Group ; $Group]
   End If
   # Add body row
   Set Variable [ $Body ; $ Body &
```

```
    Invoice::Record ID & " " &
    Invoice::Invoice Date & " " &
    Invoice::Invoice Company Name & " " &
    Invoice::Invoice Amount & "¶" ]
    Go to Record/Request/Page [ Next ; Exit after last: On ]
End Loop
# Result =
    Open
    1003 06/1/2021 Fantastic Client 4500
    1003 06/15/2021 Fantastic Client 958
    Over 30 Days
    1002 05/19/2021 Creative Company 3000
    Over 60 Days
    1001 04/15/2021 Fantastic Client 1000
    1001 04/15/2021 Fantastic Client 1000
```

Looping Through Data

A *Loop* can also be used to step through data stored in a variable. Each loop can perform operations on a paragraph of a return-delimited list of values or a key of a JSON Object, working through them one by one until complete. There are different ways of controlling the process. One method involves setting up a couple of *control variables*, one to store a *count* of values and another to keep track of the number of the *current* value which is incremented on each loop.

For example, assume a list of state abbreviations placed into a variable named *$States*. Each state listed will be used to build one find criteria request for a search of *Contact* records. If the entire list of states is entered into a single find request, there will be no resulting matches since that would instruct FileMaker to look for records with a mailing address that includes all those states. To get a result, multiple find requests need to be created, one for each state in the list. The following script assumes a variable named *$State* contains a list of abbreviated states, e.g., OH¶PA¶NY. It counts these using the *ValueCount* function and places that number into a variable named *$Count* which will control how many loops we perform. Then, it initializes another variable named *$Current* to indicate a start on the first state in the list. Next, it does the *Enter Find Mode* step and begins the *Loop* through the list of states, creating one find request for each state in the variable. With each loop, the *$Current* variable is increased by one until it exceeds *$Count* and the loop is exited. After the loop has terminated, the find is performed.

```
Set Variable [ $States ; "OH¶PA¶NY" ]
Set Variable [ $Count ; ValueCount ( $States ) ]
Set Variable [ $Current ; 1 ]
Enter Find Mode [ Pause : Off ]
Loop
   Set Field [ Contact::Contact Address State ; GetValue ( $States ;
   $Current ) ]
   Set Variable [ $Current ; $Current + 1 ]
   Exit Loop If [ $Current > $Count ]
   New Record/Request
End Loop
Perform Find [ ]
```

Another method of doing the same is to use the first value from the list on each loop but remove it from the list, repeating until the list is empty. This eliminates the need to have control variables to store the number of values and the current value. In the following example, *GetValue* is used to insert the first state into the current request. Next, the $States variable uses the *ValueCount* and *RightValues* functions to remove the first value, leaving the remaining values for future iterations. When the *$States* variable is empty, the *Exit Loop If* step terminates the loop and the find is performed.

```
Set Variable [ $States ; "OH¶PA¶NY" ]
Enter Find Mode [ Pause : Off ]
Loop
   Set Field [ Contact::Contact Address State ; GetValue ( $States ; 1 ) ]
   Set Variable [ $States ; RightValues ( $States ; ValueCount
   ( $States ) - 1 ) ]
   Exit Loop If [ $States = "" ]
   New Record/Request
End Loop
Perform Find [ ]
```

Managing Windows

There are numerous script steps that allow for the manipulation and management of windows. The *Adjust Window* step changes the visibility or size of a window based on a selection from one of five options. The *Resize to Fit* setting will adjust the dimensions of the window to the minimum size possible while continuing to display the entire content area within the confines of the maximum size allowed by the current monitor dimensions. Choosing *Maximize* will cause the step to resize the window to the full size of the computer screen, while *Minimize* will shrink the window down to an icon stored in the Dock (macOS) or taskbar (Windows). To return a window to the size and position it was when the script started, choose *Restore*. Finally, the *Hide* option will hide the window from view, placing it into the *Window* ➤ *Show Window* menu from where it can be reopened. The *Arrange all Windows* step can arrange every open window one of four ways: *Tile Horizontally, Tile Vertically, Cascade,* or *Bring All To Front*. Other steps can *Close, Refresh,* or *Scroll Window*. The *Select Window* step will bring a specific window to the front, making it the currently active context. With *Move/Resize Window*, a script can adjust the *Height, Width, Distance from Top*, and *Distance from Left* dimensions for a specified window. Change the name of a window using the *Set Window Title* step.

Creating a New Window

The *New Window* step will create a new window based on the current window's type, layout, size, positions, and other properties, unless these are specifically modified in the configuration dialog shown in Figure 25-13.

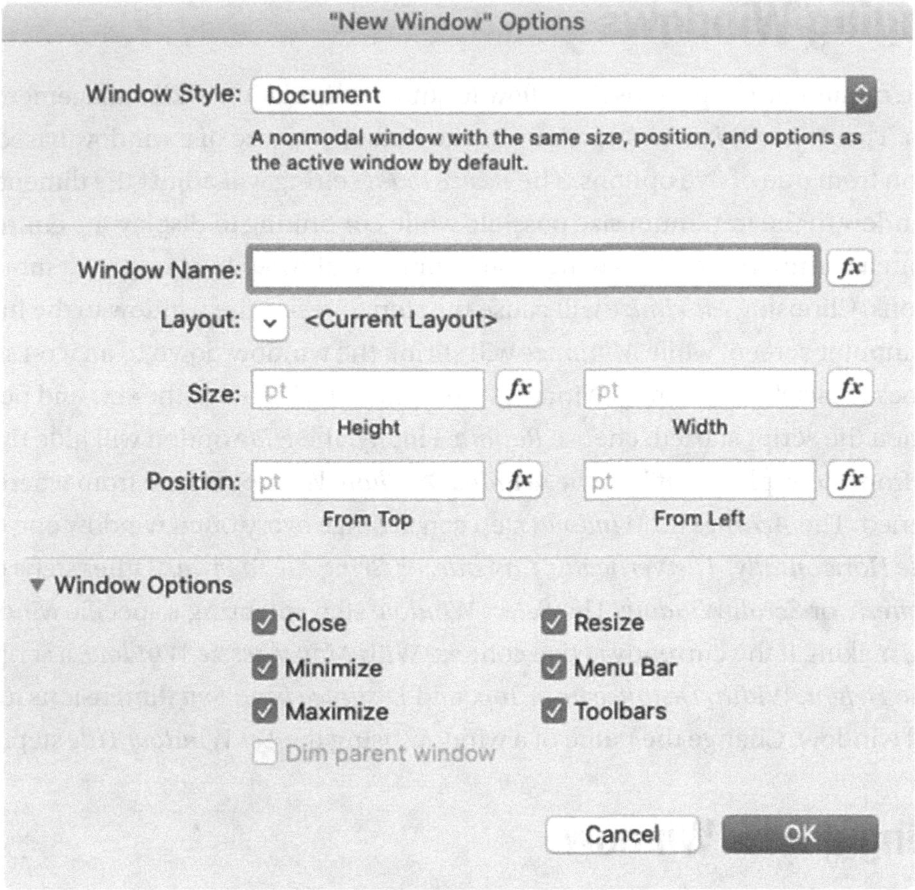

Figure 25-13. *The configuration options for creating a new window with a script*

The *Window Style* controls the type of window that will be created. The default option is a *Document* which is a standard non-modal FileMaker window. Other options are a *Floating Document* (a non-modal window that remains in front of other windows), a *Dialog* (a window that is modal to the application), or a *Card* (a window modal to and attached as an overlay to the parent window).

Note   A window is *modal* when it forces user interaction and/or dismissal before resuming other work in the affected context.

The central settings are all optional. If these are not specified, the new window will default to the settings of the window active when the step is executed. A *Window Name* can be entered in the text area or by clicking the *fx* button to generate one with a formula. If no name is specified, the new window will be named the same as the current window with a numeric suffix. Select a *Layout* that should be displayed in the new window. The *Size* and *Position* dimensions control window dimensions, each with the option to directly enter a value or a formula. The *From Top* and *From Left* positions can specify positions based on the current user's screen size. A formula can be used for precise centering or other alignments (Chapter 13, "Getting Window Dimensions").

Tip   Developers often create "staging" windows with large negative value for the *From Left* and *From Top* properties to "hide" them off-screen when performing a complex sequence of steps that would be visually distracting to a user if done in full view.

The *Window Options* checkboxes control the properties of the new window. The *Close*, *Minimize*, *Maximize,* and *Resize* options enable the ability of a user to modify the window. The *Menubar* visibility can be visible or hidden (Windows only) as can the *Toolbars*. For Card windows, the *Dim Parent Window* option will obscure the window behind the attached card window to help highlight its dimensions.

Caution   Opening a modal window without access to the close function and without a button or script to close the window will trap the user and may require a force quit of the application to escape.

Building a Custom Dialog Window

One way to overcome the limitations of the *Show Custom Dialog* step is using the *New Window* step to open a custom layout designed as a dialog. Since the dialog is really a layout, it can contain any number of any type of object formatted in any way required to accomplish the intended task. It can include lengthy instructions, any number of input fields configured with any control style, and way more than three buttons. A script can present the dialog in a new window and pause for the user action before continuing. In this section, we create a simple dialog layout and script that opens it in a new window, enters Find mode, and pauses for the user to make a selection of a state in a pop-up menu. Four buttons are included to continue the process: a choice of three types of marketing emails that would be sent to the found set and an option to cancel.

Creating a Dialog Layout

Create a new layout named "Contact – Dialog Find" and assign it to the *Contact* table. Remove other parts and shrink the Body part down to a desired dialog size, as shown in Figure 25-14. Add a text object for a heading and action prompt. Place the *Contact Address State* field formatted as pop-up menu assigned a value list of state abbreviations. Distribute four buttons along the bottom, and configure their *Autosize* settings in the *Position* tab of the *Inspector* pane to lock to the bottom right, so the window size can vary slightly without adversely affecting the appearance. Then, save the layout by returning to Browse mode and create a script.

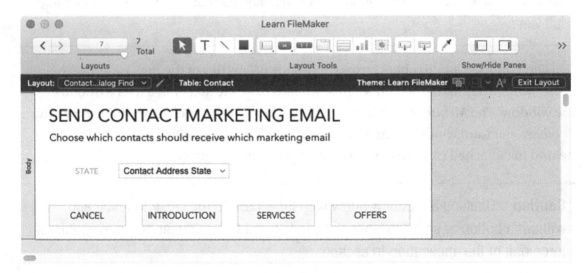

Figure 25-14. *An example of a layout designed for use as a dialog*

Creating a Dialog Layout Script

A dialog script can be configured in a variety of different ways, and your choice will vary based on the functions required. In some cases, a script can open the dialog, pause, and then continue when a button is clicked. In other cases, a group of separate scripts can be created: one to present the dialog and one for each button option. The following example uses parameters to package all the operations as separate functional sections of a single script. Start by creating a script named "Contact - Marketing Email," as shown in Figure 25-15. The script starts with a *Set Error Capture* step and then places the script parameter into a *$function* variable. It accepts one of five parameters to guide the workflow through different conditional statements: *Start (default when no parameter provided), Cancel, Introduction, Services,* and *Offers.*

A *Start* parameter will begin the process, being triggered when the user runs the script from the *Scripts* menu, a custom menu, a button, or some other triggering methods. The first portion of the conditional *If* statement allows for either a parameter of "Start" or no parameter, which opens a new window showing the dialog layout, assigns a name, and centers itself on-screen both horizontally and vertically. Then it enters Find mode and relinquishes control to the user, allowing them to select a state from the pop-up menu and make a button selection. The other four parameters will be used to perform different conditional steps depending on which of the four buttons is clicked. So, each button calls the same script but passes in a different parameter which activates a different portion of the conditional statement. When the script detects the *Cancel* parameter, it will enter Browse mode and close the dialog, returning the user to the window they had open previously. Each of the three report buttons will be handled after the first *Else* step which has a nested conditional statement. There, the *Perform Find* step executes the search and, if records are found, steps through the resulting found set. Inside the *Loop* statement is a nested condition for each of the three parameters, but with specifics omitted for simplicity. The three comments indicate where additional steps would be placed to create and send an email, or perform whatever action is required.

```
Set Error Capture [ On ]
Set Variable [ $function ; Value: Get ( ScriptParameter ) ]
If [ $function = "Start" or $function = "" ]
    New Window [ Style: Document ; Name: "Marketing Email" ; Using layout: "Contact - Dialog Find" (Contact) ;
    Height: 250 ; Width: 575 ; Top: ( Get ( WindowDesktopHeight ) / 2 ) - 125 ;
    Left: ( Get ( WindowDesktopWidth ) / 2 ) - 290 ]
    Enter Find Mode [ Pause: On ]
Else If [ $function = "Cancel" ]
    Enter Browse Mode [ Pause: Off ]
    Close Window [ Current Window ]
Else
    Perform Find [ ]
    If [ Get ( FoundCount ) > 0 ]
        Go to Record/Request/Page [ First ]
        Loop
            If [ $function = "Introduction" ]
                # <steps>
            Else If [ $function = "Services" ]
                # <steps>
            Else If [ $function = "Offers" ]
                # <steps>
            End If
            Go to Record/Request/Page [ Next ; Exit after last: On ]
        End Loop
    End If
    Close Window [ Current Window ]
End If
```

Figure 25-15. *The dialog script has conditions for each of five parameter values*

Notice that the script doesn't close the dialog until after it is finished running whichever conditional section is activated by the parameter. The new window for the dialog is being used as a temporary context which is separate from other windows the user had open when the script ran. Since the find is performed in the dialog window, the results will only exist there, and so the other steps must be performed in that context before closing the window. Alternatively, a script could gather the find criteria entered in the dialog and the name of the button clicked, store them in variables and close the window, and then reconstruct and perform the find in the original window.

Once the script is written and saved, make sure to check the box to include the script in the *Scripts* menu or provide some other interface access point where the users can start the process.

Caution   Be sure to connect the layout buttons to the script to avoid opening a window that can't be closed!

Connecting the Dialog Buttons to the Script

Each button should call the script with a parameter, as shown in Figure 25-16.

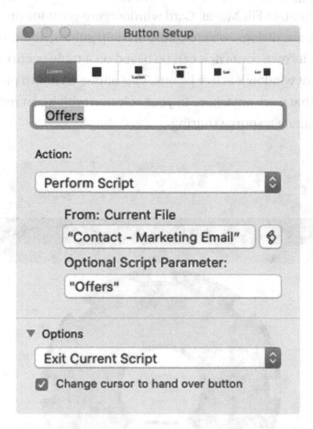

Figure 25-16. *Each button calls the script with a parameter and set to exit the current script*

Introducing the Card Window

A *Card* is a modal window that appears as an overlay connected on top of the current window's active layout, as shown in Figure 25-17. The parent window's content becomes inactive and inaccessible while the card is open. However, depending on the size of the card, the content behind may still be visible in an optionally diminished light. Unlike a *Dialog window*, which is modal to the application, a card only locks up a single window.

Cards are similar in appearance and behavior to modal windows found in other environments. For example, a macOS dialog can open as a *sheet*, attached to the top of a window. Also, web pages often display various objects like advertisements or images in a similar *lightbox* format. In FileMaker, Card windows are great for presenting navigation menus, custom toolbars, dialogs, wizards, custom help guides, and more. Since the layout displayed has its own context, it can be based on a table occurrence other than that of the parent window's active layout. This allows a card to provide universal interface "services" that work anywhere in your solution which can reduce technical redundancy and facilitate resource sharing.

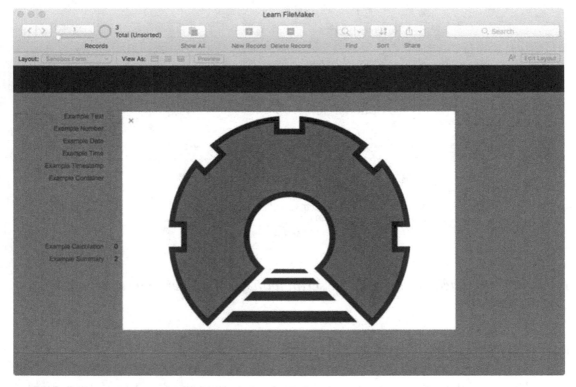

Figure 25-17. *An example of a card window*

Tip When configuring a Card in the *New Window Options* dialog, leave the *Size* and *Position* values empty to have the layout centered in the parent window at full size. Set the top position to 0 to simulate attachment to the top of the parent window.

Using Insert from URL

The *Insert from URL* step enters data from a URL into a target field or variable. The command supports the *http*, *https*, *ftp*, *ftps*, and *file* protocols and includes *cURL* options. The step's panel includes options to specify various settings, as shown in Figure 25-18.

Insert from URL [With dialog: Off] ⚙

☐ Select entire contents

☐ Target: Specify...

Specify URL   Specify...

☐ Verify SSL Certificates

Specify cURL options   Specify...

Figure 25-18. *The Insert from URL step's configuration panel*

Downloading a PDF File

Start with a simple example by downloading a PDF file from a website. First, click to specify a target container field as the destination for the file, e.g., the *Example Container* field in the *Sandbox* table. Then, click to *Specify URL* and enter the address of a PDF file, as shown in Figure 25-19. Run the script and the file should appear in the container field.

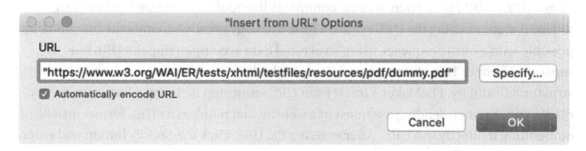

"Insert from URL" Options

URL

"https://www.w3.org/WAI/ER/tests/xhtml/testfiles/resources/pdf/dummy.pdf"   Specify...
☑ Automatically encode URL

                                        Cancel   OK

Figure 25-19. *The Insert from URL step's configuration panel*

Accessing Zip Code Information

The *Insert from URL* step can be used to access APIs such as the zip code lookup service from Datasheer, L.L.C. (`https://www.zip-codes.com/zip-code-api.asp`). The site allows a URL to request a JSON object of information about any U.S. Zip Code. You can register at the site for a free account (limited to 250 lookups/month) or purchase a variety of tiers up to 2 million lookups per month. The example below uses a limited demo API key and can be run from a *Contact* layout after a zip code is entered into a field. The script starts by placing site's API address and the current record's *Contact Address Zip* field value into a *$URL* variable. Next, the *Insert from URL* step targets a *$Data* variable and uses the *$URL* variable as it's URL. The two *Set Field* steps places the city and state values parsed from the *$Data* result into the corresponding fields.

```
Set Variable [ $URL ; Value: "https://api.zip-codes.com/ZipCodesAPI.
svc/1.0/QuickGetZipCodeDetails/" &
Contact::Contact Address Zip & "?key=DEMOAPIKEY" ]
Insert from URL [ With dialog: Off ; Target: $Data ; $URL ]
Set Field [ Contact::Contact Address City ; JSONGetElement ( $Data ; "City" ) ]
Set Field [ Contact::Contact Address State ; JSONGetElement ( $Data ; "State" ) ]
```

Tip   For the smoothest experience, use an *OnObjectValidate* script trigger (Chapter 27) to run this script after the user types into the *Contact Address Zip* field.

Using cURL Options

Client URL (cURL) is an open-source, command-line tool for data transfer between different systems using the URL syntax. The technology greatly expands the functionality possible with website requests, using structured data accompanying the URL but separated from it. This offers a more secure method of data transfer with far greater structural flexibility. FileMaker's *Insert from URL* script step includes a button to *Specify cURL Options* when sending a request to a website that requires a cURL format instead of embedding it directly in a URL. After entering the URL, click the *Specify* button and enter options, structured as required by the target website. For example, if a website requires authentication, the options might be formatted as shown in the following example. This example places a URL into one variable and cURL options in another and then uses these in the *Insert from URL* step which targets a $Data variable for the result.

```
Set Variable [ $URL ; Value: "https://www.example.com/" ]
Set Variable [ $Options ; Value: "--user name:password ]
Insert from URL [ With dialog: Off ; Target: $Data ; $URL ; cURL Options:
$Options ]
```

cURL can be used to push data to a web form as shown in the following example. A first name and last name are structured with field labels and included as the content of a data option which is then sent to a website's contact form.

```
Set Variable [ $URL ; Value: "https://www.example.com/contact.cgi" ]
Set Variable [ $Options ; Value: "--data \"firstname=Mark&lastname=Munro\"" ]
Insert from URL [ With dialog: Off ; Target: $Data ; $URL ; cURL Options:
$Options ]
```

Summary

This chapter presented many examples of scripting tasks that can be used to automate activity within a database. In the next chapter, we will look at the built-in script debugging capabilities provided as part of FileMaker's advanced tools.

CHAPTER 26

Debugging Scripts

When a simple script encounters an error, it is relatively easy to troubleshoot. As a database grows more complex, troubleshooting rapidly becomes more challenging. Script calls initiated by users, event triggers, other scripts, and external systems form complex interwoven hierarchical execution stacks. Scripts can change found sets, switch layouts, and open new windows, creating a complex web of interconnected interface contexts. When something breaks, it is often difficult to even know which script caused the error, not to mention knowing where, why, and under what contextual conditions the problem occurred. To ease this burden, modern development environments like FileMaker include a debugger. In this chapter, we introduce script debugging and cover the following topics:

- Introducing debugging

- Exploring the debugging interface

- Using custom breakpoints

Introducing Debugging

A *script debugger* is an interactive tool used by developers to visually step through a scripted process and troubleshoot or analyze performance. FileMaker's debugger makes it easy to step through scripts, monitor variables, set breakpoints, and discover errors while directly observing the corresponding actions performed in the database interface in real time. It includes an option to temporarily disable all script triggers to avoid a malfunctioning startup script or other situations. The debugger can be activated by selecting *Script Debugger* from the *Tools* menu or in the header of the *Script Workspace* (Chapter 24). Also, a *Pause on error* option can be enabled to automatically open the debugger and pause action anytime a script generates an error while working in Browse mode as a user.

© Mark Conway Munro 2021
M. C. Munro, *Learn FileMaker Pro 19*, https://doi.org/10.1007/978-1-4842-6680-9_26

When running a script in the debugger, FileMaker pauses at the start of each script in the stack and at any step that encounters an error. You can define arbitrary *breakpoints* at any step to force the script to pause for further investigation. Once paused, there is a choice to *Continue* executing the script to the next breakpoint, *Halt* to abort the script, or *Step forward* using one of four options:

- *Step Over* – Continues executing the current script, performing any subscripts *without* debugging

- *Step Into* – Continues executing the script step by step, performing any subscripts *with* debugging

- *Step Out* – Executes the remaining steps in the current subscript and then returns control up to the stack to the parent script, pausing on the line after the subscript call

- *Set Next Step* – Skips ahead to a selected step in the current script *without performing the interim steps*

Exploring the Debugging Interface

The debugging interface includes debugging options under the *Tools* menu, a *Script Debugger* window, and a *Data Viewer* window.

Debugging Options Under the Tools Menu

The *Tools* menu, shown in Figure 26-1, contains the three items at the top for debugging. The *Script Debugger* menu item will toggle the visibility of the debugging window. The *Debugging Controls* submenu contains various debugging functions for controlling the movement through an active script. Most of these are also available in the debugging window toolbar. Finally, the *Data Viewer* menu item toggles the visibility of a window used to browse variables and dynamically monitor formula results based on the current context.

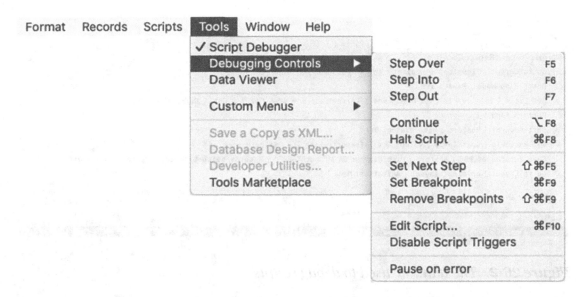

Figure 26-1. The Script Debugger menu showing the Debugging Controls submenu

Exploring the Script Debugger Window

The *Script Debugger* window, shown in Figure 26-2, is always open when debugging is active. The non-editable toolbar contains buttons for controlling the debugging process. The steps of the active script are listed in the middle with a green arrow label on the number of the paused step. Any steps with a breakpoint are similarly highlighted with a blue arrow. The *Pause on error* checkbox below opens the debugger and pauses on any steps that generate an error during regular use, including those automatically suppressed with the *Set Error Capture* script step. At the bottom is the *call stack*, a hierarchy of nested script calls that are listed up in execution order, from the current script back to the first script that started the currently active workflow.

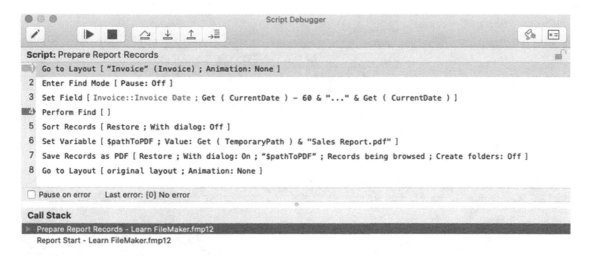

Figure 26-2. *The window used to debug scripts*

In the example shown in Figure 26-2, a script named "Report Start" was run, and it called the active script named "Prepare Report Records" which is displayed. Sensing a new script starting, the debugger automatically paused on the first step, freezing the interface in its current state. The fourth step has a breakpoint which adds an additional forced pause. The developer now has time to observe the state of the interface, review the current script steps, and decide the next option: continue running normally, stepping through the script line by line, or completely halting the entire script stack to make any required development changes.

Status Toolbar Items (Debugger Window)

The non-customizable status toolbar for the *Script Debugger* window, shown in Figure 26-3, provides control over the debugging process.

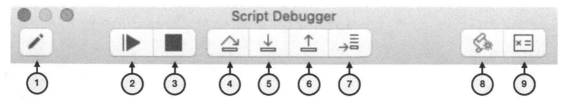

Figure 26-3. *The toolbar of the Script Debugger window*

1. *Edit Script* – Open the paused script in the *Script Workspace*.

2. *Continue* – Continue running the paused script using default stepping/pausing options.

3. *Halt Script* – Stop all scripts in the entire stack.

4. *Step Over* – Continue the current script *without* debugging subscripts.

5. *Step Into* – Continue the current script step by step *with* debugging subscripts.

6. *Step Out* – Continue the current subscript without debugging until control is returned to the parent script, and then pause.

7. *Set Next Step* – Jump ahead to the script step that is selected in the window, skipping over the interim steps.

8. *Disable Script Triggers* – Toggle the enabled status of script triggers globally in the database file.

9. *Open Data Viewer* – Open the *Data Viewer* dialog.

Exploring the Data Viewer

The *Data Viewer* is a dialog that displays a list of variables and their current value, as shown in Figure 26-4. This can be opened at any time to view global variables or to test a formula. When used in conjunction with the debugging feature or any time a script is paused, it displays the value of all variables at the moment the pause occurred. The dialog has two tabs: *Current* and *Watch*.

Figure 26-4. The dialog used to monitor the value of variables

The *Current* tab lists every variable currently defined. Global variables are always present, while local variables are only present when a script is running or paused. Double-click to open a variable into a dialog for an expanded view of its content. Observing variables at key moments during a script's execution has many uses. For example, when an *Export* or *Save as* script step fails and you suspect it might be a faulty path construction, add a breakpoint just prior to that step, and then confirm that the value in the variable contains a valid path when the debugger pauses.

The Watch tab is used to monitor values in a manually compiled list of variables, fields, or expressions. This can be used during debugging or to test new formulas before integrating them into a field, layout object, or custom function. An expression on this tab can optionally continuously evaluate a result based on the current window's context so it provides the ability to confirm a formula with real-time values.

Setting Custom Breakpoints

A *custom breakpoint* is a developer marked point in a script that pauses the debugger and is used to troubleshoot script problems. Breakpoints allow you to stop a script at any arbitrary position and provides an opportunity to see the current layout context and review current values in key variables at a frozen moment in time. Breakpoints allow you to quickly run a script up to a specific line without having to manually step through it. To add a breakpoint, open a script and click a step number. A breakpoint is indicated when the number is illuminated in a blue arrow, as shown in Figure 26-5. Breakpoints can be removed individually by clicking on the arrow icon or selecting the *Remove Breakpoints* option from the *Tools* ➤ *Debugger Controls* submenu to remove all breakpoints from the current script paused in the debugger.

```
                            Hello World
1
2  # Extract input parameter
3  Set Variable [ $State ;
   Value: Let ( [   input = Get ( ScriptParameter ) ;   state = Case ( input ≠ ""_ )
4
5  # Find all contacts by state
6  Go to Layout [ "Contact" (Contact) ]
7  Enter Find Mode [ Pause: Off ] ⊙
8  Set Field [ Contact::Contact Address State ; $State ]
9  Perform Find [ ]
10
11 # Compile a list of contact information for the found set
12 Go to Record/Request/Page [ First ]
13 Loop
14     Set Variable [ $Names ;
       Value: $Names &    Contact::Contact Name First & " " & Contact::Contact N_ ]
15     Go to Record/Request/Page [ Next ; Exit after last ]
16 End Loop
17
18 # Send list as email
19 Send Mail [ Send via E-mail Client ; With dialog: On ;
   To: "jane.accounting@widget.com" ; Subject: "Contacts from " & $State ;
   Message: $names ]
```

Figure 26-5. *A script with two breakpoints*

Summary

This chapter introduced the debugging capabilities of FileMaker. These provide an invaluable tool for troubleshooting databases with complex scripting. In the next chapter, we will learn how to trigger scripts in response to interface events.

Using Script Triggers

A script connected to a button or menu requires a user to perform a manual action to initiate the process. While this is fine for tasks that are optional or require a conscious choice, critical business functions can be forgotten. In some cases, it may be inefficient and non-intuitive to require a user to perform extra clicks to initiate mandatory actions in the interface. FileMaker allows you to design dynamically responsive interfaces that connect user events to custom scripts. A *script trigger* is a developer-defined connection between an interface event and a script process. Whenever the event occurs, the script runs automatically. FileMaker has over two dozen triggers for a variety of file, layout, and object events. Some events run the assigned script prior to the completion of the user action, allowing the script to execute custom steps and determine if the event should be performed to completion. Others run after the event, allowing the script to perform follow-up tasks. This chapter introduces script triggers, covering the following topics:

- Defining available triggers

- Understanding event precedence

- Accessing targets before event completion

- Avoiding trigger exceptions

Tip   Objects assigned a script trigger will optionally display a badge icon in Layout mode (Chapter 17, "View Menu").

© Mark Conway Munro 2021
M. C. Munro, *Learn FileMaker Pro 19*, https://doi.org/10.1007/978-1-4842-6680-9_27

Defining Available Triggers

There are three categories of script triggers: *file*, *layout*, and *object*.

File Triggers

A *file trigger* runs a script in response to a file event. These triggers are configured in the *Script Triggers* tab of the *File Options* dialog (Chapter 6), shown in Figure 27-1. This dialog can be accessed by selecting the *File* ➤ *File Options* menu. At the top of the dialog is a list of all the *file events* available. The checkbox indicates an active event that will trigger the script displayed. The bottom half displays details for the selected event. Click *Select* to specify the script that will be connected to that event.

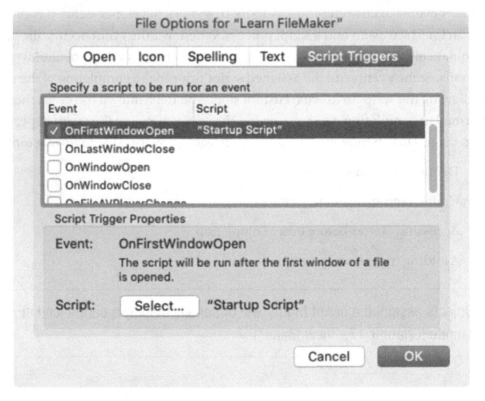

Figure 27-1. *The options dialog tab used to define triggers for the file*

OnFirstWindowOpen

The *OnFirstWindowOpen* event occurs after the first window appears when a database file opens, providing an opportunity to automatically perform setup functions prior to a user beginning work. The triggered script can initialize global variables, automatically open other windows, or perform default finds and sorts. This event only occurs when a database is opened by a user or by the *Open File* script step run from another file. It does *not* occur if the file opens as a hidden window behind another database to display resources through a relationship.

Tip   Navigation to a starting layout and hiding toolbars on file opens can be set on the *Open* tab of the *File Options* dialog without a trigger.

OnLastWindowClose

The *OnLastWindowClose* file event occurs as a file begins to close the last interface window. This provides an opportunity for a script to perform last-minute maintenance tasks. If necessary, the script can halt the closure by returning a false (0) value. For example, a script can use the *Show Custom Dialog* step can confirm that the user actually intended to close the file and give them an option to cancel. In the following example, the dialog step is configured so the first (default) button is named "Cancel," and the second is named "Close." It uses the *Get (LastMessageChoice)* function to detect which button was clicked. If the user clicks the first button to cancel, it returns a zero result which causes the triggering event to halt, thereby leaving the window and file open.

```
Show Custom Dialog [ "Really close the database?" ]
If [ Get ( LastMessageChoice ) = 1 ]
   Exit Script [ Text Result: 0 ]
End If
```

OnWindowOpen

The *OnWindowOpen* file event occurs after any new window is created by a user selecting the *Window* ➤ *New Window* menu or a script running the *New Window* step. It is also triggered when a file previously opened hidden because of a relational connection is brought forward for the first time. This provides an opportunity to perform any configuration or setup routines for the window. For example, this can be used to position the window precisely on screen, perform a default find, sort, set up control variables, or otherwise prepare the window for use.

OnWindowClose

The *OnWindowClose* file event occurs immediately *before* any window is about to close. This provides an opportunity to perform last-minute validation functions or maintenance routines to the record(s) viewed within the window. Like other events that precede an action, if the script returns a false (0) value, the process will be halted and the window will remain open.

Note   Both window open events are triggered when a file is first opened, and both window close events are triggered when closing the last window.

OnFileAVPlayerChange

The *OnFileAVPlayerChange* file event occurs after the playback state of a media file playing in a container field or URL is changed. For example, the event triggers when paused, played, or stopped or when the media stops upon reaching the end. This event is only supported in FileMaker Go on iOS devices.

Layout Triggers

A *layout trigger* runs a script in response to a layout event. These triggers are configured in the *Script Triggers* tab of the *Layout Setup* dialog (Chapter 18), shown in Figure 27-2. The dialog is similar to the *File Options* dialog with the addition of checkboxes to control which Window mode(s) the event is enabled.

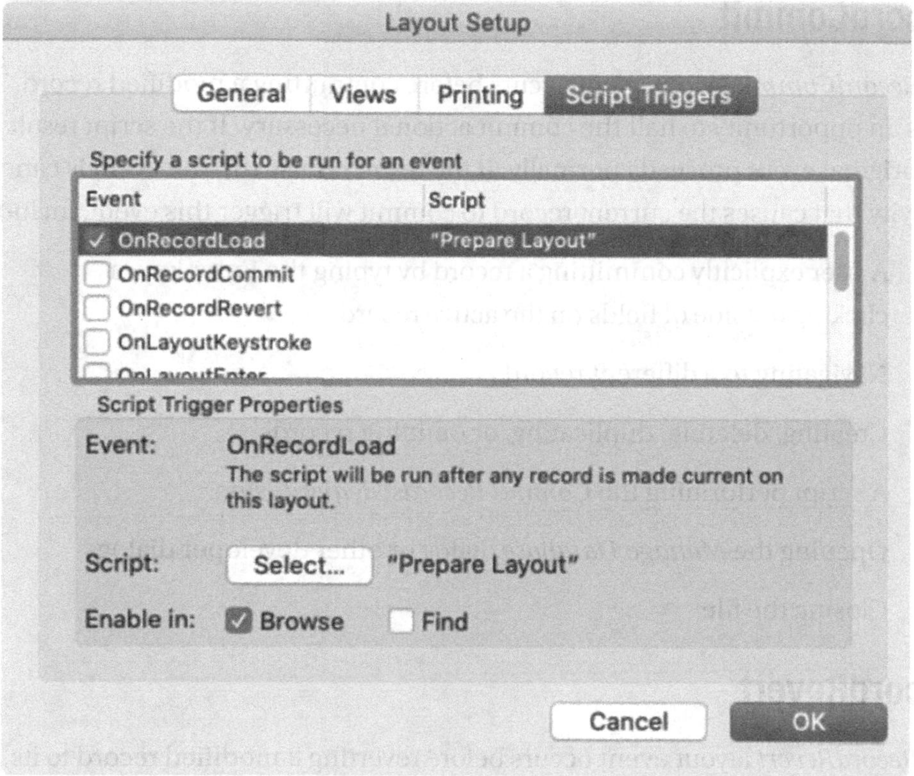

Figure 27-2. *The dialog used to configure layout script triggers*

OnRecordLoad

The *OnRecordLoad* layout event occurs after a record becomes current. This provides an opportunity to set up default field values with values too complex for auto-enter settings, create related records, or perform other custom record tasks. Any activity that causes a window to activate a record will trigger this event. This includes the following:

- Navigating to a new record within a found set
- Navigating to a different layout
- Creating a new record
- Deleting a record in a found set of more than one record
- Creating a new window showing a table with one or more records
- Displaying search results

OnRecordCommit

The *OnRecordCommit* layout event occurs before committing a modified record. This provides an opportunity to halt the commit action if necessary. If the script result is true (1), the original event proceeds normally. If the result is false (0), the event is canceled. Any activity that causes the current record to commit will trigger this event, including

- A user explicitly committing a record by typing the Enter key or clicking outside of fields on the active record

- Navigating to a different record

- Creating, deleting, duplicating, or omitting records

- A script performing the *Commit Records/Requests* step

- Opening the *Manage Database* dialog or other developer dialogs

- Closing the file

OnRecordRevert

The *OnRecordRevert* layout event occurs before reverting a modified record to its previously committed state. This event is triggered when a user selects the *Records ➤ Revert Record* menu or a script runs the *Revert Record/Request* step. It provides an opportunity to open a custom dialog confirming the action, perform other resetting actions, or halt the reversion action if necessary.

OnLayoutKeystroke

The *OnLayoutKeystroke* layout event occurs when any character is typed on the keyboard except those handled as functions by the operating system or FileMaker's active menu set. The event triggers even when no field has active focus and occurs *before* the keystroke event is sent to FileMaker. This provides an opportunity for a script to override the default error dialog with a custom message when the user begins typing before entering a field. This can also be used to run a script in response to a key combination that isn't associated with a menu or to refresh a view when typing into a portal filter (Chapter 20, "Filtering Portal Records"). Using two trigger-centric *Get* functions, the following example gets the key(s) typed and runs a script when the user types "1" while holding down the macOS Control key. The script runs the *Perform Script* step (shown undefined) and then uses the *Exit Script* with a result of 0 to halt the keystrokes. Any other keys typed are ignored by the script and continue into the active field.

```
If [ Get ( TriggerModifierKeys ) = 4 and Get ( TriggerKeystroke ) = "1" ]
    Perform Script [ ]
    Exit Script [ Text Result: 0 ]
End if
```

OnLayoutEnter

The *OnLayoutEnter* layout event occurs after a when a window switches to a different layout in Browse mode. This provides an opportunity to perform similar setup functionality as the triggers when opening a window or activating a record.

OnLayoutExit

The *OnLayoutExit* layout event occurs before navigating away from the current layout. This provides an opportunity to validate and halt the navigation change if necessary.

OnLayoutSizeChange

The *OnLayoutSizeChange* layout event occurs after the window has changed size. This happens when opening a window, resizing a window, hiding/showing the toolbar or formatting bar, and toggling an iOS device between portrait and landscape. This provides an opportunity to perform activity such as enforcing a minimum window size or repositioning a window to keep it centered perfectly within the bounds of the screen dimensions. The following formula can be used in a *Set Variable* step to establish variables for *$Height* and *$Width* using either the current window dimensions or switching to a default minimum when those values are too low. Those variables can then be used in the *Move/Resize Window* script step to enforce a minimum window size, in this case 800 x 1000.

```
Let ( [
    Height = Get ( WindowHeight ) ;
    $Height = Case ( Height < 800 ; 800 ; Height ) ;
    Width = Get ( WindowWidth ) ;
    $Width = Case ( Width < 1000 ; 1000 ; Width )
] ;
    ""
)
```

OnModeEnter

The *OnModeEnter* layout event occurs after a change to Browse, Find, or Preview mode. This provides an opportunity to prepare a window for specific activity like setting up default find criteria, initializing variables, or adjusting print setup.

OnModeExit

The *OnModeExit* layout event occurs before changing the window's mode. This provides an opportunity for a script to validate and halt the mode change if necessary.

OnViewChange

The *OnViewChange* layout event occurs after a change between Form, List, and Table view.

OnGestureTap

The *OnGestureTap* layout event occurs when a tap gesture is performed on a layout. This provides an opportunity for a script to use the *Get (TriggerGestureInfo)* function to determine details about the event and perform custom actions or halt the gesture if necessary. The event is triggered under the following conditions:

- FileMaker Go and Windows only (except Windows 7).
- Browse and Find modes only.
- Tap is not made in active web viewers or active edit boxes.
- Single tap is one, two, or three fingers (iOS).
- Double tap with one finger (iOS), which will trigger the event twice.
- Tap is with two fingers (Windows).

OnExternalCommandReceived

The *OnExternalCommandReceived* layout event occurs when a user presses a button to control playback functions on an iOS device lock screen or on an external device, e.g., *play, pause, stop, next,* and *previous*. The triggered script runs *before* the event occurs, and it can use the *Get (TriggerGestureInfo)* function to gain information about the external event.

Object Triggers

An *object trigger* runs a script in response to an event performed to or within a layout object. These can be configured in the dialog shown in Figure 27-3, which is accessed by selecting an object and choosing the *Set Script Triggers* function from the *Format* menu or an object's contextual menu. Also, the *Popover Panel Setup* dialog has a button to open this dialog (Chapter 20, "Exploring the Popover Button Setup Options").

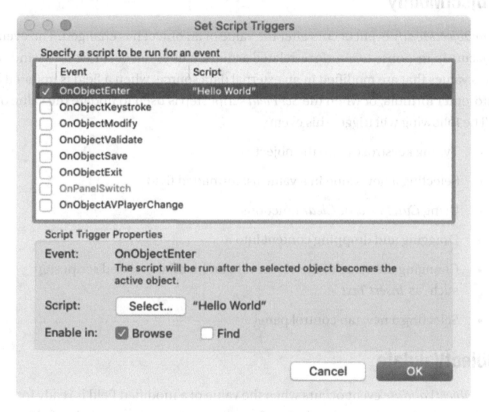

Figure 27-3. The dialog used to configure object script triggers

OnObjectEnter

The *OnObjectEnter* event occurs after a layout object receives active focus when a user clicks on the object or tabs into the object or when a script runs a step such as *Go to Object* or *Go to Next Field*.

OnObjectKeystroke

The *OnObjectKeystroke* event occurs when any character is typed into an object with focus but before the event is completed. Similar to a layout keystroke trigger, this will ignore those keystrokes handled by the operating system or the FileMaker application, and it can be halted by exiting the script with a false (0) value.

OnObjectModify

The *OnObjectModify* event occurs after the value of an object has changed. The event only occurs in response to interface-related actions. It does *not* occur when a window updates values that are modified in an external data source, when a field is updated by an auto-enter formula, or when the *Set Field* script step is used to update the value of a field. The following will trigger this event:

- Typing keystrokes into the object

- Selecting a new value in a value list formatted field

- Using *Cut*, *Paste*, or *Clear* functions

- Dragging and dropping content into it

- Changing the value of the object with an interface-related script step such as *Insert Text*

- Selecting a new tab control panel

OnObjectValidate

The *OnObjectValidate* event occurs when the value of a modified field is ready for validation just prior to being saved when focus is about to move to another field or a record is in the process of being committed. This provides an opportunity to validate the change to the object, perform any preliminary actions, and/or halt the movement to another object if necessary.

OnObjectSave

The *OnObjectSave* event occurs after a modified field has been validated but before being exited, providing another opportunity to halt the exit process.

OnObjectExit

The *OnObjectExit* event occurs anytime an object is about to lose active focus regardless of any modifications. This happens when moving to another object, portal row, or field repetition. It also occurs when any action that causes a record to commit occurs. The script is triggered before exiting the object allowing it to halt the process if necessary.

OnPanelSwitch

The *OnPanelSwitch* event occurs before the current view of a panel control is about to change and can be halted by exiting the script with a false (0) value. Built-in *Get* functions can determine the layout name of the object and the number of the current and target panels allowing a script to take specific actions pertinent to the change. The following formula can be placed into a *Show Custom Dialog* step of the target script or in the *Data Viewer* (Chapter 26) to illustrate these values, in the form of a sentence. Use them in an *If* statement to conditionally perform different sets of steps depending on which was the starting and ending panel.

```
Let ( [
    currentPanel = GetValue ( Get ( TriggerCurrentPanel ) ; 1 ) ;
    targetPanel = GetValue ( Get ( TriggerTargetPanel ) ; 1 )
] ;
    "Changing from panel " & currentPanel & " to panel " & targetPanel & "."
)
```

OnObjectAVPlayerChange

The *OnObjectAVPlayerChange* event occurs after media in an object changes state. For example, the event will trigger a script when a user pauses, plays, or stops a video in a field or when the video stops upon reaching the end. This event is only supported in FileMaker Go on iOS devices.

Understanding Event Precedence

Many user actions will trigger multiple events, and FileMaker will execute the script triggers in a specific order of precedence. The choice of where your script intercepts the action depends on the kind of action intended and whether or not the option to cancel the event is important.

Opening a Database File

When *opening a database file*, the following events will be triggered in order:

1. OnFirstWindowOpen

2. OnWindowOpen

3. OnLayoutEnter

4. OnModeEnter

5. OnRecordLoad

Caution   While not a script trigger, the file's option to *Switch to layout* when the file is opened occurs prior to all script triggers (Chapter 6, "File Options: Open").

Committing a Record with Unsaved Changes

When *committing a record with unsaved changes*, the following events will be triggered in order:

1. OnObjectValidate

2. OnObjectSave

3. OnObjectExit

4. OnRecordCommit

5. OnRecordLoad

6. OnObjectEnter

Opening a New Window

When *opening a new window*, the following events will be triggered in order:

1. OnWindowOpen

2. OnLayoutEnter

3. OnModeEnter

4.   OnRecordLoad

5.   OnLayoutSizeChange

Changing Layouts

When *changing layouts*, the following events will be triggered in this order:

1.   OnLayoutExit

2.   OnLayoutEnter

3.   OnRecordLoad

Note   When c*hanging layouts* in a window displaying a record with unsaved changes, the record commit sequence will be performed first followed by the changing layout sequence.

Accessing Targets Before Event Completion

As noted previously, many events trigger scripts *before* the event is completed, providing the option to halt the effects of the event *before* they are implemented. However, this means that the results of the action have not yet been realized and aren't discernable to the script from the interface by normal means. For example, the *OnObjectKeystroke* event is triggered when a user types a character into the field. However, the script runs before the character is entered into the field, so pulling the field value into a formula in a script step will not include the most recent keystroke which triggered the script. Similarly, the *OnPanelSwitch* event happens before the target panel is activated. Since there is no corresponding event that occurs after the switch, ascertaining the target panel may be required in order for a script to take a particular course of action.

FileMaker provides a set of built-in *Get* functions specifically designed to provide information about events so that information can be accessed and used by the triggered script. For example, the *Get (TriggerCurrentPanel)* and *Get (TriggerTargetPanel)* each return the number and name of the current and target panel as two return-delimited lists. The *Get (TriggerKeystroke)* will return the last key typed not yet in the field on a *OnObjectKeystroke* event, and the *Get (TriggerModifierKeys)* returns a number indicating any modifier key(s) the user is holding down when they typed. For example, if the user is holding the Shift key, this will return a "1," while holding the Option key will return "8." When key combinations are held, the result is the sum of the numbers representing those keys, e.g., holding Shift and Option returns "9."

For events that don't have access to target information, switch from a pre-event trigger to a post-event trigger. For example, there is no function available to determine the next target object in a script triggered by *OnObjectExit,* so try switching to *OnObjectEnter* since it happens after the change has occurred.

Caution   These target-determining functions will only work within the target script, *not* as a parameter sent to the script from the object.

Avoiding Trigger Exceptions

Some object changes will *not* trigger events. For example, most of the built-in *Spelling* and *Find/Replace* functions, especially when performed across found sets, will not trigger events such as *OnObjectModify*, *OnObjectValidate*, and *OnObjectSave*. Also, since functions like *Import Records*, *Replace Field Contents*, and *Relookup Field Contents* modify table data directly, they won't trigger interface events. Similarly, script steps like *Set Field*, *Set Field by Name*, and *Set Web Viewer* are not triggering events. Be sure to consider all possible actions that users or scripts may perform and, where necessary, lock out functions or use alternative steps in your scripts to ensure that critical functionality is triggered. For example, use the *Insert Text* or *Insert Calculated Result* script steps instead of *Set Field* if the field in question has critical triggers assigned on the layout. When non-triggering steps can't be avoided, add steps to programmatically trigger the relevant target scripts, or add steps to explicitly perform the desired functionality. Alternatively, don't use script triggers excessively, especially in situations where they aren't absolutely required and may create unnecessary complexities when excluded by these exceptions.

Summary

This chapter continued the discussion of scripting, focusing on how interface events can trigger scripts. In the next chapter, we will explore how plug-ins can extend the built-in functions and script steps available.

Extending Features with Plug-ins

A *plug-in* is a software extension package developed that extends the capabilities of FileMaker by adding new functions and script steps. They can also modify the development interface with new options. Plug-ins for FileMaker are available from third-party vendors, which means they involve an added expense and logistical considerations for installing and maintaining them over time. However, a good plug-in can be worth the effort since the features they provide would be difficult or impossible to achieve using only built-in tools. This chapter covers basic plug-in concepts including

- Finding plug-ins
- Installing plug-ins
- Accessing plug-ins

Finding Plug-ins

Plug-ins for FileMaker can be found from a variety of different vendors. Start by searching the Claris Marketplace (marketplace.claris.com), and take a look at some other prominent offerings directly available from the developer website.

MonkeyBread Software

The MBS plug-in *from Monkey Bread Software (*www.monkeybreadsoftware.com*) boasts* over 6,000 functions. The impressive feature list includes enhancements to the Script Workspace, connectivity features, OS integration, and content editing. Some highlights include

- Syntax coloring

- Search in scripts, lists, or relationships

- CURL for up/downloads, send/receive e-mail

- Accessing scanners

- Access to Address book, Calendars, and Reminders

- Window management functions

- Send user notifications

- Control printers

- Convert images, draw, and annotate

- Create, edit, or merge PDF documents

- Generate and recognize barcodes

- Read and write Excel files

- Fill Word files

Productive Computing

The *Productive Computing* plug-in offerings (`www.productivecomputing.com`) include

- *Address Book Manipulator* – Enables bidirectional data flow between a database and the macOS Contacts application

- *iCal Manipulator* – Enables bidirectional data flow between a database and the macOS Calendar application

- *Biometric Fingerprint Reader* – Adds the ability to incorporate fingerprint security and script control options to a database

Prometheus Systems Consulting

Prometheus Systems Consulting sells dozens of plug-ins (*360works.com*), including

- *360Works Email* – Send and receive email messages within a database. Supports SMTP, POP, and IMAP.

- *360Works Plastic* – Enables credit card processing within a database. Supports both Authorize.net and Verisign/PayPal Payflow.

- *360Works Web Services Manager* – Publishes your custom FileMaker scripts as XML Web Services that can be accessed by SOAP (Simple Object Access Protocol)–compatible software.

Troi Automatisering

Troi Automatisering offers several plug-ins (*www.troi.com*), including

- *Troi Dialog* – Create dynamic, feature-rich dialogs

- *Troi Encryptor* – Generate passwords and save them in the keychain

- *Troi File* – Access files and folders outside FileMaker, zip and unzip files and folders, search directories, and more

Installing Plug-ins

Each computer accessing a database with plug-in functions must have the plug-in installed locally. However, installation resources can be embedded in and installed from a database file, either in a separate installer database or directly within a database solution. Some plug-in venders deliver plug-ins embedded inside of an installer database.

To prepare a custom database to install a plug-in, create a container field for each plug-in installer. This may require more than one if the database is used in a cross-platform workflow of different operating systems. Create a script that uses the *Install Plug-in File* step like the following example which uses *Set Variable* to put a list of installed plug-ins into a variable named *$installed* and then uses the *PatternCount* function to determine if the *Troi File Plug-in* needs to be installed or updated. If so, it uses *Get (SystemPlatform)* to determine if it should install the macOS or Windows plug-in.

```
Set Variable [ $installed ; Value : Get ( InstalledFMPlugins ) ]
If [ PatternCount ( $installed ; "Troi File Plug-in;8.0.2" ) = "" ]
    If [ Get ( SystemPlatform ) = 1 ]
        Install Plug-in File [ Resources::Troi_File.fmplugin ]
```

```
Else
    Install Plug-in File [ Resources::Troi_File.fmx]
    End if
End if
```

The script can run automatically as part of a startup script triggered by an *OnFirstWindowOpen* event (Chapter 29) to ensure that each user's computer has a proper installation. The script can be expanded to check for errors to confirm that the installation process was successful and warn the user to contact a database administrator if a problem was detected. For example, the script will fail if the *Application* preference to *Allow Solutions to Install Files is not* enabled. The *Plug-ins* tab of the *Application* preferences dialog, shown in Figure 28-1, lists every installed plug-in. From here, you can confirm installation, enable, disable, and configure a plug-in.

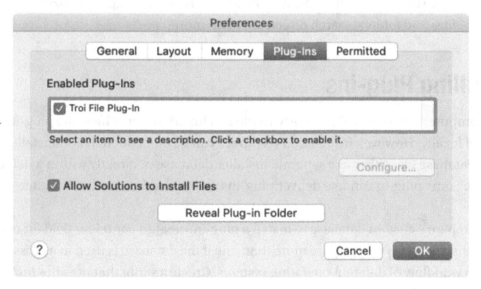

Figure 28-1. *The preference tab showing installed plug-ins must allow installation*

Accessing Plug-in Functions

Once installed, a plug-in's functions will appear as a new category in either *Functions* pane of *Specify Calculation* dialogs or the *Steps* pane of the *Script Workspace*. Some plug-ins appear in both lists, as shown in Figure 28-2. From here, plug-in functions can be easily inserted into formulas (Chapter 12) and scripts (Chapter 24) like functions or steps.

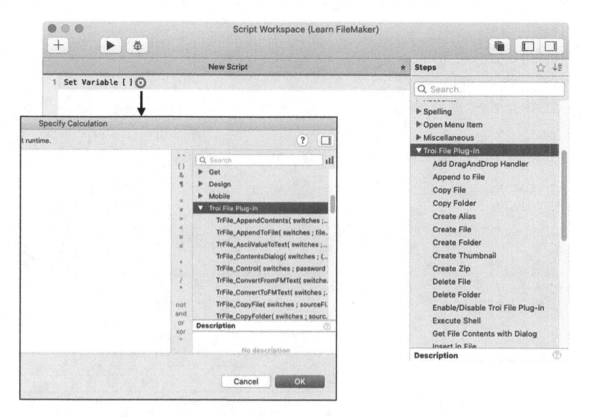

Figure 28-2. *Plug-ins appear in the Steps pane of the Script Workspace (back) and/or in the Functions pane of the Specify Calculation window (front)*

Summary

This chapter presented the basic process for finding, installing, and accessing plug-ins. In the next chapter, we begin an introduction to network sharing.

PART VI

Deploying, Securing, and Analyzing Files

These final chapters cover the basics of deploying, network sharing, security, and some advanced tools:

Deploying and Accessing Databases

When finished developing, it is time to deploy your database into the target workflow. There are three primary choices for deployment: in a *folder directory*, on an *iOS device*, or on a *host server*. Each option has different benefits, and the choice affects who can access the file, how, and from where. Each product in the FileMaker family has different capabilities for deployment and access (see Chapter 1, "Reviewing the Product Line"). In this chapter, we explore these options, introducing specific topics related to deploying and accessing a solution, including

- Deploying to a folder directory
- Deploying to an iOS device
- Sharing databases on a network
- Hosting with FileMaker Server
- Hosting with FileMaker Cloud
- Accessing solutions externally

Deploying to a Folder Directory

The easiest deployment method is to store a database in a *folder directory*. With access to the folder, the FileMaker Pro desktop application can open and use the database. This provides a lot of convenience, since the database can be moved between folders or duplicated for reuse as simply as a word processing or excel document. While this is an easy and useful option for a single user, opportunities for sharing are limited. The database can be shared by sending a copy to coworkers, but each person will have their

© Mark Conway Munro 2021
M. C. Munro, *Learn FileMaker Pro 19*, https://doi.org/10.1007/978-1-4842-6680-9_29

own isolated copy of the file without the benefits of collaborative, simultaneous use. It can be placed in a folder on a networked file server; however, this is not recommended because each copy the desktop application reading and writing to the same file at the same time will cause file corruption that may be catastrophic (Chapter 6, "Avoiding File Damage"). Similarly, services like Dropbox or Google Drive may corrupt files when syncing even with a single user. The *FileMaker Pro* desktop app can safely share a file opened from a local folder by acting as a proper host with *peer-to-peer sharing* (described later in this chapter). However, that is limited to five simultaneous connections by other users with access limited to FileMaker products. However, if sharing isn't an important consideration, using a database from a local folder is a suitable option. Just make sure the file is closed before moving it to another folder and keep it in a folder that other users can't access.

Deploying to an iOS Device

A database can be deployed directly onto an iPhone or iPad, accessed with the free FileMaker Go iOS application. Since the file is physically stored on the device, this provides the benefit of portability. The user can access the database anywhere they have their device, even when not connected to a cellular or Wi-Fi network. A deployment to an iOS device is limited to data entry related tasks only, with no option to structurally alter the file. Also, there is no option to share a database from the device for simultaneous workgroup access, so each device has an isolated copy of the file. However, this option is perfect for convenient single-user access to a database designed for smaller screens.

To install, start by downloading the Claris FileMaker Go 19 app onto the device. Then, connect the device to a computer and copy the database from a folder into the *FileMaker Go 19* folder in the device's *Files*. On macOS Catalina (10.15), this is done by following these steps, as shown in Figure 29-1:

1. Open a new Finder window and make the sidebar visible.

2. Select the target iOS device under the *Locations* sidebar group.

3. Select the *Files* tab. Then drag the database file into the *FileMaker Go 19* folder.

Note   Four Claris sample files will be automatically installed and appear in the folder with your file. These can be deleted if desired.

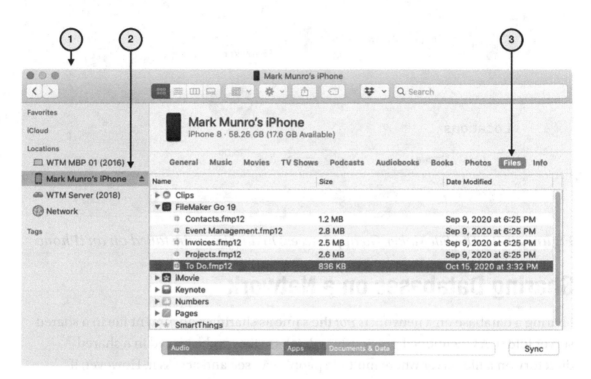

Figure 29-1. *The macOS Catalina (10.15) window for configuring an iPhone*

Once the database is installed on the device, launch the *FileMaker Go* app. Click the *My Apps* tab at the bottom, and then click *On My iPhone* under the *Locations* headings, as shown in Figure 29-2. The next screen will display a list of databases installed on the device. Click to open the desired database.

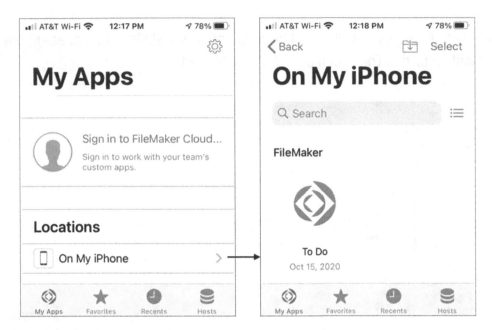

Figure 29-2. *The FileMaker Go app's access to databases installed on an iPhone*

Sharing Databases on a Network

Sharing a database on a network is *not* the same as sharing a document file in a shared server folder. As mentioned previously, a database file *can* be placed in a shared directory on a file server where multiple people can see and access it. However, if multiple users open the file at the same time, each copy of FileMaker will begin reading and writing to the file continuously as data entry tasks are performed. *This will result in file corruption and data loss!* If this happens, the file must be run through the Recovery process and may be damaged beyond repair (Chapter 6, "Avoiding File Damage").

The proper method of sharing a database across a network is *through* a share-enabled version of FileMaker software acting as a host service. This can be done using *peer-to-peer sharing* with the FileMaker Pro desktop app or using a dedicated server running FileMaker Server or FileMaker Cloud. The databases are stored in a folder hidden safely behind the host software which manages connections and coordinates conflict-free read/write processes, as illustrated in Figure 29-3.

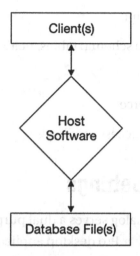

Figure 29-3. *A database with client access managed by host software*

Once the host is actively serving up a database, users can access it through their client software. In the *FileMaker Pro* desktop application, select the *File* ➤ *Hosts* ➤ *Show Hosts* menu, or click *Hosts* in an *Open File* dialog to see a dialog listing favorite and local hosts. The *Hosts* tab in the *FileMaker Go* iOS app lists the same. When databases are configured for *WebDirect*, users can also access the database from the hose through a URL in a web browser, e.g., *http://127.0.0.1/fmi/webd*. When hosting with FileMaker Server or FileMaker Cloud, it is also possible to enable incoming connections using ODBC/JBDC and *Representational State Transfer* (REST) with the *FileMaker API*. For more on those methods of connection, visit Claris' documentation website.

Understanding Collaborative Limitations

There are several limitations automatically enforced to avoid conflicts between multiple users when working in the same hosted file. The sections are each limited to a *single user* at a time. The first three can be undertaken at the same time if the users are each modifying a *different* record, layout, or script. The remaining development actions are limited to a single user at a time within the respective developer dialog, i.e., one user can edit value lists at the same time another is editing schema since they are done in different dialogs.

- Editing the *same* record

- Modifying the *same* layout

- Modifying the *same* script

- Modifying *any* database schema: tables, fields, and relationships

- Modifying *any* value list

- Modifying *any* data source

- Modifying *any* security access privileges

Configuring Network Settings

The *FileMaker Network Settings* dialog serves a dual purpose. It is used to enable network sharing capabilities of the FileMaker Pro desktop application and to configure network access settings for individual open databases. The dialog, shown in Figure 29-4, can be opened by selecting the *Share with FileMaker Clients* option from the *File* ➤ *Sharing* submenu or the toolbar's *Share* menu.

Caution   FileMaker will not host a database lacking adequate account credentials (Chapter 30).

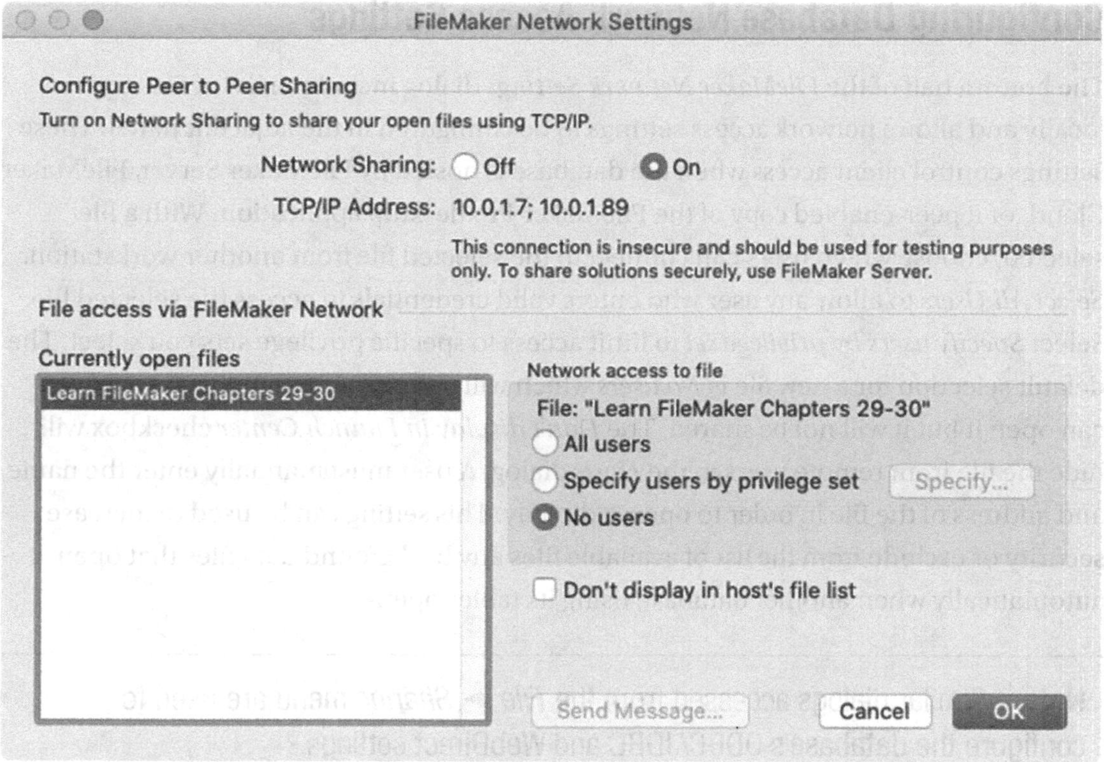

Figure 29-4. *The dialog used to configure peer-to-peer network sharing*

Enabling Peer-to-Peer Sharing

The *peer-to-peer sharing* option allows a user to open up to 125 databases with the *FileMaker Pro* desktop application and act as a host for up to five concurrent remote client connections. Since the peer host is running a client version of the software, both the host and other connected users can perform data entry and development tasks in the files, depending on their access privileges. The top half of *FileMaker Network Settings* dialog is used to enable peer sharing for the client's local application. A warning is posted here that peer sharing is not a secure network protocol since only *FileMaker Server* and *FileMaker Cloud* have options for *Secure Socket Layer* (SSL) certification to enable secure transfer across a network. While not adequate for large workgroups or where security is important, this method can be workable for sharing a database with a small group of colleagues.

Configuring Database Network Access Settings

The bottom half of the *FileMaker Network Settings* dialog includes a list of files open locally and allows network access settings to be configured in the adjacent panel. These settings control client access when the database is hosted by FileMaker Server, FileMaker Cloud, or a peer-enabled copy of the FileMaker Pro desktop application. With a file selected, choose which users can connect to the selected file from another workstation. *Select All Users* to allow any user who enters valid credentials to access the selected file. Select *Specify users by privilege set* to limit access to specific privilege sets you select. The default selection for a new file is *No users* which will deny all access to the file, i.e., you can open it but it will not be shared. The *Don't display in Launch Center* checkbox will hide the file from remote users in the *Hosts* dialog. A user must manually enter the name and address of the file in order to open it directly. This setting can be used to increase security or exclude from the list of available files any background data files that open automatically when another database using its tables opens.

Note   Similar dialogs accessed from the *File* ➤ *Sharing* menu are used to configure the database's ODBC/JDBC and WebDirect settings.

Opening a Hosted Database

To open a hosted file with the FileMaker Pro desktop application, select the *File* ➤ *Hosts* ➤ *Show Hosts* menu, or click the *Hosts* button on the *Open File* dialog. This opens a *Hosts* dialog listing files available from hosts instead of folder directories, shown in Figure 29-5. The sidebar contains three collapsible groups. Click *Claris ID* to access databases hosted on a FileMaker Cloud account. Cloud hosted files can also be opened from the *My Apps* section of the *Launch Center*. Access a local peer or FileMaker Server host by clicking on the *Local* group and selecting a database. Files from any host can be assigned a favorite status by selecting *Add to Favorites* from the contextual menu when right-clicking on a file in the list. These will appear in a list under the *Favorites* tab.

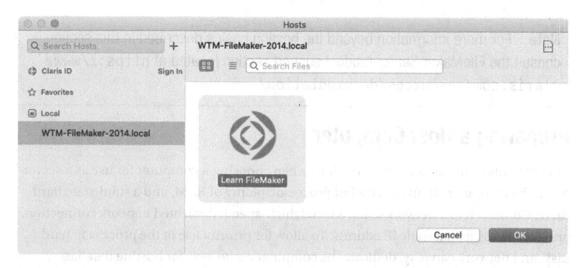

Figure 29-5. *The dialog used to open a hosted database*

Hosting with FileMaker Server

FileMaker Server is a fast, reliable, and scalable server software package that securely shares database files across a network. The server has powerful features and benefits including

- Reliable, full-time serving of databases to users of any of the FileMaker product line running on macOS, Windows, or iOS.

- Multiple, flexible licensing options that can be mixed and matched to suit the needs of your individual team members.

- Share databases on the Web without web programming using FileMaker WebDirect, or use Custom Web Publishing to create data-driven websites with PHP or XML.

- Use *Open Database Connectivity* (ODBC) and *Java Database Connectivity* (JDBC) to share hosted databases remote systems.

- Monitor and manage the server locally or remotely using either the *Admin Console* web interface or the *fmsadmin* command line.

- Automate administration tasks with automatic database backups and scheduled scripts.

- Scripts can be offloaded from the client's software to run on the server using the *Perform Script On Server* step.

Note   For more information beyond the hosting basics described in this section, consult the FileMaker Server product support section located at `https://www.claris.com/resources/documentation/`.

Preparing a Host Computer

There are many important considerations when choosing a computer for use as a server host. The computer should have a fast processor, plenty of RAM, and a solid-state hard drive. Connect it to a network using a wired, high-speed, dedicated network connection, and ideally assign it a static IP address. To allow for priority use of the processor, hard disk, and network capacity, dedicate the computer *exclusively* for hosting databases. To avoid corruption, the folder containing hosted databases should *not* be backed up directly. Instead, use FileMaker Server's built-in scheduled backup feature, and then make additional copies of those backups to other drives. Also, disable screen savers and energy-saving hibernation features in favor of monitor diming. Turn off indexing services such as the macOS Spotlight feature, and don't use antivirus software scans.

Tip   Always check the Claris website for the minimum hardware requirements for a server and other server recommendations.

Defining Installed Resources

FileMaker Server isn't a traditional application and will not appear in the computer's *Applications* folder. Instead, the following resources will be installed:

- *Database Server* – Hosts the databases, sharing them with FileMaker Pro and FileMaker Go clients.

- *Web Publishing Engine* – Handles the WebDirect services, managing traffic between a Web Server and the Database Server.

- *Web Server* – macOS uses its own copy of the Apache web server. On Windows, the Internet Information Services is enabled during installation and used as the web server.

- *PHP Engine* – Used to route calls for the FileMaker API to the Web Publishing Engine.

- *Admin Console* – Accessed through a web browser on the server or a client computer, this is used to configure and administer the server.

- *Command-Line Interface Executable* – The *fmsadmin* commands are used to administer the server through a command-line interface.

- *User Account* – Specifies an account under which the server will run. The default choice on macOS is a new *fmserver* user created by the installer, and on Windows, the *Local System*. A custom account can be specified instead, if desired.

- *User Group* – A new user group called *fmsadmin* is created and must be assigned to hosted database files.

Accessing the Admin Console

The *Admin Console* is used to administer the server and is accessible through a web browser. After installation of the server, a bookmark to the local host will be found on the server computer's desktop. The console can also be accessed by opening a web browser and entering

```
http://localhost:16001/admin-console
```

To access it from another computer, replace the localhost with the following server address:

```
https://10.0.1.20:16000/admin-console
https://10.0.1.20/admin-console
```

When the console page opens and requests authentication, enter the administrator name and password you defined during installation. Server administration controls are organized across six tabbed pages:

- *Dashboard* – Summarizes server information and status

- *Databases* – Lists all installed databases and actively connected clients, with controls to manage databases and communicate with or disconnect clients

- *Backups* – Used to schedule and view backups

- *Configuration* – Contains general settings, clients, folders, scheduled scripts, notifications, certificates, and logging

- *Connectors* – Contains settings for Web Publishing, FileMaker Data API, Plug-ins, and ODBC/JDBC connections

- *Administration* – Contains license, admin password, and external authentication settings

Uploading Files to a FileMaker Server

Database files can be added to the server by manually moving them into the *Databases* folder or uploading them from a client computer through the *FileMaker Pro* desktop application.

Moving the File into the Databases Folder

The server stores hosted files in a *Databases* subfolder of the *FileMaker Server* folder. If installed into the default location, this folder will be in one of two locations depending on the operating system, in the *Library* folder on macOS or in the *Program Files* folder on Windows, both shown in the following. To manually install files, simply drag them into the *Databases* folder. However, when adding files this way, you must manually assign them to the *fmserver* user and *fmsadmin* group.

```
/Library/FileMaker Server/Data/Databases
[drive]:\Program Files\FileMaker\FileMaker Server\Data\Databases\
```

Caution   If databases are actively hosted by the server, removing, replacing, or directly opening them with *FileMaker Pro* desktop application will cause major corruption. Confirm files are not actively hosted before performing any of these functions.

Uploading a File from a Client Computer

A database file created on a client computer can be uploaded directly to a server through the FileMaker Pro desktop application. For FileMaker Cloud, this is the only method available for uploading a file to the server. Open the *Upload to Host* dialog by selecting the *Upload to Host* option from the *Sharing* submenu or the *Sharing* icon menu in the toolbar. The dialog is similar to the Hosts dialog with a sidebar for selecting a host, as shown in Figure 29-6. Once selected, sign into the host to begin adding databases.

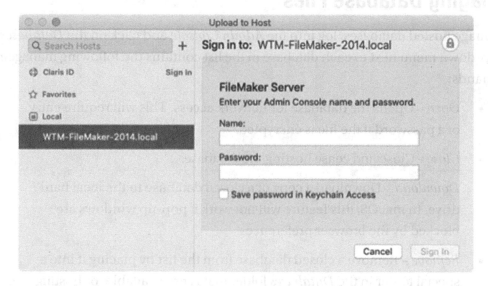

Figure 29-6. *The sign-in dialog is used to upload to a host*

After entering admin credentials for the selected host, the main panel changes to a list of database uploads, as shown in Figure 29-7. Drag database files into the list or click the *Browse* button to select them through a dialog.

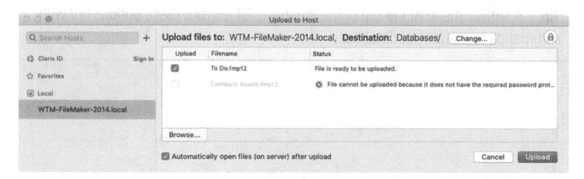

Figure 29-7. *The dialog showing database file(s) to be uploaded*

As databases are added, FileMaker runs a consistency check to determine the health of the file and checks to see if it has security adequate for hosting. In the preceding example, the first has a password-protected *Admin* account, while the second file has no password and has been rejected. Enable the checkbox next to a file to include it in the upload. The checkbox at the bottom of the dialog will cause files to automatically open on the server after the upload is complete.

Managing Database Files

To manage hosted databases, log into the *Admin Console* and click on the *Databases* tab. A drop-down menu next to each database in the list contains the following management commands:

- *Open* – Opens the database for network access. This will require entry of a password if the file is encrypted.

- *Close* – Close and cease hosting the database.

- *Download* – Download a copy of a closed database to the local hard drive. In macOS, this feature will not work if pop-up windows are blocked by the browser preferences!

- *Remove* – Remove a closed database from the list by placing it into a special folder in the *Databases* folder that is not available for hosting.

- *Verify* – Close, verify, and reopen a database.

- *Clear the Encryption Passwords* – Remove the encryption password from the selected database file(s).

Tip   A similar menu at the top of the database list mirrors these options but with commands that affect all databases.

Restarting a Server Computer

When the server is actively hosting files, it may be communicating with clients, holding recent changes in cache, or be in the middle of writing those changes to disk. A file might become corrupt if the server process is force quit or hardware is abruptly forced to shut down. To avoid damage, it is important to avoid certain risks and properly close databases. Always use an adequate uninterruptible power supply (UPS) device, and close all databases in the *Admin Console* prior to shutting down a computer. Never force quit the application or perform a hard reboot of the computer without first closing files unless absolutely necessary due to a major crash or malfunction.

Using the Command-Line Interface

The *fmsadmin* command-line tool allows administration of the server using the *Terminal* app (macOS) or the command prompt (Windows). These commands are automatically installed with the server in the following platform-specific folder(s):

```
macOS = /Library/FileMaker Server/Database Server/bin/fmsadmin
macOS (symbolic link) = /usr/bin/fmsadmin
Windows = [drive]:\Program Files\FileMaker\FileMaker Server\Database
Server\fmsadmin.exe
```

Formatting a fmsadmin Command

The formula for a command is: fmsadmin <command> <options>. For example, to get a list of all hosted databases, type the following command into the Terminal and type Enter.

```
fmsadmin list files
```

Certain functions require authentication and will prompt you to enter the server administrator username and password. Optionally, you can include credential information with the command to avoid the secondary prompt. Simply add them as shown in the pattern and example here:

```
fmsadmin <command> -u <user> -p <password>
fmsadmin list files -u Admin -p J56TF3
```

Available fmsadmin Commands

The *fmsadmin* tool contains the following commands, each with various options available:

- *autorestart* – Get or set the auto-restart feature of the server
- *backup* – Back up one database or every database in a folder
- *clearkey* – Remove saved database encryption passwords
- *close* – Close one or more databases
- *certificate* – Manage SSL certificates
- *disable* – Disable schedules or statistics logging
- *disconnect* – Disconnect one or more clients
- *enable* – Enable schedules or statistics logging
- *help* – Get help with available commands
- *list* – List clients, databases, plug-ins, or schedules
- *open* – Start hosting databases
- *pause* – Temporarily stop the database server
- *remove* – Move files out of the Databases folder
- *resetpw* – Reset the admin user password
- *restart* – Restart the server, adminserver, FMSE, WPE, or XDBC process
- *resume* – End a temporary pause of the database server
- *run* – Run a schedule
- *send* – Send a message to connected users
- *standby* – Manage standby server connections, roles, and updates
- *start* – Start the server, adminserver, FMSE, WPE, or XDBC process
- *status* – Get the status of clients or databases
- *stop* – Stop the server, adminserver, FMSE, WPE, or XDBC process
- *verify* – Check the consistency of databases

Getting Detailed Command Help

To get more information about a command, type "help" followed by the name of the command. For example, type "fmsadmin help close" to return a help page for the *close* command, as shown in Figure 29-8.

```
● ● ●                    ⌂ markmunro — bash — 80×23

Usage: fmsadmin CLOSE [FILE...] [PATH...] [options]

Description:
    Closes the specified databases (FILE) or all the hosted databases in the
    specified folders (PATH). If no FILE or PATH is specified, closes all
    hosted databases.

    To specify a database by its ID rather than its filename, first use the
    LIST FILES -s command to get a list of databases and their IDs.

Options:
    -m message, --message message
        Specifies a text message to be sent to the clients that are being
        disconnected.

    -t seconds, --gracetime seconds
        Specifies the total number of seconds to wait before forcing
        disconnection of clients. The default (and minimum) value is
        90 seconds.

    -f, --force
        Forces a database to be closed, immediately disconnecting
        clients (overrides -t option).
```

Figure 29-8. An example of the command help request

Hosting with FileMaker Cloud

FileMaker Cloud is a service by Claris that provides reliable access to cloud-hosted databases. While the use and configuration interface are nearly identical as those described earlier for *FileMaker Server*, there are some important differences with Cloud. The hardware is managed by Claris so you don't need to be concerned with hardware or energy costs. There is no way to access the folder structure directly, so interactions with the server and databases can only be performed through the *Admin Console*. To protect your information, all databases must be encrypted when uploaded to the cloud. Various maintenance tasks such as daily backups, software upgrades, automatic restarts during non-business hours, and other maintenance tasks are or can be performed automatically. Another benefit is that Claris provides round the clock support options.

Note   For more information about Claris hosting your database solution, visit `www.claris.com/filemaker/cloud/`.

Controlling FileMaker with Links, URLs, and AppleScript

There are several ways to open and perform actions within a database from outside FileMaker: *Snapshot Links, FileMaker URL,* and *AppleScript.*

Sharing Bookmarks with Snapshot Links

A *snapshot link* is an XML file that stores information about a record or a found set of records that can be used to re-create a previously existing found set. They act like a bookmark but reference a specific found set of records within a database. Opening a snapshot file will automatically open the database, navigate to the layout, and restore the found set of records, thereby re-creating the same context a user was viewing at the time they saved the snapshot. These files can be stored in folders and sent to coworkers, allowing users to exchange lists of records with other users. For example, each client folder on a company file server can include a snapshot link that instantly opens a list view of contacts for the company.

To generate a snapshot link, select the *File* ➤ *Save/Send Records As* ➤ *Snapshot Link* menu. This will open a *Save Records* dialog with snapshot configuration options, shown in Figure 29-9. Enter a name and choose a save location for the link. Select a *Save* option of *Current record* or *Records being browsed* to control which records are saved. The optional checkbox can be used to create an email with the snapshot attached. A *Send Records as Snapshot Link* script step uses the same dialog to configure a script that automates snapshot link generation.

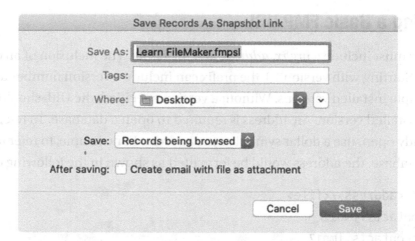

Figure 29-9. *The dialog used to configure and save a snapshot link*

Using the FileMaker URL

The *FileMaker URL* is an internet protocol registered with the FileMaker Pro client application installation that can open a database and run a script using a URL. If a user account's privilege set is explicitly granted permission to the *fmurlscript* extended privilege (Chapter 30), the following URL options become possible:

- *Typed in a Web Browser* – Type or pasted a URL into a web browser and the command will be routed to FileMaker.

- *Embedded in a Web Page* — Use a *href* tag to create a link in a web page in a browser or a web viewer on a layout in a database. Alternatively, the new *FileMaker.PerformScript* JavaScript function is a better option for web viewers (Chapter 20, "Calling a FileMaker Script with JavaScript").

- *Used in a Script* – Use the *Open URL* script step to trigger other scripts. However, the *Perform Script* step has a better option to run a script by a calculated name.

- *Used in External Applications and Scripts* – Programming languages such as AppleScript can instruct the FileMaker application to run the URL.

Formatting a Basic FMP URL

The address must include a *prefix, address,* and *file name.* The inclusion of an extension is optional. Starting with version 18, the prefix can include a version number to specify one of multiple installed versions. Without a version specified, the URL should be routed to the last installed version. An address is required to open a database. To reference a file that is already open, use a dollar symbol as the address. For example, to refer to an open *Contacts* database, the address would be formatted as shown in the following examples:

```
<prefix>://<address>/<file>
fmp://$/Contacts.fmp12
fmp18://$/Contacts.fmp12
fmp19://$/Contacts.fmp12
```

If the database is stored in the user's *Documents* folder, use a tilde as the address as shown in the following example which will automatically open the database:

```
fmp19://~/Contacts.fmp12
```

All URLs must be *percent encoded* except when using the *Open URL* script step within FileMaker. For example, a database named "Learn FileMaker" would require the space changed to "%20" as shown in the following example:

```
fmp://$/Learn%20FileMaker.fmp12
```

Tip   When building a URL in a FileMaker calculation, use the *GetAsURLEncoded* function to automatically handle encoding.

Addressing a Hosted Database

To access a database hosted on a network server, include the address to a host computer. For example, if a *Contacts* database was hosted, the FMP URL can be formatted with an IPv4 address, IPv6 address, or a DNS name as shown in these three examples:

```
FMP://10.1.0.10/Contacts.fmp12
FMP://[2001:0db8:0a0b:12f0:0000:0000:0000:0001]/Contacts.fmp12
FMP://filemaker-server.local/Contacts.fmp12
```

Including Access Credentials

To avoid a dialog requesting account credentials and achieve a seamless operation, an account and password can be specified in the URL. These can be added as colon-delimited values ahead of the address separated by an "@" sign. For example, a database with an account named "admin" that has a password of "58Jt234" can be opened without a password dialog using the address shown in the following example:

```
FMP://admin:58Jt234@10.1.0.10/Contacts.fmp12
```

Including a Script Name

The URL can also instruct FileMaker to run a script in the database. Add a question mark after the database name "script=" and include a URL encoded script name. For example, the following example will confirm a *Contacts* database is open from the specified host computer and then run a script named "Find":

```
FMP://10.1.0.10/Contacts.fmp12?script=Find
```

The account credentials are excluded in this and other examples for brevity. However, these can be included to ensure the database opens without a dialog requesting that information. When the script runs, it will be executed with the privileges and limitations of the user account used to sign into the database.

Adding a Script Parameter

When targeting a script that accepts parameters, the URL can include a *param* value by appending it after the script name and an ampersand. For example, instead of always searching for the same criteria, the *Find* script from the previous example can be modified to accept a parameter and use that value to determine which type of search to perform. The parameter used in an *If* script step can allow the script to search a *Status* field based on a value provided by the URL. Now to find records that are "Active" or "Hold," add an ampersand and *param* component to the URL, as shown in the following examples:

```
FMP://10.1.0.10/Contacts.fmp12?script=Find&param=Active
FMP://10.1.0.10/Contacts.fmp12?script=Find&param=Hold
```

Adding Script Variables

The URL can go even farther and initialize local variables within the script by adding an ampersand, the name, and value of the variables, following the pattern shown here:

```
FMP://<address>/<database>?<script>&param=<Parameter>&<$variable>=<value>
```

This example initializes a variable specifying a state name for the find script:

```
FMP://10.1.0.10/Contacts.fmp12?script=Find&param=Active&$State=Pennsylvania
```

Using AppleScript to Automate FileMaker

AppleScript is an *Open Scripting Architecture* (OSA) compliant command language that can communicate with and control macOS applications (`https://goo.gl/i7olnx`). Back in 1994 when the language was first introduced as a part of the Macintosh System 7.5, FileMaker was one of the first scriptable applications. Since then, support for the language has steadily evolved and continues to provide a great option for automating FileMaker functionality from external scripts and integrating it with data from other applications. If a user account's privilege set is explicitly granted permission to the *fmextscriptaccess* extended privilege (Chapter 30), an AppleScript will be able to control application and database actions.

Defining the Tell FileMaker Statement

AppleScripts are written using the *Script Editor* application located in the *Utilities* subfolder of the *Applications* folder. Event instructions are sent to an application using a *tell* statement that points to the application and encloses the object references and commands.

```
tell application "FileMaker Pro"
   <commands>
end tell
```

Opening FileMaker's Script Dictionary

Every macOS scriptable application has a script dictionary which can be opened by dropping the application onto the *Script Editor* application or by launching the editor and selecting the *File ➤ Open Directory* menu. This opens a window exposing the dictionary of objects and commands available for controlling the application, as shown in Figure 29-10.

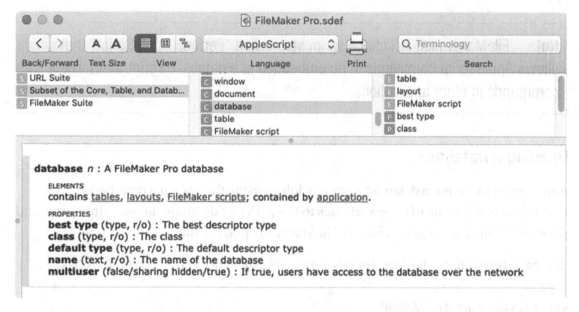

Figure 29-10. *The FileMaker Pro Advanced AppleScript dictionary window*

Caution   FileMaker's script commands use three different words to describe a database window: *database*, *document*, and *window*. Each of these can be used interchangeably but may have a slightly different effect.

Scripting Basic Tasks

As a brief introduction to automating FileMaker with scripts, this section presents a few simple examples of opening a database, activating an open database, changing layouts, performing a find, and counting records. These can be expanded with other functions to create complex scripted workflows that perform vastly more complex actions. They can also be woven with script commands sent to other applications to create powerful inter-application data transfer solutions.

Note   FileMaker also includes a script step called "Perform AppleScript" that allows AppleScript commands to be embedded in a database script that targets commands in other applications.

Opening a Database

AppleScript can open a database from any folder using the *open file* command. This example sets the value of three variables to the path to a database, an account name, and password. These are used to instruct FileMaker to open the file:

```
set pathToDatabase to "Macintosh HD:Users:shannonmiller:Learn FileMaker.
fmp12"
set textAccount to "Admin"
set textPassword to "58Jt234"
tell application "FileMaker Pro"
    open file pathToDatabase with passwords textPassword for Accounts
textAccount
end tell
```

To open a hosted database, the *getURL* command will accept a FileMaker URL described earlier in this chapter.

```
tell application "FileMaker Pro"
    getURL "fmp19://Admin:58Jt-234@10.0.1.20/Learn%20FileMaker.fmp12"
end tell
```

Activating an Open Database

To bring an open database to the front of the document window stack, this example checks if the document exists and then uses the *show* command to activate the database:

```
set nameDatabase to "Learn FileMaker"
tell application "FileMaker Pro"
    if (document nameDatabase exists) = true then
        show document nameDatabase
    end if
end tell
```

Changing Layouts

This example activates a layout named "Contact" using the *show* command:

```
tell application "FileMaker Pro"
    tell document "Learn FileMaker"
        show layout "Contact"
    end tell
end tell
```

Finding All Records

To perform the equivalent of a *Find All* command, use the *show* command with a reference of *every record*.

```
tell application "FileMaker Pro"
    tell database "Learn FileMaker"
        tell table "Contact"
            show every record
        end tell
    end tell
end tell
```

Finding Records Based on a Field Value

This example appends a *whose* clause to the *show* command to search based on a specific value within one field.

```
set nameTable to "Contact"
set nameField to "Contact Address State"
set textToFind to "NY"
tell application "FileMaker Pro"
   tell database "Learn FileMaker"
      tell table nameTable
         show every record whose cell nameField of table nameTable contains
         textToFind
      end tell
   end tell
end tell
```

The *whose* clause can use various operators for matching data in the field, including *contains*, *does not contain*, *is equal to,* and *is not equal to*. Further, clauses can be grouped with others to form compound search criteria, as shown in this example:

```
show every record
      whose cell nameField1 of table nameTable contains value1 or
      whose cell nameField1 of table nameTable is equal to value2 and
      whose cell nameField2 of table nameTable is not equal to value3
```

Counting Records in the Found Set

To count the records in the found set of the current window, a *tell window* statement is required to refer to the context displayed, regardless of the layout or table.

```
tell application "FileMaker Pro"
   tell window "Learn FileMaker"
      return the number of every record
   end tell
end tell
```

Counting Every Record in a Table

To count the total records in the table regardless of the current window's layout, use a *tell database* statement.

```
tell application "FileMaker Pro"
    tell database "Learn FileMaker"
        return the number of every record of table "Contact"
    end tell
end tell
```

Summary

This chapter introduced the methods of solution deployment and various ways to access databases. In the next chapter, we explore credentialing to restrict access to a database.

Defining Accounts and Permissions

In this modern age of global network connectivity, the need to secure a database should be glaringly obvious. News stories about data breaches, leaked information, and malicious exploitation by hackers provide us a sobering warning about the dangers of unsecured data. As important as it is to stop unauthorized access by outsiders, security permission is a far more complex subject. Even authorized users require restrictions on their activity inside the database. Limitations on the content they can create, view, modify, and use are important to consider. Also, restricting access to the *structural design* of a database can help stop careless or malicious alternations to the schema, interface, and script functions. Even a minor accidental change to a formula or script can be catastrophic to a company's workflow and may result in severe financial consequences. Only users with adequate technical skills and knowledge of business logistics should be authorized to act as a developer. This chapter explores the available credentialing features, covering the following topics:

- Defining default security
- Defining user accounts
- Exploring privilege sets
- Using credentials in formulas
- Leveraging custom extended privileges
- Controlling file access

© Mark Conway Munro 2021
M. C. Munro, *Learn FileMaker Pro 19*, https://doi.org/10.1007/978-1-4842-6680-9_30

Defining Default Security

Account credentials define who can open a file and what privileges they are granted. Every FileMaker database begins with default credential settings configured to be unobtrusive and allow anyone instant access to the full content and structure of the file. Anyone who can see the file stored in a directory or shared by another client can open it and will have *full access to everything*. The file will appear to be unlocked and will open without a login prompt. This configuration may be acceptable for situations involving personal use of a database as a document file on a local computer or in small teams where security isn't a concern. However, in most cases, credentialing is recommended to protect both sensitive content and structural programming. It is *required* when hosting a database with FileMaker Server or FileMaker Cloud.

FileMaker requires every database to have at least two default accounts setting: one active account that allows full development access and another account that provides guests read-only access. Every new database is created with both. An account named "[Guest]" allows a user to open the file *without* entering a username or password but with severely limited privileges. This account cannot be deleted but is disabled by default. When enabled, a *Sign-in As Guest* button is added to the login dialog. A second account named "Admin" is automatically enabled but has no password entered. Since the *Log in using* setting of the *File Options* dialog (Chapter 6, "Database File Options") is automatically configured to enter this account when a file is opened, it creates the illusion that new files have no access settings. In fact, new files are simply bypassing the login screen and signing in as this default full access account without a password.

Caution   When a file is configured to auto-enter a *Full Access* account or if no password is assigned it, FileMaker Server and FileMaker Cloud will refuse to host it.

Defining User Accounts

Accounts are defined in the *Manage Security* dialog, shown in Figure 30-1. This dialog is opened by selecting the *Manage* ➤ *Security* under the *File* menu. It lists the accounts defined in the file and is used to create, configure, edit, duplicate, and delete accounts. It also has a button used to access another dialog of *Advanced Settings* (discussed later in this chapter).

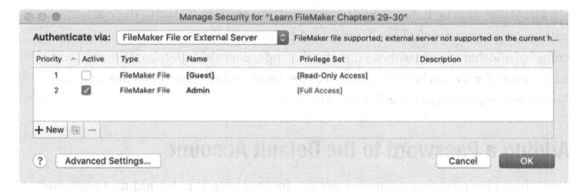

Figure 30-1. *The dialog used to manage file access credentials*

While the two default accounts are stored fully inside the database file, accounts can also be defined that authenticate a user using an external authorization system. The *Authenticate via* pop-up menu toggles the account list by the selected authentication method.

The default *FileMaker File or External Server* authentication option combines two accounts types into a single list. A *FileMaker File* account is defined with an account name and password that is fully stored inside the database file. An *External Server* account is defined in the file with only a name that references a *user account group* created externally on the host computer or on a centrally managed authentication server, such as *Apple Open Directory* or *Windows Active Directory*. This allows individual user credentials to be stored and managed at the computer level by the IT department, so personnel changes don't require modifications inside the database. One or more external user accounts can be attached to a group by the operating system or authentication server. The database account grants permissions to any user assigned to the group, allowing them to sign in using their external credentials. This is especially useful when a database solution is composed of many separate files and managing user changes across them all would be too labor intensive. External authentication only works when a database is hosted by a FileMaker Server.

The *Claris ID* option appears at the top of the authentication menu when the developer's local application is signed into a *FileMaker Cloud* account. Sign into an account by selecting the *My Apps* section of the *Launch Center* window. Then, return to the security dialog and define which cloud users will have access to this file when it is hosted on that *FileMaker Cloud*.

FileMaker also includes support for *Open Authorization* (OAuth), the open-standard authorization framework that allows a third-party system to authenticate a user on behalf of another system without directly sharing credentials. Databases hosted on a *FileMaker Server* can be configured to authenticate using credentials from a user's *Amazon*, *Google*, and *Microsoft Azure AD* account.

Adding a Password to the Default Account

To begin exploring the configuration options for accounts, start by adding a password to the default *Admin* account. Select the account in the list to open the details panel on the right, shown in Figure 30-2. Click the pencil icon to open a *Set Password* dialog and enter a new password. If desired, you can also optionally modify the *Account Name* to something more descriptive or more personal, e.g., "Developer" or your name.

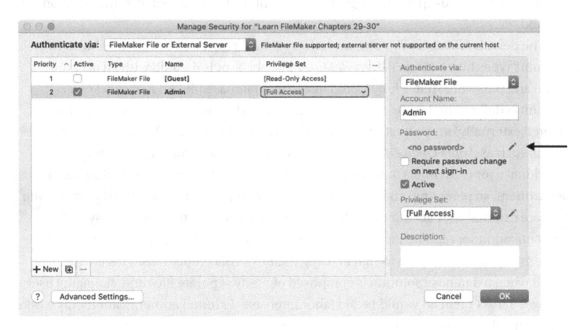

Figure 30-2. *The panel for a selected account, showing the change password button*

When closing the *Manage Security* dialog after entering a password, FileMaker will present a *Verify Access* dialog to ensure that you know an *Account Name* and *Password* that has full access privileges. This helps to ensure that you don't lose access to the file. Be sure to write down the password you enter so that you don't forget it!

The next time the database file is opened, a sign-in dialog will ask for an *Account Name* and *Password*. The *Account Name* will default to the computer's name and doesn't necessarily indicate an acceptable account for access. Enter your credentials and click *Sign In* to regain access.

Note   Passwords can be any length and may include any characters. However, to ensure compatibility with WebDirect, they should be limited to ASCII characters that don't contain accented or non-Roman characters. They are case-sensitive, so be aware of Shift-lock.

Creating a FileMaker File Account

A *FileMaker File* account defines sign-in credentials and privileges for a user that will be stored internally and can be used to access the file even when not hosted on a server. To begin, open the *Manage Security* dialog and follow the steps shown in Figure 30-3.

1. Click the *New* button to add a new account to the list. The account will be *Active* by default and selected, ready to configure.

2. Confirm that the authentication option is *FileMaker File*.

3. Enter an account name, e.g., "John Smith."

4. Click the pencil icon to enter a password. To force a user to change their password to something private, check the *Require password change on next sign-in* box.

5. Select a *Privilege Set* to determine the permissions granted to the user (discussed later in this chapter).

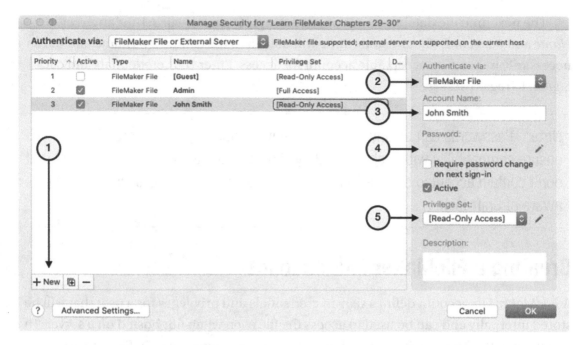

Figure 30-3. *The process for configuring an internal account*

Creating an External Server Account

An *External Server* account defines permissions for a user group. The actual user account(s) and user group are created in the operating system of the host *FileMaker Server* computer. The account inside the database identifies the group name that a user must be a member of externally in order to gain the selected level of access defined. This allows one or more users to log into the database using their externally defined credentials and gain access to specific database features based on membership in an externally defined user group. To create a new *External Server* account, open the *Manage Security* dialog, and follow the steps shown in Figure 30-4.

1. Click the *New* button to add a new account to the list.

2. Select *External Server* as the authentication method.

3. Enter a *Group Name* that is defined on the external server, remembering that these are case-sensitive.

4. Select a *Privilege Set* to determine the permissions granted to any user who signs in as a member of that group.

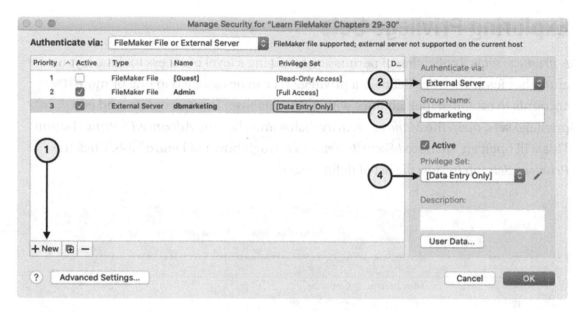

Figure 30-4. *The process for configuring an external account*

Tip   On macOS, the externally defined users can be *Sharing Only* accounts to avoid creating unnecessary directories and resources.

Enabling FileMaker Server External Authentication

Users can only log in using an external account when the database is hosted on a *FileMaker Server* or that is configured to explicitly allow authentication from external accounts. To confirm this for FileMaker Server version 19, follow these steps:

1. Open and sign into the *Admin Console* (Chapter 29).

2. Click the *Administration* tab along the top.

3. Click on *External Authentication* in the sidebar.

4. Under the *Database Sign In* heading, enable *External Server Accounts*.

Exploring Privilege Sets

A *privilege set* is a collection of permissions defining a level of access to data, layout, and other features. Once defined, a privilege set can be assigned to one or more user accounts to establish their abilities within the database. To view, create, and edit privilege sets, open the *Manage Security* dialog and click the *Advanced Settings* button. This will open an *Advanced Security Settings* dialog, shown in Figure 30-5. Click the *Privilege Sets* tab to view the list of defined sets.

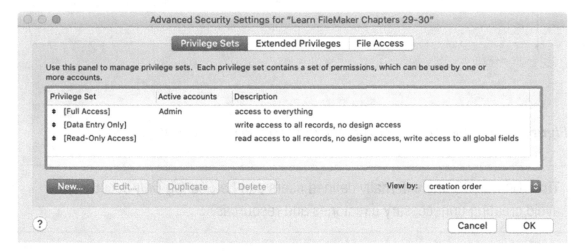

Figure 30-5. *The dialog used to define sets of access privileges for user accounts*

Default Privilege Sets

Every database will have three default privilege sets. Each of these has a square bracket around their names and are non-editable except for the ability to enable and disable *extended privileges*.

- *Full Access* – Allows unrestricted access to *every available feature* and all content. This should be reserved for developers only. FileMaker requires at least one account that allows full access.

- *Data Entry Only* – Provides limited access to only data entry work. Users assigned this set can create, edit, and delete records in every table. They can use but not structurally alter layouts, scripts, and value lists. They can print and export. They are automatically disconnected from a server when idle, and they can change their own account password.

- *Read-Only Access* – Similar to the preceding one but more with no access to modify content or structure in any way.

Creating Custom Privilege Sets

To create a new privilege set, open the *Advanced Security Settings* dialog, click on *Privilege Sets* tab, and click the *New* button. This will open a new empty set in the *Edit Privilege Set* dialog, shown in Figure 30-6. By default, a new set allows almost no access. Enter a name, optional description, and then begin enabling the desired permissions which are grouped into three categories:

- *Data Access and Design Privileges* – Allow access by resource type: *Records, Layouts, Value List,* and *Scripts*

- *Other Privilege* – A mixture of miscellaneous features

- *Extended Privileges* – Enables specific capabilities, ten default options that can be expanded

---

Caution   A custom privilege set cannot grant developer access to modify the structural schema (table, fields, and relationships). Only the default, unalterable *Full Access* privilege set allows editing these.

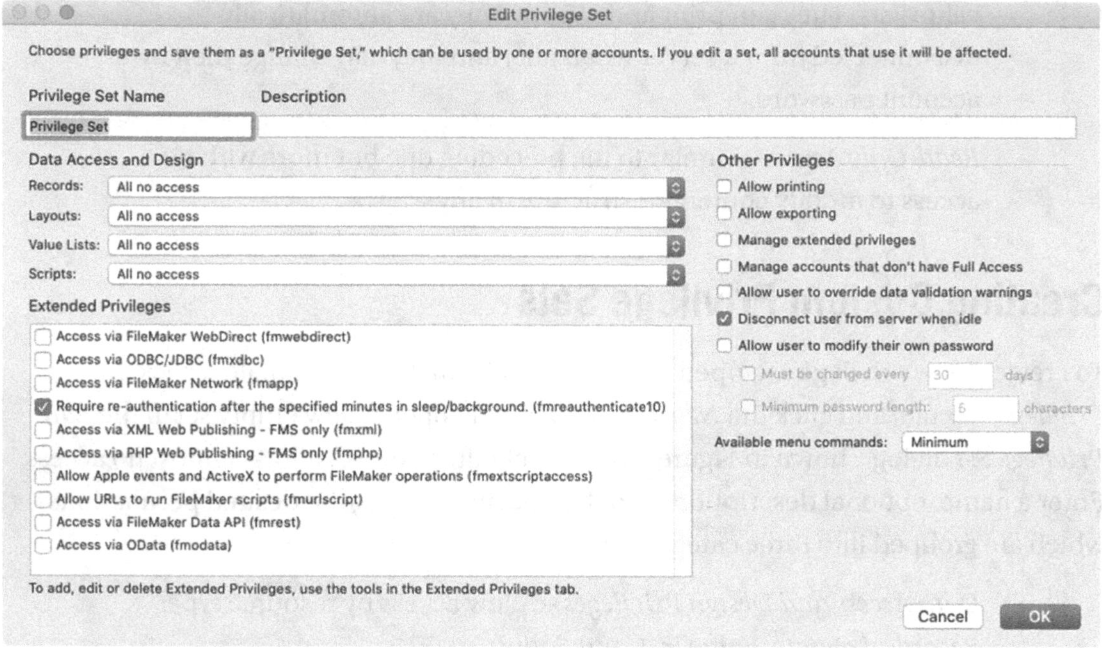

Figure 30-6. *The dialog used to edit permissions for a privilege set*

Configuring Data Access and Design Settings

The first set of privilege settings define *data access and design* permissions. These control the actions users can perform by resource type: *Records, Layouts, Value Lists,* and *Scripts.* Each has a menu of several options that control access to all entities within its class and an option to assign *custom privileges* to individual objects instead.

Controlling Record Access

The *Records* pop-up menu of the *Edit Privilege Set* dialog offers five options that control what users can do with records:

- *Create, edit, and delete in all tables*

- *Create and edit in all tables*

- *View only in all tables*

- *All no access*

- *Custom privileges*

The first four are self-descriptive and apply to records in every table. Select the *Custom Privileges* option to open the *Custom Record Privileges* dialog, shown in Figure 30-7. Every table in the database is listed with an extra row at the bottom that defines default privilege settings for any new table that is created in the future. Below the list are five pop-up menus for specifying the *View, Edit, Create, Delete,* and *Field Access* permissions for the selected table(s) in the list above.

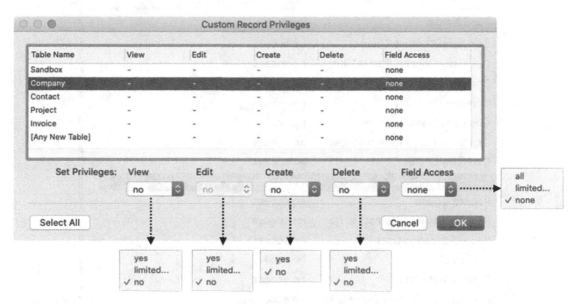

Figure 30-7. *The dialog used to control permissions for record access per table*

The settings available across all five pop-up menus are similar with only a few minor differences. The first four have a *yes* and *no* option that do exactly the same thing: enable or disable the function for the selected table. For example, to allow creation of records in the selected table(s), select *yes* under the *Create* menu. Three of these four also have a *limited* option that opens a *Specify Calculation* dialog so a formula can provide more finely tuned control over access to the function. For example, a formula can allow deletion of a record only when a specific field has a certain value, on a certain day of the week, only when a certain layout is current or any other criteria included in the formula. The *Edit* menu is disabled when the *View* option is set to not allow access, i.e., you can't grant permission to edit something that the user can't view.

The *Field Access* menu options are slightly different than the other four. Although they perform similar functionality, they are named to relate to fields instead of function. Choose *all* to allow editing access to all fields and *none* to restrict access. Select *limited* to open a *Custom Field Privileges* dialog, shown in Figure 30-8. This dialog allows each field to have a setting of either *modifiable, view only,* or *no access.* It also includes an option that defines default settings for any new fields added to the table in the future.

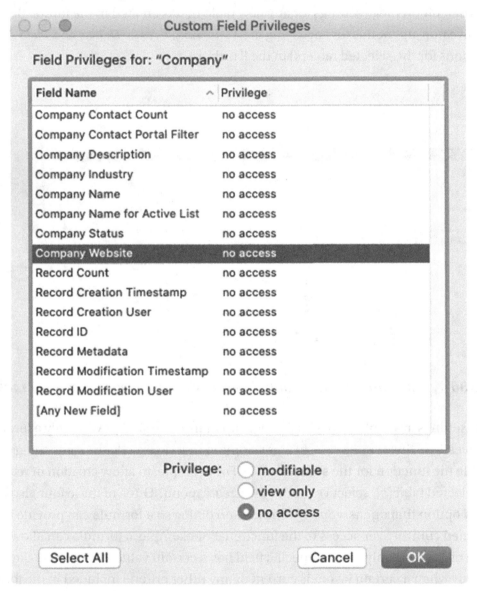

Figure 30-8. *The dialog used to control the privileges of individual fields for a table*

Controlling Layout Access

The *Layouts* pop-up menu of the *Edit Privilege Set* dialog offers four options that control what a user can do with layouts:

- *All modifiable*
- *All view only*
- *All no access*
- *Custom privileges*

Caution   If a user can't access a layout, neither can a script that runs during their session, unless it is configured to run with full access.

When you choose the *Custom Privileges* option from the *Layouts* menu, it opens the *Custom Layout Privileges* dialog, shown in Figure 30-9. Enable the *Allow creation of new layouts* checkbox at the top corner to allow users to create new layouts. Every layout in the database is listed with an extra option at the bottom that defines the default privilege settings for any new layout that is created in the future. Below the list are two sets of privilege options for the selected layout(s). The *Layout* options offer three levels of permission: *modifiable, view only,* or providing *no access.* The *Records via this layout* radio buttons control the permission for record interactions when a layout is viewable or modifiable with similarly named options, allowing you to grant layout-by-layout control over field interactions beyond the previously discussed *Record* settings for the entire table.

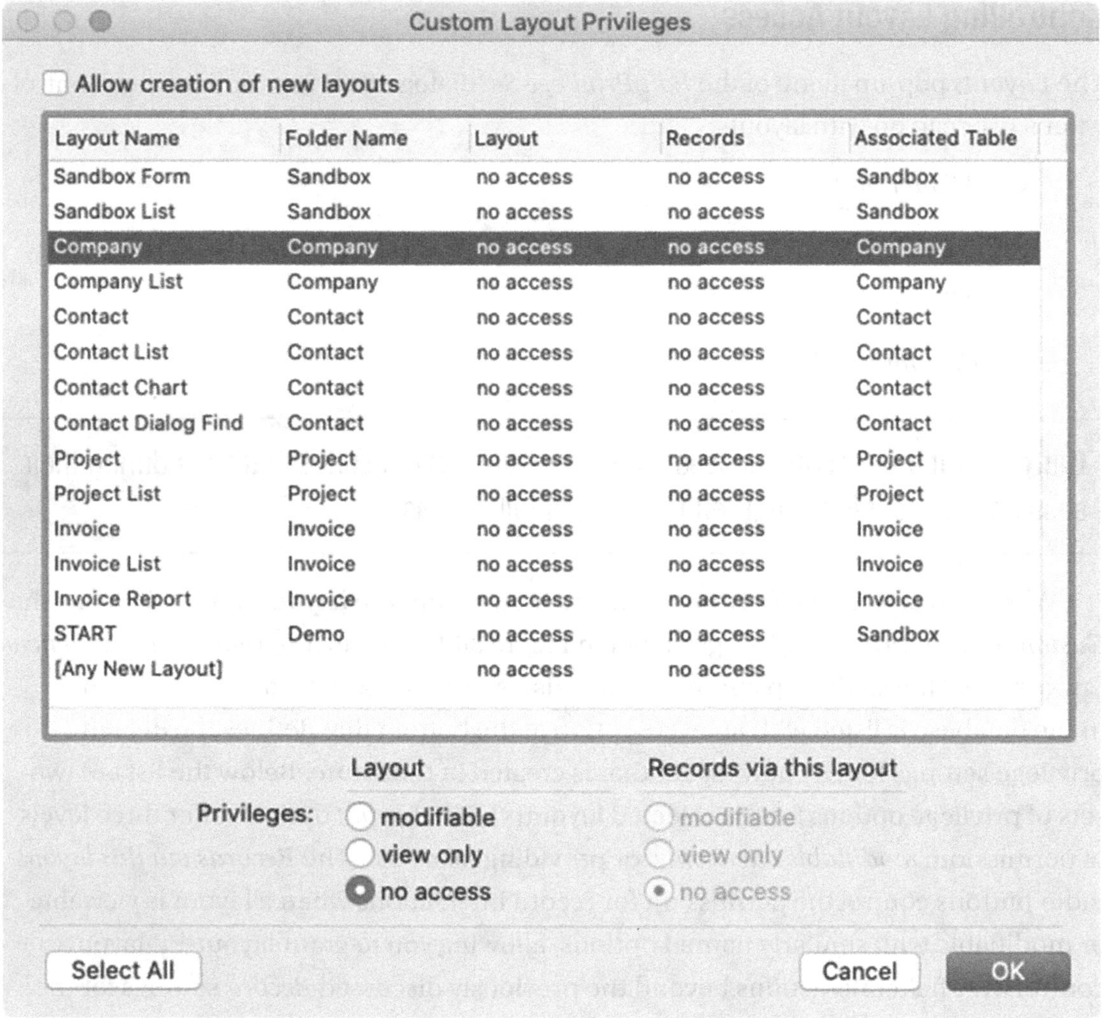

Figure 30-9. The dialog used to control permissions by layout

Controlling Value List Access

The *Value List* pop-up menu of the *Edit Privilege Set* dialog offers four options that control what users can do with value lists.

- *All modifiable*

- *All view only*

- *All no access*

- *Custom privileges*

Controlling Script Access

The *Scripts* pop-up menu of the *Edit Privilege Set* dialog offers four options that control what users can do with scripts.

- *All modifiable*

- *All executable only*

- *All no access*

- *Custom privileges*

Assigning Other Privilege Settings

On the right side of the *Edit Privilege Set* dialog are *Other Privileges*, seen previously in Figure 30-6. The functionality enabled by most of these features should be fairly obvious by their phrasing. However, a few are worth mentioning.

The *Allow exporting* option enables a variety of data output functions including exporting records, saving records as an Excel file, copying all records in the found set, and saving a copy of records. But it also enables the ability of external scripts to access and extract record information, e.g., *AppleScript* on macOS.

When the *Allow user to override data validation warnings* option is enabled, users assigned the privilege set can override any field validation warning dialog, including those that are not explicitly defined to allow it (Chapter 8, "Validation Control").

Enable the *Allow user to modify their own password* to let users change their password by selecting the *File ➤ Change Password* menu item. Two adjacent checkboxes allow you to schedule a forced password change at regular intervals and control a minimum length for any new passwords they select.

The selection from the *Available menu commands* pop-up menu controls the menus available. While access to menus can be influenced by other permissions granted to the privilege set and by the presence of custom menus (Chapter 23), this option specifies a blanket category of commands they can access. Choose *All* to grant access to the entire active menu bar. Limit them to basic editing functions by choosing *Editing Only*. Select *Minimum* to severely restrict them to menus for only the most basic functions such as open, close, and create database files, window functions, perform scripts, preferences, and help.

> **Caution**   The menu setting for new privilege sets defaults to minimal which
> provides almost no enabled functions. Be sure to change this when creating new
> accounts.

Assigning Extended Privileges

The *Extended Privileges* section of the *Edit Privilege Set* dialog seen previously in
Figure 30-6 includes a list of additional privileges that can be enabled. An *extended
privilege* is a keyword-based permission setting that can be assigned to one or more
privilege sets. These enable access to one specific type of functionality. FileMaker
includes several extended privileges that are fixed to specific functions, mostly various
types of inbound networking and scripting access.

Some extended privileges grant the ability of users to sign in via specific methods.
For example, *fmwebdirect* enables access to a server-hosted database from a web
browser, while *fmapp* allows access to the file from the *FileMaker Pro* and *FileMaker Go*
apps.

Others provide protocol-specific access to a server-hosted database by external
systems: *fmxdbc* allows incoming access with ODBC/JDBC, *fmxml* allows XML access,
fmphp allows PHP, and *fmrest* allows access from a *Representational State Transfer*
(RESTful) web service via the *FileMaker Data API*.

Two others provide scripted access: *fmextscriptaccess* allows access with *AppleScript*
(macOS) and *ActiveX* (Windows), while *fmurlscript* allows triggering a database script
from a URL (Chapter 29, "Using the FileMaker URL").

While all of the default extended privileges are hardwired to simply turn on or off
a built-in FileMaker capability, new extended privileges can be defined that control
custom features in your database (discussed later in this chapter).

Using Credentials in Formulas

Credentialing with *accounts* and *privilege sets* does a great job limiting access to the
file, built-in capabilities, and custom structural elements. Although the credentialing
interface exerts an impressive level of control over custom resources, its reach is
somewhat limited. A privilege set can control a layout's viewability but has no options

to limit access to individual objects. It can make a script executable but has no option to control individual steps within the script. It can't exert any control over the accessibility or behavior of custom menus or custom functions, and it can't reach inside of formulas. These limitations are simply due to the nature of a custom solution. At a certain point, the built-in credentialing interface simply can't *reach outward* far enough to control permissions for every object, script step, and custom configuration. Beyond that point, the custom resources must instead use formulas to *look inward* at the user's credentials and determine what limits should be imposed and which variations performed. To accommodate this, there are three *Get* functions that can be used in formulas to impose *credentials-based conditions*. Using these, a formula can identify the name of the user's *account, privilege set,* and, when using an external authentication method, *group*. These examples show hypothetical results of each.

```
Get ( AccountName )                // result = Jim Smith
Get ( AccountPrivilegeSetName )    // result = [Full Access]
Get ( AccountGroupName )           // result = dbmarketing
```

A script can use an *If* step to limit execution of a group of individual steps for a specific user. For example, an invoice report script may be run by many users but have a section of steps that generates a sensitive financial report that should only execute when the script is run by the Chief Financial Officer. The account name can be used to determine if the steps should execute or not.

```
If [ Get ( AccountName ) = "Rashida Fields" ]
   Go to Layout [ "Invoice - Special Report" ; Animation: None ]
   Sort Records [ Restore ; With dialog: Off ]
   Print [ With dialog: On ]
   Go to Layout [ Original Layout ; Animation: None ]
End if
```

Another script may navigate to a department-specific menu layout based on the user's privilege set. This example script uses a sequence of *If* and *Else If* script steps with separate steps, each targeting a single layout.

```
Set Variable [ $set ; Value: Get ( AccountPrivilegeSet ) ]
If [ $set = "human resources" ]
   Go to Layout [ "Home HR" ; Animation: None ]
Else If [ [ $set = "sales" ]
```

```
   Go to Layout [ "Home Sales" ; Animation: None ]
Else If [ [ $set = "production" ]
   Go to Layout [ "Home Production" ; Animation: None ]
End if
```

These functions can be used to create credential-specific behavior anywhere that a formula is an option. Hide layout objects or custom menus, change button or tab names, personalize a tooltip, produce different results in calculation fields, and more. *However, using this technique should be done with some hesitation.*

Understanding the Risks of Credential Embedding

Embedding credentials in formulas to create conditional functionality should be used with caution. Each change to the company workforce may require changes to employee names used in dozens, hundreds, or thousands of different formulas. Even something as simple as a coworker marrying and changing their last name can require a lot of work in a complex database. While the name of an existing account can be changed for a new employee, all the uses of the former name in formulas don't automatically update because they are literal text and not dynamic references. In a large organization with high turnover, locating and changing these could become a full-time job.

This problem can be somewhat abated by using *titles* for account names instead of employee's actual *name*. For example, Jim Smith might sign into the database as "Account Supervisor" with a unique password. Then, if a new person fills that position, they carry on with the same account name and a new password. Since the actual account name didn't change, any formulas using it wouldn't need to change either. However, this approach is problematic since it depersonalizes the user identity and can be confusing when looking at a historical list of records seeing they were all modified by the "Account Supervisor," but they span a period where three different people held that position. Ideally, users sign into the database with a personal identifier.

Conditional features can be made slightly more impervious to team changes when formulas use *privilege sets* instead of *account names.* Individual user accounts can be removed and created as needed, while the assigned privilege set continues to control the interface and behavioral conditions in formulas. Although this is a better approach, there are still elements of risk. Unless privilege sets are meticulously designed with near omniscience, it is almost inevitable that certain features will need major changes as roles and responsibilities shift within a company workflow. Also, since each user can be assigned only a single privilege set, features may require numerous compound clauses, to grant permission for a group of different privilege sets.

Using credentials in formulas does extend the ability of security settings beyond the *Manage Security* dialog, but in a potentially labor-intensive way. What may begin as a simple, ad hoc exception for one user or group can quickly become a bad habit that paralyzes developers who must constantly try to remember thousands of credential exceptions lost and forgotten in the dark corners of a crowded interface design. Fortunately, FileMaker has an amazing alternative that solves this problem by allowing custom feature exceptions to be easily wired directly into the security interface: *custom extended privileges*.

Leveraging Custom Extended Privileges

A *custom extended privilege* is a developer-defined, keyword-based permission that can be safely used in formulas to create conditional features. These can be easily linked to one or more privilege sets, making them adaptable to future changes to a company's personnel. Instead of connecting directly to changing *accounts* and *privilege sets*, conditional formulas are connected to an unchanging *custom extended privilege* by keyword. As individual user accounts are created and deleted, as privilege sets are modified and reassigned, conditional access and behavior granted by the extended privilege can be easily enabled or disabled directly in the *Manage Security* dialog. Instead of inserting credential naming into formulas, extended privileges allow you to name a custom feature of your database and insert it as a new setting in the credentialing interface.

To create a custom extended privilege, start by identifying a set of conditional features and the objects/formulas involved. For the sake of illustration, let's use a simple example: the ability to approve an *Invoice* record by clicking a button on a layout. The button will need to be conditionally hidden so unauthorized users can't see or click it. To begin, choose a name for the new privilege. The name should be a short keyword made up of two or more words that is unique and clearly indicates the function(s) it will control. For this example, a name like "InvoiceApproval" will describe the capability we are defining in our example.

Caution   Choose extended privilege names carefully before using them in many object formulas to avoid having to change it numerous times, the very problem we are trying to avoid!

Open the *Manage Security* dialog, click the *Advanced Settings* button and select the *Extended Privileges* tab. This lists all built-in and custom extended privileges defined in the file. Click the *New* button to open a new, extended privilege in an *Edit Extended Privilege* dialog, shown in Figure 30-10.

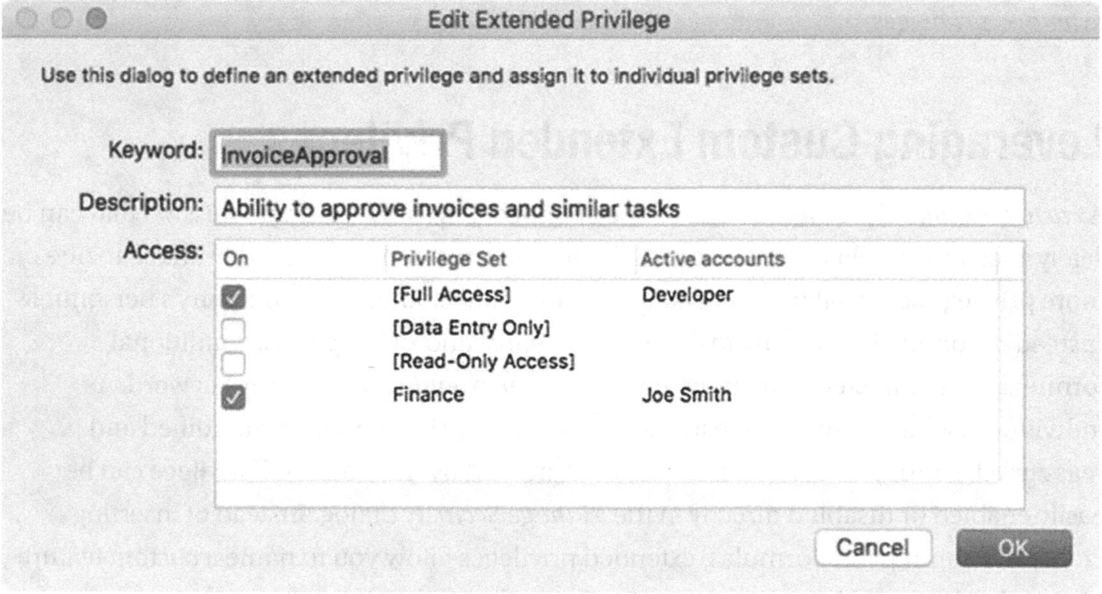

Figure 30-10.   *The dialog used to create and edit custom extended privileges*

Type the name of the privilege in the *Keyword* text box and enter a short *Description*. The *Access* list shows privilege sets with a checkbox indicating those with permission to access this custom privilege. After closing the preceding dialog, view any privilege set to see the new extended privilege listed as an option, as shown in Figure 30-11.

Extended Privileges

☐ Access via FileMaker WebDirect (fmwebdirect)
☐ Access via ODBC/JDBC (fmxdbc)
☑ Access via FileMaker Network (fmapp)
☑ Require re-authentication after the specified minutes in sleep/background. (fmreauthenticate10)
☐ Access via XML Web Publishing - FMS only (fmxml)
☐ Access via PHP Web Publishing - FMS only (fmphp)
☐ fmscriptdisabled
☐ Allow Apple events and ActiveX to perform FileMaker operations (fmextscriptaccess)
☐ Allow URLs to perform FileMaker scripts (fmurlscript)
☐ Access via FileMaker Data API - FMS only (fmrest)
☑ Ability to approve invoices and similar tasks (InvoiceApproval)

To add, edit or delete Extended Privileges, use the tools in the Extended Privileges tab.

Figure 30-11. *The new extended privilege enabled on a privilege set*

The *InvoiceApproval* privilege is now defined but doesn't actually control anything until it is used in a behavior conditioning formula somewhere in the database. For our invoice approval example, add a button to an *Invoice* layout, and enter the *Hide object when* formula (Chapter 21) shown in the following example to hide the object for any users who do not have the extended privilege enabled on their account's privilege set. The formula uses the *Get (AccountExtendedPrivileges)* function to get a list of the names of all enabled extended privileges for the user's privilege set and then checks for *InvoiceApproval* using the *FilterValues* function (Chapter 13, "Manipulating Values").

```
FilterValues ( Get ( AccountExtendedPrivileges ) ; "InvoiceApproval" ) = ""
```

Controlling File Access

The *File Access* tab of the *Advanced Security Settings* dialog lists which other FileMaker databases can access the current database. Individual databases can be *Authorized* or *Deauthorized*. A *Reset All* will reset the ID of all the files listed and require them to be reauthorized. Use this to ensure unique identifiers if a duplicate or clone of a file should be granted access along with the original.

Summary

This chapter explored the credential options for securing a database. In the next chapter, we will explore some additional advanced tools for analyzing and modifying files.

CHAPTER 31

Analyzing and Modifying Files

The *Tools* menu contains a few additional features below the *Script Debugging* options (Chapter 26) and *Custom Menus* submenu (Chapter 23). These additional tools include

- Save a Copy as XML
- Database design report
- Developer utilities
- Tools Marketplace

Save a Copy as XML

The *Save a Copy as XML* option saves a copy of the current database file as an XML file. The file includes raw structural details about the file but does not include any record content. This can be used to store and compare structural changes over time.

Generating a Database Design Report

A *database design report* is a detailed report of a database file structure, listing every table in the database with optional information about other resources. These reports can be saved as a HTML or XML file and can be used to perform the following development tasks:

- Troubleshoot structural problems by locating missing references, broken relationships, and more.

© Mark Conway Munro 2021
M. C. Munro, *Learn FileMaker Pro 19*, https://doi.org/10.1007/978-1-4842-6680-9_31

- Find obsolete elements to help maintain a clean structure.

- Locate interface elements still pointing to an old script or custom functions.

- Glimpse statistics about component counts and usage.

- Save a structural snapshot of a database at a certain point in time, which can be compared to a later structure to identify changes.

Generating a Design Report

To generate a report, open a database and select the *Tools* ➤ *Database Design Report* menu. This will open the `Database Design Report` dialog, shown in Figure 31-1. The *Available Files* area allows a selection of the currently open database files that should be included in the report. Select a file to have the option to exclude individual tables from the adjacent list. Choose from the *Include in report* checkboxes to determine what resources are included in the analysis. This scrolling list includes everything from *Accounts* to *Value Lists*. The *Report Format* option at the bottom controls which style of report will be generated.

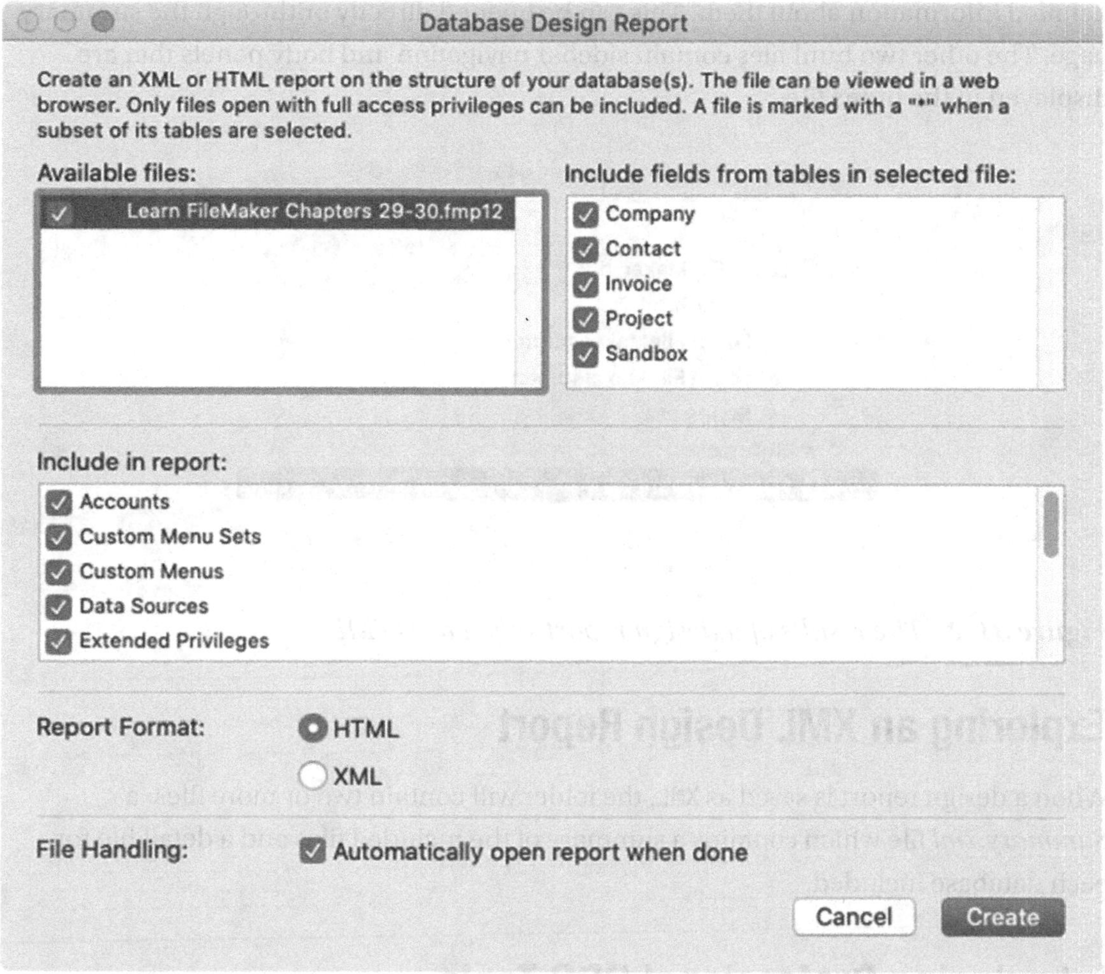

Figure 31-1. *The dialog used to create a database design report*

Exploring a HTML Design Report

An HTML design report will produce collection of pages, as shown in Figure 31-2. The *Summary.html* contains a navigable overview of each included database showing a columnar summary of its objects. The *Styles.css* files contain style information, one for the summary and one for pages inside of each database folder. Each database included in the report will be represented by a folder, in this case only a single folder for the *Learn FileMaker* database. Inside each database folder, an *Index.html* page contains a complex table structure with navigable sidebar detailing every object and lots of detailed information about them. This can be opened directly or through the summary page. The other two html files contain sidebar navigation and body panels that are displayed in the index file.

Figure 31-2.   *The results of a design report saved as HTML*

Exploring an XML Design Report

When a design report is saved as XML, the folder will contain two or more files: a *Summary.xml* file which contains a summary of the included files and a detail file for each database included.

Introducing Professional DDR Tools

Several companies offer products that import an XML design report and present the material in a more polished interface than the HTML pages provided by FileMaker. Developers who build complex databases that require a lot of analysis will appreciate the improved viewing experience of these products.

BaseElements

BaseElements is a great analysis tool for traversing the structure of a database sold by a company of the same name. The solution is available as a FileMaker file or a stand-alone application for macOS and Windows. The product has full layout access, so you can link to BaseElements Data Tables from your database's relationship graph and access the information in scripts. The product includes an open source BaseElements plug-in with many useful functions. For more information visit `www.baseelements.com`.

FMPerception

FMPerception is a utility for searching, analyzing, and maintaining databases sold by Geist Interactive. The product uses a progressive analysis technique to quickly provide current and accurate information about a database's structure. Some features include

- A high-level overview and a "Database Report Card" that summarizes the complexity of a database and lists any potential problems that were detected.

- A fast DDR import process that is nearly instantaneous.

- A graphical "call chain visualization" illustrates the flow of script calls from buttons to scripts to subscripts, helping trace the flow of complex functionality.

- Identifies layout objects that might slow down performance.

- Performs a security audit to identify vulnerabilities such as missing passwords or scripts that run with full access.

For more information visit `www.geistinteractive.com`.

InspectorPro

InspectorPro is an advanced diagnostics, analysis, and visualization tool sold by Beezwax DataTools. The product boasts over 115 different areas where it normalizes analysis information and can automatically detect problems with a database structure. For more information visit `www.beezwax.net`.

Exploring Developer Utilities

The *Developer Utilities* dialog, shown in Figure 31-3, is accessed from the *Tools* menu. Once the dialog is open, click the *Add* button to place one or more files into the *Solution Files* list. These will be batch-manipulated by the various features and options initiated in the dialog. Within the list, a red arrow designates one file as the primary which is used by the Kiosk option to denote the database containing the starting "home" interface. Below the list are controls for renaming files, selecting an output folder where modified files will be saved.

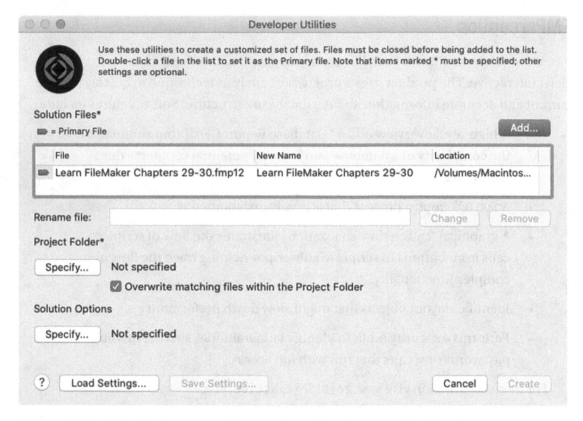

Figure 31-3. *The dialog containing various developer utility functions*

Renaming Files

To rename a file, select it in the list, enter a new name without the extension into the Rename File text field, and click the *Change* button. This is the recommended method for renaming database files in a multi-file solution since it will not only rename the selected file *but also* update all external file references to it within all other files in the list. Any new names specified will be queued into the *New Name* column of the file list. These will not take effect until a *Project Folder* is specified and the *Create* button is clicked.

Specifying a Project Folder

Before you can rename files or perform solution options, choose a *Project Folder* by clicking the *Specify* button. Since the utility dialog creates new versions of files, this setting indicates where these should be saved. Check the box below to automatically overwrite any files with the same name that exist in the selected folder.

Specifying Solution Options

This *Developer Utilities* dialog contains several utility functions that can alter the structure of the *Solution Files*. To enable one or more of these options, click the Specify button under the *Solution Options* header which opens a *Specify Solution Options* dialog. Then enable checkboxes to any of the following utility functions:

- Remove admin access from files permanently.

- Enable kiosk mode for non-admin accounts.

- Databases must have a FileMaker file extension.

- Create error log for any processing errors.

- Enable database encryption (or re-encrypt files).

- Remove database encryption.

Removing Admin Access from Files

Enable the *Remove admin access from files permanently* checkbox to save copies of the files with all admin access removed from every user account and most design and structural elements rendered read-only. This essentially prevents *anyone* from acting as a developer within the file while allowing normal data entry and other uses to continue unabated. While this can be a useful method to secure a file for sale as a product or distribution as a demo, it should be used with caution and while retaining a safe unmodified backup file.

Enabling Kiosk Mode

The *Enable Kiosk mode for non-admin accounts* option saves copies of the file with full screen mode and no menu bar enforced for all non-admin access. This is a great option for creating touch kiosks where you don't want to allow users access to anything except the interface controls you make accessible on layouts. The database must have at least one non-admin user account defined, which must be used to open in kiosk mode. Once in kiosk mode, a user's ability to navigate within the file or to close the file will be through the controls you provide on layouts. There will be *no* menu bar, and even access to operating system functions such as force quit or toggle applications will be completely disabled. When adding a button to quit the database intended to be a public kiosk, be sure to include some sort of authentication process to exclude regular users from quitting the solution and accessing the underlying operating system.

Caution   If you don't provide a button on the layout that will quit the application or close the database, the *only* option will be to perform a hard restart of the computer that may lead to file damage.

Requiring a FileMaker File Extension

The *Databases must have a FileMaker file extension* option will confirm each *Solution File* has a file extension and will add it to the new copies if missing.

Creating an Error Log of Errors

The *Create Error log for any processing errors* option will generate a log file in a *Project Folder* containing any errors that occur while processing other utility functions. This option can optionally be selected with any other utility function but is *required* when enabling encryption and will be selected by default for both encryption options. Once selected, an extra option below allows customization of the name and location of the log file by clicking the *Specify* button. The default is a file named "Logfile.txt" that will be saved in the *Project Folder*.

Exploring Encryption Features

FileMaker includes several encryption features that can be employed to protect data. Container fields using managed external storage (Chapter 11) can be configured to automatically encrypt stored files. Various built-in functions provide *Base64* and *Crypt* options for encoding/decoding and encrypting/decrypting data that is stored in fields or exchanged with other systems. *SSL Encryption* certificates installed protect data when in transit between client and server; these are encouraged by *FileMaker Server* and required by *FileMaker Cloud*. Additionally, two *Solution Options* available through the *Developer Utilities* dialog provide *Encryption at Rest* protection of an entire database file which adds a layer of protection beyond the standard credentialing for normal access (Chapter 30). An encrypted database is structurally modified to protect it from unauthorized access, tampering, or analysis while stored on disk, e.g., if someone acquires a stolen backup or archive of the database. The password you define during the encryption process *must* be entered to open a file on the desktop or to host it with *FileMaker Server*. *FileMaker Cloud* requires this and will automatically encrypt files uploaded. Once hosted, only standard credentials are required for a user access.

Caution   Be sure to keep encryption keys safely stored since there is no possibility of recovery.

Enabling Database Encryption (or Re-encrypt Files)

The *Enable Database Encryption (or Re-encrypt files)* option will create a copy of the *Solution Files* that are structurally altered with an encryption password you define. This key will require a decryption password to be entered to open the files directly or to host them on FileMaker Server. To encrypt the selected file(s), select the option in the *Specify Solution Options* dialog, and configure the settings below, shown in Figure 31-4.

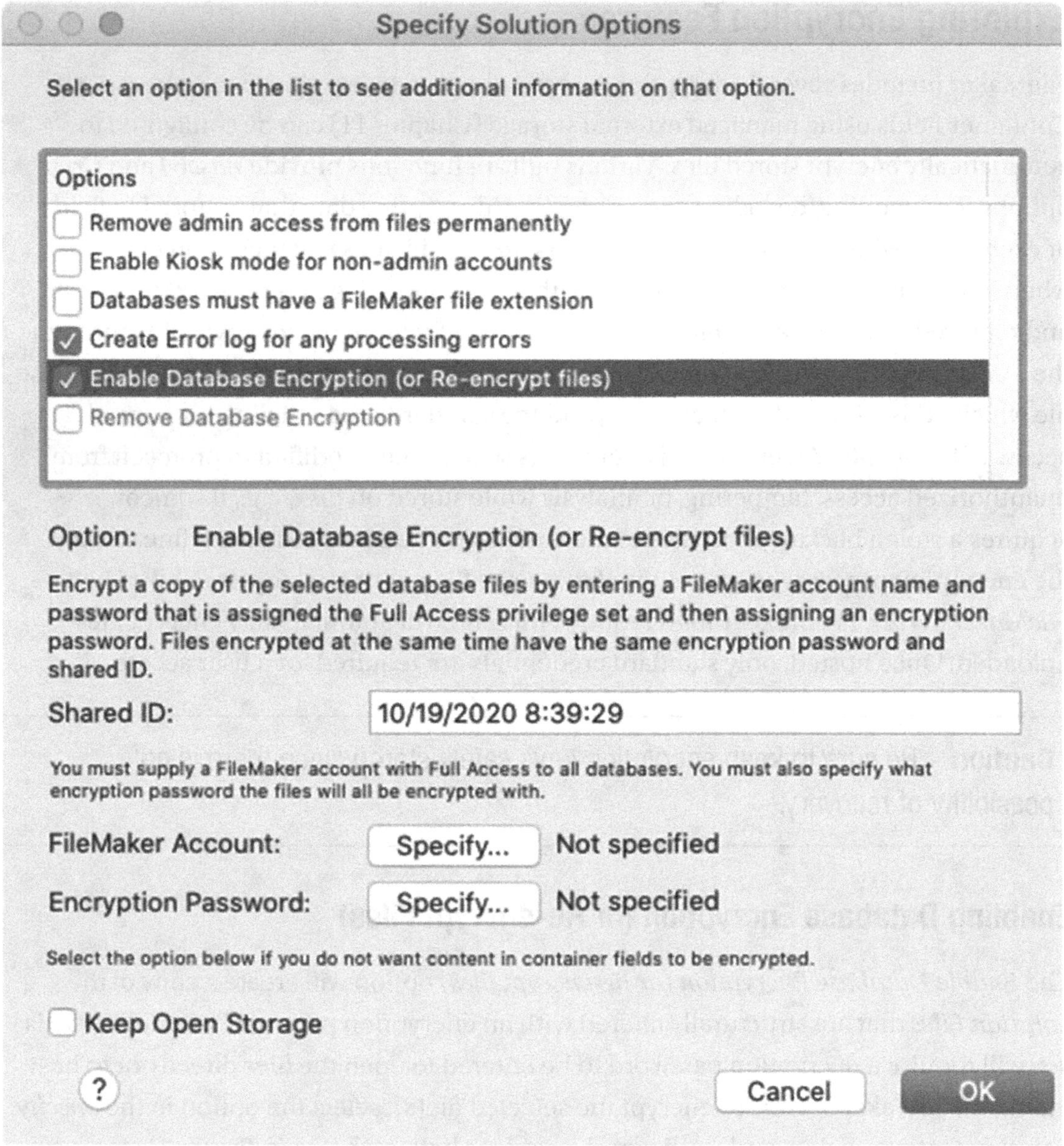

Figure 31-4. *The settings required when enabling encryption*

The *Shared ID* text field contains a case-sensitive string of up to 32 characters and is used to link all the database files in a multi-file solution. When one file is opened with the encryption password, that file can then access any other file that has been saved with the *same Shared ID* and *encryption password,* without prompting the user for the encryption password repeatedly.

Click the *Specify* button to enter credentials for a *FileMaker Account* that has full access to the file(s) being encrypted. This is required to prove that you are an authorized full-access user of the file before modifying the structure of the files.

Next, click the Specify button to enter an Encryption Password. This password will be used during encryption and will be required prior to opening a file or hosting it on a server.

The Keep Open Storage checkbox can be selected to maintain externally stored container files in an unencrypted state if desired. Leave this unchecked to automatically encrypt all container field content.

Once finished, close the *Specify Solution Options* dialog to return to the *Developer Utilities* dialog. Then, click *Create* to run the utility and create encrypted copies of the files in the specified *Project Folder*.

Now, two dialogs will appear when opening the encrypted file(s) on the desktop. First an *Open Encrypted Database* prompt requires entry of the encryption password and then the standard login prompt for user account credentials. When opening an encrypted file for hosting on a server, only the first of these will appear and users continue to see only the prompt for account credentials.

Tip   When encrypting a multi-file solution, be sure to use the same Developer Account and encryption password for every database.

Removing Database Encryption

The *Remove Database Encryption* option will save a copy of the files in an unencrypted state, restoring normal operating behavior and access methods. Select the option in the *Specify Solution Options* dialog, and enter the required settings, shown in Figure 31-5. *Type the Encryption Password* for the file(s) to prove that you have access to modify the files. Then, click the *Specify* button to enter a *FileMaker Account* with full access. Both of these should be common to *all* the selected files. Close the *Specify Solution Options* dialog to return to the *Developer Utilities* dialog. Then, click *Create* to run the utility. The decrypted files will appear in the specified *Project Folder*.

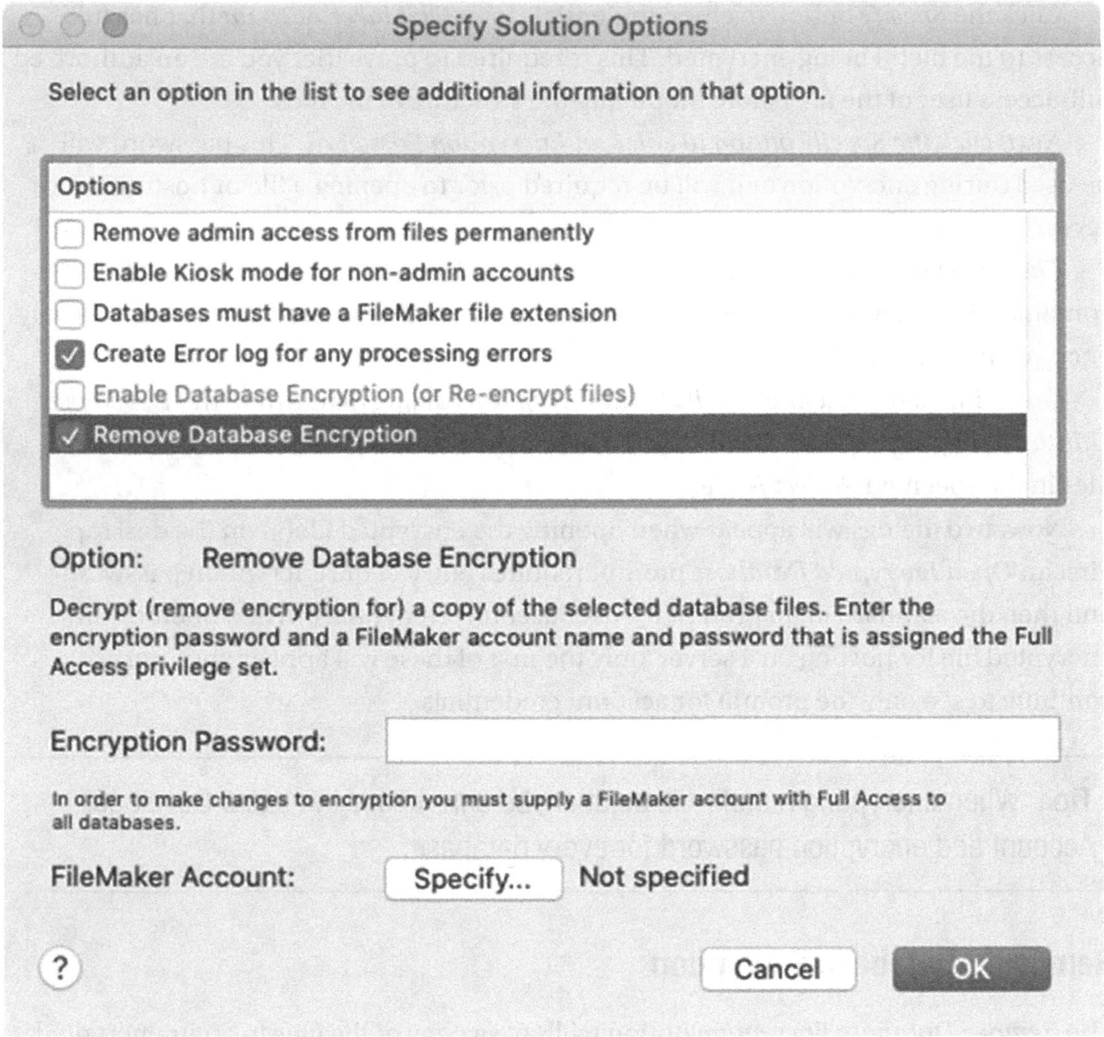

Figure 31-5. *The settings required to remove file encryption*

Tools Marketplace

The last item under the *Tools* menu is the *Tools Marketplace* which opens the *Claris Marketplace* web page. The site contains a collection of developer tools and products created by Claris Partners. This growing site includes pages of templates, tools, and plug-ins, some free and some paid, including

- Templates from *DB Services* that help integrate Square and Stripe into a FileMaker solution

- A tool for writing and troubleshooting SQL queries from *Soliant Consulting*

- Various paid products from *Productive Computing* that allow a database to manipulate or link to various external applications such as the Calendar, Address Book, and QuickBooks

- Various *Database Design Report* tools mentioned earlier in this chapter

- Various plug-ins, including some mentioned in Chapter 28

Summary

This chapter discussed advanced features accessible through the *FileMaker Pro* application's *Tools* menu.

Index

A

© Mark Conway Munro 2021
M. C. Munro, *Learn FileMaker Pro 19*, https://doi.org/10.1007/978-1-4842-6680-9

C

D

P, Q

Printed in the United States
By Bookmasters